D1320897

A COMPANION TO THE BIBLE

A COMPANION TO THE BIBLE

SECOND EDITION

ORIGINAL EDITION
EDITED BY
T. W. MANSON, D.Litt., D.D.

NEW EDITION
EDITED BY
H. H. ROWLEY, D.D., B.Litt., F.B.A.

Edinburgh: T. & T. CLARK, 38 George Street

PRINTED IN GREAT BRITAIN BY
MORRISON AND GIBB LIMITED
EDINBURGH AND LONDON
FOR
T. AND T. CLARK, EDINBURGH

First Edition 1939
Second Edition (*entirely revised and reset*) 1963

PREFACE

For nearly a quarter of a century the *Companion to the Bible* which the late Professor T. W. Manson edited has served many readers. It is much to be regretted that now that a revision is called for, to take account of new sources of knowledge and new trends and discussions, Professor Manson is no longer with us to supervise its preparation. His early death was an incalculable loss to Biblical scholarship, and one which I, who had counted it a high privilege to be his close colleague for so long, especially feel. When the publishers asked me to edit this new edition, the request came as an honour and an obligation. I cannot hope to have succeeded so well as he would have done; but I know no one who could have done that.

My own chapter has been revised, and the Appendix, for which Professor Manson was himself originally responsible, has also been revised. For the rest, the *Companion* has been completely rewritten. Substantially, its plan is the one Professor Manson gave it, though there have been some modifications. Its aim and purpose remain the same as those of the volume it replaces, and these can be stated in no better terms than those Professor Manson used in the original Preface, part of which is here quoted:

> The form and contents of this book are determined by the conviction stated in the introductory chapter: that the primary and vital interest of the Bible is that it records the authentic word of God—His gracious revelation of Himself in terms of personality and life in the midst of the life of men. It is a revelation which gives true knowledge of a real God, that is, something more than probable propositions about the Absolute.
>
> Consequently the main interests of the *Companion to the Bible* must be fixed on two matters: the content of the revelation and the historical context within which it is first given. As a matter of historical fact, the revelation is given within the framework of the History of Israel. Hence it is important to have a clear idea of the course of that history, both the outward fate of Israel as a small buffer-state between great empires, and the inward social and economic conditions, which gradually evolved from the simple code of the nomad clans to the elaborate refinements of Mishnah and Talmud. We must also take account of the physical conditions—the geography of Palestine—which had so great an influence on the course of Hebrew

history ; and we must not overlook the great mass of archaeological evidence. On the religious side, we need to know something of the cult-practices of the Hebrew people : the sacrificial system, the priesthood, and the later developments of synagogue organization and worship ; and the Christian Church with its ministry and sacraments. To complete that side of the picture, the whole must be set on the background of primitive Semitic religion, and later popular superstitions.

A most important part of this reconstruction of the historical environment of the divine revelation is the history of the documents themselves in which it is recorded. Hence we need Introductions to the Old and New Testaments and, as necessary accompaniments of these, a sketch of the extra-canonical literature, and some information about the languages in which the records have been made.

Finally, there is the supremely important business of the content of the revelation itself—that knowledge of God which is eternal life, that fear of God which is the beginning of wisdom. To focus attention on these great matters is the task that is undertaken in the chapters on the " Religion of Israel," the " Life and Teaching of Jesus Christ," and the " History and Doctrine of the Apostolic Age." The bearing of this knowledge and fear of God on the relations of man with his neighbour is the concern of Biblical ethics.

The book as a whole will have achieved its purpose if it helps students of the Bible to a fuller and deeper understanding of the Biblical revelation in its historical setting. In order to make it as widely useful as possible the contributors have eschewed the luxury of footnotes. Quotations in foreign tongues are, as far as possible, avoided, and Semitic words and phrases are transliterated.

It is my hope that this new volume will be found of service to lovers of the Bible, who desire to read it in the light of modern knowledge and to receive its message by faith into their hearts. Here and there they will find that there is some overlap between two articles and that divergent views are taken by the different authors. That is inevitable since often there can be no more than a probable solution of some questions, and different minds weigh probabilities differently. No other book has been so widely and so closely studied as the Bible, and none is so worthy of study. From this volume about the Bible, let the reader go anew to the Bible itself and find in it the " lively oracles of God," and our aim will be fulfilled.

H. H. ROWLEY.

February 1963.

CONTENTS

PAGE

PREFACE v

PART I

THE BOOK

I. THE NATURE AND AUTHORITY OF THE CANONICAL SCRIPTURES 3
By JOHN HUXTABLE, M.A., Principal of New College, London.

II. THE BIBLICAL LANGUAGES 11
A. Old Testament Languages.
By E. ULLENDORFF, M.A., D.Phil., Professor of Semitic Languages and Literatures, University of Manchester.
B. The Language of the New Testament.
By GEORGE JOHNSTON, M.A., Ph.D., D.D., Professor of New Testament in McGill University and Principal of United Theological College, Montreal.

III. INTRODUCTION TO THE OLD TESTAMENT . . . 27
By H. H. ROWLEY, M.A., D.D., F.B.A., Emeritus Professor of Hebrew Language and Literature, University of Manchester.
(i) The Law.
(ii) The Former Prophets.
(iii) The Latter Prophets.
(iv) The Writings.
(v) The Canon.

IV. THE INTER-TESTAMENTAL LITERATURE . . . 71
By MATTHEW BLACK, D.D., D.Litt., F.B.A., Professor of Biblical Criticism and Principal of St. Mary's College, University of St. Andrews.
(i) Apocrypha.
(ii) Pseudepigrapha.

V. INTRODUCTION TO THE NEW TESTAMENT . . 90
By G. R. BEASLEY-MURRAY, M.A., M.Th., Ph.D., Principal of Spurgeon's College, London.
(i) The Primitive Christian Tradition and Form Criticism.
(ii) The Synoptic Gospels.
(iii) The Pauline Epistles.

PAGE

(iv) Hebrews and the General Epistles.
(v) The Johannine Literature.
(vi) The Canon.
(vii) Early Non-Canonical Christian Writings.

VI. Literary Forms 123
A. Old Testament Forms.
By James Muilenburg, M.A., Ph.D., L.H.D., D.D., Davenport Professor of Hebrew and Cognate Languages, Union Theological Seminary, New York.
B. New Testament Forms.
By George Johnston.
(i) Categories of Books.
(ii) Form Criticism.

VII. The Transmission of the Text 144
A. Old Testament.
By Bleddyn J. Roberts, M.A., D.D., Professor of Hebrew, University College of North Wales, Bangor.
(i) The Massoretic Text.
(ii) Qumran.
(iii) The Versions.
(vi) Textual Emendation.
B. New Testament.
By Nigel Turner, Ph.D., M.Th., B.D.
(i) The Earliest Copies.
(ii) The Period of Recensions.
(iii) The " Western " Text.
(iv) Copying after Constantine.
(v) Vulgates and New Versions.
(vi) The Last Stage of the Written Text.
(vii) From Erasmus to Westcott and Hort.
(viii) B. F. Westcott and F. J. A. Hort.
(ix) Sequel and Reaction.
(x) Present and Future Editions.

PART II

THE LAND AND THE PEOPLE

VIII. The Geography of Palestine 185
By Denis Baly, B.A., Chairman, Department of Religion, Kenyon College, Gambier, Ohio.
(i) The Physical Features.
(ii) The Climate.
(iii) The Climate and the Way of Life.

PAGE

IX. THE BACKGROUND OF THE BIBLE 205

A. Israel's Neighbours.

By C. J. MULLO WEIR, M.A., D.Phil., D.D., Professor of Hebrew and Semitic Languages, University of Glasgow.

B. The Graeco-Roman World.

By H. H. SCULLARD, F.B.A., F.S.A., Professor of Ancient History, King's College, University of London.

X. BIBLICAL ARCHAEOLOGY 246

By JOHN GRAY, M.A., Ph.D., Professor of Hebrew, University of Aberdeen.

(i) Cradles of Culture: Egypt and Mesopotamia.
(ii) Neighbours of Israel.
(iii) Archaeology and Biblical Events.
(iv) Archaeology and the Culture of Israel.
(v) Archaeology and the Religion of Israel.
(vi) Archaeology and the Literature of the Bible.
(vii) Archaeology and the Text of the New Testament.

XI. THE HISTORY OF ISRAEL 281

By P. R. ACKROYD, M.A., M.Th., Ph.D., Samuel Davidson Professor of Old Testament Studies, King's College, University of London.

(i) Before the Exodus.
(ii) The Exodus and Conquest.
(iii) The Monarchy.
(iv) Exile and Restoration.
(v) The Greek and Roman Periods.

PART III

THE RELIGION OF THE BIBLE

XII. THE RELIGION OF ISRAEL 335

By WALTER HARRELSON, B.D., Th.D., Professor of Old Testament, Vanderbilt University, Nashville, Tennessee.

(i) Patriarchal Religion.
(ii) Moses and Israelite Faith.
(iii) The Tribal League.
(iv) The Kingship.
(v) The Great Prophets.
(vi) Israelite Worship.
(vii) The Wisdom Tradition.
(viii) The Second Temple.
(ix) Israelite Religion and the Christian Faith.

PAGE

XIII. JUDAISM: ITS FAITH AND WORSHIP . . . 381

By MARCEL SIMON, Docteur ès-Lettres, Professor and Dean of the Faculty of Arts, University of Strasbourg.

(i) Fundamental Beliefs.
(ii) Worship: the Temple and Priesthood.
(iii) Worship: the Synagogue.
(iv) Jewish Sects: Sadducees, Pharisees, Zealots.
(v) The Essenes.
(vi) Angelology and Demonology; Philonic Speculation.
(vii) Messianic Beliefs and Eschatology.

XIV. BIBLICAL ETHICS 418

By A. S. HERBERT, M.A., B.D., Professor of Old Testament Literature and Religion, Selly Oak Colleges, Birmingham.

XV. THE LIFE AND TEACHING OF JESUS . . . 436

By H. E. W. TURNER, D.D., Van Mildert Professor of Divinity in the University of Durham and Canon Residentiary of Durham Cathedral.

(i) Sources of Information.
(ii) Chronology.
(iii) The Life of Jesus.
(iv) The Kingdom of God in the Teaching of Jesus.
(v) The Titles of Jesus used in the Gospels.
(vi) The Ethical Teaching of Jesus.
(vii) Jesus and the Church.
(viii) Jesus and the Jewish Law.
(ix) Jesus and the Gentiles.
(x) Conclusion.

XVI. THE HISTORY AND DOCTRINE OF THE APOSTOLIC AGE. 495

By F. F. BRUCE, M.A., D.D., Rylands Professor of Biblical Criticism and Exegesis, University of Manchester.

A. Apostolic History.
(i) The Beginnings of "The Way."
(ii) The Gentile Mission.
(iii) The Gospel in the Roman Empire.
(iv) The Church Outlawed.
(v) Palestinian Christianity.

B. Apostolic Doctrine.
(i) The Primitive Preaching.
(ii) Living Between the Times.
(iii) The Teaching of Paul.
(iv) Christian Apologetic.
(v) Typological Exegesis.

PAGE

(vi) Temple and Priesthood.
(vii) The Hope of Glory.

XVII. WORSHIP IN THE OLD TESTAMENT . . . 523
By N. H. SNAITH, M.A., D.D., Litt.D., formerly Principal, Wesley College, Leeds.
(i) The Age of the Patriarchs.
(ii) The Post-Mosaic Period.
(iii) The Temple.

XVIII. THE ORGANIZATION AND WORSHIP OF THE PRIMITIVE CHURCH 546
By C. W. DUGMORE, M.A., D.D., Professor of Ecclesiastical History, King's College, London.
(i) The Nature of the Church.
(ii) Organization of the Primitive Church.
(iii) Worship in the Primitive Church.

APPENDIX 570
By the late T. W. MANSON, Litt.D., D.D., F.B.A., Rylands Professor of Biblical Criticism, University of Manchester, revised by H. H. Rowley.
Time and the Calendar.
Chronology.
Weights, Measures, and Money.

INDEXES 581
(i) Scripture References.
(ii) Authors.
(iii) General.
(iv) Latin, Greek, and Oriental Words.

MAPS . . . . *at end*

ABBREVIATIONS

ANET = *Ancient Near Eastern Texts* relating to the Old Testament, ed. by J. B. Pritchard.

A.V. = Authorized Version.

BASOR = *Bulletin of the American Schools of Oriental Research.*

BSL = *Bulletin de la Société Linguistique.*

BWANT = Beiträge zur Wissenschaft vom Alten und Neuen Testament.

CQR = *Church Quarterly Review.*

EVV = English Versions.

HAT = Handkommentar zum Alten Testament.

JAOS = *Journal of the American Oriental Society.*

JEH = *Journal of Ecclesiastical History.*

JTS = *Journal of Theological Studies.*

LXX = Septuagint.

OTMS = *The Old Testament and Modern Study*, ed. by H. H. Rowley.

R.S.V. = Revised Standard Version.

R.V. = Revised Version.

PART I
THE BOOK

I. THE NATURE AND AUTHORITY OF THE CANONICAL SCRIPTURES

BY JOHN HUXTABLE

THE Bible is a collection of writings of greatly different antiquity, which is regarded by Christians of all traditions as the standard of faith and the rule of life. The Old Testament, which the Christian Church inherited from Judaism, consists of three main groups of books: the Law, the Prophets, and the Writings. In the Greek MSS., which included also other works, several of which are now called books of the Apocrypha, the order of the books is different from that in the Hebrew. The Greek order has somewhat influenced that followed in the English Bible. It is important to observe that to the Hebrew mind the distinction between history and prophecy was not as clear as it has since seemed to later generations. The New Testament also divides into three portions: there is history, as in the Gospels and Acts; the Epistles disclose what was the apostolic teaching up to the end of the canonical period; and the Revelation stands by itself, apart from such shortish passages as Mark 13, and represents a type of literature, of which there are many non-biblical examples, in which faith in God's final victory over all evil is set forth in an almost bewildering variety of imagery.

How these books came to be regarded as canonical is a fascinating and somewhat puzzling question. The subject is discussed at length in A. Souter's *Text and Canon of the New Testament* (1912, and revised by C. S. C. Williams, 1954). The basic idea of a " canon " is that it is a list of books which may be read in public services; and with this idea necessarily goes that of other books which, though religious and edifying, are not on the list. Such a list would have been compiled as a result of a long process during which the relevant writings secured recognition as specially significant and authoritative. Indeed, such recognition in all probability long preceded canonization; and in fact discussion about the canonicity of a particular book appears to have been concerned with its exclusion from the Canon rather than the possible inclusion within the Canon of some fresh material. As far as the Old Testament is concerned, the Law (Torah) was recognized as canonical before either of the other two of its divisions. In all probability the whole of the Old Testament was so recognized by the time of Christ. The early Church inherited the Old Testament and never questioned its canonicity. Gradually it added thereto a Canon of its own. The sayings of Jesus and accounts of His life, ministry, and (especially) His passion and resurrection, and writings which were believed to derive from the Apostles enjoyed a special status ; and before the end of the second century what we now call the New Testament was widely recognized. The two tests applied in deciding whether or not a book was canonical appear to have been its regular use in public worship and its (supposed) apostolic origin. Certain documents which were eventually included in the New Testament Canon came under suspicion in certain quarters, *e.g.* Hebrews, James, Jude, 2 Peter, 2 and 3 John, and Revelation, while some others, eventually excluded, were temporarily regarded as canonical in some places. The 39th Festal letter of Athanasius (A.D. 367) is the first document we know in which the list of canonical books corresponds precisely with the New Testament as we have it. No doubt behind this lies a gradual process in which the Church believed itself to be guided to recognize as special and authoritative only part of a considerable literature. Such decisions as were made were a sort of recognition of what was already agreed, and not the initiation of any novelty.

The Bible, then, consists of a number of books which the Christian Church came to recognize and continues to recognize as particularly important. This value did not attach to the individual books of the Bible alone, but to the whole of it, in which there was believed to be a unity. This belief persisted through the Christian centuries and is still held, so that, while there is truth in saying that the Bible is more like a library than a book, there is even greater truth in saying that the books of the Bible are even more like one book than they resemble a library. The nature of this unity has been expressed in several ways. It could well be said that Jesus Christ is the unity of the Bible, in that the history recorded is the story of what led up to His coming, of what He said and accomplished, and of what immediately followed from His death and resurrection. Or it could be said that the unity of the Bible consists in its recording the story of the People of God, which is called into being from the time of Abraham to be the agent of God's purpose in the world. It is a tale of misunderstanding and failure as well as of some success, for the Jewish people often mistook their calling to be one of privilege rather than service and so failed to fulfil their missionary vocation. There was, always, however, a remnant who sought to be worthy of that calling ; and "in the fulness of the times" Jesus Christ appeared, and as a result of His ministry, passion and triumph, a New Israel emerged, the Church. Whichever of these two similar ways of describing the unity of the Bible be preferred, it will be seen that in each case there is the conviction that the Bible tells the story of salvation ; and this is taken to be the thread by which all the component parts are held together, so that each part, whatever its individual importance may be, cannot be truly understood apart from its context in the whole.

It is in fact this insistence on history which distinguishes the Bible from the sacred writings of the other great religions. Their Scriptures are indeed part of the spiritual wealth of mankind. In them may be found passages as " inspiring " as a great many in the Bible and perhaps more so than some ; and the moral precepts inculcated in them have in many cases their parallel in Christian Scripture. Yet it is not in its capacity to uplift or to provide moral exhortation that it may be claimed for the Bible that it is unique. What distinguishes it from all other religious literature is that it records the history of a people and the story of a Person through which and in Whom the character of God was revealed and human destiny altered once and for all.

The Bible, then, is important for the Christian Church in that it records the acts of God through which and by which salvation came in Jesus Christ ; and this historical element in the Bible is of the highest importance. If, for instance, it could be proved that there never had been an Exodus, still more, if it could be proved that Jesus Christ was no more than a figment of pious imagination, Christianity would cease to exist in any recognizable form. It might still be possible to maintain some religious sentiment about ideas which have value whether or not the author of them had actually existed ; but that would reduce Christianity to the level of a mystery religion. The importance of the Bible is that it provides reliable information about Jesus Christ, all that preceded Him, the milieu in which He appeared, what He said and accomplished, and what were the beginnings of the consequence of His life and work in the life of the primitive Church. It must be admitted that some doubts may be entertained about details of the general story, and there is a good deal of debate as to the way in which this or that alleged incident is to be understood. There are no grounds whatever for saying that the Bible is free from historical or literal error. What is important, however, is that as a result of thorough scrutiny of the most exacting kind the general reliability of the history recorded in the Bible is beyond real dispute ; and the extreme scepticism of some modern New Testament scholars is likely to be no more than a temporary fashion on the part of those who do not know how well off they are in comparison with those who study antiquities in other fields.

It is claimed, then, that the Bible records "religious facts" by means of which there is conveyed knowledge of God, who is known chiefly by what He has done and in the Person in Whom He was incarnate. It is equally important to recognize what the Bible is not. It makes no claim, for instance, to be a mine of scientific information; indeed, the Biblical writers inevitably and naturally used the language of their times in writing about natural phenomena, and from the point of view of modern science what they wrote is now seen to be in that sense inaccurate. Who now believes in the three-storey universe presupposed by the canonical writers? Who thinks of heaven as "up there" or supposes that Sheol is beneath the earth? Nor do the Biblical writers provide us with the sort of history we should now expect from historians. Their religious interests control their selection of events and the importance attached to them. The Old Testament, for instance, does not give to certain figures, such as Omri, the importance which would undoubtedly have been given them by the "secular" historians of the period. Each person and each event is treated according to the importance they are deemed to have in the religious history which is being recorded. There are, moreover, many facts about the life of Jesus Christ which we should have wished included in a biography of Him; but the Evangelists were not writing biography. Rather, they set out to provide evidence that He was the Saviour of men. In the best sense they were propagandists, seeking to establish a case. This does not detract from the historicity of what is recorded. It merely states the angle from which the history is told; and who can write history but from some angle?

What reason is there to suppose that this particular angle shows us the facts in a true light? How can we be sure that the Biblical writers have not in fact distorted what they set out to record?

To answer such questions we must examine the conviction, shared by Christians of all sorts, though very differently understood among them, that the Bible is inspired. For a great many Christians inspiration has been virtually understood to mean that what the inspired author wrote is free from all error. "All the books and the whole of each book which the Church receives as sacred and canonical were written at the dictation of the Holy Spirit; and so far is it from being possible that any error can co-exist with divine inspiration that not only does the latter itself exclude all error, but excludes and rejects it with the same necessity as attaches to the impossibility that God Himself, who is the supreme truth, should be the author of any error whatsoever." Those words of Pope Leo XIIIth in the Encyclical *Providentissimus Deus* (1893), which reinforce the view of the Council of Trent about three hundred and fifty years earlier, could, as they stand, equally well represent the views of the more extreme conservative Evangelicals. (It must be remembered, however, that the Romanist conception of the role of Tradition in the teaching of the Church provides a room for manoeuvre which these rigid words do not themselves provide.) Such a view of inspiration can only be held if we are prepared also to hold that the Spirit so took charge of the human authors of Scripture that they were also delivered from all error, so that they were " secretaries of the Holy Ghost." Quite apart from the very serious theological question whether the nature of the Gospel itself permits us to think of God so using human personality, most would now hold that a scientific examination of the Scriptures discloses the simple fact that the evidence does not support such a view of inspiration. Errors and inconsistencies there are ; and it seems likely that some of the estimates of population and the reckoning of years (so many thousands died or " forty years ") are inexact. This does not invalidate the general message of Scripture ; it is, however, fatal to any doctrine of inspiration which declares that the sacred writers were preserved from all error. Once this doctrine proved untenable, some fell to the opposite extreme, and held the view that the Scriptures must be inspired because they were inspiring. The spiritual value of certain great religious passages was recognized ; but the doctrine deduced from this recognition did not reckon sufficiently with the fact that as much could be said about a good deal of literature which was not notably sacred, nor did they quite know how to relate this doctrine of inspiration to the less edifying and less spiritually exciting parts of the Bible. So this reaction from inspiration understood as inerrancy raised the question whether the Bible was *uniquely* inspired and whether it was inspired in whole or in part ; and those who held the modern, more liberal, view had also to rethink in what way they could describe the Bible as unique. Were not other sacred writings " inspiring " ? Are there degrees of " inspiringness " ? How are they assessed, and by whom ? If someone claimed to find the Bhagavadgita more inspiring than the Bible, how could he be persuaded to a contrary opinion ? *Chacun à son goût.*

One way of understanding the inspiration of the Bible which avoids these two unacceptable extremes has been found by examining more closely from this point of view the idea that the Bible's purpose is to recount the mighty acts of God for man's salvation and the moral consequences of this story for all mankind. Many, as we have seen, regard this main theme as the principle of the Bible's unity ; and it has been suggested that it is within the character of this main theme that we are to find a clue as to the nature of inspiration. The theme presents a whole range of historical episodes which taken together constitute one whole ; and each episode as well as the entire story itself is so told as to be understood in a particular way. The narration of each important event is, so to say, the account of what " actually happened " and an interpretation of its significance. A young carpenter of Nazareth is nailed to a cross : of all possible interpretations of this event the one given is that this was the supreme act of God for the salvation of the world ; and it is claimed that those who so recorded and interpreted this drama of redemption were enabled to do so by divine illumination : they were given insight. This is in line with what we know of prophetic inspiration in the Old Testament. The prophet, called to speak in the name of the Lord, was given insight into the meaning of what was happening and what therefore would happen in the future. He takes an episode or a series of episodes to which a variety of interpretetations might be attached and gives the " true " interpretation of it, which had been given him from God. Thus the Exodus is regarded as a great act of divine deliverance and the Exile a clear result of divine displeasure. It is not essential to such an understanding of inspiration that the form in which the narrative is recorded should be *verbally* inspired, for what is involved lies deeper than verbal accuracy : insight into the meaning of things, into the activity and so into the nature of God is given. Moreover, the uniqueness of the Bible becomes perfectly clear. It records what is nowhere else recorded. No other sacred literature provides what is given here.

Inspiration is not only a matter of providing the essential record of God's activity with men for their salvation. The story must be read (or heard) and understood : " spiritual things are spiritually discerned." He who runs may read at a certain level of understanding, though he must not expect to understand much at a mere glance. " Full persuasion and assurance of the infallible truth and divine authority (of the Scriptures) is from the inward work of the Holy Spirit, bearing witness by and with the Word in our hearts " (Westminster Confession, art. 5). So it is that we call the Scriptures the Word of God. Through them we are told how He has acted for our salvation. He speaks through what He has done, and actions speak louder than words. We are given insight into the significance of this ancient story, so that what was done for all the world is seen as done " for me." Like Nathan, the

Scriptures can say " Thou art the man." God speaks, and we are given to hear.

Just as there have been differing views about the nature of inspiration, so there have been also about the nature of Biblical authority : the two questions are very closely related. The question of authority, of course, seeks to discover why the Scriptures are to be accepted as a true ; and to this problem there have been given four main answers. The Roman Catholic Church, which, as we have seen, officially takes the view that the Scriptures are inerrant, regards itself as the divinely appointed teacher of all Christian truth, which naturally includes the true interpretation of the Scriptures. According to Romanist teaching, the Scriptures are the written part of a Tradition the oral part of which has been handed down from the Apostles and is now guarded and interpreted by the Church. In the light of this Tradition the Church tells the faithful how to understand the puzzling written Tradition. " It is the Church, the holder of Tradition, that gives life to the dead letter of Scripture " (*A Catholic Commentary on Holy Scripture*, p. 8). On this view the authority of the Bible gives place to the authority of the Church : a man believes the Scriptures because the Church teaches him to do so. There is more truth in this view than many Protestants are prepared to admit ; but they have rejected it partly because they took another view of inspiration. They also considered that the Romanist view of the matter gave the Church an authority over the Bible which in fact the Bible should have over the Church ; for while it is true to say that the Church produced the Bible, it is still more true to say that the Church needs to be judged, reformed and given life by the Word of God, alongside which the Church can never stand *pari passu*, still less in a position of superiority. Traditional Protestantism, therefore, has taken the view that since the Scriptures are infallibly inspired they must be entirely believed. " Every book of it, every chapter of it, every verse of it, every word of it (where shall we stop ?), every letter of it, is the direct utterance of the Most High. The Bible is none other than the Word of God . . . faultless, unerring, supreme " (J. W. Burgon, *Inspiration and Interpretation* [1861], p. 89). Conservative Evangelicals are not as happy with Bishop Burgon as all their fathers were ; but, be that as it may, his words set forth a view of the authority of Scripture which was almost universally held by Protestants until the widespread acceptance of the critical study of the Bible, and in many quarters has persisted since. It is sometimes claimed that John Calvin is the origin of this rigid view of Scripture ; but deeper study of his works, particularly of his commentaries, shows that he cannot be claimed as supporting the literalist view of Scripture. A special feature of his view of authority was that the inward testimony of the Holy Spirit not only enabled men to understand the Scriptures but also led them to obedience. With the rise of the critical study of the Bible and of Liberal Protestantism such a view of the authority of the Bible became untenable for many, and in its place was set what its critics usually regarded as the more nebulous idea that the Scriptures were authoritative only as the individual reader found them so. He recognized truth for what it was in the Scriptures as elsewhere. This emphasis on personal recognition of the truth of Scripture was valuable, although it left a good many problems unsolved, to which the older views had at least given some answer. In particular, it was difficult to see how the exponent of the more modern view reckoned with the place of the Church in the interpretation of Scripture or with the special value of the Scripture as divine revelation. Some kind of reconciliation between these conflicting views may be found, if the Scriptures are regarded as the record of God's acts for man's salvation as made by those who were inspired to see and interpret what was happening, a record which is understood and accepted under the illumination of the Holy Spirit, so that the reader knows what God has done and so may be said to have heard God speak. In that case, the authority of the Bible consists in its capacity to be the vehicle through which the personal authority of God is exercised. It may be thought that the strength of this view lies in its personal quality, which is secured without undervaluing the unique quality of the Scriptures or the place of the Church in the continuing proclamation of the message of the Bible. However that may be, in the last resort what is believed about the authority of the Bible depends entirely on what is taken to be the nature of the Scriptures themselves and the nature of the God to Whom they bear witness.

BIBLIOGRAPHY

C. H. Dodd, *The Authority of the Bible*, 1929; paper-back, 1960.
C. H. Dodd, *The Bible Today*, 1946.
C. W. Dugmore (ed.), *The Interpretation of the Bible*, 1944.
H. Cunliffe-Jones, *The Authority of the Biblical Revelation*, 1945.
A. Richardson and W. Schweitzer, *Biblical Authority for Today*, 1951.
H. H. Rowley, *The Unity of the Bible*, 1953.
A. G. Hebert, *Fundamentalism and the Church of God*, 1957.
J. K. S. Reid, *The Authority of Scripture*, 1957.
R. Abba, *The Nature and Authority of the Bible*, 1958.
J. I. Packer, "*Fundamentalism*" *and the Word of God*, 1958.
J. Huxtable, *The Bible Says*, 1962.

II. BIBLICAL LANGUAGES

(A) OLD TESTAMENT LANGUAGES

By E. Ullendorff

Apart from some sporadic glosses in Aramaic and other Near Eastern languages as well as several Aramaic chapters in Daniel and Ezra, the language of the Old Testament is Hebrew. It is implicit in the naming procedure described in Gen. $2^{19f.}$ (when God brought the animals " unto the man to see what he would call them ") and in the story of the tower of Babel (Gen. 11) that the Old Testament assumed Hebrew to be the original language of mankind. Yet, while we have no knowledge of the precise nature of the language spoken by the Hebrew immigrants into Canaan, it is virtually certain that from a purely linguistic point of view the Old Testament owes more to the vanquished Canaanites than to the conquering Hebrews. The latter are called *'ibhrîm* already in the Patriarchal narratives (Gen. 14^{13}, 40^{15}, etc.), but their language, Hebrew (*'ibhrîth*), is never as such mentioned in the Old Testament. This may, of course, be sheer accident—as must indeed be expected in a corpus of such comparatively limited extent as is represented by the Hebrew Scriptures. The language of the Hebrews is called by Biblical writers either " Jewish "(*yᵉhûdhîth*, 2 Kings 18^{26} ; Isa. 36^{11} ; Neh. 13^{24} ; 2 Chron. 32^{18}) or " the language of Canaan " (*śᵉphath Kᵉna'an*, Isa. 19^{18}). Whether " Jewish " and " the language of Canaan " were really identical has not been fully established, although their identity has, as far as I know, been generally assumed. While the expression " language of Canaan " might have been chosen as the one most likely to be known to the Egyptians (who are being addressed in this Isaiah passage), it is at least conceivable that this reference is to some Canaanite *lingua franca* which may have remained in oral use but was obviously excluded from written sources.

The word " Hebrew," as indicating the language, is first attested in the prologue to Sirach ; it later appears in the New Testament as ἑβραϊστί (Rev. 9^{11} and elsewhere), in Josephus and, though sparingly, in the Talmud. Rabbinical sources prefer " the holy tongue " and similar expressions.

Hebrew has frequently been referred to as a " mixed " language. The justification of this appellation need not be disputed, but one may doubt that it contains much of linguistic value, for in the sense in which this is true of Hebrew it applies to most languages. An early form of Hebrew, or an Hebraic language, had been spoken by the Semitic inhabitants of Canaan who were conquered and partly dislodged by Joshua. This is attested by the evidence of place-names and by the so-called Canaanite glosses in the Tell el-Amarna letters (fifteenth to fourteenth century B.C.). Many of these documents were written by Canaanites and, though composed in a vulgar form of Akkadian, they are full of Canaanite expressions and forms. The data drawn from these glosses are supplemented by a group of Egyptian transcriptions belonging to the second half of the second millennium.

Other extra-biblical sources contributing to our knowledge of Hebrew include ancient Hebrew inscriptions (such as the Gezer calendar, the Siloam inscription, and the Lachish letters), cuneiform transcriptions of Hebrew proper names, comparative Semitics, and the light which later phases of Hebrew throw on the Biblical tongue. Of particular importance are the Ugaritic documents, the Ras Shamra epics of the fourteenth and thirteenth centuries B.C., whose language, style, and poetic structure closely resemble those of the Old Testament. At a much later period, the Dead Sea scrolls provide fresh evidence for palaeographic study and the historical grammar of Hebrew—quite apart, of course, from their intrinsic significance in fields outside the scope of the present survey.

The Old Testament is a book of moderate size, and though it affords us a good view of the language as it appeared in the last millennium B.C., it is, of course, clear that only a relatively small proportion of the original Hebrew literature was allowed to enter the Canon of the Old Testament. From a linguistic point of view this is an irretrievable loss, for the vocabulary of the Old Testament, though not altogether unrepresentative, by no means exhausts the resources which must have been at the disposal of the living language during that period. Even morphologically, not all forms are attested; and in the field of syntax and style, though many variegated specimens are offered, we have samples rather than an inventory of the full resources.

The text of the Old Testament was transmitted in a consonantal skeleton until, in the second half of the first millennium A.D., a body of scribes and systematizers—called Massoretes—superimposed an elaborate network of vowels and accents which have effectively disguised many of the distinctive characteristics which the living tongue must have exhibited. There is no discernible development in the Massoretic pronunciation of Hebrew, and the vocalism applied to the consonants makes Deborah talk in very much the same manner as Daniel or Esther almost a thousand years later. Attempts have at times been made to penetrate through the maze of the Massoretic system and to reconstruct Biblical Hebrew as it was spoken at the time of Isaiah or Jeremiah. While the material is by no means abundant, detailed research based on modern linguistic notions will undoubtedly be able to recover dialectal forms and colloquialisms beyond the hackneyed story of *shibboleth-sibboleth* (Judg. 12[6]). Dialect geography, the influence of social stratification on Biblical Hebrew, the pronunciation of Hebrew by the Samaritans, phonological and morphological aspects of the Dead Sea documents, and other pre-Massoretic materials may well place the study of Hebrew on a different basis altogether.

The language of the Hebrew Scriptures derives much illumination from the later phases of Hebrew which maintain speech-forms as well as lexical and syntactical elements that are accidentally absent from the Old Testament. In this connexion special significance must be ascribed to apocryphal literature, the Mishnah, and early Rabbinic writings ; nor can the poetical and exegetical literature of the Middle Ages or even Modern Hebrew be neglected altogether.

Hebrew is a Semitic language. This trite statement implies that many aspects of Hebrew can be properly evaluated only against the background of the *ensemble* of Semitics. The principal Semitic languages include Akkadian (=Assyrian and Babylonian) in Mesopotamia, Ugaritic, Amorite, Phoenician-Punic, Hebrew-Moabite, and Aramaic in the Syro-Palestinian area, Arabic and South-Arabian in central and south-west Arabia, and Ethiopic in the horn of Africa. The closeness and relationship of the classical Semitic languages to each other and their essential unity (this would not be true of the developed forms of many modern Semitic tongues) had been recognized by Muslim and Jewish grammarians as early as the tenth century.

One of the most characteristic traits of the Semitic languages (and Hebrew prominently shares the features to be enumerated in the following) lies in the special relationship between consonant and vowel. It must not, however, be supposed that the great preponderance of the consonants over the vowels is expressed in numerical terms. Cantineau has found that, while Old Testament Hebrew possesses twenty-one consonant phonemes and six vowel phonemes, their distribution over a consecutive passage is in a proportion of 63% to 37% respectively. Generally speaking, it is true to say that meaning in Semitic reposes on consonants—at least as far as primary semantic distinctions in verbal roots are concerned, for modifications of a grammatical nature are being imparted by vowels which convey meaning-variants and are, therefore, of secondary semantic significance. Thus English *tackle* and *tickle* have entirely different meanings, but Hebrew *ḳāṭal* and *ḳōṭēl* are merely variants of the same root.

Triliterality in Hebrew and Semitic appears to be largely due to the force of analogy. Historically, many triconsonantal words represent, in fact, extensions of originally biconsonantal elements. There are not only the old common Semitic nouns such as *'b* " father," *'m* " mother," *ym* " sea," *dm* " blood," but also a number of " bases " which have been expanded by an additional consonant in initial, medial, or final position: *prd* : *prš* connoting different aspects of " distinguishing," *rḥm* : *nḥm* different aspects of " having compassion," etc. To the same class belong the verbs with identical second and third radicals where the device of gemination was employed to create triconsonantals from original biradicals. This is particularly interesting because one of the fundamental trends in Hebrew and Semitic root composition prevents the appearance of identical or homorganic consonants in verb morphemes. It seems established, therefore, that the original semantic connotation reposed on two radicals and that the third acted merely as a modifier.

The Hebrew and Semitic verb occupies a much more central position within the morphological framework than is customary in other languages. It has a set of simple or derived stems in which formal changes (gemination, prefixes, infixes) correspond to certain semantic variations and express different aspects of the action denoted by the root. The semantic connexions are not always stable or readily identifiable, nor are all the stems attested for any one verb. Perhaps the most complex and disputed problem of Hebrew and Semitic linguistics is the so-called tense system. It appears, however, that the use of the term " tense " is scarcely proper, while its substitute " aspect " is too vague to convey anything of real significance. On a purely formal basis we can distinguish a prefix-conjugation (*tḳṭl*) from a suffix-conjugation (*ḳṭlt*). The former generally indicates an incomplete action, although the so-called conversive *wāw* and certain particles may neutralize even this cautious statement. The suffix-conjugation connotes most frequently completed action or simply a state or condition. The full complexity of the situation can, however, be appreciated only by a comprehensive examination of these " tense " features in all the Semitic languages.

The Hebrew noun falls into a series of patterns which are distinguished by gemination, vowel distribution, preformatives, afformatives, etc. Thus the active participle has the theme *kōtēb,** the passive participle *kātûb,* doubled medial radical denotes professions : *ṭabbāḥ* " cook," prefix *m-* describes local, temporal, instrumental, and abstract meaning-variants : *mapṭēaḥ* " key," *mišpāṭ* " judgment," etc. Hebrew possesses two " genders "—or, more properly, classes : the so-called masculine has no special endings, while the feminine is associated with the morpheme *-t* or *-āh* : *par* " ox," *pārāh* " cow," etc. Genuine feminine gender is not always marked, in relation to the corresponding masculine, by the feminine ending, but is sometimes expressed by means of lexical opposition: *ḥ^a^môr* " he-ass," *'ātôn* " she-ass." Grammatical gender does not invariably correspond either to sex or to the formal constitution of the noun. In the numerals the usual gender categories appear to be inverted.

Hebrew employs three numbers : singular, plural, and dual. The plural is formed by the attachment of external suffixes (internal plurals appear to be limited to South Semitic). The dual is used for the expression of natural pairs, but it also serves, in some Semitic languages, to indicate duality outside these narrow limits. Its extensive use in Old Akkadian, Ugaritic, and Arabic suggests that the restricted employment in Hebrew and elsewhere may be a secondary phenomenon. While the Semitic languages originally possessed three cases (nominative for the subject, genitive for the complement governed by a noun, accusative for the complement governed by a verb), in Hebrew we can discern only faint traces of this state of affairs : the ending *-āh* still denotes motion towards a place and is thus associated with the old adverbial accusative. The construct state is the special form taken by a noun when it is defined by a following genitive or pronominal suffix. In these conditions the *nomen regens* merges with the *nomen rectum* in a single complex whose principal stress falls on the *rectum, i.e.* the " genitival " element. The two nouns cannot ordinarily be separated.

Syntactically, parataxis marks the general type of Hebrew sentence structure which shuns subordination and all elements associated with it. It has sometimes been asserted that this limits the logical range of argument in Hebrew, but that would be mistaking the manner of linguistic expression for the substance of linguistic content—and there appears to be no direct and readily discernible correlation between the two. Poetic form in Hebrew is determined by parallelism and rhythm. The former is a powerful instrument of lexical research, for it illuminates the general range of meaning in parallel hemistichs.

* In this paragraph the system of transliterating certain consonants adopted elsewhere in this volume is departed from, so as to leave clear to the reader the consonants of the stem.—H. H. R.

It is very difficult to form a precise judgment about the substance and the extent of the Old Testament vocabulary. The concentration of subject-matters within a number of areas is such that many other fields are inevitably neglected in the type of literature which was admitted into the canon. This is, however, a reflection on the interest of the redactors rather than on the breadth of the Hebrew lexicon in Biblical times. The fact that words for " blessing " or " whoring " are frequent merely determines the genre of literature collected in the Old Testament, while the absence of words denoting " kitchen " or " niece " does not imply that the Hebrews ate their food uncooked and indulged in nepoticide practices. Even the few small Hebrew inscriptions discovered in Palestine have brought to light a number of words which do not happen to occur in the Old Testament, though they must have been quite common in the every-day language of the Hebrews. Similarly, the Mishnah undoubtedly contains a sizable portion of vocabulary for which the small Old Testament selection had no use. If a word is a *hapax legomenon* in the Bible, it was not necessarily rare in normal use.

It has frequently been stated that Hebrew is " deficient " in adjectives or " poor " in abstract terms, " rich " in emotional vocabulary or " abundant " in expressions for physical action. Such statements are inherently fallacious, because they contemplate one language from the viewpoint of another and judge its resources, lexical and grammatical, in terms of an entirely different linguistic structure. If Hebrew has relatively few adjectives in the Indo-European sense, it is not necessarily short of adjectival potential or equivalent means of expression. The fact that English possesses no *hithpa'ēl* does not materially affect its linguistic efficiency. Judged by its own criteria (the only valid procedure) Biblical Hebrew expresses its actions, its thoughts, and its entire *Weltanschauung* in an effective (and indeed the only possible) way.

In contrast to Hebrew, the word " Aramaic " (denoting the language) does occur in the Old Testament, especially in the well-known passage in 2 Kings 18^{26} where the Assyrian officers are invited by the Jewish negotiators to speak Aramaic rather than " Jewish " within ear-shot of the people on the wall. Several chapters of the Old Testament are written in Aramaic (Dan. 2^{4}–7^{28} ; Ezra 4^{8}–6^{18}, $7^{12\text{-}26}$), partly no doubt to quote documents originally composed in Aramaic, for it had become a language of great international standing and wide diffusion. The solitary verse in Jer. 10^{11} was, perhaps, written in Aramaic to lend authenticity to an injunction addressed to other nations. Linguistically, this verse exhibits quite a number of peculiarities (*l*^{e}*hôm*, *'arḳā'* beside *'ar'ā'*, the Hebrew *'ēlleh*).

In Gen. 31[47], Laban uses the Aramaic *y^e^gar śāh^a^dhûthā'* ("heap of witness") while Jacob calls the place *gal 'ēdh*, the precise Hebrew equivalent.

Biblical Aramaic forms part of a considerable and widespread linguistic group whose earliest manifestations go back to the beginning of the first millennium B.C. and which survives, in a few remnants, to the present day. Shortly before the Christian era Aramaic split into two main branches, West Aramaic (which appears to be a more direct continuation of Old Aramaic) and East Aramaic. Old Aramaic is the language of the inscriptions originating from Damascus, Hamath, Arpad, Sam'al, and Assyria, while classical or Imperial Aramaic (it is to this category that Biblical Aramaic belongs) was used under the Assyrian, Babylonian, and Persian empires (eighth to third century B.C.). The Elephantine and other papyri and ostraca from Egypt are of particular importance.

Hebrew and Aramaic were not mutually intelligible. The Hebrew plenipotentiaries' request (in 2 Kings 18[26]) to talk Aramaic would only have been meaningful if the people at large could not even grasp the gist of the discussion. We know, of course, that Hebrew and Aramaic are not merely "dialectally" distinguished but are each of well-established and fairly clearly delimited linguistic identity. Yet, if the Massoretic text of the Hebrew and Aramaic portions of the Old Testament were a reliable guide to the actual pronunciation of these two languages in the eighth century B.C. we might suppose that their linguistic diversity would scarcely exceed that between, say, Spanish and Italian. It is likely that we may find here further support for the view that the Massoretic redaction of the Hebrew text appears in an Aramaicized form. The Hebrew spoken about the year 700 B.C. must have been very much more sharply differentiated from Aramaic than the Biblical version would allow us to suppose.

While Hebrew and, to a much lesser extent, Aramaic are the languages of the Old Testament, there exist a few traces of other tongues, either in the form of loan-words or technical terms. The Philistines, who were probably the most important among the immigrants who settled along the coast of Canaan, were a non-Semitic people hailing from Caphtor. Among the traces of their language are: *seren* (the heads of their city-states) probably related to *τύραννος*, *ḳôbha'* or *kôbha'* "helmet," *lappîdh* "torch" (from *λαμπάς* [*λαμπάδος*]), etc.

We know a little more about the Moabite language from the famous Mesha stone which commemorates the Moabite king's victory over Israel (2 Kings 3[4]) about the year 830 B.C. From this important inscription it is clear that Hebrew and Moabite must have been mutually intelligible, for the language of the stone differs only very slightly from that of the Old Testament, while its style shows a quite remarkable resemblance with comparable Biblical narratives. A most recent study of the Mesha stele has, in fact, suggested that the inscription might be regarded as a Hebrew text, belonging to a central Palestinian dialect, and drawn up by an Israelite in the service of the king of Moab.

In some parts of the Old Testament a number of non-Semitic words may be detected: there are a few Persian expressions in the books of Esther and Daniel. Egyptian is quoted in Gen. 41[43. 45]: both phrases appear to be genuine, the former an exclamation (perhaps "attention!") and the latter the Egyptian version of Joseph's name.

The Hebrew Scriptures were originally written in the Phoenician—Old Hebrew alphabet from which all alphabetic forms are derived. Later on it came to be substituted by the familiar "square" script of Aramaean origin. Both writing systems run from right to left.

BIBLIOGRAPHY

H. Bauer and P. Leander, *Historische Grammatik der Hebräischen Sprache*, 1918.

H. Bauer and P. Leander, *Grammatik des Biblisch-Aramäischen*, 1927.

C. Brockelmann, *Hebräische Syntax*, 1956.

Brown, Driver, and Briggs, *A Hebrew and English Lexicon of the Old Testament*, Reprint 1951.

J. Cantineau, "Essai d'une phonologie de l'hébreu biblique," *BSL*, 1950.

H. Cazelles, "Hébreu," *Linguistica Semitica*, 1961.

G. R. Driver, *Problems of the Hebrew Verbal System* (Old Testament Studies II), 1936.

G. R. Driver, *Semitic Writing*, 1954.

A. Dupont-Sommer, *Les Araméens*, 1949.

Gesenius, Kautzsch, and Cowley, *Hebrew Grammar*, 1910.

J. H. Greenberg, "The Patterning of Root Morphemes in Semitic," *Word* VI, 1950.

Z. S. Harris, "Linguistic Structure of Hebrew," *JAOS*, lxi., 1941.

F. Rosenthal, *A Grammar of Biblical Aramaic*, 1961.

H. H. Rowley, *The Aramaic of the Old Testament*, 1929.

H. H. Rowley (Ed.), *The Old Testament and Modern Study*, 1951.

S. Segert, "Die Sprache der moabitischen Königsinschrift," *Archiv Orientální*, xxix., 1961.

E. Ullendorff, "What is a Semitic Language?" *Orientalia*, N.S. xxvii., 1958.

E. Ullendorff, "The Knowledge of Languages in the Old Testament," *Bulletin of the John Rylands Library*, xliv., 1961–2.

J. Weingreen, *A Practical Grammar for Classical Hebrew*, 1952.

II. BIBLICAL LANGUAGES

(B) THE LANGUAGE OF THE NEW TESTAMENT

BY GEORGE JOHNSTON

THE New Testament documents, which date from the years A.D. 50 to 150 approximately, were written in Greek, the majority of them by Christians of Jewish stock. It is possible that some portions or some of their sources may have existed originally in Aramaic. There is general agreement that Jesus taught in Aramaic and so all His words come to us in later version. There must therefore be in the New Testament what has to be called "translation-Greek," a factor that has given the language its own peculiarities. Nevertheless it must be emphasized that the language which concerns us here is Greek.

Now Greek belongs to the Indo-European family and it was spoken in various forms by a people who came southward into the land we call Greece (Hellas) and who spread also across the Aegean Sea to the islands and coastland of Asia Minor (Turkey). Later there were colonies of Greeks in Sicily and southern Italy, and as far west as Gaul and Spain. In its heyday Greek was developed by great poets, dramatists, orators, and philosophers into an unsurpassed medium for the expression of artistic and intellectual life. It is distinguished for its subtlety, a tremendous range of refinement, and for a haunting beauty.

Classical Greek is the language of the period from Homer to Aristotle, that is, from about 900 to 300 B.C. There were many dialects, the more significant being Aeolic (the tongue of Sappho the poetess), Attic (the tongue of Pericles and Demosthenes, the Athenians), Doric (the dialect of the poet Pindar), and Ionic, the Greek in which Herodotus, the Father of history, wrote. The outstanding names of this classical age are familiar to most people. There is blind Homer the Ionian, superb epic story-teller in mellifluous verse. There is that trio of tragic dramatists who penetrated so profoundly into the mystery and meaning of human life—Aeschylus, Sophocles, and Euripides. How greatly the outlook of western man has been shaped by the logic of understanding, the moral sense, and the metaphysical enquiries of Socrates, Plato, and Aristotle! But time would fail to mention them all. We recall too that peerless Athens set the tone for Greece. She it was that led the scattered city-states in the historic struggle for liberty against the hosts of Persia. By her maritime supremacy and her genius for commerce, Athens tended to dominate the Greek scene and she made her Attic dialect the most important of them all.

This classical age came to an end, however, and the era following is one during which may be discerned the birth-pangs of a western society in which Israel, Greece, and Rome would be the chief contributors to thought and religion. First the states of Greece were conquered and unified by Philip of Macedon and his greater son, Alexander. Prince Alexander led his Macedonians and Greeks eastward to overrun ancient Egypt and Persia, together with their subject peoples, and to plant the standards within India and Bactria. The inevitable result was the spread of Greek culture and language in a "common form," and that meant the exposure of Jews and others to the humanism, science, fine arts, philosophy, and intellectual liveliness of the Greek spirit. The men of the new age had to be bilingual, using Greek words and, to a lesser degree, Greek idioms in daily life. Of course, the process of acculturation worked equally on the Greek, so that he lay open to oriental customs in government and diplomacy, in human relations, in religion and philosophy. Not least among the eastern forces were those of the Synagogue and later the Church. It was quite early in the period (about 250 B.C.) that Jewish synagogues outside Palestine had to provide a translation of the Holy Scriptures in current Greek (the Septuagint). Even inside Palestine Greek was quite familiar, and Grecizing attempts led to the rebellion against the Syrians. A third element, no less important, was introduced with the emergence of Rome as a world power in the second century B.C. and the Caesars' succession to the empire of Alexander. Christianity was born into a Graeco-Roman world. Its missionaries beyond Palestine had to preach and write in contemporary Greek.

We may regard the six centuries from the death of Alexander to the founding of Constantinople (323 B.C. to A.D. 330) as a unit of history, the Hellenistic-Roman period. The language we are concerned with is called Hellenistic to distinguish it from the dominant Attic of the classical age, or *Koinē* (common) since it was the "common dialect" of Alexander's dominions. So the language of the New Testament is Hellenistic Greek.

As a *lingua franca,* spoken from southern France to the borders of India, *Koinē* was subject to many changes, with some borrowing and influence from Aramaic and Persian, the languages of the Persian Empire. Full discussion of these demands considerable acquaintance with Classical Greek, and all that can be attempted here is to indicate some of the primary differences.

The basis of Hellenistic Greek was Attic and Ionic, and dialectical idiosyncracies are flattened out (*e.g.* double *t* in Attic lost out to double *s*). There was a general simplification in grammar and syntax, although this varied a great deal from author to author. The " dual " forms disappeared. The passive " voice " of the verb tended to absorb the old " middle " (a kind of reflexive). There was considerably less use of the mood called " optative," the mood of wishing, except naturally in religious contexts (" Would God he would come ! "). There were notable changes in the use of the infinitive and it approximated more and more to a verbal noun. The superlative almost died out too.

Hellenistic Greek was freer and less complicated in its structure. Classical is very rich in small words (particles) that act as connectives or to define the different types of clauses and sentences, Hellenistic much less so. Classical prose is notable for its " periods," fairly long and highly integrated sentences, Hellenistic may produce very long sentences, but the periods are less frequent and less elegant. We can detect the influence in the later language of Semitic " parataxis " (setting statements down side by side with little or no subordination of clauses), and consequent overuse of the word " and " (*kai*). There is decided preference in the *Koinē* for reporting in direct discourse. For the intricate cross-relationships of the most sophisticated classical Greek was beyond most of those for whom Greek was a second language ; just as some Europeans cannot quite use the English subjunctive correctly, or as badly-educated British and American people make heavy weather of *should* and *would, like* (as an adverb), *too* meaning very, and so on.

The changes were indeed radical, and they were matched by innovations in vocabulary. There were many new compounds, and some loan-words. Of the latter we may note a Coptic word for *palm branch* (John 12^{13} ; cf. 1 Macc. 13^{51} ; Test. Naph. 5^{4}) ; the Persian *paradise*, and the word for *treasure* in Acts 8^{27} ; from Latin came the terms for *centurion, legion*, and the word correctly translated by the A.V. at Mark 6^{27} as executioner (*speculator*). To illustrate new formations Blass-Debrunner list in §114 of their *Grammar* the more striking compounds and their derivatives in the short letter to Titus.

Hellenistic Greek may be literary or colloquial : the former may be read in Epictetus, Polybius, Plutarch, and Strabo, as well as two important Jewish writers of the first century A.D., Philo and Josephus. The evidence for the latter is to be found in ostraca, inscriptions, and papyri. Among the papyri are accounts and receipts, political decrees, religious documents, and the quite ordinary letters of very ordinary men and women.

How are we to classify the language of the New Testament? Is it literary or colloquial? The answer is: both kinds are to be found, but the predominant linguistic features belong more to the colloquial. Few New Testament writers, if any, composed for the book trade. Few of them were gifted with literary grace, or indeed had such a mastery of Greek idiom that they could aspire to sublime style. There is considerable variety in their achievement: Luke and the author of Hebrews can write exquisite Greek; 1 Peter is well written; James shows the influence of the "diatribe" style (frequent question and answer); St. Paul, poet as well as theologian, and a man reared in the Hellenistic world, rises to superb heights but may fall into obscurity. The late writer who gave us 2 Peter has been classed with those who tried to "Atticize," that is, to imitate what they thought was a better and more classical style. Undoubtedly the worst Greek of all is that of Revelation. John writes in the most uncouth way, he is full of solecisms; at times his words hardly make any sense in Greek, for they are Aramaicized Greek. Yet even John can attain the heights in spite of hideous grammar and syntax!

It was therefore entirely proper for our predecessors to poke among the papyri, inscriptions and ostraca for new light on the usage of the Greek employed in the New Testament. Vulgar speech has provided helpful parallels and even startling new insights. For some seventy-five years scholars have harvested the results, as may be seen from a comparison of the Revised Standard Version or the New English Bible with the Authorized Version. For how many older people now living did the Moffatt New Testament transform the whole picture of the early Church by opening dark places and re-minting the colloquial tone of the sacred writings!

In the first edition of this *Companion* Dr. W. F. Howard, who was one of our foremost authorities in this field, illustrated the range and interest of the new discoveries. Take the legal and financial metaphors of the following:

Heb. 11^{1}, title-deeds (*hypostasis*); 2 Cor. 1^{22} and Eph. 1^{14}, earnest or, better still, down-payment (*arrhabōn*); Phil. $4^{8.\ 15.\ 17\text{-}18}$, reckon (*logizomai*), an account (*logos*), interest or profit (*karpos*), give a receipt (*apechō*). *Apechō* appears also at Matt. $6^{2.\ 5.\ 16}$, and in the perplexing verse, Mark 14^{41}.

Other examples are commonly cited from Acts 18^{24} (*eloquent*, rather than *learned*); 1 Pet. 1^{7}, where the word for *testing* should probably be something like *sterling quality* (but the same word in James 1^{3} clearly refers to *testing*).

Since the first papyri discoveries philologists have re-opened certain issues and returned to older positions in spite of the new evidence. For example: did Zacchaeus cheat or defraud his fellow-Jews by *exacting wrongfully* or by *accusing falsely*? (Luke 19^8). A.V. takes the latter, with support from classical usage as well as the economic and legal situation; A.V. is to be preferred. Did our Lord speak about adding a cubit to one's *height* or some length of time to the *life-span* (Matt. 6^{27})? Probably the former, as the New English Bible understands it. Again, it was once thought that inscriptions from Claros had solved a crux in Col. 2^{18}, where the A.V. translates a difficult *embateuōn* by "intruding" and inserts a negative (by accepting a poorly attested reading). R.V. has "dwelling in," but in the margin suggests "taking his stand upon," which the R.S.V. accepted. *Embateuō* in the inscriptions seems to be a technical term from the mystery cults, perhaps used by the Colossian "heretics," meaning "to enter the sanctuary after initiation." But "entrance into visions" is difficult in the Colossians passage, hence it has been proposed to translate "going into detail about what he has seen," with support from Jewish Greek (2 Macc. and Philo).

We must now return to the question of translation-Greek and to the allied matter of Septuagint (*i.e.* "Biblical") influence on New Testament Greek.

De Zwaan in the *Beginnings of Christianity*, Part I, vol. ii., p. 54 (ed. Lake and Jackson), reminds us that a person who has complete command of current *Koinē* for conversational and literary purposes will not only compose in idiomatic Greek (and may be almost "classical" in his style), but can also translate flawlessly from a Semitic tongue into Greek. Another writer whose native language is Semitic and whose command of Greek is imperfect is likely to put Semitic touches at will into a translation say from Hebrew to Greek, or in imitating (as he might very well do) an existing Semiticized Greek such as the Septuagint Bible contains. If he attempts original composition in *Koinē*, he will produce Semiticized forms. These types, from one with imperfect Greek and long familiar with the Septuagint, are "primary Semitisms" and they are bound to occur. The writer skilled in *Koinē* could also introduce a Semitic flavour, either by conscious imitation of the Greek Old Testament or by adaptation of Semitic sources or by his own sensitivity to a Semitic public. His Semitisms may be called "secondary." The Jewish Christians who wrote our New Testament were soaked in the Septuagint, and their debt to it in language and ideas is tremendous.

The Gospels, however, were composed in Greek (despite C. C. Torrey). They seem to contain translations from original Aramaic in Luke's Infancy Hymns, the Prologue to John, the sayings of Jesus and John the Baptist in John, and also the words of Jesus found to be common to Matthew and Luke. Here we follow the conclusions of Dr. M. Black, who points out how much interpretation is involved in translation (*An Aramaic Approach to the Gospels and Acts*, 2nd ed., pp. 206–11).

Secondary Semitisms abound in the Acts of the Apostles. The author may have translated for himself or incorporated existing versions; at other times the phenomena may be explained by deliberate effort to write a Biblical Greek.

In the light of all this it is evident that the language of the New Testament must be recognized as greatly under the spell of the Semiticized Greek of the Septuagint. Does it then follow that we should define the Christian vocabulary mainly in such Septuagintal terms, plus the new light revealed in and by Jesus Christ? This is the question that has sparked a debate of considerable importance at the present time.

In the first place, it is proper to see that Christian understanding has enlarged the range of meaning in many a familiar Greek expression and occasionally has poured quite new content into it. The living language came uniquely alive within the churches of the Hellenistic world, and does so (*a*) from the context of Jesus' own contribution to thought and from the apostolic interpretations of His significance, and (*b*) from appropriation of Biblical words, idioms, and tone as found in the Bible of the Synagogue. The Church came to possess its own "technical terms." This may be illustrated by the following words: *agapē*, love; *baptisma*, baptism; *charis*, grace; *ekklēsia*, assembly, meaning church; *hodos*, way, in the ethical sense derived from Christian revelation; *kosmos*, the world as an order of human life in rebellion against God; *pistis*, faith; *skandalon*, stumbling block; *skandalizō*, to discourage a possible convert or to encourage a believer to backslide. And the following phrases: *ho huios tou anthrōpou*, Son of Man (a most un-Greek piece of Greek!); *hē basileia tou theou*, the Kingdom or Rule of God (which needs a whole volume to explain it); and *hē dikaiosunē tou theou*, the righteousness of God (which requires a tome on Pauline Theology to begin to do justice to its range and glory). *Apolutrōsis*, redemption, is another distinctive term that comes readily to mind. All these are to be understood only within a truly Christological context.

But the words are still Greek! We must needs be wary lest we go too far in reaction from those who insist that New Testament Greek is fundamentally the colloquial *Koinē*. Walter Bauer, supreme among lexicographers, demonstrates how, as new evidence from contemporary, secular Greek comes in, words supposed to be Biblical turn out to be current

Koinē, lying ready to Christian hands. I take a list of words that Nigel Turner affirms to be thoroughly Christian, owing almost nothing to vulgar Greek. All of them have some currency in religious contexts, and none of them can safely be said to be purely Christian at all:
adelphos, brother (member of a religious fraternity); *parousia*, advent (of a divinity) or visit (of a king), with consequent effects on either the dating of an era or the mere imposition of taxes; *koinōnia*, fellowship or communion (*e.g.* at a common meal about one table, where "friends" assemble and yet some are too selfish to recognize the rights of the others: cf. 1 Cor. 11 and the use of "friends" in John); *aiōnios*, eternal (of God or a kingdom or of life); *apostolos*, apostle or messenger (from divine beings); *episkopos*, overseer or, technically, bishop (in the temple of Apollo at Rhodes or as officer in a cult association); *presbuteros*, elder (civic or religious official); *Sōtēr*, saviour (of many divinities and emperors; cf. "gods many, and lords many," 1 Cor. 8[5]); *euangelion*, good news or Gospel (of an imperial god). So with the verb to "proclaim good news."

Professor James Barr rightly argues that the cult of the "word-study" may have gone too far. Beware of etymological fallacies! The new religious ideas were conveyed in sentences or larger complexes. But the novelty and power of Christian faith seldom reside in the words as such (*The Semantics of Biblical Language*, 1961).

The fact is that the study of Greek is still of first-rate importance for the exegesis of Scripture. There need be no fear that the Semitic or, more exactly, the Old Testament contribution will be undervalued as a result. For the early Christian world, Palestine as well as Asia Minor and Europe, was saturated by a syncretism of Greek and Semitic language and thought. Was it not providential that the Aramaic Word became a Greek Word, with its universalism and humanism? Did it not promote Mission, and win the intellectuals? In our own generation we have a like task throughout the world and among thinkers; and for it our basic New Testament documents are Gospels, Letters, and Apocalypse in Greek.

BIBLIOGRAPHY

F. Blass and A. Debrunner, *A Greek Grammar of the New Testament and Other Early Christian Literature*, tr. and ed. by R. W. Funk, 1961. Other *Grammars* by E. G. Jay; J. G. Machen; and D. F. Hudson ("Teach Yourself").

W. Bauer, *A Greek-English Lexicon of the New Testament and Other Early Christian Literature,* tr. and ed. by W. F. Arndt and F. W. Gingrich, 1957.

A. Deissmann, *Bible Studies,* 2nd ed., 1909.

J. H. Moulton and G. Milligan, *The Vocabulary of the Greek Testament,* 1914–29.

Bible Key Words, tr. from G. Kittel and G. Friedrich, *Theologisches Wörterbuch zum Neuen Testament,* 1933-

C. H. Dodd, *The Bible and the Greeks,* 1935.

C. F. D. Moule, *An Idiom Book of New Testament Greek,* 1953.

M. Black, *An Aramaic Approach to the Gospels and Acts,* 2nd ed., 1954.

T. Boman, *Hebrew Thought Compared with Greek,* 1960.

J. Barr, *The Semantics of Biblical Language,* 1961.

B. M. Metzger, art. on the Language of the New Testament, in *The Interpreter's Bible,* vol. vii., 1951.

N. Turner, art. on the Language of the New Testament, in *Peake's Commentary on the Bible,* ed. by M. Black and H. H. Rowley, 1962.

III. INTRODUCTION TO THE OLD TESTAMENT

By H. H. Rowley

The collection of literature which we know as the Old Testament came into existence over a long period, and the task of defining the date of origin and the process of compilation of the various books is by no means easy, and cannot be carried through with certainty. The arrangement of the books in our Bible is different from that of the Hebrew Bible, and since it was in the Hebrew form that the collection came into existence, we shall follow the order of the Hebrew Bible. Here they are divided into the Torah, or Law, the Prophets (sub-divided into the Former and the Latter Prophets), and the Writings. The Law consists of the five books of the Pentateuch ; the Former Prophets of Joshua, Judges, Samuel, and Kings ; the Latter Prophets of Isaiah, Jeremiah, Ezekiel, and the Twelve (*i.e.* the Minor Prophets) ; the Writings of Psalms, Proverbs, Job, the Five Rolls (Song of Songs, Ruth, Lamentations, Ecclesiastes, Esther), Daniel, Ezra-Nehemiah, Chronicles. Some variations of order within one of the major divisions are found in the manuscripts.

(i) THE LAW

Traditionally the first five books of the Bible were believed to have been written by Moses, but the Bible itself nowhere in the text of these books makes any claim that the Pentateuch was composed by Moses, and there are few scholars today who accept the tradition. The reasons for its rejection can only be briefly indicated.

(a) *Anachronisms*. The death of Moses is recorded in Deut. 34, while the statement that " the Canaanite was then in the land " (Gen. 12^{6} ; cf. 13^{7}) implies a later age. Gen. 14^{14} refers to the city of Dan, which did not receive its name until after the death of Moses (Judg. 18^{29}). Gen. $36^{31ff.}$, which record the kings of Edom before there was a king in Israel, carry us down to the time of Saul. All of these passages could be regarded as later glosses and additions.

(b) *Doublets*. Beersheba is said to have received its name from a covenant between Abraham and Abimelech (Gen. 21^{31}), and again from a covenant between Isaac and Abimelech (26^{33}) ;

Luz is twice renamed Bethel by Jacob (28^{19} and 35^{15}), and his own name is twice divinely changed to Israel (32^{28} and 35^{10}). Hagar twice leaves her mistress, once before Ishmael's birth ($16^{6ff.}$) and once after Isaac's ($21^{10ff.}$). On both occasions Sarah's jealousy was the cause, and on both the crisis came near a well in the wilderness, where an angel appeared and promised greatness for Ishmael. Abram passed his wife off as his sister in Egypt ($12^{10ff.}$) and again in Gerar ($20^{1ff.}$), and later Isaac deceived the same king of Gerar in the same way ($26^{6ff.}$). It is more probable that these are variant traditions of single incidents than that the incidents were duplicated.

(c) *The Divine Names in Genesis.* In Ex. $6^{2f.}$ we read "I am Yahweh, and I appeared unto Abraham, unto Isaac, and unto Jacob as El Shaddai, but by my name Yahweh was I not known unto them." In agreement with this we find in Gen. 17^{1} and 35^{11} the divine announcement to Abraham and Jacob "I am El Shaddai"; but in disagreement with it there are other passages where the name Yahweh is put into the mouth of the patriarchs and others ($15^{2, 8}$, 16^{2}, 24^{31}), of angels (18^{14}, 19^{13}), or of God Himself in addressing Abram (15^{7}) and Jacob (28^{13}).

(d) *Discrepant Narratives.* There are several cases of disagreement in Genesis. Some are found in separate narratives and some in what appears to be a single account. In Gen. 1 and 2 we have two irreconcilable accounts of creation. According to the first, God created heaven and earth, then vegetation and animal life, and lastly man. According to the second, Yahweh God formed man out of the dust of the ground and set him in the Garden of Eden. Then He formed all the animals, and lastly woman. In the one case man and woman are said to have been created together, after the animals, and in the other separately, the one before, and the other after, the animals. Again, in the account of the Flood, we read in Gen. $6^{19ff.}$, $7^{8f.}$ that all the animals were taken into the Ark in pairs for their preservation, while in $7^{2f.}$ Noah is bidden to choose the clean beasts and birds by sevens and the unclean by twos; and in 7^{12} the waters are said to have lasted forty days, whereas in 7^{24} the period is a hundred and fifty days. In the narrative of Joseph's expulsion, his brothers are said to have sold him to a caravan of Ishmaelites ($37^{27, 28b}$) and beside this we are told that he was kidnapped by Midianites (37^{28a}). Both Midianites (37^{36}) and Ishmaelites (39^{1}) are said to have sold him to Potiphar.

Nor are disagreements limited to Genesis. In Ex. 25–31 Moses is instructed to make the Tabernacle, and in 35–40 he repeats the instructions and it is made. But in the interval we read of another Tent (33^{7-11}), of an altogether simpler character. That this was not a temporary Tent, to be used till the other was prepared, is clear from the fact that it continues to figure in the subsequent history (Num. 11^{16-30}, 12^{4}). According to the one account, the Tent was elaborate in construction and furnishing, requiring for its care more than 8,000 Levites (Num. 1^{49-53}, 3, 4), while its position was always in the centre of the camp, both in travelling and in resting (Num. 2); according to the other, it was simple, requiring for its care a single Ephraimite, while its position was outside the camp and afar off. Again, in Num. 13f. we have two accounts of the spying of Canaan combined. In the one the spies went to Rehob, in the extreme north (13^{21}), and reported that the land was impoverished (13^{32}), while two spies, Joshua and Caleb, calmed the people ($14^{6f.}$) and were excepted from the punishment (14^{30}); in the other, the spies reached only Hebron (13^{22}), and reported that the land was fertile (13^{27}, $14^{8f.}$), while only Caleb is mentioned as dissenting from the majority (13^{30}, 14^{24}).

(e) *Discrepant Laws.* Disagreements are also found in the legal sections of the Pentateuch. Thus, Ex. 20^{24} commands that an altar shall be erected to Yahweh in every place which He shall appoint, while Deut. 12^{14} limits the offerings of sacrifice to one sanctuary. According to Deut. 18^{7} any Levite might offer sacrifice, whereas Ex. 28^{1} limits the right to Aaron's descendants. The Feast of Tabernacles is a seven-day feast in Deut. 16^{15}, but an eight-day feast in Lev. 23^{36}. In Ex. $21^{2ff.}$ it is enacted that a Hebrew male slave must be released in the seventh year, but it is explicitly stated (v.^{7}) that a female slave is not entitled to release, while Deut. 15^{12} declares her equally entitled to release.

(f) *Theological Differences.* Some passages are marked by a naïve anthropomorphism. Anthropomorphism is nowhere entirely eliminated in the Bible, and God is represented as speaking to men, and hearing and seeing men. What is here referred to, however, is the naïve anthropomorphism, which represents God as forming man from the dust of the ground and breathing into his nostrils (Gen. 2^{7}), planting a garden (2^{8}), in which He later walks in the cool of the day (3^{8}), building woman from the man's rib ($2^{21f.}$), and making coats of skin and clothing the first couple (3^{21}). In the Flood narrative He shuts Noah in the Ark (7^{16}), and smells the sweet savour of his sacrifice (8^{21}). All this is alien to the first account of the creation, which avoids anthropomorphism, save for the reference to the image of God ($1^{26f.}$), and represents creation as achieved by the mere fiat of God. There are also passages which avoid the cruder anthropomorphism, but represent divine revelation as given through dreams (Gen. 20^{3}, 28^{12},

$31^{11.\,24}$, $37^{5.\,9}$, 40^{5}, 41^{1}), and angels (Gen. 21^{17}, 22^{11}, 28^{12}, 31^{11}, 32^{1}).

(g) *Stylistic Differences.* Deuteronomy is marked by an ornate, rhetorical style absent elsewhere from the Pentateuch. In the other four books there are many passages marked by an equally strongly characterized formal and repetitious style, and others by great simplicity. Even the reader of the Old Testament in translation can appreciate these differences, but in Hebrew there are lexical differences which make still more distinct these three main styles. Lesser differences can be found within the simpler narratives, though their general similarity makes separation much harder.

If we confined our view to Genesis, we might suppose that this evidence is not irreconcilable with Mosaic authorship, but that Moses could have used older diverse traditions or documents. Against this we may note : (*a*) that the same literary styles as are found in Genesis appear in the later books of the Pentateuch ; (*b*) that if Moses found the name Yahweh freely used in older sources, he could hardly have supposed that it first came to Israel through himself ; (*c*) that the disagreements concern not only the pre-Mosaic period, but the Mosaic, including events in which Moses appears as a leading actor ; (*d*) that contradictions are found in the laws Moses is represented as issuing.

It is often supposed that the case of Pentateuchal criticism can be shattered by the demonstration that we cannot depend on the accuracy of the transmission of the divine names in the Hebrew text. This supposition ignores the considerations (*a*) that whether we have sufficient evidence to *analyse* the sources or not, Ex. $6^{2f.}$ and the texts above cited clearly demonstrate the *use* of at least two sources ; and (*b*) that the clue of the divine names forms but one of many clues, and that it cannot be employed beyond Ex. 6, since all the sources employ the name Yahweh thereafter. It should be added that the general reliability of the transmission has been established by Skinner (*Divine Names in Genesis*, 1914).

Reference has been made to the repetitious formality of style that marks much of the Pentateuch. Using this clue, we can separate a group of passages, containing most of the genealogical sections of Genesis, the first account of creation, and a large portion of the legal and ritual sections of the Pentateuch. Owing to this last characteristic, it is usually called the Priestly Code, or P. With the exception of one instance at Bethel (Gen. $35^{9ff.}$), it contains no stories of theophanies, and knows nothing of angels to mediate between God and man. It records no erection of altars by the patriarchs, and contains no evidence of sacrifice having been offered before the consecration of Aaron. Its author apparently regarded sacrifice, not as man's spontaneous offering to God, but as God's ordinance, which could not rightly be offered before the ordinance had been given. It represents Moses as having received the revelation of the name Yahweh as the name of Israel's God, and hence does not use the name in the earlier narrative.

Having separated this source, we find in the remaining material some of the pairs of stories above referred to. Separating these by the clue of divine names, we find other differences of vocabulary and style marking the two groups of narratives, despite their general similarity. We also find differences of outlook and interest. The source that uses the name Yahweh in Genesis is called the Yahwistic (Jehovistic), or J source, while that which, like P, uses only Elohim (God) in Genesis, but that is distinguished from P by its style, is called the Elohistic, or E source. The J source gives a sketch of human history from the creation, and represents the patriarchs as sacrificing, without the need of priest, under sacred trees, by wells or stones. Simple anthropomorphism abounds in it, and though occasionally angels represent Yahweh they are not characteristic of this source. It betrays a special interest in the south. It is Judah who takes the lead in the Joseph story, and Abraham's residence is at Hebron.

The E source is much shorter, and begins with Abraham. Like P, it dates the beginning of God's worship under the name Yahweh among the Israelites in the days of Moses (Ex. 3^{15}), and thereafter, though there is still a preference for Elohim, Yahweh is freely used in its narrative. Its anthropomorphism is less strongly marked than J's, and there is a greater fondness for dreams and angels. It delights in scenes of blessing and farewell (Gen. 27, 48, 50), and represents the patriarchs as offering sacrifice, and presents them somewhat more grandly than does J. It appears to be chiefly interested in the north. Reuben takes the lead in the Joseph story, and in the Mosaic age the Ephraimite Joshua is particularly prominent. In the Jacob stories Bethel and Shechem figure largely, and while in the Abraham story the patriarch is associated with the southern Beersheba, we learn from Am. 5^5, 8^{14} that in the eighth century B.C. northern Israelites still went thither on pilgrimage. Hebron, on the contrary, is unmentioned. It should, however, be emphasized that it is often very difficult to separate J and E, and the symbol JE is employed when it is impossible, or unnecessary, to effect the separation.

The remaining source to which we have referred is confined to Deuteronomy, which consists almost wholly of material from this source. Hence it is called the Deuteronomic, or D source. Apart from its rhetorical style, concern for the purity of Yahwism marks it. It demands the elmination of all shrines save one, and limits priestly rights to the Levites, though it knows no distinctions within the tribe. It delights in historical retrospect, but only as a basis for moral exhortation. It has deep humanitarian interest, and frequently commends the poor and helpless to the mercy of men.

In determining the order and date of these sources we begin with D. 2 Kings 22 f. record the finding of a Law-book in the Temple in the eighteenth year of Josiah (621 B.C.), and the religious reform that followed. The book apparently contained legal sections and exhortations, and curses on those who disregarded it. The reforms it led to were the centralization of worship, the destruction of idols, sacred pillars (*maṣṣēbhôth*), and posts (*'ᵃshērîm*), the suppression of sacred prostitution, and the celebration of the Passover in Jerusalem. The Law-book would appear to have been smaller than the Pentateuch, and it was almost certainly Deuteronomy, or a part of it, since here alone do we find sufficient to account for every item of the story. If we examine the history from the Conquest to Josiah's reign, we find no evidence of acquaintance with the special provisions of Deuteronomy. In the premonarchical period sanctuaries were common, and even Samuel was conscious of no impropriety in sacrificing in several places. Nor did the building of Solomon's Temple bring any attempt at centralization, while Elijah, so far from advocating such a policy, complained that Yahweh altars had been broken down, and himself repaired one on Carmel. In Hezekiah's reign, indeed, there was an attempt at centralization, and Sellin at one time held that Deuteronomy was the basis of that attempt. Since there is no mention of any book as the basis of that reform, however, it is more likely that Deuteronomy was written later, during Manasseh's reign, and that it embodied the lessons of the earlier failure, and thought out the implications of centralization. During this long reign, which was a period of reaction, providing no opportunity for reform, the book was lost and forgotten until it was discovered in 621 B.C. Some scholars (including Sellin at a later date) have thought it was written in Josiah's days, shortly before its "discovery." This is unlikely, since its provision that the country Levites could share in the ministry at the central sanctuary (Deut. 18^{7}) was not put into effect (2 Kings 23^{9}), and it is improbable that the Temple authorities had any hand in the preparation of a law which they successfully resisted.

That J and E are earlier than D can hardly be disputed, while P is as certainly later. It was formerly held that P was the oldest of the sources, but Graf, Wellhausen, and Kuenen so firmly established the view that it is the youngest that it has not been seriously challenged since. As E displays a special interest in northern Israel, it was probably composed before the fall of that kingdom. Moreover, we find by a comparison of the narrative sections of the sources that D shows a knowledge of JE, but ignorance of P. Thus, whereas in Num. 13 f. P represents the spies as journeying to Rehob, and Joshua and Caleb are exempted from the general punishment, while JE represents the spies as reaching only Eshcol, near Hebron, and Caleb alone is exempted, in D we find Eshcol given as the limit of the spies' journey, and Caleb alone is exempted (Deut. $1^{24, 36}$).

Even clearer is D's acquaintance with the legal sections of JE and ignorance of P's. Indeed, D seems to be largely a revision of the laws of JE (often quoted verbatim) in the interests of the centralization of the cultus. It is to be noted that JE allows many altars (Ex. 20^{24-26}), and this was the unchallenged practice until Josiah's reform, save for the brief duration of Hezekiah's reform. D contends for the principle of centralization, and enjoins the destruction of all rival shrines. P assumes the centralization for which D contends. On the priesthood JE says nothing, since neither J nor E recognizes a priestly tribe. D, however, recognizes only Levites as priests, but places all members of the tribe on the same footing. In P we find a distinction between ordinary Levites, who occupy a subordinate place in the Temple service, and the family of Aaron, which alone is entitled to specifically priestly privileges, while at their head stands a hereditary high priest, who nowhere appears in D. The legislation of P was followed in post-exilic times, down to the fall of the Jewish state, and we may therefore say that the known development of practice confirms the conclusion to which the study of the codes leads, that D is intermediate between JE and P.

It has been noted above that in one particular the law of D was not put into effect. The book of Ezekiel rationalizes this violation of D's law. In its sketch of the ideal state of the future, only the priests the Levites, *the sons of Zadok,* are allowed full priestly rights in the sanctuary, because they kept the sanctuary of Yahweh when Israel went astray, while the Levites who went astray are punished by being reduced to menial service in the Temple. By non-Zadokites Ezekiel plainly means the country priests, who had failed to establish their equality with the Zadokite, or Jerusalem, priesthood, but who were now to be brought in on a lower footing. Equally plainly Ezekiel was unacquainted with the law of P, but provides a stepping-stone between D and P. This means that not only was P's law regulative only of post-exilic practice, but that it was of post-exilic promulgation. This does not mean that everything in it was of post-exilic origin, since in any re-codification of usage much that is ancient will inevitably survive, the older usage being eliminated only where it conflicts with the principles the re-codification is intended to serve.

It is generally believed that the law of P was first promulgated by Ezra (Neh. 8) in 444 B.C. or 397 B.C. (see below, pp. 66f.). Ezra's law appears to have agreed with P's in requiring an eight-day celebration of the Feast of Tabernacles (Neh. 8^{14-18}), instead of D's seven-day celebration (Deut. 16^{13}), while the arrangement of worship set forth in Neh. 10^{34} is that of P, and the Temple tax (Neh. 10^{32}) appears only in P (Ex. $30^{11ff.}$). How long before Ezra brought this code to Jerusalem it had been composed we have no means of knowing, save that it was later than Ezekiel. It may have been known for some time before he brought it, but first put into effect by Ezra under the authority of the Persian king.

As between J and E, the former seems the more primitive; yet it cannot be earlier than the days of the monarchy. For it was not until the period of the monarchy that Judah and Israel came into the stream of a common life, and while J appears to have been written in Judah, and to display a special interest in the south, it is a corpus of Israelite, and not merely Judahite, traditions. Moreover, Gen. 15^{18} refers to the traditional boundaries of Solomon's kingdom (cf. 1 Kings 4^{21}). Further, the J source seems to be continued in Joshua, and to have contained an extract from the book of Jashar (Josh. 10^{13}). Since this book was not compiled before the days of David (cf. 2 Sam 1^{18}), the J source was at least as late, while the language of Josh. 6^{26}, which is also assigned to J, would seem to point to the ninth century B.C., when Jericho was rebuilt in the days of Ahab (1 Kings 16^{34}). Hence J is commonly dated 900–850 B.C.

That E is younger is generally agreed, though it is certainly older than the fall of Samaria. Joseph's dreams reflect the sovereignty of his house, while Balaam's oracles imply Israel's prosperity. Moreover, the Gilead covenant (Gen. $31^{44ff.}$) between Israel and Aram would suggest that the long struggle between the two peoples was past. On these grounds E is commonly assigned to the prosperous reign of Jeroboam II., *c.* 800–750 B.C.

The process of combination of the sources can only be conjectured. J and E may have been first combined, and D added at a later date, the material of this work then having been inserted in a framework which P supplied, and the whole process having been completed soon after Ezra's promulgation of the law. At each stage, the editor's hand was responsible for slight additions or modifications, and especially for the joins. It is not to be supposed that it is possible to be certain to which source every verse of the Pentateuch belongs. Scholars earlier essayed the meticulous and exact analysis of every word. But no writer's peculiarities of style, or special ideas, are displayed in every sentence he writes. Nor should we forget, in our dissection of sources, the final compiler of the Pentateuch, who used these sources to trace the divine hand in the story of the establishment of his people and to express his faith that the sacred law of his own day expressed the will of God for his people, and that it derived from the God Who revealed Himself to Moses on Sinai.

We must not omit to observe that each of these four sources itself had a history, and the compilers of each drew on older sources which carry us back much nearer to the time of Moses than the earliest of the four. The many poetical fragments which were incorporated in them were doubtless taken over from other sources, written or oral, and beyond these J, E, D, and P seem to have embodied other older sections, or to have received later additions. It is usual to distinguish in J an older element, J_1, and a younger element, J_2. Eissfeldt argued for an expanded J_1 as a separate source, which he called the Lay source, or L. Morgenstern and Pfeiffer differently delimited what they separated as the earliest source, the one regarding it as a Kenite source, or K, dating from *c.* 900 B.C., and the other regarding it as an Edomite source, or S, dating from the tenth century B.C. To the original D, which probably consisted of Deut. 12–26, 28 only, successive additions were made by other members of the same school, especially chaps. 5–11 and 1–4. P, on the other hand, embodied a considerable earlier section, called the Holiness Code, or H. This stands in Lev. 17–26. It is generally held to be slightly later than D, but Oesterley and Robinson regard it as slightly earlier. H and D are independent of one another, and H has affinities with Ezekiel. Von Rad analysed the whole of P into two separate strands.

Something more should be said about the poetical passages embodied in the Pentateuch. Some of these may have been taken over from oral tradition (cf. Num. $21^{27ff.}$), but it is specifically stated that one was extracted from a book (Num. $21^{14f.}$). The poems preserved are of various kinds: (*a*) tribal and local songs, as the Song of Lamech (Gen. $4^{23f.}$), the Moabite Sites (Num. $21^{14f.}$), the Song of the Well (Num. $21^{17f.}$), the Song of Heshbon and Sihon (Num. $21^{27ff.}$); (*b*) blessings and curses, as the Blessing and Curse of Noah (Gen. 9^{25-27}), the Blessing of Melchizedek (Gen. $14^{19f.}$), the

Blessing of Rebekah (Gen. 24^{60}), Isaac's Blessing of Jacob (Gen. $27^{27ff.}$), Isaac's Curse of Esau (Gen. $27^{39f.}$), Jacob's Blessing of Joseph's Sons (Gen. $48^{15f.}$), the Blessing of Jacob (Gen. 49), the Priestly Blessing (Num. $6^{24ff.}$), the Ark Formula (Num. $10^{35f.}$), the Balaam Oracles (Num. 23 f.), the Oracle on Amalek (Num. 24^{20}), the Oracle on the Kenites (Num. $24^{21f.}$), the Oracle on Assyria (Num. $24^{23f.}$), the Blessing of Moses (Deut. 33) ; (*c*) sundry oracles, as Rebekah's Oracle (Gen. 25^{23}), the Oracle on Moses (Num. 12^{6-8}) ; (*d*) national songs, as The Song of Moses (Ex. 15^{1-19}) and Miriam (Ex. 15^{21}), the Oath against Amalek (Ex. 17^{16}) ; (*e*) a prophetic lyric, the Song of Moses (Deut. 32).

The Blessing of Melchizedek is embodied in a chapter which stands outside the main Pentateuchal documents, and it has been held to be a late addition to the Pentateuch. Recent writers have tended to find in it an ancient fragment which was taken into the work, and it has been held that it dates from the time of David's capture of Jerusalem from the Jebusites.

The Blessing of Jacob is in part a very ancient poem. It consists probably of material from more than one source, since a double motif appears in the various oracles, sometimes emblematic and sometimes etymological. Neither runs through the whole, and in some parts we find one and in some another, and in yet others we find both or neither. Parts of this composition may go back to the pre-monarchical period. The Blessing of Moses, on the other hand, is younger. It is commonly ascribed to the period of Jeroboam II., though Jeroboam I. has also been suggested. Sellin ascribed it to the period of the Judges, but the present writer thinks rather of the period of Saul. For the reference to Benjamin (v.^{12}) which is often taken to refer to the Temple as situated within the borders of the tribe of Benjamin, seems more likely to refer to Saul as the leader supplied by that tribe. It is unlikely that a poem written after the Disruption would glory in Benjamin's possession of the Temple and at the same time lament Judah's isolation from the other tribes (v.^{7}), since Jerusalem was then reckoned to belong to Judah and not to Benjamin. But until the emergence of Saul Judah had not been brought into the stream of the life of the northern tribes, though its kinship with these tribes was recognized.

The Balaam Oracles have often been held to be post-exilic, but again opinion is moving to earlier dates, and Albright has maintained that they may be the work of a twelfth century diviner.

The Song of Miriam is generally held to be a contemporary song of triumph composed at the time of the crossing of the Red Sea, but the Song of Moses which precedes it is thought to be a later expansion of it. Its Deuteronomic phraseology and the thought of a single sanctuary (v.[17]) would seem to carry us to the period of Deuteronomy, or at least to that of Hezekiah.

The Song of Moses is commonly assigned to the period of the exile, since its phraseology is reminiscent of Jeremiah, Ezekiel, and Deutero-Isaiah, and its thought is characteristic of the prophets. It is clearly long after the time of Moses, since Israel is settled in Canaan and demoralized by Canaanite religious influence and chastised by calamity for its defection. The value of the poem lies in its religious message, rather than in its date and authorship.

That a history lies behind the legal sections of the Pentateuch may be particularly readily supposed, since much ancient usage is embodied in any codification. Modern study, analogous to that of the *Formgeschichte* school in New Testament criticism, has attempted to get behind our present codes by studying the forms of the commands. Thus Alt has argued that the casuistic law stems from a Canaanite background, while the apodictic law is essentially Israelite and Yahwistic.

To this whole conception of the development of the Pentateuch there have been a number of challenges, though none can be said to have secured any considerable following. From two sides there was a strong attempt to overthrow the seventh century dating of Deuteronomy, Oestreicher and Welch arguing that it was much older than is generally allowed, and Hölscher and Kennett seeking to bring it down to the post-exilic age. Robertson attributed the compilation of the Pentateuch to the time of Samuel, supposing that the first four books were compiled from materials drawn from the various shrines, while Deuteronomy was composed by a committee presided over by Samuel. Löhr argued that there was never an independent source P, and Volz and Rudolph that there was never an independent source E. Mowinckel, on the other hand, would carry the E source back to the beginning of Genesis, instead of to the time of Abram only.

Noth detached Deuteronomy from the Pentateuch, and in this he has been followed by a number of writers, who regard Deuteronomy as the opening part of the Deuteronomic history contained in the Former Prophets. That these historical books were edited by men who were influenced by Deuteronomy has long been recognized, but there is no evidence that Deuteronomy and these books were ever issued as a single whole, and the long interval between the composition of Deuteronomy in the early part of the reign of Manasseh and the compilation of the books comprising the Former Prophets does not favour the view that the one was written to be the introduction to the others.

Certain Scandinavian writers, and particularly Engnell, have not only followed Noth in detaching Deuteronomy, but have condemned the literary criticism of the Pentateuch root and branch. They have emphasized oral tradition, and have maintained that the materials of the Tetrateuch were orally transmitted until the post-exilic period, when this work received its final form. Engnell recognizes various strata of tradition, but holds that they were so interwoven together that it is impossible to separate them. He attributes to oral tradition a fixity comparable with that of written literature. All this carries us less far from literary criticism than it would seem to promise, and C. R. North observes that " if we bury the ' documents,' we shall have to resurrect them—or something very like them." That oral tradition continued after documents were written down is doubtless true, but it would seem to be more important to recognize that the main documents themselves, whose approximate age may be taken as reasonably established, rested on older written sources, which are occasionally explicitly cited, and on oral tradition, which carries us back beyond our sources a great deal nearer the events they record.

(ii) THE FORMER PROPHETS

1. *Joshua.* The book of Joshua is manifestly not by its hero, nor could it have been written until long after his time. For (*a*) in 10^{13} the book of Jashar, which included David's elegy on Saul and Jonathan (2 Sam. 1^{18}), is quoted ; (*b*) in 9^{27}, 15^{63}, the age of the Conquest is looked back upon, over an obviously long interval ; (*c*) in 19^{47} events which did not take place until much later than the age of the Conquest (cf. Judg. 18) are already described ; (*d*) the dominant view of the book is that the conquest was achieved in a single generation, with the almost complete extermination of the inhabitants, whereas there are fragments of an older view (13^{13}, $15^{13-19.\ 63}$, 16^{10}, $17^{11-13.\ 16-18}$, 19^{47}), also represented in Judg. 1, showing that this is not to be trusted.

That the book is a compilation from different sources is indicated by further duplications and discrepancies. Joshua gives two farewell addresses (23, 24) ; 4^{9} says he set up twelve stones in the midst of Jordan, while $4^{8.\ 20}$ say the Israelites carried twelve stones from Jordan and erected them in Gilgal ; in 3^{17} the people cross the river, and again in 4^{11} ; the king of Hebron appears to have been twice killed ($10^{26.\ 37}$), and while Hebron is captured and its inhabitants destroyed in chap. 10, in 14^{12} it is still in Canaanite hands, and in 15^{14} it is taken by Caleb.

The sources of Joshua are generally held to continue the

Pentateuchal sources, and hence many writers speak of the Hexateuch, to include the Pentateuch and Joshua. This, however, is misleading. For while the sources may overlap, there is no evidence that the Hexateuch ever formed a single work. Moreover, the process of compilation was different. Joshua's framework belongs to a writer of the Deuteronomic school, and not to P, as in the Pentateuch, and it is generally held that into it were fitted extracts from an already combined JE narrative, though some scholars deny any use of JE here, and widely varying views as to the sources of Joshua have been expressed. (Note that Eissfeldt finds his additional source, L, continued in Joshua 2–7, 24.) In the first half of the book there is little from P, but in the second half, which deals with the division of the land, there was ample scope for the geographical and statistical details in which the P school delighted. Noth denies the use of any P source, but there are expressions which indicate the hand of P. These are, indeed, few, but in such lists of names we could not expect to find many, and most scholars think these chapters were taken from a P source, though this is not to deny that the materials drawn on were much older.

The issue of the Deuteronomic book of Joshua could not have been earlier than the end of the seventh century B.C., and in its present form, with the insertion of the P material, it must come from a time subsequent to Ezra's mission. Of the antiquity of some of the material, however, and especially the poem from the book of Jashar, there can be no doubt.

2. *Judges*. The book of Judges falls into three parts: (*a*) 1^1–2^5, briefly recounting the story of the partial conquest of Canaan; (*b*) 2^6–16^{31}, relating the stories of the Judges; (*c*) 17–21, an appendix, telling of the Danite migration and the founding of the sanctuary of Dan (17 f.), and of the Benjamite outrage and the rape of the maidens of Shiloh (19–21).

Turning first to (*b*) we observe that the narratives stand in a schematic framework, resting on a philosophy of history. Disloyalty to Yahweh brings foreign oppression, until the raising up of a Judge, who brings deliverance and peace, until fresh defection from Yahweh starts the circle again.

The religious pragmatism of the editor's philosophy of history reveals him as a member of the Deuteronomic school. But the stories he incorporated in his framework were much older. Most of them prove on examination to be composite, and they are believed to have belonged to two collections of Hero stories, connected, perhaps, with the J and E cycles, in the sense that they issued from writers of the same school, though not, probably, standing in continuous documents with the Pentateuchal sources. (Eissfeldt once more finds a third cycle, akin to his source L.) More ancient than any of these cycles is the Song of Deborah (Judg. 5), which is perhaps the oldest surviving considerable literary composition in Hebrew, and which may reasonably be regarded as contemporary with the events it describes.

The chronological scheme is usually considered in relation to 1 Kings 6[1], which dates the building of the Temple 480 years after the Exodus. Since the figures are too high as they stand, it is sometimes supposed that the years of foreign domination are included in the period of each Judge, while the years of the usurpers, Abimelech and Saul (according to the later view of him) are to be disregarded. (For other proposed ways of dealing with this problem, see H. H. Rowley, *From Joseph to Joshua*, 1950, pp. 86 ff.) It is probable that the Judges were local heroes, whose periods may have synchronized, or overlapped, and the chronological framework is of little historical value.

Reverting to (*a*), we find an account quite inconsistent with the dominant view of the book of Joshua. For here the division of the land takes place before the Conquest, and not after, and instead of the tribes fighting as a single unit, under Joshua, they fight each for themselves, or in local combinations. Moreover, instead of the extermination of the Canaanites, we learn of the failure of the newcomers to dislodge them from many places. Much of this material is found, indeed, scattered in the book of Joshua (see above), and it is generally regarded as an extract from the J cycle.

As for (*c*), it consists of manifestly old narratives, which became attached to the book subsequently to the compilation of the main portion. They stand outside the chronological and pragmatic scheme, and are not concerned with Judges. Each of these stories appears itself to be composite.

It is sometimes thought that the original Deuteronomic book consisted only of (*b*), with the exception of the Abimelech story, and that the rest of the book was subsequently added. It should be remembered, however, that the story of the founding of the sanctuary of Dan accords well with the Deuteronomic polemic against that sanctuary in the books of Kings, and that the second of the stories in the appendix to Judges is relevant to the story of Saul, since it explains why the city of Jabesh-gilead should appeal to Benjamin for help. It may therefore be that the Deuteronomic compiler of Judges placed these stories here because they belonged to the period of the Judges, though no Judge figured in them.

3. *Samuel*. In Hebrew MSS. the books of Samuel stand as one book, but in the Septuagint they are divided and called 1 and 2 Kingdoms, our books of Kings being called 3 and 4 Kingdoms.

That Samuel cannot have been the author of the work is clear from the fact that he dies in 1 Sam. 25. Equally clearly these books rest on earlier sources, for they contain duplicate and discrepant accounts of several events. There are two accounts of the establishment of the monarchy, marked not alone by disagreement of detail, but by a totally different attitude to the monarchy as an institution. In 1 Sam. 9^{1}–10^{16}, 11^{1-11}, Samuel is a local seer who, acting under divine guidance, privately anoints Saul to deliver the people from the Philistines. Saul later brilliantly leads the Israelites against the Ammonites, and the tribes thereupon acclaim him as king. But according to 7^{2-17}, 8, 10^{17-24}, 12, the desire for a king proceeds from the people, and is displeasing to Samuel and to God. It is an act of rebellion against God and wholly unnecessary, since they have already been completely and permanently delivered from the Philistines (7^{13}). In this account Samuel is a national figure, by whose means the desired king is chosen by lot. Similarly, there are two stories of David's introduction to Saul (16^{14-23} and 17^{55}–18^{5}), two of David's sparing Saul's life (24 and 26), two of David's flight to Gath (21^{10-15} and 27^{2-12}), and two of Saul's death (1 Sam. 31^{1-7} and 2 Sam. 1^{1-16}).

At least a double strand, therefore, runs through much of the work, and Cornill and Budde analysed the whole on a two-source theory, connecting the stories with the J and E cycles. The stories of Samuel's infancy they connected with E, and the long continuous section in 2 Sam. 9–20 with J. They found a few Deuteronomic additions, and a few redactor's insertions. Eissfeldt analysed the work on the basis of a three-source theory, and found here, as in the Pentateuch, an additional source. The evidence for a third source is often very strong, and there is certainly much that does not fit easily into a two-source theory.

Kennedy found the analysis even less simple, and traced the material to a number of sources. He assigned the infancy stories of Samuel to a separate source, which was unconnected with the main body of what Cornill and Budde called E, and the passages dealing with the Ark to a lost History of the Ark. Further, he ascribed 2 Sam. 9–20 to a Court History of David, and believed it formed the oldest piece of continuous prose narrative in the Old Testament. The later of the two sources dealing with the establishment of the monarchy he connected with D. He believed the earlier of the accounts of the establishment of the monarchy and the Court History of David formed the earliest nucleus of the book, but that towards the end of the exile a Deuteronomistic writer prepared a second account of the establishment of the monarchy, marked by an attitude of hostility to the institution. Later a redactor combined these two works, prefixing sections from an old account of Samuel's infancy and from a History of the Ark. This redactor, Kennedy believed, omitted what is now 2 Sam. 9–20, but it was subsequently restored.

In this last particular Kennedy is not alone, for other scholars believe the Chronicler's omission of all material contained in this section, despite his close following of much of the narrative of Samuel, is to be explained by the excision and subsequent restoration of these chapters. Sellin further held that what is now an appendix to Samuel (see below) contains material that once stood in the body of the work, but that was later omitted, and still later reinstated. He believed that 2 Sam. 8 was composed to take the place of these excluded sections. On this view the appendix was restored earlier than 2 Sam. 9–20, since the Chronicler makes use of the former. It is by no means certain, however, that the Chronicler's non-use of 2 Sam. 9–20 implies that it did not lie before him. It is equally likely that he refrained from recording David's sins and family misfortunes, because these narratives would not serve to point the lessons in which he was interested.

What Kennedy calls the Court History of David is continued in 1 Kings 1 f., and it is more commonly treated as a Succession History, because it is concerned with the family intrigues for the succession to David's throne. That Kennedy is right in finding a variety of sources for the books of Samuel is held by other scholars, but it is doubtful if his account of the course of the growth of the book is right. It is improbable that the Deuteronomic edition of Samuel should be placed so late as he puts it, since the books of Kings give evidence of Deuteronomic editing, and they take up the story where the books of Samuel lay it down.

The appendix (2 Sam. 21–24) appears to have had a history of its own. It contains six sections, of which the first and last are connected, and similarly the second and the fifth, and the third and the fourth. Apparently there were two successive insertions in the appendix. The material of the appendix is certainly old. However the rest of the appendix may be related to the other sources of the work, the two poems (22, 23^{1-7}) have a separate origin, and the same may be said of the other poems that lie in the work. That David's laments over Saul (2 Sam. 1^{19-27}) and Abner (2 Sam. $3^{33f.}$) are genuinely Davidic is agreed by most, though Hannah's Song (1 Sam. 2^{1-10}) can hardly be attributed to Hannah. It may be noted that some scholars believe the narratives of the infancy of Samuel belonged originally to the life of Saul. But despite the fact that the name Saul would suit the etymology of 1 Sam. 1^{20} better than Samuel's, the view is improbable.

It is clear that the books of Samuel have had a complicated history, any assured recovery of which is difficult to secure. It certainly contains much early and historically valuable material, and equally certainly the material that shows a bias against the monarchy is relatively late.

4. *Kings*. The books of Kings, like those of Samuel, form a single book in Hebrew MSS., and are treated in the Septuagint as a continuation of the preceding work, whose story they certainly carry on.

The method of compilation of the two works is quite different, however, and this would suggest that while the one was written to continue the record of the other, it was compiled by another hand. Here we find a compiler's framework, into which narratives from various sources have been fitted. The framework consists of the formulae with which the various kings are introduced and dismissed. Throughout the period of the divided monarchy we find this framework with only minor variations. The opening formula records (*a*) the synchronism of the accession with the regnal year in the sister kingdom, (*b*) the length of the reign, and (*c*) a judgment on the reign. In the case of the Judahite kings we have further (*d*) the age of the king at his accession, and (*e*) his mother's name. At the close of the reign the formula indicates where further information may be obtained, and records the king's death and burial, and his successor's name.

The judgments on the kings are significant for the dating of the compiler. For in the case of the Israelite kings, they are usually comparisons with Jeroboam, who is condemned for creating rival sanctuaries to the Jerusalem shrine, while in the case of the Judahite kings, they are also always from the standpoint of the centralization of worship. Uniformly, therefore, we find the Deuteronomic standpoint. Moreover, the religious pragmatism of Deuteronomy is stamped on the compiler. He endeavours to show the connexion between the prosperity or adversity of the kings and their religious attitude. In the case of Solomon he arranges his material to show a connexion between the troubles Solomon suffered and his love of foreign wives and their cults. His phraseology is also influenced by Deuteronomy, so that we may say with confidence that he was acquainted with the spirit, outlook, and style of Deuteronomy.

Since the last event recorded in the work is the release of Jehoiachin, on the accession of Evil-merodach, in 561 B.C., it might appear to have been written not earlier than this. But possibly it received an appendix after it was first compiled, and many scholars believe that the verses recording Jehoiachin's release are such an addition. Indeed, since the regular formula ceases with Jehoiachin's reign (597 B.C.), it may be that the original work ended here. There are some slight indications that the final editing was done in Babylon.

Into the framework extracts from older sources were inserted. Some are named, and others may be detected. (*a*) 1 Kings 1^{1}–2^{11} is quite certainly from the same source as 2 Sam. 9–20. (*b*) For Solomon's reign the compiler used an Acts of Solomon (1 Kings 11^{41}), which Oesterley and Robinson assign to the early ninth century B.C. There are references to (*c*) a Royal History of Judah, and (*d*) a Royal History of Israel. These are quite unconnected with the books of Chronicles, and they do not appear to have been court records, since the extracts seem to have been of too informal a character. (*e*) Oesterley and Robinson believe there was a separate source dealing with Ahab's reign, which they call Acts of Ahab. As this was principally concerned with Ahab's wars with Aram, others think rather of a History of the Syrian Wars. (*f*) The compiler seems to have had access to a Temple History. Finally, (*g*) there are several stories concerning prophets, and it is probable that the compiler used prophetic biographies. There are three principal cycles of stories, dealing with Elijah, Elisha, and Isaiah. Lesser extracts from prophetic sources, such as the story of Micaiah, may have been taken from a collection of prophetic stories.

(iii) THE LATTER PROPHETS

The method of compilation of the prophetic books was wholly different from that of the books so far examined. Most of the actual oracles spoken by the prophets were short poems. How far the prophets compiled collections of their own oracles we cannot tell, but we know that Jeremiah prepared a collection of his and that they were read in the Temple (Jer. 36). The manuscript was taken to the king and read to him, and as it was read he cut it off from the roll, section by section, and cast it into the fire. Jeremiah thereafter re-dictated the contents of the roll, and added to them. Whether other prophets similarly collected their oracles, or whether that was left to their disciples, we have no means of knowing. The fragmentary and incomplete state of some of the oracles suggests that they were written on ostraca, which subsequently became broken.

The principles on which such collections as have survived were made, by whomsoever they were made, are far from clear. Sometimes we find a collection of utterances on foreign nations; sometimes several oracles with the same opening word stand side by side; sometimes the occurrence of a particular word, which was treated as a catchword, appears to have determined the arrangement, and quite unrelated oracles that contained it were set side by side. Frequently it is difficult to tell when one oracle ends and another begins, and the lack of any chronological or other clear arrangement makes it hard to determine at what point in a prophet's life a given oracle was uttered.

Nor is oracular matter the only type contained in these books. There is autobiography, usually in prose, recounting the prophet's experiences. Much material of this type stands in Jeremiah and Ezekiel ; and some in Amos, Hosea, and other prophets. Most of this almost certainly issued from the prophets themselves. Beyond this, we find biographical prose written in the third person about the prophets. In the case of Jeremiah, it is often thought this may have been written by Baruch ; in general it may have come from the disciples of the prophets. Both autobiographical and biographical sections often contain oracles, and give their setting.

That the prophets did not compile their own books, in the form they now have, is therefore clear, since they contain material of these various kinds woven together. This is made still clearer by the attribution of some oracles to two different prophets (cf. Isa. 2^{2-4} and Mic. 4^{1-3} ; Obad. $^{1-4. 5f.}$ and Jer. $49^{14-16. 9. 10a}$).

1. *Isaiah*. The book of Isaiah falls into two main divisions, chaps. 1–39 and 40–66. The first contains a number of prophetic oracles and four chapters of biographical matter, substantially repeated in 2 Kings, and it frequently mentions Isaiah's name. The second contains oracles alone, with no biographical matter and no mention of Isaiah's name. It is improbable that the second comes from Isaiah.

Confining ourselves first to chaps. 1–39, we find in the first five chapters oracles only datable on internal grounds, with a general heading to the book in 1^1, and a fresh heading, either to a particular oracle, or to a small collection of oracles, in 2^1, while the prophet's call is not recorded till we reach chap. 6. In chaps. 7 and 8 are oracles arising out of a defined and dated historical situation, though we cannot assume that all in the chapters belongs to that date. The next four chapters contain oracles with only internal indications of date, while chaps. 13–23 form a collection of oracles on foreign nations. Chaps. 24–27 are an apocalyptic section, and chaps. 28–35 consist of undated oracles, some of which resemble in character those found in the early chapters. Chaps. 36–39 form the historical appendix to the whole.

From the historical and biographical sections, as well as from 1^1, we learn that Isaiah prophesied in Jerusalem in the latter part of the eighth century B.C., and that he pronounced oracles on the royal policies of Ahaz and Hezekiah, particularly in connexion with the Syro-Ephraimite attack in 735–4 B.C., and the events that led up to Sennacherib's expedition of 701 B.C., while chap. 20 tells us he both acted and uttered oracles referring to the capture of Ashdod in 711 B.C. We therefore have a historical background into which many undated oracles fit, while others yield an insight into the social conditions of the age. Many oracles, however, not only cannot be related to the conditions of this age, but point definitely to another. Thus, 13^{1}–14^{23} (unless, as some hold, 14^{4b-23} is an independent poem, originally belonging to another context) presupposes that Babylon is an oppressive imperial power, and is doubtless of exilic origin; 21^{1-10} comes from the same age, and looks forward to the downfall of Babylon; 24–27 reflect post-exilic conditions and hopes of a divine breaking into history and world judgment, and are generally recognized to be not earlier than the age of Alexander; 34 f. come from the exilic or post-exilic age and look forward to the return of the Jews, either from Babylon or from the Dispersion, and to their triumph over the Edomites, whose cruelty at the time of the exile aroused undying hatred. Further, 11^{10-16} is commonly held to be post-exilic, as are the Psalm-fragments in 12. The messianic passages 9^{2-7} and 11^{1-9} are held by some scholars to be non-Isaianic, but there is a growing readiness to accept them, and especially the former, as Isaianic. Much non-Isaianic material has been incorporated in the book, therefore; and to the passages noted others might be added. That the collection is of late compilation would seem certain, since it appears to rest on earlier collections, which themselves contain post-Isaianic material.

Turning to the second part of the book, we find that the historical background here presupposed is quite different. The people are in exile (47^{6}), and Jerusalem is in ruins ($44^{26ff.}$), but the exiles will shortly return (48^{20}, 51^{11}, $52^{11f.}$), and Jerusalem will be delivered (52^{2}, 54), while Babylon will be overthrown (48^{14}, 47^{1-5}). Deliverance and destruction are alike to be achieved by the hand of Cyrus, who is twice named (44^{28}, 45^{1}).

The prophets did not transport themselves to a future age and predict the future that should arise out of that future; they predicted the future from the standpoint of their own age, which is therefore to be discovered by studying the conditions which they presuppose. By this test we recognize these chapters to come, not from Isaiah of Jerusalem, but from an anonymous prophet who lived in Babylonia in the latter part of the exilic period. He is commonly referred to as Deutero-Isaiah.

It is improbable, however, that his work extends to the whole of chaps. 40–66. Chaps. 56–66 are probably not his work, though Torrey would attach 34 f. to 40–66 and regard the whole as the work of a single author, who lived, however, not in the exilic period, but *c.* 400 B.C.

Embedded in 40–55 are four poems, generally known as the Servant Songs (42^{1-4}, 49^{1-6}, 50^{4-9}, 52^{13}–53^{12}), around which endless discussion has taken place. It is not agreed whether they are by Deutero-Isaiah, or whether they were taken from some other work; nor is there agreement on their interpretation. The traditional view was that though in other passages in Deutero-Isaiah Israel is called the Servant of Yahweh (41^{8}, $44^{1f. 21}$, 48^{20}), the Servant of these poems, and especially of 53, was the Messiah. This was followed by the collective interpretation of the Servant (the empirical Israel, the ideal Israel, or the faithful remnant), and this by the interpretation in terms of a historical individual, either past or contemporary with the prophet (Jeremiah, Zerubabbel, Jehoiachin, Uzziah, Moses, an unknown leprous Rabbi, or the prophet himself). None of these is entirely satisfactory, and it is more probable that there is fluidity in the conception, and the Servant is both Israel and an individual who both represents it and embodies its mission in himself. It is thus understood in terms of what Wheeler Robinson termed the concept of corporate personality. But whereas he believed the oscillation was between Israel and the prophet himself, it is more likely that it was between Israel and a future individual. On this view the concept is not unrelated to messianic prophecy.

Chaps. 56–66 are commonly referred to as Trito-Isaiah, but whereas Deutero-Isaiah was undoubtedly a single individual, it is improbable that Trito-Isaiah was. The passages here preserved are so miscellaneous that they probably come from more than one hand, though several may come from a single author. They were written under the influence of Deutero-Isaiah's work, and reflect the conditions of the post-exilic age. The background appears to be Palestinian (57^{3-7}), and while the walls of Jerusalem are not yet built (60^{10}), the Temple is already standing (56^{5-7}, 60^{7}). The period is therefore between the Return and the time of Nehemiah.

2. *Jeremiah.* The book of Jeremiah contains relatively little that is unconnected with Jeremiah, though it cannot have reached its present form until long after his day. There are four main divisions: (*a*) chaps. 1–25, consisting largely of poetic oracles dealing with Judah, interspersed with prose, mainly autobiographical; (*b*) chaps. 26–45, consisting largely of prose, biographical and autobiographical, but containing some poetic oracles; (*c*) chaps. 46–51, consisting almost wholly

of poetic oracles dealing with foreign nations ; and (*d*) chap. 52, consisting of a historical appendix, which is duplicated in 2 Kings. In the Septuagint the oracles on foreign nations are transferred to follow 25^{13}, and their order is different.

The period of Jeremiah's prophetic activity was from 626 B.C. until shortly after the fall of Jerusalem in 586 B.C., and we have an unusually full account of his life and experiences. While it is not always easy to determine with confidence when the undated oracles were uttered, there are few which cannot be attributed to Jeremiah. It is generally agreed, however, that 10^{1-16} is non-Jeremianic and of later origin, while 17^{21-27} is commonly believed to be un-Jeremianic in its standpoint, and to recall the age of Nehemiah. Some have denied 30 f. to Jeremiah, but parts of them, and especially 31^{27-34}, on insufficient grounds. On the other hand, 50^{1}–51^{58}, which looks forward to the imminent fall of Babylon, is almost certainly non-Jeremianic.

It is not to be supposed, however, that with the exception of these passages the book came from Jeremiah's hand. In 605 B.C. Baruch prepared a roll at Jeremiah's dictation (36^{32}), and this was perhaps later added to. It was evidently a scroll consisting primarily of oracles, and it was probably one of the sources drawn on for our present book. The biographical and autobiographical material probably came from separate collections, and the present work does not appear to have reached the form we now have until the post-exilic period.

3. *Ezekiel*. The book of Ezekiel was long regarded, even by critical scholars, as unique in its unity and authenticity, representing the work of one of the exiles of 597 B.C., who received his call and exercised his ministry in Babylonia. Its divisions are : (*a*) chaps. 1–24, a chronologically ordered collection of prophecies delivered before the fall of Jerusalem ; (*b*) chaps. 25–32, prophecies on foreign peoples ; (*c*) chaps. 33–39, prophecies of the restoration of Jerusalem ; and (*d*) chaps. 40–48, the ideal picture of the restored community and its worship.

The unity of the book was disputed by Kraetzschmar in 1900, but with little effect. In 1924 Hölscher renewed the challenge, but vitiated his work by the arbitrariness of the canon with which he started. For he held that Ezekiel wrote only poetry, and that all that was not poetry was not genuine. This left Ezekiel only 170 verses. Irwin was less radical than Hölscher, but left the prophet only some 250 verses. Torrey in 1930 held that the book was a pseudepigraph, written *c.* 230 B.C., purporting to have been written in the reign of Manasseh, and addressed to a Palestinian circle, but that it was later recast by an editor, who transferred it to the exilic age. More recently van den Born has presented the view that the book is a pseudepigraph of the fifth century B.C.

James Smith, writing independently of Torrey, argued in 1931 that Ezekiel belonged to northern Israel in the time of Manasseh, while in the following year Herntrich maintained that Ezekiel prophesied in Jerusalem until 586 B.C., and not in Babylonia, but that his work was edited by a disciple, who added 40–48. A number of scholars have believed that Ezekiel's ministry was first exercised in Palestine and later in Babylonia. Messel brought his ministry down to *c.* 400 B.C., and L. E. Browne to the period of Alexander the Great.

None of these views has secured any wide following, and opinion is now moving back more nearly to the traditional view. This movement is represented by Cooke, Howie, and Fohrer, who accept the substantial unity and authenticity of the book and a Babylonian setting for the ministry of Ezekiel, while recognizing a limited number of passages to be secondary.

4. *Hosea.* Hosea prophesied in the northern kingdom during the last years before the fall of Samaria. His ministry began *c.* 740 B.C., and appears to have ended before 722 B.C., since there is no reference to the fall of Samaria. The book consists of a number of prophetic oracles, whose text is badly preserved, together with biographical and autobiographical narratives. The most discussed question connected with the book is the relation between the biographical account of Hosea's marriage in chap. 1 and the autobiographical account in chap. 3, and there is no agreement as to whether we have two accounts of a single event or whether chap. 3 is the sequel to chap. 1. Some argue that the story of the marriage is simply an allegory, but most believe Gomer was a real person, who was unfaithful to her husband, and that from his bitter experience Hosea was led to a deeper understanding of the divine love.

Editors have often suspected of being later additions all the hopeful passages in the book, but this is unnecessary. The authenticity of 11^8f. is secure, and this expresses hope. The passages referring to Judah may be secondary, or in some cases the name Judah may have been scribally substituted for Israel.

Whether the Minor Prophets already existed in their present form before they were brought together in the collection of the Twelve, or whether they were compiled from their sources for that collection cannot be known, but in any case it is improbable that the book was compiled before the exile.

5. *Joel.* This little book contains no explicit indication of date, and older writers regarded it as coming from the period of the minority of Joash, or from the age of Jeremiah. The

latter view is still maintained by Kapelrud. A pre-exilic date is now generally abandoned for a post-exilic on the grounds that (*a*) there is no reference to the northern kingdom, but Israel is synonymous with Judah (2^{27}, $3^{2.\ 16}$) ; (*b*) $3^{2.\ 17}$ clearly imply a date after the fall of Jerusalem and the dispersion of the Jews, while the fact that the Temple is used ($1^{13f.}$) would carry us down beyond 516 B.C. ; (*c*) there is no mention of a king, but the priests and elders are the leaders of the community ; (*d*) there is no reference to the Assyrians or Babylonians, as in all other pre-exilic prophets, though there are references to other foreign oppressors, and also to the Greeks (3^{6}) ; (*e*) there is no mention of the sins that prevailed in pre-exilic Israel, while the frequent allusions to priests and offerings, and the assembly of the whole people for fasting, weeping, and mourning (2^{12}) suggests post-exilic Judaism ; and (*f*) the reference to " the meal offering and the drink offering " ($1^{9.\ 13}$, 2^{14}) points definitely to the post-exilic period.

It remains to be considered whether the book is a unity. Its first two chapters treat of a plague of locusts which devastated the land, but from 2^{28} to the end it treats of an apocalyptic Day of Yahweh, when He will bless the Jews, but will assemble the nations in the Valley of Jehoshaphat and punish them for their treatment of His people. Some writers have argued that these two parts are of independent origin, while others think the devastation of the locusts could well suggest to the prophet the Day of Yahweh.

6. *Amos*. The book of Amos contains the oracles of the earliest of the prophets represented in the prophetic books. Though himself a southerner he delivered his prophecies in the northern kingdom in the reign of Jeroboam II., *c*. 760 B.C. There is a short biographical section in 7^{10-17}, and some autobiographical material in 7–9. The fact that we have the three types of material suggests that it was compiled after Amos's time, and this conclusion is reinforced by other considerations. The book falls into three divisions : (*a*) chaps. 1 f., consisting of seven oracles on the peoples surrounding Israel, followed by one on Israel itself, all introduced by a similar formula ; (*b*) chaps. 3–6, a collection of oracles denouncing the social abuses that prevailed in Israel ; (*c*) chaps. 7–9, a series of visions, in which some other oracles have been incorporated. The oracle against Judah in $2^{4f.}$ is commonly believed to come from a later hand, but the fact that it is introduced by the same formula as the surrounding oracles suggests that it was already written when the book was compiled. This formula may be due to the compiler of the book or to the compiler of the source from which he drew. Doubts have been raised against a few other passages, and especially against the closing verses of the

book. Many scholars date 9^{11-15} after the fall of Jerusalem, and 9^{8b-10}, which ill accord with 9^{1-4}, are often attributed to another hand.

7. *Obadiah.* This is the smallest book in the Old Testament, and it gives no explicit information as to the prophet's period. From $v.^{11}$ we see that the fall of Jerusalem is past, but it is disputed whether the book is a unity. About a quarter of it is duplicated in Jeremiah ($vv.^{1-4}$ = Jer. 49^{14-16}; $vv.^{5f.}$ = Jer. $49^{9.\ 10a}$), and it is probable that the editor of Jeremiah borrowed from the book of Obadiah. But in view of our uncertainty as to when Jer. 49 was compiled, this proves nothing for the date of Obadiah. Sellin believed $vv.^{1-10}$ refer to Edom's revolt against Jehoram (852 B.C.), while $vv.^{11-14}$ were added during the exile, and $vv.^{15-21}$ in the age of Malachi. Rudolph finds the whole to be by one hand, shortly after 586 B.C., with the exception of $vv.^{19-21}$, while Pfeiffer assigns $vv.^{1-14}$ to the time of Malachi, $vv.^{16-18}$ to half a century later, and $vv.^{19-21}$ to the early part of the fourth century B.C.

8. *Jonah.* This book is unique in the prophetic Canon in that it contains no oracular matter, but, with the exception of the psalm in chap. 2, consists wholly of biographical matter. In 2 Kings 14^{25} we read of a prophet Jonah, the son of Amittai, who lived in the time of Jeroboam II., shortly before Amos, and the book doubtless purports to tell his story. But it was not written until long after his time. This view rests partly on the fact that in 3^{3} the fall of Nineveh (612 B.C.) is looked back on as long past, but more securely on the evidence of the language, which marks it as definitely post-exilic, and probably not earlier than the fourth century B.C.

Though it contains no oracles similar to those found in the other prophets, it rightly stands in the prophetic Canon, for its unknown author delivers a truly prophetic message through the medium of this story. It is probably to be read as allegory, and not as history. Jonah, swallowed by the fish for his disobedience and vomited out to fulfil his divinely appointed mission of converting the heathen, symbolizes the Jewish people, swallowed up in the Babylonian exile for their disloyalty to God, but brought forth again in the Return that they might lead the nations to God.

Apart from the psalm in 2^{2-9}, the book is a unity. That psalm, however, has no relevance to its context. It is not a prayer for deliverance, but a psalm of thanksgiving for deliverance from some peril in the sea, and it is doubtless an interpolation into the text.

9. *Micah.* Micah was a contemporary of Isaiah's, as we learn from the heading of the book and from Jer. 26^{18}, but we know little about him, as the book consists only of oracles.

It falls into three sections: (*a*) chaps. 1–3, which deal with the social injustices rampant in Judah, and close with the prophecy of doom upon Jerusalem, cited in Jeremiah; (*b*) chaps. 4 f., which contain promises of restoration; (*c*) chaps. 6 f., which contain miscellaneous oracles.

It is agreed that chaps. 1–3 are the work of Micah, but the rest of the book is commonly denied him. By some a genuine core is found in 4 f., but there are several indications of a date not earlier than the exile, which must then be treated as glosses. In chaps. 6 f. there are oracles which might be Micah's, though there is little to establish that they were. The great passage 6^{1-8} is held to come from the reign of Manasseh, or, with less likelihood, from that of Ahaz. It is often denied to Micah on the ground that its spirit and temper differ so widely from those of chaps. 1–3. Micah may well have survived to the reign of Manasseh, though the heading of the book does not indicate this, while there would be nothing surprising in the prophet uttering a mellower note in old age than in youth. Chap. 7^{7-20} is held by many to be exilic or post-exilic.

10. *Nahum*. The book of Nahum opens with a mutilated acrostic poem (1^2–2^2), generally held to be of post-exilic origin, followed by oracles against Assyria (2^3–3^{19}). It is the latter which constitute the work of Nahum, whose date can be determined only on the internal evidence of his oracles. These look forward to the destruction of Nineveh (612 B.C.), and since in 3^8 there is a reference to the sack of Thebes (663 B.C.), we can define the period of their origin broadly as between these dates. Since the fall of Nineveh seems to have been imminently expected, it is probable that their date is very close to that event. Humbert has suggested that the book is a liturgy prepared for the festival that celebrated the fall of Nineveh. The brilliance of Nahum's poetry is noteworthy.

11. *Habakkuk*. This little book has raised problems which have received the most varied solutions. It contains oracles in chaps. 1 f., and a psalm in chap. 3. The oracles represent the Chaldaeans as the instrument of justice on the wicked oppressor, and then seem to go on to pronounce judgment upon the Chaldaeans, who now appear to be identified with the oppressors. The period is apparently the end of the seventh century B.C., when the Neo-Babylonian empire was rapidly rising, but Duhm, by substituting *Kittîm* for *Kasdîm* in 1^6, and *hay*^{e}*wānî* (the Greek) for *hayyayin* (wine) in 2^5, transferred the oracles to the period of Alexander. Most scholars feel it is precarious to base a theory on a conjectural emendation. The commentary on Habakkuk found amongst the Dead Sea Scrolls interprets the Chaldaeans as the Kittim, but offers no evidence

for a change of reading in the text. Budde varied the arrangement of the book, and Marti assumed that it had received many interpolations, but Cannon showed that it is possible to accept the whole of chaps. 1 f. as the work of Habakkuk, who first hailed the Chaldaeans as God's instrument of justice, and later, after experience of their ruthlessness, looked for vengeance upon them. The psalm in chap. 3, which Duhm regarded as integral to the text, is held by most to be of post-exilic origin. A liturgical view of the book was proposed by Balla, and this view has been followed by Humbert, who dates it in the year 602–1 B.C., and who thinks the oppressor throughout was Jehoiakim.

12. *Zephaniah.* The prophet Zephaniah, who may have been a descendant of king Hezekiah (1^{1}), appears to have prophesied *c.* 626 B.C., at the time of the Scythian peril, and his emergence would then be contemporary with Jeremiah's. He believed that the inroads of the Scythians heralded a Day of Yahweh that should bring a general judgment on all the nations. The anticipation of the destruction of Nineveh in 2^{13} has led to the suggestion that the prophecies should be carried down nearer to 612 B.C., but it is not necessary to suppose that all the oracles in the collection, brief as it is, come from a single year. A few verses (*e.g.* 2^{15}, $3^{14\text{-}20}$) have been held to be later additions, and Pfeiffer doubted if any of chap. 3 is from Zephaniah.

13. *Haggai.* The book of Haggai contains brief addresses uttered on various occasions, the exact date of each being recorded in its heading. All the dates fall within a single year, the second year of Darius Hystaspis, 520 B.C. There is no reason to doubt the authenticity of the utterances, and Haggai thus belongs to the immediately post-exilic period. It is probable that he did not compile the book himself, since he is consistently referred to in the third person, but it was doubtless prepared very shortly after 520 B.C.

14. *Zechariah.* That the book of Zechariah is not a unity is now generally agreed. The prophet Zechariah, who was contemporary with Haggai, and whose genuine prophecies are supplied with dates, ranging from 520 to 518 B.C., is concerned only with chaps. 1–8, while chaps. 9–14 form a wholly independent collection. The reasons for this view are: (*a*) whereas in 1–8 the background of the early Persian period is clear, in 9–14 there is nothing whatever of this; (*b*) whereas in 1–8 the land is at peace and the interest is in rebuilding the Temple, in 9–14 we find pictures of war and Jerusalem is besieged; (*c*) whereas in 1–8 the leaders of the community, Zerubbabel and Joshua, are named, in 9–14 we find only references to unnamed shepherds. In addition, the literary style and the

theological ideas of the second part are quite different from those of the first.

The work of Zechariah consists of eight Night Visions, related in the first person, to which are attached introductory notes ($1^{1.7}$, 7^{1}) in the third person. These visions, which are filled with messianic hopes, centering in Zerubabbel, may without hesitation be ascribed to Zechariah.

The remaining chapters have called forth less agreement. Earlier writers thought they were pre-exilic, but most moderns have recognized them to be post-exilic. A third view has distinguished between 9–11 and 12–14, finding the former to be mainly pre-exilic and the latter post-exilic. Oesterley and Robinson held that these chapters consisted of seven different sections, coming from dates ranging from 218 B.C. to 134 B.C. More recently P. Lamarche has examined the structure of chaps. 9–14 and without any rearrangement of the text finds a careful chiastic arrangement throughout. This would argue the unity of these chapters. He would date them in the fifth century B.C., but the reference to Greece in 9^{14} points to a late post-exilic period, and this would far better fit the conditions.

15. *Malachi*. It is doubtful if Malachi, which means *my messenger*, is a proper name at all. But it is possible to determine within narrow limits the author's date. The land is ruled by a *peḥāh*, or governor (1^{8}), and it is therefore after the fall of Jerusalem; and since the Temple is standing (1^{10}, $3^{1.10}$) it is after 516 B.C., and probably a long time after. On the other hand, no distinction is drawn between priests and Levites (2^{4-9}, 3^{3}), and therefore it is before Ezra's promulgation of P. Its agreement with P (cf. 3^{10} with Num. 18^{21-33}) in the matter of the tithe (D's tithe law was quite different) shows that in some respects the usage codified in P is older than its promulgation (cf. above, p. 34). As the condemnation of mixed marriages (2^{10-16}) indicates that Nehemiah's work was not yet done (cf. Neh. 13^{23-27}), we should probably assign the oracles to *c*. 460 B.C.

(iv) THE WRITINGS

1. *Psalms*. The book of Psalms consists of 150 poems, but 9 and 10 were originally one, as were 42 and 43, while in several cases two poems have been combined in a single psalm. The collection is divided into five books: 1–41, 42–72, 73–89, 90–106, 107–50; but probably books 2 and 3 were originally one, and so books 4 and 5.

Several psalms are duplicated. Thus 14 = 53, 40^{14-18} = 70, 108 = 57^{8-12} and 60^{7-14}. By comparing 14 and 53 we find that Elohim (God) stands in 53 in four places where 14 has Yahweh. Similarly 70 substitutes Elohim for Yahweh three times, while retaining the latter twice. This appears to be no accident, for we find Yahweh 272 times in book 1 and Elohim used absolutely 15 times, while in Pss. 42–83 Yahweh stands 40 times and Elohim 200 times. Book 1 is attributed almost wholly to David, only Pss. 1 and 2 (introductory to the entire book), 10 (the completion of 9), and 33 being without ascription to him. Book 1 was therefore a Davidic Yahwistic Psalter, while books 2 and 3 formed an Elohistic Psalter, attributed to various authors. To this latter an appendix (84–9) was added, but without the editorial change of Yahweh to Elohim. Books 4 and 5 are again Yahwistic, the poems bearing various ascriptions or none. Altogether 50 psalms have no ascription, of which 34 are "orphans" (*i.e.* without heading at all).

Book 1 is generally recognized to be the oldest of the three collections, though it is improbable that it was made before the exile. The other collections must have been completed by *c.* 100 B.C., so that the compilation of the Psalter may be placed broadly between the Return and 100 B.C. The recognition of this formerly led to the assignment of an increasing number of individual psalms to the post-exilic period, and especially to the Maccabaean age. This tendency reached its climax in Duhm, who held that no psalm is pre-exilic, that perhaps two are from the Persian period and the rest from the Greek period, the vast majority being Maccabaean. From this there has been a reaction, and today it is recognized that while the compilations are post-exilic, the contents may be largely pre-exilic.

It is, however, extremely difficult to date the individual psalms, and students today are less concerned to define the date than to discuss the form and use of the psalms. It is many years since Smend argued that many of the psalms which read like individual prayers were really national prayers, and that where the Psalmist uses "I," it should be understood collectively. This view was disputed by Balla, and is rejected by Gunkel. Wheeler Robinson argued that here, as in the case of the Servant of Yahweh, we should find a fluidity which passes from the individual to the collective without difficulty.

There is less inclination today than formerly to think of the Psalter as a Hymn-book, in our sense of the term. Instead, it is thought of as a book of ritual poems, to be used in ritual acts, whether public or private. Mowinckel sought to define the purpose in many cases. He held that the references to "workers of iniquity" are to sorcerers, whose wiles the worshipper tried to counter by ritual acts and prayers. Other psalms he believed to belong to an annual Enthronement Festival, similar to the Babylonian New Year Festival. Johnson has interpreted the royal psalms in terms of the new year rites of the Jerusalem Temple, and thinks the messianic psalms set before the king the ideal king of the future as his model.

Another characteristic modern approach to the Psalter is associated with the name of Gunkel, who studied their forms and types, and classified their use on this basis. This approach has been widely followed, and the principal groups of psalms distinguished are: Hymns, Communal Laments, Communal Thanksgivings, Individual Laments, Individual Thanksgivings, and Royal Psalms. Gunkel stressed the cultic associations of the psalms less than Mowinckel, and in particular thought the individual laments were sung by the suffering in their homes with no cultic association.

The headings of the psalms have attracted much discussion. The personal ascriptions were doubtless early understood to imply authorship, but it is impossible to accept them as authentic in that sense. A common view has been that they indicate earlier collections from which they were taken, but it is difficult to think there was a collection of psalms bearing the name of Moses from which only one (90) was taken. Beyond these personal ascriptions there are terms such as Miktam, Maskil, "For the Chief Musician" (the last standing at the head of fifty-five psalms). The cryptic phrases over Pss. 22, 56 have been thought to indicate tunes. Kennett held that all the terms in the headings indicated the mode of their accompaniment, while Mowinckel thought they had cultic significance, and indicated the nature of the cultic acts they accompanied.

2. *Proverbs*. The book of Proverbs is a collection of Wisdom writings of very varied character. The title ascribes the work to Solomon, and again in 10^{1} he is named as the author of the collection that follows, while 25^{1}, though ascribing the following sayings to him, states that they were collected by the men of Hezekiah. Clearly, therefore, Solomon cannot have prepared the work in its present form. Moreover, it contains some admittedly non-Solomonic material. Thus 24^{23} attributes the sayings that follow to "the wise men"; 30^{1} the sayings that follow to Agur; 31^{1} the section that follows to Lemuel.

The book is commonly analysed into eight sections, but Oesterley subdivides one of them to yield a total of ten. These are: (*a*) 1^{1}–9^{18}, of which 1^{1-6} are an introduction to the whole book: (*b*) 10^{1}–22^{16}; (*c*) 22^{17}–23^{14}; (*d*) 23^{15}–24^{22}; (*e*) 24^{23-34}; (*f*) 25–29; (*g*) 30^{1-14}; (*h*) 30^{15-33}; (*i*) 31^{1-9}; (*j*) 31^{10-31}.

The characteristic of the first section is the personification of Wisdom which reaches its climax in chap. 8. It presents its material, moreover, not in brief aphorisms, such as we find in most of the book, but in connected sections, developing each a single theme. It is generally agreed that this is the latest part of the book, and it is commonly assigned to the fourth or third century B.C.

Section (*b*) is probably the oldest in the book. It is most likely of pre-exilic origin. This view rests on the consideration that " the wise " are already referred to in pre-exilic writers as a separate class, who might therefore be presumed to have left some deposit of their wisdom, and on the undeveloped literary character of the sayings. For each verse is commonly an independent couplet. Further, there are frequent references to the king, which, despite Gray's reminder that Ben Sira could also refer to the king, are thought to point to the time of the monarchy.

Section (*c*) has many points of connexion with the Egyptian text, The Wisdom of Amen-em-ope, and it is on this ground that Oesterley separates it from the two short sections which follow. The fresh heading in 24^{23} accounts for the separation of section (*e*). These three sections Oesterley regards as of approximately the same date and closely connected with one another. We may here observe that Hebrew Wisdom literature, like Hebrew psalmody, has parallels in other ancient literatures, and especially in Egyptian, whose oldest known fragment of this kind, the Teaching of Ptah-hotep, goes back to the third millennium B.C. But Hebrew literature, though it grew from a common stock, developed a quality of its own. In the case of The Wisdom of Amen-em-ope, however, the case for the literary dependence of the author of Prov. 22^{17}-23^{14} would appear to be established, though there are differences of outlook between the two works. The date of the Egyptian work is probably the eighth or seventh century B.C., and Oesterley assigns these three sections of Proverbs to the seventh century B.C.

The ascription of 25–29 to the age of Hezekiah rests, according to Sellin, on a sound tradition, so far, at any rate, as its kernel is concerned. While he recognizes it to be later than 10^{1}–22^{16}, marked by a spirit of scepticism instead of the confidence of the earlier section, he finds a definitely pre-exilic nucleus in it, and in this Oesterley concurs.

The remaining sections are all short, and impossible to date, though they are probably late. We do not know who Agur or Lemuel were. The final section is an alphabetic acrostic poem in praise of the virtuous woman, and its language marks it as post-exilic. These four sections stand in relatively different positions in the Septuagint, and are distinguishable in contents.

3. *Job.* The book of Job is one of the world's masterpieces, superb as literature and wrestling with a great and enduring problem. It consists of a prologue and epilogue in prose,

between which stands a dialogue in poetry. It has been held by many that the prologue and epilogue are older than the rest of the book and from a different hand. But while it is probable that the work rests on a traditional story of a good man who suffered, both prologue and epilogue are integral to it, and a separate literary origin need not be assumed.

The book has gathered some accretions, however, and has probably suffered some loss. The chief accretion is the Elihu section. After Job's dialogue with his three friends, Elihu suddenly appears without introduction, delivers his speeches (32–37) without interruption, and is thereafter ignored. The fact that his speeches can be dropped from the book without disturbing its structure, indicates that he is in no way integral to its conception, and despite the effort of Cornill and Budde to defend this section, it may be regarded as an attempted solution of the problem of the book by a later writer, who failed to perceive the author's real message.

The second speech of Yahweh (40^{6}–41^{34}) is also commonly regarded as an accretion. Cheyne and Van Hoonacker rejected both Yahweh speeches, but this mars the structure and plan of the book. It is asserted that these speeches are inconsistent with the epilogue, since here Job is rebuked, while there he is pronounced in the right. But, as Gray observes, the difference of judgment is not on the same issue. He is vindicated as against the Satan's charge, made in the prologue, but rebuked for his ignorant criticism of God's ways. The second speech of Yahweh, however, with its lengthy descriptions of Behemoth and Leviathan, contributes nothing material to the work, and falls below the level of brilliance of the first speech. Moreover, as Peake says, after Job has unreservedly thrown up his case ($40^{4f.}$), the second speech of Yahweh comes perilously near nagging.

Chap. 28 is also generally recognized to be an addition, though possibly by the author of Job. Its affinities are with the first section of Proverbs. If Job had already reached this insight into the limitations of human achievement, compared with the inscrutable wisdom of God, he had already reached his goal, and the ironical tone of Yahweh's speech would be uncalled for. On the other hand, it is impossible to attribute the chapter to any of Job's friends.

The loss from the book would appear to be in the third round of the dialogue. The scheme of the dialogue is as follows : following an opening soliloquy of Job's, each of the three friends speaks in turn, and after each speech Job replies ; a second cycle follows the first, and a third is begun, but not completed before Job makes his final soliloquy. It is probable that the third cycle was once complete, but that part of it has been lost and part misplaced, so that part of chap. 27, now attributed to Job, once belonged to Zophar's third speech. Various reconstructions of this part of the book have been attempted.

The complete integration of the book is then clear. The dialogue deals with the question of innocent suffering, which the friends, fortified by the current orthodoxy, hold to be unthinkable, since suffering is held to be the proof of divine disfavour. Job, however, maintains his integrity, and insists that there is a problem. But the explanation of his suffering cannot be deduced from the human side. The intellectual problem therefore remains, and the book in no sense claims to solve it. It declares that there is an explanation, though the sufferer cannot discern it. In the case of Job it is given to the reader in the prologue, which is vital to the book. It was essential that the reader should know that Job was genuinely innocent, and equally so that Job should never know the cause of his suffering. Had he been granted a knowledge which is denied to other sufferers, the book could have brought no message to them. What the explanation is in any given case is not ascertainable by the sufferer, but, as in the case of Job, there is a reason hidden in the heart of God and worthy of God. God had staked Himself upon Job, and in his suffering Job was not merely vindicating himself, but also God. It is for impugning God's justice on the basis of human ignorance that Job is condemned in the divine speech, which is the climax of the book, and whose burden is that the human mind cannot comprehend God and therefore humble trust is wiser than the effort to comprehend. Hence, though reason cannot solve the problem, faith can transcend it. This carries the further consequence that since suffering may be innocent, and not the mark of divine disfavour, communion with God is not necessarily broken by it, and faith can maintain that communion. It is this point that Job reaches, resting in God even in his suffering. The epilogue then comes, not as the anti-climax so often supposed, but as the inevitable sequel to the prologue. It belongs less to the message of the book than to its artistry. God's confidence in Job is vindicated and the Satan discomfited. Clearly, then, the trial must end, and the suffering, which is the form of the trial, must terminate. Job's renewed prosperity is not the reward of his righteousness and the giving away of the case to the friends, but the sign that the test is finished.

We may then accept the work, shorn of the passages noted, as a unity. It is generally recognized to be a product of the post-exilic age, and is probably to be dated *c.* 400 B.C. It has been suggested that a Babylonian text, sometimes called the "Babylonian Job," provided the source of the book of Job. But the Babylonian sufferer, while unconscious of the sin that has caused his suffering, is far from certain that his sin has not brought it on him. This is in marked contrast with the rectitude of Job, announced in the prologue, and confirmed by his own conscience.

4. *The Song of Songs*. The Song of Songs is ascribed in its title to Solomon, but on linguistic grounds alone it is certain that the work is post-exilic, though its precise date cannot be fixed. Some would date it *c.* 400 B.C., and others somewhat later. No book in the Bible has given rise to greater varieties of interpretation, and there is no agreement even as to the class of literature to which it belongs.

The traditional rabbinical interpretation held it to be an allegory, treating under the figures of human love God's dealings with Israel, and this view has been defended by some Christian scholars. In general, however, Christian exegesis has traced Christ's dealings with the Church in all the imagery of the book, and the most fanciful interpretations have been given. In modern times this view has been generally abandoned, and in the nineteenth century the book was treated as a dialogue or drama. One school, following Delitzsch, found in it two main characters, Solomon and the Shulammite, who was wooed and won by the king. Another, following Ewald, found three principal characters, Solomon, the Shulammite maiden, and her rustic lover. According to this view, the maiden resisted the royal advances, and finally returned to her true love. A further development of this view adds a chorus. The chief difficulty about this view is the absence of rubrics, which the interpreters must liberally supply.

For many years the most popular view was that the book consists of a collection of wedding songs. In 1873 Wetzstein published a study of modern marriage customs in Syria, and in the light of these customs Budde attractively presented the view that we have in the Song a selection from a single cycle of songs in honour of the bride and bridegroom during the seven days of the wedding celebration. This view has today yielded to the more general interpretation of the Song as a collection of love lyrics.

Meek propounded the view that in the Song we have a liturgy of the Adonis-Tammuz cult, but reinterpreted and absorbed into the faith of Judaism. There is little clear trace of the Yahwism into the service of which any revision was made, and it seems more likely that we have songs expressing the pure love of a man and a woman in language which is reminiscent of the Adonis-Tammuz rites.

5. *Ruth*. The book of Ruth tells a simple story, laid in the age of the Judges, and to that fact it owes its transfer in Greek

MSS. to follow Judges. It presents no history of public events, and instead of revealing the turmoil and strife reflected in Judges it gives a picture of humble village life. While the author has doubtless worked with old traditions, the book is of post-exilic origin. For the opening verse suggests that the author was familiar with the Deuteronomistic editor's book of Judges, and the way in which old customs are explained implies that they were now obsolete. In Deut. 25^{9} it is laid down that the brother-in-law who declines the duty of levirate marriage should have his shoe publicly drawn off by the wronged woman, who should spit in his face. While in Ruth 4^{9} it is not the brother-in-law, but a more distant next-of-kin, who declines the duty, the drawing off of the shoe figures in the ceremony. But here he draws off his own shoe and there is no spitting, and the woman is not present. Either we have a later modification of the custom or, as is more probable, the modification is due to the more distant relationship of the *gō'ēl*.

Many scholars believe the book was written in the period of Nehemiah and Ezra, to protest against their attitudes to mixed marriages by its quiet reminder that even David had a Moabite ancestress. Sellin, who at one time dated the book in the time of Zerubbabel, later adopted this view. While this date may be correct, it is doubtful if a polemic purpose inspired the book. The closing genealogy appears to be a later addition.

6. *Lamentations*. In the book of Lamentations we have five separate poems, of which the first four are acrostic. The fifth, though containing the same number of verses as the letters of the alphabet, is not acrostic. Moreover, its rhythm differs from that of the others.

Traditionally the book has been assigned to Jeremiah, but the reasons against this are decisive. For (*a*) the statement in 2^{9} suggests that the author was not one of the prophets; (*b*) 4^{17} suggests that the author had vainly looked for help from Egypt, whereas Jeremiah consistently declared that hope to be vain; (*c*) 5^{7} presents a view against which Jeremiah had explicitly protested (Jer. $31^{29f.}$); (*d*) the expectation that trouble was about to fall on the Chaldaeans (3^{64-66}) is in disagreement with Jeremiah's point of view; (*e*) the linguistic evidence is against it.

It is unlikely that all the poems are from one hand. For (*a*) the order of the letters of the alphabet differs in chap. 1 from that of chaps. 2–4; (*b*) from a literary standpoint there are differences in the quality of the chapters, chaps. 2 and 4 being superior to the others and chap. 3, which appears to have been written with Jeremiah in mind, being the poorest.

There is no reason to doubt that the poems date from the period of the exile, save perhaps chap. 3, which may be somewhat later, and chaps. 2 and 4, which may be from a single author, were probably written by an eye-witness of the fall of Jerusalem. Gottwald has persuasively examined their religious significance and their influence on Deutero- and Trito-Isaiah.

7. *Ecclesiastes*. Traditionally the book of Ecclesiastes, like the Song of Songs, has been attributed to Solomon, since it purports to have been written by a king who is a son of David. Luther rejected the tradition, which is now generally abandoned. For (*a*) the author frequently writes from the standpoint of the subject, condemning the iniquities of the regime under which he lives (3^{16}, 4^{1}); (*b*) he appears to be living in a province of a great empire, and warns against the activity of the common spy (10^{20}); (*c*) the anarchy that appears to prevail in the land (4^{13-16}, 10^{16-20}) suggests either the last century of Persian rule or the period of the later Seleucids and Ptolemies; (*d*) the linguistic evidence is so strong that Delitzsch could say: "If the book of Ḳoheleth be as old as Solomon, then there can be no history of the Hebrew language." It was probably written in the Greek period, in the third century B.C.

Concerning the integrity of the book, widely differing views have been expressed. Its inner contradictions led Herder to see in it a dialogue between two persons, while Cornill thought it reflected the varying moods of a single person. Others have assigned it to more than one author, Siegfried finding no less than eight hands. McNeile argued that the original work had been interpolated by two hands, the one, whom he called the *Ḥasid* interpolator, introducing the glosses breathing orthodox religious conviction, and the other, whom he called the *Ḥokmah* interpolator, adding the maxims of wordly wisdom. Galling maintained the unity of the work, arguing that it contains the casual jottings of the author, who sometimes quoted a current maxim to add his own mordant observation as a corrective. More recently Gordis has defended the unity of the work. Ginsberg has argued that it was composed in Aramaic and translated into Hebrew in the Maccabaean age.

A much-discussed question is the relation of Ecclesiastes to foreign thought. Langdon argued for Babylonian influence, and Dahood for Canaanite-Phoenician influence. More commonly Greek influence has been maintained. Sellin found the influence of Epicurean, Stoic and Heracleitean philosophy confusedly mixed, while Ranston argued for the influence of the early Gnomic writers, Hesiod and Theognis. Others, including McNeile, denied the alleged Greek influence, while Galling explains much in the book from Egyptian influence.

8. *Esther*. The book of Esther enjoyed extraordinary popularity among the Jews, but its origin is very obscure. In the ὕμνος πατέρων in Sir. 44–49 there is no reference to Esther or Mordecai, though most of the greater heroes of Old Testament story figure in it. From this it is generally regarded as probable that the book is later than Ecclesiasticus (*c*. 180 B.C.). Esther is the only book of the Old Testament not represented amongst the Qumran scrolls, though we should be cautious in drawing conclusions from this. We may perhaps date Esther *c*. 150 B.C.

It is impossible to maintain the historicity of the story. Ahasuerus is generally identified with Xerxes (485–465 B.C.), and since Mordecai is represented as having been carried into captivity in 597 B.C., he would be somewhat elderly 120 years later. Moreover, Xerxes did not have a queen named Esther. Hoschander transferred the story to the reign of Artaxerxes II. (404–359 B.C.), and maintained that a basis of history underlies it. The book shows acquaintance with Persian customs, and its author had access to good sources of information.

Cornill found in it a reflection back into history of the Maccabaean struggle. This seems unlikely, though the fact of that struggle may have influenced the author to present in a Jewish dress older legends gathering round the feast of Purim, and to give a nationalistic significance to the feast.

Most scholars explain the book from eastern mythology. The feast of Purim has a non-Jewish name, and it was probably of foreign origin. Zimmern found its source in the Babylonian New Year's festival in honour of Marduk (=Mordecai), when the gods gathered in an assembly, or *puḫru* (whence Purim). Jensen, on the other hand, connected Esther with the Babylonian goddess Ishtar, Haman with the Elamite god Hamman, Vashti with an Elamite goddess Mashti, and resolved the story into the presentation in the dress of history of a mythological conflict between the Babylonian and the Elamite gods. Lagarde, again, looked to the Persian festival of Farwardigan for the origin of Purim, and Meissner modified this by pointing to the Persian festival of Sacaea, in which elements of Farwardigan were combined with elements from the Babylonian New Year festival. Pfeiffer held that the book is pure fiction, and that the author invented both the feast of Purim and its name. It is clear that no final answer to the question of the sources of the book can yet be given.

9. *Daniel*. The book of Daniel is partly in Hebrew and partly in Aramaic. The first six chapters contain narratives about Daniel, and the last six Daniel's visions. But the change of language does not coincide with the change of character, the Aramaic section being 2^{4b}–7^{28}.

That the book is not the work of one who lived in the sixth century B.C. is certain. For (*a*) there was no siege and capture of Jerusalem in the third year of Jehoiakim (1^1) ; (*b*) Belshazzar was neither the son of Nebuchadnezzar nor the king of Babylon, but the son of Nabonidus, the last king of the neo-Babylonian empire ; he was, however, charged for many years with the administration of Babylon, while his father dwelt in Têma ; (*c*) Darius the Mede is an unhistorical figure, for whom history allows no room, since Cyrus annexed the empire of Nabonidus after having previously annexed the Median kingdom ; (*d*) the use of the word "Chaldaeans" in a non-ethnic sense, to denote a learned, priestly class, though amply paralleled in later classical authors, is unknown in the sixth century, while it is inconsistent with all that we know of the exclusiveness of the Babylonian priesthood that a Hebrew should have been admitted to its membership, and inconsistent with the rigid loyalty of character ascribed to Daniel that he should have consented to become such a heathen priest.

To these decisive considerations others might be added, such as the position of the book in the final division of the Canon ; the non-mention of Daniel in the *ὕμνος πατέρων* in Sir. 44–49 ; and the character of the language. For the Aramaic sections are not in Babylonian Aramaic of the sixth century B.C., but in Aramaic which is later than that of Ezra, which is itself later than that of the fifth century Aramaic papyri from Elephantine, while the Hebrew, which is inferior to the Aramaic in style, is late. In both parts there are Persian loan-words, suggesting by their number a long period of Persian influence, and in the Aramaic there are a few Greek loan-words including one which is not attested in Greek literature in the sense it here has until the second century B.C.

The interest of the book culminates in the reign of Antiochus Epiphanes and his persecution of the Jews, which became acute in 168 B.C. In chaps. 2 and 7 the interest is centred in the fourth kingdom, which is clearly the same in both cases, while the "little horn" of $7^{8.\ 25}$ is the same as the "little horn" of $8^{9\text{ff.}}$, to which is attached an interpretation that definitely locates it in the Greek period that followed Alexander. So also chap. 9 culminates in a similar attack upon the Jews, while the vision of the last three chapters enters with such detail into the history of the Seleucids and the Ptolemies as to be an important historical source for the period, and it, too, culminates in the reign of Antiochus Epiphanes, whose death, however, did not take place in Palestine (11^{45}), but in Persia. The phrase "abomination of desolation," or the like, is found in 8^{13}, 9^{27}, 11^{31}, 12^{11}, where the reference is doubtless the same, binding the chapters together once more in their point of climax. In 1 Macc. 1^{54} the heathen altar which Antiochus set up in Jerusalem is called " the abomination of desolation." The Temple was desecrated and so lay for three years, after which it was cleansed and reconsecrated. It is probably to this period that the half week (9^{27}), and the time and times and half a time (7^{25}; cf. 12^{7}) refer.

In view of the inaccuracy of the knowledge of the sixth century and the remarkable accuracy of the knowledge of the third and early part of the second centuries, it has been generally held that the book was a pseudepigraph, written in the time of Antiochus Epiphanes. That the accuracy of its knowledge falls short of the death of Antiochus, which took place in 164 B.C., has led scholars to date it with precision just before that date. The purpose of the book was then to hearten the persecuted people and to promise them deliverance. All the other considerations noted are consistent with this date, as also is the theology of the book, where we find the resurrection of just and unjust expected (12^{2}), and a developed angelology revealed.

While all of these positions are still challenged by upholders of traditional views (cf. H. H. Rowley, *Darius the Mede*, reprinted 1959), in recent years they are being modified by many critical scholars, who hold that the book is composite. Many years ago Meinhold held the Aramaic part to be extracted by the author of the visions from an older work, while Dalman held the stories and the visions to come from two different hands, a redactor combining the two works by translating the beginning of one into Hebrew and the beginning of the other into Aramaic. Torrey advanced a similar view, save that he believed chaps. 7–12 were written definitely to be attached to chaps. 1–6, the author of 7–12 translating 1^{1}–2^{4a} into Hebrew and writing 7 in Aramaic. Kent and Montgomery followed Torrey, who dated the stories in the middle of the third century B.C. Baumgartner assigned the stories to the Persian period, and Welch thought chaps. 1–6 and probably 7 had a Babylonian origin, and had already taken literary shape before they were adopted by the writer of the present book. Hölscher believed 1–6 to come from the third century B.C., with 7 as a later appendix, and maintained that this work was glossed in the Maccabaean age, when 8–12 were added to it. Haller was in substantial agreement with this, save that he held chap. 7 to be the oldest in the book. There is thus no agreement among those who divide the book as to where chap. 7 belongs, and it is held to be glossed or not according as it is connected with the first part or the second. The present writer believes these views to be mistaken and maintains the unity of the book (cf. H. H. Rowley, *The Servant of the Lord*, 1952, pp. 237–68).

This is not, of course, to deny that the author used older traditions and stories which he reshaped for his purpose.

10. *Chronicles-Ezra-Nehemiah*. In the Hebrew MSS. the two books of Chronicles are combined, as also are Ezra and Nehemiah, but the latter work stands before the former, which closes the Canon. Originally all seem to have formed a single work, whose second part was probably added to the sacred collection before the first, which covered the ground of Samuel and Kings, and was therefore less essential. The reasons for the view that we have a single work are: (*a*) the concluding verses of Chronicles are identical with the opening verses of Ezra, but the passage is mutilated in Chronicles; (*b*) the style of those parts of the two works which come from the editor, as distinct from his sources, is the same; (*c*) the outlook and interests of the editor are identical in the two works, and include a love of genealogies and statistics, and veneration for the Temple and all that pertains to its service.

The date of the work cannot therefore be earlier than the period of Ezra and Nehemiah. This conclusion is reinforced by other considerations: (*a*) the work is written under the influence of P, and the history is frequently rewritten in its light, *e.g.* the Carites of 2 Kings 11 are changed into Levites in 2 Chron. 23, and similarly in 1 Chron. 15 Levites are supplied to carry the Ark into Jerusalem, and the first failure explained by their absence then, whereas 2 Sam. 6 does not mention them on either occasion; (*b*) not only is the account of Chronicles carried down to the reign of Cyrus (537 B.C.), but the genealogy of 1 Chron. 3 carries the Davidic line down to the sixth (Septuagint eleventh) generation after Zerubbabel (*c*. 520 B.C.); (*c*) in Neh. $12^{11.\,22}$ the high-priestly line is carried down to Jaddua, who was high-priest in the time of Alexander; (*d*) in 1 Chron. 29^{7} there is mention of the daric, a coin which was perhaps (but cf. H. H. Rowley, *Darius the Mede*, pp. 45 f.) first coined in the reign of Darius Hystaspis, and which was certainly not circulated in Palestine until post-exilic times; (*e*) the references to "the king of Persia" (Ezra 1^{1}, 3^{7}, 4^{3}, 7^{1}) imply that the Persian empire no longer exists (in Haggai, Zechariah, the *sources* of Ezra-Nehemiah, and the fifth-century Aramaic papyri, we find simply "the king"). We are therefore carried down to a date not earlier than 300 B.C. for the work.

The reader of the work would suppose that Ezra and Nehemiah were contemporaries, but many scholars hold that Nehemiah preceded Ezra. Some ascribe Ezra to the end of the reign of Artaxerxes I., and others think that whereas Nehemiah belonged to the reign of Artaxerxes I., Ezra belonged to the reign of Artaxerxes II., and came to Jerusalem in 397 B.C.

The reasons for this are : (*a*) the absence of reference to either in the other's memoirs, and the fact that on the rare occasions when both names stand in a single context, there is independent reason to suspect the text ; (*b*) the fact that Ezra finds the wall already built (Ezra 9^{9}) ; (*c*) the fact that whereas Nehemiah was contemporary with the high-priest Eliashib (Neh. 3^{1}), Ezra was contemporary with Johanan (Ezra 10^{6}), the grandson of Eliashib (Neh. $12^{11.\,22}$) ; (*d*) the evidence of the Elephantine papyri that Johanan was high-priest in 408 B.C. ; (*e*) the evidence of the same papyri that whereas the Elephantine Jews sent to Jerusalem to ask the high-priest's aid, they sent simultaneously to Samaria to ask the help of Sanballat's sons, probably because Sanballat, the governor and the enemy of Nehemiah, was now aged and the administration was left to his sons.

For the period of the divided monarchy the Chronicler ignores the northern kingdom, and he also deals scantily with Saul. For him the Davidic dynasty is alone legitimate. He does not mention David's sin or family misfortunes or the succession trouble on Solomon's accession. The history is treated with great freedom to suit his interests, and little historical value can be attached to statements on his unsupported authority when they appear to accord with his favourite ideas. He may well, however, have had access to good sources of information now lost to us, and there is a tendency today to credit his narratives, where they do not appear to be dictated by his theories.

Of his sources, in addition to our books of (*a*) Samuel and (*b*) Kings, and probably (*c*) Isaiah, he names several in Chronicles, but it is probable that the same work is separately named for the several sections from the prophets who appear in it, and that for most of Chronicles his extra-biblical sources did not exceed two, (*d*) the " Midrash of the book of Kings " and (*e*) the " Midrash of Iddo the Seer " (so Oesterley and Robinson, though some would identify these two). For Ezra-Nehemiah he used (*f*) Memoirs of Nehemiah and (*g*) Memoirs of Ezra, sometimes quoting verbatim, most probably, but sometimes working over his extracts. In the Aramaic sections in Ezra (4^{8}–6^{18}, $7^{12\text{-}26}$) he quotes documents which purport to be official documents sent to, or from, the Persian monarchs. These doubtless rest on (*h*) an older Aramaic source. Further, he had access to (*i*) Temple records and trustworthy genealogical lists.

It should be added that some writers have denied the unity of Chronicles-Ezra-Nehemiah. Von Rad argued that the work came from two hands, one writing under the influence of D and the other under that of P. Welch, too, found a double recension, assigning the first, consisting of Chronicles (save chaps. 1–9), to *c.* 520 B.C., and the second to a writer influenced by P. He assigned Neh. 10 to shortly after 586 B.C. Rothstein and Hänel dated the groundwork of the Chronicler *c.* 432 B.C. and its revision *c.* 400 B.C., but thought there had been later additions. Similarly Rudolph, who dates the work of the Chronicler *c.* 400 B.C., thinks there were additions over the next two centuries, and Granild includes the account of the work of Nehemiah among the additions. Pfeiffer would bring down the date of the Chronicler to *c.* 250 B.C., but Galling's date, *c.* 300 B.C. seems more probable. The radical view of Torrey, that Ezra was the fictitious creation of the Chronicler, and that there was no Return of the exiles, has secured no significant following.

(v) THE CANON

It is necessary to consider not only the processes which brought the individual books of the Old Testament into existence, but the processes whereby the books were collected and recognized as a sacred corpus, or Canon.

It has commonly been supposed that the three divisions of the Hebrew Canon, to which reference was made at the beginning of this article, correspond to three stages in the growth of the Canon. This view is accepted by Pfeiffer, who assigns the canonization of the Law to *c.* 400 B.C., that of the Prophets to *c.* 200 B.C., and that of the Writings to *c.* A.D. 90, when the Rabbis met at Jamnia and when discussions as to whether certain books rightly belonged to the sacred collection took place. Oesterley and Robinson dispute this and hold that the canonicity of all the books was first declared at Jamnia. It is to be noted, however, that at Jamnia not only the Writings, but also Ezekiel, came under discussion, and the only issue was whether certain books should be excluded from the collection. Moreover, the Samaritans regard the Pentateuch, and only the Pentateuch, as canonical. They were not concerned in the Council of Jamnia, and it would seem certain that the acceptance of the Pentateuch as sacred antedated the final breach between the Jews and the Samaritans. That breach is probably to be dated in the fourth century B.C. There is thus every reason to suppose that the Law was the first part of the Bible to be accepted as canonical. This was not by any decree of a council, however, but because it had become so venerated that it was regarded as inviolable.

The New Testament gives evidence that before the Council of Jamnia most of the Old Testament could be appealed to as authoritative, and its threefold division was accepted (Luke 24^{44}).

It is probable that the process of canonization was a gradual one, and that the different divisions of the Hebrew Canon reached relative fixity at different times. Before the books of Ezra-Nehemiah-Chronicles and Esther had secured veneration, the Former Prophets had already achieved such esteem that nothing could be added to them ; and before Daniel, who is referred to in the New Testament as a prophet, had secured veneration, the collection of the Latter Prophets had achieved the same esteem. We need not suppose that none of the books of the Writings had begun to be collected until after the other parts of the Canon had secured general recognition. The processes for the different parts of the Bible probably overlapped, but the terminus of the process was reached first for the Law, then for the Former Prophets, then for the Latter Prophets, and finally for the Writings, and therefore any works which had not secured widespread recognition as sacred before the terminus of the earlier divisions was treasured with the more miscellaneous collection whose limits were still fluid.

There is no evidence that any books outside the Hebrew Canon were considered for inclusion in the Canon of the Jews. Certain books were challenged, but the fact that they were unsuccessfully challenged shows that they had already gained a position from which they could not be dislodged. In Greek manuscripts of the Old Testament, however, other books are found interspersed among the translations of the Jewish sacred Scriptures. Many writers speak of the Alexandrian Canon, but this is without warrant. No two of the early Greek MSS. which contain such works contain the same selection, and it is therefore out of the question to speak of a "Canon." Some of the early Fathers of the Church denied that they should be accepted as canonical. As they are Jewish works, it is probable that their veneration by Jews led to their being taken over by Christians, but none was considered for inclusion in the Hebrew Canon at Jamnia, and it may be supposed that the process of growth in esteem had not gone very far, and was checked by that Council.

Among Christians, however, many of these works gradually secured an esteem from which they had not been dislodged, and they are accepted by the Roman Church as "deutero-canonical." In Protestant Bibles they are placed in the separate collection of the Apocrypha. Some Protestant Churches have accepted them as profitable for edification, and some Roman writers, both before and since the official acceptance of them in the Canon, have raised their voices against them. It is most instructive to see how from the fluidity of the early Christian acceptance of these additional works, as represented by the great fourth and fifth century uncial MSS., fixity was gradually achieved in spite of opposition, until with the Council of Trent final fixity for the Roman Church was attained. For the process of the canonization of the books of the Hebrew Canon was probably similarly gradual, until the Council of Jamnia gave a recognition which it was powerless to withhold.

BIBLIOGRAPHY

G. W. Anderson, *A Critical Introduction to the Old Testament*, 1959.
A. Bentzen, *Introduction to the Old Testament*, 2nd ed., 1952.
J. A. Bewer, *The Literature of the Old Testament*, 3rd ed., revised by E. G. Kraeling, 1962.
S. R. Driver, *Introduction to the Literature of the Old Testament*, 9th ed., 1913.
O. Eissfeldt, *Einleitung in das Alte Testament*, 2nd ed., 1956.
H. F. Hahn, *Old Testament in Modern Research*, 1954.
W. O. E. Oesterley and T. H. Robinson, *An Introduction to the Books of the Old Testament*, 1934.
R. H. Pfeiffer, *Introduction to the Old Testament*, 2nd ed., 1952.
H. H. Rowley, *The Growth of the Old Testament*, 1950.
H. H. Rowley (ed. by), *The Old Testament and Modern Study*, 1951.
A. Weiser, *Introduction to the Old Testament*, Eng. trans. by D. M. Barton, 1961.

IV. THE INTER-TESTAMENTAL LITERATURE

By M. Black

By the "inter-testamental" literature we mean the body of Jewish writings which were produced "between the Testaments," *i.e.*, roughly from 200 B.C. to A.D. 100. The books of this literature are usually referred to as the *Apocrypha and Pseudepigrapha* of the Old Testament. The Apocrypha are available in some editions of the Revised Version of the English Bible, and the new American Revised Standard Version is specially recommended. The so-called Pseudepigrapha are collected in English translation with notes in the large two-volume work of R. H. Charles entitled *The Apocrypha and Pseudepigrapha of the Old Testament* (1913).

The term "apocrypha," "apocryphal," as applied to the books so described, has a curious history, and is, in fact, something of a misnomer. The Greek word means "hidden away" and was probably originally a rendering of the Hebrew *gānûz* (pass. partc. of *gānaz*) "hidden" which, when applied to books, referred to books which were either banned or discarded, since it was customary to hide such books away in a *Genizah* (a hiding-place) in the Synagogue rather than to destroy them, for fear of desecrating the sacred name which most of them contained. (Later they might be removed from the Genizah and solemnly interred.) The term "apocrypha" was first applied not to the books which now go by that name but to the collection which we now call "pseudepigrapha" (with the inclusion of 4 Esdras). It was these "apocalypses"—as they mostly are—known in Hebrew as *hag-gilyônîm* from *gālāh*, "to reveal," or as *siphrê hammînîm*, books of the heretics, which were first called "apocrypha," "hidden away," *i.e.* banned. Thus the word is so used to describe this literature in Origen's time, though it may also have been understood to mean "books with hidden (esoteric) meanings." The books now called apocrypha were then known as "ecclesiastical books" (*libri ecclesiastici*) to distinguish them from "canonical books" (*libri canonici*). (See further below under *Ecclesiasticus*.) It was St. Jerome who first applied the term "apocryphal" to these books, appropriating it from the "apocalypses." Jerome's new use was not generally approved (St. Augustine still uses "apocryphal" in the old sense, *de Civ. Dei* xv. 23), but the new usage eventually established itself, though there was nothing either esoteric or "heretical" about the books so described. The "apocalypses" came to be known as "pseudepigrapha" (lit. false titles) since they were generally falsely attributed to an author such as Enoch or Solomon, the real author remaining anonymous.

(i) APOCRYPHA

In general the *apocrypha* are on a higher plane, both as literature and for their religious contents, than the *pseudepigrapha*.

The order which is here followed is a roughly chronological one, though it is, of course, at times impossible to be certain about the date or dates of a writing; and one of the main features of this literature is its composite character, with elements coming from widely different periods.

1. The so-called *Letter of Jeremiah* may be the earliest of the apocrypha, but its date is not certain, and it may have been written any time between 323 and 100 B.C. (*i.e.* within the Greek period of Hebrew history). It purports to be a letter of Jeremiah to his fellow-countrymen who were about to be led into Babylonian exile, warning them against the dangers of idolatry. It is obviously an imitation of the genuine Epistle of Jeremiah (29^{1-23}) with even sharper warnings against false gods. Though it has reached us in a Christian redaction only, it was basically a Jewish work originally composed in Hebrew or Aramaic (it has survived in Greek, Syriac, and Latin versions). It is no more a letter than the genuine epistle, but a homily or tractate, written in a somewhat florid and rhetorical style, against idolatry; its text is Jer. 11^{10}.

2. *I Esdras* (or the Greek Ezra) was written about 200 B.C., again originally in Hebrew or Aramaic, but it is now preserved in a free Greek version. The nomenclature and order of the various writings attributed to Ezra the Scribe are puzzling since they differ in different traditions. 1 Esdras is the designation of the Septuagint (=Old Latin, Syriac) for this book, though it is also known as "the Greek Ezra," apparently to distinguish this freer Greek version from the more literal Greek translation of the canonical Ezra-Nehemiah, designated 2 Esdras in the Septuagint. (Lucian gave priority to the canonical books and reversed the order.) The book is known as 3 Esdras in the Vulgate where the book of Ezra = 1 Esdras, and Nehemiah = 2 Esdras. The Apocalypse of Esdras (see below, page 81)—is variously known as 4 or 2 Esdras, according as one is following Vulgate or another Latin order.

The book recounts the history of Israel from Josiah (621 B.C.) to Ezra, basing itself substantially, with minor differences in underlying recension, order of stories, etc., on the Chronicles-Ezra-Nehemiah account. The only new story is that of King Darius and the three young Jews of his bodyguard who entered into a contest in wise sayings, the winner, Zerubbabel, being permitted as a reward to lead the Jews back to Jerusalem. The main purpose of the book is to show how the Temple came to be rebuilt and its cultus reinaugurated.

3. The *Book of Tobit* (also *c.* 200 B.C.) was likewise originally in Hebrew, though it may also have circulated at an early period in Aramaic—both Hebrew and Aramaic fragments have been found at Qumran.* Tobit is a pious Jewish folk-tale, one of the earliest forms of the literary genre from which the novel has developed (the story of Joseph in Genesis is similar in character). The Tobit tale resembles the story of the Persian sage Ahikar, with which the writer appears even to have been familiar, and, like many examples of Jewish writings from the Greek period, shows traces of marked foreign influence, mostly Persian in inspiration, though the book itself may first have appeared in Egypt.

Tobit is a strict Galilaean Jew living in the eighth century B.C., devoted to the meticulous observance of the Law in both its moral code and ceremonial aspects, given to charitable deeds, and thus held up as an exemplar of Jewish piety. Along with his wife and sons he is carried off into captivity to Babylon in 721 B.C. (cf. 2 Kings $18^{9ff.}$). There his extraordinary piety is rewarded by a position of trust as a purchasing agent of King Shalmaneser. In the course of one of his trips in Media he left ten talents of silver in trust with a friend of his in Rages, named Gabael. After the accession of Sennacherib, Tobit's fortunes took a turn for the worse, and he was banished from Nineveh. Sennacherib, however, was assassinated and Tobit was permitted to return to Nineveh, but, for all his piety, his fortune did not mend—he was blinded in an accident and forced to live on his wife's earnings as a dressmaker—and in his anguish Tobit prays to be released from his sufferings by death itself.

Meantime, in far away Ecbatana, Sarah, the daughter of Raguel, a kinsman of Tobit, was also praying for death : Sarah had been married seven times, but on each occasion her husband had died before the marriage could be consummated. Sarah was accused by her hand-maidens of having murdered her husbands : in fact they had died as the result of the evil machinations of a wicked demon Asmodaeus, himself in love with Sarah.

Tobit, preparing for death, gives instructions to his son

* Editions of these fragments have not yet been published, so that their relationship to the later versions is not known.

Tobias, admonishing him " Remember the Lord our God all your days, my son, and refuse to sin and transgress His commandments " (chap. 4) and " what you hate, do not do to anyone " (4^{15}), the first occurrence in Jewish literature of the negative form of the Golden Rule. Tobias is given a commission to go to Tobit's friend in Rages to recover the ten talents of silver once left in trust with him.

Then there follows the best-known part of the story—the tale of Tobias and the Angel.

Tobias sets out with a certain Azarias as his travelling companion, the latter, in fact, being the angel Raphael. While washing in the Tigris on their journey Tobias is attacked by a great fish which he seizes and throws up on the land. On the advice of Azarias, he cuts the fish open and removes and keeps the heart, gall and liver, being informed by his guide that smoke from them would drive away any molesting demon or evil spirit. As they approach the city where Sarah lives the angel informs Tobias that Sarah is destined to be his bride. Tobias, who had heard of Sarah's previous matrimonial misfortunes, is not very happy at the prospect, but the wedding is arranged, and while Sarah's mother is making the preparations for the wedding feast, her father, of a less sanguine turn of mind, sets about digging Tobias's grave.

But all ends happily, for Tobias follows the angel Raphael's advice, smokes the entrails of the fish, and the wicked Asmodaeus flees to the remotest parts of Egypt where the angel binds him. With the help of Azarias, Tobias completes his commission and returns to Nineveh with his bride and the ten talents of silver.

The book ends on a peaceful note. Tobit dies full of years and Tobias provides a magnificent funeral for his aged father, returning to live with his bride in Ecbatana, and Tobias lives on to the ripe age of 127, learning with rejoicing before his death of the destruction of Nineveh.

4. The *Book of Ecclesiasticus*, or the Wisdom of Jesus, son of Sirach, is one of the longest books of the Apocrypha, and possibly the best known. It was written in Hebrew *c.* 200 B.C. and is one of the few inter-testamental books of which substantial portions of the original (some two-thirds of the whole book) have been preserved. Four fragmentary manuscripts were discovered in an Old Cairo Synagogue just before the beginning of this century: they had been in the possession of a famous Jewish sect (the Qaraites), and though the manuscripts belong to the eleventh and twelfth centuries, it is now virtually certain that their archetype came from the Qumran Essene sect. A few Hebrew fragments were discovered at Qumran in 1952. The book fell into disuse in rabbinical Judaism,

possibly because of its popularity among Christians or sectarian Jews.

The title Ecclesiasticus comes from the Latin version "(Liber) ecclesiasticus" and is usually explained as meaning "the Church Book." Why it came to be so called is less easy to explain: it has been suggested that it got this name as a book which, though not canonical, was nevertheless regarded as suitable for reading in Church. It is preserved in Greek, Syriac, and Latin translations, and in a number of secondary versions.

Ecclesiasticus belongs to the category of Hebrew Wisdom literature, though its contents are a strange blend of profound *sententiae* of the type familiar in the Book of Proverbs along with prudential maxims, including advice which we would rather associate with craftsmanship or business dealing, as well as the praise of wisdom, self-control, discretion—all that comes under the general heading of right living, and all culminating in the fear of the Lord.

Ecclesiasticus is the only book in the Apocrypha where the author's name is known: he tells us (50^{27}) that he is Jesus, the son of Sirach, the son of Eleazar, of Jerusalem; he probably belonged to the professional scribes or *ḥᵃkhāmîm*, and, as such, he may have been of priestly family. Some fifty years after the book appeared a grandson of the author translated it into Greek, mainly for distribution among Alexandrian Jews.

The material of the book is not arranged according to any discernible system or sequence. At times it rises to poetic heights, as, for instance, in the description of God's work in nature ($43^{13f.}$). The longest connected section in the book is the celebrated chapter in praise of famous men, the introductory words of which are among the best-known in the Apocrypha:

> Let us now praise famous men,
> and our fathers in their generations.
> The Lord appointed to them great glory,
> his majesty from the beginning.

Theologically the book seems to show Sadducaean influences: there is no doctrine of the resurrection and rewards and punishments are meted out here on earth. An interest in the worship of the Temple and in its priesthood may also suggest Sadducaean connexions, and Ezra, the scribe *par excellence* and the spiritual father of Pharisaism, is passed over when Ben Sira enumerates the Fathers of old.

5. The so-called *Song of the Three Children* is an addition inserted into Daniel after 3^{23} in the Septuagint, providing one of the three condemned youths who had been bound and thrown into the fiery furnace with a prayer, possibly in order

to avoid the impression given by the unadorned narrative that it was the pagan King Nebuchadnezzar who had been the first to recognize and bless the God of Israel; it may also have been added to indicate that the deliverance from the fire was an answer to prayer. It may have come from a collection of hymns, and it appears to have been translated from Hebrew; there is a certain similarity in detail with Ps. 148. The addition is usually dated, on internal grounds, to a period after the persecutions of Antiochus Epiphanes, *i.e. c.* 170–165 B.C.

6. The *Book of Judith* is a pious fiction in the style and manner of Tobit, told with great skill and with its unfolding drama vividly presented. Judith's thanksgiving prayer (16^{17}) has been compared, for its literary qualities, with the Song of Deborah. The date of composition of the original Hebrew is usually set about the middle of the second century B.C., possibly during the Maccabaean struggles.

The book falls into two parts. The first describes the war of the Assyrians and the Jews. Nebuchadnezzar's commander-in-chief Holofernes invests Jerusalem in the course of a great punitive expedition against Assyria's western enemies. Part 2 goes on to narrate how Judith, a Jewish patriot, by sheer audacity and cunning, brought about Holofernes' death and raised the siege. Judith was a wealthy widow of great beauty matched only by her deep piety. Dressed in her finest clothes and adorning her person with jewels and cosmetics "to entice the eyes of all men who might see her" (10^{4}) she made her way to Holofernes' camp and, by pretending to be a Jewess fleeing from the city, won her way into the presence-chamber of the commander-in-chief. Holofernes was captivated and at a banquet at which he had arranged to entertain his beautiful and treacherous visitor, he was murdered by her, and his head carried off, as a ghastly trophy, to her fellow-countrymen. The enemy, panic-stricken when they discovered that their general had been murdered, fled at the first resolute onslaught of the besieged.

The story was no doubt a tract for the times, when the times were evil in the days of the Maccabees. Patriotism and devotion to God are identical and the chief virtues are those of the dedicated warrior.

7. The *Prayer of Manasseh*, which has been described as a "classic of penitential devotion," is usually dated to approximately the same period as Judith, *i.e.* mid-second century B.C. The purpose of the prayer appears to have been to show that the divine mercy goes out even to the worst offenders, since it was extended to Manasseh, reputedly one of the wickedest of the kings of Judah. The composition of the prayer was suggested by the statement at 2 Chron. 33^{18} that Manasseh's

penitential prayer was recorded in "the book of the Kings of Israel." No such source has survived, and a devout Jew of the second century supplied the lack by our apocryphal prayer. The prayer never formed part of the Septuagint text of 2 Chron. 33, but it found a permanent place in Christian liturgical tradition.

8. The Septuagint of the *Book of Esther* has six additional chapters, originally composed in Greek about 130–25 B.C. Their evident purpose was to give to a book otherwise devoid of religious meaning and message some kind of religious justification. They are usually found at the end of the canonical books, where they make little consecutive sense: originally, however, they were interpolations at different points in the book, intended by their Greek composer to give some religious point to the episodes narrated. When St. Jerome prepared his Vulgate Version on the basis of the Hebrew he extracted these additional sections and collected them together at the end, with explanatory notes. The last step towards our present position for these chapters was taken when Stephen Langton, Archbishop of Canterbury († 1228), numbered the chapters of Esther consecutively with the apocryphal additions at the end *as six additional chapters, but without Jerome's explanations.* A typical addition is the prayer of Mordecai and Esther originally inserted at chaps. 13^{8}–14^{19}. An excellent discussion of the additions is to be found in Professor B. M. Metzger's *Introduction to the Apocrypha*.

9. The apocryphal writing which goes under the name of *Susanna* (or *Susanna and the Elders*) is one of several additions to the Book of Daniel and it is deservedly the most widely known, for it is one of the best short folk-tales of Jewish imaginative piety.* It was originally written in Greek, possibly in Alexandria, though the author may have been a Palestinian Jew; its date is uncertain and is usually set in the second or first century B.C. Susanna was the wife of a Babylonian Jew, by name Joachim, as beautiful as she was virtuous. It was her custom to walk in her husband's garden each day at noon, where she was observed by two elders accustomed to attend daily Joachim's court house. They both became infatuated with the beautiful Jewess, and, making known their illicit passion to each other, set a plot to seduce her. As she was bathing alone one day in the garden pool she was approached by the elders: "Look," they said, "the garden doors are shut, no one sees us, and we are in love with you;

* In her volume entitled *Omnibus of Crime* Miss Dorothy Sayers places the story, along with its companion-piece Bel and the Dragon (another folk-tale addition to Daniel) at the beginning of her classics of detective or mystery tories.

so give your consent, and lie with us. If you refuse, we will testify against you that a young man was with you, and this was why you sent your maids away" (vv.[20-21]). Susanna called for help and the elders did as they had threatened. Susanna was condemned to death by stoning as an adulteress, but, just as she was being led away for execution, the young man Daniel demanded the right to cross-examine the false witnesses. He put the same question to each separately: "Under what tree did you see them being intimate with each other?" The one elder replied: "Under a mastic tree." The other replied: "Under an evergreen oak." The case against the lying elders was proved: Susanna was acquitted and the two elders were promptly put to death under the law of Deut. 19[18-21] ". . . and from that day onward Daniel had a great reputation among the people" (v.[64]).

10. The little book known as *Bel and the Dragon* is another apocryphal addition to the Book of Daniel, of uncertain date but of the same period as Susanna (second to first century B.C.). It was probably originally composed in Hebrew. Its purpose is to ridicule idolatry and heathen priestcraft. The title is misleading since there are two separate stories, not a single story, in this apocryphal addition to Daniel. The first is the story of Bel (vv.[1-22]), the patron deity of Babylonia which Daniel refused to acknowledge, declaring that the immense quantity of food which the idol daily consumed was never eaten by the god. Cyrus the king then commanded the priests of Bel to seal off the image so that none of them could have access to it overnight. This they did, knowing well that they had a trap-door underneath by which they could secretly reach the food and drink which they and their families nightly consumed. But Daniel gave instructions for a fine dust to be sprinkled on the floor overnight. When the king arrived the deceit of the priests was disclosed by the marks of their footsteps on the Temple floor. Daniel was vindicated and the priests of Bel put to death by order of the king.

The story of the *Dragon* or Serpent is a sequel to the story of Bel. The Serpent (apparently a live snake) was also an object of veneration in Babylon, but Daniel again refused the king's command to worship it, declaring, "I will worship the Lord my God, for he is the living God. But if you, O king, will give me permission, I will slay the dragon without sword or club." King Cyrus, believing in the dragon's immortality, granted permission, and Daniel slew the serpent by feeding it a concoction of pitch, fat and hair, boiled into cakes (vv.[23-27]). As a retaliation for his destruction of Bel, the slaying of its priests and of the dragon, Daniel (according to the apocryphal addition) was thrown into the den of lions.

11. *1 Maccabees* is the most famous of the inter-testamental historical books, written originally in Hebrew about the year 90–70 B.C.; the book antedates the Roman occupation of Palestine, and is subsequent to the reign of John Hyrcanus († 104–103 B.C.). Though the book was best known in its Greek translation (Josephus knew it in this version) Hebrew copies are said to have survived to the time of St. Jerome; there are also two Latin and two Syriac versions. Like most of the historical writings of the period, 1 Maccabees makes use of earlier sources: this is clear from such passages as 9^{22} and 16^{24} (which mentions the chronicles of Hyrcanus's high-priesthood) as well as at $11^{3.\ 7}$, $14^{18.\ 27}$. One of these sources was a collection of psalms and hymns, e.g. at $1^{25ff.\ 36ff.}$, $2^{8ff.\ 44}$, 9^{41}, $14^{16ff.}$; 7^{17} draws on the canonical Psalm 79^{2-3}, so that these hymns may derive from the Maccabaean hymns and psalms, some of which have survived in our Psalter. A similar collection of hymns and psalms has now been found at Qumran, and they resemble in some points the hymns preserved in 1 Maccabees.

The book gives a sober and reliable account of the story of the Maccabaean uprising and the establishment of the Hasmonaean dynasty. It takes its name from the central figure of the Jewish revolt against Syria, Judas, nicknamed Maccabaeus, usually explained to mean "the hammerer (of the Gentiles)." It begins with the accession to the Syrian throne of Antiochus known as Epiphanes ("manifest," *i.e.* deity manifest), a name which the Jews turned into Epimanes (the madman), and, after a description of the Syrian attempts to hellenize Judaism, goes on to recount the victorious exploits of the Maccabaean heroes.

12. *2 Maccabees*, composed in Greek, possibly by an Alexandrian Jew, sometime during the first half of the second century B.C., is a quite different type of book, historical in form but religious in outlook and purpose. The author himself informs us (2^{23}) that his work is an epitome of the five books of a certain Jason of Cyrene. The book purports to cover the same historical period as the first book, but there is no proper sequence of events. Judas Maccabaeus and his exploits are described, but otherwise the Hasmonaean house is ignored: the author was, in all probability, a Pharisee and anti-Hasmonaean. In the place of sober history we are given tales of the miraculous and of supernatural apparitions. The book has been well described as a romanticized melodrama rather than a history—even as history was written in that period.

13. Like Ecclesiasticus, the Book known as the *Wisdom of Solomon* belongs to the category of Jewish sapiential literature.

The work was originally written in Greek by an unknown hellenistic Jew, probably from Alexandria; its date is uncertain, but it is usually assigned to the second half of the last century B.C. or the first half of the first Christian century. It was issued in the name of Solomon, like the canonical Book of Proverbs, and no doubt in order to give it a standing and place in the Wisdom tradition of Judaism. Its unity and literary integrity have been called in question, in view of the marked differences between chaps. 1^{1}–2^{1} and 11^{2-19}, but the differences may reflect nothing more than a change in outlook and attitude of the writer; the two parts may have been written at different periods of his life.

In contrast to Ecclesiasticus with its interest in practical ethics and manners Wisdom is more of the nature of a theological treatise in which Jewish orthodox piety is united with the Greek philosophical spirit. A special feature of the book is the way in which it carries forward the personification of Wisdom begun in Proverbs and developed in Ecclesiasticus to its highest point: Wisdom is identified with the power of God (1^{3}), the spirit of God (9^{17}), and the hand of God (14^{6}). Chap. 2 appear sto be combating what is regarded as the erroneous teaching of Ecclesiasticus.

Wisdom was held in high esteem by the early Church and is possibly the most quoted of the Apocrypha. The reasons for this are readily understood: 2^{12-20} were taken to be prophecies of the sufferings of Christ; 5^{1-9} describe, in a classic passage, the blessedness of the righteous departed (and the condign punishment of the wicked).

14. The book of *Baruch* (*1 Baruch*) is modelled on Old Testament prophecy and purports to be a prophecy and exhortation of Baruch, the son of Neriah, companion and amanuensis of Jeremiah, addressed to the exiled Jews and their deposed king Jeconiah five years after the destruction of Jerusalem (586 B.C.).

Internal criticism has established that the book consists of three separate and independent sections, written by different authors, 1^{1}–3^{8}; 3^{9}–4^{4}; 4^{5}–5^{9}. The first section is in prose, the second and third in poetic form. The language was originally Hebrew, and this is confirmed by the tradition that the book at one time was used in the Jewish liturgy (some scholars argue that some portions were originally composed in Greek). The first part is dated after A.D. 70, the second and third parts towards the end of the first century A.D.

In the first prose section Baruch calls the exiles to repentance for the sins of Israel "for we have sinned against the Lord our God, and to this day the anger of the Lord and His wrath have not turned away from us" (1^{13}). The prescription is then laid down that the book is to be read publicly on feast days and at certain appointed times. Then follows the confession of sin and prayer for the divine mercy. The same general theme is continued in the second part, in poetic style, and the third part concludes with words of comfort, encouragement, and hope for the restoration of Jerusalem. The book is quoted as Scripture by some of the early Fathers.

15. *4* (*2*) *Esdras* is a composite work, the latest in the Apocrypha, containing Christian elements in the first two chapters: in their present form these introductory chapters belong to the second century A.D., and were obviously added by a later editor for they were clearly originally composed in Greek. The concluding two chaps. 15 and 16 were also added, in Greek, by a later editorial hand, possibly the same editor as composed the Introduction. The main Jewish portion of the book is the so-called Ezra Apocalypse (3–14), written about A.D. 100, and possibly originally composed in Aramaic. The Apocalypse consists of seven visions to Ezra in Babylon; the main burden of these "revelations" given to Ezra by an *angelus interpres* is to give some explanation of Israel's sufferings. The most famous of the visions is the sixth—the man from the sea, symbolic of the appearance of the Messiah, who is to annihilate his enemies and gather together again the lost tribes of Israel.

The book survives in secondary versions only: there are several Old Latin versions, for the book appears to have enjoyed considerable popularity in the West (it is published as 4 Esdras in the Vulgate*): there are also Syriac, Coptic, Ethiopic, Arabic (two versions), Armenian, and Georgian translations. All that has survived of the Greek version (the original Aramaic has completely perished) are three verses of chap. 15 which were found in a leaf from an Egyptian manuscript (*Papyrus Oxyrhynchus* VII, 1001).

(ii) PSEUDEPIGRAPHA

1. We turn now to the remaining inter-testamental books known as the *Pseudepigrapha*, and begin with the oldest, and certainly the most important from the theological point of view, namely the *Book of Enoch* or 1 *Enoch*, which, like 1 Baruch, was quoted as Scripture in the early Church (*e.g.* by the author of Jude, v.[14]). The book is a composite one, made up, in the redaction which has reached us, of a mixture of many disparate elements of different periods and dates. It appears, in fact,

* The Vulgate text is defective at 7^{35} where in most Latin manuscripts some of the verses had been lost. The missing verses were supplied from an Amiens manuscript of the ninth century discovered in 1874 by Robert L. Bensly of Cambridge.

to be a collection of pieces from a whole apocalyptic tradition subsumed under the name of Enoch and carried on, for instance, in 2 Enoch and in the Hebrew 3 Enoch.

The whole of the 101 chapters known as 1 Enoch have been preserved in an Ethiopic version only—in manuscripts not earlier than the fifteenth or sixteenth centuries—but substantial portions of the Greek version have also survived. Fragments in Aramaic, in some eight different recensions, from almost every chapter except chaps. 37–71, have been found at Qumran. They have not yet been published and their connexion, therefore, with the Greek version, is still unknown: it seems fairly certain, however, that the Aramaic was the original of the Greek.

According to our main authority, R. H. Charles, the oldest parts are chaps. 12–36 and the so-called Apocalypse of Weeks (91^{12-17}, 93), both of which are dated by him *c.* 200 B.C. Fragments of a "Book of Noah," which have been incorporated in 1 Enoch, are, likewise, pre-Maccabaean. Chaps. 83-90, the "Dream Visions" are dated *c.* 160 B.C.; chaps. 72–82, the "Book of the Heavenly Luminaries" or the "Book of Astronomy," *c.* 100 B.C. The Parables or Similitudes (chaps. 37–71) are assigned by Charles to the first half of the first century B.C. So too are chaps. 91–104. Chaps. 1–5, the introduction, are, according to Charles, the latest section of the book.

The most important chapters theologically are those known as the Similitudes of Enoch, where the Danielic symbol of the Son of Man (Dan. 7^{13}, a figure for Israel) reappears as a supernatural being who is to act as viceregent of God in the forthcoming judgment of mankind. It has been generally assumed, till recently, that this section of 1 Enoch is Jewish and pre-Christian. But, like 2 Enoch, now conclusively shown to be a syncretistic work with Christian elements, the Similitudes have not been freed of all suspicion of Christian influence or tampering; no trace of these chapters of 1 Enoch has been found at Qumran. It may be too (even granted a pre-Christian Jewish book) that earlier interpretation was wrong in assuming too hastily that the central figure was an individual, not, as in Daniel, corporate and symbolic of Israel; perhaps the idea of the Son of Man in Enoch, like the idea of the Servant of the Lord in Second Isaiah, was both individual and corporate. An older tradition of Son of Man belief appears too to be embedded in chaps. 70–71, where the Son of Man is unmistakably identified with the glorified patriarch Enoch himself. In that case we may require to assume a pre-Christian form of Jewish mystic "gnosticism," where the figure of Enoch was the centre of belief in a divine-human mediator, and coming world Judge. But such a "mysticism" may well all be post-Christian and derivative, as much in the mysticism of the Hebrew 3 Enoch appears to be.

2. The so-called *Sibylline Oracles* is a collection of prophecies or pseudo-prophecies, composed in Greek, probably in Alexandria, by a hellenistic Jew, an imitation of the famous pagan collection of oracular utterances of this kind. There appear originally to have been fourteen books of these writings, twelve of which have survived. Different parts of the collection come from different dates: the *Prooemium* and Book III are the oldest parts, and are dated to the middle of the second century B.C. Books IV and V are next in point of antiquity, dating from the second half of the first century A.D. Though the work is originally Jewish, it has been preserved by Christians, and there is evidence in different places of Christian influence and interpolation.

3. The *Testaments of the Twelve Patriarchs* was originally written in Hebrew and Aramaic, possibly about 100 B.C. The book has survived in a Greek recension which shows frequent Christian interpolations. Aramaic fragments have been found, including fragments from Qumran; comparison with the corresponding passages in the Greek version reveals a very extensive reworking of the original—in its Greek form it is virtually a Christian writing.

The book purports to give the last words of each of the twelve patriarchs to his sons, each "testament" being modelled on Jacob's last words at Gen. 49. Each patriarch delivers his parting advice to his descendants, dwelling on his own virtues and sins. The sins against which the patriarchs give their most urgent warnings are sexual vice, envy, hatred, anger, covetousness, intemperance, falsehood. Brotherly love, compassion and forgiveness are particularly stressed, and, in this respect, the moral teaching is on a very high level, though it may owe something to Christian influences.

There is an important apocalyptic element. Beliar, the prince of evil, is to be bound and cast into the fires of Gehenna (T. Lev. 18^{12}, T. Judah 25^{3}) by the Messiah descended from Levi. The book also appears to envisage a Messiah from Judah, and in its doctrine of two Messiahs, as in other respects, such as its teaching on the two ways (T. Asher 1^{3}) and the two spirits (T. Judah 20), resemblances have been noted with the Qumran writings.

4. The *Book of Jubilees* is one of the longest of the Pseudepigrapha, and next in importance to Enoch. It was originally written in Aramaic some time in the second century B.C. but is now, like 1 Enoch, preserved mainly in an Ethiopic version, the translation of a Greek version which enjoyed a very wide currency and of which a fair number of fragments have been

preserved by the Fathers. Fragments of the original are also reported to have been found at Qumran.

Jubilees is a haggadic or expository commentary on Genesis (it is sometimes known as " the little Genesis "), and represents an interpretation of the story of the Genesis narrative from the creation to the giving of the Law on Mount Sinai. The name Jubilees derives from the divisions of the history into " Jubilee " periods each of 49 years. The author was probably a Pharisee.

Jubilees is a typical product of the midrashic treatment of Biblical history. The author does for Genesis what the Chronicler did for the history of Samuel and Kings : one of his main purposes is to show that the Torah had been meticulously observed by the Patriarchs and he passes over in silence any facts or incidents which could be understood as breaches of the divine Law.

The form given to this midrash is that of a special revelation made to Moses on Mount Sinai by " the angel of the Presence " who refers to " heavenly tablets." In this way there is traced back long before Moses traditional observances of the Law which the Patriarch represents as first revealed by Moses. Thus the Feast of Weeks (Pentecost) was celebrated in Heaven from the Creation to Noah (6^{18}) and on earth by Noah and Abraham ($6^{17ff.}$). The ritual of the Feasts is described in great detail, and the author follows a calendar peculiar to himself which may have represented an attempt in certain circles to reform the Jewish festal calendar. (It has been suggested that the Calendar of Jubilees is identical with the sectarian calendar observed at Qumran.) In a number of other instances the " law " which the author regards as valid differs from the later interpretation and practices of the rabbis and may, therefore, represent a pre-Christian sectarian school of Torah.

5. *3 Maccabees* is a Greek composition, variously dated by scholars to the last century B.C. or the first century A.D. Though it purports to be a history, it is, in fact, pious fiction for the glorification of the Jews : but it is apologetic fiction, with the underlying purpose of showing that the Jews, however much they were despised for their religion, were nevertheless good citizens and loyal to the State authorities ; and God was always on their side : " the God of heaven surely protects the Jews, fighting on their side continually as a father for his children " (7^{6}). The style of writing is rhetorical and bombastic to a degree and the work has been described as " a specimen of the worst kind of pseudo-classicalism." The title is a misnomer, for the book has nothing to do with the Maccabees : it has probably arisen through the collocation of the book with the books of the Maccabees in the manuscripts, or possibly through a superficial resemblance to 2 Maccabees.

6. The *Psalms of Solomon* have been attributed to Solomon for the same reason as is the Wisdom of Solomon, though possibly also their author thought that, as David had written so many psalms, his example must have been followed by his son. They consist of eighteen psalms, the work of a Pharisee writing in the middle of the first century B.C., originally written in Hebrew though preserved only in Greek; they may have had a place at some time in the service of the Synagogue. There is every reason to believe that they are of Palestinian origin.

It is in these psalms that classic expression is given in the inter-testamental literature to the Pharisaic form of the doctrine of the Davidic Messiah. There is nothing superhuman or supernatural about this figure: the Anointed Lord (or the Anointed of the Lord) is to reign as an actual king of David's line in a restored Israel. Nevertheless, he is to be raised up by God Himself, to whom alone is known the time of his coming ($17^{23.\,47}$, 18^{6}). His rule is to be spiritual, holy, wise, and just. He is not to be an aggressive conqueror trusting in force of arms, but in Yahweh (cf. Isa. 9^{6}; Zech. 9^{11}; Mic. 4^{1}). At the same time, he is to overthrow the supremacy of the Gentile rule and to destroy them utterly from Jerusalem and the borders of Israel ($17^{25.\,27.\,31}$), driving out also the renegades of Israel itself who have obtained unlawful possession of the land. In general, the figure may be described as "Solomonic," but it is the figure of one "greater than Solomon," King David's "greater son," who is to restore Israel and gather the dispersion into a new Jerusalem.

It is in its ethical features that this ideal of a personal Messiah of Pharisaism constitutes a remarkable *praeparatio evangelica*: the ideal Messianic king's personal purity from sin, *e.g.* is to be the measure of his authority (17^{41}); and under him all his subjects shall become holy and "sons of God" (17^{30}; cf. Rom. 8^{15}; Matt. 5^{45}, etc.).

7. *4 Maccabees* is a Greek work, written in the first century A.D., probably in Alexandria, the main purpose of which is to commend and inculcate "pious reason," a characteristically Hebrew form of philosophy. This is done by an elaboration of the story, taken from 2 Maccabees, of the martyrdom of the aged priest Eleazar and of an unnamed mother and her seven sons, martyred under Antiochus Epiphanes. The book reads like a sermon, and it may have been originally delivered orally; it has been suggested that it was first composed and delivered as a kind of memorial address on the Feast of Dedication, to commemorate the Maccabaean martyrs.

8. The *Assumption of Moses* is a short apocalypse preserved in one Old Latin palimpsest manuscript only and bearing this

title. The apocryphal lists know of a *Testament of Moses*, and since our apocalypse is a testament of Moses, similar to the Testaments of the Twelve Patriarchs, these lists are probably referring to the same book. The Latin is a translation of a lost Greek text: the original was in Hebrew or Aramaic and is believed to have been the work of a Pharisee possibly of the first part of the first century A.D. Chap. 10^{1-10} is in poetry and may come from an earlier work; doctrinally it is an important passage: the reign of God will be established by a judgment (and destruction) of men and nations. Evil is conceived as a cosmic force and the world as the Kingdom of Satan and his demonic powers (an idea found also in the new Hebrew scrolls); and the final triumph of the reign of God will bring the total destruction of the reign of Satan.

And then his Kingdom shall appear throughout all His creation,
And then Satan shall be no more
And sorrow shall depart with him . . .
For the Heavenly One will arise from His royal throne,
And He will go forth from His Holy habitation
With indignation and wrath on account of His sons . . .
For the Most High will arise, the Eternal God alone,
And He will appear to punish the Gentiles,
And He will destroy all idols.
And thou, Israel, shalt be happy, . . .
And God will exalt thee,
And He will cause thee to approach to the heaven of the stars.

9. *2 Enoch* or the *Slavonic Enoch*, so called because it has survived only in that language, is a very different type of apocalypse from 1 Enoch, though it belongs to the same literary *genre* (from its contents it is also known as the "Secrets of Enoch"). Like 1 Enoch the book appears to be a composite production: while some portions may go back to a pre-Christian Hebrew original, the bulk of the book was written in Greek, probably about the middle of the first century A.D., but before A.D. 70. (Chap. 59^{2} seems to refer to the Temple cultus as still in operation.) The author is thought to have been an Alexandrian Jew for he is familiar with Greek and Egyptian ideas; at the same time he is loyal to the Mosaic Law. Two apocalyptic features of special interest are the author's doctrine of the millennium and his teaching about the seven heavens.

In his recent edition of the Slavonic text Professor A. Vaillant inclines to the view that the book may have been a product of a syncretistic type of Judaism and that the book contains a Christian element, *e.g.* the Beatitudes at 22^{6-16} may owe not a little to the Synoptic Beatitudes (Matt. 5^{3-10}).

10. The Syriac *Apocalypse of Baruch* (2 Baruch) is so called because it is best known in its Syriac version (though there is

also a Latin translation extant), and to distinguish it from the Greek apocalypse of that name. The Syriac is itself a translation of a lost Greek version of an original Hebrew. The work is a composite one, and is believed to have been written in the last century B.C. and the first century A.D. It shows marked resemblances with 4 Esdras; it was at one time thought that both were the work of the same author. Some kind of inter-dependence certainly exists between the two writings, and it is now generally held that it is the Ezra Apocalypse which is dependent on Baruch.

The book purports to be a series of special revelations about the future given to Baruch, the scribe of Jeremiah, and its aim was to give comfort and encouragement to Jews suffering under Roman persecution. Like 4 Esdras it contains apocalyptic and theological material of some importance for an understanding of the Judaism of the Roman period, such as its doctrine of the Messiah, or original sin, justification by works, and the resurrection.

11. The *Testament of Abraham,* to be distinguished from the Apocalypse of Abraham (see below) is a Greek apocalypse, possibly to be dated as late as the second century A.D. Scholars are divided on the question whether it is a Christian or a Jewish writing. There are certainly unmistakable Christian interpolations, but there may have been a Hebrew original. There are two different Greek recensions.

12. *The Ascension of Isaiah* is a composite writing made up of three distinct portions: *The Martyrdom of Isaiah* (1^{1}–3^{12} and 5^{1-14}). *The Testament of Hezekiah* (3^{13}–5^{1}), and *The Vision of Isaiah* (or The Ascension of Isaiah) (6^{1}–11^{40}). The first part is Jewish, but the remaining two sections of the book are Christian. The first part, which is legend, is older than the other two parts which are usually set in the second century A.D. and are genuine apocalypses. The book has been preserved in the Ethiopic version only, though fragments have survived in Greek, Latin, and Slavonic.

13. *The Apocalypse of Abraham* is a late Jewish work of the end of the first or the beginning of the second century A.D. It has two distinct parts, the second of which (chaps. 9–22) is the apocalyptic part, containing a revelation to Abraham about the future of the Jewish race.

14. *The Books of Adam and Eve* (sometimes erroneously entitled the Apocalypse of Moses) belong to a cycle of legends about Adam of which the Jews were very fond, and which Christians took over and developed. This particular legend begins with the expulsion from Eden and concludes with the death of Adam. The book has doctrinal value, especially for its doctrine of sin and the fall.

15. *The Greek Apocalypse of Baruch* (or 3 Baruch) seems to be a later sequel to the Syriac apocalypse. In 2 Baruch 76^3 God promises to grant Baruch cosmic visions, *i.e.* revelations of earth and sea and sky. These are not mentioned again in that book, but they do form the theme of the Greek apocalypse. Otherwise, however, 2 and 3 Baruch are two quite independent writings. The book has been preserved by Christians and has Christian elements.

16. The Greek *Book of Joseph and Asenath* is a Jewish legendary romance, written (probably in Alexandria) in the second century A.D., and based on the references to Asenath, the beautiful wife of Potiphera, priest of On, whom Pharaoh gave to Joseph to wife and who was the mother of Manasseh and Ephraim (Gen. 41^{45}; 46^{20}). Again the present book is a Christian recension of earlier Jewish material, but the original Greek writing appears to have been first published as propaganda for Judaism.

17. Mention has been made more than once of the *Dead Sea Scrolls* in the course of this article. In these writings we have the remains of a whole library of inter-testamental writings, preserved in their original Hebrew or Aramaic. The earliest discoveries consisted of both Biblical and non-biblical documents, two scrolls of Isaiah, a commentary on the text of Habakkuk of a very peculiar type, a document which has proved to be the rule of a Jewish sect and has been given the name *The Manual of Discipline,* a collection of ancient Hebrew psalms or "hymns," and a scroll describing a kind of Armageddon, and given the title by its first editor "The War of the Sons of Light with the Sons of Darkness." A second harvest of manuscripts was yielded by later exploration, and numerous fragments of documents are at present deposited, for the most part, in the Palestine Museum; they cover most of the books of the Hebrew canon, and include other commentaries of the same type as the Habakkuk commentary, with, in addition, Hebrew and Aramaic fragments of the inter-testamental Apocrypha and Pseudepigrapha (Enoch, Jubilees, Tobit, the Testaments of the Twelve Patriarchs, and similar writings), together with fragments of the Greek Old Testament. A copper scroll, containing what appears to be an inventory of Temple treasure, has also been discovered.

The Biblical manuscripts are of great importance for our knowledge of the ancient Hebrew text of the Bible. The Hebrew Old Testament scrolls, of which the most famous are the two scrolls of Isaiah, ante-date extant Hebrew manuscripts by a millennium. Examination of them by experts has revealed relatively few important deviations from the received Old Testament text. That of itself is a remarkable testimony, not only to the conscientious accuracy of Hebrew scribes, but to the integrity of the text of Holy Scripture. The value of the tradition of the Greek translators of the Bible, known as the Septuagint, is also vindicated by the new discoveries. For the Biblical scholar the Dead Sea Scrolls have come to occupy a position next to the Septuagint, and indeed taking priority of it, for the study and interpretation of the Old Testament.

Much has been written on the theological significance of the new discoveries. In this respect, they share many ideas with the other inter-testamental books, such as their doctrine of the two Messiahs, the two spirits, and the two ways (see above p. 83). The so-called Damascus Document, now known to have belonged to this sect, shows that an even stricter legalism was observed by this group of non-Pharisaic Jews than among the Pharisees themselves. Their hymns of thanksgiving are classic utterances of Hebrew piety comparable with many of the canonical Psalms. A particularly interesting connexion has been traced between the Qumran *Book of Discipline* and the Johannine writings—their dualism, light in conflict with darkness, the spirit of truth striving with the spirit of error—and a common terminology has been noted. In general, it seems probable that it was from this side of Judaism that Christianity sprang.

BIBLIOGRAPHY

R. H. Charles, *Religious Development between the Old and the New Testaments*, 1919.

R. H. Charles (ed. by), *Apocrypha and Pseudepigrapha of the Old Testament*, 2 vols., 1913.

B. M. Metzger, *An Introduction to the Apocrypha*, 1957.

Robert H. Pfeiffer, *History of New Testament Times with an Introduction to the Apocrypha*, 1949 (contains a valuable select bibliography on individual books of *Apocrypha* (pp. 533 ff.) and *Pseudepigrapha* (pp. 538 ff.).

H. H. Rowley, *The Relevance of Apocalyptic : A Study of Jewish and Christian Apocalypses from Daniel to the Revelation*, 3rd ed., 1963.

Articles on *Apocrypha* and on *Pseudepigrapha* in *Hastings' Dictionary of the Bible*, 2nd ed., pp. 39 ff., 820 ff.

V. INTRODUCTION TO THE NEW TESTAMENT

By G. R. Beasley-Murray

(i) THE PRIMITIVE CHRISTIAN TRADITION AND FORM CRITICISM

Long before any document of the New Testament was composed the early Church was occupied in formulating its message to the world and teaching its adherents the elements of the Christian Faith. Through constant repetition the traditions of the Good News and the instruction bound up with it assumed firm lineaments, often crystallizing into brief summaries of doctrine and ethics. Great importance was attached to the preservation of these traditions, as is evidenced by 2 Tim. 2^2: "What you have heard from me through many witnesses entrust to faithful men who will be able to teach others also": that which Paul has gained through the original witnesses of Jesus he had handed on to Timothy; the latter must secure it to reliable teachers who will be able to instruct others in turn, so ensuring the continuity of a living chain of testimony from the fountain head of faith.

The prime element of tradition consisted of a declaration of historic facts enshrining the heart of the gospel (the *kerygmatic* tradition—from *kērygma*, "proclamation"). It is preserved in briefest statement in 1 Cor. $15^{3f.}$: "Christ died for our sins, in accordance with the scriptures . . . he was buried . . . he was raised to life on the third day, according to the scriptures . . . he appeared to Cephas (Peter)." This primitive proclamation could be represented simply as "witness to the resurrection of the Lord Jesus" (Acts 4^{33}); in part, that was due to the fact that the death of the Lord could be presumed as a well-known fact in Jerusalem, but also because the resurrection revealed who Jesus was and the redemptive nature of His death; hence this emphasis on the resurrection remained even when the Gospel was preached in Gentile areas (cf. Rom. $10^{9f.}$). The sermons in the early chapters of Acts indicate that Gospel preaching also commonly included a narration of the story of Jesus, leading up to His crucifixion and resurrection; the best example of this fuller preaching is the address of Peter to Cornelius (Acts $10^{36ff.}$).

The tendency to crystallize the Gospel into pithy statements is witnessed by the presence of many *confessional* traditions in the Epistles. In Rom 10^{9} the Christian creed is summed up by Paul in the simple declaration, "Jesus is Lord." In 1 Cor. 8^{6} it is conjoined with an affirmation of the one Creator-God, such as might be taught to converts from paganism. An early variant tradition of Acts 8^{37} renders it, "Jesus is the son of God"; this, too, is primitive messianic language, reflecting the ancient idea of the king as the (adopted) son of God. The beginnings of trinitarian confessional language can be discerned in the sonorous tones of 1 Cor. 12^{4-6}.

Some confessional statements have been preserved to us in the form of hymns, the best known examples being Phil. 2^{6-11}, Col. 1^{15-20}. They indicate to us the powerful effect of Christian *worship* on the preservation and development of the traditions. There is a surprising number of such hymn fragments in the Epistles (see *e.g.* Eph. 5^{14}, 1 Tim. 3^{16}, 2 Tim. 2^{11-13}) and the Book of Revelation (chaps. 4, 5, 15). The tradition of the Last Supper in 1 Cor. $11^{23\text{ff.}}$ provides a hint that the Passion narratives of our present Gospels would have been repeated and preserved in the constant celebration of the Lord's Supper.

The basic ethics of the New Testament appear to have been derived from a common stock of teaching, the so-called *paraenetic* tradition (from *parainesis* = "exhortation"). Allusion is made to it in 1 Thess. $4^{1\text{ff.}}$ and 2 Thess. 3^{6}; its content forms the bulk of the "practical" sections of Paul's Epistles, but it is also apparent in the Catholic Epistles (especially James and 1 Peter). It is in this connexion, more than in any other, that we find preserved in the Epistles reminiscences of sayings of the Lord Jesus (see especially Rom 12–13 and the Epistle of James).

It will be recalled that the statement of the kerygma in 1 Cor. 15^{3} twice contains the phrase, "according to the scriptures." One of the earliest tasks of the primitive Church was to assemble passages of the Old Testament that bore testimony to Christ (hence the name "testimonies"). Examination has shown that portions of Isaiah, Jeremiah, certain Minor Prophets and Psalms were regarded as particularly significant in this respect; apart from their apologetic importance in preaching to Jews, this governed to no small degree the apostolic interpretation of the Gospel events and ensured a continuity between the writings of the Old Covenant and those of the New.

This context of the Church's activity in mission teaching, worship and controversy, which shaped and preserved its doctrinal and ethical instruction, also operated in the shaping and preservation of the traditions of the words and deeds of

Jesus. The study of this process has come to be termed "Form Criticism," since its pioneers paid special attention to the forms of the evangelic traditions ; on the analogy of laws of tradition, ascertainable in other literary fields, they sought to arrive at the original forms of the Gospel material. For the purpose of this study it is axiomatic that tradition prior to the formation of the Gospels consisted largely of isolated units of sayings and narratives without indication of time and place ; the position that the latter now occupy in the Gospel story is believed to be mainly due to the evangelists themselves. The sayings tradition consists of utterances of Jesus, whether poetic or in prose, and parables ; the narratives are chiefly stories about Jesus, many of which have a miracle as their chief point of interest ; between the two there are narratives whose significance wholly attaches to a saying embedded in or attached to them (the so-called "pronouncement stories," see for example at Mark $2^{15ff.}$, $10^{13ff.}$, $12^{13ff.}$).

Form criticism has made a valuable contribution to our understanding of the first three Gospels. In particular it has recalled us to recognize the living process by which the Gospel material was preserved by the Churches (the material was not maintained in a vacuum) and it has enabled us intelligibly to classify and compare it. The subjectivity of the method can lead to a sceptical estimate of the trustworthiness of the Gospels, but that is not at all a necessary conclusion. The traditions of the life of Jesus were shaped in the Churches of Palestine, at a time when eye-witnesses of the ministry of the Lord were active ; that presumes the presence of people who were able to check as well as inform on the ministry of Jesus. There are signs in the Gospels that our Lord used the Rabbinical method of requiring disciples to learn teaching by heart ; it is possible to demonstrate a variety of poetic forms in the traditions of His sayings (the Beatitudes, for example, when retroverted into Aramaic show rhyme as well as rhythm). There are at least some indications of primitive order in the disposition of Gospel narratives and sayings ; this applies above all to the Passion Narratives, the independence yet congruence of which presume a fairly fixed form of the Passion story at an early date. It has further been pointed out that if comparison be made of the groupings of the material according to form (*i.e.* parables, poetical sayings, dialogues, pronouncement stories) each group yields a picture of the ministry of Jesus from a particular standpoint ; while these viewpoints naturally differ, they leave an unavoidable impression that it is *one* picture that is portrayed ; the self-consistency of the portrayals strengthens the presumption of their authenticity (see Dodd, *History and the Gospel*, pp. 91 ff.).

(ii) THE SYNOPTIC GOSPELS

1. *Their Relations.* The first three Gospels have been accorded the name "synoptic" through the practice of arranging their texts in parallel columns to form a "synopsis," that they may be "seen together." The so-called "synoptic problem" is that of accounting for the relationship suggested by the parallelism and divergences of these Gospels.

A comparison of the synoptic Gospels shows that the *content* of Mark is almost entirely reproduced in Matthew and Luke; his *wording* is generally supported by the other two, either alternatively or both together; his relative *order* of events and sections is followed by them; his *style and grammar* are constantly improved by them. Accordingly it is agreed by most critics that Mark was prior to Matthew and Luke and was employed in their composition.

When the material taken from Mark is abstracted from Matthew and Luke, there remains a considerable body of some two hundred verses which they have in common; this is generally designated "Q" (=German *Quelle*, "source"). Most of this material consists of sayings, of which the language and order is so uniform as to make it probable that either one Gospel copied from another or both used a common source. The latter is the more likely, since each Gospel has much more material that would be of value to the other; moreover the original version of a saying appears sometimes in one Gospel, sometimes in another, and they differ in the contexts in which they are set. The chief items of the passages denoted by Q are: (i) The preaching of John the Baptist, baptism and temptation of Jesus; (ii) the Great Sermon, John's message to Jesus, mission charge; (iii) the Beelzebub controversy, sign of Jonah, Queen of Sheba and Ninevites, woes against Pharisees and lawyers; (iv) eschatological parables (watching servants, drunken servant, mustard seed and leaven), lament over Jerusalem, portents of the End (="Q apocalypse," Luke $17^{23ff.}$).

When material due to Mark and Q is taken from Matthew and Luke, each Gospel is left with a substantial collection peculiar to itself; for convenience they are designated M and L. It follows that Matthew = Mark + Q + M, Luke = Mark + Q + L. But there is a difference in the way the two evangelists employ Mark: whereas Matthew is fundamentally an expanded version of Mark, Luke distributes Mark in blocks through his Gospel; where Luke's sources overlap he seems to prefer Q and L to Mark. It has been suggested therefore that Luke combined Q and L as a preliminary draft of a Gospel before he saw Mark; this theory is known as the "Proto-Luke" hypothesis; it is vigorously championed by some and as vigorously opposed by others.

2. *Mark*. Papias, a Christian writer in the first half of the second century A.D., cited the testimony of a presbyter who flourished about A.D. 100: " This also the presbyter used to say: Mark indeed, who became the interpreter of Peter, wrote accurately, as far as he remembered them, the things said or done by the Lord, but not however in order." This witness is generally regarded with favour, for there is no sufficient reason to discredit it. On the basis of it the Gospel of Mark has been described as the " reminiscences of Jesus as told by Peter to his friend John Mark " ; this is perhaps claiming too much, since form criticism teaches us that Mark embodies much of the traditional preaching of the Churches; nevertheless there is much to support the contention that not a little of Peter's testimony is embodied in Mark's Gospel (observe for example the candour regarding the failings of Peter and the rest of the Twelve in Mark, a feature lessened by Matthew and Luke but which is likely to have come from one of the Twelve).

The date of Mark is uncertain. Irenaeus puts it after the deaths of Peter and Paul, thereby reproducing (probably) the tradition of the Church of Rome in his day. There is no reason to place it after the destruction of Jerusalem (A.D. 70). It could have been written in Rome about A.D. 65–7.

The purpose of the Gospel is clear: to give an account of the redemptive acts of Christ by which the Church was called into being. This is its supreme contribution, for while Mark could almost certainly have reproduced more of the teaching of Jesus than he has done, he has strictly subordinated it to making the essentials of the kerygma plain. His vividness of style, realism in descriptions of Jesus and those about him are well known. More important is his clear delineation of the Messiahship of Jesus, the reserve with which Jesus makes it known, and its association with the doctrine of redemption through suffering: the Messiah must suffer, and so must all who would follow Him (Mark $8^{34f.}$). This was a grimly pertinent message to the Church and enquirers after the Faith in the Rome of Mark's day.

3. *Matthew*. Papias has handed on another tradition that has become famous: " Matthew compiled the oracles in the Hebrew language, but everyone translated them as he was able." This is a puzzling statement if applied to the Gospel of Matthew, since the latter is an expanded edition of the Greek Gospel of Mark and does not give evidence of having been originally written in a Semitic language, whether Hebrew or Aramaic. Since the description would perfectly fit Q, an important source in Matthew, it is a plausible conjecture that

the tradition of Matthew's authorship originally attached to Q. The Gospel itself is anonymous.

The date of Matthew is determined on the one hand by its use of Mark and on the other by its employment by the authors of the Book of Revelation and the early Christian writing, the Didache (A.D. 110 ?). There are indications that Matthew was written as a kind of revised Gospel book for use in the services of the Church, the author utilizing to good effect experience gained by the use of the earlier sources in Christian worship. That would give some credence to the guess that the Gospel should be dated about A.D. 85, but we are in the realm of conjecture here.

A feature of the Gospel is its employment of Old Testament citations, introduced by a formula, " This happened that what was spoken by the Lord through the prophet might be fulfilled " (1^{23}, $2^{6.\ 15f.\ 23}$, 3^{2}, 4^{14}, 8^{17}, 12^{17}, 13^{35}, 21^{4}, 27^{9}). These citations are in harmony with the author's marked concern for the Jewish people. Indeed, the theme of Matthew has been defined as " Jesus has fulfilled Jewish prophecy." Matthew is notable for his so-called Judaistic emphasis (see *e.g.* 5^{17-20}, $10^{5ff.}$, 10^{23}, $23^{2f.}$), his interest in the Church (16^{18}, 18^{12-20}) and in eschatology (cf. the parables of the Kingdom, chap. 13, and the discourse of chaps. 24–25). Paradoxically, Matthew also lays stress on the universality of the Kingdom and Gospel (see above all 28^{18-20}). This twofold and apparently contradictory emphasis has been accounted for by the suggestion that the evangelist has harmonized the emphases of the followers of James, the champion of the Jews, and of Paul, the missionary to the nations. It is more likely that it represents an insight into the mind of Jesus, who knew Himself sent to Israel for the fulfilment of Deutero-Isaiah's vision that the world might receive redemption through Israel, and that Matthew framed his Gospel as an implicit appeal to his nation to rise to their vocation to be the Servant of the Lord for the nations. Matthew further wrote with a view to amplifying the presentation of the kerygma given by Mark and to systematize the material in the other sources, to make the whole of utmost service in the worship of the Church. Its success in this direction is evidenced by the ease with which passages occurring in all three synoptic Gospels can be found in Matthew and its proved usefulness in the Church for exposition. Matthew's Gospel became *the* Gospel of the Church.

4. *Luke-Acts.* It is necessary to treat these two books together, since they form two parts of a single work. Luke 1^{1-4} is a preface to the whole composition, and Acts 1^{1} is a secondary preface with a backward reference to Luke 1^{1-4}. Luke's purpose in writing has thus to be deduced from the whole work: it was to explain the origins of Christianity in the life, death

and resurrection of Jesus and its spread from the city of the Messiah to the capital of the Roman empire.

From the end of the second century the tradition is uniform that the author of these two volumes was Luke, the "beloved physician." Even more than in the case of Mark, the insignificance of this writer tells in favour of the tradition. From the passages in Acts written in the first person plural ($16^{9.\ 18}$, 20^{4-16}, 21^{1-18}, 27^{1}–28^{16}), it is evident that a diary has been incorporated in the book; the uniformity of style in these "we-passages," as they are termed, and the rest of Acts and the Gospel indicate that the whole was written by a companion of Paul. There is also evidence to show that the author was familiar with expression concerning ailments and their cure such as a physician would use.

The date of the work is bound up with its purpose. No book in the New Testament has so clear an apologetic purpose as Acts (it has been called the first Christian Apology). Luke is concerned to demonstrate that Rome has not always persecuted Christians: Paul's sufferings were usually due to Jewish jealousy or indignation ($14^{2ff.}$, $17^{5ff.}$, $18^{12ff.}$, $21^{27ff.}$) or to Gentile unreasonableness ($19^{23ff.}$, $16^{20ff.}$); time and again Roman authority intervened to ensure that Paul received just treatment ($18^{12f.}$, $21^{32f.}$, $23^{12f.}$.) and even tended to acquit him ($26^{31f.}$). This emphasis could have had in view either a desire to vindicate the Church in the eyes of Roman society, or more specifically to secure a favourable hearing of Paul's case. Harnack strongly insisted on the latter alternative: in his view the only plausible explanation of Luke's failure to tell of Paul's fate, after concentrating attention on it on page after page of Acts, is that it had not been settled at the time of writing. This would demand a date for the book of about A.D. 63. Most critics are unwilling to bring the Gospels of Mark and Matthew forward to so early a date as this would involve, for Luke has used Mark and Matthew and Luke must be roughly contemporary; they therefore favour a date about A.D. 80.

The most conspicuous feature of Luke's Gospel is its universalism. It is the least Jewish of the Gospels and manifests a striking interest in the under-privileged of society and every intimation of the relation of the Gospel to all peoples (cf. 2^{32}, 3^{6}, $4^{14ff.}$, 13^{29}, $15^{11ff.}$, 24^{47}). The writer's concern for the whole world, together with the fact that he writes the story of the Church as well as of its Founder, has extended the centre of gravity from the cross and resurrection to include the ascension and Pentecostal gift of the Spirit. The tragedy of the Jewish rejection has been swallowed up in the joy that salvation has come to the Gentiles: "*They will listen*" (Acts 28^{28}).

(iii) THE PAULINE EPISTLES

Writers on New Testament Introduction commonly place the Epistles ascribed to Paul in their supposed chronological order of writing. It has the merit of making plain the living development of Paul's theological thought and makes for ease of reference to the narrative of Acts. So much uncertainty attaches to the dating of a number of the letters, however, as to make any such assignment of order tentative. We shall therefore deal with them in the order of their appearance in the Bible.

1. *The Epistle to the Romans.* This letter has not always stood at the head of the New Testament collection of apostolic letters, but there is no doubt that it is first in importance. Its occasion is reasonably clear: Paul plans a visit to Jerusalem, to present a gift of money from the Gentile churches for the poor of the Jerusalem community, and from there to journey to Spain via Rome (Rom. $15^{23\text{ff.}}$); he desires to become acquainted with the church in Rome, first for its own sake and then to secure its co-operation in his projected mission to Spain ($1^{9\text{ff.}}$, 15^{24}). This situation is narrated by Luke in Acts ($19^{21\text{f.}}$, $20^{1\text{ff.}}$). The letter was probably despatched to Rome during Paul's three months' stay in Greece (Corinth? Acts 20^{3}), *i.e.* about A.D. 57.

So much is clear. But the question has been raised whether this was the sole occasion when the letter, in its present or in a modified form, was sent by Paul to a church. The query is due to a series of related phenomena connected with the letter; (i) its references to Rome are omitted from 1^{7} and 1^{15} in the Greek MS. G (Codex Boernerianus) and by Origen; (ii) the doxology set in our Bibles at $16^{25\text{-}27}$ comes at the end of chap. 14 in most Greek MSS. of the letter, after chap. 15 in the Chester Beatty papyrus, after chap. 16 in several of our earliest Greek MSS., and after both 14^{23} and 16^{24} in Codex Alexandrinus; (iii) Origen reports that Marcion (active about A.D. 144) in his edition omitted chaps. 15 and 16; (iv) the earliest paragraph marking in the Latin tradition does not extend beyond the end of chap. 14. Accordingly it is suggested that the letter was extant in recensions ending at three different points—at the conclusion of chap. 14, of chap. 15, and of chap. 16. Some have objected that Paul could never have finished the letter at 14^{23}, since his argument continues unbroken to 15^{13}: it must be confessed, however, that $15^{1\text{-}13}$ looks more like an application of chap. 14 than a completion of its argument; moreover Zahn was convinced that theologically the doxology followed chap. 14 perfectly. Two further points call for notice: from $1^{16\text{f.}}$ (the "text" of which the letter is exposition) to 15^{13} there is nothing personal in the letter; on the other hand, chap. 16 contains an extraordinary number of greetings sent by Paul to a church he has never visited, and in which are numbered Priscilla and Aquila, whom he had left in *Ephesus* (Acts 18^{26}), and Epaenetus, his first convert in *Asia* (Rom. 16^{3-5}).

It has been conjectured, therefore, that the letter Paul sent to the church at Rome ended at chap. 15; that 1–14+16 was sent to Ephesus, the last chapter forming a note of introduction to that church for Phoebe (Rom. $16^{1f.}$); and that Paul despatched 1–14 to yet other churches as a summary of his Gospel (those of Antioch and of Asia Minor have been cited in this connexion). It is impossible to tell for whom the letter was composed in the first instance—whether for Rome first and then for Ephesus, a copy of the letter being bequeathed by Paul to the church when he left the city, or for Ephesus first (cf. Acts 18^{18-21}?) and then for Rome, or for some other church or group of churches. The issue is not important; the argument of Romans was not first enunciated when the letter was written, for it is passionately expounded in Galatians and whole sections of the letter reflect Paul's habitual preaching in the synagogue (cf. chaps. 2 and 9–11).

Consequently it is insufficient to limit the intention of this letter to Paul's desire to secure the co-operation of the Roman Church in his mission to Spain, although that was undoubtedly its immediate end; its wider purpose was to provide "an exposition of the kerygma, viewed particularly from the vantage point of Paul's experience, with a brief hint of its application in life" (C. H. Dodd). Its dominant theme is the saving righteousness of God: the need for it in face of the universality of sin (1^{1}–3^{20}), its revelation in the redemption of Christ (3^{21}–8^{39}), its activity in the history of Israel and the nations (9–11), its expression in the life of the Church (12–15).

2. *The Epistles to the Corinthians.* Paul's ministry in Corinth is recorded in Acts 18^{1-18}. His correspondence with the Corinthian church began during his stay in Ephesus (1 Cor. 16^{8}) and was concluded in Macedonia (2 Cor. 2^{13}). While precise dating is uncertain this indicates that it belongs to the period A.D. 54–6.

The nature of Paul's correspondence with the church at Corinth is more complex than appears from the simple label "1 and 2 Corinthians."

(*a*) In 1 Cor. 5^{9} reference is made to a letter in which Paul had appealed for a more complete break with pagan ways than the Corinthians had effected. Their laxity had meant that "the church was in the world as it had to be, but the world was in the church as it ought not to be" (Moffatt). Paul wrote in order to correct this defect. (*b*) The Corinthians evidently replied to this letter. They not only addressed themselves to this point but raised questions on others for Paul's judgment. The outline of this letter may be reconstructed from Paul's comments in 1 Corinthians: (1) As to "worldliness," was not Paul being too restrictive in his view? How could one avoid contact with outsiders in this world? (chap. 5). (2) What did Paul think as to the wisdom of marriage? (Gnostic scruples lay behind this question.) In particular, if a Christian couple were able to live in continence ought they not to remain unmarried? (chap. 7). (3) What should their attitude be to meat that had been dedicated in idol sacrifice? Since there is only one God in heaven, what harm could there be in eating it? (chaps. 8–10). (4) Should women still wear veils in services? And how would Paul propose that they should exercise their many gifts in worship, notably the gift *par excellence* of "speaking in tongues"? (chaps. 11–14). (5) Paul had earlier referred to "resurrection from the dead"; but some of their number maintained that dead men don't rise; would he say a little more on the subject? (chap. 15). (6) What did he want them to do about the collection for Palestine? (chap. 16). Paul answered these queries, but first took up two matters that the Corinthians had tactfully omitted to mention: (7) Members of Chloe's household had told him that the church was bitterly divided over personal loyalties; this, urged Paul, contradicted the very nature of the Church and must cease (chaps. 1–4). (8) Their moral laxity had led to ignoring a case of incest and to law suits against one another; these matters, too, had to be remedied (chaps. 5–6). (*c*) Not long after this letter Paul apparently paid a painful visit to Corinth (2 Cor. 2^{1}, 12^{14}, 13^{1}). His allusions to one who had committed an offence that caused him much grief ($2^{5ff.}$, 8^{12}) are best interpreted of a violent insult against Paul that occurred during this visit. The letter written "out of much affliction and anguish of heart" ($2^{3f.}$), accordingly, was not 1 Corinthians but one sent after his return from the last visit. If it be asked, "What happened to that letter?" the answer now given runs, "It is preserved, in part at least, in 2 Cor. 10–13."

Among the reasons for this, at first sight, extraordinary suggestion the following may be mentioned: the otherwise inexplicable change of tone at 10^{1}; the psychological maladroitness, as Plummer terms it, of allowing the torrent of reproaches and warnings in chaps. 10–13 to follow the longing for reconciliation voiced in 1–9; the logical inconsistency of expressions of fears for the Corinthians' apostasy coming after earlier assurances of confidence (*e.g.* 7^{16}); the evident citations of chaps. 10–13 in 1–9 (cf. 13^{2} with 1^{23}, and 13^{10} with 2^{3}).

It is therefore concluded that chaps. 10–13 preceded in time 1–9. There is much in chaps. 10–13 that could have been written with "anguish and tears," and it is comprehensible that Paul wrote with such manifest relief in the early chapters of 2 Corinthians.

(*d*) 2 Cor. 6^{14}–7^{1}, having the theme "The Church has walls" (Strachan), is generally considered to intrude in its present context and to come from an earlier letter (observe how well the passage reads without it). Many identify it as part of the letter referred to in 1 Cor. 5^{9}; as the latter dealt with erring members of the church and 2 Cor. $6^{14ff.}$ unambiguously relates to outsiders, that is a doubtful identification. (*e*) the above analysis of 2 Corinthians is accepted by a majority of scholars. It has been further suggested that 2 Cor. 2^{14}–7^{4}, an "apology of the apostolic office," may have been written before the rest of 1–9, when as yet the church had not yielded to the persuasions of Paul's opponents; it was the failure of this more gentle letter to have its desired effect that prompted the "painful visit." While a confident decision on this issue is difficult, it remains an interesting possibility.

In view of the discredit which much of 2 Corinthians throws on the church at Corinth it is not surprising that a considerable delay elapsed before this correspondence was made known, and by that time the original sequence had been forgotten. It has been hazarded that the present order of chapters reflects the custom of setting warnings against false teachers at the end of an epistle, a procedure which itself was due to the conviction that false prophets are a sign of the end of the age; by placing 10–13 at the close of the letter the editor characterized Paul's opponents as false prophets of the last times (so G. Bornkamm).

3. *The Epistle to the Galatians.* The identity of the "churches of Galatia" (Gal. 1^{2}) has been interminably discussed. As may be expected, the evidence is unclear and the choice involves balancing probabilities. The problem arises from the ambiguity of the term "Galatia"; originally it designated an area, controlled by Galatian settlers, extending north to south in the centre of Asia Minor; after its conquest by the Romans in 25 B.C. the southern section of this territory, together with adjacent portions of Lycaonia, Pisidia and Phrygia, became the province of Galatia. The "churches of Galatia" therefore could denote: (*a*) the churches of south Galatia founded on Paul's first missionary journey, in Derbe, Iconium and Antioch, Acts 13–14; or (*b*) churches in old Galatia, founded presumably on the second journey, Acts 16^{6}. The second alternative used to predominate, on the ground that "Galatians" most naturally designates Gauls by descent

(in Latin *Galatai* = *Galli*), therefore descendants of the settlers of north Galatia. Most moderns favour the former, since Paul seems to have used geographical terms officially recognized by the Roman government. He grouped his churches in their Roman political divisions and called them by the name of the Roman province in which they were situated (*e.g.* the churches of Macedonia, Asia, Achaia). In 1 Cor. 16^1 the "churches of Galatia" are mentioned in connexion with the collection; other references to this collection group the churches in provinces (cf. Rom. 15^{26}) and in Acts 20^4 Gaius and Timothy are named as delegates for south Galatia; this is perhaps the strongest pointer to the Galatian churches of our letter being those of the southern province.

The date of the letter is even more uncertain than its destination. It is further complicated by the relation supposed to exist between Gal. 2 and Acts 15. If these two passages refer to the same event, Galatians certainly falls after the Council of Jerusalem. Such is the common opinion. It is urged: (*a*) the resemblance between the two narratives is so strong as to make it difficult to believe that they refer to different occasions; (*b*) the conflict between Paul and Judaizers could not have occurred twice, the second conducted as though the first had never taken place; (*c*) the thought of Galatians is closely related to 2 Corinthians and Romans, indicating a similar time of composition; (*d*) Gal. 4^{13} implies that Paul visited the Galatian churches twice before the letter; therefore it must come after Acts 16^6. Those who hold to an early date for the letter maintain: (*a*) the identification of Gal. 2 and Acts 15 raises too many difficulties to be probable. Paul represents the former occasion as his second visit to Jerusalem after his conversion, Luke makes the visit of Acts 15 his third (cf. Acts $9^{26ff.}$, 11^{20}, and 12^{25}). Paul states in Gal. 2 that the subject of discussion was "my gospel," a matter he never would have submitted to a Jewish-Christian assembly; and he reports that Titus was circumcised—a compromise understandable on behalf of preaching undertaken by Titus in the synagogues, but an unthinkable one before the church on the grounds of faith. (*b*) It is not an impossible notion that the problem of Gentile admission into the Church was raised more than once: on the theory of a later date for Galatians the Judaizing Christians accepted neither the decision of the Council regarding admission nor the decrees, but they continued to fight Paul tooth and nail to gain their point in the churches of his foundation; if these Judaizers, who initiated the conference at Jerusalem, yet rejected its findings, they certainly would not have accepted decisions made privately between Peter and James and Paul. (*c*) It is doubtful how far correspondence of thought and language between Galatians, Romans and 2 Corinthians should be pressed, in view of the possibility that Romans is a final draft of an earlier letter, and in any case reflects the pattern of Paul's regular preaching, and 2 Corinthians was written over a period of months. (*d*) As to the two "visits" implied in Gal. 4^{13}, why should they not be the formation of the churches recorded in Acts 13^{14}–14^{21a}, and the consolidation described in 14^{21b-23}? Moreover if Galatians was written after the Council of Jerusalem, why did Paul not cite the decision of the Jerusalem Council in Gal. 2 and thereby settle the Galatian problem at a stroke? Many answers to this have been propounded: *e.g.* that Acts 11^{30} and 15^{2} refer to one visit only to Jerusalem, of which Luke had two reports but which he wrongly made into two visits; that the apostolic decrees were later than the Council; that Acts 15^{2} and 18^{22} refer to one visit only; that Gal. 2^{1} was prior to Acts 15 but not mentioned by Luke. Any of these is conceivable, and none may be right. It is at least possible that Luke was not incorrect, that the Gal. 2 story belongs to the visit described in Acts 11^{27-30}, and that Galatians is to be dated before the Council of Jerusalem, *i.e.* in A.D. 48. If so, it is the earliest extant letter of Paul. If a later date be preferred, some time in the Ephesian ministry is the most plausible guess.

The occasion of Galatians, whatever its date, was an attempt of Judaizing Christians to win the Galatian churches away from Paul's gospel. To achieve this end they had to deny Paul's apostleship, and so his right to found churches. Paul therefore defended both his apostleship and his gospel, for they were inseparably connected. In so doing he gave us a valuable piece of autobiography and a view from within of the controversy between upholders of the narrow Jewish view of the Christian faith and those who, like Paul, fought for broader conceptions. Acts gives us the picture of a later and independent observer, Galatians is a voice out of the conflict itself. Its insistence on the freedom of the Christian from legalism and on faith and love as the heart of the moral life makes this letter "epochal": "It is tragic that its contentions were so soon lost to the Church" (Burton).

4. *The Place of Origin of the Pauline Prison Epistles*. The Prison Epistles are Ephesians, Colossians, Philemon, and Philippians. (*a*) Traditionally it has been assumed that these letters were written during Paul's imprisonment in Rome. The *praitōrion* of Phil. 1^{13} is most easily explained as the *Praetorian* guard in Rome and the "saints of Caesar's household" (Phil. 4^{22}) as members of the Imperial palace. An escaped slave would naturally flee to the capital city, where he could easily be lost, hence the flight of Onesimus to Rome after

leaving Philemon. Acts $28^{30f.}$ shows that Paul had freedom to preach the Gospel when imprisoned in Rome, and Phil. $1^{14ff.}$ suits that situation perfectly. The advanced theology of Colossians and Ephesians, with its slower movement and style, suits a later date in Paul's ministry better than an earlier.

(*b*) Against the Roman origin of the letters weighty arguments can be adduced. Paul intended to evangelize Spain after being in Rome (Rom. $15^{24ff.}$); this plan would not have been affected by his being transported thither as a prisoner instead of paying his own fare, but in Phil. 1^{26}, 2^{24} Paul speaks of his intention to return to Macedonia when freed and makes no mention of Spain. Communications between Paul and Philippi are so frequent, it is difficult to think that he could have been in Rome when he wrote the Philippian letter. Paul mentions in Phil. 4^{10} that the gift sent by the Philippians was the first for a very long time, for they had had no opportunity of helping him; but if Paul had been imprisoned in Rome for two years, it is twelve years since his mission in Macedonia and ten years since his stay in Corinth; he had been three years in Ephesus and imprisoned two years in Caesarea; it can hardly be said, then, that the Philippians had lacked opportunity of assisting Paul—indeed, in view of their affection for him, it is strange that through that long period they had failed to do so. It is also urged that Paul's request for a lodging with Philemon in Colossae (Philem.^{22}) is more likely to have come from a period of working in that area than when he was imprisoned in Rome.

(*c*) Caesarea has been proposed as a possible place of writing the letters, since Paul was there imprisoned for two years. Apart from objections to the Roman origin that are pertinent here, it cannot be shown that Paul was in danger of death at Caesarea as he was when he wrote Philippians (2^{17}); and after his appeal to Caesar he could not have planned journeys to Philippi and to Philemon.

(*d*) Ephesus is considered by not a few as the most likely place of writing the prison letters. While there is no evidence to prove that Paul was imprisoned in this city it is highly probable that he suffered this fate. 1 Cor. $15^{30ff.}$ refers to Paul fighting with wild beasts in Ephesus and enduring daily dangers there, 2 Cor. $1^{8ff.}$ to a rescue from terrible death in Asia, and Acts 20^{19} to Jewish plots against him in Ephesus; it is clear therefore that Paul experienced intense opposition during his ministry in that city, of which Luke's account provides not a hint. This is of importance when considering 2 Cor. 11^{23}: Paul has suffered many prison sentences, but Acts records to this time only his imprisonment in Philippi;

Ephesus is the most likely scene for at least *one* such imprisonment. The Marcionite prologue to Colossians says that Colossians was written from Ephesus while the apostle was bound, and Origen assigned Philippians to the period between 1 and 2 Corinthians—*i.e.* while he was in Ephesus. We know that there were Praetorian troops in Ephesus, though Duncan points out that *praitōrion* can also apply to those attached to the official residence of a proconsul; similarly "Caesar's household" could denote the civil service that managed Imperial property and interests in the Empire. On the hypothesis of an Ephesian imprisonment the communications between Paul and the Philippians are comprehensible; the gift sent from the Philippians to Paul is more intelligible; and the reference in Philippians, 1 Corinthians and Acts to plans and actual journeys of Paul and Timothy dovetail remarkably well (cf. Phil. 2^{19} with Acts 19^{22}, 1 Cor. 4^{17}, 16^{10f}.; Phil. 1^{26}, 2^{24}, with Acts 19^{21}, 1 Cor. $16^{3ff.}$). It is also maintained that the flight of Onesimus from Philemon is more likely to have been to nearby Ephesus than to distant Rome.

In the light of these considerations there is a growing conviction that Philippians at least was written from Ephesus (the strongest evidence occurs in relation to this letter), but that the case for a similar origin for Ephesians, Colossians, and Philemon is insufficient to warrant abandoning the traditional ascription of these letters to the later imprisonment in Rome.

5. *The Epistle to the Ephesians.* The authenticity of Ephesians is one of the most keenly debated problems of New Testament criticism, and in recent years there has been a marked swing away from belief in its Pauline authorship. The difficulties of accepting its Pauline origin are by no means equal. Differences from acknowledged Pauline letters in vocabulary and style are apparent; sentences are sometimes so long as to lose their grammatical structure, genitives following genitives in profusion. Appeal could be made, however, to the employment of an amanuensis to account for features such as these. It is the literary relationships and the doctrine that cause chief concern.

The claim has been made that no less than three-fifths of Colossians are embodied in Ephesians. This is not so much by direct citation as by the combination in Ephesians of phrases that appear in separate passages in Colossians. Moffatt described Ephesians as "a set of variations played by a master hand upon one or two themes suggested by Colossians" (*Introduction*, p. 375). A peculiar difficulty arises through modifications in Ephesians of the meaning of key terms in Colossians: *e.g.* it is maintained that *sōma* (body) in Col. 2^{19} relates to the cosmos, in Eph, 4^{16} to the Church; *mystērion* (secret) in Col. 1^{27} concerns Christ the word of God, in Eph. $3^{3ff.}$ the nature of the Church as uniting Jew and Gentile; *plērōma* (fulness) in Col. 2^{9} resides in Christ, in Eph. 1^{23} in the Church. The dilemma is therefore proposed that the literary relationship requires Ephesians to be written immediately after Colossians but the doctrinal relationship indicated by these changes requires a long interval (Mitton). Other doctrinal developments beyond Paul in Ephesians have been found in its emphasis on the exaltation of Christ rather than on his death; its high doctrine of Church and ministry; its advanced Christology; its modified eschatology, anticipating a gradual advance to the consummation rather than a speedy return of Christ; its noble conception of marriage as compared with the comparatively low estimate in 1 Cor. 7. The most popular explanation of these phenomena is that of Goodspeed. He put forward the hypothesis that a Christian of Asia Minor (Onesimus?) read Colossians so often that he learned it by heart; on securing five other letters of Paul he determined to make them known to the Church; he prepared a comprehensive statement of Paul's thought to form an introduction to the collection; this introduction is our Ephesians; it echoes Colossians more than the other letters because the writer knew Colossians so well.

What have defenders of its authenticity to say in reply to all this? They hold that while the divergences between Colossians and Ephesians are real enough, too much has been made of their significance. The linguistic problem is not so acute as is represented: *mystērion* (secret) in Col. 1^{27} is not so much Christ the word of God as Christ among the Gentiles (Christ in *you*!), and therefore is similar in meaning to its use in Eph. $3^{3ff.}$; if *sōma* (body) in Col. 2^{10} refers to the cosmic hierarchy of being, in Col. 1^{18} it is explicitly related to the Church, as in Eph. 4^{16}; the attribution of *plērōma* (fulness) to the Church in Eph. 1^{23} is comprehensible on the basis of the doctrine, expounded even in Colossians, that Christ is the Head of the Body, for the Church is the fulness of Christ as Christ is the fulness of God. It is maintained that none of the doctrinal developments in Ephesians is incompatible with the teaching in Colossians and the earlier Pauline letters. The notion that Ephesians was written as an introduction to the Pauline letters is queried in view of the little made in the letter of justification by faith, the typical Pauline eschatology, and (in its hortatory sections) the Spirit-dominated life; it is one thing for Paul to write in this strain, another for an independent person to represent it as an adequate introduction to Paul's most characteristic thought. The theological developments manifest in Ephesians raise other queries than those mentioned above: for example, it is agreed that the Christology, soteriology, and ecclesiology of Ephesians represent a genuine advance on the Pauline teaching, albeit in the same direction; is this advance more likely to have come from a later Paulinist or from Paul in his maturer years? Ephesians is "the crown of Paulinism" (Dodd); is it really conceivable that Onesimus was a greater theologian than Paul? These questions are admittedly capable of more than one answer, but they illustrate the ambiguity of the problems surrounding this letter and scarcely justify dogmatism. The issues are, in fact, delicately balanced. Provisionally the present author considers the ascription to Paul to be the more likely solution.

The reference to Ephesus in the address of the letter (1^1) is absent from many of our earliest MSS., and should be regarded as a later insertion. Yet the text reads strangely without a place name! Either the original name has been accidentally omitted or, more probably, a space was left for the filling in of names and the letter was intended to be an encyclical.

Ephesians has been described by one of its interpreters as "a non-controversial exposition of the great doctrine of his (Paul's) life—the unity of mankind in Christ and the purpose of God for the world through the Church" (J. A. Robinson). As such it is an implicit appeal to the Church to rise to its vocation to be the agent of this reconciliation and to exemplify it in its life.

6. *The Epistle to the Philippians.* For the place of origin of this letter see the discussion on pp. 102 ff. On the hypothesis that it was written in Rome, a date shortly before Paul's death is frequently favoured, in view of the apostle's anticipations of martyrdom; Lightfoot preferred an early date in the Roman imprisonment, since the letter has more in common with Paul's earlier correspondence than with Ephesians and Colossians. If the Ephesian period is preferred, and it is accepted that Paul's plans for travel ($2^{19ff.}$) are identical with those mentioned in 1 Cor. 4^{17}, $16^{10f.}$, these two letters will have been written in fairly close proximity; as Paul's sufferings in Ephesus are presumably known to the Corinthians (1 Cor. 15^{32}), Philippians comes first, *i.e.* about A.D. 54.

The occasion of the letter is clear. The Philippians had sent a gift to Paul through Epaphroditus, who was to minister to the Apostle's needs on their behalf ($2^{25ff.}$, $4^{10ff.}$). The letter was Paul's thanks for their kindness. Information is supplied concerning the unexpected advance of the Gospel during Paul's present imprisonment ($1^{12ff.}$) and of an illness that had overtaken Epaphroditus ($2^{25ff.}$). Warm encouragement is given to the Philippians themselves, for they were enduring sufferings for Christ's sake as Paul was ($1^{29f.}$). Lohmeyer even characterized the letter as a tractate on martyrdom, written by a martyr to a church of martyrs, accounting thereby both for the joyous tone of the letter and its references to division ($4^{22ff.}$): martyrdom brings pride as well as peace! While this feature can be exaggerated, there is no doubt that the Philippians had been refined in the crucible of suffering and that Apostle and church were closely drawn to each other through their common experience. The divisiveness of the Philippians should not be exaggerated; there is no shadow over this fellowship such as that which darkened the life of the Corinthian community.

From time to time the unity of this letter has been questioned, above all on account of the abrupt change of tone at 3^2 and the " finally " of 3^1, indicating that Paul intended to close the letter without having expressed thanks to the Philippians, which was its real purpose. Those who maintain this theory largely agree in recognizing the unity of the first two chapters and in beginning a second letter at 3^{1b} or 3^2, but they differ as to where the second letter ends; Lake, for example, adds 4^{4-23} to chaps. 1–2 and makes the second letter 3^2–4^3, but the most recent advocate of the partition theory finds a second letter in 3^1–4^9 and a *third* in 4^{10-20} (B. D. Rahtjen, *New Testament Studies*, vi., 1959–60, pp. 169 ff.). While the possibility of a composite origin of Philippians may not be ruled out as impossible, there is no such compelling evidence for it as in 2 Corinthians; a similar occurrence of " finally " is in 1 Thess. 4^1 (but it probably ought to be rendered " as to the rest," " and now "—a mere means of transition from one point to another), and an underlying homogeneity of ideas pervades the entire letter, particularly the note of rejoicing and calm in face of the future, which the polemical note of $3^{2ff.}$ cannot dispel. Most critics, therefore, hold to the unity of the letter.

7. *The Epistles to the Colossians and to Philemon.* These two letters belong together. Both include Timothy with Paul in the address and both mention Aristarchus, Demas, Epaphras, Mark and Luke in the conclusion. The theme of Philemon is the return of the runaway slave Onesimus; in Col. 4^{19} it is said that Onesimus will provide the Colossians with further information about Paul. It is reasonable to assume, therefore, that the two letters were written at the same time.

Colossae lay eighty miles east of Ephesus in the Lycus valley. The church had been founded by a colleague of Paul, one Epaphras, probably during Paul's ministry in Ephesus when " the whole population of the province of Asia heard the word of the Lord " (Acts 19^{10}, Col. $1^{7f.}$). Its members had fallen prey to advocates of one of the many forms of syncretism popular in their day. From Col. 2^8–3^4 it appears that this included Jewish and Gnostic elements. The former are evident in the stress laid on Jewish legal rites ($2^{11.\ 14.\ 16}$), the latter by indications of the philosophic dualism that was fundamental to this world view ($2^{8\text{ff.}}$). From the basic postulate of the evil of matter the Gnostics deduced the total removal of God from the material creation, the existence of a hierarchy of spirits who mediated between God and the universe, sin as entanglement in the material world and redemption as emancipation from it. Hence the references to asceticism and reverence of angels in $2^{18\text{f.}}$ and the prominence given to the " elemental spirits " and the like in $2^{8\text{ff.}}$.

Paul answered this heresy by an exposition of the significance of Christ. His aim was " to restate the absolute adequacy of Jesus in relation to the world and the Church, to show how faith in Him requires no outside philosophic or esoteric cult in order to perfect itself, and to expose the absurdity of any mystical supplement to Christian experience of Jesus as Redeemer " (Moffatt, op. cit., p. 151). It is in Christ that " fulness " of life is found, not in inferior mediators, for the " fulness " of God dwells in Him ($2^{9\text{f.}}$).

The authenticity of Colossians has been questioned, first on account of its likeness to Ephesians, but now that its priority to Ephesians is universally accepted, attention is focussed on its peculiarities of style and vocabulary and its relation to Gnosticism. It is true that there are many unusual terms in the letter and the style is ponderous ; most are satisfied that these are accounted for by the nature of the subject (controversy with Gnostic instead of Judaistic perverters of Christianity) and the greater use of the liturgical hymn style, of which examples may be found in other Pauline letters. Objection ought no longer to be made on the ground of the polemic against Gnosticism, for we now know (what was formerly doubted) that this type of thought is pre-Christian. It is no more surprising that Paul should employ Gnostic categories in refuting a Gnostic perversion of the Gospel than that he should use Rabbinic concepts in refuting Judaistic perversions of the Faith.

The letter to Philemon was written as a commendation of Onesimus to his former master and to entreat that forgiveness and a welcome might be accorded to him. It is a masterpiece of tact, with greater implications than perhaps even Paul envisaged : the idea that a master should receive a slave, no longer as a slave but as a " brother beloved " (v.^{16}), entails an outlook that in the end must destroy slavery.

8. *The Epistles to the Thessalonians.* The founding of the Church at Thessalonica, immediately following on that of nearby Philippi, is briefly recounted by Luke in Acts ($17^{1\text{ff.}}$).

After settling down at Corinth Paul sent Timothy to find out how the infant community was faring (1 Thess. $3^{1ff.}$). The news was mainly cheering, but evidently aspersions had been cast on Paul's behaviour by certain Jews, sufficient to awaken suspicion in some of the converts ($2^{1ff. 15f.}$). Paul had to defend both himself against the charge of working for gain and the Gospel he preached. Difficulties had also arisen within the church owing to its lack of experience. It has been plausibly suggested that these difficulties sprang from three types of Christians, mentioned in 5^{14}: (*a*) the "weak," who looked on immorality as a matter of indifference; they needed to learn the meaning of consecration in daily life (4^{1-10}); (*b*) the "faint-hearted," anxious as to the destiny of their departed friends and their own salvation; such needed to understand the significance of the return of Christ (4^{13}–5^{11}); (*c*) the "unruly" or "idle," whose distorted view of the parousia led them to abandon work; they had to be exhorted to work or starve ($5^{12ff.}$). The letter was written from Corinth *c.* A.D. 50.

Apparently it did not achieve all it was hoped to do. Further trouble arose from the "faint-hearted" and the "idle." They had somehow drawn the deduction from the first letter that the day of the Lord was now dawning (2 Thess. 2^2). This had but aggravated their own peculiar notions. The second letter was written to make Paul's meaning plain and to inculcate a proper attitude to the coming of the Lord. It is not necessary to postulate a long interval between the two letters; five to seven weeks are enough to account for the new situation (Frame).

While the authenticity of the first letter has not seriously been challenged, doubts have been raised from time to time about the second, above all owing to a difference of eschatological view in the second letter; this teaches that the parousia of Christ must be preceded by that of Antichrist (chap. 2), whereas 1 Thess. 4–5 represents the parousia as coming unexpectedly; appeal has also been made to an unwarranted repetition of ideas and phrases of the first letter in the second. Most critics are unconvinced by these arguments. The twofold expectation of the parousia as heralded by premonitory signs and yet unknowable as to time is common throughout the New Testament and is even implied in 1 Thess. $5^{1ff.}$, which assumes that Paul's teaching on signs of the end is known to the Thessalonians. The changed emphasis in 2 Thess. 2 is solely due to the pastoral intention of putting a stop to the fanaticism to which the belief in the immediate consummation was giving rise (McGiffert).

A few scholars incline to place the second letter before the first in time, believing that the situation presupposed in the first thereby becomes more intelligible. This has not commanded general assent. The misunderstanding of Paul's eschatological teaching and the correction it received is more comprehensible on the present order, as also the references in 1 Thess. 2^{17}–3^{6} to events that had taken place since Paul's departure from Thessalonica and the warning against a letter or letters purporting to come from him (2 Thess. 3^{17}).

9. *The Pastoral Epistles.* The origin of the letters to Timothy and Titus is still the most complicated problem of the New Testament Epistles. Criticism tends to a decisive rejection of their authenticity, but strong protestations continue to be made in their defence. The points at issue may be reduced to four. (*a*) The historical situation assumed in the Pastorals cannot be fitted into the Acts narrative, and there is little evidence for a release of Paul from his Roman imprisonment. It is doubtful, however, if this ought to be pressed. Clement of Rome speaks of Paul coming to "the limit of the west," *i.e.* Spain; this may reflect a reliable tradition of Paul's release from prison for a period of freedom. (*b*) The organization of the Church is believed to be advanced, beyond that known in Paul's lifetime. This, too, is debatable. Phil. 1^{1} mentions *episkopoi* and *diakonoi*; if it was written in the Ephesian period there was time for the development presupposed in the Pastorals. (*c*) The theology is more formal and stereotyped than that of the authentic Paulines. Denney voices the judgment of many: "Paul was inspired, the Pastor was only orthodox." If it is argued that this is a purely subjective judgment, the lack of emphasis on the Holy Spirit is yet significant, and the ethical teaching has a Hellenistic accent (love is one virtue among others rather than supreme). (*d*) The style and language are very distinctive; most consider them impossible to Paul. The former is characterized as stilted and prim in its preciseness. Harrison, after an intensive study of the vocabulary of these letters, urged that it shows a greater approximation to that of second-century writings than to earlier letters. Lock, who also devoted many years to the Pastorals, believed that the argument from style favoured Pauline authorship but, on Harrison's evidence, that from vocabulary was "strongly, though not quite conclusively, against it." Battle is still waged over the legitimacy of Harrison's methods. Some hold that mathematical calculations of this sort can never prove linguistic affinity (Guthrie). Others insist that the principles of structural linguistics have established themselves and that if Harrison misapplied them, his conclusions are nevertheless vindicated by a right application of the method (Grayston and Herdan). Still others

contend that this is a secondary issue : all is accounted for if greater freedom was given to the amanuensis (Jeremias). Those who reject the authenticity of the letters either consider them to be pseudonymous or compositions embodying authentic Pauline fragments. The latter alternative is altogether preferable, but the " fragments " are probably more extensive than is commonly allowed. Whoever wrote them up was well acquainted with the mind of Paul and it is impossible to say where the limits of Paul's authority end. More than one critic has suggested that Timothy, with perhaps some assistance from Luke, drafted the collection, but this is naturally speculative.

The occasion of the letters may be gathered from their common concern for " healthy teaching," *i.e.* sound faith (2 Tim. $1^{13ff.}$) and healthy morals (Tit. $2^{1f.}$). The emphasis on this theme, unique in these letters, reflects the uprising of a wave of " unhealthy " teaching, *i.e.* heretical faith and bad living. In 1 Tim. $4^{1ff.}$ the false teachers are said to forbid men to marry and to demand abstention from foods ; this identifies them as Gnostic. In face of such a corruption of Christianity the author recalls his readers to the " healthy teaching " of the great apostle and its outworking in the life of the Church.

The date of the Epistles is uncertain. Nothing in them demands a date beyond the outgoings of the first century, and they could be earlier.

(iv) HEBREWS AND THE GENERAL EPISTLES

1. *The Epistle to the Hebrews.* It has been paradoxically maintained that " Hebrews " was written to Gentiles, chiefly because the letter does not mention the Temple ; the background of the book is said to be the Tabernacle and the Pentateuch, *i.e.* the study and not experience (Moffatt). The traditional interpretation is surely more likely. The letter reflects the sense of crisis, when war clouds gathered over Palestine, *c.* A.D. 66, and appeal was made for Jews to stand together for faith and fatherland. " These ' philosophic liberals,' who had never thoroughly embraced the Christian tradition, were being moved by the appeal. . . . In the wavering doubt as to whether the new faith was worth the breaking of the unity of the ancient Church he (the author) called them to grasp that faith more whole-heartedly and learn at last what it really was " (Nairne).

An attempt has lately been made to identify the recipients of the letter as Jews who formerly belonged to the Qumran sect. Yadin points out that the " Covenanters " looked for the appearance of a last prophet who would be like Moses

(Deut. 18^{18}); Hebrews affirms that Jesus was God's final word to man and argues for his superiority to Moses ($8^{6ff.}$). The sect assigned to the "Angel of Light" (Michael) a greater role in the eschatological process and the world to come than that of the Messiahs; Hebrews emphasizes the superiority of Jesus over the angels and asserts that God has *not* placed the world to come under the control of angels (Heb. 2^5). The sect apparently looked for two Messiahs, one priestly the other royal, the former superior to the latter; Hebrews seeks to demonstrate that Jesus Christ is the only eschatological High Priest, and his priesthood is of the order of Melchizedek, not Aaron. The sect organized itself to be a replica of Israel in the wilderness; the constant reference of Hebrews to the Pentateuch would therefore especially appeal to its adherents. This is a plausible thesis. If accepted it would strengthen the view that the letter was written shortly before the Jewish war. (Those who favour a later date usually put it in the eighties of the first century.)

As to the author, the main suggestions are Paul, Barnabas, Apollos, Luke, Silas, Clement of Rome, Priscilla. The most doubtful of the list is the first. The most compelling view is that of Origen: God alone knows who wrote it.

The letter, by its contrast of Judaism with Christianity, invites comparison with Paul's teaching. This has never been better represented than by William Manson. He views Paul's argument as an ellipse with two focal centres: (*a*) the promise of God to Abraham came before the Mosaic Law and was not annulled by it; (*b*) if the Law had power to communicate life, righteousness would have come through it. The argument of Hebrews also has two foci: (*a*) the high priesthood of Melchizedek was announced to Abraham before the Levitical priesthood existed and its order was not cancelled by the latter; (*b*) if complete access to God were possible through the Levitical priesthood, no other priest (cf. Ps. 110^4) would have arisen. For Paul therefore the abrogation of the Law as a source of rightness with God carries with it the fall of the cultus; in Hebrews the supersession of the cultus involves the repeal of the Law.

2. *The Epistle of James.* The writer of this letter has been traditionally regarded as James the Lord's brother. The identification has been disputed, owing to the slowness with which the letter was accepted in the Church, its lack of specifically Christian elements (observe the absence of any mention of the cross and resurrection) and its uncommonly good Greek. The atmosphere of the letter is clearly Jewish and the setting Palestine; there only in ancient times did farmers employ hired labour rather than slaves (cf. 5^4), and

the Dead Sea was noted for vapours that caused gold and silver to become discoloured (cf. 5^3). There is no allusion to the Jewish war of A.D. 70, and the uncertainties of life are those of peaceful times; accordingly the writing must either be very early or come from the end of the first century A.D. A number of recent critics prefer the latter alternative and consider the letter was written by an unknown James, or even pseudonymous. Certain indications, however, favour the earlier date. The allusions to violence in $4^{1ff.}$ fit none so well as the Zealots in Palestine prior to A.D. 70. If $2^{1ff.}$ refers to Christian participation in the Jewish synagogue worship (" assembly " in 2^2 is " synagogue "), this would suit the first generation of the Church rather than later. Many passages appear to be addressed to non-Christian Jews rather than Christians (notably $4^{1ff.}$ and $5^{1ff.}$, but cf. also $1^{19ff.}$, $2^{10ff.}$, $2^{14ff.}$, $3^{6ff.}$, $3^{13ff.}$). The strangely indecisive Christian tone of the letter is explicable if it was written to Christian Jews, to exhort them to manifest a conduct worthy of their faith, and to non-Christian Jews, to commend this " pure religion " (1^{27}) to them. Herein lies a curious parallel with the Q source of the Gospels: T. W. Manson long ago suggested that this source was compiled both for the instruction of Christians acquainted with the Gospel and as an exposition of Christian beliefs and practices for the benefit of the Jews, in the conviction that a better hearing would be secured by positive statement than by any form of disputation. This would have been particularly applicable in the early years of the Church in Palestine, when Judaism had rejected the Gospel but would listen to prophetic religion. The writer of our letter was a Jew of Jews, soaked in the teaching of Jesus and conscious of a mission to his people. That describes none better than the Lord's brother. We cannot insist on the identification, in view of the frequency of the name James (=Jacob); if it be accepted, a free hand must be postulated for the amanuensis who gave the letter its form.

3. *The First Epistle of Peter*. The persons addressed (1^1) were inhabitants of the region of Asia Minor north-west of the Taurus mountains. From 2^{10}, 4^3 it is clear that they were converted pagans; their description as " exiles of the dispersion " (1^1) therefore must be figurative: they are the " new Israel," scattered through the world, citizens of the Kingdom of God.

The letter claims to be written by the apostle Peter (1^1). Objections have been lodged to this on three grounds: (*a*) the language is too refined for a Galilean fisherman who is said to have required Mark as an interpreter; (*b*) it manifests considerable dependence on Pauline thought; (*c*) its references to persecution reflect a time when profession of Christianity was a capital crime, and this did not occur till after Peter's death. Defenders of the letter contest all three points: (*a*) the writer explicitly refers to Silvanus as his amanuensis (5^{12}); (*b*) the so-called "Paulinism" is the primitive Christianity on which Paul depended as well as others (though as Silvanus was a companion of Paul, it would not be surprising if there were some echoes of genuine Paulinism); (*c*) the persecution referred to seems to be privately instigated, "pogroms," such as are reflected elsewhere in the New Testament (Mark $13^{9ff.}$, Heb. $10^{32ff.}$). Positively it may be held that the primitiveness of the Christianity contained in the letter, its indications of eye-witness (*e.g.* $2^{21ff.}$), its echoes of the teaching of Jesus and coincidences with Peter's speeches in Acts all tell in favour of its authenticity.

It has been observed that no other writing of the New Testament contains baptismal material in comparable proportions to 1 Pet. 1^{3}–4^{11}; it may well reflect the pattern of baptismal instruction followed by the writer, or even an address given by him to newly baptized converts. Its incorporation in a letter written in time of persecution recalls to suffering Christians the meaning of their baptism as union with the Christ of the cross and resurrection.

The date of the letter is uncertain. Written from Rome (5^{13}), a time not long before the Neronian persecution of A.D. 64 would suit its authorship by Peter.

4. *The Second Epistle of Peter and the Epistle of Jude.* These two letters fall to be considered together; 2 Pet. 2 and Jude $^{4-16}$ are so closely parallel, one writer must have copied the other. The priority of Jude over 2 Peter is universally accepted. Of the many reasons for this conclusion it suffices to quote one: it is easier to explain the dependence of 2 Peter on Jude than vice versa (cf. *e.g.* 2 Pet. 2^{4} with Jude ^{6}, 2 Pet. $2^{10b.\ 11}$ with Jude ^{9}). Is it possible that Peter the Apostle used Jude's letter? Hardly. Jude is a tract against heretics, "a sort of fiery cross sent through the churches to rally the faithful" (Moffatt). Whether the designation "brother of James" (Jude ^{1}) means that he was a brother of Jesus (Mark 6^{3}), as tradition asserts, is uncertain. In any case the letter was written late, after the death of the Apostles (v.^{17}), late enough for the Gnostics to have become active in the churches, and long enough after the fall of Jerusalem for it no longer to dominate the horizon of Jewish Christians; this indicates a date *c.* A.D. 80. By that time Peter had long been a martyr. 2 Peter therefore is a pseudepigraph. Observe, it should not be called a *forgery*; that is a misnomer in relation to religious works in the Hebrew-Christian tradition, for some of the noblest Jewish writings of the inter-testamental period were

written in the name of another; pseudonymity was a device by which men effaced their identity to gain a hearing for the word of the Lord. Of the author of 2 Peter, Schlatter stated: "He chose this manner in which to speak to the Christian world, with the earnest endeavour that the Church should not depart from the way which the Apostles had shown her, but keep that which she had received from them. Hence he set Peter's name at the head of the letter, rather than that of another Apostle, for Jesus had made Peter his first messenger and the Church had arisen through his testimony. The Church remains in the way of Jesus, as it has been shown her from the beginning, when she does not lose that which Peter had proclaimed to her."

2 Peter is commonly regarded as the latest book in the New Testament and dated *c.* A.D. 150. Since, however, its situation is closely similar to that depicted by Jude there is no need to set it much later than Jude itself.

(V) THE JOHANNINE LITERATURE

1. *The Fourth Gospel.* The earliest testimony to the authorship of this Gospel occurs at its conclusion: "It is this same disciple who attests what has here been written. It is in fact he who wrote it, and we know that his testimony is true" (21^{24}). The reference is to the beloved disciple, John the son of Zebedee. The identity of the guarantors of the Gospel is unknown. Is their testimony reliable?

The classical defence for an affirmative answer came from Westcott. He presented the internal evidence in a series of concentric circles, arguing that (*a*) the author was a Jew, (*b*) he was a Jew of Palestine, (*c*) he was an eye-witness, (*d*) he was an Apostle, (*e*) he was the Apostle John. Investigations since his time may be said to have vindicated (*a*) and (*b*), and there is much to be said for (*c*), at least in respect to some of the ministry of Jesus. Over (*d*) and (*e*) there is sharp disagreement, but that a connexion of some kind did exist between the Gospel and the Apostle John is generally admitted.

The relations between the Synoptic Gospels and the Fourth Gospel are not easily defined. Undoubtedly there are striking differences. The teaching of Jesus in the Synoptics is direct and abounds in illustrations; in John it is more akin to Rabbinical argumentation, and parable is replaced by allegory; yet most of the discourses of John have a synagogue or Temple setting and much of their instruction corresponds with their festal context; there may be authentic material here of which the Synoptists knew nothing. The miracles in the Synoptics are acts of power done out of pity, in John they are signs and are primarily evidential; but this is a matter of emphasis and should not be regarded as contradictory. Eschatology in the Synoptics is strongly futurist, in John it is primarily realized, but again this can no longer be viewed as opposition: realized eschatology is of vital importance in the Synoptics and futurist eschatology appears in John. The messiahship of Jesus in Mark is gradually revealed, in John it is divined at once and not hidden; this is a real divergence, though a development of messianic revelation of a different kind occurs in John. The milieu of the Synoptics is of Palestine and Jewish; it used to be maintained that that of John is of the Diaspora and Hellenistic, but that, too, has to be modified, above all in the light of the affinities between this Gospel and the outlook of the Qumran sectaries. The Synoptic Gospels and the Fourth Gospel must be regarded as positively related and complementary, rather than as standing in irreconcilable opposition. Moreover, whereas it was formerly unanimously held that the author of the Fourth Gospel used Mark and Luke, and possibly Matthew also, there is a widespread conviction that the fourth Evangelist wrote independently of our canonical Gospels but with knowledge of traditions parallel to those on which those Gospels were based (see especially Gardner-Smith, *St. John and the Synoptic Gospels*).

The authorship of the Fourth Gospel is therefore an open question. If we hold that it was written by the Apostle John, we must concur with R. H. Lightfoot that he will have moved with the times and become acquainted with Rabbinic teaching and attempts of writers like Philo to reconcile Jewish and Greek thought (this applies above all to the Logos-doctrine of the prologue); but it must also be confessed that much of this material will have been available in Palestine itself, as the Qumran literature shows. The once fashionable belief that the Gospel was written by John the Elder is less popular; never was a more ambiguous statement penned than that of Papias, cited by Eusebius, on which the notion is based, and since the man may have never existed, too much confidence ought not to be placed in the conjecture. If the writer was not the Apostle John he was in close touch with him, probably as a disciple, and the tradition he expounded was that of his beloved master.

The purpose of the evangelist is stated in the conclusion proper of the Gospel: "These are written that you may believe that Jesus is the Christ, the son of God, and that through this faith you may possess eternal life by his name." It is unlikely that he wrote to supplant the other Gospels, but in view of the high degree of selectivity he exercised it is probable that he desired to elucidate the significance of the evangelic traditions current in his area.

The date of the Gospel is unknown. The discovery of the Rylands papyrus 457, dated *c.* A.D. 130, makes improbable the once popular belief that it was written in the second quarter of the second century. Traditionally considered to be the latest of the four Gospels and written at the end of the first century, it could as well have been written prior to the Jewish war. Any date between A.D. 60 and 100 is possible.

2. *The Epistles of John.* Traditionally it has been believed that these three writings were of common authorship and that they were written by the fourth Evangelist. Modern criticism has generally accepted this conclusion in view of their common themes, theological standpoint, vocabulary, and style. Precisely, however, on the basis of alleged differences in theology, vocabulary and style, the unity of Epistles and Gospel has been challenged of late. Most critics still adhere to common authorship, believing that such divergencies as do exist may be accounted for by the different nature of the Gospel and Epistles and their different purposes. On the least estimate they must have come from the same circle of Christian belief. Since the earliest references to the letters come from writers of the province of Asia (Polycarp and Papias) the tradition that they emanated from that area may be right. There is little indication of date, beyond the improbability of their being written after the end of the first century A.D.

The first letter is the most important of the three. It seems to have been called forth by a threat of major schism in the Church. Certain teachers had led out believers from the churches (2^{19}); they possessed prophetic gifts ($4^{1ff.}$) and secured a large following (4^{5}). Their chief error concerned the person of Christ: they would not confess that Jesus Christ has come in the flesh (4^{2}). This is the docetic heresy and is a hallmark of Gnosticism. Characteristic claims of the Gnostics to superior knowledge and life are cited: " We have fellowship with him " (1^{6}), " I know him " (2^{4}), " I abide in him " (2^{6}), " We have a chrism " (2^{20}), " We have seen God " (4^{12}), and even " We have no sin " (1^{8}). The writer describes the kind of life that should proceed from such enlightenment, and where it is missing he refutes the claims, bluntly calling those who falsely make them liars (2^{4}). He calls for a recognition of the indissolubility of the Gospel and the command of God; in the faith and love of Christ they are one (3^{23}, $4^{10ff.}$).

The second letter is sent to a church, not an individual (vv. $^{8-10}$). The address to the elect lady in v.^{1}, therefore, is a picturesque mode of speaking to a congregation (cf. 2 Cor. 11^{2}), and the elect sister of v.^{13} is the writer's own church. The letter appears to be a warning against the same kind of heresy as that described in the first letter.

The third letter has a personal address but it concerns church matters, notably the recalcitrant behaviour of one Diotrephes, who refused to welcome visiting missionaries and excommunicated those who wished to do so (vv.$^{9f.}$). Dodd observes that Diotrephes is either the first "monarchical bishop" known to history in the province of Asia, or he is a symptom of the disease which the quasi-apostolic ministry of monarchical bishops was designed to relieve. In any case there are better examples in the Church for Gaius, and all subsequent readers, to follow (v.^{11}).

3. *The Book of Revelation.* The author calls himself John (1^{4}), with no title beyond brother (1^{9}) and prophet (22^{9}). Though exiled in Patmos, his connexion with the churches of Roman Asia indicates that he was normally resident there. In view of the tradition that the Apostle John migrated to Ephesus, it was natural that the John of Revelation became identified with the Apostle of that name. The weightiest support for this is the manner in which the prophet refers to himself simply as John, as though there were no other Christian leader in that area with whom he could be confused. There are also sufficient affinities of thought and diction between the Revelation and the Gospel to demand some connexion between the two works. On the other hand the thought, style, and diction of the Revelation differ so greatly from the Gospel as to make it difficult to attribute both to a single author. Admittedly, some critics still accept a common authorship of all five Johannine writings. In the eyes of most the differences between the Revelation and the other four are so great, the matter would be dismissed were it not for the view, learnedly advocated by C. C. Torrey, that the Revelation was written in Aramaic and translated into Greek with extreme literalness. If another writer was responsible for this translation the difficulties connected with vocabulary and style would fall to the ground. The question, however, whether an apocalyptist would express his thought in so unapocalyptic a fashion as the fourth Gospel remains; it is hard to believe that he would. It is, of course, possible to attribute the Revelation to the Apostle and the Gospel to another, or both works to different disciples of the one Apostle, but this must be weighed in the light of the discussion on the authorship of the fourth Gospel.

It is generally considered that the Revelation was written towards the close of Domitian's reign, as his persecution was beginning, *c.* A.D. 96. Some favour an earlier date, in the reign of Nero or in Galba's short rule, A.D. 68. This is based on a literal interpretation of Rev. 11$^{1-2}$, 17$^{9ff.}$, but in view of the frequent employment by the writer of earlier sources it is questionable (note that 11$^{3-13}$, immediately following the short oracle 11^{1-2}, is almost certainly a reapplication of an earlier writing). The fact that John, a prominent Christian leader, has already been exiled points to an official determination to eradicate the Church, and compulsion in respect of emperor worship is believed to be imminent: this accords with conditions in Roman Asia during the Domitianic persecution but not during the reign of Nero.

The modes of interpreting Revelation are legion, but it makes sense when it is related to other similar writings and to its historical setting. The writer sees in his experience the threat of universal persecution for the Church through the enforcement of Caesar worship. No man who confessed "Jesus is Lord" (Rom. 10^{9}) could also affirm "Caesar is Lord," as was being demanded in Roman Asia. John saw the consummation of such tendencies as mankind divided to the obedience of Christ or Antichrist. On the canvas of his age he pictured a final crisis of cosmic proportions, the outcome of which should be the advent of Christ in glory. The book is a trumpet call to faith in view of the sure triumph of the Kingdom of Christ and of God.

(vi) THE CANON

The idea of a collection of authoritative works setting forth God's acts for men and His will for men was natural to a Church cradled in Judaism and nurtured on the Old Testament. Not that the earliest Christians thought of adding to the Old Testament or of forming a complement to it in the New. The factors which actually caused this to happen were (*a*) the authority of the words of Jesus, greater even than that of the Old Testament Law (Matt. 5^{17-48}); (*b*) the authority of the apostolic teaching, itself an explication and development of the Lord's teaching and of the significance of His life; (*c*) the use of writings concerning Jesus Christ and of epistles from apostolic men in the services of the Church; (*d*) the publication by heretics of writings that claimed to embody secret traditions from the apostles. This last feature provided a powerful incitement to the Church to action: the literary output of the Gnostics, the issuing by Marcion of his own canon of authoritative writings (an abbreviated edition of Luke + ten epistles of Paul), and the claim of the Montanists to immediate inspiration caused the Church to evaluate its treasures handed down from apostolic men and to pronounce judgment on those which were of lesser worth or which did not accord with their teaching. On this basis Origen divided the "books of the Church" into two groups: (*a*) those recognized everywhere (*homologoumena*) and (*b*) those disputed. The latter included Hebrews (owing to doubt as to its Pauline authorship) and the five lesser Catholic epistles (James, 2 Peter, 2 and 3 John, Jude). Eusebius of Caesarea, after ascertaining the usage of all the churches, went a stage further and divided the books into three: (*a*) 22 acknowledged books, *i.e.*, 4 Gospels, 14 Epistles of Paul (including Hebrews), 1 John, 1 Peter, Revelation; (*b*) 5 disputed works—James, 2 Peter, 2 and 3 John; (*c*) 5 spurious—Acts of Paul, Hermas, Apocalypse of Peter, Barnabas, Didache: "to these perhaps the Revelation should be added, as some reject while others accept it" (Eusebius would cheerfully have rejected it had it been possible!). It will be observed that this is virtually our canon. The Festal letter of Athanasius, written A.D. 367 to clear up ambiguities relating to the canon, gives our New Testament in its present order (except that Acts is followed by the Catholic epistles).

(vii) EARLY NON-CANONICAL CHRISTIAN WRITINGS

Among the works valued by the Church but which did not ultimately find a place in the New Testament canon, the group designated as the Apostolic Fathers is best known. They are contained in a single volume edited by J. B. Lightfoot, and more recently in two volumes edited by K. Lake in the Loeb Library.

1. *The first Epistle of Clement* was written to the church of Corinth on account of disorders in that church. Its opening paragraph contains an apology for delay in writing, occasioned by "sudden and repeated calamities which have befallen us"; if this refers to the persecution of Domitian, as most think, the letter is to be dated *c.* A.D. 95 and so contemporary with the Book of Revelation. Clement wrote in the name of the church at Rome to rebuke a "detestable and unholy sedition" that had deposed presbyters in Corinth. The writer is led to dilate on the nature of the office of presbyter-bishop and to expound the idea of an apostolic succession of presbyters. Subsequent tradition regarded Clement as the presiding *episcopos* in the church of Rome; this has been contested, but possibly he had such a position tacitly rather than explicitly.

2. *The second Epistle of Clement* follows immediately on the first in early MSS., and was apparently ascribed to Clement, although no such claim is made for it in the document, neither is it really a letter. It is our earliest extant Christian homily, and is generally dated about the middle of the second century A.D. The writing is not particularly valuable but displays a high moral tone and unfaltering faith.

3. *The Epistles of Ignatius*, bishop of Antioch, were written in the early years of the second century, possibly *c.* A.D. 115. Ignatius had been condemned to death and was on his way to Rome, expecting to die there in the amphitheatre. During a

halt at Smyrna he wrote to the churches at Ephesus, Magnesia, Tralles, and Rome; stopping later at Alexandria Troas he wrote to the churches of Philadelphia and Smyrna and a letter to Polycarp. The letters reveal the ardour of a martyr and reflect an extraordinary reverence for order, above all as embodied in the bishop ("Follow your bishop as Jesus Christ followed the Father, and the presbytery as the Apostles; and to the deacons pay respect as to God's commandments"). The writer also inveighs against purveyors of the docetic heresy.

4. *The Epistle of Polycarp* was written by the famous bishop of Smyrna in reply to a letter from the Philippian church. They had invited him to send them a homily, asked him to pass on a letter to the Syrian church, and requested that he forward to them any letters from Ignatius that he possessed. Polycarp's reply is directed to these three matters. His letter belongs to the same period as the Ignatian epistles, *c.* A.D. 115.

5. *The Martyrdom of Polycarp*, as its name implies, gives an account of Polycarp's death in a letter from the church of Smyrna to the church of Philomelium. The letter was written shortly after the martyrdom, which took place *c.* A.D. 155.

6. *The Didache*, or "Teaching of the Twelve Apostles," was compiled from a Jewish work called "The Two Ways" and the Bible. The Two Ways was used even more extensively than the Didache; it describes the paths of righteousness and unrighteousness, of life and death, and is a moral treatise for catechumens. The remaining part of the work gives directions relating to the worship and organization of the Church. Its primitive church order has caused some to suspect it to be a Montanist reaction to developing episcopacy, but it is more likely to be of early date, perhaps *c.* A.D. 110 or even *c.* A.D. 95.

7. *The Epistle of Barnabas* does not, in fact, claim to be by Barnabas, though it is so cited by Clement of Alexandria and Origen. The work is violently anti-Jewish but cites the Old Testament at length and abounds in allegorical interpretation. Its date is unknown; Lightfoot sets its limits A.D. 70–132.

8. *The Shepherd of Hermas* is an apocalyptic writing in three parts—"Visions," "Mandates" (precepts), and "Similitudes." The Shepherd is the divine teacher who instructs Hermas for the benefit of the whole Church. The great theme of the book is sin in the Church and repentance—a burning issue in the second and third centuries. Its date is uncertain; the Muratorian Canon states that it was written during the episcopate of Pius I. of Rome, *i.e.* A.D. 140–55, but the book mentions Clement of Rome as a contemporary, implying a date *c.* A.D. 100. Possibly the book was composed at intervals between the two dates.

9. *The Epistle to Diognetus* is " one of the noblest and most impressive of early Christian apologies " (Lightfoot). The person addressed may be the tutor of Marcus Aurelius, who is represented as an enquirer after truth. The simplicity of the work and its absence of reference to heresies is notable and favours a relatively early date, *i.e. c.* A.D. 150, though it may be considerably later.

BIBLIOGRAPHY

J. Moffatt, *An Introduction to the Literature of the New Testament*, 3rd ed., 1913.
K. Lake and S. Lake, *An Introduction to the New Testament*, 1938.
F. B. Clogg, *An Introduction to the New Testament*, 2nd ed., 1940.
T. Henshaw, *New Testament Literature*, 1952.
H. F. D. Sparks, *The Formation of the New Testament*, 1952.
A. H. M'Neile, *An Introduction to the Study of the New Testament*, revised by C. S. C. Williams, 1953.
G. S. Duncan, *St. Paul's Ephesian Ministry*, 1929.
Vincent Taylor, *The Formation of the Gospel Tradition*, 1933.
Vincent Taylor, *The Gospels : A Short Introduction*, 8th ed., 1956.
P. Gardner-Smith, *Saint John and the Synoptic Gospels*, 1938.
A. M. Hunter, *Interpreting the New Testament, 1900-50*, 1951.

VI. LITERARY FORMS

(A) OLD TESTAMENT FORMS

BY JAMES MUILENBURG

NOT only the animating spirit of a people but also the way that it comprehends its existence is reflected in the manner of its speaking, in the ways it employs words and articulates them into forms and structures, in the conventions whereby thought is symbolized into language. If it is true that *le style c'est de l'homme,* then it is also true that the styles and modes of speaking of a people are in some profound sense a transcription of its interior nature. They may reflect, for example, how its daily habits and practices, its social customs and institutions, its mores and values are understood and then transmitted to the community. Or they may be the means whereby the orders of a society or its chosen representatives (military leader, judge, king, priest, poet, etc.) relate themselves to the people. The content of what is said is intimately connected with the manner in which it is said; the two must not be separated. Similar situations evoke similar forms of speech. In a society where the types and styles of language are first transmitted orally and where the power and vitality of the spoken word are deeply felt and discerned, where thought becomes alive and effectual in its being bodied forth in being spoken, where the self extends itself by naming, addressing, calling, telling, etc., there, it goes without saying, the forms and structures which words assume will prove an interior disclosure of the fabric of a people's consciousness.

1. *Poetry.* Only in relatively modern times have we come to an understanding of the types and forms of speech in the Old Testament. Hebrew poetry, like the poetry of other peoples of the ancient Near East, is governed by the principle of *parallelismus membrorum.* The individual line is paralleled by a second, and sometimes by a third, which re-states, completes, contrasts, or develops in some other way what has been stated (cf. Ps. 1^{6}, 8^{3-6}, 15^{1}, 19^{1}, etc.). Meter is determined, not by the measured succession of syllables (iambic, anapaestic, trochaic, etc.), but rather by sense or meaning. Generally the Hebrew poem can be divided into strophes or stanzas. Literary forms can be most readily recognized by the way they begin and end, but also by typical phraseology and terminology. In spite of the sense for form which characterizes most Hebrew

literary compositions, spontaneity, passion, sense of immediacy, and concreteness are equally apparent. The Hebrew seldom reduces his literary forms to stereotype. Fluidity is apparent almost everywhere. This is to be observed in the variety and complexity of the parallelism, in the diverse length of the strophes, in the " break " of the structure and pattern, and in manifold other ways. The same fluidity and diversity is illustrated in the use of words. The Hebrew is sensitive to the connotations of words, and he uses them with great versatility. One has always to recognize the context in which a word is used to determine its particular meaning or nuance. The Hebrew did not feel himself so much bound and fettered to formal patterns as is often thought. Form there is indeed, but it must not be reduced to rigidity or too great conformity. There is freedom and creativity within the conventions and patterns. The same type may assume different guises.

It is evident from the Old Testament itself that ancient Israel possessed a substantial secular " literature," and this is not at all surprising because its religious faith constantly enters into conversation with the vicissitudes of daily existence. So we have the formal greetings or *salutations* (Ruth 2^{4}, Ps. 129^{8}, Judg. 18^{6}) and the *acclamations* on the occasion of the king's accession to the throne (1 Sam. 10^{24}, 1 Kings $1^{34.\,39}$, 2 Kings 11^{12}, etc.). Then there are the formal expressions of *good wishes*, sometimes almost oracular in character, as on the occasion of a child's birth (Gen. 35^{17}, 1 Sam. 4^{20}). Not unrelated to these are the sententious *birth pronouncements* which appear in identically formulated contexts (Gen. 29^{31}–30^{24}, Hos. 1^{4-8}; cf. Isa. 7^{14}, Matt. 1^{23}). *Drinking songs* have been preserved (Isa. 22^{13b}; cf. Isa. 56^{12} and Wisd. 2^{1-9}). We hear the enigmatic words of the watchman (Isa 21^{11-12}; cf. Hab. 2^{1-4}, Ezek. $3^{16ff.}$, 33^{7-9}). The Song of the Well in Num. $21^{17f.}$ is probably a *worker's song*, the words of which lightened the burden of labour and were probably believed to have magical power. In Egypt too such songs were sung. The song of the harlot in Isa. 23^{16} is a model of Hebrew literary composition with two triads in 2′ 2′ meter. *Dirges* too were intoned, with their cry, " Ho! Ho! " (Am. 5^{16} or " Ah, my brother " (*hôy 'āḥî*) or " Ah, sister " (*hôy 'āḥôth*) or " Ah, lord " (*hôy 'ādhôn*) (Jer. 22^{18}; cf. 34^{5}). There were professional mourners in Israel, especially the mourning women, like those represented on the Ahiram sarcophagus (Jer. 9^{17-22}). David indited a magnificent dirge over Saul and Jonathan (2 Sam. 1^{19-27}); it is an excellent specimen of early Hebrew lamenting with its repetition of the key-line, " How are the mighty fallen " (cf. Am. 5^{2}). The first word *'êkhāh* is one of the central features of the dirge or lament. Such forms were imitated by the prophets (Am. 5^{2},

Isa. $14^{4ff.}$, Ezek. 30^{2b-4}). One of the most characteristic features of this literature of lamentation is the contrast between life and death, what the person once was and what he is now. The comparative literature from the other peoples of the ancient Near East is abundant.

As among all peoples, men *boasted* of their prowess and sought to daunt the enemy by their proud vaunting. The early Song of Lamech (Gen. 4^{23-24}) is a passionate outburst of nomadic braggadocio, but shows extraordinary sense of form and structure. Samson's boast (Judg. 15^{16}) is notable for its striking assonance and paronomasia (cf. 1 Sam. 14^{12}, 17^{44}). In the prophets we hear the arrogant boasts of the king of Tyre (Ezek. 27^{3}, 28^{1}) and of Babylon (Isa. 47^{7}). Not unrelated to the boast is the *mocking saying*, a good example of which is the song to be sung by the ballad singers in Num. 21^{27-30} (cf. Judg. 5^{15b-17}). More highly developed forms are seen in the taunt songs against Sennacherib (Isa 37^{22-29}) and Babylon (Isa. 47). Israel, like most peoples, delighted in the *riddle*. A beautiful example is preserved in Samson's riddle on the occasion of a feast, though the solution is by no means clear (Judg. 14^{12-18}). Apparently riddles were cultivated among the sages (Prov. 1^{6}).

Warfare played a great role in the life of ancient Israel and gave rise to a considerable literature. On the occasion of a military engagement *war-cries* were shouted to urge the soldiers into battle (Judg. $7^{8b.\ 20b}$). In times of discontent shouts of revolt were raised (2 Sam. 20^{1}, 1 Kings 12^{16}). The songs of the Ark (Num. 10^{35-36}) were surely of a military nature, and the echoes of these songs continue to resound in the celebrations of the cult in the cry for divine intervention in the laments of the Psalter. Women greeted the returning heroes with their songs (1 Sam. 18^{7}; cf. Judg. 11^{34}). The Song of Miriam (Ex. 15^{21}) is a song of victory, while the Song of the Sea (Ex. 15^{1-18}) is a superbly wrought liturgy designed to celebrate the event of Yahweh's mighty triumph at the Sea of Reeds. Similarly the Song of Deborah (Judg. 5) celebrates the great victory of the tribes of Israel in the Plain of Esdraelon. The two early collections, the Book of the Wars of Yahweh (Num. 21^{14}) and the Book of Jashar (the Brave? 2 Sam. 1^{18}), may have been compilations of war-songs. A very early military oath by the throne (?) of Yahweh is preserved in Ex. 17^{16}. It is a portentous word.

The *oath* is a solemn asseveration that what one is saying is true. It is common among the Semitic peoples and played a conspicuous role in Israel's life. Perhaps the most familiar form is the adjuration "As the Lord lives" (1 Sam. $14^{39.\ 45}$, 19^{6}, 25^{34}) or "As the Lord and you yourself live" (1 Sam. 20^{3},

25^{36}) or " As you live " (2 Sam. 11^{11}). Another common form of the oath was " May the Lord do so to me and more also " (Ruth 1^{17}, 1 Sam. 3^{17}, 14^{44}, 2 Sam. 3^{35} ; cf. also 1 Sam. 20^{13}). Or the oath may invoke the divine witness, as in " God is witness between you and me " (Gen. 31^{50} [see vv. $^{44-52}$]; cf. 1 Sam. 12^{5f}?, 20^{12}, Mic. 1^{2}). As holy words, oaths were naturally associated with the sanctuaries ; there the divine name was invoked (Hos. 4^{15}). The covenant in Israel was sealed by mutual oaths as were covenants between persons (cf. Gen. 31^{49}). The oath was naturally related to the curse, as we see in such conditionals as Job 31 ; Ps. 7^{4-5}, 137^{5-6}.

Love poetry is not abundant in the Old Testament, with the notable exception of the Song of Songs, a collection of voluptuous lyrics, passionate in mood and profuse in its imagery. Like so much of the rest of Israel's literature, it has affinity with the other literatures of ancient Near Eastern peoples, the Sumerian love-songs, the Tammuz fertility cult-songs, and Egyptian poems. Weddings in Israel were occasions for rejoicing and festival. We may be confident that there was much singing at such times. Congratulations were offered (Gen. 24^{60}, Ruth 4^{11}), the beauty of the bride was extolled, and it was a time of jubilation.

Songs of the harvest (Isa. 9^{3}) and of the vintage (Isa. 16^{10}) were sung in Israel. Annually at Shiloh there was dancing among the vineyards (Judg. 21^{12}), and it is not improbable that it was accompanied by singing. Jeremiah speaks of the shouts of those who tread the grapes. Such celebrations are of course common among many peoples, ancient and modern. The prophet Isaiah employs the form of a vineyard song as a kind of parable or allegory (Isa. 5^{1-7}). It may seem surprising that none of the harvest and vintage songs has been handed down to us. The reason may well be that they were too much bound up with the fertility cult celebrations and so were an offence to the worshippers of Yahweh. This may account in part too for the paucity of *fables*. Only two have been preserved, the first the fable of Jotham in Judg. 9^{7-15} which swarms with Canaanite affinities (cf. Baal and Anath in *ANET*, 134*a*, 135*a*, 140), the second the fable of the thistle and the cedar in 2 Kings 14^{9}. Yet it is clear that the fable did exercise an influence upon later writers, as in Ezekiel's allegory (Ezek. 17^{3-10} ; cf. also 19^{2-9} and 10^{14}). Parabolic contexts are not infrequent in the Old Testament ; the best example of the *parable* is Nathan's story of the little ewe lamb (2 Sam. 12^{1-6}).

We may now undertake to explore somewhat more systematically the regions in which the literary types and forms come to expression and, more particularly, to enquire into the seminal forces which gave rise to them. Perhaps first place should be assigned to the role of singing in the life of Israel. From earliest times there were those who responded to the elemental rhythms of life by composing *songs*, and it is doubtless to these that we are to look for the origins of Hebrew poetry. The parallelism of successive lines may well have originated in antiphonal singing. To be sure Israel is by no means unique in this. The other peoples of the ancient Near East also employed this poetic form, and Israel borrowed from them, above all from Canaan and Aram, not only in this but in many other ways. It is striking that already in the earliest compositions we have the summons to sing in the opening introit: "Let me sing" or "I will sing" or "Sing to Yahweh!" But what is more, this proclivity to sing attends Israel's historical life throughout the whole Old Testament, whether in hymn or lament or battle-song. But with the singers of Israel were the narrators, and these, too, often recounted the mighty deeds of Yahweh in poetry and song. That narrative occupies so large a place in the Old Testament is not at all surprising, for those who were most representative of Israel told of the mighty deeds of Yahweh; above all in worship they rehearsed the events that belonged to their life (Josh. $24^{2ff.}$, 1 Sam. $12^{7ff.}$, Deut. 6^{20}, Pss. 78, 105, 136).

2. *Narratives.* Most primitive of the narrative forms in the Old Testament is the *folk-tale*, drawn originally from the world of magic. Yet nowhere do we encounter this type in a pure form, for magic has been altered by the presence of the personal will, human or divine. Folk-tale motifs are nevertheless abundant as in the case of the speaking serpent (Gen. $3^{1ff.}$), or the speaking ass (Num. $22^{21ff.}$), or the ravens which feed Elijah (1 Kings 17^{1-6}), or the great fish in Jonah (Jon. 2^{1-10}), or the lions in Daniel (Dan. $6^{23ff.}$). The *legends* of the Old Testament have frequently been influenced by Near Eastern prototypes. An aetiological interest is apparent in many of them, as in the cursing of Canaan (Gen. 9^{24-27}), or the birth of Moab and Ammon (Gen. $19^{30ff.}$), or of Jacob and Esau (Gen. $25^{19ff.}$). The legend also recounts the origin of circumcision (Ex. $4^{24ff.}$, Josh. $5^{2ff.}$, Gen. 17), as also of the serpent of brass (Num. $21^{4ff.}$; cf. 2 Kings 18^{4}). Cultic legends associated with the founding of sanctuaries appear not infrequently: Bethel (Gen. 28^{10-22} JE), Beersheba (Gen. 26^{23-25}), and Penuel (Gen. 32^{22-32}). Legends gathered not only about places but also persons, like Elijah and Elisha (1 Kings 17–18, 2 Kings 1^{2-17}, 2^{1-5}, $4^{1-7.\ 11-31}$, 6^{1-7}). *Hero tales* belong to another genre. These are to be found in the account of Joshua's victory over the Amorites (Josh. 10), in the exploits of the "judges" (Judg. 3^{15}–16^{31} with the deletion of the frameworks), and in David's slaying of Goliath (1 Sam. 17). Brief reference may be made to the

anecdotes, in which a small episode centres in the "hero" (Judg. 1^{22-26}, 2 Kings 4^{1-7}). Much more elaborate and stylistically more finished is the *novella,* the classical example of which is Joseph and his Brothers (Gen. 37, 39–45). The books of Ruth and Esther and the apocryphal book of Judith belong to the same genre. *Myth* occupies a position of considerable importance in the Old Testament, yet it nowhere appears unbroken or unchanged. If we define myth as a story of the gods, then we should not expect Israel to incorporate it into her traditions. Yet mythological contexts are by no means infrequent. One recalls the torso of the myth of the sons of God in Gen. 6^{1-4} or the oracles against the prince of Tyre (Ezek. $28^{2-10.\ 11-19}$) or of the morning star (Isa. 14^{12-20}). The flood stories also reflect an early myth (Gen. 6^{11}–8^{22}; cf. Gilgamesh Epic, Tablet XI, *ANET*, pp. 93–7; also the Atrahasis Epic, *ibid.*, pp. 104–06). By far the most prominent and theologically the most significant is, of course, the myth of the chaos-dragon (Isa. 27^{1}, $51^{9f.}$, Ps. $89^{9f.}$; cf. Job 40^{15}–41^{34}).

Israel achieved an undisputed pre-eminence among the peoples of the ancient Near East in the *historical narrative.* There were, to be sure, the court annals, like the Book of the Acts of Solomon (1 Kings 11^{41}) or the Chronicles of the Kings of Israel and Judah (1 Kings 14^{19-29}), similar to those in other royal courts such as Assyria, and excerpts from these are doubtless preserved in the Old Testament (1 Kings 3^{4-28}, 4^{1-19}, 5^{7-8}, etc.). But it is rather to the court history of 2 Sam. 9–20, 1 Kings 1–2 that we must look for what is distinctively Israelite. Here we discern historical connexions and causes, and the account has every claim to trustworthiness. The historical narratives of 1–2 Kings are controlled by and large by prophetic and Deuteronomic interests, but they are drawn from a diversity of literary forms and types. Perhaps it is not out of place here to refer to *biographical narrative,* best illustrated by Baruch's prose accounts of the fortunes of Jeremiah (Jer. 26–29, 32–45). *Autobiography* is represented in the somewhat confessional memoirs of Nehemiah (Neh. 1–7, 12^{31}–13^{31}).

3. *Other prose forms.* The Old Testament contains a considerable variety of other literary types in prose. Consider, for example, the *address* or speech. Before his death Joshua delivers a long charge to Israel (Josh. 23^{2-16}); similarly David before his death gives a final charge to Solomon (1 Kings 2^{1-9}). Of quite a different order is the speech of the Rabshekeh to Hezekiah (2 Kings 18^{19-25} = Isa. 36^{4-10}) and to the people (2 Kings 18^{28-35} = Isa. 36^{13-20}). Notable, too, are the speeches of the covenant mediators (Joshua in Josh. 24^{2-15} and Samuel

in 1 Sam. 12^{1-18}). Related to these are the *sermons*, often both in form and in content (Deut. 1^{1}–4^{43}, 5^{1}–11^{32}, Jer. 7^{1-15} (–8^{3} ?) ; Ezek. 20). The *monologue* is well represented in Job 29–31 ; the influence of sacral law is manifest in the great conditionals of Job's oath of clearance in chap. 31. Solomon's prayer of dedication (1 Kings 8^{22-53}) is the finest specimen of the *prayer in prose* in the Old Testament (cf. John 17), but there is the brief outcry of Samson (Judg. 16^{28}) and the moving utterance of Jehoshaphat (2 Chron. 20^{5-12}).

Many *treaties* have come down to us from the peoples of the Ancient Near East (*e.g.* Sumerians, Akkadians, Egyptians, Hittites, Aramaeans), and the Old Testament refers to not a few such transactions (Josh. 9^{15}, 1 Kings 5^{16-23}). Perhaps the first actual treaty to be preserved for us, however, appears in 1 Macc. 8^{22-32}. It is probable, however, that the *covenant* (treaty) account in Ex. 19–24 has been modelled after the Hittite suzerainty treaty. Many *letters* from Israel's neighbours are extant (Mari, Alalakh, Tell el-Amarna, Ugarit, Lachish), and the Old Testament contains a number (1 Kings 21^{8-10}, Jer. 29^{1-23}, 29^{24-28}, Dan. 4^{1-18} [Aram. 3^{31}–4^{17}]). The documents quoted in Ezra $4^{7-16.\ 17-22}$, 7^{12-26} reflect the formal epistolary style of the Persian court. It is clear that the letter as a formal type has influenced many of the prophetic oracles and other contexts (Gen. 32^{3b-5}, Num. 20^{14-19}). Several *royal edicts* are preserved (Ezra 1^{2-4}, 6^{2b-12}, Dan. $4^{1ff.}$ [Aram. $3^{31ff.}$]) ; these may be compared to some of the records from Elephantine. Finally, attention may be called to the large number of *lists* of various kinds : genealogies (1 Chron. 1–9), lists of towns allotted to the tribes (Josh. 15–19), inventory of votive offerings (Ex. 35^{21-29}), booty (Num. 31^{32-47}), David's bodyguard (2 Sam. 23^{24-39}).

4. *Laws*. As among other peoples of the ancient world, the communal life of Israel was regulated by law. The recovery of Sumerian, Akkadian, Hittite, Assyrian, and other legal collections has made it possible for us to arrive at a better understanding of Israelite law. In the Old Testament several *legal corpora* appear : the Covenant Code (Ex. 20^{23}–23^{33}), the Deuteronomic Code (Deut. 12–26), the Holiness Code (Lev. 17–26), the Priestly Code (Ex. 25–40, etc.). The two major types of law are the casuistic or case law and the apodictic or categorical law. The former appears in the style of the conditional sentence with its protasis and apodosis (if . . . then) ; the concrete situation or offence is described and is then followed by its consequence (Ex. 21^{1}–22^{16}). The latter, on the other hand, is formulated succinctly and categorically : *Thou shalt not* (Ex. 20^{1-17}, Deut. 5^{6-21}). Or it may be stated in the participial style as in the original Hebrew of Ex. $21^{12.\ 15.\ 16.\ 17}$,

etc. A further variant may be the curse or malediction (Deut. 27^{15-26}). A third literary form of law is the priestly *tôrāh* or law, the oral direction of the priest who speaks in the name of Yahweh on matters of cult or to the individual. This formulation is preserved in some of the prophets (Isa. 1^{10-17}, Am. 4^{4-5}, 5^{4-5}). A fourth type has been described as the ritual, which is particularly common in Ex. 25–Lev. 16 (Ex. 25^{10-31}, $26^{7-15. 29-37}$, 27^{1-8}, Lev. 1–4). The ritual was used as a kind of cult aetiology designed to legitimize the correct rites. The laws of Israel left their impression both upon the prophets and the wise men.

5. *Prophetic literature.* The prophetic books of the Old Testament contain a great variety of literary types. But we may begin with the *oracular* saying. In early Israel men "inquired of the Lord," whether by lot or by urim and thummin or by ephod. The responses were brief, probably a "yes" or "no" or another word (2 Sam. 2^{1}) or a sentence (Judg. 1^{2}, 1 Sam. $23^{2. 4}$) or a poetic oracle (Gen. 25^{23}). Already in Elijah we discern a striking change. Yahweh communicates his word to the prophet without mechanical devices, though the word is still characteristically brief (1 Kings $17^{2-3. 9}$, 18^{1}, $19^{9. 13}$). The style of the *messenger's report* such as we have in the Mari letters exercised a profound influence upon prophetic literary types, especially in their opening and closing words: "Thus says the Lord" and "says the Lord." Jeremiah's oracles about the foe from the north (Jer. 4^{5}–6^{30}) and the poems of Second Isaiah (40^{1-11}, 52^{7-10}) have also been influenced by the messenger's style. This same style has influenced the *invective* and *threat,* which belong together as a single literary unit, even though one or the other has at times been lost in transmission. This type is the most common as it is the most characteristic prophetic type. It appears in many guises, most classically perhaps in the *Woe-therefore* manner (Isa. 5^{8-25}, Am. 6^{1-7}, Zeph. 3^{1-8}), but also in other ways (cf. Am. 1^{3}–2^{16}, Ezek. 13^{2b-15}, $25^{3b-7. 8-11. 12-14. 15-17}$). Another literary type often used by the prophets was the *lawsuit* (*rîbh*) and for good reason, for better than any other type it reminded Israel of her accountability to a transcendent Judge (Isa. 3^{13-15}, 41^{1}–42^{4}, Jer. 2^{5b-13}, Mic. 6^{1-8}). The *exhortation* was still another favourite form (Am. 5^{6}, Zeph. 2^{3}). The *visions* of the prophets also conform to conventional style (Jer. $1^{11-12. 13-14}$, 24^{2b-10}, Am. $7^{1-3. 4-6. 7-9}$). It seems that the *symbolic prophecies* were also viewed as a special literary form (2 Kings 13^{13-19}, Jer. 13^{1-11}, 16^{1-9}, Ezek. 3^{16}, $4^{1-3. 7}$, 5^{1-17}). The prophet Ezekiel offers us several examples of the *allegory* (Ezek. 17^{2-24}, 19^{2-14}, 23^{2-35}). Second Isaiah, more than any other prophet, employs the *oracle of salvation* (41^{8-13}, 43^{1-7}, 45^{1-7}), though it should be

pointed out that he usually combines them with other types. The same prophet offers us the best example of the *satire* in the Old Testament (44^{9-20}). It is he, too, who gives us the *confession* (Isa. 50^{4-9}, 53^{1-9}). Many other literary types are present in the prophetic literature, but these may be said to be the most representative.

6. *Cultic Speech.* The religious vitality of the worship of ancient Israel receives ample documentation in the great variety of literary types which seek to body forth the thoughts, feelings, and attitudes of the worshipping community and of the individual devotee in the presence of God. The religious literatures of the other peoples of the ancient Near East demonstrate the close cultural affinities of Israel with her neighbours, but the Old Testament also shows where Israel was distinctive, that is, how she transforms what she borrows in the light of her own unique heritage. It is significant that nearly all of the literature of worship is transmitted in poetic form, and it is apparent that music, whether vocal or instrumental, has left its impression upon not a few literary types. The stylistic diversity of the various ways of expression is to be explained, in part at least, by the diversity of the situations which evoked them. It is also to be explained by the persons who participate in worship: priest, Levite, cultic prophet, teacher, king, and surely not least of all, the people. Wisdom, law, court speech, the nature myths, and the sacred history of the past, especially of the Mosaic age—all have left their stamp upon Israel's cultic speaking. Similarly, the national festivals, the celebrations of the royal courts, times of national peril, and the offering of sacrifices influenced in various ways the forms and styles which the cultic life of Israel assumed. Some of the types we have already examined are drawn from the cult. We shall now present a brief survey of other cultic types.

We may begin with two of the most ancient formulations: the *blessing* and the *curse*. To be sure, these do not always appear in cultic situations, but they certainly came to find their home there. These forms have their origin in the realm of magic, but, as in the case of the oracle, magic has given way to something radically different. In the early period of Israel's life blessings and curses were spoken by those who were charismatically endowed (Gen. $27^{27-29.\ 39-40}$, 2 Sam. 6^{18}, 1 Kings $8^{14-16.\ 55-61}$). The word is very powerful, depending in part upon the speaker and in part upon the occasion upon which it is spoken, as in the hour of death (Gen. 48^{14-16}). Naturally, the words of the priest were of great effect (Num. 6^{24-26}). Blessing and curse are not infrequently associated (Num. 24^{9b}, Deut. 28^{1-19}, Jer. 17^{5-8}). Blessings are numerous in the Psalter but are always combined with other types (Pss. 1^{1-3}, 2^{11b}, 32^{1-2}, 41^{1-3}, 119^{1-2}) ; curses are to all intents and purposes absent (cf. Ps. 137^{9}).

One of the most important of all the literary types in the Old Testament is the *hymn*. It has its own characteristic construction with the opening summons to praise or rejoice, its address to the persons who are to participate, its line of motivation giving the reasons why one should praise, usually introduced by the word " for " or " because," and the conclusion. All these forms are employed with great versatility. There are hymns outside the Psalter (Isa. 6^{3}, 12^{1-2}, 42^{10-13}), but of course most of them are to be found there (Pss. 8, 19, 103, 104, 105, 145–150). Related to the hymn is the so-called *hymn of the divine enthronement* (Pss. 47, 93, 96–99), the most distinctive feature of which is " the acclamation," " Yahweh reigns " or " Yahweh has become king " (Pss. 93^{1}, 96^{10}, 97^{1}, 99^{1}). A third type of special importance is the *royal psalm* (Pss. 2, 18, 20, 21, 45, 72, 101, 110, 132) ; the Israelite king plays a central role in these psalms. The style is often that of the royal courts of the ancient Near East, as for example, the oracular words, probably spoken by a prophet (Pss. 2^{7-9}, 132^{11-18}). In the same general classification of literary types we may place the *song of thanksgiving* ; the affinities of this latter type to the hymn are very close. The following have been ascribed to this category : Pss. 30, 32, 34, 40^{1-11}, 41, 66, 92, etc.). Still another type has been identified, *viz.* the *songs of Zion* (Pss. 46, 48, 76, 87 and the songs of ascent, Pss. 120–134). The presence of other literary types associated with the House of David and the sacred hill of Zion has been proposed, but the foregoing will suggest the great impetus to cultic composition which was inspired by the kingship in Israel.

Important as is the hymn in the worship of Israel, it is surpassed in extent at least by the *communal lament*. This type appears in numerous prophetic contexts (*e.g.* Isa. $26^{8-14. 16-19a}$, Jer. 14^{2-9}, Mic. $7^{7-10. 14-17}$, Hab. 1^{2-4}), in lamentations, and in the liturgies. Representative examples are Pss. 44, 74, 79, 80, 125. Many of these laments were doubtless employed on the occasion of the national day of mourning. They are of course closely connected with the dirge. In the same general class is the *personal lament*, which appears in profusion in the Old Testament. One thinks at once of the " confessions " of Jeremiah, which are probably to be assigned to this type (Jer. 15^{10-21}, 17^{12-18}, 18^{18-25}, $20^{7ff.}$). The most familiar examples in the Psalter are Pss. 3, 5, 13, 22, 42–43, 51, and 102. The marks of this literary type are easily recognized, and the parallels in the cognate literatures are often very striking. On the communal lament, for example, the Lamentation over the Destruction of Ur (transl. by S. N. Kramer in *Assyriological Studies*, No. 12, Chicago) provides many interesting parallels. One feature of the lament is that it sometimes closes with an expression of *certainty that God has heard* the suppliant's cry (Pss. 5^{12}, $7^{10f.}$, 13^{6}, 52^{10}; cf. 22^{22-31}). Upon occasion the assurance of being heard will be accompanied by a *vow*, as also in the Babylonian laments (Pss. 54^{6}, 56^{12}, 61^{8}). Allied with the personal lament is the *psalm of trust*, the classical example of which is Ps. 23 (cf. also 4, 11, 16, 62, 131).

Songs of pilgrimage were sung on the occasions when the Israelite visited the sanctuary (cf. Ex. 23^{17}, 34^{23}, Deut. 16^{16}, 1 Sam. 1^{3}, Isa. 2^{3} = Mic. 4^{2}). The one complete specimen of this type is Ps. 122 (cf. Ps. 84). A final cultic type deserves attention, one that has assumed ever-increasing importance in modern Old Testament research. It is the *liturgy*. We have referred to the two prophetic liturgies, Isa. 33 and Mic. 7^{6-20} (cf. also Isa. 63^{7}–64^{12}). The Song of Moses (Ex. 15^{1-18}) is certainly a liturgy employed at the celebration of the Passover. It has been held that Joel 1^{1}–2^{27}, the Book of Habakkuk, and the Book of Nahum also belong to this type. Similarly, Pss. 75, 85, and 126 have been assigned to the same form. Jer. 14^{1}–15^{3} most likely falls into this classification. In many respects our two best examples are the Torah liturgies of Pss. 15 and 24. In the liturgy the pious Israelite enters into dialogue and thus participates in an interior way in the grace that is proffered him.

7. *Wisdom speech.* In no area of Israel's life was the influence of foreign peoples brought to bear more strikingly than in the literature of wisdom. It seems clear that Prov. 21^{17}–23^{11} is largely dependent upon the Wisdom book of Amenemope, and the Aramaic Ahikar, an example of Assyrian wisdom, has also influenced our Book of Proverbs. To be sure, there were popular *proverbs* which are the property of all peoples, crisply formulated lines like " Is Saul also among the prophets " (1 Sam. 10^{11b}) or " Out of the wicked comes forth wickedness " (1 Sam. 24^{13}; cf. Judg. 14^{14}) or " Let not him that girds on his armour boast himself as he that puts it off " (1 Kings 20^{11}) or " The fathers have eaten sour grapes, and the teeth of the children are set on edge " (Jer. 31^{29} = Ezek. 18^{2b}) or " Like mother, like daughter " (Ezek. 16^{44b}) (cf. also Ecc. 9^{4b}, Hos. 8^{7a}, Isa. 10^{15}, Jer. 23^{28b}). The elaboration of the wisdom style was doubtless fostered by the court of Solomon, and it may well be that Egyptian influence was a major force in this stylistic development. The individual sententious saying is formulated in many different ways: contrast, comparison, alliteration or assonance, personification, rhyme, etc. On the other hand, we have a number of hypotactic expansions, as in Prov. 1–9

(1^{10-18}, 2^{1-22}) or autobiographical vignettes (4^{3-9}) or the *māshāl* about the harlot (Prov. 7^{6-27}) or the extended hypostasis (Prov. 8^{22-31}) or the wisdom poem (Job 28). The Book of Job combines many literary types in a remarkable way. When one takes into account in addition the numerous forms represented in Proverbs, Ecclesiastes, and the Wisdom of Ben Sirach, he can readily begin to appreciate both the wide range of wisdom reflection and the diversity of literary types which were employed to give it adequate expression.

BIBLIOGRAPHY

A. Alt, *Die Ursprünge des israelitischen Rechts*, 1934.
W. Baumgartner, "The Wisdom Literature," *OTMS*, 1951, pp. 210–37.
J. Begrich, *Studien zu Deuterojesaja* (BWANT), 1938.
A. Bentzen, *Introduction to the Old Testament*, 2nd ed., vol. i., 1952.
O. Eissfeldt, *Einleitung in das Alte Testament*, 2nd ed., 1956.
H. Gunkel, "Die israelitische Literatur," *Kultur der Gegenwart* (Teil I., Abt. VII.), 2nd ed., 1925.
Die Genesis, HAT, 3rd ed., 1922;
Das Märchen im Alten Testament, 1921;
What Remains of the Old Testament, 1928;
H. Gunkel and J. Begrich, *Einleitung in die Psalmen* in HAT, 1933.
J. Hempel, *Die althebräische Literatur und ihr hellenistisch-jüdisches Nachleben*, 1930.
A. R. Johnson, "The Psalms," OTMS, 1951, pp. 162–209.
C. Kuhl, *The Old Testament: its Origins and Development*, 1961.
A. Weiser, *Introduction to the Old Testament*, Eng. trans., 1961.

VI. LITERARY FORMS

(B) NEW TESTAMENT FORMS

By George Johnston

The documents of the New Testament are a selection from the domestic literature of the early Church, accepted as suitable for use in worship and instruction because they were (*a*) the record of God's final revelation and redemption in Christ, and (*b*) the authoritative deposit of the original apostolic tradition (cf. 2 Thess. 2^{15}, Heb. 13^{9}, 1 John 2^{27}). They may be classified as Gospels, History, Letters, Homilies, Tracts, and an Apocalypse. We shall look first at their more obvious features.

(i) CATEGORIES OF BOOKS

1. *Gospels.* As Justin Martyr said, a gospel-book is a "Memoir" of sorts, for it purports to give a connected account of the life and teaching of Jesus (cf. Luke 1^{3}). In Matthew, after the genealogical tree (1^{1-17}) and stories of His birth and early years (1^{18}–2^{23}), we read about the baptism, call and temptations of Jesus, His preaching, dynamic works, calling and training of disciples, His controversies and at last His betrayal and death (3^{1}–27^{66}). In chap. 28 is narrated the strange tale of the resurrection. Here is a Gospel well arranged for teaching and lectionary purposes.

Mark as a unit corresponds to Matt. 3–28 but is far shorter. Nowadays we cannot follow St. Augustine in thinking that Mark abbreviated Matthew; it is the other way round. Notable characteristics of Mark are its speed and vividness. The structure is, on the whole, tightly integrated (8^{1-26} seems to be a doublet of 6^{30}–7^{23}).

Luke more closely resembles Matthew in having Infancy Stories and a genealogy prior to the history of the public ministry. He too has used and edited much of Mark, and added material that is found nowhere else (*e.g.* many parables). Luke is enriched by the inclusion of magnificent canticles, the *Benedictus*, *Magnificat*, and *Nunc Dimittis*; and his version of the resurrection has some striking elements (*e.g.* the Emmaus story, 24).

It is generally agreed that these three Gospels are related as follows: Mark is a primary source of the others, and his narrative provides backbone to the outline of Jesus' career. Luke and Matthew have employed for the Sayings of Jesus a common source or different editions of it (usually cited as "Q"); and each has incorporated fresh materials exclusive to his book ("Special Luke" and "Special Matthew"). The Lucan and Matthaean sources of the teaching of Jesus are sometimes designated "L" and "M" respectively. How far such sources were written is still much debated.

When we turn to John, we find a quite different atmosphere. He starts with a prose poem to the *Logos* or divine Word and the witness of John the Baptist (1). Then in the "Book of Signs," as C. H. Dodd describes 2–12, he proceeds with narratives of seven miracles, dialogues and debates, and monologues. This is followed by the profoundly moving "Night of the Upper Room" (13–17) and the story of the final days (18–20). Chap. 21 is an appendix to the original Gospel, which may have been published posthumously. John is a literary unity (we follow Dodd in this), marked by dramatic power. Perhaps the long discourses of Jesus may have originated in prophetic sermons or eucharistic meditations delivered under the Paraclete's influence.

It will be convenient here to point out that Jesus wrote nothing and yet His words were treasured and passed on by His disciples. This was aided by the fact that Jesus was one of the great poets who used traditional Jewish parallelism—synonymous (Mark 4^{22}), antithetic (Matt. 7^{17}), synthetic (Luke 12^{49}) and climactic (Mark 9^{37}). He did not disdain puns, rhyme, alliteration and assonance, but the flavour of this must be found in retranslation into Aramaic. Dr. T. W. Manson attributed to Jesus a "strophic" parallelism which was "the most distinctive characteristic of his poetry and his special contribution to the forms of poetry in general" (*The Teaching of Jesus*, p. 56). For examples see Luke $11^{31f.}$, 12^{24-28}, 17^{26-30}. Dr. M. Black describes the grandeur of Jesus' language as Isaianic, "cast in a medium which can express in appropriate and modulated sound the underlying beauty of the sentiment or the passion out of which the thought arose" (*An Aramaic Approach to the Gospels and Acts*, p. 142). Besides the poetry, we should observe the humour of Jesus (Mark 7^{27-29}, 10^{25}) and His superb gifts as a story-teller. (John the Baptist too may have uttered his oracles in poetic form: Mark $1^{7f.}$, Matt. 3^{12}, John 3^{27-36}.)

But now we must ask whether the four Gospels are really biographies of Jesus, and the answer must be No, not as we would use the term. They are quite brief and seem to have no interest in the personal details that we expect from a *Life*. They are not scholarly or scientific, complete with references and a bibliography of the sources. On the contrary, they are all religious documents, avowedly partisan and missionary in purpose (Luke 1^4, John 20^{31}). Each one is a peculiar blend of history and theology and as literature they constitute a special class. The title "Gospel" may have been derived from its use in Mark 1^1.

2. *History*. The Acts of the Apostles, at first sight a history of the expansion of the early Church, is really the second instalment of Luke's Gospel. It includes (*a*) summaries of sermons (the *kērygma*), (*b*) what may be an eye-witness record from 16^{11} to the end. The latter contains the poignant Farewell Discourse to the Ephesian elders (20^{18-35}), which may be compared with 1 Sam. 12, Mark 13, John 14–16, and the *Phaedo* of Plato.

As a literary type, the Acts has affinities with Greek and Jewish models. The speeches may be partly editorial compositions, but they depend also on earlier sources, oral and written. The author wished to present the Christian "way" so that it might shine in clear, inoffensive light to Theophilus and the Roman public. He must also have wanted to satisfy the concerns of the Church itself, because following Paul's death (Acts 20^{35}) and the fall of Jerusalem in A.D. 70 Christians needed authentic news of the Apostles' missions and teaching.

3. *Letters*. Letters in the New Testament are ascribed to James, John, Jude, Paul, and Peter. Most scholars agree that Paul did not write Hebrews, nor did Peter write 2 Peter. Hebrews is a *homily* (13^{22}), with a closing greeting. 2 Peter may be dated about A.D. 125, and it re-writes most of Jude. James is an encyclical in the style of a diatribe (questions and answers on themes loosely brought together). 1 John and Jude are *tracts* for the times; 2, 3 John are anonymous notes. 1, 2 Timothy and Titus are probably second century compilations, with some genuine Pauline scraps within 2 Timothy. Some scholars, including the writer, would argue that Ephesians is artificially constructed out of the collected letters of Paul, on the massive topics of cosmic salvation and the universal Church as body, bride, and temple.*

These collected Paulines have special importance, for they reveal the man Paul, missionary *par excellence*, teacher, saint, and martyr. He wrote to churches he had founded, or (Romans and Colossians) those with which he had personal connexions. Even Philemon went to a house church (Laodicea? cf. Col. 4^{16}). I take Rom. 16^{1-23} to be a testimonial for Phoebe, sent to Ephesus (cf. 1 Cor. 16^3, 2 Cor. 3^1). Paul himself gave the letters a special place in the life of his congregations (Col. 4^{16}, 2 Thess. $3^{14f.}$). Before long (*c*. A.D. 90, in Corinth or Ephesus) they were collected and edited, with resulting changes in their form (see *e.g.* 2 Cor. 10–13, 1–9, Phil. 3^{2-21}, Rom. 16^{25-27});

* For another view cf. above, pp. 104 ff.—H. H. R.

and they are not in chronological order. At a later time, Marcion tampered with them.

Even when colleagues are mentioned in the salutation, the letters are in substance Paul's own. Frequently, if not invariably, they were dictated (Rom. 16^{22}), with effects on the style! but the Apostle may authenticate them with his own handwritten greeting (1 Cor. 16^{21}, Gal. 6^{11}, Col. 4^{18}, 2 Thess. 2^{2}, 3^{17}). Whenever he could, Paul visited the churches (2 Cor. 13^{1}) and there may have been some preference for face to face encounters (cf. 2 John ^{12}; 3 John ^{13}; and Papias quoted by Eusebius, *Church History*, III. xxxix. 4). The first churchesc ontained members from diverse cultural and economic strata, and on average were not highly literate. So the letters were truly occasional correspondence, composed in the midst of a busy and dangerous life and written in the living *Koinē* Greek of the time. Seldom does the style attain the heights of literary excellence. Nevertheless they were not simply casual pieces. For Paul wrote his expositions of the mind of Christ with authority, and it was as a prophet of the Spirit that he laid down decisive utterances on significant ethical issues. Such letters are also "Epistles."

4. *Apocalypse.* St. John's Revelation, or Apocalypse, begins with seven letters to churches in Asia Minor, possibly on the model of the Pauline Corpus. Most of the book consists, however, of a series of prophetic visions intended to nerve Christians to resist the idolatry of Emperor-worship. The type is Daniel and similar Jewish apocalypses. John wrote execrable Greek, and yet his literary qualities are considerable.

(ii) FORM CRITICISM

All the documents thus far described may be dated between A.D. 65 (Mark) and 125 (2 Peter). They emerged from the worship, missions, and educational enterprise of early congregations, and presumably these concerns had much to do with the precise form and contents of the literature. Yet it was the historic life of Jesus and the miracle of His resurrection that remained, and remain, of primary importance in the Tradition (cf. 1 Cor. 15^{3-8}). Hence it was entirely natural for scholars to enquire if it might be possible to penetrate into the time before the composition of Mark. Just how far back could the historian go? It was not enough, following the ancient Fathers, to interpret John Mark as a translator of Peter's preaching and so look for Petrine elements in his Gospel. There were sceptics who discounted Paul's claim to possess a tradition " from the Lord " regarding the sacrament which was central in worship (1 Cor. 11^{23}). For Paul could be pictured as belonging to a Hellenistic form of the Faith and his sacrament as a radical innovation in which Jesus' death received a theological explanation as the means of the atonement. A few scholars went farther and discovered in Paul and John clear traces of a Gnostic redeemer-myth (the dying and rising god; the descending and ascending saviour). Were the practice and teaching of the post-crucifixion Church so different from that of Jesus; and if so, have the New Testament documents, especially the Gospels, been manipulated in the Christian community in order to justify their worship, ethics, and Christology?

1. *In Gospels.* Further analysis of literary forms, *e.g.* in the Gospels, must not be counted a luxury of the critics. For the manhood of the Lord, His teaching, and the works with which he is credited, must always be central and must be investigated with every tool we possess. Similarly, the life and procedures of the ancient Church give precedents to the ongoing Church of today, since Christianity is bound in history to the apostolic tradition. Devotionally, politically, and theologically, Christians in modern times seek through personal fellowship in God to learn from the classical first century and from the New Testament Canon as an authoritative exposition.

The method of advance in literary analysis was borrowed from that already fruitful for the study of the Old Testament and of folklore. This had shown that in a primitive age traditions circulated orally in short units (*pericopae*) patterned according to definite laws, subject to development but, to begin with, quite simple and non-literary in style. Such *pericopae* reflect the needs, interests and problems within the community, rather than objective, historical curiosity. Hence we have to seek imaginatively for the life-setting (*Sitz im Leben*) of the traditions. The name for such investigation is " Form History " (German *Formgeschichte*) or, following Hermann Gunkel, it may be called " Analysis and History of Literary Types " (*Gattungsgeschichte*).

Such analysis has produced a crop of classifications, but they may all be reduced to (*a*) Words of Jesus; (*b*) Stories about Jesus; and (*c*) Stories about persons associated with Jesus.

(*a*) We have already seen that the *sayings* of Jesus include memorable poetry. In addition, there are riddles and parables that tease and challenge the listener into spiritual alertness, and provoke a response to a destiny-laden message. Some words are prophetic and eschatological (*e.g.* Luke 6^{20-26}), some are apocalyptic (*e.g.* Mark $13^{7f.\ 14-20.\ 24-27}$), some deal with the Jewish Torah and its authority (*e.g.* Matt. 5^{21-37}). A few are epigrams or proverbs (*e.g.* Matt. 24^{28}).

An interesting sub-division here is what Dr. Vincent Taylor has called the Pronouncement Story (*Paradigm* or *Apophthegma* in German studies). This is a short unit which has been preserved because it ends with a pronouncement by Jesus that gives some direction to the earliest churches (*e.g.* Mark $2^{1-12.\ 23-28}$, 3^{1-6}).

Jesus' words in general have survived through their use in missionary preaching and the exhortation given to the faithful. When applied to post-resurrection situations, many have been subtly modified (see *e.g.* the private instruction of disciples in Mark). We know from Acts 20^{35}, 1 Cor. 7^{10}, 9^{14}, and other passages that the words had unique authority for the young Church. But is it proper to argue, as Form historians do, that words are retained only if they could be made relevant to the particular problems before the Church ? If so, why are some of the most perplexing situations left without a word ? Again, it is more than hinted that the community was not above inventing a word and ascribing it to Jesus. But once more, why did it fail to invent words to suit the situations otherwise left bare, so to speak ? This is a sociological heresy and really absurd. It was the genius of the prophet Jesus that produced the profound sayings. Dr. Bultmann and his school tend to limit the genuine words to the sheerly eschatological, as though Jesus could not have asserted for Himself a special role in the coming of the Kingdom or even a divine role.

(*b*) *Stories about Jesus* are called *Novellen* (wonder tales or miracle stories) and *Myths*. The former relate remarkable dealings with Nature, death, and disease (heightened to an extreme form in the Johannine signs) ; the latter are narratives like those of the baptism, temptations, transfiguration, and resurrection of Jesus. In a myth God appears like a character on the stage of history ; the transcendent from the beyond is shown on this side of reality as immanent. Even if historical elements lie buried within them, what matters in myths is the theological truth to be communicated. " Form " in a healing story is very simple : a statement of the sickness, then the marvel of the cure, and lastly the reactions of bystanders and patient. As such it is comparable to many similar non-Christian tales, and for that reason some critics jump to the conclusion that identity of form involves fabrication. What other form could be expected from a human mind ?

(*c*) *Stories about people* in the entourage of Jesus (disciples like Philip, Zacchaeus, Mary, Martha, Nathanael, Cleopas, Lazarus, and Mary of Magdala), or about those who had some contact with Jesus (Simeon, Anna, Pilate's wife, Nicodemus) are classed as *Legends, i.e.* edifying tales which may or may not be historically authentic. The appearance of actual names is said to mean that the tradition has become more literary and sophisticated.

In 1919 K. L. Schmidt asserted that the separate *pericopae* were strung together by Mark without rhyme or reason, but surely the outline or pattern of the most primitive preaching is just the string that lay to his hand (cf. C. H. Dodd's argument in *The Apostolic Preaching and Its Developments*). John's framework of Jesus' ministry is remarkably like Mark's in essentials, and is indeed superior. From 1 Cor. 11^{26} we may deduce that the Church required a Passion Narrative plus an account of Jesus' words and works. This is precisely what Paul could have learned from Peter in Jerusalem (Gal. 1^{18}) or from several other eye-witnesses (1 Cor. 15^{6}). Moreover, the incidents in all four Gospels generally fit a Palestinian situation and it is quite gratuitous to affirm that the first Christians were interested only in the future Advent of the Son of Man and not at all in the historic career of Jesus. We need not be unduly affected by the discovery that every document and many oral traditions have come from persons of Christian faith, as if this meant that Jesus of Nazareth is smothered in the cult or the theology of the Church! It is an historic Mind that we encounter in the Sayings, and a real human person in whom we see what divine love is like.

It is necessary, however, to insist that *Gattungsgeschichte* is a legitimate and valuable tool for research into the pre-literary period. Used with caution, it enables us to see the growth of the Gospels within churches that worshipped through the *Kyrios* Jesus, and in His Name carried on His ministry and mission. At different stages and in different centres sayings and narratives may have been combined before any of the Evangelists came to integrate them into the gospel-books that became canonical (so W. L. Knox).

2. *Outside Gospels*. Can we discover literary forms in the New Testament outside the Gospels and Acts? Recent research suggests that four basic types can be isolated: poems or hymns, credal formulae, liturgical material, and a common Christian paraenetic tradition.

(i) Phil. 2^{6-11} is a glorious *hymn* on the theme of the Last Adam as the suffering Servant of the Lord; E. Lohmeyer proposed that it was pre-Pauline, but more probably it is Paul's own. So is Col. 1^{15-20}, praising the divine Son (C. Masson), while Eph. 1^{3-14} is a *Jubilate* to the electing God, the Father of our Lord Jesus Christ. Eph. 5^{14} may be a fragment from a song (cf. Col. 3^{16}). The Servant motif re-appears in the rhythmic passage 1 Pet. 2^{21-24}. More doubtful is Heb. 7^{26-28}. Hymns may be reflected in Rev. 7^{15-17}, 13^{10}, $15^{3f.}$, and 18. (For 1 Tim. 3^{16} see below.)

(ii) *Credal pericopae* have been uncovered in Rom. $1^{3f.}$, 10^{9}, 1 Cor. 12^{3} (" Jesus Christ as *Kyrios* "), 1 Cor. 15^{3-6} (not, in my judgment, a pre-baptismal summary so much as a statement of the primary points in Paul's evangelical preaching); 1 Pet. 1^{20} (very dubious), $3^{18f.\ 22}$ (the case for this as a credal formula is pretty weak); 2 Tim. $2^{11f.}$ (the " sure saying "), to which we should perhaps add 1 Tim. 3^{16} and (more doubtfully) Tit. 2^{13f}. Note also the Western text of Acts 8^{37}, " I believe that Jesus Christ is the Son of God." Provided we do not press them too far, some of the above may indeed represent the sort of confession demanded from converts.

(iii) *Gattungsgeschichte* associates many oral and written forms with Christian worship and of course with Baptism and the Eucharist; and *liturgical* bits and pieces can be identified with some imagination (outside the canticles, hymns, poems, and credal types) in such places as Rev. $4^{8.\ 11}$, $5^{9f.\ 13f.}$, 7^{12}, $11^{17f.}$, $19^{1.\ 4-6}$, 22^{20}. At any rate, these were quarried later for liturgical purposes.

The arguments of Streeter for 1 Peter as a sermon combined with a letter (1^{3}–4^{11}, and 4^{12}–5^{11}) are unconvincing. So is Preisker's theory that the first part was based on the Roman baptismal liturgy; and still more far-fetched is Cross's attempt to derive it from the celebrant's part of a baptismal Eucharist on Passover Eve. What adequate evidence is there for such Christian celebrations of Vigils or for such baptismal liturgies? We have to wait till Justin Martyr for the association of Baptism with a Eucharist following at once. If we come to 1 Peter not looking for liturgical material, we can explain it as the stitching of two epistles (C. F. D. Moule) or the writer's repetition of his own ideas (van Unnik).

There are hints, however, that synagogue lectionaries may have influenced our documents. Hence my colleague, J. C. Kirby, has suggested in a doctor's thesis that Ephesians may have been built on a covenant-renewal ceremony at Pentecost, with the use of such traditional Psalms as 68 (cf. also the Qumran practice).

(iv) The *paraenetic* tradition is said to be represented in several ways: (*a*) The lists of vices and virtues in Rom 1^{29-31}, 1 Cor. $5^{10f.}$, Gal. $5^{19f.\ 22f.}$, 1 Tim. 6^{11}, and 2 Pet. 1^{5-7}. Models can be found in Hellenistic moral teaching or in the Qumran *Manual of Discipline* (the fruits in man of the evil and the good spirits). (*b*) The so-called *Haustafeln* or Tables of Household Duties in Col. 3^{18}–4^{1}, Eph. 5^{22}–6^{9}, 1 Tim. 2^{8-15}, $6^{1f.}$, supplemented by passages on bishops, elders, deacons and widows, 3^{1-15}, 5^{3-22}, and Tit. 1^{5}–2^{10}. (*c*) The " neo-Levitical code " of Christian Holiness in 1 Thess. 4^{1-12}, 1 Cor. 6^{1-11}, and 1 Pet. 1^{15-22}, 2^{12} (cf. Matt. 5–7). In these may be seen the picture of

Jesus as a New Moses, or as Himself the New Torah (Rom 6[17]; so W. D. Davies).

Adequate discussion of this catechetical tradition would take much more space than is available. Its proponents have reacted against former theories of literary dependence (*e.g.* of 1 Peter on Romans and Ephesians), and find agreeable the thought of a long oral tradition or written forms of little ethical manuals. It is, however, possible that the evidence of manuscript copying at Qumran may cause the critical pendulum to swing back toward literary dependence, especially for the period after A.D. 70. It should be remembered, too, that worship may have remained "charismatic" and free far longer than is presently thought, at least in Greek-speaking areas. Did the synagogue influence the Church as much before 1 Clement as after?

It is exciting to see so much attention being directed to the life-situations of the early churches. Christian imagination is thus coming to the aid of textual, theological, and archaeological study! This is all to the good. I propound one large question with which to close:

What difference does it make to the theological exegesis of the New Testament to be aware that its material contains myths, poetry, hymns, parables, miracle stories, and real letters written in the heat of controversy, as well as stately homilies and the doctrinal epistle?

BIBLIOGRAPHY

M. Dibelius, *Die Formgeschichte des Evangeliums*, 1919 (E.T., *From Tradition to Gospel*, 1934).
K. L. Schmidt, *Der Rahmen der Geschichte Jesu*, 1919.
R. Bultmann, *Die Geschichte der synoptischen Tradition*, 3rd ed., 1957 (E.T., 1962).
V. Taylor, *The Formation of the Gospel Tradition*, 1933.
F. C. Grant, *The Growth of the Gospels*, 1933.
E. Fascher, *Die formgeschichtliche Methode*, 1924 (critical of the method).
R. H. Lightfoot, *History and Interpretation in the Gospels*, 1934.
C. H. Dodd, *The Parables of the Kingdom*, 1935.
C. H. Dodd, *The Apostolic Preaching and its Developments*, 1936.
E. B. Redlich, *Form Criticism, its value and limitations*, 1939.
T. W. Manson, *The Teaching of Jesus*, 1931.
M. Black, *An Aramaic Approach to the Gospels and Acts*, 2nd ed., 1954.
O. Cullmann, *The Early Christian Confessions*, 1953.
H. Riesenfeld, *The Gospel Tradition and its Beginnings*, 1957.
W. L. Knox, *The Sources of the Synoptic Gospels*, I (1953), II (1957).
A. M. Hunter, *Paul and His Predecessors*, 2nd ed., 1961.
E. G. Selwyn, *1 Peter* (1946).

VII. THE TRANSMISSION OF THE TEXT

(A) OLD TESTAMENT

By Bleddyn J. Roberts

In recent years the study of the Old Testament Hebrew text and its early versions has taken rather a new turn, for although scholars are still concerned with textual corruptions and variant readings, it is now becoming clear that the history of the transmission has its own special part to play. New information is becoming available, and sensational discoveries such as the Dead Sea Scrolls have forced the issue in unexpected ways. They have provided more material for the specialist to assess, but they have also provoked a popular curiosity about the early history of the text. Questions are asked that come within the province of the Grammar School and Sunday School teacher, and consequently the textual specialist, hitherto one of the lesser-known types of Old Testament scholar, has had to popularize his topic. One result has been to put the history of the transmission in a position to control more effectively than hitherto the activities of the non-textualist who was inclined to emend the text regardless of exact textual considerations. Readings once thought to be textually irregular have frequently been ironed out in this way, and others once assumed to be corrupt have been shown to be legitimate.

It is impossible to say when the text of the Old Testament was given its present form; indeed the question is one on which both the textualist and the literary critic join forces. It is at once admitted that the current text abundantly shows the existence of divergent forms in a way which the textualist alone is not able to explain. In passages which are duplicated, namely 2 Sam. 22 and Ps. 18, 2 Kings 18^{13}–20^{19} and Isa. 36–39, 2 Kings 23^{3}–25^{30} and Jer. 52, Isa. 2^{2-4} and Mic. 4^{1-4}, Pss. 14 and 53, Pss. 40^{14-18} and 70, and in lengthy portions of Sam.–Kings and Chron., along with innumerable short quotations—in all these passages it can be seen how the textual divergences reveal deliberate interference with the original text according to an identifiable pattern. A simple instance can be found in Pss. 14 and 53, and again in Pss. 40^{14-18} and 70, where there is a change in the use of the Divine Name in accordance with the characteristics of the Yahwistic and Elohistic Psalters.

Additional evidence for the conclusion that the textual transmission was fluid comes from the Qumran scrolls and the Septuagint, as we shall see later.

Despite this lack of uniformity in the early transmission, however, the emphasis of Rabbinic teaching from earliest times is that great care was to be taken with the transmission, and that all copies of the text were to be corrected and made uniform. The text came to be known as the Massoretic Text, with the word *Massorah* drawing attention to the "tradition," and the word *Massoretes* denoting the Scholars responsible for its transmission. Ultimately, the Massorah came to denote the collections (*Massôrôth*) of scribal data, with a vast number of annotations and items of information, but before we arrive at this phase, there is a long and rather complicated story of how the text fared in the earlier periods of manuscript transmission.

Alongside the Massoretic text we place the Biblical manuscripts from Qumran, the Greek translations in the Septuagint and other versions, Aramaic translations and still further sources. The result of a comparison of these sources shows that although Judaism itself insisted on a uniform transmission it is obvious that about the time of Christ the text existed in a variety of forms, technically known to us as recensions. One purpose of reconstructing the recensions is to regain the early forms of the text and thereby elucidate and emend the standard Massoretic text. Nevertheless, for all practical purposes, especially that of translating the text, it is the Massoretic text that provides the basis of study, and consequently we begin our survey with it.

(i) THE MASSORETIC TEXT

The oldest extant witness to this text-form comes from the Dead Sea Scrolls; not, however, in the well-known Qumran manuscripts but in the few fragments of Biblical texts found, along with other manuscripts, in the caves at Murabba'at, about the same time as the Qumran scrolls. They form part of the writings left behind by Jewish insurgents during the last rebellion against Rome led by Bar Cochba in A.D. 132–5. The Biblical texts agree with the Massoretic text. It is generally thought that Rabbi Akiba early in the second century was responsible for producing the Massoretic text, but although it is obvious from what is said about him in Rabbinic writings that he was a great authority on this text, it is probable that the actual text was current before his time.

The main line of evidence for the subsequent history of the Massoretic text, however, is to be reconstructed from Rabbinic Writings, mainly the Mishnah and Talmuds, and from actual manuscripts from a somewhat later period. The history of

Judaism forms a controlling factor, and from it we learn that after Jerusalem fell to the Romans in A.D. 70 Judaism flourished for centuries in two main centres, Babylon and Palestine. The Rabbis have always recognized two main strands in their tradition, reflecting the two centres, and they call them the Eastern (*i.e.* Babylonian) and Western (*i.e.* Palestinian). The traditions were not wholly independent of each other, but they emerge in two divergent codifications of teaching, namely the Babylonian and Palestinian Talmuds, and in two transmissions of Massoretic text. In both cases the divergent developments are based on common material, for the former the Mishnah, and for the latter the Massoretic text. There are no actual Biblical manuscripts from these earlier stages, and we are therefore dependent on information about them from the Mishnah and the two Talmuds, together with incidental details from other Rabbinic writings.

From them we learn that the Massoretes were scrupulously careful about the copying of manuscripts, and were fully instructed about details. The script was the square, Aramaic alphabet and not the earlier script, which is sometimes called the archaic or palaeo-Hebrew script. Leather—later parchment—scrolls were prepared in a prescribed way. The scrutiny of manuscripts, on the basis of a prototype, was a special responsibility, and there is an account—given in a number of places—of how three manuscripts in the Temple with divergent readings were resolved by majority counts. The scribes reckoned the number of letters in each book, and state that a consonant in Lev. 11^{42}, a word in Lev. 10^{16} and a verse, Lev. 13^{13}, stand at the middle of the Pentateuch. They also reckoned the number and nature of paragraphs (some " open " and others " closed ") which regulated the lectionary divisions of the text—incidentally the East and West diverged considerably on this point. Gradually these and other items of information came to be written on the margins of those manuscripts which were not intended for public worship in the synagogue, and in the course of time the collections of data became a major element in scribal activity and were produced in independent collections, the *Massôrôth*. The annotation was not uniform, but varied from centre to centre, and especially reflected the distinction between East and West.

There are other early items of textual interest mentioned in Rabbinic writings. *Siphrê*, a commentary on the book of Numbers from the third century A.D., gives a list of fifteen passages where dots (*puncta extraordinaria*) are placed over letters in the text where the Rabbis doubted their correctness. Another mark used by the scribes is the *pāsēḳ* (divider) which occurs nearly 500 times in the whole of the text but whose exact significance is not clear. In other cases the Massoretes listed instances of interference with the text though the actual passages were not marked; the lists include *tikkûnê has-sōphᵉrîm* (" emendations of the scribes "), *'iṭṭûrê has-sōphᵉrîm* (" omissions of the scribes "), *sᵉbhîrîn* (" unexpected," *i.e.* the form was unusual if not incorrect).

In these and other ways the Massoretes made a constructive contribution to the transmission of the text in the early centuries of the Christian era, and we see that in their concern for the correct transmission the Massoretes produced much more than carefully copied manuscripts.

At some time before the end of the seventh century an important development took place, namely the introduction of vowel marks to control the correct recitation of the text in the synagogue ritual. Hitherto the text had been consonantal though occasionally certain consonants were used to give vocalic values, and even a cursory study of some of the Biblical scrolls from Qumran will show that this custom was more frequently followed in some manuscripts than in others. The process of adding vocalic signs, however, has its own history, but it is well to remember that it was not an " official " feature, for even today the texts intended for use in the synagogue are not vocalized. The absence of private manuscripts with vocalization throughout the centuries deprived scholars of the means of reconstructing the history, but, as we shall see, the position was improved by the discovery of a great number of relevant manuscripts in a synagogue in Cairo. The actual details of the history still remain to be worked out, but the main stages can be outlined.

Possibly under the influence of developments in Syriac literature, two independent schemes of indicating vowels emerged in Babylon and Palestine respectively. In the former it consisted of dots and dashes (the technical word for vocalizing is *niḳḳēdh*—" pointing ") which then was replaced by letters of the square Hebrew alphabet written horizontally. In the latter it remained a scheme of dots. In both transmissions, however, a much more refined scheme was substituted, introduced by a Jewish sect called Qaraites, who emerged in Babylon *c.* A.D. 760 and later flourished in Jerusalem. They were violently anti-Rabbinic, but quickly gained dominance as Biblical scholars, and it was their detailed vocalization and accentuation which became normative. In Babylon, the basis was still provided by letters of the alphabet and the pointing was introduced supralineally. In Palestine the number of dots and dashes was increased to produce the system now in common usage, and known as the Tiberian vocalization. The supremacy of the latter scheme was the result of the collapse of Babylonian

Judaism in the ninth century A.D. and its virtual disappearance. Even so, the Tiberian vocalization was still not quite standardized, for there was a conflict between two schools, or rather families, of Massoretes. On the one hand we have a family of five generations called Ben Asher and on the other Ben Naphtali ; ultimately the former became supreme. As already mentioned, the main period of the growth of vocalization is covered by an important collection of Hebrew manuscripts, discovered in recent times. Soon after 1890 the contents of a Genizah in an ancient synagogue in Cairo became available. Many of the manuscripts had been taken from it by a Russian Qaraite Jew, Firkowitch, some twenty years earlier and housed in Leningrad, where it forms part of what is claimed to be the largest collection of Hebrew manuscripts in the world. The major collection of the Cairo Genizah, however, came to this country, and is now mainly divided between the University Library of Cambridge, the British Museum, the Bodleian Library at Oxford and the John Rylands Library at Manchester, but there are also other important collections. It is estimated that there are some 200,000 fragments in all, and much work remains to be done on them. Not all are Biblical manuscripts ; in fact everything that had to do with the religious and even secular life of the synagogue is represented in these manuscripts.

Of the Biblical fragments the most interesting are those which provide specimens of vocalized texts, with Palestinian, early and later Babylonian, and, of course, Tiberian pointings. But there are also others, with divergent texts which suggest, for instance, that the Rabbinic transmission of the Ineffable Name was far from uniform. Others contain lists of Massoretic notes, and yet others provide copies of Aramaic translations, Targums, to which we shall return. It is difficult to assess the upper limit of the period covered by the Genizah fragments, but they certainly ante-date the ninth century when the building, previously a Christian Church, came into the possession of the Jews. Specialists argue that some fragments go back as far as the fifth century ; others, however, dispute this date.

Mention should be made here of one other collection of Massoretic data which relates more immediately to the vocalization of the text but which actually belongs to the whole history of the transmission. It is the variation known as *ḳ*^{e}*rê* and *k*^{e}*thîbh* (" what is read " and " what is written "). They can be explained—in an over-simplified way—as cases of divergences between the vocalization and the consonantal text, where each reflects variant traditions of the text-form, only one of which had been transmitted in the consonantal text of the Massoretes whereas the other (and, possibly, more than one) had been transmitted orally until it finally found its way into the vocalization.

Later Biblical manuscripts from the Cairo Genizah lose some of their interest because of the existence, from the tenth and eleventh centuries, of large manuscripts which form part of the actual history of the Massoretic transmission. They are especially important because of their claim to be the work of the Ben Asher family already mentioned as the Massoretes responsible for the final form of vocalization. They include the very valuable British Museum Manuscript, *Or* 4445, which is the earliest of the collection but contains only the Pentateuch, the Cairo Codex of the Prophets dated A.D. 895, the Aleppo Codex, from the first half of the tenth century, the Leningrad Codex of the Prophets from A.D. 916 ; the Leningrad Codex of A.D. 1008. Two of them, the Aleppo Codex and the Leningrad will turn up again in our discussion. Whether the claim that they are Ben Asher texts is substantiated for all four is in dispute, but the tradition represented here is, largely, that of Ben Asher, whereas that of Ben Naphtali is ignored. On the other hand, Ben Naphtali was also a living force even at a much later period, for we know that about the year 1000 Mishael ben Uzziel composed a lengthy treatise consisting of the variants between the two traditions, and even as late as 1493–4, in a codex recently edited, the Aberdeen Codex, a number of columns are included which list the variants. Incidentally, this same codex provides an excellent example of the Massoretic notes being rendered in an artistic design—a development which signifies that long before the fifteenth century the notes had lost all their earlier significance and were included in manuscripts only for convention.

The invention of the printing press soon resulted in the publication of printed Hebrew Bibles, but for us the main interest centres on the Rabbinic Bible printed by Daniel Bomberg in 1524–5 and edited by Jacob ben Chayyim. It was this Bible that provided the basic text for most printed editions of the Hebrew Bible down to our own times, a phenomenon which now appears quite inexplicable. Ben Chayyim himself admitted that the manuscripts on which he based the edition were recent and lacked importance, but the attitude of scholarship, even during the height of Biblical criticism in the nineteenth century was one of complacency to Ben Chayyim's admission. It was always assumed that the Rabbinic transmission was so uniform and scrupulous that even the Rabbinic disputes themselves were irrelevant. It was the discovery of the Cairo Genizah, and the masterly interpretation of the fragments under the inspiration of Professor Paul Kahle, that produced a more correct approach and the result has been to bring the early history of the transmission and of Massoretic activity into focus. The immediate result was that Kahle himself became responsible for the new edition of the Hebrew text now in general use by scholars everywhere, namely the third edition of *Biblia Hebraica*. This Bible was first edited by Rudolf Kittel in 1905 and 1912, and used, as did most other editions, the text of Ben Chayyim. When, in 1936, Kahle produced the third edition, the Leningrad Codex of 1008 was, used, and subsequent editions have likewise used this codex.

A new and possibly significant advance has recently been reported from the Hebrew University of Jerusalem, and brings into prominence the Aleppo Codex mentioned above. This ancient manuscript, generally acknowledged to be a genuine Ben Asher text from the early tenth century, had throughout the centuries been kept in Aleppo, and permission to examine it was granted only very occasionally. In 1887 a facsimile of a single page was published; otherwise little was known of its contents, and in 1948 it was reported destroyed. Ten years later, however, the news broke that the major part had been recovered and purchased by the Hebrew University. In 1961 a new technical annual, called *Textus*, was published in Jerusalem, and in the first number an account is given of a projected production of a new edition of the Massoretic text based on the Aleppo Codex. The text will be accompanied by an *apparatus criticus* for which manuscript evidence, Rabbinic writings, as well as the usual versions, will be utilized, and the work as a whole will mark an important step forward in the scientific study of the Hebrew text. The editors claim that it might well replace the Leningrad manuscript, as used in *Biblia Hebraica*[3], but this remains to be seen. At the same time, a completely new edition of *Biblia Hebraica* is being prepared, again based on the Leningrad Codex.

Finally, reference might be made to the 1958 edition of the Hebrew Bible by the British and Foreign Bible Society. The edition claims to provide a genuine Ben Asher text, but it is reconstructed from manuscripts which are much later than the tenth century, and consequently the claim is inevitably subject to query. Scholars are not unanimous in accepting the basic assumptions, and, although the edition is valuable in that it draws attention to some remarkably interesting manuscripts from Spain and elsewhere, it is unlikely that its reception by scholars will be commensurate with the trouble involved in its preparation.

(ii) QUMRAN

It will have become clear that, apart from the fragments in the Cairo Genizah, all important extant manuscripts of the Hebrew Bible come from the tenth century A.D. and later, and that the scientific study of the actual Massoretic text is confined to that of the Ben Asher family with its variants. When the Qumran manuscripts were discovered in 1947, and especially since the continued publication of later material, it was realized that, whatever the precise date might be, the evidence they provide relates to the text as it was current about a thousand years before Ben Asher. It was natural for scholars to become excited about them, and the public response to reports was so enthusiastic that exaggerated claims were far too readily accepted. A more responsible attitude is now adopted, and though the discovery still merits superlatives, the general picture is being presented with a better perspective.

It is the Biblical scrolls from Qumran that demand our main interest in the present context, and they contain texts of all the Old Testament books with the exception of Esther. There are some books of the Apocrypha here, and also of those known as Pseudepigrapha. It is also to be noted that some of the books occur in a number of manuscripts. The other, non-biblical, scrolls however are also relevant to the present study. They provide the background, and it is from them and from the excavations of the ruined monastery at Qumran, that we learn how the scrolls came to be written. Some time in the second half of the second century B.C. a dissident community of Jews settled in the wilderness around the northern part of the Dead Sea and lived in caves in the neighbourhood of the monastery where they exercised their devotions by pious living. Among other things they copied the Scriptures, and the number of fragments of Biblical manuscripts which have been discovered shows that considerable importance was attached to this aspect of their piety. On the other hand, there is nothing to indicate that they attempted to standardize the text or in any way set a pattern similar to that adopted by scribes and Massoretes in orthodox Judaism. An important point to remember is that the community at Qumran differed in many essential respects from that element in Judaism which we can call orthodoxy, or at least which was the one practised in the Temple during the period of the Qumran secession. Indeed, it has been argued that at an early stage it was the Jerusalem priesthood, and even the High Priest himself, that constituted the most dangerous threat to their existence. The festival calendar followed at Qumran differed essentially from that of the Jerusalem Temple. Again, a peculiar method of interpreting Scripture was followed at Qumran. In view of these, and other rather more complicated divergences, it might be argued that the method of transmitting Scripture among the Qumranites was not characteristic of Judaism as a whole, and does not, strictly speaking, provide direct evidence for the history of what might be called the pre-Massoretic Hebrew text. At least, we might find here the explanation of the difference between the amorphous scribal character of Qumran manuscripts and the rigid uniformity of the Massoretic transmission.

The absence of uniformity in Qumran Scriptures can be inferred on the following grounds. First and foremost, where there are a comparatively large number of manuscripts of the same book no two are exactly alike, and some vary considerably. Secondly, where comparison is possible between the text of various books, *e.g.* in the matter of orthography, there is again no consistency; indeed, in the well-known scroll of Isaiah (*1QIsa*) there are at least two distinct schemes in the one manuscript. Thirdly, the numerous quotations of Scripture in the other, non-biblical, scrolls show a fluidity of transmission. Fourthly, a comparison of the scrolls with other comparatively free transmissions, for instance the Septuagint, shows that affinities lie with them rather than with the rigid text-form which was perpetuated by the Massoretes.

Consequently, it is necessary to qualify somewhat the generally accepted view that the scrolls directly confirm the Massoretic text, and to state that the confirmation is indirect and by implication only. In order to demonstrate the point, three manuscripts are chosen for brief review. Firstly, a scroll of the book of Isaiah, known technically as 1*QIsb*, shows a text-form which is practically identical with the Massoretic text. It is not a complete text of the book, since the greater part of proto-Isaiah is missing, and in other sections there are some lengthy passages where damage to the scroll prevents definite conclusions. Nevertheless the text of chaps. 41–66 is sufficiently complete to offer the conclusion that here we have a text so similar to that of the Massoretes that identification can be claimed between the two. Moreover, this is not the only case of a text identical with the Massoretic, for many others, especially Pentateuchal texts, carry the same measure of agreement.

The choice of this Isaiah text, however, serves to draw attention to the next one in our list, namely the well known and virtually complete scroll of Isaiah, *1QIsa*, which figured prominently in the first publications of Qumran texts. This scroll is not by any means identical with the Massoretic text, and its variations are significant. Firstly, the vocabulary shows instances where words in the Massoretic text are replaced by common words, and others where—at least some scholars think—some of the peculiar creeds of the community are reflected in the readings. Secondly the orthography of the scroll varies from that of the Massoretes, especially in the more common use of vowel letters. But, as has been mentioned, the scrolls in general allow a fluidity in the matter of orthography, and even in *1QIsa* there are clear traces of two distinct orthographies. It is significant that there is nothing to indicate that of the two Isaiah scrolls the one nearer the Massoretic text stood higher in the esteem of the community than the other; indeed, it looks as if *1QIsa* was more often read than *1QIsb*. This implies that similarity with the Massoretic text meant nothing to the sect of the scrolls. At the same time, it is also significant that where *1QIsa* varies from Massoretic text the variations are such as to indicate the qualitative priority of the latter. It is for this reason that it is correct to say that the Massoretic text receives confirmation more by implication than by the actual evidence itself.

The third manuscript comes from the collection of fragments in Cave Four and not, as do the others previously mentioned, from Cave One. It contains quite extensive portions of the text of Samuel (*4QSama*), and, according to a report by Professor F. M. Cross, who is an expert on the Biblical texts from Qumran, 47 out of the 57 columns in the original manuscript have been partially preserved in the scroll. The significance of this manuscript is that it approximates to the one underlying the Septuagint, and not the Massoretic text. Nor is this an isolated instance, for three scrolls of Samuel from Cave Four agree, to varying degrees, with the Septuagint rather than with the Massoretic text. Furthermore, there are other fragments, especially of Deuteronomy (amongst the most frequently copied of all Old Testament books) and of Jeremiah, where the obviously divergent Septuagint receives support from Qumran.

Consequently, despite the affirmation, with which qualified agreement has been expressed here, that the Massoretic text receives support from Qumran manuscripts, the discovery has by no means answered all the questions raised by the early history of the Hebrew text. Indeed, on the contrary, it has also supported the view that alongside the Massoretic text there existed, at least in some movements within Judaism, text-forms for which Rabbinic Judaism had given us little or no actual evidence. This is particularly true of the Septuagint.

There are other interesting features to the Qumran scrolls. There are texts which date back to early periods, apparently considerably earlier than the settlement in Qumran; some, possibly, are from the third century B.C., and others only a generation or so after the original was composed. Some manuscripts are written in the palaeo-Hebrew script, in direct contradiction to later Rabbinic injunctions. From the standpoint of the history of the text, however, these manuscripts do not provide any significant new evidence in addition to that exemplified in the three scrolls already mentioned.

(iii) THE VERSIONS

Throughout the history of the Christian Church there has been one version of Hebrew Old Testament which has been of paramount importance; indeed, for many centuries, it claimed official priority over the Massoretic text itself. It is the Greek version called the *Septuagint,* or the LXX. The version, however, is only one of a number of renderings which play an important part in the history and criticism of the Old Testament text, and in the present survey only certain aspects of this vast field of study can be included. Unfortunately, it means that we omit other aspects, each of which has its own importance for a full appreciation of the study of the versions as a whole.

In order to place the versions in perspective we look once more at the history of the Bible transmission. After the fourth century B.C. Judaism flourished both inside Palestine and also outside in what is known as the Hellenistic diaspora. In the former, Hebrew continued to survive, but alongside it the official language of the western part of the Persian Empire, namely Aramaic, also flourished. In due course the Old Testament came to be interpreted and also translated into Aramaic, producing what is known as the Targums. In the Hellenistic diaspora on the other hand the prevailing language was Greek, and, again, Greek became a vehicle for renderings of the Old Testament. From them grew the Septuagint and also other Greek renderings. The LXX, in turn, became the Bible of the Early Church, and played a formative part in the production of Latin Versions, namely Old Latin, and of so-called Daughter Translations such as Coptic, Ethiopic, Armenian and others. Jerome's Vulgate was based on the Hebrew text; the Syriac branch of Christendom produced the Peshitta, but scholars still dispute whether this version is based directly on the Hebrew text or the LXX or is a conflation of both.

Obviously it is the Greek (LXX) transmission that receives priority. From the second century B.C. comes the letter of Aristeas, which describes how a Greek translation of the Pentateuch was produced a hundred years previously, for inclusion in the royal library at Alexandria. It was the work of seventy-two men, six from each tribe (hence, for convenience, *Septuaginta* and LXX). The letter, and its later elaborations, contains a large element of legend and a factual basis. But there is considerable disagreement about many aspects of the early history of the Version; in fact the controversy seems to resolve itself into two schools of thought. On the one hand some scholars claim that, apart from the Pentateuch, the LXX is essentially a Christian work, and that prior to a standardization of its text during the early Christian era and for Christian usage, there existed a number of renderings which can only very roughly be called a Version. On the other hand, other scholars insist that the actual Version which we know as the Septuagint was produced in the late pre-Christian era, and that during its transmission within the Church it suffered considerable textual changes, as did also the New Testament text, but that it is nevertheless possible to assume the existence of an original LXX text. For the purposes of textual criticism this division of opinion has far-reaching effects, for if the former view is correct, then the appeal to the LXX for the purpose of reconstructing the early pre-Massoretic Hebrew text is considerably weaker than if we accept the view that the LXX, despite its loose transmission, contains on the whole an authentic text from pre-Christian times. This is not the place to discuss the problem in any detail, but it is relevant to note that the discovery of the Samuel manuscript in Qumran (the above-mentioned *4QSama*), with its text closely approximating to the LXX, is an important factor in favour of the authenticity of the version. Furthermore in Cave Four, actual fragments of the LXX have been found.

There are, however, other Greek renderings from the second century A.D. which must be fitted into the picture. *Aquila* produced a slavish translation of the Massoretic text; *Symmachus* rendered the Hebrew text into a more readable Greek form; *Theodotion* revised an earlier Greek text which diverged from the LXX. At least, many scholars argue in this way. On the other hand, the discovery of yet another Dead Sea Scroll may provide fresh information. From an unidentified source—not Qumran—the beduin in 1952 brought a manuscript with portions of the Minor Prophets in Greek, which belongs, say the experts, to the first century A.D., and this may well be evidence of an early effort to bring the LXX into line with the Massoretic text. But the manuscript has also been used to support the contrary view, that there existed in pre-Christian times, not a version (LXX) but a number of semi-independent Greek translations.

The next step to note in the actual history of the LXX is the production of Origen's *Hexapla*, a rendering of the whole of the Old Testament in six columns in the following order: Hebrew, Greek transliteration, Aquila, Symmachus, Septuagint, Theodotion, with the occasional addition of other columns. Its purpose was to bring the text of the LXX into line with the Hebrew, and in accordance with this purpose the LXX column received *sigla* (asterisk, obelus, and others) to indicate additions and omissions which were made to and from the Hebrew text. The result was the Origen, or Hexaplaric, recension of the LXX. Another work, the *Tetrapla*, having the texts without the two Hebrew columns, is also attributed to Origen. The Hexapla was produced about A.D. 230–40 in Caesarea, but after the Islamic conquests it disappeared. Other copies had been in circulation, especially of col. V, and a fragment with five of the six columns of some Psalms was discovered at the end of the last century. It is known as the Mercati Palimpsest and was written in the tenth century. Manuscripts known to contain the Hexaplaric recension are obviously important, and the main edition of the LXX now in production, the *Göttingen*, gives Hexaplaric readings in a special section of its *apparatus criticus*. It partly replaces the 1875 edition of Field's collection of Hexaplaric remains.

After Origen, other recensions were produced, and from early Church historians we learn that around A.D. 400 there were three in circulation, that of Hesychius in North Africa, Lucian in Syria and Constantinople, and in Palestine that of Origen, qualified by the work of later Fathers such as Eusebius and Pamphilus, which bring us down to the fifth century.

Extant fragments of the LXX itself, however, cover the period during which the above recensions were composed, but it is not easy to bring the two activities together. There are two fragments of the LXX from the pre-Christian era, and another three from Qumran ; all of them texts of the Pentateuch. From the early Christian era comes the very important collection of papyri from a Christian library probably in the Fayyum in Upper Egypt, and now mainly but not wholly in the collection of Sir Alfred Chester Beatty in Dublin. They belong to the second to fourth century A.D., and provide representative texts of parts of the Old Testament. They became available for use after being edited by Sir Frederic Kenyon in 1933–7.

Then comes the period from which lengthy, virtually complete texts are derived. There are four Great Codices (containing the whole Christian Bible, together with some books of the Apocrypha), namely *Codex Vaticanus* (fourth century), now in Rome, *Codex Sinaiticus* (fourth century) and *Codex Alexandrinus* (fifth century), both now in the British Museum (a small portion of the former, however, is in Leipzig), and finally, *Codex Ephraemi* (fifth century), now in Paris. An important historical fact in connexion with the Great Codices is that they were produced after the Edict of Milan, when Christianity was accorded official status in the Roman Empire and its Bible received a measure of textual standardization.

Along with these major manuscripts there are hundreds

from later dates, some written in capital letters (uncials) until about the eighth century and others in cursive (minuscles), and it is the task of the LXX textual critic to evaluate the manuscripts, since they all show the divergencies so characteristic of Christian textual transmission. And the invention of the printing press did nothing to check the flow of still more divergent texts.

Out of this chaos, attempts have been made to produce editions which could be used by scholars with some degree of confidence. One of two methods of reconstruction and editing could be used, and both have been tried. For the first, the best known early manuscript (*Codex Vaticanus*) becomes the basic text with gaps filled in from other " established " manuscripts and the variant readings are arranged schematically in footnotes. For the two editions associated with British scholarship this was the plan adopted, namely the Swete edition (1887–91, with later editions of some books), and the larger Brooke-McLean-Thackeray edition known as the Cambridge Septuagint (1906–). The most recent volume appeared in 1940, and afterwards the late Professor T. W. Manson took charge of the project.) The second method is much more ambitious. After collating all available sources—manuscripts, versions and quotations, the editor chooses what he thinks is the " best " reading, and thus produces an eclectic text which, he can claim, approximates most closely to the original text. The book of Joshua was elaborately worked out according to such a scheme by Margolis in America (1931–8), but the best known edition along these lines is the *Göttingen Septuagint* (1931–). The principles were laid down by Lagarde in the last century, but the work has been conducted mainly by Rahlfs, Kappler, and now Ziegler. The publication of the text continues and will be completed in the foreseeable future.

A compromise edition, inclining to the first alternative, and resulting in a most useful text, is that edited by Rahlfs (*Septuaginta*, 1935 and later) and based on the three codices, *Vaticanus*, *Sinaiticus* and *Alexandrinus*, with other readings embodied in the *apparatus criticus*.

The history of the Septuagint is essentially one of a Christian transmission ; consequently, for the more orthodox Jewish translations we turn to the Aramaic Targums, and, as might be expected, the most fruitful source for this kind of text is the synagogue and the Polyglotts. Consequently the Cairo Genizah manuscripts play an important part, especially in the way they have helped scholars to reconstruct the history of the transmission. Another important discovery made in 1957 comes from the Vatican Library. It is known as Neofiti 1. and contains the whole of the Pentateuch Targum.

The Targums fall into two types. There are those which are free, with interpretations and even legends inserted in the rendering. They include nearly all the books of the Old Testament, and, where different versions exist of the same books, as they do for instance for the Pentateuch, there is no uniformity between them. Pride of place, nowadays, goes to the above-mentioned Neofiti I., which replaces some fragments of the same Targum which had long since been known as the Fragment Targum. Here, although the actual manuscript is medieval, the text is pre-Christian. A second contains the fragmentary remains of an old Palestinian Targum ; and a third is known as Pseudo-Jonathan because its abbreviated initials T. J., *Targum Jerushalmi*, were misinterpreted as Targum Jonathan. The second type of Targum has a more fixed text and uniform transmission, and bears the marks of an official rendering produced for use in synagogue services. This characteristic, too, explains the fact that these Targums exist only for the Pentateuch and the Prophets (Former and Latter), which provide the lectionary for the synagogue services. The Pentateuch is given in Targum Onkelos, which is a literal rendering and whose text, in its present form, derives from Babylon in the fifth century A.D. and somewhat later from Palestine. Targum Jonathan, for the Prophets, has a much greater element of interpretation and this, in part, goes back to pre-Christian times ; the present form of the text, however, was achieved in Babylon about the same time as Onkelos. Nineteenth century editions of these two Targums, which are basic sources for the textual critic, were produced by A. Berliner (*Targum Onkelos*, 1884–6) and Lagarde (*Prophetae Chaldaice*, 1872) and others ; they are now, however, replaced by A. Sperber's monumental work, *The Bible in Aramaic*. Vol. i., the Pentateuch (*Targum Onkelos*) and vols. ii., the Former Prophets (*Targum Jonathan*) appeared in 1959 ; vol. iii., the Latter Prophets (*Targum Jonathan*) in 1962 ; and vol. iv., general conclusions, which is eagerly awaited.

We now turn to two other Versions which, though they are Christian works, reflect also the direct influence of the Hebrew text. They are the Latin *Vulgate* and the Syriac *Peshitta*. The former is, of course, Jerome's translation of the Hebrew text into Latin during the fourth century, but it needs to be stressed that we cannot always regard the Vulgate as sound evidence for Hebrew readings at that time. The Vulgate had a stormy passage, and from the outset the text became Christianized by the substitution of Old Latin variants. A recent attempt by the Benedictines to reconstruct the Vulgate text and its history shows how impossible it is to arrive at an original text form. The first volume of the text appeared in

1926 and the work is still in progress. The textual value of the Peshitta is still more difficult to assess. Firstly, it is a matter of dispute whether or not it was originally a Christian production ; secondly, the possible influence of the Septuagint is always to be borne in mind ; and thirdly, the textualist is seriously handicapped by the absence of a good, scholarly edition of the Peshitta text. This situation will be remedied, it is hoped, in the near future by a definitive text. A band of European scholars are busily engaged on the collation of the vast number of manuscripts available, especially in the British Museum, and on the preparation of the edition.

Finally, mention must be made of the *Samaritan Pentateuch,* which has recently entered a period of considerable difficulty. For many years it has claimed an important place in textual criticism, chiefly by virtue of the Abisha Scroll which traditionally enjoyed great antiquity. Indeed, it was held by prominent critics to provide the best pre-Christian witness to the text of the Pentateuch. The Abisha Scroll, however, has in recent years been twice photographed in Nablus, where it has lain throughout the centuries, and the later of the two photographs forms the basis of an edition of the text by Pérez Castro (*Sefer Abisha,* 1959). The editor has shown that the scroll is merely a patchwork of medieval manuscripts, and further comments by the leading Samaritan scholar in this country, Edward Robertson, have confirmed this conclusion. It is too early to assess the exact significance of the publication, but it is bound to detract from the authority usually attributed to this version.

(iv) TEXTUAL EMENDATION

With this massive information about the nature of the text and the versions of the Old Testament at his disposal the textual critic of today is much better placed than were his predecessors ; but for the same reason he also realizes that the emendation of a word, and especially of a phrase in the text, is much more difficult to justify. Nevertheless such a duty is inevitable, and to conclude the present survey an attempt will be made to show just how the work is conducted.

The critic realizes firstly how inadequate is the *apparatus criticus* of *Biblia Hebraica,* especially of the third edition. It is seriously antiquated and despite the attempt to distinguish, in two sets of annotations, between incidental variants and those which actually concern his task, it cannot be of great use to him. It is strangely anomalous that the notes in this edition concur in the vast majority of places with those produced for earlier editions long before the main points of the history of the transmission were reconstructed, though this was the *raison d'etre* for the edition itself. The results of important work on the Versions, especially on the LXX, have also largely been ignored. The new edition of *Biblia Hebraica* now in preparation, and the new project of the Hebrew University will obviously rectify this defect. The same criticism holds for many standard commentaries, especially those in which conjectural emendations of the text figure prominently.

Of course, the presence in the text of the usual type of scribal error is immediately recognizable. There are cases of dittography (words written twice where one is correct), haplography (words written once where they should have been twice), and homoeoteleuton (where two words have a similar ending and the text between them is dropped). But there are other cases where the history of the transmission is more readily related to its emendations. They include the following: at an early stage in transmission, the use of textual abbreviations was common, and in due course the contracted forms came to be incorporated in the text, producing either misleading particles such as prepositions or suffixes, or confusing the sense altogether. Again, it is thought that liturgical instructions became embedded in the text and later interfered with its correct transmission. Among more common, and better exemplified cases of corruption are those where vocalization provides a clue; as we have seen, vocalization was not only a late invention but also became the vehicle for transmitting divergent traditions. The variants of *Ḳ*ᵉ*rê* and *K*ᵉ*thîbh* account for a number of the corruptions, but there are other cases where the accepted vocalization itself calls for emendation. On the other hand, the uniformity of transmission throughout the Massoretic period makes the scholar very cautious about interference with the actual consonantal text itself. Where he has reason to doubt the text, he also realizes that the reading might be capable of confirmation through a more thorough knowledge of cognate languages, or a better understanding of the exegesis of the passage itself. In any case, there is little justification for mere guess-work and conjectural emendation, and fortunately there are but few today who practise it. The results of ingenuity might be interesting, and even illuminating, but they are never authoritative.

The best sources of possible emendations are, of course, supplied by the Versions, especially the LXX. The reasons for its priority are two-fold; firstly, it is based on a text-form which diverges from the Massoretic text, and secondly it is an early rendering. The drawbacks of the LXX, however, are also to be seriously considered, and they also are two-fold. Firstly, it is always possible that the divergence points to interpretation rather than to a different text; secondly, the history of its transmission shows a lack of uniformity which tends to minimize the authenticity of its renderings. The Qumran scrolls are rather less valuable than the LXX because they testify, on the whole, to the Massoretic text and the truly divergent manuscripts among them, so far as we know at present, support mainly the LXX recension. The Targums again reflect the Massoretic text and deviations from it must be carefully scrutinized. The Vulgate and Peshitta, despite occasional readings which affect the Massoretic text, are of greater use for reconstructing the LXX and this fact is still more true of the daughter translations of the Version, such as the Coptic and Ethiopic translations.

Recent discoveries, and especially the Qumran scrolls have resulted in checking at least one form of textual emendation which was earlier frequently used. It is that textual corruption arose from the confusion of similar letters. The scrolls give, now for the first time, the form of script used in pre-Christian and early Christian times, and it is possible to study the history of palaeography with reasonable certainty. Many well-established theories have been disproved; others will now probably replace them. But the trend is obviously to stress caution in the resort to palaeography and script for cases of scribal errors: it is not denied that this is a possible source of error, but we do not know enough about the history of the script to appeal to it indiscriminately.

As we assess the modern practice of textual criticism of the Old Testament, we note two outstanding features. Firstly, it shares with all other approaches to the Old Testament a tendency to caution and conservatism. Reasons are adduced for preserving the standard Massoretic text rather than for its emendation; and it may be noted that the acuity practised to this end is just as ingenious as that shown by previous generations to quite the opposite end. Secondly, it is much more concerned than previously with the history of the transmission both of the Massoretic text and of the Versions. To this extent, it is more squarely based on scientific criteria and it is certainly a more satisfying and more informative study.

BIBLIOGRAPHY

For a general introduction see Articles in:

Twentieth Century Encyclopedia of Religious Knowledge, 1956.

Peake's Commentary on the Bible, ed. by M. Black and H. H. Rowley, 1962.

The Interpreter's Dictionary of the Bible, 4 vols., 1962.

Hastings' *Dictionary of the Bible*, one volume edition, ed. by F. C. Grant and H. H. Rowley, 1963.

For a more detailed study of major aspect the following will be of use :

F. F. Bruce, *The Books and the Parchments*, 3rd ed., 1962.
B. J. Roberts, *The Old Testament Text and Versions*, 1951.
H. G. May, *Our English Bible in the Making*, 1952.
H. W. Robinson (ed.), *The Bible in its Ancient and English Versions*, 2nd ed., 1954.
I. M. Price (rev. by W. A. Irwin and A. P. Wikgren), *The Ancestry of our English Bible*, 3rd ed., 1956.
E. Würthwein (Eng. trans. by P. R. Ackroyd), *The Text of the Old Testament*, 1957.
F. M. Cross, *The Ancient Library of Qumran and Modern Biblical Studies*, 1958.
F. G. Kenyon, *Our Bible and the Ancient Manuscripts*, 5th ed., revised by A. W. Adams, 1958.
H. G. G. Herklots, *How the Bible came to us : Its Texts and Versions*, 1959.
P. E. Kahle, *The Cairo Geniza*, 2nd ed., 1959.

VII. THE TRANSMISSION OF THE TEXT

(B) NEW TESTAMENT

BY NIGEL TURNER

(i) THE EARLIEST COPIES

IT is scarcely credible that the original writings of the New Testament, known as the autographs, have survived. Nevertheless, much papyrus material in Egypt has been recovered, for all its brittleness, notably the tiny fragment p^{52} (*c.* A.D. 125), and future discoveries may include equally early copies of parts of the New Testament.

Copying in the first days was not accurate. We know that marginal notes and words between the lines were incorporated in the text; difficulties of interpretation were eased; and discrepancies between previous copies were resolved. Harmonizers felt the time to be ripe for a revision of the wording of the Gospels and St. Paul's letters even before the individual books began to be collected into a single corpus. This was happening before Origen complained about it in the third century, and some variants in the text, especially in Mark, must have originated when the books circulated separately.

Problems of this period invite investigation: how far did Marcion in the second century corrupt the text of Paul and Luke? Comparison of Marcion's readings with those surviving in the Old Latin versions and the *Diatessarōn* of Tatian has made the extent of his influence apparent. Although Marcion was expelled from the Roman Church for heresy in A.D. 144, his Canon of Scripture was soon rendered into Latin and its peculiarities obviously influenced the Old Syriac as well as the Old Latin versions. His influences reached to the fourth-century Codex Vaticanus which in Rom 1[16] omits *first* from the phrase *to the Jew first*. But wherever we can be sure that Marcion's peculiar readings are not tendentious and if they have support elsewhere, he is a representative of the text of Luke and Paul in Rome at this very early time. It was strongly "Western" in type, resembling Tatian's *Diatessarōn* and the Old Syriac.

Tatian too found Rome unfriendly. Here is another crux. Did he compile his Gospel harmony, the *Diatessarōn,* in Greek from a Roman text and then put it into Syriac when he fled to Assyria in A.D. 172 ? Or has it a Syriac origin (as Vööbus) ? Did it become, in separated four-fold form, the official Syriac Gospel, and is its influence traceable in the Syriac writers Aphraates and Ephraem (A.D. 350) and in medieval Gospel harmonies like the Persian *Diatessarōn* edited by Messina in 1951 ? How far did "Tatianisms" spread ? Strangely, Clement, Origen, Irenaeus, and Jerome did not mention the *Diatessarōn*. Are its resemblances with Greek MSS., the Old Latin, Old Syriac, Armenian and Georgian versions, due to Tatian's influence ? Doubtless there is a just reaction to von Soden and Vogels who exaggerated the influence of Tatian, but these recensions of Marcion and Tatian, and perhaps earlier ones, contributed to the textual contamination which appeared everywhere about A.D. 200. Our earliest papyrus fragments, during this period, differ from each other at the rate of about one variant per verse.

Recent attempts to probe the pre-Tatian text in Rome by studying Justin Martyr's quotations lead us to think it was strongly "Western" (see below), resembling EFGHKMSV *ΔΘΠΩ*, Old Latin (*h, f*), Peshitta, Palestinian and Harklean Syriac, Armenian, Ethiopic.

The expanding Church needed *versions in Latin* as well as Syriac from about A.D. 150. The value of versions can be overestimated, especially when we now have so much Greek papyrus material as old as any version. Moreover, the versions may be targumic rather than literal translations. Pre-Vulgate Latin readings are inestimable, nevertheless, not only for the great age of their text, emerging perhaps at Rome from a Latin Gospel-harmony based on Tatian's—and in any case translated from very early Greek MSS. now lost—but because they are often servile renderings of the Greek. They reflect a wide area : Africa, Spain, Gaul, North Italy, and Rome. Some of the eccentricities common to these fifty or so texts are found in Tatian's *Diatessarōn*, Old Syriac and Ethiopic (even in Arabic) versions and in Scripture quotations by Hippolytus (Italy, A.D. 220), Irenaeus (Gaul, 190), Cyprian (Carthage, 250), and Clement (Alexandria, 200). Such a text is not only ancient but widespread. A Spanish Old Latin is now distinguished from the European and African. The most important codices belonging to the postulated African branch (the *Afra*) are Bobiensis (*k*) resembling Cyprian's text, Palatinus (*e*), Floriacensis (*h*), and the Freising fragments (*r*).

The European texts (the *Itala*) are supposed to be Vercellensis (*a*), Veronensis (*b*), Colbertinus (*c*), the only complete Gospel MS., Cantabrigiensis (*d*), Brixianus (*f*), related somehow to the Gothic version, Rehdigeranus (*l*), Monacensis (*q*), Corbeiensis II (*ff*²), Gigas (*gig*), and the *Speculum de divinis*

Scripturis (*m*). They vary in date from the fourth century to the Middle Ages, but all contain a text more or less uncontaminated by Jerome's revision. It is not likely that one group influenced the other, but probable that both originate in a Latin version of the *Diatessarōn*. Their readings when they differ from the Greek MSS. normally deserve notice, since they will be based on "Western" Greek MSS. which disappeared as soon as Italian churchmen went over to Latin. The exceptions are obvious harmonizations, targums, bad translation, or tendentious Marcionisms. The Old Latin MSS. were serviceably edited by A. Jülicher: Matthew 1938, Mark 1940, Luke 1954 (with W. Matzkow). John (by W. Matzkow and K. Aland) is in preparation.

Tatian influenced *the Syriac versions* but we do not know whether their Tatianisms accrue from the translators or from subsequent revision of the Syriac versions. We have a MS. of this old version known as the Curetonian (syr^{cur}), and another known as the Sinaitic (syr^{sin}), both fifth century, but we are not sure if either influenced the other. Translation into Syriac is likely to have started as early as A.D. 150 and to have been made from the Greek text current at Antioch. But a revision followed, as is apparent from a study of syr^{cur}. As a whole, the Old Syriac forms an independent text-type—the "Eastern" text—parallel with the Old Latin and Coptic, and influenced by Tatian. Recent research makes it clear that syr^{sin} and syr^{cur} form but a fractional part of an Old Syriac text-type that was popular around Edessa for many centuries. Unfortunately, we have the greatest misgiving that the Old Syriac, more than any version, is *targumin* rather than faithful translation.

Somewhat resembling the Old Latin and Syriac, especially in the Gospels, is *the Coptic*. The Sahidic, according to P. E. Kahle, Jr., is the earlier and more official version. Our MSS. are fragmentary, but all books are represented in our extant Bohairic (lower Egyptian) texts. They are separate translations, made from different Greek MSS. The publication of Bodmer papyrus III containing John in Bohairic in 1958 provides valuable fourth-century evidence for the early date of a Bohairic Bible. The importance of other Coptic dialects is now appreciated. The sub-Achmimic has a fourth-century MS. of John, the Qau. A fragment of Luke in the Achmimic was discovered in 1953. Kahle in 1954 published the Bodleian texts discovered in 1907 at Deir el-Bala'izah in the subdialects. The archetypes of the Coptic version originate from at least A.D. 275—probably earlier.

Critics have attempted to restore the local texts, to forestall the recensions of the third and fourth centuries and unearth the divergent types of text current in Syria and Palestine, in Rome, and in Egypt, because our oldest Greek MSS. in varying degree are redressed by the great recensions. Indeed, recent discovery of new MSS.—we have twenty-five papyrus fragments from the third century—and research into the quotations of Church writers have suspended the classification of witnesses into rigid types belonging to particular recensions. " Recension " itself may be too strong a word for a development of revision which was rather more gradual than is now thought, as research and discovery fill the gaps to let us see the full development. The " recension " at worst may have been simply a large-scale collation of corruptions in various copies over a period. Although text-types did exist, resulting from some kind of revision, our MSS. show signs of several types in their text. Sharp and consistent cleavage between MSS. is less easy to maintain.

(ii) THE PERIOD OF RECENSIONS (THIRD TO FOURTH CENTURY)

There were, Jerome said, three kinds of Bible MS. at the end of the fourth century: (1) those resulting from the recension of Hesychius, existing chiefly in Egypt, (2) those of the recension of Lucian, prevalent in the north-east of the Mediterranean world, and (3) those circulating in Palestine, which were due to the critical work of Pamphilus, Origen's disciple. Origen was admired by Jerome who decidedly preferred the third type of text.

1. *The Egyptian Recension.* Would that we knew more about Hesychius. He produced the Alexandrian recension of the Septuagint, but did he revise the New Testament too? More probably there was a series of revisers. Whoever it was, the work was not original or unified. Certain characteristics are clear: the aim was to find the oldest readings, to eliminate accretions to the text, and to purge what were thought to be grammatical errors in transmission. Such scholarly solicitude may already have operated at Alexandria in the second century. We have moved away from Hort who named this text " Neutral," even from Kenyon, and the modern inference is that Vaticanus (B), the chief mirror of careful Alexandrian-Caesarean revision and our most valuable MS., is not the product of an almost pure textual tradition. We see in its text, and in that of other members of the same group, including Sinaiticus (א), some harmonizations and additions and even tendentious corrections in the interests of interpretation. In Acts the revision may—so many critics judge—have ruthlessly suppressed sentences and verses which are genuine. Representatives of the recension include third- or fourth-century

papyrus fragments numbered 1, 3, 5, 6, 8, 9, 13, 27, 29, 35, 41, 43, and important uncial MSS. : Alexandrinus (A) except for the Gospels, Vaticanus (B), Sinaiticus, Ephraemi (C) for the Gospels, Regius (L), and the Freer Gospels (W) in part. Also M Δ (Mark) Ξ Ψ 059 and several minuscule MSS. (33, 81, 579 except Matt., 892, etc.), the Bohairic version and most of the Sahidic, with quotations in Didymus, Athanasius, and Cyril. For the Epistles, the copyist of the important 1739 claims that its text agrees with that of Origen. The Egyptian is the best text-type for study because conditions in Egypt favoured careful preservation and correction of a Greek text. It was a land of Greek scholars and sound Christians. All our uncials and papyri of the fourth century and earlier are Egyptian, or Caesarean, which encourages the reconstruction of this early text-type. It will be discussed more fully when we consider the Palestinian recension and the " Western " text.

2. " *Lucian's* " *Recension* (*the Syro-Byzantine*). The fourth-century text resulting from this revision in Syria, according to Hort and Streeter, was later revised repeatedly. Chrysostom and other Syrian incumbents of the see of Constantinople (Byzantium) understandably did much to disseminate the product of the Syrian recension, until it became in about the ninth century the Byzantine text of the majority of our MSS., and on it was based the *Textus Receptus*—the Greek edition behind the Authorized Version and generally used until Lachmann, Tischendorf, Tregelles, and supremely Westcott-Hort produced more acceptable redactions. The Antioch revision favoured virtuosity, intelligibility, and the fullest possible wording. " Lucian " had at least one eye on the cultured reader and produced a clear, smooth, comprehensive text, such as is most clearly found in EVΩ in the Gospels of A, in a group which has some Caesarean variants (MUΛ 71, 1071, 1424, 1604), in Matthew and Luke $8^{13\text{-end}}$ in W, in FGHKΠ 028, 031, and in a more revised form in the mass of uncials and minuscules, and the neglected and servile Gothic version (Ulfilas was made bishop of the Goths at Antioch A.D. 341). Indeed, almost all MSS.—even the best representatives of their own recension, like Θ—have succumbed to some extent to the Byzantine pattern.

No longer can we assume with Hort that the Byzantine text was uniform from the time of Chrysostom. Kirsopp and Silva Lake suggested the ninth century for its origin, but later investigation of quotations in a ninth-century patriarch of Constantinople, Photius, indicates that the text he used was still at this period mixed, not Byzantine (J. N. Birdsall, *Journal of Theological Studies*, vii., 1956, pp. 42–55, 190–98, ix., 1958, pp. 278–91). Even the Byzantine or ecclesiastical text is not to be despised and will be increasingly studied, as it probably contains elements of all the older text-types. While a reading peculiar to the average Byzantine MS., no less than a reading peculiar to the " Western " text, has little value, nevertheless when these two agree, it can be postulated that the reading goes back to the second century and precedes the Alexandrian reading (ℵB).

3. *The Palestinian Recension.* A third revision is connected with the names of Origen and Eusebius. A century later Jerome described the recensions of Hesychius and Lucian as " poor," and his admiration for the scholarly work of Origen inspires the thought that the highly valued and ancient MSS. which Jerome used really belonged to Pamphilus's recension. Pamphilus, the Origen enthusiast and master of the famous school at Caesarea in Palestine, may have edited the Bible copies which Origen had corrected and left there. Origen was a renowned exegete and doubtless created a revival of interest in the sacred text in the latter half of the third century, leading to fresh revisions. We do not know how radically these changed the text which Origen used in Palestine, but a group of MSS. has been segregated by B. H. Streeter and subsequent critics, because all its members to some extent have affinities with the text of Mark used in Palestine by Origen and by Pamphilus's disciple, Eusebius. This group was named " Caesarean," in spite of Burkitt's opposition, and includes the eighth-century Codex Koridethi (Θ), " discovered " in 1913, and Mark 5^{31}–16^{8} in the Freer Gospels (W), a fourth-century text purchased by C. L. Freer in 1906, besides 0188, p^{45} (Mark), a third-century papyrus fragment from Egypt acquired by Sir Alfred Chester Beatty in 1933, and the semi-uncials 28, 565, 700, minuscules 1071, 1275, and groups known as " family 1 " and " family 13." The test for a Caesarean text outside Mark is proceeding. G. Zuntz (Schweich Lectures 1946) examined Chester Beatty's p^{46} for 1 Corinthians and Hebrews and found not so much a Caesarean text-type as a " proto-Alexandrian," a foreshadowing of the great Egyptian text-type, additional witnesses being B, 1739, Sahidic and Bohairic versions, and quotations in Clement and Origen. R. V. G. Tasker had already found (1936) that Origen's text of Matthew, Luke and John was not definitely Caesarean, and another blow to the solidarity of Caesarean witnesses has been dealt by an investigation of Eusebius's text of Matthew and John. The Matthew-text is not supported mainly by Caesarean, but by " Western " witnesses, notably the African Old Latin; and the mixture of all the recensions in Eusebius's Matthew " makes it impossible to describe his text as belonging to any of the conventional categories " (M. J. Suggs, *Novum Testa-*

mentum, i., 1956, pp. 233–45). The John-text is partly Alexandrian, partly "Western" (*Journal of Biblical Literature*, lxxv., 1956, pp. 137–42).

However, although the so-called Caesarean witnesses often conflict, and many of their readings appear to have been introduced by way of the Syro-Byzantine recension, some modern writers concede to Streeter that there is a family likeness, though not so clear-cut. Their common characteristics appear to be a tendency to waver between the text of the Egyptian recension and Origen's text (Caesarea, *c.* A.D. 250), and harmonization between the Gospels, with attempt at style and clarity. Further study may identify more members of this group, but at best the Caesarean is a derivative of a very old Egyptian text-type. The difficulty is: what text was Origen using when he settled at Caesarea? The Lakes and Blake, who addressed themselves to the problem, concluded that it was an Alexandrian text. The Caesarean, which he used later on, can hardly hold its own on independent terms with the Egyptian and "Western" text-types in age and excellence, because, rather than the text which he found at Caesarea, it may simply be a compromise in Egypt between an Alexandrian and "Western" text-type, revised subsequently at Caesarea! Not to beg a question, "Group Theta" is a better title than "Caesarean."

There is now a tendency to subdivide these witnesses, restricting Group *Θ* to a strictly Caesarean text-type (*Θ*, 565, 700, Origen, Eusebius), and discerning in p[45], W, 28, fam. 1 and fam. 13, with Georgian support, a pre-Caesarean or Egyptian variety of the same text. J. H. Greenlee, having investigated Cyril of Jerusalem's quotations, finds the Markan agreeing closely with the pre-Caesarean sub-type. The inclusion of Cyril really indicates that this sub-type ought to be named "Palestinian," not "Caesarean." There was much rivalry between the sees of Jerusalem and Caesarea *c.* A.D. 300–50 and Cyril would not have used a Caesarean text that had not already become well established throughout Palestine (*The Gospel Text of Cyril of Jerusalem*, 1955).

(iii) THE "WESTERN" TEXT

Apart from peculiarities of text identified in the recensions mentioned by Jerome, there remain other variants in many MSS., versions and Fathers. It is always possible that the archetypes of these texts preserve readings which entirely escaped the attentions of editors, and which would therefore be primitive and valuable. Are these the readings which have provisionally been grouped into a badly named text-type, the "Western"—so-called by Griesbach because these readings were first observed in the Old Latin version of *western* Christendom?

Patristic research proves that such readings were widely diffused geographically and are of very ancient date. They may have entered the East by way of Tatian's *Diatessarōn*. There is not too obvious a family likeness among the witnesses, but this may be due to the different provenances of the various subdivisions of the text-type. Chief witnesses in which such readings occur are as follows: papyrus fragments (29, 37, 38, 48), uncials (DEFG, 0171, W. for Mark 1–5^{30}), minuscules (383, 614 for Acts), versions (Old Latin, Old Syriac, margin of Harklean Syriac, part of Sahidic, Old Slavic sometimes), quotations in Greek and Latin Fathers (Marcion, Justin, Irenaeus, Clement, Origen; Tertullian, Cyprian, Ambrosiaster, Pelagius, etc.), Syriac writers (Tatian, and consequently Aphraates and Ephraem). There is a wide field of circulation, from Rome and Carthage to Egypt, Palestine, Edessa, and beyond. It is quoted in Church Fathers much earlier than representatives of the Egyptian recension. Its respectable age takes us back to A.D. 140, even to the period of the *Didache, Gospel of Peter, Epistola Apostolorum*, and *Epistle of Barnabas*. Doubtless even to the first century, for it might be shown that Matthew and Luke used a "Western" text of Mark. Many critics consider it the most ancient and reliable New Testament text that we are likely to possess. However, in its present form it shows signs of revision, which is why Hort dubbed it a corrupt text. The question bristles with controversy. Some of the additions and omissions, embellishments, doctrinal alterations, harmonizations of Old Testament quotations with the LXX forms, and transpositions, stand out conspicuously. Apocryphal (uncanonical) matter may have entered the "Western" text by way of the *Diatessarōn* in the embryonic period of textual transmission, if deviations in the newly discovered Coptic *Gospel of Thomas* were incorporated in the *Diatessarōn*, as is suspected. So much attention has been devoted to the "Western" text since Hort that with modest certainty we may tell where revisions were made—Italy, Gaul, Spain, Carthage, Egypt, Syria, and Palestine—and we may distinguish an Eastern and Western subdivision.

The value of such a text lies in the contrast it affords with the other revised texts, Egyptian and Palestinian. Comparisons will eliminate targumic material, errors of accident, and refinements. Involved though the discussion has become, the "Western" text to its moderate enthusiasts—and even to J. H. Ropes—reflects a very early period of textual transmission, the second century, and its errors are older than the errors of the other great text-types.

Codex Bezae (D) is probably not a safe guide to the quality of this text-type, being a late manifestation of it. On the other hand, its language is first-century *Koinē*, and even Septuagintal. The reasons for its extensive additions in Acts and omissions in the Gospels still elude investigators. In Acts, A. C. Clark had thought the D-text primary ; Ropes the ℵB-text. But the choice is now felt to be not so simple ; each reading must be considered on its merits, and the other MSS. considered more carefully. However, there is hardly any doubt that the "Western" text reveals that Luke's language was a more typically Biblical, Jewish or Septuagintal Greek than is indicated by the other text-types, and therefore is more original.

Some, owing to the presence of the "Western" text in Egypt very early, submit that even Vaticanus and Sinaiticus represent a recension of the "Western" text. But we need to know more about the text that Clement and his contemporaries used in Alexandria before the revision there, as distinct from any "Western" text which Clement may have brought from Italy, and to compare it both with the great uncials and with the "Western" text. For this reason consideration must be given to the Chester Beatty papyrus (p^{45}), belonging to Egypt in the third century, often independent of the influence of the Egyptian recension and sometimes displaying "Western" readings. However, it does also give Alexandrian "corrections" and one might guess therefore that it was made in a transition period about A.D. 250 just after Origen left Egypt for Palestine —a period in which the preliminary revision of Origen's text may have begun, a little time before Alexandrian scholarship completed it. The papyrus represents a mixed kind of text which has recently been named "pre-Caesarean." "Mixed" is used from the standpoint of text-types accepted before these early MSS. were examined and is entirely provisional.

As to p^{46} (Chester Beatty for Epistles), in the Schweich lectures 1946 G. Zuntz examined the papyrus for 1 Corinthians and Hebrews in connexion with this complex problem, the relation of the "Western" and Alexandrian text-types in Egypt, finding that the earlier one goes in the Egyptian tradition the more often one encounters "Western" elements. The "Western" text is thus even earlier than the "proto-Alexandrian." Further, the investigation appears to reveal that when the "Western" text is found to be supported most strongly by Byzantine readings, at that point it gains all the more support from the "oldest Alexandrians." Zuntz urged that such readings have an excellent claim to originality and consequently the investigator is taken "back deep into the second century" to a popular text, of which Marcion is the fullest extant witness, before the divergence of "Eastern" and "Western" text-types.

Older still by fifty years and probably originating also in Egypt is Bodmer papyrus II (p^{66}), including part of John, published after Zuntz's publication. Like p^{45} it has a "mixed" text, from the standpoint of our previous classifications, but provisionally speaking, less mixed.

These two early witnesses have seventy verses in common, in which unfortunately they differ some seventy-three times fairly substantially! Bodmer II is essentially more Alexandrian than "Western," exacerbating the problem for those who think in terms of an Egyptian revision tending gradually from "Western" to Alexandrian (אB) type. This papyrus, dated before p^{45}, seems to indicate the contrary direction, but its antecedent date need not mean that its text-type was older than that of p^{45}. Probably there was both a "Western" and an Alexandrian text-type in Egypt side by side about A.D. 200. And so the examination of a further Bodmer papyrus (XIV–XV), p^{75}, published in 1961, reflecting the textual position in Egypt at this date, is awaited with interest. As far as can be seen, p^{66} and p^{75} often support BW against א in John, but sometimes B stands apart, and p^{66} and p^{75} do not always agree. No one text-type was authoritatively recognized at this early time in Egypt.

What then do we see provisionally on this side of the recensional veil, which modern scholarship tries so assiduously to pierce? At least four distinct text-types, early in the third century, each probably the result of a process begun much earlier: (1) Egyptian, (2) Syriac, (3) Caesarean, (4) European and North African. A text-type might be defined, with E. C. Colwell, as a group of witnesses which agree together in most of the readings where the witnesses are divided. A "family" is the smallest and tightest form of subdivision, like fam. 1, and each member usually contains the same pattern of mixture in its text—unlike the members of a text-type. Somewhere in between we may speak of a "sub-text-type." Thus, some critics are inclined to class (2) and (3) together as a text-type called "Eastern," with "Antiochian" and "Caesarean" as sub-text-types. Others prefer to class (2) and (4) together as a "Western" text-type in view of their similarities. We need to know more about the influence of Marcion and Tatian on (2) and (4), and about the texts used by Origen both before and after his move to Caesarea. The importance of Patristic study is evident.

(iv) COPYING AFTER CONSTANTINE

Moving forward from A.D. 325 one notices that after the great recensions the witnesses rapidly become textually diverse.

Constantine gave the Church a period of peace in which she became conscious of her Bible in greater detail, and evangelism seemed less important than the combating of heresy by means of verbal precision. Better materials were used and the text was divided into sections, notably by Eusebius, to facilitate quick reference to Gospel parallels. There is the sixth-century Codex Coislinianus or Euthalianus (H_3), which comprises forty-three leaves divided between Paris, Turin, Leningrad, Mt. Athos, Moscow, and Kiev. It is thought to resemble an edition of Acts and the Epistles prepared in the fourth century by Euthalius, written in unequal lines to assist public reading and divided into chapters and sub-sections. For this part of the New Testament it may represent the culmination of the Alexandrian recension.

Lists of passages for reading aloud, and lectionaries, were made, providing the critic with additional material. Nearly nineteen hundred have been catalogued and recent research on them (published at Chicago, 1933 on) has helped in the more precise tracing of the provenance of text-types and families. They are not all Byzantine in type. They show hundreds of variants from that text-type in the lections from Mark alone.

In this period the text-types were increasingly contaminated by repeated copying, especially by the influence of the MSS. of one type upon those of another, until the need of fresh recensions became urgent. Despite this, Vaticanus displays an early and uncontaminated text more consistently than any other large MS. known to us. Sinaiticus itself suffered numerous corrections from the fifth to the seventh century in Palestine, and may even have been improved in odd passages, so that sometimes it is superior to B. The Freer codex (W) presents a seriously diversified text, and grammar-conscious scribes have wrought havoc in the eighth-century codex Regius (L) or its antecedents, which thus but imperfectly represents the Egyptian text-type.

(v) VULGATES AND NEW VERSIONS

Outside the Greek-speaking areas of the Empire the Greek text of the important sees was being used as a norm to correct the deviations of Syriac, Egyptian, and Latin versions and these revisions resulted in the Vulgates: notably the Latin of the fourth century and the Syriac Peshitta of the fourth or early fifth.

1. *The Latin Vulgate.* Much has been written of Jerome's revision, undertaken at the behest of Pope Damasus in A.D. 382, correcting the chaotic deviations of the current Latin versions of the Gospels, but too little has been discovered concerning the Greek and Latin MSS. which he used. Pre-Jerome Latin

texts are scarce. It is difficult even to arrive at the true Jerome behind the many revisions of the Vulgate itself: Cassiodorus, Alcuin, Theodulf, and so on. When the Vulgate appeared, zealous scribes used it to correct the old Latin texts and sometimes only half-heartedly, or only half-way through, and contrariwise the Vulgate itself was later corrected by means of Old Latin MSS.—apart from normal errors due to hand-copying down the centuries. The work of patient unravelling must proceed. The importance of Vulgate study lies in the hope that it will lead us to an ancient Latin text which we can confidently set beside the Greek text-types of the Gospels. One can be even more sanguine on turning from the Vulgate Gospels to the rest of the New Testament. Much work remains to be done on Jerome's commentaries, but probably this part of the Vulgate was not nearly so thorough a revision as the Gospels and may give us the Old Latin text not even revised by Jerome at all.

2. *The Peshitta* (*syr^{pesh}*). In spite of patent errors and paraphrases the Peshitta, unlike the Vulgate, was previously thought to have been transmitted in a fairly pure state in its 250 or so MSS., and until recently the only importance the critic saw in this recension—probably (Burkitt) by Rabbula, bishop of Edessa 411–435, more likely earlier and by several hands—was (*a*) that it was inclined to be reverentially conservative and allowed many Old Syriac readings to stand, and (*b*) it was thought to have brought the Syriac into conformity with Lucian's Greek text and therefore to be a pointer in reconstituting the original text of the Antiochian recension which in turn lay behind the Byzantine text. Now Burkitt is considered to be mistaken. There was no recension, but a gradual development. Old Syriac and Peshitta-type texts were co-existent for a long time. If Rabbula took any part, it was as one link in the chain of revision, and somewhere in the middle, but Vööbus (against Black) thinks he did not, for the Peshitta is older than Rabbula and both he and later writers used the Old Syriac. However, the text is Byzantine mixed with Alexandrian and " Western " elements.

3. Some have over-estimated the Aramaic *Syro-Palestinian* version (syr^{pal}), because it resembles somewhat the text of Origen at Caesarea and because it is independent of the Syriac versions and of the text of the Egyptian and Antiochian recensions, but this Gospel lectionary may be as late as the Byzantine emperors Justinian and Heraclius, intended for the forcibly Christianized Jews of Palestine.

4. The *Philoxenian* version (syr^{ph}) was an attempt at a more accurate work than the Peshitta, *c.* A.D. 508. Another version of the Monophysites was the *Harklean* (syr^{hk}) a century

later, but (according to McHardy, not Zuntz) it was not greatly different except that it contained obeli and asterisks which now puzzle us and it had marginal notes giving the collated variants made by the translator from Greek and Syriac MSS. The margin is more valuable than the text, which is almost entirely Byzantine, because while the Syriac MSS. resemble syr^{sin}, the Greek MSS. belong to the Egyptian, Caesarean and " Western " text-types, resembling D for Acts. According to some scholars the influence of the " Western " type can be traced in the Harklean text of Acts.

The Syriac story is continued still further in the new versions made from it. Study of them proceeds, and questions are outstanding. How and why has that sixth-century version, the *Ethiopic*, derived from the Syriac (according to tradition, corroborated by Vööbus), as many as fifty striking readings in common with the pre-Caesarean or " proto-Alexandrian " Chester Beatty papyrus (p^{46}) ? Can this version owe its origin to Frumentius, the Syrian whom Athanasius consecrated bishop of Ethiopia about A.D. 340 ? The version of nearby *Nubia* awaits investigation. Was the *Sogdian* version made from the Peshitta ? Some questions about the Armenian and Georgian versions can, however, be answered.

5. *The Armenian*. Was this version, dating from the days of the patriarch Sahak (fifth century), translated from the Syriac or the Greek ? A Caesarean Greek was widely affirmed until the research of S. Lyonnet (1950) made Syriac more likely, although whether it was the *Diatessarōn* or the four-fold Old Syriac is still unsettled. Under the impression either that an original Armenian version was made from Caesarean Greek MSS., or that our present Armenian vulgate was a revision effected by this means, scholars were once over-sanguine that the Armenian would help them to reconstitute the exiguously represented Caesarean recension, but since Lyonnet has contended that the Old Armenian only gradually assumed the shape of the vulgate it is recognized that the Caesarean elements in the version may be due to the Old Syriac text from which it was translated.

6. *The Old Georgian*. R. P. Blake considered that this version too has a Caesarean text-type, having been translated from the Armenian. But Joseph Molitor (1953) thought the Adysh Gospels were close to the Old Syriac and *Diatessarōn*. We now have a study of the Old Georgian outside the Gospels, for Père Garitte (1955) has edited a text of Acts which resembles the ninth-century Adysh MS. more than the usually printed Gospel text. This was indeed translated from Armenian (fifth century ?), but not the Armenian Vulgate. The importance of Garitte's work is that without this text we know

nothing of the alleged Caesarean text-type in Acts. Nevertheless here too its helpfulness is diminished by the possibility that the Caesarean elements derive, not directly, but from the Old Syriac text behind the Armenian. Otherwise this might be reckoned one of the best witnesses to the Caesarean text-type. Not that the discussion of the influence of Caesarean, *Diatessarōn,* or Old Syriac upon the Armenian and Georgian is by any means closed yet.

(vi) THE LAST STAGE OF THE WRITTEN TEXT (NINTH TO SIXTEENTH CENTURY)

A period without critical activity but rich in productivity and conservatism as to Greek MSS. and versions saw transition to minuscule (cursive) lettering for economy in parchment and was prolific in lectionaries and commentaries. Varieties of text existed; not all the two thousand extant MSS. of this date had been made to conform to the Byzantine pattern which sprang from the Lucianic recension and was now dominant in the East and much of the West. For instance, codex 33 represents the Alexandrian and 28 the Caesarean text-type of much earlier periods. Minuscules as well as uncials of this Byzantine period are often worthy of study and will no longer be neglected by editors and critics. They have a mixed text. Degeneration was now rapid and would have proceeded much further, but for the invention of printing.

(vii) FROM ERASMUS TO WESTCOTT AND HORT (1516–1881)

Half a century after the invention of printing a Greek Testament was published by Erasmus in 1516 in an unscholarly rush to beat Cardinal Ximenes in Spain who printed his Polyglot edition (Greek and Vulgate) before Erasmus, but did not publish it in time. Neither text is worth very much, but they terminated the long supremacy of the Latin Bible in the West. Unfortunately the edition of Erasmus, based on a few minuscules no earlier than the tenth century, became an important constituent of the *Textus Receptus.* Little was accomplished in Paris by Simon de Colines and Robert Estienne (Stephanus), mid-sixteenth century, beyond correcting Erasmus's text by means of Ximenes's and a few late MSS. Beza's editions in Geneva show no improvement on Estienne in spite of possession of the MS. which bears his name (D). In 1624 the brothers Elzevir in Leiden reproduced Beza, and the name *Textus Receptus* became attached to this edition through the bookseller's blurb. It was soon popular and enthroned in scholarship by seven editions; yet, being solidly based on Erasmus, it is little more than the late Byzantine text current in the Orthodox Church after the sack of Constantinople, 1453, and brought to Europe in many copies by refugees. Adulation of a text on the mere ground that it was Greek did, however, incite the scholars of the Counter-Reformation to get to work on the Vulgate and the resulting standard edition produced in 1592 under Clement VIII. checked the spread of corruptions.

The ascendancy of *Textus Receptus*, printed but less respected as more MSS. were collated, lasted until 1831. Versions and Fathers were examined and consequently the manuscript material was divided into groups. John Fell made some advance in 1660 when he put the collations of a hundred MSS. and of early versions (Bohairic and Gothic) in an *apparatus criticus*. John Mill (1645–1707) improved on this, with nearly thirty thousand variants and even ventured to correct the *Textus Receptus* in thirty-one places. It was R. Bentley's bold and far-sighted plan (1662–1742), which he abandoned, to edit the text of the fourth century from Greek and Latin MSS.

The sixth-century Codex Alexandrinus had been presented to England in 1627, and the Greek text behind fifth-century Codex Ephraemi Rescriptus was discovered about 1700. But even in 1734 J. A. Bengel kept largely to the received text, while attempting to classify MSS. into families, tribes and nations, and to weigh them rather than count them. The lead was followed by J. S. Semler and J. J. Griesbach who saw that even our oldest MSS. were the result of recensions—Western, Alexandrian, and Constantinopolitan. J. L. Hug followed, dating the degeneration about A.D. 250 and naming the recensions: Origen's (Palestine), Hesychius's, Lucian's.

From K. Lachmann (1831) until Hort there was an increasing tendency to base editions on the oldest uncials, neglecting the Western text— mistaken, but it dethroned the *Textus Receptus*. L. F. K. Tischendorf first made available the fourth-century codices, Vaticanus and Sinaiticus, and his admirable 8th edition follows the latter closely (1869–72). His *apparatus* is still gratefully used, and we are heeding once again his caution that Greek MSS. are better than versions and that a reading which corresponds linguistically with the author's style or with first-century *Koinē* is to be preferred.

(viii) B. F. WESTCOTT AND F. J. A. HORT

The Revised Version was born of discontent with the received text engendered by the accumulated evidence of Lachmann and Tischendorf, and its Greek *Vorlage* owes much to the labour and perspicacity of two English scholars. They gave direction to all subsequent textual study and still Hort's *Introduction* is a standard work. A system of arriving at the original text was carefully evolved from an examination of all available variants, although for their edition they relied mainly on the more ancient MSS.

They observed that in many New Testament passages there are two short forms of reading and one longer form which is something of a combination. The groups of witnesses were approximately: (1) B א L Bohairic, (2) D and older forms of the Latin version, with Old Syriac and Sahidic often changing sides, and (3) all the rest, *e.g.* AC in Gospels, EFKMS, minuscules, and Peshitta. The conflate readings (3) were presumed to be later than the others, especially as they were supported by Fathers not earlier than the fourth century, and in fact most writers from Chrysostom on.

These conflate readings they described as a "Syrian" text-type; this was given the symbol α and it was rejected. Hort supposed that the text-type originated at Antioch with Lucian's recension, was taken to Byzantium, became official in the Orthodox Church and was made the basis of most of the later MSS.; the remaining late MSS., if based on a different text, are corrected by the Byzantine standard but are valuable in the parts not so corrected.

(1) and (2) above were considered "pre-Syrian" types, and (1) was subdivided into a "Neutral" (β) and an "Alexandrian" (γ) type. The term "Neutral" is question-begging but Westcott and Hort thought that the type manifested no special tendency, being basically the primitive text preserved relatively free from all early corruptions, represented mainly by B (except in Paul and Revelation), by א and often by LRTZ 33, Bohairic, Origen, sometimes by Sahidic; and, except in the Gospels, by AC. The "Alexandrian" is found, not in one MS., but in some of the B-MSS. when they differ among themselves and especially when they differ from B, all this being due to slight linguistic corruptions of third-century scholarly copyists of Alexandria.

The "Western" (δ) they considered to be another early text-type, originating in Syria and found everywhere in the second century, but with an unsatisfactory internal character. It had been retouched, and Hort suggested that it owes its peculiarities to second-century scribes who made free with the text by paraphrasing, harmonizing, interpolating for completeness, changing or inserting conjunctions, pronouns, and prepositional phrases. Its many representatives include DEFG, 28, 473 (gosp), 565, Old Latin (especially *k*), syr^{sin}, Sahidic, Irenaeus, Justin, Tertullian, Cyprian, Clement. Hort considered it a fundamentally corrupted text, whatever the merits of individual readings.

The most original part of their work was the formulation of rules to evaluate the four groups. First, they rejected all

Syrian readings, *i.e.* all except Neutral, Alexandrian, or Western. Secondly, they rejected a Western or Alexandrian reading unsupported by Neutral. Thirdly, even some Neutral readings were suspect if unsupported in δ; all the instances except Matt. 27^{49} were in the last three chapters of Luke, but now critics acknowledge a larger number of passages where the Western text-type alone has escaped corruption.

(ix) SEQUEL AND REACTION

Majority opinion still favours the Neutral text but serious defects have been revealed by subsequent study of the pre-third-century Fathers. Rendel Harris and Kenyon did much to commend the " Western " text, and C. H. Turner noted, for instance, that the " Western " readings in Mark show themselves oftentimes peculiarly Markan in language. Minuscules were grouped by Lake and Ferrar into families representing in part very early texts, " family 1 " (1, 118, 131, 209), and " family 13 " (13, 69, 124, 346).

The most controversial names have been H. von Soden and B. H. Streeter. The former's helpers searched the libraries of Europe and the Middle East with the ambition of replacing both Tischendorf's *apparatus* and Hort's critical theories. But even specialists have found von Soden's notation of the documents too tiresome. He seems to have neglected the versions overmuch for modern liking, and his theory that behind the recensions of Hesychius (H), Origen at Caesarea, including the " Western " text (I), and Lucian (K) is an archetype I-H-K which may be recovered by comparing the revised texts with one another and with earlier witnesses, such as the versions and Fathers, is too facile. Corruptions must have entered before this, and we cannot account for them all by the *Diatessarōn's* influence, as von Soden attempted. However, his *apparatus* is particularly useful for its detailed information about minuscules. Moreover, his family grouping has been broadly confirmed.

Streeter's new classification of Gospel MSS. presupposed five large " families " which were the local texts of Alexandria (CL 33 as one branch; Bℵ Sahidic as another), Caesarea (non-Byzantine readings in fam. Θ), Antioch ($syr^{sin, cur}$, syr^{pal} when not Byzantine), Carthage (W^{Mk}, *k*, *e*, Cyprian), Italy-Gaul (D, *a*, *b*, *d*, Tatian, Irenaeus). He conceived the aim of the critic to be the recovery of these primitive texts, outflanking the great recensions of Lucian and Hesychius with the help of versions, Fathers, and later vulgates. They were living Bibles, used in the local churches round the eastern Mediterranean—and the delineation of the Caesarean was Streeter's particular contribution—beside which the text-types of Hort and von

Soden seem like phantom myths. No family is perfect, but the Alexandrian is the best.

Streeter has been significantly modified in detail since 1924, as our survey has shown, and in general we think his local text-types, especially the Caesarean, are too precisely defined. We scruple even to classify MSS. by families, for their texts are mixed. Our method is eclectic when faced with a problem. We are prepared to look everywhere for the right reading in each instance. Great names of individual MSS. and of textual groups no longer constrain us, and in this respect we have travelled far from Hort. Our danger perhaps is that we shall treat the third-century papyri (Chester Beatty and Bodmer) with the same excessive reverence that Hort gave to the fourth-century vellum codices.

Intrinsic probability—the likelihood of harmonization, haplography, dittography—still avails. One variant may account for the rise of the others. It is even more important to know the tendencies of a given scribe or of the text-type to which his MS. belongs. Does he usually abbreviate, expand, correct the grammar? To that extent genealogy is still important. Then, do the linguistic patterns of the New Testament author help us to decide the intrinsic probability?

As to external criticisms of a reading, we are trying to classify variants according to the text-types which have already been identified, and to pay heed to the age and quality of the text-type rather than the age of the MS. itself.

In short, our aim today is to take each variant in turn and enquire its age and amplitude of diffusion, as well as its attestation among the witnesses. In the rare situation where we suspect that every single witness exhibits an error which occurred before the oldest attainable text-type, we will have recourse to textual emendation (*e.g.* John 19^{29}, 1 Pet. 3^{19}?).

(x.) PRESENT AND FUTURE EDITIONS

A desiderated critical tool is a comprehensive *apparatus criticus*. The text itself should be the *Textus Receptus* or the Byzantine, with which the bulk of MSS. agree, to reveal more clearly the older text-types which differ from it; but the *apparatus* must be full. Such an undertaking was the Oxford edition by S. C. E. Legg in which Mark and Matthew appeared (1935, 1940), but it refers to only six papyri! Its incompleteness and inaccuracy have been studiously criticized (*JTS*, xliii., 1942, pp. 30–34, 83–92; *Classical Philology*, xxxiii., 1938, pp. 112–15), and yet it meets a need. Failing that, one must enlist von Soden and Tischendorf. Of the other editions, Souter's is inadequate, and the deficiencies of each of the pocket editions will have to be supplied from the others:

(1) J. M. Bover, S.J. (4th ed., 1959), (2) A. Merk, S.J. (7th ed., 1951)—von Soden's sigla and classification at present, but this is to be simplified, (3) H. J. Vogels (3rd ed., 1949–50)—good for Syriac and Latin, (4) British and Foreign Bible Society (G. D. Kilpatrick, 1958; a new edition preparing), (5) Stuttgart (E. Nestle and K. Aland, 24th ed., 1960)—more detailed in *apparatus*. Even so, the picture is incomplete. Perhaps the Stuttgart is best, especially as in the present editions each variant is being checked with the MS. itself by a committee of collators, and as many as fifty-five papyri were used in the 23rd ed. The 24th, mainly a reprint of the 23rd but utilizing p^{66} and p^{72}, with a new collation of codex C, has appeared, but the 25th, a large and completely new edition to mark the 150th anniversary of the *Bibelanstalt* of Württemberg, had been promised for 1962.

Eventually the need for a comprehensive *apparatus* may be met by members of the International Greek New Testament project which was formed in 1948 to collect and check variants from MSS., versions, and quotations in the Fathers. The *Textus Receptus* will be the text, and all papyri, uncials, and three hundred minuscules, many lectionaries, all versions made before A.D. 1000, and a store of Patristic quotations will be used for the *apparatus*, beginning with Luke. Its realization would promote the construction of an eclectic text in which all might repose their trust.

Less ambitious is the projected Greek text of the American Bible Society, National Bible Society of Scotland, and the Württemberg *Bibelanstalt*, begun in 1956, to be based on Westcott-Hort, supplemented from Tischendorf, von Soden, Bover, Merk, Vogels, and Nestle-Aland, with an *apparatus* which is to be confined to variants of exegetical importance—with Bible translators especially in mind. In such passages exclusively it will provide a full *apparatus*.

Meanwhile fresh material is discovered, the old is reassessed, the versions are being critically edited. Theories are propounded. And the end of textual criticism is not even in sight.

BIBLIOGRAPHY

B. F. Westcott and F. J. A. Hort, *The New Testament in Greek, II. Introduction*, 1896.

K. Lake, *The Text of the New Testament*, 6th ed., 1928.

A. Vaganay, *An Introduction to the Textual Criticism of the New Testament* (Eng. tr.), 1937.

A. F. J. Klijn, *A Survey of the Researches into the Western Text of Gospels and Acts*, 1949.

A. F. J. Klijn, " A Survey . . .", in *Novum Testamentum*, iii., 1959, pp. 1–27, 161–73 (the above brought up to date).
M. M. Parvis and A. P. Wikgren, *New Testament Manuscript Studies*, 1950.
F. G. Kenyon, *Our Bible and the Ancient Manuscripts*, 5th ed., revised by A. W. Adams, 1958.
F. G. Kenyon, *The Text of the Greek Bible* (revised), 1949.
G. Zuntz, *The Text of the Epistles*, 1953.
A. Souter, *The Text and Canon of the New Testament*, 2nd ed., edited by C. S. C. Williams, 1954.
A. Vööbus, *Early Versions of the New Testament* (Papers of Estonian Theol. Soc. in Exile, No. 6), 1954.
Vincent Taylor, *The Text of the New Testament*, 1961.

PART II

THE LAND AND THE PEOPLE

VIII. THE GEOGRAPHY OF PALESTINE

BY DENIS BALY

(i) THE PHYSICAL FEATURES

THE word Palestine is derived from the Philistines, a people who occupied part of the coast plain south of the Carmel headland during much of the Old Testament period. The name is often applied to the territory covered by the present countries of Israel and Jordan, though it has also been used for both a larger and a smaller area than this. In order to understand Biblical history it is necessary to consider the whole region of the Levant Coast, that is to say the section of the Mediterranean coast extending from the southern border of modern Turkey to the north-eastern corner of the Sinai peninsula. Structurally this forms the edge of the great Archaean block of Arabia, which underlies the whole area, and is exposed in the extreme south of Palestine on either side of the Gulf of 'Aqaba. To the north of this block are the mountain ranges and the high inter-montane plateaux of Anatolia and Persia. The convulsions which brought these mountains into being during the Alpine mountain-building period also fractured the resistant Archaean block of Arabia, and produced the great rift valley which runs parallel to the whole length of the Levant Coast. This rift valley is part of an enormous system of rifts extending along the Red Sea and through the lakes of East Africa into Nyasaland; and on either side of these rifts the tendency was for the land to be pushed up into block mountains, which together with the rift valleys form the dominant structural characteristic of the Levant coastal region.

It is customary to divide the whole area into four very clearly recognizable north-south strips: the *Coast Plain*, the *Western Highlands*, the *Central Valley*, and the *Eastern Highlands or Plateau*. However, equally important is the transverse division of the region by a series of depressions running inland from west to east. The most northerly of these lies in the vicinity of Antioch and Aleppo, and south of this is the Tripoli-Homs depression. Further south again is the Galilee depression, and finally the Beersheba-Sodom line. There are therefore five major transverse zones: (i) the *Anatolian Piedmont* zone in the extreme north, (ii) the *Hamath* zone, (iii) the *Phoenician-Syrian* zone, (iv) the *Israelite* zone, and (v) the *Edomite* zone, each of these being divided longitudinally into the north-south strips mentioned above. The situation is further complicated by the fact that there are two major tendencies which determine the direction of the structural lines, either N.-S. or NE.-SW. Faulting may develop in either of these directions or else at right angles to them, and so the physical regions of the Levant have been governed by the fact that over the whole area a NE.-SW. rectangular grid has been imposed obliquely upon a N.-S. one. Since beyond question the heart of the Levant is the great central massif of the Lebanon and Anti-Lebanon mountains, both rising to over 9,000 feet, it is necessary to consider first the Phoenician-Syrian transverse zone, and then those to the north and south of it.

1. *The Phoenician-Syrian Zone.* The most striking features of this region are the great height to which it has been elevated, and the very strongly marked NE.-SW. trend of the structural features. So dominant is this tendency, in fact, that it is continued south-westwards into the Galilee depression, where it greatly complicates the landscape, and north-eastwards far beyond the Tripoli-Homs depression into the east of the Hamath zone. Here it may be traced in Jebel Bishri, which approaches the Euphrates not far from the modern Deir ez-Zor.

The coast plain is very narrow and rocky, and the mountains of Lebanon rise almost directly out of the sea. In the centre is the headland of Beirut, the ancient Berytus; to the north lay Byblos and Tripolis (1 Macc. 14[1]), and to the south Sidon and Tyre. The rocky coast with its excellent harbours, the lack of level land for agriculture, and the forbidding mountain barrier of the Lebanon mountains, all combined to force the inhabitants of this region to turn their backs upon Arabia and direct their attention to the West. Throughout history this has always been the most westernized part of the country and in Old Testament times it was the home of the Phoenicians, famous for their maritime empire. The western slopes of the mountains were rich in forests which the Phoenicians exploited, and which were coveted by the rulers of the treeless plains of Egypt and Mesopotamia. As early as the third millennium B.C., in fact, there was a fair-sized Egyptian commercial colony at Byblos.

The interior valley stands at a considerable height above sea-level and in its central section, near Baalbek, it exceeds 3,000 feet. Here rise the two major rivers of the northern half of the Levant, the Orontes and the Litani. The Orontes flows to the north, though its way is blocked by a great dam of volcanic basalt in the Tripoli-Homs gap, causing it to make a big curve to the east before returning to the rift valley in the Ghab. The Litani flows south-westwards along the rift until it makes a sudden turn to the west, and flows out to the Mediterranean just north of Tyre. This central valley is the region known today as the *Beqa'a* and in ancient times as Coele-Syria. Its appearance on the map is deceptive, for it would appear to offer an opportunity for communication between the north and the south, and to be more open to the east than to the west, since the Anti-Lebanon mountains are broken by the valley of the Abana, while the Lebanon range is an unbreached barrier. Of course, all three entrances to the Beqa'a were used continually, but they are none of them easy and the valley remained curiously isolated, and more often under the influence of the dwellers on the coast than of Damascus (Judg. 18[7]). In the north movement was difficult because of the basalt dam, and even more so in the south where the terrain is thoroughly confused by the crossing of the two structural patterns ; in the east as well the valley of the Abana is narrow and precipitous. Moreover, despite the limitations of rainfall behind the climatic barrier of the Lebanon the way of life is Mediterranean rather than that of the steppe, with which Damascus is more intimately concerned.

The two great mountain walls dominate the region, and when they are covered with snow in winter can be seen for a tremendous distance. The Anti-Lebanon do not reach quite the height of the Lebanon, and are divided into two blocks by the Abana gap. South of the gap is Mount Hermon, rising to over 9,000 feet and towering above the low-lying Huleh basin to the south-west of it. To the north of the gap the mountain ridges splay out like the fingers of a hand, and it is this fact which helps to channel all the routes from the north towards the city of Damascus, which in many senses is the key to the Levant, and claims to be the oldest continuously occupied city in the world. It stands at a position in which there must be a city if there are men at all, for not only do all the routes come together at this point, but also it has an admirable water supply. This is particularly important in that the surrounding region is semi-desert or dry steppe, for the huge double barrier between Damascus and the sea has meant that rainfall in the vicinity averages less than the eight inches necessary for agriculture. However, thanks especially to the Abana (the modern Barada) Damascus is the centre of a magnificent oasis, the Ghouta, famous throughout the Levant for the quality and variety of its fruit. Chief of the routes from the north, which collect at this historic city is the great Trunk Road, coming southwards from Hamath and swinging round the eastern edges of the Anti-Lebanon. The road opens out again towards the south of Damascus, the Trunk Road leading south-westwards into Galilee, while other important roads continue directly southwards across the plateau of Bashan.

2. *The Galilee Depression.* This is a very complex area, since here the imposition of one grid upon another is particularly evident. The line of the Anti-Lebanon mountains is continued south-westwards in the uplifted plateau of Upper Galilee, but it is cut by two important lines of structural weakness. One of these runs at right-angles to it, from north-west to south-east, and may be traced from Sidon on the Mediterranean coast to the Wadi Sirhan far to the south-east in what is now Saudi Arabia. It is this line which forms the sudden end to the Lebanon and Anti-Lebanon mountains, and has created the tiny plain of Merj Ayoun (the Biblical Plain of Ijon). It is followed today by the Trans-Arabian Pipeline. Parallel to it farther south is the line which marks the southern end of Galilee, and can be clearly seen in the lowland corridor which leads from Accho to Beth-shan, and in the precipitous slope of the Carmel ridge which overlooks it on the south-western side. The same line of the Mount Carmel fault may be traced farther to the south-east in the rift valley of the Wadi Fari'a, which leads down from Tirzah to the Jordan at Adam, and even beyond into the Plains of Moab, where the eastern plateau edge is recessed by faulting at the north-eastern corner of the Dead Sea.

This region of Galilee is complicated by the presence of the great north-south rift valley which extends through the whole length of Palestine proper and may be traced far to the north in the headland of Beirut, and by the west-east faults which lie at right-angles to this. The most northerly of these is the steep gorge by which the River Litani flows from the central valley of the Beqa'a to the sea, but not far south of it, in the latitude of Tyre, is the transverse step, over a thousand feet in height, which separates the Plain of Ijon in the north from the Huleh basin to the south. Here was the territory of Dan, an outpost of the Israelite territory, and here on the northern frontier of Israel were the three cult centres of Abel-beth-maacah, Dan and Caesarea Philippi, where one of the sources of the Jordan gushes out in a tremendous spring. This basin was remote and isolated, both by reason of the high plateaux which enclose it on the west and east, and because of the impenetrable marshes which cover the valley floor. Only with difficulty does a road make its way southwards from Abel-beth-maacah along the foot of the Galilean plateau on the west, but south of Lake Huleh near Hazor it is joined by the Trunk Road which crosses the Jordan at the Bridge of Jacob's Daughters, a little south of the Lake.

Somewhat farther to the south again, in the latitude of Accho, is another major transverse fault marking the northern boundary of the normal Israelite territory. To the north of this fault is the high plateau of Upper Galilee, some 3,000 feet above sea-level, and in Biblical times forested and inaccessible. The village of Merom, it is true, stood on the edge of this great scarp, but the Waters of Merom, where the battle took place (Josh. 11[7]) must refer to the point where the Trunk Road crosses the Wadi Lemmun, flowing down from Merom to the Lake of Galilee. Even in the New Testament "Galilee" refers exclusively to Lower Galilee in the south. Where this faultline crosses the central rift valley there is a huge basalt dam, which greatly impedes the passage of the river. On this mass of black basalt, overlooking the waters of the Lake, stood Chorazin, "exalted to heaven," but destined to be cast down to Hell (Luke 10[13]).

Galilee proper lay south of the fault scarp in what is known today as Lower Galilee. Here the coast plain remains no more than five miles in width, but the western highlands form a low plateau, less than 1,500 feet in height and much dissected by transverse fault basins. This is a fertile and attractive region, in which the three staples of Israelite life, wheat and grapes and olives, can be grown in profusion, and in the New Testament period it carried a heavy traffic of fish from the Lake and grain from Bashan to the port of Ptolemais, the Old Testament Accho. Nazareth, the home of Jesus, stands on the edge of the hills overlooking the Accho–Beth-shan corridor, though in His day it can have been no more than a village. The Lake of Galilee, which was the scene of most of His ministry, occupies the Central Rift Valley, and only on the north-western side is there a small area of level land, the Plain of Gennesaret. Here the Trunk Road left the lakeside at the town of Magdala and climbed up on to the plateau by way of the Valley of the Robbers and the Horns of Hattin, later the site of Saladin's victory over the Crusaders. The Lake itself is only twelve miles long by about five miles wide, and its surface is some 600 feet below sea-level. The warmth of the winter climate in this region, and the presence of a number of hot springs, suggest a reason for the high proportion of invalids indicated in the Gospel accounts of Jesus' work here.

Beyond the Lake is the broad plateau of Bashan, standing mainly about 2,000 feet above the level of the sea, and interrupted by the deep valley of the Yarmuq, which marks a continuation of the west-east faulting which is characteristic of this section of the country. The plateau itself is broad and fertile, famous in history both for its wealth of cattle and the richness of its grain. However, it is singularly exposed to invasion and every Biblical account of fighting in this region is a record of an army sweeping almost unopposed across the level plain. Farther to the east still are the volcanic mountains of Jebel Druze, which are only part of a vast outflow of basalt extending to the north-west and south-east of them. The difficulty of the terrain has made this a region of refuge and isolation, known in the New Testament as Trachonitis, and the home today of the secret sect of the Druzes.

The Accho–Beth-shan corridor, which forms the most southerly part of the Galilee Depression, has played a continuously important part in the history of the country, for not only does it provide an important lowland route from the Mediterranean to the Jordan Valley and up on to the Eastern Plateau, but it is crossed by the Trunk Road in its passage from Magdala to the Coast Plain south of Carmel. It forms, therefore, a major crossroads in Palestinian commerce, and throughout the Old Testament was one of the two great battlefields of the Jewish people. It may be divided into three clearly recognizable sections: the *Plain of Accho*, the *Plain of Esdraelon*, and the *Valley of Jezreel*. The Valley of Jezreel is the narrow corridor leading down to the Jordan Valley between Mount Moreh on the north and the Mountains of Gilboa on the south. The north-western entrance is held by the town of Jezreel, and the south-eastern entrance by the important fortress of Beth-shan, which stands upon the sudden step by which the valley debouches into the main rift. In New Testament times this city was called Scythopolis, and was the only member of the Decapolis on the western side of the river. The Valley of Jezreel was the scene of Gideon's battle with the Midianites (Judg. $6^{33ff.}$), Saul's defeat by the Philistines (1 Sam. 28^{4}, 31^{1-13}), and Jehu's dramatic drive to seize the throne of Israel (2 Kings 9).

The Plain of Esdraelon in the centre is the widest part of the corridor, and forms a large triangular plain with its base at the foot of the Carmel ridge and its apex near the solitary hill of Mount Tabor, where Barak assembled his army for the defeat of Sisera. The significance of this part of the plain rests in the ineffectiveness of its drainage, for the River Kishon makes its way only with difficulty through the narrow gap in the north-west which leads to the Plain of Asher, and consequently it floods easily, and during the whole winter the plain is water-logged and impassable. However, an important causeway of basalt crosses the plain in a south-westerly direction, and this explains the ancient importance of Megiddo, which stands at a crossroads, controlling this causeway, one of the four passes across the Carmel ridge, and the road from Accho to Beth-shan, as it hugs the foot of Carmel between the forests of the hill country and the marshes of the plain.

3. *The Israelite Zone.* This is the section of the country lying between Mount Carmel and the Beersheba Depression, and is the real core of the Israelite territory. Here the structure is very much simpler, for the north-south direction is dominant and the division into the four north-south strips is very evident. However, the NE.-SW. tendency is also present, and has been responsible for a broad uplifted area extending from the Hebron district north-eastwards into Gilead. This long, cigar-shaped " dome " has been sharply interrupted by the Jordan Rift Valley, and is not immediately apparent on most general maps of the country, but it is important structurally, for it is responsible for three significant geographical features : (i) the greater height of the Judaean and Gilead regions, both of which exceed 3,000 feet, (ii) the narrow " waist " in the centre of the Jordan Valley, dividing the better-watered northern part from the desert section to the south, and (iii) the structural difference between the northern and southern sections of the Western Highlands.

It is often stated that there was no geographical difference between the northern and southern kingdoms in ancient Israel, but this is untrue, for not only does this canting of the main line of highlands towards the north-east mean that different rocks predominate in the two kingdoms, but there is also an important line of weakness striking almost due eastwards across the country immediately north of Jerusalem, and this has played a major part in separating the two districts. We must, therefore, distinguish a northern and southern section separated by this line of weakness, which we may call the " Zone of Movement." However, before considering these sections two points need to be made : (i) both sections exhibit a very similar general pattern, that is to say a broad coast plain, a strip of western highlands, a deep rift valley well below sea-level, and an eastern plateau which is everywhere higher than the western highlands ; (ii) there are three major rocks of the highland areas, the *Cenomanian limestone,* with above it the *Senonian chalk,* and above that again the *Eocene limestone.* Both limestones tend to stand up as highlands, but the Cenomanian is characterized by more precipitous slopes than the Eocene, and it breaks down, moreover, into a very fertile soil, the *terra rossa,* whereas the Eocene is relatively infertile and consequently unproductive. The Senonian chalk is usually a narrow outcrop, except on the western side of the Dead Sea, and it is everywhere extremely porous and infertile. It is very easily eroded into smooth, low-lying valleys, which have provided the roads along which the Palestinian traffic throughout the centuries has moved.

(a) *The Northern Section.* The core of this section lies in the Western Highlands, which must again be divided into two parts. To the south is the high dome of Ephraim, entirely formed of Cenomanian limestone, which means that in consequence it was steep-sided, forested and well-defended. When the forests were cleared the fertile soil lent itself to the development of extensive olive groves. To the north, however, is Manasseh, which has a basin-like structure, in the centre of which the less attractive Eocene limestone forms the two prominent hills of Ebal and Gerizim, with Shechem guarding the cleft between them. Within the rim of the basin there are many chalk valleys, and so, in distinction from Ephraim, Manasseh was ill-defended and accessible. She was tempted, as a result, to expand until she controlled all the approaches and could feel secure. The lack of a strong defensive centre also meant that there was no obvious capital (both Shechem and Tirzah having proved unsatisfactory) until Omri fortified the hitherto unoccupied hill of Samaria.

The coast plain here is the region known as *Sharon,* which in Old Testament times was thickly forested and very often marshy. Although today it is drained and famous for the rich orange groves, it was then almost completely uninhabited and a barrier to movement, the Trunk Road from the Carmel passes hugging the foothills as far south as the great spring of Aphek. On the other side of the hill country an easy route led down from Tirzah by the Wadi Far'a to the Jordan Valley at Adam, where also the Jabbok joins it from the highland of Gilead on the eastern side. Here the plateau has been considerably uplifted in a domelike structure in which again Cenomanian limestone is the predominant rock, with, in consequence, a forested rocky landscape not unlike that of Ephraim. It is the only part of the eastern plateau where the three Israelite products of wheat, grapes and olives can all be easily grown, and it was at an early stage absorbed by Manasseh.

(b) *The Zone of Movement.* This is a line of enormous strategic importance because here fault valleys cutting back into the steep mountain slopes provide easy access to the highlands. That on the west is the Valley of Aijalon, or the Ascent of Beth-horon, the Achilles' heel of the Judaean defences, by which every major attack was made upon the kingdom, and along which both Joshua and Jonathan are reported to have made dramatic pursuits of their enemies. On the opposite side of the highlands are the valleys leading down to Jericho and to an important ford across the Jordan. The ascent to the eastern plateau is facilitated by the embayment in the plateau edge known as the Plains of Moab. From this it is possible to make one's way through Heshbon to Rabbath Ammon, which commands the headwaters of the River Jabbok.

(c) *The Southern Section.* The coast plain here is the country of the Philistines, a region of increasing drought in which the chief crop was barley. Freed from the necessity of avoiding the marshes, the Trunk Road in this section of the country follows the coast and passes through the three Philistine coastal towns of Ashkelon, Ashdod, and Gaza, whence it continues along the coast to Egypt through the desert of Sinai. This is "the Way of the Philistines," which the Israelites avoided after their escape from Pharaoh, and was the main trade route between Egypt and the north. The two other main Philistine towns were Gath and Ekron which guarded the eastern frontier of the Philistine territory. This lay on the edge of the Shephelah, a rough hilly section which lies between the coast plain and the Western Highlands, from which it is divided by a narrow but important moat of Senonian chalk. The Shephelah is formed of Eocene limestone, and contrary to most reports, is not fertile or attractive, and can never at any time have supported a large population. Its importance was essentially strategic for it lay between the Philistines and the people of Judah, and was coveted by both of them as a defensive apron in advance of their own territory. It is crossed by several broad valleys, one of which is the Valley of Elah, which was the scene of the contest between David and Goliath, and was guarded by the strong fortress of Libnah. Another, rather further north, is the Valley of Sorek, the scene of many of Samson's exploits. The Senonian "moat" is a narrow valley lying at the foot of the steep slopes of the Judaean hills, and greatly assisting their defence. An important road ran down it, and it is marked by a line of towns which receive frequent mention in the Old Testament, Azekah, Timnah, Beth-shemesh, Lachish, etc. Together with the Shephelah it formed a region apart, and those who were "wanted" by the authorities often took refuge in these towns, knowing that if the government should pursue them, it would not be difficult to slip over into the protection of the Philistine territory.

The Judaean highlands are well defended not only on their western slopes but on the east as well, for here a broad expanse of the porous chalk has combined with the drought natural to the eastern slopes to produce a sudden desolation which is difficult to imagine. This is Jeshimon, or the Wilderness of Judaea, which starts almost immediately after the crest of the highland has been passed, and has never been inhabited at any time in history, save by those who would flee society, whether for reasons of faith or from political necessity. On the top of the plateau is the territory of Judah, less rich than any of the other highland regions west of the Jordan, but better protected than any of them. Its natural centre has always been Hebron, which commands an important but difficult route leading down to Engedi on the Dead Sea, and another which leads up from Lachish to the west. However, after the capture of Jebus by David Hebron had to take a second place to Jerusalem, which lies to the north on the edge of the territory of Benjamin and of the strategic Zone of Movement. Jerusalem holds a strongly fortified position on the very edge of Jeshimon and was more central to the country as a whole and more in touch with international trade than was Hebron. However, after the division of the country, it was dangerously close also to the main line of attack, which always came by way of the Valley of Aijalon, and as a result it was besieged again and again in the course of its history.

The Central Rift Valley is here entirely occupied by the Dead Sea, the most saline body of water in the world, whose surface is 1,300 feet below the level of the Mediterranean, and whose greatest depth is 1,300 feet below that again. The valley walls climb up steeply out of the sea on either side for over four thousand feet, that on the east being considerably higher. On the eastern side the slopes are especially precipitous, though they are cleft at one point by the great canyon of the Arnon, and in the south-east are sufficiently recessed to leave a fertile little plain between the mountains and the sea. This is watered at its southern end by the River Zered coming down through another of the eastern canyons, and since the Dead Sea is very shallow south of the Lisan Peninsula, it seems reasonable to look here for Sodom and Gomorrah, and the region which was held to have been once like the " garden of the Lord." It must be admitted, however, that there is as yet not one jot of evidence in support of this, or any other, theory of the site of the Cities of the Plain. The western shore of the Sea is much drier, though there is one very important spring at Engedi, not far from which stood the grim fortress of Masada, and along this shore caravans made their way southward to the copper mines of the Arabah. At the south-western corner of the sea is Jebel Usdum, a vast hill of rock salt, which tradition has inevitably associated with the name of Lot's wife.

The plateau to the east of the Dead Sea was the ancient territory of Moab, a huge level plain rising steadily towards the south and cut in two by the Arnon canyon, on the northern edge of which stood the town of Dibon. The chief fortress of Moab was Kir-hareseth, the modern Kerak, which holds an extremely strong position in the higher southern section where it can command the route up from the Lisan Peninsula and the Dead Sea. It is remarkable today for the ruins of a gigantic Crusaders' castle.

4. *The Beersheba-Sodom Line.* This has been responsible for the broad valley in which Beersheba lies, the shape of the southern end of the Dead Sea, and the direction taken by the canyon of the Zered. It will be recollected that the traditional description of the country was "from Dan to Beersheba," and west of the Central Rift this is the southern limit of the normally settled country.

5. *The Edomite Zone.* South of the Beersheba-Sodom line a striking change takes place in the relative heights of the two sides of the Central Rift. On the east the plateau, though interrupted by the Zered fault, continues to rise until the whole plateau edge is more than 5,000 feet above the level of the sea, but to the west, in the region of the Negeb, the crest of the hills touches 2,000 feet only in places, and is sometimes below 1,500. Not until the Egyptian border does it again attain 3,000 feet. This has meant that the Mediterranean storms, increasingly rare here in the south, pass easily across the uplands, where the average rainfall is less than eight inches, but are forced to deposit their moisture of the towering scarp of the Eastern Plateau. It is true that this does not average much above sixteen inches, and soon dies away to the east, but it was sufficient for a narrow line of villages and even for woodland, which was still worth cutting in World War I. Consequently, here stood the kingdom of Edom, and here in New Testament times was the even more important kingdom of the Nabataeans, with its capital in the fabulous city of Petra, and frequently in history the people of this exalted plateau were strong enough to dominate the Negeb Uplands to the west.

At the foot of the plateau is the Central Rift Valley, which climbs southward from the Dead Sea until in its central section the valley floor stands more than 1,000 feet above sea-level. Then it descends again to the Red Sea port of Ezion-geber, once believed to have been the site of an important copper industry in the time of Solomon, though this now appears not to have been the case. Copper, however, was important in the Arabah, being mined in the Nubian sandstone which underlies the Cenomanian limestone, and is exposed mainly on the eastern side. Here the main centre was Punon, probably the place where occurred the incident of Moses and the brazen serpent.

The Negeb Uplands to the west may be divided into three unequal sections. The main backbone of the Negeb follows once again a NE.-SW. line, and on the seaward side of it we may distinguish an arid coast plain, much blocked with drifting sand, and the gentle western slopes, where some cultivation was possible, though with care and difficulty. The main Nabataean and Byzantine sites, *e.g.* Subeita and Abda, occupied positions on these slopes. To the south-east of the backbone, however, the land drops down to the Arabah in a fantastic and desolate region, with the *buttes* and *mesas* which are so characteristic of a desert landscape, and sharply plunging strata, such as those which mark the Ascent of the Scorpions near Kurnab. In the centre the uplands are cleft by the great sickle-shaped depression known as Wadi Murra. This forms an important pass across the hills, and has been followed throughout history by a much used caravan route, which is known to the Bedouin today as *Darb es-Sultan*.

The transverse zones which lie north of the Lebanon Massif may be dealt with more rapidly, since they lie outside the true Israelite territory. They are :

6. *The Tripoli-Homs Depression.* This is a very extensive line of weakness, which may be traced through Palmyra to the east of Mari (where it is followed for some miles by the Euphrates) and even into the mountain ranges which mark the edge of Persia. It has been of immense importance for trade, as the names of the towns already mentioned indicate, and where it crosses the NE.-SW. line of the Anti-Lebanon–Jebel Bishri hills the gap was controlled by the town of Hazar-enan. At the entrance to the Beqa'a from this depression stood the two towns of Riblah, where Pharaah Necho had his camp in 609 B.C., and Qarqar, where the Assyrian advance was checked in 853 B.C. In the plateau region the depression is reinforced on the northern side by the hills of Jebel Buweida and Jebel Bishri, and it seems to have formed an effective frontier between the better watered Hamath steppe and the more arid plateau of Damascus. The effectiveness of this division between the two ways of life can be seen today in the fact that the "beehive dwellings" which are so characteristic of the Hamath steppe are not found to the south of the Palmyra depression. In the Old Testament period some of the more expansive political thinkers in Israel appear to have thought of this line as the proper northern frontier for the Israelite dominions, and there is more than one reference to this in the Old Testament writings.

7. *The Hamath Zone.* The dominant region in this part of the country is undoubtedly the Eastern Plateau, which, as we have already seen, is divided from the Plateau of Damascus farther south by the combined barrier of the Jebel Buweida-Bishri line and the prolongation of the Tripoli-Homs-Palmyra Depression. This deflection of the Eastern Highlands has left the Central Rift Valley without a clearly defined eastern wall,

and the plateau on this side only occasionally rises above 1,500 feet. On the western side of the rift, however, the Nuseiriyeh mountains rise sharply for as much as 3,000 feet above the valley floor, and their precipitous, forested slopes formed a very important barrier to movement between the plateau and the coast. This was reinforced by the nature of the Ghab itself, for it is excessively marshy, and even now has not been properly drained. The coastal region, therefore, tended to be a region apart, but in the north, where the valley of the Wadi Kabir makes possible a route round the northern end of the mountains, there was the important coastal site of Ugarit.

8. *The Antioch-Aleppo Depression.* With the near approach to the Anatolian mountains the structure once more becomes confused. The Ghab and the Nuseiriyeh mountains just described follow a generally N.-S. line, but here the NE.-SW. line reasserts itself in the Amanus and Casius mountains, with a narrow rift valley between them. They are really the beginning of the true folded mountains of Anatolia, and continue in fact the line of the mountain ranges of Cyprus. The pattern is complicated, however, by the west-east depression which runs across them and may be traced through Antioch, Aleppo and the course of the Euphrates, which here flows in an eastward direction. This stretch of generally lower-lying land is sometimes known as the "Syrian Saddle," and has always been of great commercial and military importance. The near approach of the Euphrates to the coast (a distance of no more than 40 miles), the greater and more assured rainfall of the north, the access by the Cilician Gates to the Anatolian Plateau, have all made this northern region into a great route centre, Aleppo having today taken the place of the ancient Antioch. The Trunk Road followed the Euphrates northward to the very foot of the mountains before swinging southward through Hamath and Hazar-enan to Damascus, and here in the far north is Carchemish, the scene of the decisive battle which marked the final defeat of the great Assyrian empire.

9. *The Anatolian Piedmont Zone.* Carchemish lies at the very foot of the mountains, where the Euphrates valley opens out into the plain. Here the river is flowing almost due south, and parallel to it is the Balikh, which joins the Euphrates after it has swung eastwards along the Aleppo Depression. This is the region of Aram Naharaim (Aram of the Two Rivers), or Paddan-aram, which was the ancient homeland of the family of Abraham.

(ii) THE CLIMATE

The climate of the Levant is in a sense the result of a conflict between the desert and the sea. During the winter months the major wind belts of the world are shifted southward, following the apparent movement of the sun, and this brings the whole Mediterranean region within the area of cyclonic rains. During the summer months, however, the northward shift of the wind belts permits the influence of the deserts to extend further north, and the summer climate is therefore one of drought. The summer season is characterized by extreme regularity, starting in the middle of May and ending about the middle of September. The absence of rain dries up the vegetation, and the land becomes increasingly parched and dusty. Close to the sea a sea-breeze develops regularly every day at about nine in the morning, and during the course of the day it builds up enough strength to extend far into the interior. It is a very steady wind, and is used by the farmer for winnowing his grain. It greatly moderates the effect of the summer heat, and causes a heavy dew on the coast and the seaward slopes of the highlands, providing valuable additional moisture, which helps to swell the grapes.

At each end of the summer, marking the change to and from the rainy season, are two brief transitional seasons, each lasting no more than about six weeks, but of great importance, because it is during the course of these two six-week periods that the dreaded *sirocco* may blow. This is a very hot, and excessively dry, wind blowing off the desert, and notorious in the Biblical literature for the destruction it may cause to the vegetation, especially during the spring. It is too gusty to be used for winnowing, and curiously exhausting to the energy and irritating to the nerves, " a hot wind from the bare heights in the desert toward the daughter of my people, not to winnow or cleanse " (Jer. 4^{11}). The closer to the desert one is, the more severe are the effects.

The first rains of winter may occur as early as the first week in October, or be postponed until the beginning of January, and this uncertainty distinguishes the winter season from the regularity of the summer. Not only is the farmer left guessing each year in what month the vitally needed rain will begin, but also where it will begin. The first storms are often convectional as the damp air moves in over the still superheated land, and sudden torrential thunderstorms may develop, with all the limitation in area which characterizes such phenomena. " One field would be rained upon, and the field on which it did not rain withered ; so two or three cities wandered to one city to drink water, and were not satisfied " (Am. 4^{7}). Moreover, once the rain has begun, its distribution is still not certain. During a very good year there will be a storm lasting about three days, occurring with surprising regularity every week, but in a bad year, the passage of the cyclones along the

Mediterranean trough may be interrupted by high pressures forming over the European peninsulas, and there may be no rain for as long as a month or six weeks. This can sometimes be quite disastrous for the farmer, who is left in continuous doubt, from the beginning of the season till its end, whether he will or will not have a sufficient harvest.

It is upon the rain that the whole life of the Levant depends, for irrigation from rivers is possible only in a few places, and "the land which you are entering to take possession of it is not like the land of Egypt, from which you have come, where you sowed your seed and watered it with your foot, like a garden of vegetables; but the land which you are going over to possess is a land of hills and valleys, which drinks water by the rain from heaven" (Deut. $11^{10\text{-}11}$). Consequently, the urgent necessity of rain, and the rejoicing when it does come, are constantly reflected in the Old Testament. The "former and the latter rains," which are mentioned so frequently, are probably not merely the beginning and end of the rainy season, as most commentators suggest, but those uncovenanted mercies, an exceptionally early storm in October or an exceptionally late rain just before the harvest in April, for only when the rainfall is unusually extended and very regular in distribution throughout the year is it possible for the harvest to be a truly bumper one.

The winters are not cold on the coast, where snow is a quite exceptional event, but they can be icy on the higher land, especially on the Eastern Plateau, where the wind can be like a whetted knife, even when the sun is shining brightly. Snow persists throughout the winter on the Lebanon and Anti-Lebanon mountains, and for most of the winter on the Jebel Druze. It occurs almost every year on the higher parts of the Eastern Plateau, even as far south as Edom, but less often west of the Jordan, where the moderating effect of the sea is more apparent. Nevertheless, an occasional fall of snow is not uncommon in Jerusalem, and there may be a heavy snowstorm about once every five or ten years.

The rain is usually torrential, and the gentle rain characteristic of much of Western Europe is unknown. Hail is common, particularly on the Coast Plain, and can often do serious damage to crops, especially if it comes late in the year.

The varieties of climate found in the different parts of the country depend upon certain quite simple, but very nearly absolute, rules: (*a*) Rainfall increases both in amount and certainty towards the north, where the summer drought is shorter, and the attainment of the yearly average more assured, than it is in the south. (*b*) Rainfall decreases towards the east, and the eastern side of any hill or mountain is in a marked rain-shadow. This may be seen especially clearly in the Central Rift Valley and the Damascus area behind the Anti-Lebanon mountains. It should be noticed that evaporation is greater on the southern side of any hill, and so the northern and western sides, even of a mere hillock, have a noticeably denser vegetation. (*c*) Temperature decreases with elevation, but this may be somewhat modified by the fact that the temperature range increases with distance from the sea. Consequently, places on the Eastern Plateau may often have higher daily maxima than places 3,000 feet below them on the Coast Plain. It is therefore possible to distinguish the following climatic regions :—

(i) *The Phoenician Coast Type.* The winters are mild and wet, and the rain is not only torrential in character, but often prolonged, so that a week, or even two weeks, of continuous rain is possible. The summers are hot and very humid, for the Coast Plain is narrow and enclosed by high mountains, especially in the south round Sidon and Byblos, and the period without rain may be as short as two months in the north. The region is protected from the fury of the siroccos by the barrier of the mountains.

(ii) *The Sharon Coast Type,* characteristic of the coast of the modern state of Israel. The decrease in rainfall is very marked, for the summer drought lasts for at least five months, and the winter storms seldom continue for more than three days, bringing continuous rain on the first two days and intermittent squalls on the third. Naturally, the rain continues to decrease towards the south, and beyond Gaza the climate could properly be classed as desert. Along the whole coast the winters are usually mild, although snow has been known to fall on very rare occasions (*e.g.* February 1950), and the summers are hot and rather humid. The temperature is moderated in summer by the strong sea-breeze, and the humidity rapidly declines as one proceeds inland.

(iii) *The Lebanon Mountain Type,* characteristic of the Lebanon and Anti-Lebanon mountains, and in a modified form of the Nuseiriyeh mountains and the Jebel Druze. The summers are cool, with very heavy dew near the coast, but the winters are very cold, and are marked by heavy falls of snow. On the Lebanon mountains the snow is thick enough for the establishment in the modern era of ski resorts, and the highest passes are closed in winter.

(iv) *The Israelite Hill Type,* characteristic of the Western Highlands south of the Central Massif, and of the edge of the Trans-jordan Plateau. The winters are still cold, and there is often frost at night during the coldest period, which fortunately is fairly brief. However, the sun is warm, and out of the wind the temperature during the day can be very agreeable. In summer the days are hot, but the effect of this is moderated by the dryness of the atmosphere and the fairly constant wind, while the summer nights are cool or even chilly. The rainy days in winter can be very unpleasant, since they are always accompanied by very strong winds. Rainfall everywhere (except only on the eastward slopes) is above 16 inches, and at Jerusalem it averages 25 inches, which is about the same as the average for London. However, Jerusalem has only about fifty rainy days in the year, and so when the rain does fall it is very heavy.

(v) *The Hamath Steppe Type,* characteristic of the region north of Jebel Buweida. This is transitional between the climate of the Mediterranean and that of the desert, the rainfall for the year averaging between 10 and 20 inches. This is sufficient for agriculture, but pastoral farming is also common. The winters are surprisingly cold because the plateau is exposed to the bitter winds from the interior of Arabia, and the summers are hot.

(vi) *The Syrian Steppe Type,* characteristic of the Damascus region, and a zone lying between the edge of the Eastern Plateau and the desert. Rainfall here is less than it is in the Hamath zone and averages about eight inches, which is barely sufficient for agriculture. Moreover, the farther south one goes the less assured is the rainfall, and so this region is essentially pastoral. As in the previous region there is a large temperature range between summer and winter. The western section of the Negeb Uplands may be said to fall into this type, though there is a heavier dew.

(vii) *The Arabian Desert Type.* This lies east of the steppe and extends as far north as the Jebel Buweida line. In the south it sweeps round to the west as far as the ridge of the Negeb Uplands (and in Sinai to the sea), while in the Central Rift Valley it extends a long tongue northwards as far as the narrow Jordan "waist." The Wilderness of Judaea is also to be included in this type. It is a "tame" desert, with a certain amount of rain each year, usually coming in brief storms at the beginning and end of the winter, though in a good year there will be showers throughout the winter season. In such a year the rich carpet of flowers extending far into the desert has to be seen to be believed. The rain is often very limited in area, and the nomadic pastoral system depends upon man's ability to go with his animals to where the rain has fallen. There is, as may be expected, a considerable temperature range.

It should be noticed that the area of effective agriculture is very narrow, and does not normally extend more than fifty miles from the coast, exceeding this only in the north and in the Jebel Druze region. It is the greater rainfall of the north, and the fact that the Euphrates here approaches closest to the sea, that has produced the vitally important link between Mesopotamia and the Levant Coast, and directed the course of the great Trunk Road. Really plentiful rainfall, that is to say an average of over thirty inches a year, is found only in the northern coastal regions and the northern mountains, though Upper Galilee, and the higher parts of Ephraim and Gilead also surpass this figure.

(iii) THE CLIMATE AND THE WAY OF LIFE

The way of life adopted by any group is the response to the total environment within which the group lives, and it is a mistake to assume, as many scholars have done, that the physical features alone constitute the "geography" of an area. Thus, it is important to recognize that the four tremendous canyons which cleave the Trans-jordan Plateau (the Yarmuq, the Jabbok, the Arnon, and the Zered) are not necessarily the barriers to movement which they appear to be, only the Zered in fact having formed a constant political frontier between Moab to the north and Edom to the south. The northern frontier of Moab coincided with the Arnon only during periods of Moabite weakness, and normally extended beyond it to the beginning of the Gilead Dome. Gilead itself was divided by the Jabbok canyon, just as Bashan was divided by that of the Yarmuq. Consequently, it is necessary to distinguish four regions on the Trans-jordan Plateau, the limits of which are determined not by the river canyons, but by the extent to which the particular way of life was possible. Thus the flat plateau of Bashan in the north, with its adequate winter rainfall, and its fertile volcanic soil, was agricultural, and the way of life may be described as that of the farmer. The principal product was wheat, the region being less suited to the growth of olives and vines. All three, however, may be grown on the Gilead Dome, which in this respect may be compared to the highlands west of the Jordan. Here the hilly character of the landscape and the denser forest cover meant that wheat could be cultivated only in relatively small patches, and the villager produced in addition the olives and vines which are the agricultural equivalents of the trees and shrubs so characteristic of Gilead. This is the only part of the Eastern Plateau in which these two staples are at home.

The south-westerly direction of the dome structure has meant that Gilead extends in an ever-narrowing segment south of the Jabbok as far as the north-eastern corner of the Dead Sea, where it comes to an end. Here the possibility of the Gilead way of life also comes to an end, and its place is taken by the pastoral farming more suited to the great open spaces of Moab and Ammon, where the rainfall is much more precarious than on the somewhat similar level plateau of Bashan. Old Testament terminology appears to distinguish three different regional names for this part of the plateau: the broad level plateau itself is known as the *Mishor,* but the *Pisgah* is the sharp edge to the plateau on the west, as it drops away suddenly to the Central Rift Valley and the Dead Sea. The *Abarim* on the other hand signifies the edge of the rift north of the Dead Sea, where it forms the edge, not of the plateau, but of the southward extension of Gilead. There is not here the sharp distinction between the flat plateau surface and the precipitous scarp, and though the fault scarp is still very evident, the region is both more hilly and more accidented. This is also apparently the region which the Romans knew as *Peraea.*

The plateau rises steadily towards the south, and so a long tongue of better watered land extends southward along the plateau edge. Beyond the Zered canyon the elevation is more than 5,000 feet above sea-level, and settlement is confined to a very narrow line along this edge. This was a region apart in which people dwelt in clefts in the rocks (Obad. [3]). They were unable to live from their agriculture, or from the huge flocks of sheep which roamed the Moabite plateau, and so they became traders rather than farmers or herdsmen. Their wealth came from the copper mines at the foot of the scarp, and from their control of the trade-routes leading to southern Arabia. In this they were followed by the Nabataeans, who, after an interval of some 300 years, succeeded them in the same region. It was their interest in trade that gave the inhabitants of these highlands so often control over the Negeb farther west, though in point of distance the Negeb was closer to Judah than it was to Edom.

West of the Jordan similar distinctions may be drawn, for it seems to be true that Israelite colonization was confined to those hilly regions in which it was possible to produce wheat, olives, and vines together, and to descend from these hills was for the Israelites to encounter an alien culture in a foreign land. They could, it is true, manage to make a small down-faulted plain among the mountains part of their agricultural system, and the largest of these plains that they conquered and settled was the triangular plain of Esdraelon. Any plain, however, which was bounded on even one side by some feature other than mountains they could not incorporate, and it remained in consequence outside their effective colonization. This explains their inability to bring the Coast Plain properly within their orbit during the Old Testament period, and the failure to extend outwards from Gilead on the Eastern Plateau.

They might, admittedly, extend their empire temporarily for political and strategic reasons, but they never colonized such areas, and as a result they never managed to hold on to them.

This explains also the role of the Shephelah, which is rocky and infertile, and unsuited either to the Israelite system of cultivating wheat and olives and vines together, or to the open barley fields of the Philistine territory. The Shephelah, therefore, became the property of neither side, and though the Philistines and the people of Judah constantly overran this region, it could never be incorporated fully into either one system or the other.

It is probable that similar differences are reflected in the various tribal territories. Each tribe seems to have gradually absorbed land to the extent of that type of agriculture to which it was accustomed, and the various tribal areas could be recognized by the modifications, rendered necessary by the environment, in the general wheat-olives-grapes pattern. Thus, on the plateau of Judah where, because of its southern position, the rainfall is less assured, forest tends to give way to scrub, and olives therefore to the vine, which is here the dominant member of the trio. Further north, however, on the great Cenomanian dome of Ephraim, with its rich *terra rossa*, olive groves are to be found in abundance, and the olive now takes the place of the vine in importance. Further north still the Eocene hills of Manasseh offer less possibility for either vines or olives, but the down-faulted basins floored with fertile alluvium are admirably suited to the production of wheat, which here takes the lead. The farmer knows exactly where one type of agriculture ends and another begins, and so it was always possible for him to say whether a village, which was in the control of one of the stronger tribes, did in fact belong to that tribe, or whether it formed part of another type of terrain (Josh. 17[11]).

BIBLIOGRAPHY

Denis Baly, *The Geography of the Bible*, 1957.
F.-M. Abel, *Géographie de la Palestine*, 2 vols., 1933.
M. du Buit, *Géographie de la Terre Sainte*, 2 vols., 1958.
W. B. Fisher, *The Middle East*, 4th ed., 1961.
G. A. Smith, *The Historical Geography of the Holy Land*, 25th ed., 1931.
The following Bible Atlases will be found valuable :
G. E. Wright and F. V. Filson, *The Westminister Historical Atlas to the Bible*, revised edition, 1956.
L. H. Grollenberg, *Atlas of the Bible*, Eng. trans., 1956.
E. G. Kraeling, *Rand McNally Bible Atlas*, 1956.
P. Lemaire and D. Baldi, *Atlas Biblique*, French trans., 1960.
H. G. May, *Oxford Bible Atlas*, 1962.

IX. THE BACKGROUND OF THE BIBLE

(A) ISRAEL'S NEIGHBOURS

By C. J. Mullo Weir

Palestine was dominated, politically and culturally, in Biblical times, first by Egypt and then successively by Assyria, Babylonia, and Persia. Much more is known of them than of Israel's nearer neighbours whose cultural and political influence, although not negligible, were less important.

Genesis places the cradle of civilization in Mesopotamia, the valleys of the Tigris and Euphrates, and here written records begin—after a succession of village and small urban cultures going back to before 5000 B.C.—with the Sumerians, a people of agglutinative speech who immigrated into South Babylonia (Sumer), probably from the east, shortly before 3000 B.C., mingling with the earlier inhabitants and with successive waves of Semitic (Akkadian)-speaking immigrants from the Arabian steppes who settled chiefly in North Babylonia (Akkad). The Sumerians maintained a complex system of drainage and irrigation canals, created a large number of city states each under a priest-king and introduced a form of picture-writing which developed gradually into the cuneiform scripts of Babylonia and Assyria. Their culture was the foundation of later Mesopotamian civilizations.

Earlier attempts at leadership (*c.* 2600–2350 B.C.), especially by the cities of Kish, Ur, Lagash, and Umma, were ended by Sargon I. who founded in Akkad a Semitic dynasty (the Old Akkadian) which rapidly extended its control from the Persian Gulf to the borders of Anatolia but was displaced *c.* 2250 B.C. by the Gutians, uncultured invaders from the plateau of Iran to the east. Sumerian dominion was restored *c.* 2100 B.C. by Dynasty III of Ur, when art and letters reached their climax, but their rule was finally extinguished when, *c.* 1950 B.C., Semitic Amorites from the north-west and Elamites, Iranian plainsmen from the head of the Persian Gulf, overran Babylonia.

Sumerian historical records (chiefly votive and building inscriptions), business documents—inventories, accounts, contracts, etc.—and fragments of three law-codes (one in Akkadian) reveal an agricultural and pastoral economy in which theoretically the land belonged to the gods, the people being their servants and the king and priests their officials, but in course of time much of the land passed to the crown and to private owners. The king was commander of the citizen-army, legislator and chief judge, but his primary duty was to secure the fertility of the soil by managing the canal-system and by performing the due religious rites including the celebration of stated seasonal festivals. Rivers and canals were also used for internal communication and for foreign trade in metals and semi-precious stones. Owing to scarcity of building-stone almost all constructions were of mud-brick, baked or sun-dried. High city-walls whose gates were shut at night enclosed narrow streets of small, windowless houses consisting of one or more open courts surrounded by living-rooms. Overlooking the scene were the temples, tall brick buildings, sometimes painted, standing on brick platforms, sometimes with a temple-tower (*ziqqurat*) of two or more tiers. Surrounding the shrine with its altar and divine image were storerooms and accommodation for the priests. The temples also served as banks, record offices, and centres of learning and art. Among the numerous classes of priests were singers, diviners, and exorcists; priestesses included wailers and temple-prostitutes. Priestly scribes compiled hymns, prayers, laments, wise sayings, fables, and mythological poems. Artistic skill, usually with a practical aim, was exemplified in relief-carvings on stone stelae, plaques or cylinder seals, chiefly of religious, military, and ceremonial scenes, and in statues, mosaics, frescoes, metal-chasing, and jewellery.

Although every city had its patron-god, often pastoral or agricultural, other deities also had temples or chapels, their status varying with the political situation. Most are known only by name but universally worshipped were An (Akkadian Anu), sky-god of Uruk (Erech), Enlil, wind-god of Nippur (a major cult-centre but never a political capital), Enki (Ea), water-god of Eridu, Utu (also Babbar), sun-god of Larsa and Sippar, Nanna, moon-god of Ur, and Inanna (Akkadian Ishtar), identified with the planet Venus and worshipped as earth and fertility goddess in conjunction with Dumuzi (Tammuz) whose annual death and rebirth were celebrated in myth and ritual. Incantations and magic were used extensively, both nationally and on behalf of private persons, to remove calamities such as sickness which were attributed to the actions of angered gods, demons, ghosts or witches. The supernatural inspired fear and uncertainty rather than joy and the future life was regarded as a cheerless existence in a gloomy, dusty underworld where all were equal.

Civilization developed a little later and more slowly in Egypt, but by 3000 B.C. a series of agricultural communities settled in small towns and villages, after combining into two kingdoms, one in the Nile delta (Lower Egypt), the other in the long, narrow river valley to the south (Upper Egypt), united under one king. All later pharaohs used the double title of king of Upper and Lower Egypt and wore a double crown. Although the two areas were dissimilar—the Delta being more open to European and Asiatic cultural impacts and having a different mixture of races—the Nile, whose fructifying but potentially destructive annual flood required control, made a single strong government a practical need. The great fertility of the soil and the isolation by environing deserts made the Egyptians cheerful, optimistic, lazily tolerant of differing local customs and beliefs, indisposed to changes and contemptuous of neighbouring peoples with inferior achievements and advantages. Punitive raids had to be conducted regularly against Asiatics to the east, semi-nomadic Libyan coastal tribes to the west and negroid peoples in the upper Nile valley but these produced a supply of slaves and mercenaries and the inflow of foreign commodities by tribute and trade. Egyptian policy was to assume possession of Nubia (Cush) but merely to exact obedience and tribute from Palestine, Phoenicia, and Syria. No serious attempt was made to Egyptianize Asiatic territories (where Semitic and Mesopotamian patterns continued to predominate) but continuous trading by sea with Phoenician coastal towns led to their partial Egyptianization and to some diffusion of Egyptian culture, chiefly artistic, into Palestine, Syria and Anatolia.

Egyptian history, distributed over thirty-one so-called Dynasties (*c.* 2800–30 B.C.), is conventionally arranged into an Old, a Middle and a New Kingdom, with two Intermediate Periods of foreign and internal political weakness, followed, after *c.* 1100 B.C., by a Late Dynastic Period of almost uninterrupted decline ending in temporary, then final, loss of independence.

Under the Old Kingdom (Dynasties III–VI, *c.* 2800–2200 B.C.) the fiction was established that the king was an incarnation of the supreme god Re and a vast part of the country's resources in wealth and labour was employed in erecting monumental royal tombs which evolved from mastabas through step-pyramids to true pyramids, the largest arising during Dynasty IV; but in the two succeeding Dynasties royal power was so encroached upon by the priesthood and local governors that the indiscipline and disorders of the First Intermediate Period ensued. Prosperity revived under the Middle Kingdom (Dynasties XI-XII, *c.* 2000–1700 B.C.), centred near Memphis, when expeditions against Nubia, Libya, Palestine, and Syria were resumed but during the Second Intermediate Period invaders from Palestine, mostly Semitic but sometimes led by Hurrians using swift war-chariots, occupied Egypt under rulers known as Hyksos ("rulers of foreign lands") with Avaris in the Delta as their capital until expelled by Dynasty XVIII which founded the New Kingdom (*c.* 1600–1100 B.C.) based on Thebes. Thutmosis I. (*c.* 1520 B.C.) penetrated to the Euphrates and Thutmosis III. (*c.* 1450 B.C.) beyond it, Egyptian residents and garrisons being posted in selected Palestinian and Syrian towns to keep the peace and exact tribute while non-aggression treaties were concluded with the major powers—Hittites, Mitannians, Assyrians, and Babylonians. The situation is elucidated by the Amarna letters written in Akkadian by Asiatic kings and princelings to Amenophis III. (*c.* 1405–1367 B.C.) and Amenophis IV. (*c.* 1367–1350 B.C.). The latter, who changed his name to Akhenaton, was the heretic-king who imposed on Egypt a form of solar monotheism which was discarded soon after his death. Dynasty XVIII ended in confusion *c.* 1314 B.C. but Dynasty XIX reasserted Egyptian power in Palestine. Rameses II., defeated at Qadesh in Syria by the Hittites, negotiated a treaty securing to himself Palestine, South Syria, and South Phoenicia. His successor, Merneptah (*c.* 1234–1224 B.C.) had to chastise Israelites in Palestine and to beat off raids of Sea Peoples from the eastern Mediterranean. By *c.* 1200 B.C. incursions of Sea Peoples had settled the Philistines on the Palestine coast and destroyed the Hittite empire in Anatolia. By *c.* 1100 B.C. the Egyptians had vacated Asia and the New Kingdom came to an end. Thereafter the land was torn by dissension with changing dynasties, sometimes foreign (Libyan or Ethiopian). Shoshenq I. (Shishak, Dynasty XXII) raided Judah, *c.* 925 B.C., after Solomon's death, and a later pharaoh withstood Sennacherib in Hezekiah's reign, but between 674 B.C. and 671 B.C. Esarhaddon of Assyria conquered and occupied Egypt. Psammetichus I. (663–609 B.C.) of Dynasty XXVI regained independence, reigning at Sais, but Necho II. (609–594 B.C.), advancing into Asia on the fall of the Assyrian empire, was defeated by Nebuchadrezzar at Carchemish on the Euphrates and, like Apries (Hophra, 588–568 B.C.), had to abandon the defence of Palestine. The reign of Amasis (568–526 B.C.) was peaceful but Cambyses of Persia conquered Egypt in 525 B.C. from Psammetichus III. and Persian dominion continued, except from 404–343 B.C., until Alexander the Great of Macedon won Egypt in 332 B.C. His successors, the Ptolemies, ruled until it became a Roman province in 30 B.C.

The bulk of Egyptian literature, inscribed in ink on papyrus, is lost, but tomb-inscriptions, royal annals, narratives such as those of Sinuhe and Wenamon and fanciful tales like The

Shipwrecked Sailor furnish valuable historical, geographical, and psychological information. Besides hymns, prayers and rituals there are maxims, soliloquies on the evils of life, letters, and some fine love poetry. The absence of law-codes is partly atoned for by accounts of legal processes. Science is poorly represented by word-lists and astronomical, mathematical, and medical texts. Reminiscent of Old Testament passages are part of the Tale of the Two Brothers (cf. Gen. 39^{7-19}), a hymn to the Sun-god (cf. Ps. 104), and the Instruction of Amenemopet (cf. Prov. 22^{17}–23^{11}).

Daily life in town and country is illustrated by frescoes and reliefs in mastabas, pyramids, and rock-tombs. Painted wooden models, furniture, and other funerary articles supplement the picture which is one of prosperity, elegance, and contentment. Houses had an outer court leading through a central hall to the more intimate apartments; temples, built of stone, followed a similar arrangement, with embellishments such as avenues of sphinxes, obelisks, and lofty pylons and columns sometimes engraved with ceremonial and battle scenes, including interesting representations of foreign peoples. Memorial statues of kings and notables reproduce personal features and qualities; exquisite taste is displayed in ornaments and jewellery.

Religion concentrated mainly on the future life conceived as a more blissful continuation of the present; bodies were mummified so that the soul could return from time to time. The dead were believed to undergo a trial before Osiris, so magic formulas to ensure a favourable verdict were inscribed on the walls of early tombs and were eventually collected into the so-called "Book of the Dead" deposited with the mummy; it includes a repudiation ("negative confession") of sins which throws light on Egyptian ethical ideas.

Of the innumerable deities, the chief were the sun-gods Amon, Re, and Horus, with Ptah the Creator. Although conceived in human fashion, some were represented in animal or partly animal form—a survival from prehistoric times when certain animals were worshipped. Attempts to arrange the gods in order of precedence resulted in rival theologies which existed side by side. Akhenaton's endeavour to abolish the worship of all gods except Aten (symbolized by a solar disk) had no chance of permanent success in view of the popularity of tutelary household gods like Bes and Tueris and the hostility of the powerful organized priesthoods of Thebes, Memphis, and Heliopolis. The statutory daily worship included, besides hymns, bathing and dressing the statue of the temple god and offering food before it. On certain festivals images were carried in procession; sometimes ritual dramas were enacted. Magic and exorcism played a large part in popular religious practice. An amazing variety of mythological themes, often mutually contradictory, is found in funerary texts, including divergent accounts of Creation and of the future life. The most interesting myth was that of Osiris (a vegetation-god), slain by Seth (representing the summer sun) but bewailed and resurrected by his sister Isis to become king of the dead.

In Mesopotamia, the elimination of Sumerian rule was soon followed by the emergence of two rival Semitic states, Assyria in the north (with its capital at Ashur on the Tigris) and Babylonia in the south (based at Babylon on the Euphrates). Both spoke Akkadian and they shared a common culture derived from the Sumerians but Babylonia possessed a strong Amorite and, from *c.* 1100 B.C., also a decided Aramaean, racial infusion while the Assyrians had an extensive admixture of non-Semitic Hurrian blood. The harsher climate, poorer soil, and more disturbed frontiers made the Assyrians tougher, more aggressive and more cruel than their Babylonian brothers.

At the time of the fall of Ur, Ashur, although maintaining trading colonies on the borders of Anatolia, was of little significance. New Semitic arrivals, Amorites, from the desert, had recently formed towns along the Euphrates, to the west, the most powerful being Mari. The conquerors of Ur were Elamites who occupied Larsa and Amorites who settled in Isin and at about 1900 B.C. these towns, with Eshnunna in eastern Babylonia, dominated the scene. At about 1800 B.C. an Amorite king, Shamshi-Adad I., ruled at Ashur and made Mari an Assyrian dependency, but *c.* 1750 B.C. Hammurabi, sixth king of the hitherto unimportant Amorite town of Babylon, possessed himself in turn of Isin, Larsa, Eshnunna, and finally Mari (recently emancipated from Ashur). Assyria also fell within his sphere of control but regained independence when, *c.* 1600 B.C., after a destructive Hittite long-distance raid on Babylon, the Kassites, an Iranian people with an Aryan aristocracy, established themselves as rulers of Babylonia until *c.* 1150 B.C. Hurrians were now infiltrating into northern and north-western Mesopotamia and a Hurrian state, Mitanni, on the upper Euphrates, gained ascendancy over Assyria in the fifteenth century, but its destruction by the Hittites *c.* 1350 B.C. enabled Ashur-uballit I. to rebuild a strong state which negotiated on equal terms with the Hittites, Babylonians, and Egyptians. In the following centuries wars were waged continually, in the name of the national god, Ashur, against mountain-peoples of Iran, the Caucasus, and Armenia, and there were frequent border conflicts with Babylonia, usually to Assyrian advantage. The main force, however, was more and more directed to the west where Aramaean tribes settling in the upper Euphrates valley astride the Assyrian trade-routes were ravaged by the thirteenth-century monarchs Adad-nirari I., Shalmaneser I., and Tukulti-Ninurta I., and especially by Tiglath-pileser I. who, *c.* 1100 B.C., exacted tribute as far as the Mediterranean. Babylonia was less fortunate ; Aramaeans—particularly, in the south, Chaldaeans—flooded in to become a considerable part of the population.

Assyria was weak for most of the tenth century but Ashurnazirpal (883–858 B.C.), most ruthless of Assyrian kings, resumed the conquest of the west. Shalmaneser III. (858–823 B.C.) was checked at Qarqar in north Syria (853 B.C.) by a coalition led by Damascus and including Ahab of Israel, but returned to receive tribute in Jehu's reign. Succeeding Assyrian kings were occupied on other frontiers but Tiglath-pileser III. (744–726 B.C.), in spite of wars with Urartu (Ararat, later Armenia) now at the height of its power, and with Babylonia (which he finally annexed), decided to pacify the west by interchanging conquered populations and subdued south Syria, Ammon, Moab, Edom, the Philistines, Israel, and Judah. Damascus was destroyed in 732 B.C. ; Samaria, besieged by Shalmaneser V. (726–722 B.C.), fell to Sargon II. (721–705 B.C.). After quelling a revolt in Babylonia by Merodach-Baladan II., a Chaldaean usurper who with Elamite help held out for twelve years, Sargon subjugated the arch-enemy, Urartu, weakened by attacks of Cimmerians from the north. Sennacherib (704–681 B.C.), who made Nineveh his capital, put down several revolts in Babylonia, fomented by Merodach-Baladan and the Elamites, before razing Babylon to the ground in 689 B.C. The west, instigated by Merodach-Baladan and Egypt, had rebelled and in 701 B.C. Sennacherib pacified Phoenicia and overcame an alliance of Hezekiah with Ammon, Moab, and Edom ; he then marched to the Egyptian border but withdrew and was later assassinated in his own country. Esarhaddon (680–668 B.C.) rebuilt Babylon and after repelling attacks of Medes and Cimmerians in the north and destroying Sidon invaded Egypt and, defeating Tirhakah, made it an Assyrian province. It recovered its freedom, by a revolt, from Ashurbanipal (668–626 B.C.), whose later years were occupied by wars with the Elamites and with his brother Shamash-shum-ukin who had asserted Babylonian independence. He regained control of Babylon in 648 B.C. and destroyed Elam in 639 B.C. It is from his library at Nineveh that most extant Assyrian literary works have been recovered. His death seems to have been followed by throne-disputes between Sin-sharra-ishkun, Ashur-etil-ilani and Sin-shum-lishir. Nabopolassar, a Chaldaean, seized the Babylonian throne in 626 B.C., founding the Chaldaean or New Babylonian empire, and

Cyaxares the Mede, in alliance with him, sacked Ashur (614 B.C.), then Nineveh (612 B.C.), and, pursuing Ashur-uballit II., the last Assyrian king, to the west, destroyed the Assyrian army in 606 B.C. The Medes fell heir to the northern part of the empire, the Babylonians to the southern. Necho II. of Egypt, advancing north, was defeated at Carchemish on the Euphrates by Nebuchadrezzar who succeeded his father on the Babylonian throne in the same year (605 B.C.), and after attacking Egypt unsuccessfully occupied Jerusalem in 597 B.C. and destroyed it in 586 B.C. He took Tyre in 572 B.C. Under his long reign (605–561 B.C.) Babylonia prospered, but his successors Amel-Marduk (Evil-merodach), Neriglissar, and Labashi-Marduk, faced internal troubles until Nabonidus, a priest, was chosen king in 555 B.C. By favouring the god Sin and by absenting himself for several years at Tema (Teman) fighting the Arabians, leaving Babylon to the care of his son Belshazzar, he offended the Babylonian priests and people who surrendered the city to Cyrus the Persian in 539 B.C. Nabonidus was exiled ; Babylonia became a Persian province.

The Old Babylonian period is particularly well documented by official letters from Mari and Babylon, legal and business documents, and the juridical code of Hammurabi whose prescriptions often resemble in form and content Sumerian, Old and Middle Assyrian, Hittite, Neo-Babylonian and Old Testament laws. Society consisted of three strata—patricians, commoners, and slaves. Marriage was normally monogamous (with concubinage) and either party could divorce. Children were often adopted where there was no heir ; slaves could, like women, hold and administer property ; legal penalties included money compensation graded according to the social rank of those involved. To this period belong the composition, from Sumerian sources, of the Creation Epic (*enuma elish*) and the Epic of Gilgamesh (with its Flood legend, prototype of the Hebrew) and Akkadian adaptations of Sumerian myths such as the Descent of Ishtar (Inanna) to the Underworld. Assyrian historical annals give detailed information about the whole of western Asia. Great collections, in named and numbered series, of lexical, mathematical, astronomical, medical, and, especially, religious texts witness to the industry of the priests. Hymns, penitential prayers, and rituals often recall Old Testament passages. Wisdom literature includes fables, proverbs, and complaints about the misfortunes of the pious. The gloomy Sumerian beliefs about the future life and the malign power of demons, ghosts, and witches persisted and vast collections were made of omens (from celestial phenomena, animal livers, etc.) to predict the future and of apotropaic ceremonies to avert evils, especially sickness ; symbolic and sympathetic magic play a large part, *e.g.* the substitution of an image for a witch or of an animal for a sick man. Besides Anu, Enlil, and Ea, the sun and moon gods Shamash and Sin enjoyed superior status, but supremacy was accorded to the national deities, Marduk (Bel) in Babylonia and Ashur in Assyria. Conspicuous also were Nabu (Nebo, god of wisdom and writing), Adad (Amorite weather-god), Ninurta (a war-god), Ishtar (now also a war-goddess), and Tammuz. The New Year (spring) festival at Babylon included the recitation of *enuma elish,* a drama of the death and resurrection of Marduk and a procession of images ; the king relinquished the royal insignia and received them back from the high priest ; atoning sacrifices were made for the nation ; the gods were believed to decree the fates for the coming year. In Assyria, stone was used for monumental human-headed animal colossi at palace gates and for wall-friezes portraying in relief battle, hunting, and religious scenes. Mythological topics and formal designs appeared in wall-paintings and on engraved cylinder-seals. Relief bronzes, coloured tiles and jewellery (including amulets) were among minor artistic products.

The terms " Canaanites " and " Amorites " are often applied indiscriminately in the Old Testament to all non-Israelite Semitic inhabitants of Palestine, but sometimes they distinguish those of the plains (coastal and Jordan) from those of the mountains. Modern scholars use the terms (largely in accordance with ancient extra-Biblical usage) to differentiate two successive waves of Semites who emerged from the desert into settled lands—the Canaanites in and before the third millennium, the Amorites about the beginning of the second. A third wave, the Aramaean, appeared late in the second. The word " Amorite " is derived from Amurru (" westland "), an Assyrian geographical term for north-west Mesopotamia and north Syria where Semitic tribes (Amorites) settled, *c.* 2000 B.C., around Mari, Aleppo, and Qatna, and from *c.* 1950 B.C. onwards conquered Babylonia and created disorder in Syria, Palestine, and Transjordan, restricting Canaanite rule to the coastal zone (Phoenicia).

The Phoenicians, mainly Canaanites, occupied a series of independent seaport towns trading with Egypt and the Aegean, the most outstanding early in the second millennium being Gebal (Byblos) and Ugarit (Ras Shamra). Egypt usually exercised political suzerainty down to *c.* 1100 B.C., but Ugarit fell within the Hittite domain from *c.* 1350 B.C. to its destruction by the Sea Peoples a century and a half later. After 1100 B.C. Sidon and then Tyre gained the pre-eminence, protecting their southerly trade-routes by alliances with Israel. Hiram of Tyre provided materials and workmen for Solomon's

Temple and joined in his Red Sea maritime commerce; Jezebel, daughter of Ethbaal of Tyre, married Ahab. The occupation of the northerly trade-routes by Aramaean states forced the Phoenicians to depend more on trading-colonies overseas of which the chief, Carthage, was founded by Tyre *c.* 814 B.C. Assyrian westward penetration from the ninth to the seventh century led to the successive subjugation of Phoenician cities; those with island-fortresses held out longest but Arvad fell in 743 B.C., Sidon in 675 B.C., and Tyre (to Nebuchadrezzar) in 572 B.C.

Phoenician exports were chiefly cedar-wood and purple cloth. Ugarit invented a cuneiform alphabet; Gebal, after introducing semi-pictographic writing, devised (or perfected) the script from which almost all later alphabets are descended. Most Phoenician literature, being written on papyrus, has perished but from Ugarit have been recovered, on clay tablets, fragments of mythological and legendary poetry, besides liturgical, juridical, and commercial texts. Religious texts have often close similarities in motives, structure, and language to Old Testament passages in the poetical and prophetical books and they confirm Biblical descriptions of Canaanite religion. The most important is a mythological poem, probably used in a fertility-ritual, telling how Baal (son of El and god of rain) was slain by Mot (representing the destructive power of the summer sun), but after lamentation by his sister Anat was revived, whereupon fertility returned to the earth. Another theme is his slaughter of Lotan (Leviathan, the dragon of the primeval sea of chaos). The supreme god was El; his wife was Asherah. Other gods and the goddesses Anat and Ashtart (Ashtoreth) also appear. Rites were conducted both in the open air ("high places") and in large temples; the varied temple-personnel included sacred prostitutes. Phoenician art, although basically Semitic, shows pronounced Egyptian and sometimes Aegean traits.

The Amorite invasions of Syria and Palestine were made chiefly in conjunction with other wandering groups—Hurrians and perhaps Hittites, often under Indo-Iranian leadership—who formed part of the Hyksos invaders of Egypt and of the aggressors mentioned in the Amarna letters; wherever they settled in Palestine they mingled with the local populations and adopted Canaanite speech. Documents sometimes refer to them as Hapiru (or Habiru?) which is not an ethnic term but was used all over western Asia to denote stateless persons migrating, peaceably or otherwise, into settled lands; the word seems to be the same as "Hebrew" (and Egyptian 'Apiru). Abraham, Isaac, and Jacob were presumably Amorites (and Hapiru). The Mari texts of *c.* 1750 B.C. mention marauding Benjaminites a title of whose chiefs was *dawidum* (cf. the Hebrew name David).

The Old Testament also refers to Hittites and Horites (perhaps Hurrians). The Hittites were Indo-Europeans who invaded central and eastern Anatolia from the north *c.* 2000 B.C., dispossessing the earlier inhabitants (Hatti). Later, they federated at Hattusas (Boghazköi) under a king and, expanding westwards and southwards, were able under Mursilis I. to sack Babylon *c.* 1600 B.C. They were rivals of the Hurrians and Assyrians and in the fourteenth century peace was preserved with these and with Babylonia and Egypt by treaties (a favourite Hittite device). Their greatest king, Suppiluliumas, crippled Mitannian power *c.* 1350 B.C. and assumed control of North Syria and north Phoenicia. Rameses II. of Egypt was beaten off by Muwatallis at Qadesh *c.* 1290 B.C. and a subsequent treaty with Hattusilis III. confirmed Hittite rule in these territories but by *c.* 1200 B.C. Sea Peoples and other migrating groups from the north and west overwhelmed and destroyed the Hittite empire. Independent " Neo-Hittite " (largely Hurrian) states using a southern Hittite (Luwian) dialect and a " Hittite-hieroglyphic " script continued in north Mesopotamia and North Syria but most, including Ya'diya (Sam'al), Arpad and Hamath, soon became preponderatingly Aramaean with Aramaic speech and religion. Later, they fell one by one to Assyria, among the last being Carchemish (717 B.C.) and Milid (Malatya, 709 B.C.). Hittite culture never became completely unified, several dialects and local cults existing together. Prominent among the numerous deities were Teshub (storm-god), the Assyrian Anu, Enlil, Ea and Ishtar, and the Hurrian goddess Hebat. Assyrian influence is traceable in ritual, magic and divination but disposal of the dead was sometimes by cremation. Subjects of mythological texts include the slaying of a dragon by the storm-god, the disappearance and return of the (vegetation) god Telepinus and parts of a Gilgamesh cycle. Hymns, prayers, and sections of a law-code have also been recovered. Annals (or royal autobiographies) contain apologetic passages, as in the " testament " of Hattusilis I. and the self-justification of Muwatallis. In the Old Testament, " land of the Hittites " and " kings of the Hittites " refer to the Neo-Hittite states but other mentions of Hittites may relate to individuals or small groups who entered Palestine at various times as merchants, mercenaries, or freebooters.

The Hurrians were a mountain-people of agglutinative speech who swarmed gradually southwards from the Caspian region from *c.* 2000 B.C., partly merging with the Akkadians in Assyria, partly forming independent states to the west, notably Mitanni, a feudal monarchy on the Euphrates which, led by Indo-Iranian chiefs using composite bows and horse-drawn two-wheeled chariots, became, soon after 1500 B.C., the most powerful state in western Asia, maintaining treaty relations with its neighbours and with Egypt, until overthrown by the Hittites a century later. Hurrian religion, literature, and art were largely borrowed from Assyria. The chief deities were Kumarbi (sky-god), Teshub (storm-god), and the goddess Hebat, but the pantheon also contained Assyrian deities, such as Ishtar, and the Indo-Iranian gods Mithras, Indra, and Varuna. Only fragments of their literature remain, *e.g.* a myth relating Ishtar's conquest of a dragon and some Gilgamesh poems. Groups of Hurrians participated in the invasions of Palestine in the Hyksos and "Amarna" periods and some Egyptian texts called Palestine Huru; many scholars therefore consider that the Old Testament Horites, Hivites (perhaps a textual corruption for Horites), and possibly Girgashites, Perizzites, and Jebusites may represent isolated Hurrian groups in Palestine.

The Philistines were one of the Sea Peoples who attacked Egypt in the thirteenth and twelfth centuries B.C. Driven off by Rameses II. (*c.* 1198–1166 B.C.) they settled on the coast of Palestine, probably at first as Egyptian mercenaries, their chief cities being Gaza, Ashkelon, Ashdod, Ekron, and Gath. Afterwards they expanded into the Jordan valley (Bethshan) whence David expelled them. They owed their supremacy to the use of iron (as against bronze) weapons. They practised cremation, were perhaps Indo-Europeans, and may have been the destroyers of the Minoan empire in Crete *c.* 1400 B.C.

The migrations of the Aramaeans followed roughly the tracks of the Amorites. Their close associates, the Akhlamu, were raiding Mesopotamia by the fourteenth century and after the fall of the Hittite empire Aramaean tribes poured into the Neo-Hittite lands and established small federations in North Syria and in the Khabur and Euphrates region. These were absorbed by Assyrian kings between the eleventh and the ninth century but the Babylonians could not prevent Aramaean (especially, in the south, Chaldaean) bands from infiltrating into their territories where they formed, as early as the eleventh century, a substantial proportion of the population; an Aramaean, Adad-apla-iddin, attained to the throne of Babylon by *c.* 1070 B.C. and the Neo-Babylonian empire was Chaldaean. In South Syria, Aramaic states such as Zobah, Beth-Rehob, Maacah, Geshur, and Damascus were established by the time of David and some or all paid tribute to him or to Solomon but thereafter Damascus became head of a coalition and was usually successful in its frequent wars with Israel. Ben-Hadad II. co-operated with Ahab against Shalmaneser III. at Qarqar in 853 B.C. and Rezin with Pekah against Tiglath-pileser III. in 735–4 B.C. but Damascus was destroyed in 732 B.C. and Samaria in 721 B.C. The Aramaean states remained, owing to their position on the edge of the desert, poor and uncultured, largely borrowing their religion and art from their neighbours, Mesopotamian and Canaanite. Isolated from one another by mountains or wastelands, they continued small, disunited and intensely nationalistic, mostly worshipping, along with other gods, a local Baal, usually a form of Hadad the rain-god. Surviving documents are confined to a few historical inscriptions, *e.g.* of Ben-Hadad I. of Damascus, Bar-Rekub of Sam'al, and Zakir of Hamath; but Aramaic was extensively used throughout western Asia from the seventh century for commercial purposes and became the diplomatic and business language of the Persian empire in western Asia and Egypt. Important collections of Aramaic papyri (chiefly letters and legal documents) have been found in Egypt of which the most interesting and varied are the Elephantine Papyri (fifth century B.C.) which include the sayings of Ahikar. Later, Aramaic became the vernacular of Syria and Palestine.

South of Damascus lay Ammon, beyond it Moab (east of the Dead Sea), and south of that Edom. All these kingdoms were probably founded early in the thirteenth century by mainly Aramaic tribes who adopted Canaanite speech. Edom was important for its copper-mines, but all controlled caravan routes. The Israelites frequently fought them with varying success until the closing years of the monarchy. In the fourth century the Edomites were driven by Nabataean Arabs into southern Judah and John Hyrcanus, the Hasmonaean king, forced them to accept Judaism in 109 B.C. Herod the Great was of Edomite (Idumaean) origin. The Moabite Stone was set up by Mesha, a contemporary of Ahab. Chemosh was the chief god of Moab, Milcom that of Ammon.

Almost nothing is known of the Midianite and Amalekite bedouin (Ishmaelite) tribes who harried Palestine and Transjordan from the east and south. The Kenizzites coalesced with Judah; the Jerahmeelites and Kenites had friendly relations with them.

The Medes and Persians were closely associated Indo-Iranian (Aryan) peoples from the Caspian area. The Medes were a constant menace to Assyria and Urartu during the seventh century B.C. in whose closing years Cyaxares, in alliance with Babylonia, destroyed the Assyrian empire, the Medes receiving its northern territories as their reward; he was unsuccessful in an attack on Lydia in Anatolia. The Persians, who had moved south into central Iran, were under Median suzerainty but *c.* 550 B.C. their king Cyrus II. (afterwards "the Great") of the Achaemenid dynasty deposed Astyages of Media and in 546 B.C. conquered Lydia. In 539 B.C. he made himself master of Babylonia without a battle, and the Babylonian dominions, including Palestine, devolved to Persia. The success of Cyrus was in great part due to his tolerance in preserving and protecting local customs and religions; in Babylonia he proclaimed Marduk as his patron and he allowed displaced Jews to return to Palestine. His son, Cambyses II. (530–522 B.C.) conquered Egypt. Darius I. (522–486 B.C.), after overcoming Gaumata, a usurper, and suppressing widespread revolts, organized the empire into a number of satrapies connected by arterial roads. Ruling as an autocrat, he maintained supervision over the satraps by resident secretaries and travelling inspectors responsible to himself. In Europe, the Greeks defeated Darius at Marathon (490 B.C.) and his successor, Xerxes I., at Salamis (480 B.C.). Nehemiah visited Jerusalem under Artaxerxes I. (465–424 B.C.); Ezra did so probably under Artaxerxes II. (404–358 B.C.); but the empire was already in decline owing to the weakness of the central government. Alexander the Great of Macedon invaded Asia Minor with his Greeks in 334 B.C. and after defeating Darius III. occupied Palestine and Egypt before marching to Iran to enter into possession of the rest of the Persian empire in 331 B.C.

Persian religion was polytheistic with nature deities such as Mithras (sun-god), but at some time between 1000 B.C. and 600 B.C. Zarathustra (Zoroaster) preached an ethical monotheism with Ahura-mazda as sole god and with belief in a future divine judgment and a paradise for the righteous. Darius I. worshipped Ahura-mazda with other deities; Xerxes I. may have been a true Zoroastrian. Jewish beliefs about angels and demons perhaps derived something from this religion which was, however, corrupted later into a dualism by its Magian priesthood. Extant Achaemenid literature, apart (perhaps) from early Gathas of the Avesta, is virtually confined to historical inscriptions in Old Persian, Elamite, or Akkadian and letters and business documents in Elamite and Aramaic. Architecture and art were eclectic but based on Mesopotamian.

Asiatic Greece is sometimes referred to in the Old Testament as Javan or as "the isles" but the Hellenistic Asiatic empire which, with its partially Greek culture, replaced the Persian, was the legacy of Alexander the Great. After his death at Babylon in 323 B.C. his empire fell into three parts and there was frequent conflict between the Seleucid kings of Babylonia and the Ptolemies of Egypt. Palestine formed part of the Seleucid province of Syria until 301 B.C. but thereafter usually belonged to Egypt until Antiochus III. regained it in 198 B.C. Antagonism between Judaism and Hellenism led to the Maccabaean revolt (166–165 B.C.) and to subsequent Jewish independence under the Hasmonaean dynasty until the Roman general Pompey annexed the country in 63 B.C.

BIBLIOGRAPHY

The Cambridge Ancient History, 2nd ed., 1924–36.
Sabatino Moscati, *The Face of the Ancient Orient*, 1960.
Georges Contenau, *Everyday Life in Babylon and Assyria*, 1954.
J. H. Breasted, *History of Egypt*, 1906 and reissues.
Adolf Erman, *Life in Ancient Egypt*, Eng. trans. by H. M. Tirard, 1894.
Roger T. O'Callaghan, *Aram-Naharaim* (Analecta Orientalia, 26), 1948.
A. T. Olmstead, *History of the Persian Empire*, 1948.
James B. Pritchard, *Ancient Near Eastern Texts Relating to the Old Testament*, 2nd ed., 1955.
Martin A. Beek, *Atlas of Mesopotamia*, Eng. trans., 1962.

IX. THE BACKGROUND OF THE BIBLE

(B) THE GRAECO-ROMAN WORLD

By H. H. Scullard

Behind the world of the Old Testament stood the older empires of the East, behind the New Testament world was the Roman Empire. The older kingdoms had been nurtured by rivers, the Tigris, Euphrates, and Nile; by contrast the Roman Empire owed its geographical unity essentially to a sea, the Mediterranean, around whose shores a varied but basically homogeneous civilization had developed. Of this Empire Palestine formed a small section at the eastern end of the Mediterranean, but what was thought and done there in New Testament times clearly cannot be fully appreciated unless viewed in the wider context of the larger world of which it formed a part. Why for instance was Joseph affected by "a decree from Caesar Augustus that all the world should be taxed"? Why was a Jew advised to "render unto Caesar the things that are Caesar's"? Why did St. Paul appeal to Caesar by virtue of his possession of Roman citizenship? Some understanding of the Graeco-Roman world is thus obviously necessary for a proper appreciation of the later parts of the Bible.

The Roman Empire was an amalgam of many peoples and traditions, but it comprised essentially two elements, the Latin West and the Greek East. Its political and administrative structure was chiefly the work of Rome, but its culture and thought were to a great extent the gift of Greece, inherited and adapted by the Romans. Thus in the time of Christ the traditions of the East and West had blended sufficiently to enable us to speak of a Graeco-Roman world, whose main features we must shortly examine. But we must first turn to the Hellenistic world in the eastern Mediterranean, into whose political structure the Jews of Palestine found themselves incorporated; their contacts with the Romans followed later.

The political life of classical Greece had rested upon small independent units, city-states, but despite their immense cultural achievements they had failed to live at peace: torn by internal feuds and interstate wars, they had finally succumbed to the external authority of Alexander the Great of

Macedon, who had forced peace and unity upon them. With his overthrow of the Persian empire and his establishment of an empire which stretched from Egypt to North-west India, the ancient world entered upon a new phase, the Hellenistic age, in which the basic political unit was no longer the independent city-state, but the larger national state. After Alexander's death in 323 B.C. his empire was gradually torn asunder by his generals, the Successors (Diadochoi), who in mutual rivalry sought power and territory for themselves. After an era of struggle three monarchies emerged, the Antigonids in Macedon, the Seleucids in Syria, and the Ptolemies in Egypt. Throughout the third century B.C. these kingdoms continued in a precarious balance of power, often at war with one another.

Alexander's conquests changed the face of the ancient world not least because of the resultant spread of Hellenism: Greek colonists and Greek merchants followed closely on the heels of his armies, taking with them their ways of life and thought. Great numbers of Greek settlers were established throughout Asia and Egypt in places of strategic or economic importance. Alexander himself had shown the way and provided a prototype in his greatest colony, Alexandria in Egypt, together with many other Alexandrias as far east as the Jaxartes. The Ptolemies, and still more the Seleucids, followed his lead, creating new military colonies, especially in Asia Minor and Syria. These settlements, when reinforced by Greek civilians and by foreigners, developed into self-governing cities with normal Greek institutions; Greeks alone usually formed the citizen-body, however much the native population might increase, and the official language was Greek. Thus, within the framework of the large Hellenistic monarchies, Hellenism was widely diffused, and political organisation was based on municipal communities which reflected the tradition of the early independent city-states.

This development naturally affected the Jews of Palestine, since many cities on the Greek model were established on its soil, and Judaea thus came to be surrounded by numerous Greek cities. Soon after Alexander's death Palestine fell to Ptolemy and it remained under Egyptian control for the next century. Despite the fact that Egypt and Syria were frequently at war, the Palestinian Jews appear to have enjoyed a period of quiet under Ptolemaic rule, although they had to pay taxes to their overlords: the book of Daniel, by its silence, confirms the absence of serious abuses. In 201 B.C. Antiochus III. (the Great) of Syria started a Fifth Syrian War against Egypt and wrested Coele-Syria (southern Syria) from the Ptolemies; thus Palestine came under Seleucid control. Although treated less favourably than by the Ptolemies, the Jews at first did not suffer seriously until Antiochus IV. Epiphanes, in an attempt to increase the unity and loyalty of all his subjects, began to force Hellenic customs on them, though not without the support of a Hellenizing party within the governing class ("the ungodly") in Judaea itself. In 167 B.C. he occupied Jerusalem and rededicated the Temple of Yahweh to Zeus Olympius ("the abomination that maketh desolate," Dan. 11^{31}). This provoked the revolt led by Judas Maccabaeus, which culminated in the expulsion of the Seleucid garrison by Simon Maccabaeus in 142 B.C. Then for more than half a century his descendants, the Hasmonaeans, ruled Palestine and enlarged its territory, adding Samaria, Idumaea, Galilee, and the Peraea, and converting many of the inhabitants of these districts to Judaism. But this dynasty became unpopular, Alexander Jannaeus (104–76 B.C.) developed into a cruel tyrant, and civil disturbances and religious differences followed. This unhappy period culminated in the protracted quarrel of his two sons, Aristobulus and Hyrcanus, but before this war was fought out a Roman general, Pompey, intervened and reduced Judaea to dependence upon the newly established Roman province of Syria (63 B.C.).

The Jews were not, of course, confined to Palestine. Not all the exiles in Babylon returned to Jerusalem after the Captivity (Jonah, composed probably about 300 B.C., reflects the thought of one of these eastern Jews) and in the Hellenistic period many migrated from Babylon and from Palestine itself all over the eastern Mediterranean. This Dispersion (Diaspora) had started long before the Hellenistic period. In Egypt a colony of Jewish mercenaries had been settled at Elephantine since the seventh century, and Jeremiah (ch. 44) attests a colony at Memphis in his day. Of these Jewish centres in Egypt Alexandria later became the most important; many Jews were settled there by Ptolemy I., and others continued to come to Egypt during the third century when Palestine was included in the realm of the Ptolemies. Other Jews found homes in Asia and Syria: thus Antiochus III. is said to have settled 2,000 families in Lydia and Phrygia. Of this great movement our fullest information refers to the community in Alexandria which by Roman times occupied two-fifths of the city, while the Jews in all Egypt numbered a million. These Egyptian Jews spoke Greek and as they gradually forgot their Semitic speech, their Hebrew Scriptures were translated into Greek (the Septuagint). This adaptation to a Greek environment was facilitated by the lack of racial feelings in the ancient world: anti-Semitism was not rife before Roman times. Culture was the touchstone, and if men of other races acquired Greek ways, they could be accepted. Thus when as a result of Alexander's conquests Greek culture spread widely over the East from Asia Minor to NW. India, men of varied races naturally sought to emulate this new way of life. So when the authors of Maccabees speak of Greeks, they mean Hellenized Syrians, not men of Greek blood. A people as intelligent and industrious as the Jews would readily turn to the culture of its conquerors, not least because that offered a path to co-operation with the governing class. Even among the Jews of Palestine there was a Hellenizing group (led by Jason *c.* 175 B.C.), which was denounced and hated by their more orthodox compatriots, but among the Jews of the Dispersion Hellenization was naturally easier, although the question how deeply or superficially it affected their lives cannot be discussed here. The Jews thus spread and prospered, often encouraged by the Hellenistic kings, and by the first century B.C. most cities in the eastern Mediterranean had their Jewish communities, which began to spread also to the larger centres in the West.

Whether such Jewish communities were full citizens of the Greek cities in which they lived is a question that has been much debated, but on the whole it seems unlikely that they were (*inter alia*, would they have been willing to worship the city gods ?). Individuals of course might be granted citizenship, while all enjoyed considerable privileges. Their private associations for worship, under the "rulers of the synagogues," often received public recognition, while in many cities they were allowed to form corporations (*politeumata*) which gave them semi-autonomy in managing their own internal and religious matters. It may be these *politeumata* that Paul had in mind when he wrote to the Philippians (3^{20}) that "our community (*politeuma*) is in heaven." Thus, for instance, in Alexandria the Jewish community ranked below the Greek citizens, but above both other resident aliens and the unenfranchized native Egyptians who had no civic organization of their own, and in practice, apart from prestige, the difference between Jew and Greek may have been small. Yet despite close political ties, despite much social and economic interaction, and despite even occasional religious imitation (as when in Asia Minor Yahweh was given a Greek name, Theos Hypsistos), nevertheless the great majority of the Jews of the Dispersion still felt their unity which was reflected in their worship of Yahweh and their recognition of Jerusalem as the Holy City to which every pious Jew sent annually his half-shekel for the service of the Temple.

Roman policy towards the Jews, like that of the earlier Hellenistic monarchs, was at first tolerant and even friendly. The first official contact was in 161 B.C. when Judas Maccabaeus, in his struggle for Jewish independence from Syria, appealed to Rome for help. The Roman Senate, hoping to weaken Demetrius of Syria, made an alliance on equal terms with the Jews, but in the event gave them no practical support, and before the next hundred years had passed Judaea lay completely at Rome's mercy. Thus it may be well to glance at the growth of Roman power. By 264 B.C. the Romans dominated all Italy which they had united within the framework of a political confederacy. They then clashed with Carthage, the predominant naval power in the western Mediterranean, and had crushed her by 200 B.C. Thereafter, Rome came into conflict with the Hellenistic monarchies in the East, who within a decade or two were brought under her control. At first Rome was somewhat reluctant to add to her responsibilities by undertaking the administration of any territories outside Italy, but as the result of her struggles with Carthage and the Hellenistic world she had by 133 B.C. acquired an overseas empire comprising seven provinces: Sicily, Corsica and Sardinia, Spain (divided into two provinces), Africa (roughly modern Tunisia), Macedonia, and Asia (the western part of Asia Minor). Since she did not create an adequate civil service or a professional army, the problems of administration began to over-tax her constitutional machinery and allowed ambitious generals to overshadow the Republic. We cannot follow the process here, but by 63 B.C. Rome had been threatened by the power of two men, Pompey and Crassus, who were soon joined by a third, Julius Caesar. One of Pompey's stepping stones to power was the popularity that he had gained by sweeping the Mediterranean clear of piracy, and the subsequent military command that he was granted to deal with Mithridates, the king of Pontus in Asia Minor south of the Black Sea. During this campaign he not only conquered his enemy, but he also redrew the map of the Near East. The outstanding change was to make Syria a Roman province (with the capital at Antioch: Acts 11^{19-27}), while at the same time (63 B.C.) Pompey put an end to the fighting between the Pharisee Hyrcanus and his Sadducee brother Aristobulus (see above). He captured Jerusalem, which Aristobulus failed to hold, entered the Holy of Holies, left the treasure untouched, and set up Hyrcanus as High Priest and ruler of Judaea but tributary to Rome. The Jewish state, now subordinate to the Roman governor of Syria, thus continued to survive, but reduced in size and as a sacerdotal rather than a political entity. After a period of some confusion Judaea was settled by Julius Caesar, who had defeated Pompey and controlled Rome's destinies. He re-established the civil power of Hyrcanus, who received the title of Ethnarch of the Jews, but Caesar also recognized the Idumaean Antipater, father of Herod the Great, as administrator of Judaea in return for the help that he had given to Caesar at Alexandria in 48–47 B.C. Caesar then granted the Jews especial privileges: taxation was remitted (at least temporarily); they were allowed the free practice of their religion (thus, for instance, being exempted from attending court on the Sabbath); they were excused military service, and Roman troops were withdrawn from their territory. The privileges of the Jews in Alexandria and throughout the Dispersion were confirmed, and they could send their annual Temple tax to Jerusalem. Thus Caesar conciliated the Jews both in Palestine and throughout the Empire, so that at his funeral in 44 B.C. they were prominent in mourning the loss of their benefactor.

The murder of Caesar by a group of short-sighted Republicans, so far from leading to a restoration of liberties after his dictatorship, merely plunged the Roman world into another thirteen years of civil war. This developed into a struggle between Caesar's adopted son, Octavian, who was later named Augustus, and his rival Antony. Octavian emerged victorious at the battle of Actium (31 B.C.) and reasserted the supremacy of Italy and the western tradition over the Hellenistic-oriental monarchy to which Antony was turning. He faced a daunting task: not only were peace and order to be restored to a war-weary world, but the whole system of government and administration must be reorganized in such a way as to guarantee security in the future. This involved not merely reshaping the provincial system and safeguarding the frontiers of the empire, but also creating a strong central government that would both maintain its own authority and also avoid too sharp a break with the old Republican traditions. Caesar's attitude to the Senate, which had been the effective government of Rome for centuries, had been too brusque: Augustus must seek its co-operation and yet he must himself retain sole command of the army or else civil war might return. His solution of these problems was a masterly compromise, worked out by a process of trial and error. In name the Republic was restored with Augustus as its Princeps or First Citizen, but in fact the emperor was virtually a constitutional monarch, however tactfully he might disguise the fact by modesty of conduct. His complex reforms in Rome and Italy, constitutional, administrative, social, and religious, cannot even be mentioned here, but rather we must turn to those reforms which affected provincial government in general and Palestine in particular.

The provinces fall into two groups, one administered by the Senate (as under the Republic) and the other by the emperor. The Senate was responsible for the more peaceful ones, and Augustus for the frontier provinces where military activity might be necessary. At the time of his death the senatorial provinces were Baetica (southern Spain), Gallia Narbonensis (southern France), Macedonia, Achaea, Asia, Bithynia, Cyprus, Crete and Cyrene, Africa, Sicily; of these Asia and Africa were the most important. The imperial provinces were Hispania Tarraconensis, Upper and Lower Germany (military areas on the west bank of the Rhine), Pannonia (roughly Hungary), Dalmatia, Moesia (roughly Bulgaria), Syria, Egypt (all these provinces had legions stationed in them), together with the non-legionary Lusitania (roughly Portugal), Gallia Lugdunensis, Aquitania, Belgica, and Galatia. In addition there were four lesser imperial provinces: Rhaetia (roughly Austria), Noricum (east of Rhaetia), Sardinia-Corsica, and (after A.D. 6) Judaea. The senatorial provinces were governed by proconsuls, who had previously held either the consulship or praetorship in Rome, *e.g.* Sergius Paulus of Cyprus or Gallio of Achaea (Acts 13[7], 18[12]). The imperial provinces were administered by men appointed directly by the emperor to whom they were responsible. These legates in the larger provinces (*e.g.* Syria) were called *legati Augusti propraetore* (irrespective of whether they were ex-praetors or ex-consuls). In the four smaller imperial provinces mentioned above (*e.g.* Judaea) the governors were called procurators or prefects, while Egypt also was under a prefect. The proconsuls of the senatorial provinces normally held office only for a year, but the imperial governors held their posts for several years. The proconsuls and *legati* alike were chosen from the aristocratic senatorial class in Rome, while the procurators and prefects were Knights (*Equites*), a lower social grade, rich business men and merchants who hitherto had been excluded from the governing class although often exerting much influence upon it. But both the equestrian and senatorial Orders had been reformed by Augustus in order to secure men of personal integrity and efficiency for the administration of the Empire. During the late Republic there had been much provincial maladministration, and many governors, sometimes hand-in-glove with the Knights, had plundered the unfortunate provincials, but now they had less chance or inducement. They were salaried professional administrators (unlike the unpaid amateurs of the Republic), and they wielded considerably less power than their predecessors. In the more peaceful provinces their duties were mainly civilian. They all depended indirectly upon the favour of the emperor, and a large proportion were directly responsible to him. It is true that they exercised independent jurisdiction, but this was limited by the right of Roman citizens in the provinces to appeal to Caesar when faced with capital charges, while ex-governors of senatorial provinces could be impeached for extortion before the Senate in Rome which now became a high court of justice. Further, the civil authority of governors was limited by the fact that in the imperial provinces, financial matters were largely in the hands of an equestrian procurator directly responsible to the emperor. Thus many of the abuses that the provinces had suffered during the last century of the Republic were checked or removed.

Administration required money, and that meant taxation. But the Empire could not be equitably taxed unless its resources were accurately known ; then the amount to be raised must be fairly apportioned and just methods of collection be devised. It was necessary to hold a census of all the provincials like the census of Roman citizens which had been conducted periodically under the Republic ; this was probably carried out chiefly by provincial governors. It is unlikely that Augustus ordered a *simultaneous* census throughout all the provinces (Luke 2[1] is sometimes thought to imply this, but in fact the passage may only refer to the local application to Judaea on its annexation of a general rule that applied to the whole Empire), but he will have acted with characteristic thoroughness. Thus he himself held a census in Gaul in 27 B.C. and again in 12 B.C., while the famous assessment of Judaea by Quirinius, the governor of Syria, in A.D. 6 was undertaken immediately Judaea was formed into a Roman province (on this see below). An Augustan edict from Cyrene shows how detailed was the information that such surveys could provide about the extent and ownership of land and about other forms of wealth.

Such returns provided the basis for fair taxation. This took many forms. Direct taxes comprised a land tax (*tributum soli*) and a property tax (*tributum capitis*) levied on other forms of property, which might take the more simple form of a poll-tax in some districts, as Egypt and Judaea. Indirect taxes included customs, tolls and harbour dues, while some provincials might also have to pay local taxes. The method of collection, if not strictly controlled, might give even more offence than the tax itself. Under the Republic the government had allowed private citizens, either as individuals or companies, to help collect the provincial revenues. These publicans (*publicani*), when not checked by the governor, often managed to fleece the unfortunate provincials, despite some excellent laws designed to protect them. Augustus did not find it possible to abolish the *publicani* completely or at once ; they continued to contract for the indirect taxes in the imperial provinces, but they were more carefully supervised and could exercise little political influence. The numerous publicans of the New Testament were comparatively humble men and were natives of Palestine. Further, the direct taxes in the imperial provinces were collected by newly established financial officers called procurators, who were the emperor's agents and were largely independent of the governor, between whom and the procurator there might be friction or hostility. (These financial procurators must be distinguished from the procurators who served as governors of the smaller imperial provinces, as Judaea.) Thus many of the abuses that taxation may create were eliminated, and Augustus subjected all financial operations to scrutiny and control.

The provinces however could not prosper if their frontiers were menaced by barbarian tribes beyond. To safeguard the Empire therefore Augustus created a standing army, to whose upkeep part of the provincial revenues was devoted. The troops were stationed in permanent camps in the frontier provinces, particularly those that were liable to attack. One weak spot in the Empire was the northern frontier, which had been advanced to the Rhine as a result of Caesar's conquest of Gaul. Augustus decided that the protection of Italy and the Balkans required a frontier along the Danube that would link up with the Rhine frontier; this he achieved by conquest and by the creation of four new provinces, namely Rhaetia, Noricum, Pannonia, and Moesia. This long frontier needed constant vigilance: no less than eight legions had to be quartered permanently along the Rhine alone. This new permanent army was in fact none too large in relation to the length of the frontiers. It consisted of two distinct groups: the legions, of which there were 25 at the time of Augustus' death, amounting to about 150,000 men, and the *auxilia* who numbered about the same. The legions were recruited from Roman citizens, normally from volunteers (though conscription could be applied). The *auxilia* were raised from non-citizens in the less Romanized (*i.e.* the imperial) provinces, but on discharge after twenty-five years' service they received Roman citizenship; thus service in the *auxilia* became one of the main channels to citizenship. Further, soldiers tended, on discharge, to settle in the districts where they had served, and thus they helped to Romanize the more distant parts of the Empire. A legion comprised 5,500 infantry (divided into ten cohorts) and 120 cavalry. The *auxilia* consisted of *alae* and cohorts (either 500 or 1,000 strong); the *alae* were cavalry, the cohorts either infantry or mixed. A legion was commanded by a senatorial *legatus*, who had under him 6 tribunes (officers) and 60 centurions. The senior centurions, most of whom had risen from the ranks, were men of considerable authority, and the chief centurion of a legion received equestrian rank on discharge. The auxiliary troops came under the command of the legionary legate, but their cohorts were commanded by prefects (if 1,000 strong, by tribunes; cf. Acts 21[33], 25[33]), who were sometimes tribal chiefs or former senior legionary centurions and who had under them centurions and decurions. These centurions in the *auxilia* either rose from the ranks and were therefore not Roman citizens or else were Roman citizens who had been transferred from legionary service; thus the status of the centurions mentioned in the New Testament must remain uncertain.

The legions were stationed in the strategically important provinces where they could defend the less important neighbouring provinces, in which a few auxiliary troops might suffice to maintain internal order. Thus the four legions and numerous *auxilia* stationed in Syria not only guarded a crucial point in the whole defensive system of the Empire, but also afforded protection to the neighbouring Judaea. Here there were no legions, but only some four or five auxiliary infantry cohorts and one *ala*; they were mainly Syrians, recruited locally from the non-Jewish population and officered by Romans. Their headquarters was Caesarea, not Jerusalem, but some could be drafted for use as garrison troops in Jerusalem; the number of the garrison doubtless varied according to need (cf. Acts 23[23]). There are two difficult references to these auxiliary forces in Acts. The "Italian band" of Acts 10[1] was a *cohors Italica civium Romanorum* (this was a unit whose members must on some occasion in the past either have been freedmen or received citizenship before their discharge); their centurion, Cornelius, was presumably a Roman citizen, but whether born so or not we do not know. "Augustus' band" (*speira Sebastē*) of Acts 27[1] has been interpreted as a *cohors Sebastenorum* (*i.e.* of Samaritans), but the Greek really means *cohors Augusta,* and we do know of units with this title in Syria. Finally, mention should be made of the nine cohorts of the Praetorian Guard which Augustus created as a crack corps in Italy and which from the time of Tiberius had their barracks in Rome itself.

So far the government of the Empire has been regarded from the viewpoint of the central administration, but local government survived and flourished. Indeed it was one of the greatest achievements of the Principate to extend to the provinces the principle which had been evolved in Italy that the narrower loyalties of a man to his own town were not incompatible with loyalty to Rome. Thus by promoting healthy local government among the provincials, the Romans made them better and not worse citizens of the world-empire, Roman civilization was based on city life which took various forms, but it is not possible here to discuss the differing status of colonies, municipalities and native towns, beyond noting that members of municipalities and colonies possessed Roman citizenship; the former were towns incorporated into the Roman state, while colonies were settlements of Roman citizens, normally veteran soldiers (*e.g.* Philippi in Macedon, settled by Caesar and Augustus). Rather, some basic principles may be mentioned.

Rome respected local custom and, especially in the East, old forms of municipal self-government endured for centuries. Further, cities eager to share the privileges granted by Rome would tend to imitate the methods by which Rome itself had been governed. In general, Rome made agreements with individual towns in the provinces, granted them charters that stated their rights, and thereafter seldom interfered. The towns had their own magistrates and assemblies, they taxed themselves, issued their own copper coinage, built their own public works, and had their own law courts. In the less civilized districts, especially in the West, where city life was less developed, Rome used the native tribe as the unit of government, as shown by the conditions in Malta when Paul was shipwrecked there. Thus a great variety of local officials appear in the New Testament: not only the "chief man of the island" of Malta but also the "two men" or *duoviri* of the Roman colony of Philippi, the politarchs of the "free" city of Thessalonica which was the seat of the proconsul of Macedonia, the town clerk of Ephesus, the Areopagites of Athens (Acts 28^{7}, 16^{20}, 17^{6}, 19^{35}, 17^{19}). It was these local units, whether cities or tribes, that formed the whole basis of the administration, and the officials who represented Rome in the provinces have been described as "a mere superstructure added to self-governing communities." When, however, we move from the wider world of Acts to the simpler scene of Galilee and Judaea depicted in the Gospels, we find both under the Herods and the later Roman procurators a system of villages grouped into areas known as toparchies, with a large village acting as the capital of a toparchy (*e.g.* Gadara); there were very few self-governing cities (as Tiberias and Sepphoris in Galilee). Many of the villages might be of quite considerable size (*e.g.* some 15,000 souls), but they did not develop into municipalities or self-governing cities, although the local synagogue might exercise some sway. Thus the faithful servant in the parable, who was given rule over five or ten cities (Luke 19^{17-20}), was in fact made the commandant of a toparchy.

Another important feature of provincial life was the formation of Councils (*Koina* or *Concilia*) for the maintenance of the imperial cult. The divine honours that had been accorded to some of the Hellenistic kings were alien to the Roman tradition, but gradually Roman generals serving in the

East, and then Roman emperors, received dedications in which they were given the same extravagant titles as earlier kings. Thus Jesus' reference to the kings of the Gentiles who "are called benefactors" (Luke 22^{25}) could be applied to Roman emperors, and in fact dedications to Augustus as Euergetes (Benefactor) are not uncommon in the East. Augustus sensibly deprecated any worship of himself in Rome and Italy, and tried to limit such sentiment to sacrifices to his "genius," but such moderation was impossible in the eastern provinces where he allowed a cult of "Rome (*i.e.* the goddess Roma) and Augustus." He saw in this institution a valuable bond of unity for the Empire and such cults spread before long to the western provinces also. The cult with its priests was organized by groups of cities which sent delegates to an annual council-meeting where religious ceremonies, games, and festivals were held in the emperor's honour. The president was the chief priest of the cult, called, *e.g.* "the chief priest of Asia." The title Asiarch (Acts 19^{31}) was given to wealthy magnates in the province and in course of time was closely associated with that of "chief priest." These Councils, although private rather than public bodies, became a valuable means of expressing provincial opinion (as in criticising or praising the Roman governor), while their attitude might often help a governor to mould his policy (as later, for instance, whether to tolerate or persecute the Christians in his province).

During her long history Rome had made frequent use of political units, such as native rulers, to act as buffer states between the frontiers of her Empire and the barbarian tribes beyond. Such client kingdoms, when they became more civilized, might ultimately be annexed as part of the provincial system (thus when Amyntas, king of Galatia, died in 25 B.C., Augustus made his realm a Roman province), but in the meantime they provided a means by which backward or unruly areas could be trained in the responsibilities of government and in loyalty to Rome. Rome was thus saved from much tiresome administration. The native ruler surrendered his foreign policy, and sometimes was liable to tribute or had to provide troops, but he retained internal freedom ; only exceptionally did he receive the title of king. These client princes were often educated at Rome and promoted Roman and Hellenistic fashions in their realms, yet often they retained some Oriental feelings. Their knowledge of their own people and customs might often make them more acceptable than a Roman governor would have proved (cf. Luke 23^{7}). An excellent example of such a client-king is Herod the Great, whose career brings us back to Rome's relations with the Jews (see above, pp. 223 ff.).

After Caesar's death disturbances broke out in Palestine. After Antipater's murder in 43 B.C. his son Herod before long skilfully seized power and received Roman recognition as king of Judaea, where he ruled as a client king for thirty-three years (37–4 B.C.). His stormy and exciting reign cannot be described here. As "friend and ally of the Roman people" (he officially called himself the Friend of Caesar), he had to retain Rome's goodwill as well as that of his Jewish and non-Jewish subjects, although his policy of Hellenization was bound to alienate many. When he transformed his country by founding Hellenistic cities, he carefully showed his loyalty to Rome: his great new seaport was named Caesarea and the rebuilt city of Samaria was called Sebaste (the Greek for Augusta). In the non-Jewish parts of his kingdom he established the imperial cult; daily sacrifice for the emperor was offered in a magnificent new temple at Sebaste, and even in Jerusalem quadrennial games in honour of Augustus were established. But these good relations gradually deteriorated and were not mended even when Herod disregarded Moses' prohibition of images and placed the golden figure of an eagle over the Temple gate. Further, Herod's domestic quarrels increased and his cruelty is reflected in the story of the "massacre of the innocents." When he died in 4 B.C. his will, under which his kingdom was divided between his three sons, required the approval of Augustus who decided to enforce it and maintain the client kingdom, despite a Jewish deputation that came to Rome to seek the abolition of the monarchy and the organization of the country as a Roman province. We must now see how the three sons fared.

Archelaus received Judaea, Samaria, and Idumaea with the title of ethnarch and the promise of that of king if he ruled well (Matt. 2^{22}). Although he restored the Temple colonnades which had been burnt in riots after his father's death, he was often tactless and harsh. Against the "Law of the fathers" he married his deceased half-brother's widow; he arbitrarily removed the High Priest on two occasions; and his repressive rule drove the Jews and Samaritans to forget their differences and to join in an appeal to Augustus to abolish the monarchy. In A.D. 6 Augustus summoned Archelaus to Rome, deposed him, and banished him to Gaul. Since the client-kingdom had proved unsatisfactory Augustus annexed the ethnarchy and transformed it into the Roman province of Judaea.

Meantime Archelaus' brother Philip was proving more successful as tetrarch of Ituraea and Trachonitis, his share of his father's kingdom (Luke 3^{1}); his title had once meant ruler of a fourth part, but was now applied loosely. He reigned for thirty-seven years until his death in A.D. 34. Since he had few Jews in his principality, he could more easily adopt a policy of Hellenization and even venture to issue coins bearing the emperor's head (an offence to Jews). According to the Jewish historian Josephus, Philip "showed a mild and peaceable spirit in governing." He rebuilt the village of Bethsaida on the Sea of Galilee and named it Julias in honour of Augustus' daughter Julia; the Apostle Philip was one of its citizens. He built a new city Caesarea Philippi or Panias, which had only a small Jewish population and enjoyed self-government over a fairly large area. The peaceful state of his territory enabled Jesus to take refuge there when the Pharisees and Herodians were plotting against Him. Soon after Philip's death the emperor Gaius (Caligula) in A.D. 37 gave the kingdom to Agrippa, a grandson of Herod the Great.

The third son, Antipas, became tetrarch of Galilee and Peraea, and modelled his rule on that of his father, Herod the Great, whose name he took (he is called Herod in the Gospels: "Herod the tetrarch" in Matt. 14^{1}, Luke 9^{7}; Mark 6^{14} names him "king Herod," reflecting popular usage). Besides rebuilding Betharamphtha as Livias in honour of Livia, the wife of Augustus, Antipas made the interesting experiment of founding two autonomous Jewish cities in contrast to the pagan cities or non-autonomous towns that Herod the Great had founded. These were Sepphoris and Tiberias; the latter, on the Lake of Galilee, was founded in honour of the emperor Tiberius who had succeeded Augustus in A.D. 14 (but since it was built on an old cemetery, stricter Jews avoided it). The population of these two towns, however, was predominantly Jewish, and Tiberias at any rate had a normal Greek constitution (a Council of 500 and various magistrates). Although their freedom was circumscribed by the presence of a royal commandant and they did not control any territory beyond their walls (as did most classical cities), their creation marked a further stage in the Hellenization of the Jews. In general, Antipas gained the support of the upper and middle classes, both Pharisees and the pro-Roman Herodians, but the lower classes were restless, affected by the religious revivals led by John the Baptist and Jesus. Antipas may have welcomed the excuse, offered by John's denunciation of his marriage with Herodias, to imprison John, even if he put him to death with reluctance, but he avoided any direct responsibility for the death of Jesus. When Pilate tried to involve him on the ground that Jesus was a Galilean, Antipas refused to act, although he may have welcomed Pilate's subsequent action. Domestic troubles soon followed: the Arabian king Aretas, father of the woman Antipas had divorced in order to marry Herodias, invaded his territory. When Antipas appealed to

Tiberius, Lucius Vitellius, the governor of Syria, was ordered to eject Aretas, but Vitellius, who had earlier been insulted by Antipas, acted slowly and withdrew altogether when news reached him of Tiberius' death in A.D. 37. Tiberius' successor, Gaius, soon became suspicious of Antipas and banished him to Gaul in A.D. 39. The kingdom of the "fox" (Luke 13[32]) was then given to Agrippa, who two years before had received Philip's realm.

We may now return to the history of Judaea which, with the deposition of Archelaus, was freed from the hated Herodian dynasty at the cost of accepting Roman rule. The decision of Augustus that it should be administered by an equestrian governor had the advantage that these men came from the business class and so might be well adapted to work the complicated Herodian system of government. On the other hand, they lacked the diplomatic tradition enjoyed by the aristocratic senatorial governors of larger provinces, while the lower status of their ruler might offend the Jews' dignity and the stormy history of Palestine might tend to make good administrators chary of appointment there. In the pre-Claudian period the governor appears to have been called *praefectus*, not *procurator*; this view, which several scholars had advanced, is now confirmed by the recently discovered inscription from Caesarea which names Pontius Pilate "(praef)ectus Iud(aea)e." The governor resided at Caesarea and not Jerusalem, had judicial authority and was responsible for the preservation of law and order. He commanded the small body of local troops already mentioned, but since these were drawn from the anti-Jewish Greek cities of Sebaste and Caesarea, their attitude to the Jewish population might not always be conciliatory. The procurator had a garrison in the Antonia, the old citadel of Jerusalem which Herod had rebuilt, and policed the Temple at festival time. In case of need he could seek the help of the legions of the governors of Syria. Although he assumed the right that Herod had exercised of appointing the High Priests and controlling the Temple funds, yet in some matters the Jews regained powers that they had lost under Herod, who had restricted the jurisdiction of the Sanhedrin to religious questions and had created a new secular privy Council, modelled on those of the Hellenistic kings. The Romans now abolished this Royal Council and made the old Sanhedrin of seventy-one members an advisory body to the procurators. It recovered some of its judicial authority in religious cases: it could execute judgment on minor offenders; it could also try capital cases but (and here the evidence is very controversial) it could not itself inflict the death penalty without reference to the procurator who could either sanction or annul it. Thus establishment of direct Roman rule was effected with considerable tact, and Augustus upheld for all Jews, in Palestine or of the Dispersion, those privileges already granted by Julius Caesar. Though the Jews were not very popular in Roman eyes (Cicero, for instance, had remarked that the Jewish religion was alien to the Roman spirit), their importance (and their potential restlessness) in the eastern provinces was very great. Augustus had therefore to choose between protecting or suppressing them (the latter policy might make them turn for help to the Parthian empire beyond the Euphrates): he chose the more generous course.

The annexation of Judaea in A.D. 6 was effected not by its first governor but by the legate of Syria, Publius Sulpicius Quirinius, who carried out a census for taxation purposes. The implication of Luke (2^2) that Quirinius (Cyrenius) held a census at the time of the birth of Jesus has given rise to much discussion, but it is now generally agreed that Quirinius, who had been consul in 12 B.C., was not governor of Syria at the time of the Nativity (he had been governor of Galatia-Pamphylia) and that the Judaean census was held only in A.D. 6. This view agrees with the reference to "*the* census" in Acts 5^{37} and the evidence of Josephus(Ant. xx. v. 2 [102]), while Quirinius' census is mentioned in an inscription which records: "I, Quintus Aemilius Secundus . . . have held a census of the 117,000 citizens of the town of Apamea (in Syria) under the command of Quirinius." Its object was to re-assess the basis of a poll-tax of one *denarius* (Mark 12^{13-17}) which may have been levied under the Herods; the method of assessment was probably that used by the Romans in Egypt. The only serious outcry against this taxation was in Gaulanitis, east of the Jordan, where Judas of Gamala, who had fomented an earlier rising, was joined by a Pharisee called Zadok. Together they led an extremist party, the Zealots, and started a campaign of terrorism against both Romans and loyal Jews. Beside the poll-tax the Jews had to pay 12½% on the corn harvest (*tributum soli*) and apparently a house tax in Jerusalem, but the Romans did not interfere with their Temple tax and tried to avoid friction by using native tax-collectors, such as Zacchaeus, who was responsible for the tolls at the crossing of the Jordan near Jericho (Luke 19^{1-2}), or Levi, a tax-gatherer of Capernaum on Lake Tiberias concerned with port duties or fishing tolls (Mark 2^{14}).

One symbol of the emperor's authority was coinage. While allowing the Senate to mint copper coins, Augustus himself retained control of the gold and silver. At this time Roman coinage comprised the golden *aureus*, the silver *denarius* (the day wage of a labourer), the fine brass *sestertius* (¼ denarius), the copper *as* ($\frac{1}{16}$ *den.*), and smaller copper coins. The procurators issued local copper coins in the emperor's name, probably at Caesarea, while a great variety of small local currencies will have circulated in Palestine; the "thirty pieces of silver" (Matt. 26^{15}) were probably either tetradrachms of the Greek cities of Syria or Greek imperial staters of Antioch or Caesarea. With so many coins in circulation, money-changers were certainly needed in Jerusalem.

We may now look briefly at the fortunes of the Jews, both in and outside Palestine, under the Julio-Claudian emperors who followed Augustus from A.D. 14–68. Tiberius (A.D. 14–37) was an efficient administrator and the provinces were in general well governed under him: he told a governor who had exacted too much taxation: "you should shear my sheep, not flay them." A scandal among the local Jewish community in Rome induced him to persuade the Senate to expel the Jews from Rome and to send 4,000 of them on military service to Sardinia. This isolated episode was probably due in part to Tiberius' dislike of Jewish proselytizing activities in Rome and also perhaps to the malevolence of his friend and minister, Sejanus. During the last eight years of Augustus' principate Judaea had three governors (Coponius, Marcus Ambivius, and Annius Rufus), but only two under Tiberius. Valerius Gratus (A.D. 15–26) made himself unpopular by deposing the High Priest whom Quirinius had appointed, and establishing five others, of whom the last was Caiaphas. His successor, Pontius Pilate (A.D. 26–36), was even more tactless. Unlike his predecessors he insisted that troops entering Jerusalem should carry their standards which bore the emperor's image; only a storm of protest forced him to rescind this order. He dedicated some golden shields in the royal palace at Jerusalem; this was his official residence and the shields bore merely his own and the emperor's names, but a protest was sent to Tiberius who ordered him to move the offending shields to the temple of Rome and Augustus at Caesarea. His proposal to use some Temple funds to improve the water supply led to further disturbance, which was suppressed only with bloodshed; some Galileans participated, apparently at a festival, and their blood was "mingled with their sacrifices" (Luke 13$^{1-2}$). It may have been in connexion with constructing Pilate's aqueduct that eighteen workmen were crushed by the falling masonry of the tower of Siloam (13^{4}). Then followed the Crucifixion. Condemned to death by the Sanhedrin on religious grounds, Jesus was remanded to Pilate with a political charge added: Jesus was King of the Jews, a messianic rebel, and His acquittal would prove Pilate no friend of Caesar's. On the ground that Jesus was a Galilean, Pilate tried but failed to transfer the case to Antipas. Though unconvinced of Jesus' guilt, he finally confirmed the Sanhedrin's condemnation in order to avoid political complications with the emperor and further rioting in Jerusalem. Threat of a later riot led to his downfall. He scattered with bloodshed an armed mob of Samaritans whom an impostor had gathered at Mount Gerizim where he alleged Moses' sacred vessels were buried: Pilate feared the emergence of another would-be Messiah. The Samaritans appealed to Vitellius, the legate of Syria, who happened to be in Jerusalem, and Pilate was ordered to render an account of himself before Tiberius in Rome. His fate is not known. Vitellius, however, acted with tact and even obtained Tiberius' permission to restore to the Jews the High Priest's vestments which were held by the Romans.

Gaius (nicknamed Caligula), the successor of Tiberius, was or became after an illness a capricious tyrant and created disorder in many provinces. He abandoned the policy of toleration towards the Jews that his predecessors had followed. Quarrels between Jews and Greeks in Alexandria came to a head in A.D. 38 when anti-Semitic rioting took place, led by Greeks who were also anti-Roman. These nationalist leaders were jealous of the privileges that the Romans allowed the Jews who had an ethnarch and senate, while the municipal rights of the Greeks were limited. This anti-Roman movement developed a literature of its own, the so-called "Acts of the Pagan Martyrs," which survives only in fragmentary papyri. While Gaius recalled the Prefect of Egypt, both Jews and Greeks in Alexandria sent deputations to the emperor, that of the Jews being led by the philosopher and theologian Philo. Meantime Gaius had outraged all Jews by demanding that they should recognize his divinity and had provoked the Palestinian Jews to the verge of revolt by demanding that his statue should be set up in the Temple at Jerusalem. The situation was saved by his murder in A.D. 41.

His successor, Claudius (A.D. 41–54), might be eccentric but he pursued an enlightened policy. He developed the imperial administrative services in Rome, granted Roman citizenship liberally to provincials, and decided to replace client-kings by direct rule in some areas, thus adding five new provinces (two in Mauretania, Britain, Thrace, and Lycia) to the Empire. To the Jews in general he restored freedom of worship throughout the Empire and exemption from the imperial cult. Towards the Alexandrian Jews and Greeks he was firm; after receiving deputations which sought new privileges he sensibly warned both parties to keep the peace: otherwise they might expect sterner measures. He was more severe in Rome where, despite Tiberius' expulsion order, a large Jewish colony had re-established itself. In A.D. 41 he denied them the right to hold meetings (perhaps other than the individual synagogues), presumably as a result of some disturbances, since he charged the Alexandrine Jews this same year with "fomenting a universal plague." In A.D. 49 a further clash resulted apparently in their expulsion (Acts 18[2]). It is uncertain whether the emerging new religion of Christianity had any influence on these events, but Suetonius records that a riot arose *impulsore Chresto*. If Chrestus is not an unknown Jewish agitator but refers to Jesus Christ, the latter may have been a cause in that news of Christianity, reaching the Jewish community in Rome, may have led to internal dissensions. Another controversial piece of evidence is an inscription from Nazareth embodying an imperial rescript which threatened with death those who violated tombs. Some scholars, who date this to Claudius, suggest that it records his action after an enquiry that revealed the anti-Christian version of the Resurrection (Matt. 27[12-15]), that the disciples had taken the body of Jesus from the tomb: the rescript then aimed at preventing similar troubles in the future.

However that may be, Claudius made a temporary change in Palestine, partly in order to reward his friend (Herod) Agrippa, the grandson of Herod the Great, who had already won the favour of Gaius (see pp. 233 and 237). Agrippa, who like many another client prince had spent his youth at the imperial court in Rome, was visiting the city when Gaius was murdered, and he gave Claudius considerable help in gaining the succession. The new emperor repaid him by installing him as king of Judaea, since the restoration of independence under a king of their own might also help to pacify the outraged feelings of the Jews. Agrippa, who with great courage had previously resisted the attempt of Gaius to desecrate the Temple, proved a popular ruler, and as a supporter of Jewish orthodoxy he took severe action against the Christians: he executed James, the son of Zebedee, and arrested Peter who soon managed to escape (Acts 12[1-5]). But in A.D. 44 when he was attending the quadrennial games in honour of Augustus at Caesarea, where he was hailed as a god, Agrippa died (Acts 12[20-23]). Claudius felt that any other native ruler might be unreliable, and so Judaea reverted to its provincial status under procurators.

The procurators had to face increasing difficulties. Not only did the hostility of Jews and Gentiles lead to frequent disturbances, but religious outbreaks and lawlessness increased and armed bands roved the land, not to mention famine (Acts 11[28]). Thus Cuspius Fadus had to crush the rising of a false Messiah named Theudas (Acts 5[36]). Ventidius Cumanus

(A.D. 48–52) had to deal with fighting between Jews and Samaritans which became so ugly that the legate of Syria, Ummidius Quadratus, held an enquiry. The issue was referred to Rome, where Claudius decided for the Jews and deposed Cumanus from his procuratorship. This humiliation would not strengthen the hands of his successors. Of these Felix and Festus are well known from Acts. Felix, unlike his predecessors was a freedman, not an *eques*, and a brother of Claudius' influential freedman minister, Pallas ; his third wife was a Jewess, Drusilla, a daughter of Agrippa I. (Acts 24[24]). He had to face still more troubles, including an extreme section of the Zealots called Knifemen (Sicarii) who added to the disorders (cf. Acts 21[38]). Paul's adventures in Jerusalem illustrate the efficiency of Roman rule. Saved by Claudius Lysias, the commander of the small force in the Antonia, first from the mob and later from the Jewish plot to assassinate him, saved also from investigation by scourging by his declaration of his Roman citizenship, Paul was formally handed over to the governor Felix in Caesarea. That he was kept in custody for two years may be due less to Felix's hope of a bribe than to his fear that Paul's release would entail further rioting. The matter was resolved under the next procurator, Porcius Festus (A.D. 60–62), who brought Paul to trial and very properly sent him to Rome when Paul decided to use his right as a Roman citizen to appeal to Caesar. As is well known, Festus was perplexed how to frame the charge in his report to the emperor (Nero, who had succeeded Claudius in A.D. 54), and so sought the co-operation of Agrippa II., who had been brought up in Rome, had been made king of Chalcis in the Lebanon area and soon afterwards had received the tetrarchies of Philip and Lysanias (A.D. 50). Festus' successors faced such disorders that the situation was rapidly getting out of hand. The crisis came under Gessius Florus, who owed his procuratorship in A.D. 64 to Nero's wife Poppaea who was interested in the Jews. A spark set the whole country ablaze in the great Jewish war which ended in the siege and destruction of Jerusalem by Titus in A.D. 70. Roman patience and tolerance were at last ended. The Temple was destroyed, the Sanhedrin and High Priesthood were abolished, the annual Temple tax was diverted from Yahweh to Jupiter Capitolinus, and the Jewish state died as a political entity. But Judaism as a religion continued and was even protected as in the past, since its followers were still allowed their Sabbath, freedom from military service and exemption from the imperial cult. Judaea remained a Roman province, but the equestrian procurator now became the subordinate to a senatorial legate who commanded the Tenth Legion which henceforth garrisoned Jerusalem.

The Jewish war was only one of many troubles that darkened the later years of Nero's principate (A.D. 54–68). The great fire that had destroyed a considerable part of Rome in A.D. 64 had increased his unpopularity, so that he had sought a scapegoat by blaming the new sect of the Christians against whom he took such savage action that it defeated his purpose: the sight of some torn to pieces by beasts in the amphitheatre, of others used as living torches to light the imperial gardens, excited pity and emphasized Nero's cruel tyranny. The legal basis of his action has been endlessly debated, but it is not now widely believed that he passed a general law against Christians as such. More probably Christianity was proscribed by magisterial edict because of the supposed crimes it involved, and this would lead to formal enquiry by magistrates against individuals who were charged. The persecution was local and limited: what happened in Rome would not affect the provinces. No less controversial is the tradition that two of Nero's victims were Peter and Paul. The recent excavations under the Basilica of St. Peter's in the Vatican city have not established that Peter was buried beneath it near the Circus of Nero where he is alleged to have perished, but they have shown that the Christians in Rome about a hundred years later connected this site with him.

When Paul had arrived in Rome he was handed over to the "commandant of the camp" (Acts 28^{16}). The latter may not have been the Prefect of the Praetorian Guard, but a subordinate officer called the *princeps castrorum* who was the chief administrator of the Guard. Thereafter Paul "remained for two whole years in a private lodging" (28^{30}), during which he was not brought to trial. The reasons are obscure: perhaps his accusers did not follow up their charge at Rome, or the court lists may have been so overcrowded as to result in long delay, or outstanding charges that were in arrears may have been cancelled by the emperor in the interests of clemency or of administrative efficiency. Any way Paul was able to continue his evangelism until his final fate, which may be linked with the Neronian persecution of 64.

The story cannot be taken much further here. Nero's death was followed by a brief period of Civil War (the Year of the Four Emperors) out of which Vespasian emerged victorious and then gave stability and confidence to a shaken world. From A.D. 69 to 96 Rome was governed by the three Flavian emperors, Vespasian and his sons Titus (A.D. 79–81; his mistress, Bernice, was the sister of Agrippa II., mentioned in Acts 25^{13}) and Domitian (A.D. 81–96). Their rule, though enlightened in many ways, tended to greater autocracy, and more importance was attached to the imperial cult. This was popular in some provinces, as Asia, where cities were glad to show their loyalty to the emperor, but the book of Revelation shows how it affected Christians who would not conform. Antipas the martyr died in Pergamum, " where Satan's throne is," rather than deny his faith, and others were to suffer at Smyrna (Rev. $2^{13, 10}$). Men refused to bow down to " an image to the beast who hath the stroke of the sword" (Rev. 13^{14}). Thus two pictures emerge: Rome, the upholder of law and good government in Acts, has become for the writer of Revelation " the woman drunken with the blood of saints."

No balance sheet of Rome's virtues and vices can be attempted here, but some further aspects of the complex life of the Empire must be mentioned. First, it should be emphasized that Judaea was not a typical province and that therefore undue concentration upon it tends to distort the picture of the Empire as a whole. Most other provinces were free from such strong internal tensions and consequently enjoyed much greater peace and prosperity. Peace, the *pax Romana*, was in fact the greatest blessing that a war-weary world received from Augustus. But it was bought at a great price: curtailment of Republican liberties. Yet even this would be felt most by the small minority that formed the governing class rather than by the toiling millions in the provinces, and in any case a free and lively municipal life flourished. The tyranny of a Nero was limited in its effects, while the Flavian emperors introduced a much higher code of behaviour and public service; for the next century emperors were humane and benevolent rulers, at worst paternalistic. In other respects men enjoyed great personal freedom. They were subject to taxation, but it was not severe. They were liable to military service, but seldom conscripted. They could move through the length and breadth of the Empire, from Newcastle to the Sahara, from Cadiz to the Euphrates or beyond, along the vast network of roads or by sea, not threatened by piracy or hampered by national frontiers. A man would meet with little or no racial prejudice. He could use his own language and preserve his native customs. He had complete intellectual and religious liberty, except in those cases where the authorities regarded any religious rite as a danger to public safety or order.

Roman citizens throughout the Empire naturally enjoyed greater privileges than did the provincials, but Rome had always been liberal in granting her citizenship to others and the process continued: thus in the year A.D. 70 a Roman general could tell an audience of Gauls, " you yourselves often rule over Roman provinces or command Roman legions; nothing is excluded or shut off from you." Citizenship may have lost the political value that it had under the Republic, but its social importance was unchanged, while its practical benefits are seen in Paul's right of appeal and immunity before condemnation from flogging (though in fact he was not always saved from this). And if there were abuses, there were also courts where redress might be sought. In fact the establishment of one general system for the administration of justice, based upon Roman law, was a gift, no less valuable than that of peace, that Rome gave to its Empire. Roman law, both civil and criminal, had been developed over the centuries and became increasingly sensible, flexible, and humane. It was marked by a strong sense of equity and fairness. Thus the jurists developed new notions such as Intention, while a legate could be told, " When in doubt, you must follow the law of the local city." And justice was open and equal for all citizens (see Acts 25^{16}). Of the content of Roman law, one of the greatest achievements of the human mind, obviously nothing can be said here.

Nor can much be said about the extremely varied social and economic life of the Empire. While peaceful conditions encouraged thriving industrial and commercial activities, there were great contrasts of wealth and poverty, between civilized urban life and more backward agricultural areas, and between freeman and slave. Slavery was, of course, accepted as a normal and unquestioned feature of organized society. Here generalization is dangerous and there were very great contrasts in treatment, from revolting cruelty and degradation to consideration and even friendship. On the whole the number of slaves began to diminish and legislation regarding slavery became more humane. Further, the Romans had always been most generous, judged by ancient standards, in their readiness to free slaves, so that a large class of freedmen was to be found in Italy ; many of them prospered and some became very influential, especially from the time of Claudius (*e.g.* Felix). By A.D. 100 a very high proportion (some would put it at 90%) of the population of Rome were non-Italians of slave origin. Here in the capital men increasingly demanded an idle life, to be fed and amused by the state, by means of " bread and circuses." The gladiatorial and animal combats in the amphitheatre remind us that even the earlier Romans had a strong streak of cruelty in their nature, which now found much wider expression in these revolting and degrading spectacles. But neither these nor the fulminations of satirists such as Juvenal should obscure the fact that in most of the Empire life must have been very much healthier and simpler than in the great cities, and agriculture remained the basic industry.

The great achievements in art and architecture, to which all the cities of the Empire could bear increasing witness as the benefactions of emperors or rich citizens added to their temples, theatres, amphitheatres, circuses, baths, aqueducts, these achievements must be passed by here, together with all the great works of poets and writers. But a final word may be added about philosophy and religion, where, as in these other spheres, the Romans were the heirs of the Greeks. During the late Republic educated Romans read the classical Greek writers, but they were even more conscious of the Hellenistic world. Thus Plato may have had less influence upon Cicero than did the Stoic philosopher Posidonius (135–50 B.C.). It was Cicero through his philosophic writings that made Greek philosophical thought easily accessible to his fellow-countrymen (and later to the Church fathers, Italian humanists, and French Revolutionaries). The two systems that appealed most to Rome were products of the Hellenistic age, Stoicism, and Epicureanism. While the Epicureans tried to ease life by removing fear of death, the Stoics were increasingly concerned with social ethics. While Epicureans withdrew from public life, the Stoics became linked during the early Empire with practical politics, since many of the men who opposed the tyranny of rulers like Nero and admired the lost Republic found their inspiration in this creed. How far Stoicism influenced Christian thought is a problem that has received many answers. Other philosophers included the Cynics who sought independence by renouncing worldly obligations: some became itinerant beggars who preached anarchy. Other men turned to Neo-Pythagoreanism and in a common cult hoped to purify the soul and free it from the burden of the body. Thus in the early Empire philosophy had come down to earth, being less concerned with metaphysical thought and more with providing a way of life in face of the oppressions of the world; its emphasis was more ethical and religious.

Early Roman religion was polytheistic and divorced from ethics: as long as the formal cults of the State were maintained in order to assure the goodwill of the gods, a man could believe and act as he wished, provided always that such action did not involve public disorder. In early days the Romans had assimilated the gods and mythology of Greece, and then cults from further east began to reach Italy (*e.g.* Magna Mater from Phrygia in 204 B.C.). Some of these were regarded with a certain reserve, but Rome did not persecute religions as such (the cult of Bacchus had been checked in 186 B.C. because of the crime-wave that it provoked; Claudius checked Druidism because it involved human-sacrifice). In general a polytheistic society would not object to other gods, provided such recognition was mutual ; trouble only arose when Rome faced monotheistic peoples who would not recognize the gods of the Roman State, as the Jews and Christians. Thus by the time of the Empire the religious scene at Rome was highly cosmopolitan : Egyptian Isis vied with Cappadocian Ma, Phrygian Cybele, and later with Persian Mithras for men's allegiance. Beside these well-known cults, many smaller and semi-secret worships flourished, which by initiation offered the member hopes of personal immortality : one such cult was celebrated at Pompeii in the Villa of the Mysteries whose painted walls depict some initiation-rites, or at the Porta Maggiore chapel at Rome. Other men turned for help to astrology, which despite periodic expulsions of its professional practitioners from Rome, flourished and received almost official patronage since several emperors (*e.g.* Tiberius) were interested in it (note also Sergius Paulus and Elymas : Acts 13^7). In the countryside the older and simpler forms of worship of an agricultural people continued to inspire belief. Thus the turning to the older gods of household and field, to magic and superstition, to mystery religion and eastern cult, or to philosophy, alike testified to the need men felt for spiritual comfort. The Roman world might offer security in many ways, but each man also lived in his small private world, which was often terrifying or disheartening : he needed help and strength. To such Christianity was to offer a Gospel and another way of life.

BIBLIOGRAPHY

Hellenistic World.

Two excellent introductory volumes are W. W. Tarn, *Hellenistic Civilisation*, 3rd ed., by G. T. Griffith, 1952, and M. Cary, *A History of the Greek World from 323 to 146 B.C.*, 2nd ed., 1951. M. Rostovtzeff's great work, *The Social and Economic History of the Hellenistic World*, 1941, should be mentioned. Full bibliographies in *Cambridge Ancient History*, vi., 1927, etc.

Roman World.

Three general histories are M. Cary, *A History of Rome*, 2nd ed., 1954 ; H. H. Scullard, *From the Gracchi to Nero*, 2nd ed., 1963 ; E. T. Salmon, *A History of the Roman World from 30 B.C. to A.D. 138*, 3rd ed., 1957. For fuller treatment see *Cambridge Ancient History*, especially vols. x. and xi., 1934–6, and M. Rostovtzeff, *The Social and Economic History of Roman Empire*, 2nd ed., 1957. Much detailed material will be found in A. H. M. Jones, *The Cities of the Eastern Roman Provinces*, 1937, and in *An Economic Survey of Ancient Rome*, edited by Tenney Frank, iv., 1938, which covers

Syria, Asia, and Greece. At the other extreme M. P. Charlesworth, *The Roman Empire*, 1951, provides a splendid little introduction, and M. Grant, *The World of Rome*, 1960, a fine sketch. See also A. N. Sherwin-White, *Roman Society and Roman Law in the New Testament*, 1963.

Jewish World.

W. O. E. Oesterley and T. H. Robinson, *A History of Israel*, ii., 1932. V. Tcherikover, *Hellenistic Civilization and the Jews*, 1959. A. H. M. Jones, *The Herods of Judaea*, 1938. H. J. Leon, *The Jews of Ancient Rome*, 1960.

X. BIBLICAL ARCHAEOLOGY

By John Gray

The modern science of archaeology, even where it bears on the Bible, goes far beyond it in time and in scope. In the wider setting of the ancient Near East archaeology has made a significant contribution to the history of Israel, both corroborating certain details of the Biblical record and presenting an objective view which enables us to assess the essentially theological presentation of history in the Old Testament. The recovery of evidence both material and documentary from this whole cultural area makes possible a juster assessment of the culture of Israel, often opening the way to a fuller appreciation of the implications of Israelite institutions than was formerly possible on the sole evidence of the Old Testament, and generally emphasizing by contrast the distinctive ethos of Israel. The discovery of new literatures too and the fuller understanding of Mesopotamian literary and ritual texts recovered since the discovery of Ashurbanipal's royal library at Nineveh a century ago has given us a new appreciation of literary types and their formal and linguistic conventions, and has enabled us to detect sources behind the main literary sources in the Old Testament and to determine their relevance to situations in the life of ancient Israel. Recent archaeology too has made its contribution to the restoration of the text of the Bible. Certain words doubtful, obscure, or corrupt have been recovered in the light of new Semitic dialects or Semitic or Greek words in new contexts. New instruments have been discovered for the control of the tradition of the accepted text of the New and Old Testaments. As a result there is not an aspect of Biblical scholarship which is not affected by progress in the science of archaeology.

(i) CRADLES OF CULTURE: EGYPT AND MESOPOTAMIA

In the first edition of the *Companion to the Bible* it was pointed out that the Biblical period was a relatively late phase in human history in the ancient Near East, where urban civilization in Mesopotamia and Egypt predated the main Hebrew settlement in Palestine by over two millennia. Stratified excavation in the prehistoric periods by Miss D. Garrod in the caves on the west slopes of Carmel and by Dr. Kathleen Kenyon at Jericho now carry the story of man in the Near East back for over a hundred millennia. As a result Palestine emerges as an important centre in the development of agriculture and communal life as late as *c.* 7000–5000 B.C. But the fact remains that in the historical period as the result of climatic changes Palestine was culturally and politically of secondary importance to the great seats of civilization and empire on the Nile and the Euphrates.

Affinities with material from Egypt first gave the clue to a relative chronology in Palestinian archaeology as the result of the comparative study of pottery and unspectacular objects, often fragmentary and of no intrinsic value, promoted by Sir W. Flinders Petrie and applied in his excavation of Tell el-Hesy in 1890. From this time archaeologists became increasingly interested in the whole context of the various strata of sites as apart from spectacular museum pieces. It is this less spectacular matter which is now acknowledged to provide the clue to the cultural affinity or independence of any site in the ancient Near East, and Palestinian archaeology particularly depends upon such comparative material in the general default of more spectacular remains.

Besides this, Egyptian archaeology and such Egyptian material as has been found in Syria and Palestine has subserved Biblical study first in furnishing inscriptions which elucidate Israel's settlement in Palestine from the first infiltrations of the Habiru of the el-Amarna tablets, whom we associate with the older Jacob tribes involved with the Canaanites at Shechem (Gen. 34), to the time of Tirhakah, the contemporary of Hezekiah. Apart from such historical inscriptions, texts which concern the ritual and ideology of kingship in Egypt, which continue to be studied and brought into fresh focus, are of especial value in the study of the Hebrew monarchy, particularly in Judah, and papyri dealing with Wisdom themes show quite distinctly, as in the Wisdom of Amen-em-ope at least (extant in a papyrus from the period of the Hebrew monarchy), the direct influence of Egyptian letters on Hebrew humanism. In the Jewish Diaspora too and in the early centuries of the Christian era Egyptian archaeology has much to contribute to the study of the Bible from the communities settled in the Delta and on the Sudanese frontier at Assouan on the collapse of the Jewish state till Roman times. The mundane and often trivial correspondence and business notes on papyrus and potsherds, which illustrate the society and the common Greek language (*koinē*) of the Graeco-Roman world of the early Christian period, have set the Pauline letters in particular in true perspective. The literary deposits of these Egyptian Jewish communities has also conserved early fragments of the Bible, the Nash Papyrus in Hebrew containing a collection of commandments from Exod. $20^{2\text{ff.}}$ and Deut. $5^{6\text{ff.}}$

together with the *sh^ema'* (Deut. 6^4ff.), which has been dated variously from the first century B.C. (Albright) to the first century A.D. (Kahle), papyrus fragments of the Old Testament in Greek (the Septuagint) from the first century B.C. (the Rylands fragment of part of Deut.) to the third century A.D. (the Freer collection of fragments from the Minor Prophets, the Berlin Genesis, and Genesis, Isaiah, Jeremiah, Ezekiel, Daniel, and Esther in the Chester Beatty Papyri), and New Testament fragments, which will be considered later.

Significant though Egyptian archaeology may be for Biblical study, Mesopotamian archaeology is even more so because of the cultural and ethnic affinities of Israel with the Semitic East.

Our account of Mesopotamian archaeology begins in the fourth millennium, by which time Lower Mesopotamia, called Sumer in later Mesopotamian documents, was settled by a race, probably from the south Iranian highlands, called after this name the Sumerians. Bringing political and technical organization to canalize the waters and drain the rich alluvial land of south Mesopotamia, they developed an advanced urban civilization there, which is attested by the remains of cities with temples and *ziqqurats* (or staged towers; cf. the Tower of Babel), and other extensive buildings for residence and administration at Ur, Warka (Biblical Erech), Tell Fara (ancient Shuruppak), Khafajeh, Nippur, and Kish, where stylized pictographic inscriptions on clay tablets—the ancestors of syllabic cuneiform—were found by the joint expedition of Oxford University and the Chicago Field Museum (1923–33) dating *c.* 3500. Thus by the third millennium the Sumerians in their autonomous city-states were the protagonists of civilization in Mesopotamia as the now unified kingdom of Egypt was on the Nile.

Sumerian influence on Israel was not direct, in spite of the tradition which associates the family of Abraham with Ur. There is no good reason to doubt that cosmological and aetiological myths, epics, ritual myths and liturgies, as well as wisdom literature were developed by the Sumerians early in the third millennium, though in its extant state this matter is either transmitted in Sumerian texts from the end of the third millennium or in Semitic (Akkadian) adaptations from the second millennium, mostly recovered from the library of Ashurbanipal (664–626 B.C.) at Nineveh a century ago. It is through the latter medium that the Sumerian tradition was transmitted to the Hebrews.

In this matter and in seal motifs we find the tradition of the Flood well established among the Sumerians, though it is the Akkadian version of the Gilgamesh epic known to us from Nineveh that is adapted in Genesis. The south Mesopotamian setting, however, suggests Sumerian antecedents. Besides Utnapishtim, the "Noah" of this myth, another Sumerian "Noah" was Ziusudra, Xisuthros of Berossus, who records ancient Mesopotamian traditions in the third century B.C., and yet another is Atrahasis. The survivor of the Flood is commonly depicted in his "ark" or boat in Sumerian cylinder seals from the second millennium. Sumerian king-lists also mention a Flood as the demarcation between history and pre-history, where, few names having survived in long dark ages, the Sumerian antediluvians surpass even Methuselah.

Evidence of the Flood has been claimed in excavations in Lower Mesopotamia, notably Woolley's discovery of a clean stratum of eight feet between two occupation levels early in the fourth millennium, which on soil analysis proves to have been laid by wind and not water. The fundamental continuity in technical tradition between these strata, however, does not suggest a universal cataclysm. Other "Flood" strata, *e.g.* at Kish, Warka, and Tell Fara (ancient Shuruppak, the home of Utnapishtim in the Gilgamesh epic), do not correspond chronologically to the Ur stratum, and no corresponding stratum was found at Ubaid four miles from Ur. The Flood theme, then, in Sumerian literature, like the conflict between the high god and the monsters of the deep in the Babylonian Creation-myth (*enuma elish*) reflects the struggle of the Sumerian settlers to reclaim the swamps of Lower Mesopotamia and to maintain the canals for drainage and irrigation against the continual menace of the spring floods of the two rivers. Such local floods as may be attested by archaeology were occasioned probably by the neglect of canals and embankments when the political power of the sundry city-states was in eclipse.

Towards the end of the third millennium the whole of Mesopotamia, the Semitic north and the Sumerian south, was dominated by the Semitic rulers of Akkad, a city some twenty miles south-west of Baghdad. Sargon (now dated *c.* 2300) and his sons and grandson Naramsin, probably the first great imperialists in history, ruled from the Persian Gulf to North Syria. Akkad, however, fell before barbarians from the Iranian highlands, a chronic menace in Mesopotamian history, and about a century after their domination there was a political revival under a Sumerian dynasty (IIIrd) in Ur. This is the Ur traditionally associated with Abraham's family and for this reason it generally bulks large in popular accounts of archaeology and the Bible, a pretext for lavish illustration from the wealth of objects of art in precious metals from the royal tombs. These, however, come from about a millennium before, and they have no relevance except to illustrate the high degree of culture attained by the Sumerians in remote antiquity. There is no evidence that the Hebrews were influenced directly by Sumerian culture. The actual evidence of Genesis, the patriarchal genealogies, associates them with Aramaeans about Harran, which, like Ur, was a centre of the cult of Sin, the Moon-god, and other localities in north Mesopotamia. Archaeology attests the diffusion of Sumerian wares and motifs in pottery, seals, and metal-work from Ur under the IIIrd Dynasty through Mesopotamia and Syria into Anatolia, the source of metals and precious stones, in which Mesopotamia was entirely deficient. Stability in Mesopotamia was constantly menaced by the warlike people from Iran and the next two centuries saw the collapse of Ur and the temporary hegemony of other Sumerian cities such as Isin and Larsa before the Semitic Amorites from the steppes of the north-west came to power in the land, and Babylon eventually emerged as the most powerful city-state in Mesopotamia until by diplomacy and force it reduced all neighbouring city-states which disputed its hegemony. This phase of history is illustrated in a mass of legal inscriptions from Babylon in Akkadian cuneiform and in the political correspondence which forms a very small part of the 25,000 tablets from Mari (Tell Hariri) on the mid-Euphrates, and by the ruin of the palace of Hammurabi's contemporary and vassal Zimrilim (*c.* 1700).

The Semites served themselves heir to the ancient Sumerian culture including the syllabic cuneiform script, now used to express the same syllables in Semitic words. The Sumerian language survived in ancient liturgies as the province of scholars and of priests, and appeared in syllabaries and word-lists along with Canaanite alphabetic texts in Ras Shamra in the fourteenth and thirteenth centuries. It is what is distinctively Semitic in this mixed culture and its literary deposit which is of direct value in the comparative study of the culture and literature of Israel in the ancient Near East.

The contribution of Mesopotamian archaeology to Old Testament studies is Akkadian texts such as the Flood narrative in the Gilgamesh epic—the conflict of Marduk with the chaotic waters (Tiamat and her allies), resulting in the ordering of nature and the creation of man in the Babylonian myth *enuma elish* ("When on high . . .") from the liturgy of the Spring New Year festival, extant in the form in which it was recovered from Ashurbanipal's library, but believed on grounds of language and literary style to date from early in the second millennium—a wisdom text which poses the same problem as the Book of Job and ends much as the epilogue of Job, law-codes—chiefly that of Hammurabi and the Middle-Assyrian code from the ancient capital of Ashur (*c.* twelfth century)—

and various incantations, counter-incantations, prayers, and laments appropriate to fasts, both from south Mesopotamia in the second millennium and from Assyria from the ninth to the seventh century. Most of these except the legal texts and legal, economic, ritual, and political texts from Mari, and deeds from domestic archives at Nuzu (Yorghan Tepe, *c.* 100 miles from Kirkuk), and historical texts, which keep emerging from north Mesopotamia, were recovered long ago from Ashurbanipal's library at Nineveh. Fresh matter from this great store, however, is continually being deciphered and discovered with other cuneiform texts in the museums of the world, and the significance of others, the general purport of which was already known, is being freshly discovered and brought into relation with the emergent pattern of civilization in the world of the Old Testament. Many historical texts, royal inscriptions and annals, stelae and foundation-inscriptions giving résumés of the achievements of the kings of Assyria, and the Neo-Babylonian Empire, and her Persian conqueror Cyrus the Great, lists of Assyrian kings and the length of their reigns, annals dated by the annual eponym (*limmu*), have long been known. Certain of these have been duplicated and supplemented by more recent excavations in the mounds of Assyria or from hitherto unworked material, like the British Museum Babylonian Chronicle of the reigns of Nabopolassar and Nebuchadrezzar, which in its comprehensive sweep of the history of the times gives some impression of what the synchronistic histories of the kingdoms of Israel and Judah underlying the Books of Kings may have looked like, and elucidates the Biblical record of the end of the kingdom of Judah in its wider historical context from the death of Josiah to the fall of Jerusalem in 597 B.C. The relevance of these historical texts together with the historical texts from the Amorite city of Mari, which are one of the major discoveries relevant to Hebrew origins in recent times, will be considered more particularly in the context of the history of Israel.

With the appraisal of the spectacular discoveries of the middle of last century a pan-Babylonian school came into being, which, with some measure of justification, roused keen opposition, though not always from those best qualified to criticize. Now we may attempt a more just appraisal of the contribution of Mesopotamian archaeology to the study of the Old Testament.

The exposure of Mesopotamia, like Syria and Palestine, to seasonal migration of nomadic shepherds and occasionally to invasion by the same Semitic stock from the Arabian steppes, which eventually brought the Amorites to supreme power in Mesopotamia, prepares us to expect that the Hebrews and their

Canaanite and Aramaean neighbours would share much with the Mesopotamian Semites in social conventions and institutions, and in religion, both in oral and ritual expression. This is notably exemplified in the code of Hammurabi on the famous black diorite stele recovered from Susa, where it had been taken as the spoils of some Elamite victory, and by the Assyrian laws in comparison with Hebrew social law in the Book of the Covenant (Ex. 20^{22}–23^{33}).

Here, however, in spite of important fundamental affinities, there are notable differences. The Mesopotamian codes, for instance, reflect the complexities of urban society and are ultimately a development of Sumerian law, known from earlier codes more recently discovered, such as the code of Ur-Nammu, founder of the IIIrd Dynasty of Ur (*c.* 2050 B.C.), which was found in 1952, and that of Lipit-Ishtar on excerpts from tablets from Nippur about a century before Hammurabi, and that of the city of Eshnunna from Tell Abu Hirmil east of Baghdad. The Mesopotamian laws reflect a keen property sense and a class consciousness that occasionally result in inhuman severity. Hebrew law, while to a certain degree an adaptation of the law of urban Canaanite society, which had a fundamental affinity in form and content with Mesopotamian law, as the late Professor Alt ably contended, is informed throughout with a respect for human dignity in a virtually classless society conscious of its solidarity as the covenanted people of God. The native Israelite element, which Alt distinguished by form-criticism as " apodeictic law " in contrast with what he terms the " casuistic law " familiar in Mesopotamian, and conceivably also characteristic of Canaanite, law, differs markedly from Mesopotamian law in its presentation of the principles of morality as God's categorical imperative. This instance is illustrative of the great service archaeology has done to the study of the Bible. It has been occasionally alleged that archaeologists in adducing so many foreign affinities have lost the sense of the distinctive character of the word of God to Israel. On the contrary the comparative method of archaeology, precisely in adducing so many affinities, has particularized the distinctive character of Israel and her revelation and her adaptation of those very elements, and has thrown them into high relief. This is evidenced in law ; it is also evidenced in mythology, in the writing of history, and in the Flood narratives, where the two discrepant versions in Genesis reproduce the broad theme of the Mesopotamian Flood episode in the Gilgamesh epic. The latter, however, has no moral point, whereas in the Hebrew adaptation the details are really quite insignificant in comparison with the central theological theme that man's sin occasions the catastrophic wrath of God. The

Hebrew writers who reproduced with certain modifications the Mesopotamian Flood-tradition used it, moreover, as an episode in the story of God's saving act in the election and preservation of a people bound to Himself by covenant as a people of destiny. This sense of election and progressive guidance in adversity and prosperity towards a Divinely-appointed destiny characterizes Hebrew historical writing throughout the Old Testament. The royal annals of Assyria are much more meticulous and detailed in their accounts of the marches, victories, spoils, and casualties in the campaigns of the warrior-kings of Assyria, or of their building projects or settlements of deported peoples. The neo-Babylonian chronicles pay less attention to detail, but show more appreciation of the broader significance of the events they record. Neither, however, shows any consciousness of the universal significance of these events or the trend of history towards an appointed destiny in which the protagonists were involved in victory or defeat. This distinction was reserved for Israel, who in this particular far outstripped her neighbours in Mesopotamia or Egypt.

Before passing on to the history of Israel in the light of archaeology it is appropriate to note the contribution of Mesopotamian archaeology to the chronology of antiquity, which is vital to the intelligible understanding of the concatenation of cause and effect which is history. We have already mentioned Assyrian lists of the names and titles of eponym officials (*limmu*). There are also records of events which occurred in their year of office. Cross-references may then be made to royal annals, which makes relative dating possible. The necessary supplement is king-lists giving the sequence and duration of the reigns of the kings of Assyria. The most significant is that found by the expedition of the Oriental Institute of the University of Chicago in 1932–3 at Khorsabad (ancient Dur-Sharrukin) but published only in 1942. It is dated in 738 B.C. and gives a complete list of Assyrian kings down to Ashurnirari V. (755–745 B.C.), being corroborated, in spite of minor variations, by another king-list of uncertain provenance bought in Mosul and published in 1954. In the earlier periods only the names of the kings are noted without the length of their reigns, but for the rest the lists are full. The key to the system is the note of a solar eclipse in the month of Simanu in the *limmu*-ship of Pur-Shagale, which may be astronomically dated to 15th June 763 B.C. Since the office of Pur-Shagale coincided with the ninth year of Ashurdan III., we may reckon back and forward by the aid of king-lists and *limmu*-chronicles, and, at least, for the period of the history of Israel, establish a firm chronology. The period covered by the Khorsabad king-list and the somewhat later period to which the *limmu*-canons extend are overlapped by the canon of Ptolemy, the great Alexandrine astronomer, geographer, historian, and chronologist, which extends to Roman imperial times. Within this framework we find certain synchronisms between the history of Israel, Assyria, Babylon, Persia, and the Greek dynasties which ruled in Egypt and Asia after Alexander the Great, so that a reconstruction of a firm chronology for the history of Israel and the Jews is possible throughout the Biblical period.

(ii) NEIGHBOURS OF ISRAEL

Though the elucidation of the identity and culture of Hurrians and Hittites is one of the major achievements of recent archaeology, we cannot regard them as more than peripheral to the history of Israel, and so limit our treatment.

The Hurrians, first recognized through their peculiar names in Akkadian texts from Mesopotamia, where they were associated with the state of Mitanni with its capital on a tributary of the Khabur, where an Aryan military aristocracy ruled over a Hurrian subject-people, appeared again in texts from the Hittite capital at Boghaz-köi. They are now recognized as a definite ethnic element of Armenoid stock from Lake Van to Syria, and from the occurrence of such names on cuneiform tablets from Qatna east of the Upper Orontes and Taanach and Shechem in Palestine and in the Amarna Tablets they seem to have been present there in the second half of the second millennium, when the majority of cylinder seals from Palestine are of Hurrian design. While those were possibly the Hurrians (Horites) of whom the Old Testament speaks, we question whether they were more than a minority of feudal commanders and their retainers in the Egyptian domination. At Ras Shamra in North Syria, where we expect them to be more numerous, administrative texts indicate that they were professional soldiers behind the native dynasty. Their numbers here are further indicated by Hurrian word-lists and even whole texts in the Hurrian language.

As the result of former and more recent research the Hittites are increasingly well known both from their material remains and from their documents until the collapse of their empire *c.* 1200 B.C. before the influx of " sea-peoples," including the Philistines, whom Hittite and Egyptian records attest as mercenaries of both powers for about three centuries. Egyptian records of the XVIIIth and XIXth Dynasties attest the development of a struggle with the Hittites for control of Syria, which culminated in a *modus vivendi*, with inland Syria a sphere of Hittite influence as far south as Qadesh on the Upper Orontes and Palestine and the Syrian coast under

Egyptian influence. This tension is reflected in Akkadian documents from Ras Shamra till its destruction *c.* 1200 B.C. Ugarit apparently strove hard to maintain good relations with both Egypt and the Hittites, and the latter apparently considered the city-state so important that they did not as a rule venture to interfere too blatantly in her politics. These facts should prevent us from accepting too literally the reference to " Hittites " in pre-Israelite Palestine, as in the tradition of Abraham and Ephron " the Hittite " at Hebron. Various attempts have been made to demonstrate the literal truth of this. It is, for instance, pointed out that Abraham's transaction, in which he was obliged to acquire with the cave the adjoining land and trees, is paralleled by Hittite practice in conveyance of land. Here, however, as in the use of Akkadian script and language and in feudal procedure in general, the Hittites were probably but conforming to general usage in the contemporary Near East. Apart from a deposit of Hittite arms from a thirteenth-century temple at Bethshan, possibly a votive trophy, archaeology can adduce no material evidence of the Hittites in Palestine.

The "kings of the Hittites," the contemporaries of Solomon (1 Kings 10^{29}), may have been descended from Anatolian refugees or powerful feudal barons in their Syrian fiefs who survived the fall of the Hittite empire, but here the situation is complicated by the settlement of Aramaean tribesmen from the beginning of the first millennium. This situation may yet be satisfactorily elucidated by the decipherment of the so-called " Hittite hieroglyphs," which are a feature of certain Syrian sites like Hamath, which the now famous bi-lingual inscription of Karatepe north of the Plain of Adana in such hieroglyphs and in the linear Phoenician alphabet and certain bilingual seals from the palace of Ras Shamra have now made possible. In view of the Semitic element in the Syrian states these inscriptions are potentially important for Bible study.

Uriah the Hittite may have been such a " displaced person," either a Hittite or perhaps a Hurrian, the name strongly suggesting the Hurrian *ewir*, found in the Ras Shamra texts as a military title. The Assyrian records, as we know, used the term " Hittite " loosely to denote Syrians and even Palestinians, who were predominantly Semitic. So " Hittites " referring to people in pre-Israelite Palestine may be a case of such loose usage, though here the term may have a little more precision, referring to non-Semitic Hurrians from the north, who, as we have pointed out, are attested in Palestine in texts from the Amarna Age.

There is a good deal of interesting archaeological evidence

of the violent irruption into Palestine of the Philistines just after the final decisive stage of the Hebrew settlement *c.* 1225 B.C., and of their occupation mainly in the coastal plain south of Jaffa, especially in a debased type of late Mycenaean painted pottery. The various Aegean influences by which Mycenaean motifs are contaminated reflect the wanderings of the Philistines and their associates before they settled in Palestine. This ware is current in Palestine in the coastal plain and at certain strategic places in the interior from the twelfth to the end of the eleventh century, which is also the period of the clay "slipper" coffins with features moulded on the lid over the face with head-dress which suggests the hair helmet-crest distinctive of these warriors in Egyptian sculptures. Such information is supplemented by Egyptian inscriptions which note their coming and claim that Rameses III. settled them in fortresses in Palestine as garrison troops, which may well be true. The Egyptian papyrus of the envoy Wenamon (*c.* 1100 B.C.) also mentions them at the seaport of Dor in the north of the Plain of Sharon. Since their political contact with Israel was limited in time and scope in the latter period of the Judges and the early monarchy and they made no known cultural contribution, but were in fact themselves assimilated as the tradition of their worship of the Semitic Dagon and the disappearance of their distinctive pottery suggests, the subject need not detain us.

The natural influence on Israel was the culture of the Semitic Amorites, Canaanites, and Aramaeans.

Mesopotamian texts of the late third millennium refer to the people of North Syria and the North Arabian steppes as *Amurru*, hence the term Amorite, and the Amorites as we have seen came to dominate Mesopotamia from the beginning of the second millennium. The destruction of most urban sites in Syria and Palestine towards the end of the third millennium and the eclipse of Egypt at that time in what is known as the First Intermediate Period is associated with the irruption of tribesmen from the steppes. After the recovery of Egypt certain texts which ceremonially curse the enemies of the Pharaoh in Syria and Palestine among others suggest by the names that they were Amorites of the same stock as predominated in Mesopotamia. The fact that in many cases several chiefs are named in the same locality, such as Ashkelon and Jerusalem, which had respectively three and two chiefs, has suggested to Albright that they were still at a tribal stage of social and political development. This is borne out by Dr. Kenyon's discovery of five different types of burial at the same period at this time at Jericho. Certain of these tribal groups were apparently absorbed in other, probably older, elements culturally much more advanced, especially in settlements on the coast and along the trunk highways through Palestine and Syria, which expanded and flourished again after the recovery of the protecting power of Egypt. These were the Canaanites. As for the Amorites, whom the Old Testament mentions and locates specifically in the mountains (Num. 13^{29}), they may well be those rude tribal elements who, through their intense tribal particularism, or because of the poorer, more isolated areas they occupied, remained aloof and less open to the influence of the urban centres on the coast and more favoured sites in the plains, where archaeology demonstrates a cultural recovery from the nineteenth century, especially in the royal tombs at Byblos and sphinxes of the royal Egyptian family at Ras Shamra and at Qatna east of the Upper Orontes.

Canaan, in Akkadian *Kinaḫna,* is used of the cities on the Syrian coast in Mesopotamian texts from the second millennium, being probably derived from *kinaḫḫu,* purple dye, one of the notable products of the region in which Mesopotamian merchants were particularly interested, as we know from the correspondence of a business house at Ras Shamra. The term is used in the Amarna texts to denote this region and also Palestine in general, and this corresponds to Biblical usage, Canaan denoting primarily the great urban centres on the Syrian coast, Sidon (Josh. 13^{4}) and Tyre (Isa. 23^{11}), and secondarily areas in the plains of Palestine influenced directly by these centres culturally or politically. The term has a cultural rather than an ethnic connotation, the general unity of culture in Palestine and coastal Syria conveyed by the terms Canaan and the Canaanites being well attested by archaeology both in material remains and in the myths and legends from Ras Shamra (fourteenth to thirteenth century), which illumine Biblical references to the Canaanite way of life and indeed often modify them. In our treatment of the history of Israel, especially with reference to her institutions, and of her religion, we shall indicate the great influence of Canaan on Israel.

Contemporary with Israel in her historical period were the kingdoms of Edom, Moab, and Ammon, respectively east of the Arabah, the Dead Sea, and Jordan. Edom and Moab at least, according to Hebrew tradition, were consolidated before the final decisive stage of the Hebrew settlement in Palestine *c.* 1225 B.C., Gen. 36^{31-39} noting that there were eight kings in Edom before there was a king in Israel. This is corroborated by Glueck's surface exploration of the region, which demonstrates a recession of sedentary occupation between *c.* 1900 and 1300 B.C., after which the natural frontiers between Edom and Moab and the Amorite principality of Heshbon are heavily defended at passages over the ravines of Wadi el-Hesa (Zered) and Wadi Mujib (Arnon) by well-built fortresses. Ammon to the north apparently did not possess any walled settlements like Edom and Moab, but, as Glueck and, more recently, the Germans Gese and Hentschke have demonstrated by surface exploration, consisted of open villages in agricultural areas protected by very strong towers. As the Biblical name Bene Ammon suggests, the Ammonites maintained their tribal organization, their one large settlement Rabbath Ammon (modern ʿAmman) being the seat of the king and government. In certain seals of " servants " of kings of Ammon, which have recently come to notice or have been found in royal tombs from the vicinity of ʿAmman, there is some evidence that there were crown estates as in Judah. On the evidence from these tombs, however, and from certain pieces of rather crude statuary we must not overrate the economic or cultural status of Ammon. It has been pointed out that the royal correspondence, probably of Esarhaddon, mentions the tribute of Ammon as almost twice that of Judah. In the absence of knowledge of the particular political situation at the time the tribute was levied we cannot make any deduction regarding the relative strength of these kingdoms. It may, however, reflect Ammon's control of the caravan route from South Arabia to Damascus.

Neither Edom nor Ammon produced any inscription beyond personal names, but from Diban in Moab the famous inscription of Mesha gives direct contact with 2 Kings 3, and as well as indicating the extent of the realm of Omri and Ahab and illustrating the style, idiom, and language of royal annals contemporary with certain sources of the Books of Kings it attests the practice of the ban in a holy war, thus giving a valuable point of contact with the religion of Israel at an early stage in its development (cf. Josh. 6^{17-19}, 1 Sam. $15^{3.\ 13ff.}$).

The Aramaean states of Damascus, Hamath, Arpad, Ya'udi, and others in north Mesopotamia familiar in the Old Testament and in Assyrian records originated with the invasion of strong tribal confederacies, which Albright feasibly associates with the domestication of the camel *c.* 1200 B.C., though the Amarna Tablets and earlier Assyrian records refer to such movements from the steppe to the sown land as early as the fifteenth and fourteenth centuries. Accounts of Israel's contacts with the Aramaeans in David's reign (2 Sam. 8^{3-8}, 10^{6-19}) indicate that their migration and settlement was about two centuries after that of Israel. This is substantiated by Ingholt's excavation of Hama, which shows a cultural break *c.* 1000 B.C. The history of these states may be traced in Assyrian official records from their settlement in Mesopotamia, the Anatolian foothills, and inland Syria through the various phases of their stubborn resistance to Assyria to their final liquidation in the second half of the eighth century. From the Aramaean strata in excavations at Tell Halaf (Biblical Gozan) in the Khabur region of north Mesopotamia and at Hama on the Orontes, it is apparent that the Aramaeans made no distinctive cultural contribution, but played an assimilative role. About a dozen alphabetic inscriptions in the Canaanite (Phoenician) and Aramaic dialects occasionally supplement the information of the Assyrian records and passages in Kings. They attest the deities worshipped, Baal Shamain ("Lord of the Sky"), the Canaanite Hadad, Baal Melkart ("Lord of the City"), El, the senior god of the Canaanite pantheon, Elyon ("the Exalted"), Shamash (the Sun), Sin (the Moon-god), called Sahar ("the Bright"), his consort Nikkal, Athtar, the Venus-star, Reshef, the Canaanite god who slew men in mass by pestilence or war, and Yaw, which as a theophoric name from Ya'udi in North Syria suggests, may be a form of Yahweh.

In view of such inscriptions we may well suppose that the Aramaeans, like Israel and Judah, also kept annals. These, however, have perished, and the fact that, by contrast, those of Israel were preserved in the self-critical Deuteronomic history is but one more instance of the distinction of Israel which archaeology repeatedly emphasizes.

(iii) ARCHAEOLOGY AND BIBLICAL EVENTS

Archaeology defines the horizons of the patriarchal period in attesting the recession of civilization in Palestine and Syria towards the end of the third millennium and the Amorite, or proto-Aramaean, settlement of the early second millennium. The settlements, named in the Egyptian Execration Texts, including Jerusalem, now named for the first time in history, were fairly thinly distributed, especially in the mountains south and east of Shechem, where the Hebrew patriarchs are depicted as wandering. The distribution of the particular theophoric names in the Execration Texts and of the patriarchs at this time from the south to the north of Mesopotamia and southwards through Palestine reflects the traditional wanderings of Abraham and his kindred. More particularly Terah, Nahor and Serug, which appear in Genesis as personal names of Abraham's kindred in the vicinity of Haran in north Mesopotamia, are named in tablets of a colony of Mesopotamian merchants at Kanesh (Kara Huyuk) in Anatolia, the Cappadocian Tablets, in the twentieth century and in the political texts from Mari in the eighteenth century as towns in that region, which may well perpetuate the sheikh or ancestor of the tribes who settled the area. The term *Beni-iamini*, however, which has been hailed as a sensational mention of the

Israelite tribe Benjamin in the Mari texts, means simply "southerners" (lit. "sons of the right hand") in contrast to "northerners" (*Beni-shamali*), who are also mentioned. Certain features of Mesopotamian law, *e.g.* licensed concubinage in the event of childlessness, as in the code of Hammurabi, indicate the verisimilitude of the tradition associating Abraham with Mesopotamia. Domestic archives from Nuzu in north Mesopotamia *c.* 1400 B.C., then a predominantly Hurrian community, confirm this convention, and in forbidding the expulsion of the concubine who has borne a child, give an even closer parallel to the tradition of Abraham and Hagar (Gen. $21^{10ff.}$). They suggest similar conclusions in the case of Jacob, possession of *teraphim* (household images) giving the right of inheritance, even in preference to a son of the house (cf. Gen. 31^{32-35}). Archaeology, however, cannot particularize further concerning the Hebrew patriarchs.

It is often suggested that the occupation of Egypt by the alien Hyksos *c.* 1730 B.C. accounts for the promotion of Joseph, and that the revival of native Egyptian power and the expulsion of the Hyksos *c.* 1580 B.C. explains the persecution of the Hebrews by "a Pharaoh who knew not Joseph." The matter is not quite so simple, and the accumulation of archaeological evidence definitely excludes a date for the Exodus in the XVIIIth Dynasty. Actually a recently discovered papyrus in the Brooklyn Museum, New York, lists a number of Semites in Egypt, certain of whom, like Joseph, were chamberlains in native households, but this was before the Hyksos period. Later texts again attest Semites in Egypt, including one Arisu, a Syrian, who was vizier in the eleventh century. Actually the inscription of Horemheb, the founder of the XIXth Dynasty, recording his relief of Asiatics in the east Delta "after the manner of their fathers from the beginning" suggests many descents to Egypt and doubtless many cases of Exodus also. In the conflicting data regarding the route and other details source analysis suggests a conflation of various traditions.

Archaeology, if unable to furnish evidence for a fixed date for the Hebrew conquest of Palestine which would support the account of the combined operations in the Book of Joshua, has confirmed the account in Judg. $1^{9ff.}$ of a sporadic settlement mainly confined to the hills of the interior and effected by the tribes acting for the most part independently. Certain sites, such as Bethel and Tell Beit Mirsim (probably Kiriath-sepher, also known as Debir), were destroyed about the beginning of the Iron Age (thirteenth century) and rebuilt on a meaner scale. Other settlements in the hills, such as Tell el-Ful (Gibeah of Saul) and Seilun (Shiloh) took their origin now.

Various sites associated with the Israelite settlement have been excavated, and the result of earlier excavations checked in the light of more accurate knowledge of Palestinian ceramics. Ai ("Ruined Mound"), it is found, lay derelict between 2000 and *c.* 1150 B.C., and the only explanation of the role it plays in Hebrew tradition is that the site was occupied by the men of Bethel to resist the advance of Israel from Jericho. Recent work at Jericho compels a drastic revision of the too positive findings of Garstang, the very scanty evidence of the Late Bronze Age city suggesting *c.* 1350–1325 B.C. as the latest date of occupation. Experienced archaeologists are now very chary of using evidence from this badly eroded mound for this period. Bethel was destroyed just before or just after 1300, and about the same time inscriptions of Seti I. at Bethshan attest the activity of *'Apirw* in the hills, probably north of the city. These may be Hebrews of the tribe of Naphtali, those who later penetrated to Upper Galilee and defeated the local Canaanites under the hegemony of Hazor at the Waters of Merom, possibly Meirun by Safed at the head of the Wadi el-Amud. After this battle Hazor was destroyed, an event which the recent excavations of Professor Yadin have dated *c.* 1200 B.C. This is roughly the date of the destruction of Tell Beit Mirsim and Tell ed-Duweir in the south, but here we must reckon with the independent action of Othniel the Kenizzite, while Lachish may have been destroyed by the Philistines and other "sea-peoples" early in the twelfth century. The surface exploration of Glueck in Transjordan gives *c.* 1300 B.C. as the *terminus a quo* for the wandering of the Israelites in the Arabah and Transjordan, there being no kingdoms of Edom and Moab to oppose their progress before that time. The question is still open, however, as to the proportion of the Israelites involved in this great trek. The mention of "Israel" in Palestine in the stele of Merneptah (1223 B.C.) suggests that some at least of the Israelites were already settled, and we regard these as a tribal confederacy of the older Jacob (or Leah) tribes, who had, we believe, settled in the Amarna Age. The problem of the date and manner of the Exodus and settlement, however, is one for literary criticism perhaps even more than for archaeology.

Besides the destruction or dereliction of certain sites and their rebuilding on a much less pretentious scale, the settlement of Israel seems to be marked by the building and fortification of hill-towns in districts hitherto thinly populated. A fortress of this period was excavated by Albright at Tell el-Ful. Having first served as a Philistine garrison-post (I Sam. 13 after LXX), its casemate-walled fort was the headquarters of Saul and his striking-force including David.

Material remains of David's reign are rare and uncertain. The material developments of Solomon's reign, however, are evidenced in the copper-mines of the Arabah and Glueck's excavation of Tell el-Kheleifeh, Solomon's seaport of Ezion-geber on the Gulf of ʿAqaba, where a certain amount of ship-building was also indicated (1 Kings 9^{26}). The fortifications of Megiddo (fourth level), Lachish, Gezer, and Hazor, with their heavily fortified double gates, illustrate fortified cities in the new state of Israel, though the Megiddo fortification is later than the time of Solomon and that of Lachish possibly the work of Rehoboam. The famous stables at Megiddo now prove not to have been all from the time of Solomon. Those on the north side of the city were proved by the excavation of Dr. Yadin to have been built over a fort of Solomon's time, which has a counterpart on the south side of the city. The stable-complex in conjunction with the latter may be Solomonic.

Archaeology has also shed light on the disruption of the kingdom. The recovery of the fragment of a stele of Shoshenq I. at Megiddo bears out his inscription at Karnak (Thebes), formerly disputed, where the mention of towns in north Israel (cf. 1 Kings 14^{25-26}) suggests that, whatever Jeroboam's relations with Shoshenq may have been, the Pharaoh was determined to maintain control over the trunk road through Palestine and probably regarded Israel as a vassal state. Judah was now on the defensive against Israel and Egypt, and the excavations at Tell ed-Duweir in the south and at Tell en-Nasbeh (one of the Mizpahs) on the north frontier of Judah revealed very strong fortifications from this period (cf. 1 Kings 15^{16-22}, 2 Chron. 11^{9}). Excavations at Tell el-Farʿa, seven miles north-east of Shechem, prove that this considerable Bronze Age city, once the capital of Israel, flourished until *c.* 900 B.C., when it was partially destroyed, possibly in the civil strife which brought Omri to the fore. The subsequent reduction in the status of the town coincides with the building of the new capital Samaria on a virtually virgin site.

At Samaria the remains of the Israelite palaces on the top of the hill have been familiar since Reisner's excavations in 1908–10. Now the work of J. W. Crowfoot from 1931 to 1935 compels a revision of Reisner's dates. No differentiation is made between the palaces of Omri and Ahab ; the famous ivory inlays are dated to Ahab's time ; and the fiscal dockets, which illustrate the agricultural economy and religious syncretism of Israel in Hosea's time are dated in the reign of Jeroboam II.

Assyrian annals supplement Palestinian archaeology with objective evidence for the history of Israel. From the records of Shalmaneser III. we learn that Ahab took a leading part in an alliance with the Aramaean states of Syria in opposing the Assyrian advance to the west at Qarqar on the Orontes in 853 B.C., where he put 2,000 chariots into the field, actually the largest chariot-contingent in the alliance. This has a threefold significance. It bears out the Old Testament statement that Solomon built up a large chariot-force, most of which would be the foundation of Ahab's strength; taken in conjunction with Shalmaneser's recording of Jehu's tribute in 841 B.C., it fixes the date of Ahab's death in 853 B.C. and the first year of Jehu's reign in 841 B.C., and makes possible a firm chronology of the Hebrew monarchy by a critical use of the numbers in Kings; in mentioning one of the most significant political events of the time in the history of Western Asia, which is entirely ignored in the Old Testament, it reminds us of the fact that the Deuteronomic compilation of Kings is not a secular history, but a theological work, the strictly historical sources being used selectively in the interests of the major theological theme of God's guidance of the destiny of His people through favour and discipline, the final element predominating.

Besides references in Assyrian inscriptions to the history of the Aramaean state of Damascus, which indirectly elucidate the account of Israel's wars with Damascus in Kings, the vassal status of Menahem and Hoshea is corroborated by Assyrian records which name both, and from the annals of Tiglath-pileser III. we learn that in 732 B.C. Galilee, Transjordan and the Plain of Sharon were annexed to the Assyrian Empire as the provinces of Megiddo, Gilzau (Gilead), Du'ru (Dor) (cf. 2 Kings 15[29] and possibly Isa. 9[1]). This campaign was marked by the destruction of the third level at Megiddo and the rebuilding of the city as the administrative centre of the province, with a large fort commanding a view of Esdraelon and the Galilaean foothills. Dr. Yadin's recent excavations at the great frontier-city of Hazor have given further evidence of the campaign of Tiglath-pileser.

The end of the last remnant of Israel, the district of Samaria, and the deportation of 27,290 inhabitants is attested in an inscription of Sargon II., unfortunately rather summary and in long retrospect. Assyrian inscriptions recording rebellions and campaigns in the coastal plain south of the Yarkon (Nahr Auja) associated with the Philistines give evidence of Assyria's interest in the road to Egypt, the ultimate goal of her imperial expansion. This she secured by placing vassals in office and even military colonists. Further evidence of this phase of history has been supplied by a distinctive pottery peculiar to the period at Samaria, Tell el-Far'a (Tirzah),

Dothan, and in a tomb at ʻAmman, and at the frontier fortress of Tell Jemmeh in the Wadi Ghazzeh, which is common in the ruins of the Assyrian palace at Nineveh. Two deeds of conveyance in Assyrian cuneiform from Gezer, dated 649 B.C., are further evidence of Assyrian control of the trunk road to Egypt.

The eventful reign of Hezekiah is well elucidated by archaeology. The famous Siloam tunnel in Jerusalem, which brought water from the Spring of Gihon in the Kidron ravine east of the city wall to the pool within the city is almost certainly the work ascribed to Hezekiah in 2 Kings 20^{20} and 2 Chron. 32^{30}, and his unsuccessful revolt in 701 B.C. is also noted in more detail in Sennacherib's inscriptions than in the Old Testament, since we learn only in the Assyrian sources that Hezekiah was stripped of all his realm except Jerusalem and the neighbourhood, probably his personal crown lands. The apparent discrepancy in Kings as to the reason for Sennacherib's sudden withdrawal suggested to critics that there is a conflation of the traditions of two expeditions. Laming Macadam's recent discovery of an inscription of Tirhakah from the Sudan clearly demonstrates that he would have been too young for action in 701 B.C., so that, if the Scriptural reference to Tirhakah is accurate, a second expedition would seem to be indicated before the death of Sennacherib in 681 B.C. and of Hezekiah in 686 B.C., though there is no explicit Assyrian record of this.

The reign of Hezekiah's son Manasseh, who is branded in Hebrew tradition as a notorious apostate to the astral cults of Assyria, is known from Assyrian inscriptions to have been so strictly under Assyrian control that he was obliged with other vassal kings from Syria, Edom, and Moab to be present in Nineveh as a supervisor, or even as a hostage, while his subjects served in labour gangs on Esarhaddon's public works, and an inscription of Ashurbanipal mentions him as present in his campaign in Egypt in 668 B.C.

It is generally recognized that the reformation under Josiah was a gesture of defiance to Assyria reaching beyond Jerusalem and Judah to the zone of Assyrian control in the west and in the district of Samaria as Assyria was more and more involved in the homeland and unable to keep control in Palestine. The question of the extent of Josiah's power in the coastal plain is a matter of dispute, but the view of Alt and Noth that the topographical lists in the tribal boundaries in Joshua really described the extent of the realm as visualized in Josiah's programme finds corroboration in a Hebrew letter of the time from a Judaean fortress in the maritime settlement of Yabneh, the appeal of a peasant against the commander Hoshaiah who against the law in the Book of the Covenant (Ex. 22^{26}; cf. Deut. 24^{10-13} and Am. 2^{8}) has distrained the poor man's cloak for default in contribution of corn.

The decline of the Jewish state is now much elucidated by the publication of later parts of the Babylonian Chronicle by D. J. Wiseman (1956), the earlier parts having been published by C. J. Gadd (1923), and Sidney Smith (1924). This chronicle shows that after the fall of Nineveh (612 B.C.) and Harran (610 B.C.) an Egyptian army crossed the Euphrates and made a great, but unsuccessful, effort to retake Harran. On his way the Pharaoh (Necho) encountered Josiah at Megiddo and blasted hopes of a revival of the glories of David's kingdom. This encounter may now be dated in or just before Tammuz (June-July) 609 B.C., and Necho's deposition of Josiah's son Jehoahaz and his elevation of Jehoiakim to the throne may by the same evidence be dated to the autumn of that year. The subsequent conflict of Babylon and Egypt in the coastal plain of Palestine and the periodic involvement of Judah is lucidly documented in the Babylonian Chronicle, which dates the siege of Jerusalem precisely from December (Chislev) 598 B.C. to March (Adar) 597 B.C., when the city fell and Jehoiachin was captured with his family after a reign of three months (2 Kings 24^{8}).

The last phase of the history of the kingdom of Judah is graphically illustrated by the excavations at Tell ed-Duweir (Lachish), especially by the famous Lachish letters. These, however, must be used soberly, only five of them being more than hopelessly fragmentary. They attest divided counsels in Judah (cf. Jer. 38^{4}), with suspicion and state espionage, men of doubtful loyalty or pacifist tendencies being taken into custody (cf. Jer. 38^{13-21}). Since the fall of Azekah, mentioned with Jerusalem and Lachish in Jeremiah, is indicated, the Lachish dispatches from a military officer or perhaps a political agent may well be from the last days of the kingdom. They are, however, advisedly cryptic, and we may not particularize on events or personnel. They are, notwithstanding, an excellent commentary on Jeremiah, and the script enables us to visualize Baruch's record of the oracles of Jeremiah (Jer. 36), and is an important instrument of textual criticism.

Two seals of this period have a peculiar interest as probably relics of protagonists in the drama of the fall of Judah. The seal-impression of "Gedaliah who is over the House" denotes a royal chamberlain, probably that Gedaliah who was appointed native governor or steward over Judah at Mizpah by the Babylonians in 586 B.C. A seal found at Tell en-Nasbeh with a fine engraving of a gamecock and the legend "Belonging to Yaazaniah" would well accord with the status and calling of the commander Yaazaniah, the associate of Ishmael in the assassination of Gedaliah at Mizpah (2 Kings 24[23]).

The Babylonian Exile, such an important period in the development of the literature and religion of Israel, still remains comparatively obscure. Mizpah apparently served as the provincial capital after the destruction of Jerusalem, its location at Tell en-Nasbeh being suggested by the fact that, though almost every site explored in Judah now shows traces of destruction, Tell en-Nasbeh was undisturbed. Neither local archaeology nor Babylonian documents give any hint of the administration of Palestine. A few cuneiform tablets, brief fiscal dockets from the basement of Nebuchadrezzar's citadel in Babylon, published in 1939, actually mention rations to the captive king Jehoiachin and his family (2 Kings 25[30]). They mention others from Palestine and Syria, including Philistines, and refer specifically to certain craftsmen, who are also mentioned as being deported with Jehoiachin (2 Kings 24[14]).

Much more is known of the Persian administration of Palestine after the victory of Cyrus the Great in 539 B.C., when Palestine became part of the fifth satrapy " Beyond the River." Judah was one administrative district, Samaria, Ammon beyond Jordan, Ashdod in the coastal plain, and Arabia extending as far north as Hebron, with Lachish probably as its administrative centre, being other districts. Here the site of the old Jewish palace-fort was occupied by a much more modest residence of the Persian period, possibly the seat of " Gashmu the Arabian," with Sanballat of Samaria and Tobiah of Ammon the antagonist of Nehemiah (Neh. 2[19]) in his fortification of Jerusalem. In view of the mention of Gishem, or Geshem, in an inscription on a votive silver bowl of his son Qainu (Cain) the king of Kedar in a shrine of the North Arabian goddess han-Allat at Tell Maskhutah (Succoth of the Exodus), however, Nehemiah's antagonist Gashmu may have been not the provincial governor of south Palestine but the ruler of an Arabian province. Sanballat is mentioned as governor of Samaria in a letter from the Jewish-Aramaean military colony at Elephantine dated in 410 B.C., by which time Sanballat seems to have left the administration in the hands of his sons, which would accord with the statement in Nehemiah that he actively opposed Nehemiah's programme in Jerusalem in *c.* 444 B.C. While there is no clear reference to the individual Tobiah, there is certain evidence of the influence of his family in Ammon in a papyrus letter from an Ammonite governor Tobiah to one Zeno, a fiscal official of Ptolemy II. (285–246 B.C.) in Egypt, and from the family tomb at Iraq el-Amir some twenty miles north-east of Jericho, which is inscribed with the name Tobiah in Aramaic characters which have been dated in the third century B.C. The district of Ashdod had a very mixed population. Military colonists from Mesopotamia had been planted by Assyria; more recently Edomites, including the family of Herod the Great, had migrated from the East; and excavations by the Mandatory Department of Antiquities near Haifa at Tell Abu Hawam and Athlit, together with a Phoenician inscription from the sarcophagus of Eshmunazzar of Sidon (*c.* 300 B.C.) attest Phoenician settlement through the district. Hence the region was less conservative than Judah in Hellenistic times and was eventually the field of Philip the Evangelist. The province of Judah, called Yehud on official stamps and jar-handles (as in the Book of Ezra), was under a Persian governor, at least from the end of the fifth century, as we know from one of the papyri of the Jewish military colony at Elephantine. What official status, if any, Zerubbabel had is uncertain, but the Jewish High Priest was eventually admitted as an assessor to the Persian governor, his name actually appearing on coins, such as one found at Bethsur, the frontier town just north of Hebron.

The Diaspora of Israel is attested mainly by documents. In cuneiform texts from Nippur in south Mesopotamia, from the business archives of the Murashu firm of bankers and estate brokers in the Persian period various Jewish names indicate that some at least of the descendants of the exiles had risen to affluence. The numbers and influence, economic and intellectual, of the Jews in lower Egypt is familiar from Roman history and from papyri as well as from the writings of Philo. The papyri from Elephantine have long been known. In the royal directory regarding the festival of Unleavened Bread the influence of a Jewish commissioner for religious affairs is apparent, suggesting the status and commission of Ezra (Ezra $7^{12ff.}$). The story of this interesting community is carried a little further with the recent publication of more of these documents, and it is interesting to note that the ruined temple, regarding which the local elders had corresponded with the Persian governor and the High Priest in Jerusalem, was apparently restored. Inscriptions from Asia Minor and references in Latin writers of the early Empire indicate a wide dispersion of Jews throughout the Mediterranean, which, as indicated in the Acts and Pauline Epistles, had already begun, presumably in the Greek period. A synagogue was discovered at Delos as early as the second century B.C., and others with inscriptions at Miletus, Priene, and Aegina may be as early. We have published new epigraphic evidence for Jewish settlement in Cyrenaica in the Ptolemaic and early Roman periods which we found in a cemetery at Tocra near Benghazi.

The story of the resurgence of Jewish nationalism in the second century B.C. may be traced in the vicissitudes of strategic settlements at the head and foot of passes from the coastal plain to the mountains of Judah, such as Bethsur at the head of the pass from Marissa commanding access to the interior by the Wadi el-Afranj and the Vale of Elah, Gezer, which commanded access to Judah by the Vale of Sorek, and Samaria, commanding the pass from the coastal plain to the Jordan valley north of Judah. The heavy fortification of these places attests the intensity of the struggle by Jews and Seleucid forces, while their subsequent decay attests the final Jewish triumph when with the establishment of the Hasmonaean monarchy they ceased to have strategic significance either as bastions of Jewish defence, as Bethsur, or as Seleucid bases, like Marissa, where the presence of the Seleucid forces is attested by a town-plan with a quite un-Oriental regularity and by a great number of stamped handles from wine jars imported from Rhodes.

The most significant discovery from this period is the monastic settlement, probably Essene, at Khirbet Qumran and ʿAin Feshkha, which illustrates a phase in the life of Israel between the Jewish and the Christian eras. The Manual of Discipline of this "Sect of the New Covenant" illustrates the piety of a not inconsiderable element in the population of Palestine before and during the lifetime of our Lord until the fall of Jerusalem in A.D. 70. If, as the evidence seems to indicate, the sect was Essene, and if, as Josephus states, their members were found "in almost every city" in the land we may well imagine much in the Sermon on the Mount specially directed to them among those who heard Jesus in Galilee. John the Baptist, who baptized in the Jordan not very far from Qumran, would certainly have knowledge of this sect and their ethic, and may himself have once been a member or a probationer of the sect, the limitations of whose life and ritual are implied in his mission. Among the non-biblical texts in the Qumran MSS. tendentious "commentaries" on Biblical texts, especially the Prophets, exemplify what we should regard as very questionable ways of using Scripture, such as are familiar in Rabbinic usage, best exemplified in the New Testament in the doctrinal sections of the Pauline Epistles. The "commentaries" reflect also the internal tension in Judaism which developed during the Seleucid supremacy and broke out into open hostility when Jewish independence was won under Judas Maccabaeus and his brothers, who went on to gratify their personal ambitions as secular rulers and, in the eyes of many, illegitimate High Priests. The same writings and the scroll of the "War of the Sons of Light against the

Sons of Darkness" reflects the mood of expectancy of the consummation of an age and the Divine inbreaking into history which characterized the eve of the Messianic advent. The "War" scroll and the Psalms reflect the ethical dualism with its concomitant angelology, which became a feature of Pharisaism and was developed in Judaism possibly under Persian Zoroastrian influence, and is presupposed in apocalyptic both Jewish and Christian.

With the advent of Rome as suzerain power in the East in 63 B.C. accurate and detailed history, including the *Antiquities* and *War* of Josephus, which must be critically used, make us independent of archaeology, which is so valuable in the earlier periods, and what archaeology adduces from this period is in the nature of a supplement to what is already well known.

With the Romans came Herod the Great, who became king over all Palestine, called Judaea, by decree of the Senate in 40 B.C., occupied Jerusalem in 37 B.C., and reigned till 4 B.C. Many monuments in the Graeco-Roman style and with distinctive marginal-drafted masonry and often with Greek or Latin inscriptions survive from his time. In Samaria, now the personal estate of Herod by gift of the Emperor Augustus, the acropolis, where the palaces of the Kings of Israel had once stood, was crowned with a temple to Herod's imperial patron, the podium of which still remains. A palace with ornamental gardens and bath-house at Jericho, where Herod died, has been excavated, and grim palace-forts in the desert and remote regions, prepared in case of orthodox Jewish risings against the Roman puppet of Edomite ancestry, are conspicuous, such as Kypros by Jericho, Machaerus overlooking the Dead Sea from the East, where, according to Josephus (*Ant.* XVIII. v. 2 [19]), John the Baptist was beheaded, Herodium (modern Jebel Fureidis) the conspicuous, volcano-like cone south-east of Bethlehem, Qarn Sartaba 15 miles south-east of Nablus, and the grimmest of all, Masada on the precipitous mountain-top overlooking the south end of the Dead Sea from the west, the scene of the last desperate resistance of the Jewish insurgents after the fall of Jerusalem in A.D. 70. Recent archaeological survey work there by the Israeli Department of Antiquities has identified Herod's palace-fort built like an eagle's nest on a rock platform in three stages isolated at the edge of a precipice. Aqueducts and cisterns are also clearly traced, and as much of the hill-top as was possible and practicable was left clear for cultivation in view of siege.

Herod rebuilt the sacred precinct at the reputed site of Abraham's oak at Mamre about two miles north of Hebron at Ramat el-Khalil, and also the Temple. Nothing of this survives but the south extension of the esplanade supported on vaults erroneously identified by the Crusaders as Solomon's stables and the boundary wall on the south and west. The large stones with marginal drafting in the lower courses of the latter, the famous Wailing Wall, are almost certainly Herod's work. Other works of his, conspicuous features of Jerusalem in Jesus' day, were the fortress of Antonia commanding the Temple area from the north-west, where Jesus was probably condemned before Pilate, and the palace-fort at the west angle of Jerusalem at that time, standing on the highest part of the city, which, according to certain scholars, was the headquarters of Pilate rather than the Antonia at that eventful Passover. The limestone pavement, scored for games of dice and rutted by chariot-wheels, which, according to Père H. Vincent, covered the rock platform (*Gabbatha*) in the Antonia may still be seen under the present Convent of the Sisters of Zion, and the foundations of the three great towers of Herod's palace-fort have been excavated under the Turkish citadel by the Jaffa Gate. Another site possibly associated with the death of Jesus is the large villa on the east slope of the west hill of Jerusalem, with its own mill, presses, and underground rock-hewn cells, accessible from the lower city by a stone stairway. This site, now occupied by the Church of St. Peter of the Cockcrow, was possibly the house of Caiaphas where Jesus was tried on the night He was betrayed, scourged, and detained in one of the cells till the morning. The steps and the house at least are contemporary with these events.

Just north-east of Sepphoris (Seffuriyeh) at the site of Cana of Galilee, Khirbet Qana (not Kefr Kenna on the main road from Nazareth to Tiberias), lime-plastered cisterns may be seen. On the steep detached hill south of Tiberias the remains of the palace of Herod Antipas are still visible. The sites of Capernaum (Tell Hum), Chorazin (Khirbet Kerazeh), Bethsaida (et-Tabigha), and Magdala are fairly certainly located, though the existing monuments here, including the celebrated restored synagogue at Capernaum, are all of a much later date. The Link Expedition of the Princeton Theological Seminary in 1960, which explored the Lake of Galilee under water, established the fact that the shore-line of the lake at the beginning of our era has been submerged to a considerable distance. At Majdal (Magdala), for instance, a pavement in Roman cement about 30 feet wide and 300 feet long was found at a depth of 15 feet and about 20 yards from the present shore.

In connexion with the burial of our Lord there will probably never be complete agreement on the authenticity of the site of the Holy Sepulchre, but the known facts of the location of the Antonia and Herod's palace-fort and such fragments of walls of the period as have been detected between the two indicate that the traditional Golgotha could have been just outside the north wall. In connexion with the burial and resurrection a certain inscription from Nazareth, which has been dated *c.* A.D. 10 is of peculiar interest inasmuch as it rates tomb-violation as a capital offence. In the light of this official regulation we may well understand Pilate's picket on the tomb of Jesus, and the consternation of the disciples (Matt. 28^{11-15}) on finding the tomb empty and being thus in the position of suspects in a capital offence.

About Jerusalem many family tombs from the first century B.C. to the second century A.D. have been cleared. They yielded nothing of interest except bone-caskets of limestone. The simple inscriptions on these, however, afforded the late E. L. Sukenik a clue to the script in the Dead Sea Scrolls, a working hypothesis which was in the main substantiated by the coins and pottery from the excavation of the monastery of Khirbet Qumran by G. L. Harding and R. de Vaux between 1951 and 1956. On these ossuaries there is interest in the names Jairus, Miriam (Mary), Martha, Simon bar Jonah, etc., all of which are good Jewish names, though known to us also as the names of Christians of the first generation. Such caskets, however, found recently on the west slope of the Mount of Olives in excavations from the new Church of Dominus Flevit, marked with the sign of a cross, may have a more particular significance.

The centre of Roman administration in Palestine was Caesarea, built between 25 and 13 B.C. by Herod the Great on the site of an older Phoenician settlement Straton's Tower, with all the aspect of a Graeco-Roman city of the age, forum, stadium, amphitheatre, and theatre, and a temple to Augustus. Caesarea is a wide and rich ruinfield, but nothing has yet been identified from the Herodian age except remains of the two moles which Herod ran out into the sea to make a harbour where there was no natural moorage.

The Graeco-Roman world of Paul's mission in Cyprus, Asia Minor, Greece, and Italy, with its great Roman roads, its buildings, institutions, religions, and literature is well known from Latin literature, from Egyptian papyri, from monuments of cities of the time, and from inscriptions. Occasionally among these relics an interesting point of contact with early Christianity is established, and it may be said that the evidence of official titles in inscriptions of the period confirms the accuracy of the Acts of the Apostles. Cyprus was, in fact, made a pro-consular province in 22 B.C., thus confirming the accuracy of the reference in Acts 13^{7} to Sergius

Paulus as proconsul in Paul's time; he may be actually mentioned in an inscription from Paphos dated "in the time of the proconsul Paulus." A similar inscription from Thessalonica referring to the local council as "politarchs" confirms the accuracy of the reference to "politarchs" in Paul's sojourn there (Acts 17[6]).

The inscription in the name of Claudius from Delphi referring to Lucius Junius Gallio the proconsul of Achaea does more than confirm the accuracy of the reference in Acts 18[12] to Gallio as proconsul of Achaea; it indicates the date of Paul's arrival in Corinth (see below, pp. 500 f.).

In the rostrum uncovered in the public place, or *agora*, of Corinth of that day we may have the *bēma* (A.V. "tribunal") where Paul appeared before Gallio. Erastus the *aedile*, or curator of public works, mentioned in an inscription referring to certain public works may possibly be that Erastus mentioned in 2 Tim. 4[20] as staying in Corinth, or Erastus in Rom. 16[23], who is designated as "the city chamberlain" (A.V.), though this is but a possibility.

(iv) ARCHAEOLOGY AND THE CULTURE OF ISRAEL

Apart from the political development of Israel, her culture is much elucidated by the more intensive study of documents from Babylon, Mari, and Assyria, and especially by the Ras Shamra texts discovered by C. F. A. Schaeffer since 1929 and published by C. Virolleaud and, recently, by J. Nougayrol. As a result of the latter particularly Canaan on the eve of the Hebrew settlement is known in detail far exceeding the most sanguine hopes of scholars of a generation ago. Excavations of Bronze Age settlements such as Megiddo, Taanach, Bethshan, Tell Beit Mirsim, Tell ed-Duweir, Tell el-Ajjul, Tell Jemmeh, Tell el-Far'a in the Wadi Ghazzeh, Tell el-Far'a by Nablus, and now Hazor had already given their material evidence. At Tell ed-Duweir, Megiddo, Hazor, and particularly at Bethshan temples of the deities of the fertility-cult, Baal-Hadad, Anath, and Astarte have been excavated and we are familiar with the features of these deities from reliefs and figurines in metal and clay. The Canaanite Baal is particularly well illustrated from a stele from Ras Shamra and from bronze figurines from there and from Minet el-Beida. The Canaanite shrine is also familiar in its local variations, and the plan of Solomon's Temple in conjunction with the palace is demonstrated in the somewhat later Iron Age temple at Tell Tainat near Aleppo. A Late Bronze Age temple at Hazor exemplifies the same plan of outer and inner court and inmost shrine, or "holy of holies." Altars for burnt offerings and incense have been found, and occasionally standing stones as signs of the divine presence or memorials of ancestors of the community. The citadels, fortified gateways, and walls of Canaanite cities, the houses of the inhabitants, workshops, tombs and their grave-deposits in rockhewn tombs, usually in some adjacent wadi, and the earthenware utensils of the inhabitants and weapons of the warriors are well known and conveniently accessible in several excellent manuals. Epigraphic fragments in alphabetic script from Sinai and Byblos and cuneiform tablets from Shechem and Taanach indicate that written records were kept in Canaan as early as *c.* 1500 B.C., and the Golenischeff Papyrus (*c.* 1100 B.C.), which describes the misadventures of an Egyptian envoy in Palestine and Syria, in referring to royal records at Byblos, confirms this. From the fourteenth century and just before, the Amarna Tablets have long been valued as evidence of the political situation and geography of Palestine, and contain indirect evidence of local religion and culture. The value of this matter, however, is far outweighed by the direct evidence of the Ras Shamra texts, the greatest contribution which archaeology has made to the study of the subject-matter of the Old Testament.

These texts, from the eve of the Hebrew settlement in Palestine, are most valuable because of their variety and fulness. Administrative texts in alphabetic and syllabic cuneiform from the palace—the largest outside Mesopotamia—elucidate the relative status of the king and various classes of subject, and the fiscal system. Legal texts in syllabic cuneiform, though disappointing in that they do not illustrate the full range of Canaanite law, supplement the administrative texts with respect to royal authority, feudal status and obligations, and the conditions of land-tenure, matter which is vitally relevant to the development of the Hebrew constitution in the early monarchy.

Legends of epic style and near-epic proportions concerning ancient kings (Keret and Dan'el) and anthropomorphisms in the very graphic and extensive mythology admirably illustrate Canaanite society and social conventions such as marriage, funeral, and birth rites, hospitality, asylum, etc., and supply the living context in which Hebrew society may be more fully studied.

Mesopotamian texts and others from Canaan and Egypt provide valuable material for the study of the ideology of kingship and its peculiar adaptation in Israel. The Israelite institution was closer to the Assyrian than to the Egyptian one. The king in Assyria was the personal embodiment of his people before God, as well as the channel of divine blessing to the community. He was a social figure, a protagonist in vital acts of worship and the representative of his people in fasts and humiliation, liturgies relevant to which are of peculiar interest as elucidating certain Hebrew psalms in the category of the Plaint of the Sufferer. In Egypt, on the contrary, the Pharaoh was regarded as the incarnation of the fertility-god Horus. Study of royal texts from Egypt indicate that there was a certain borrowing of their extravagant phraseology in the Hebrew Psalms, which also appears in the Ras Shamra texts. This was doubtless one of Solomon's innovations, but we must beware of literalism, and treat such language rather as courtly convention, *Hofstil*, as Gunkel termed it.

In Israel, however, the king could not rely on the halo of sanctity. The foundation of David's dynasty was certainly the crown estate of Jerusalem and the feudal retinues of the king, and only by the acquisition of Samaria did Omri succeed in founding a dynasty. Israel, however, as distinct from Judah, was reluctant to abandon the idea that the possession of the spirit, or *charisma*, in response to a crisis made the ruler and not heredity. The study of kingship in the wider context of Canaan and the ancient Near East makes it possible to emphasize features in the monarchy in Israel, both by analogy and contrast, which were not so apparent when the Israelite monarchy was studied in isolation.

(v) ARCHAEOLOGY AND THE RELIGION OF ISRAEL

The Ras Shamra myths, besides illustrating Canaanite poetry, the conventions and possibly also the language of which were freely adopted by the Hebrews, are of great importance as the verbal expression of Canaanite religion with which the Hebrews were confronted in settling in Palestine. The main body of Canaanite mythology describes the vicissitudes of Baal ("lord"), the title of Hadad ("the thunderer"), the god of the rainstorms of autumn and winter, and secondarily the god of the vegetation thereby promoted. As god of the vital winter rain Baal is the champion of Order in nature. He engages the unruly waters, triumphs, and is acclaimed king. This theme, with its language and imagery and characteristic motifs, was appropriated by Israel, and in passages in the prophets and certain psalms we may trace the adaptation of this theme in the light of Israel's experience of God in history. The Ras Shamra evidence, however, strongly suggests that the theme of God as King was peculiarly at home in the liturgy of the autumnal New Year.

The rest of the Baal-mythology describes the vicissitudes of Baal in conflict with Mot (Death, Sterility). Baal is the dying and rising vegetation god, the local variation of Tammuz, Osiris, or Dionysus. The building of a "house" for Baal on the eve of the thunder and "early rains" of autumn recalls

Solomon's dedication of the Temple at that season (1 Kings 8[2]), and the destruction of Mot by sickle, winnowing-shovel, fire, and millstone is obviously the rite of the desacralization of the first sheaf (Lev. 2[14]). Such correspondences suggest the functional nature of these myths, which we should relate to the autumnal New Year festival in anticipation of seasonal rituals in the coming agricultural year. In view of similar rituals in Israel, such as those just cited, it is significant that the ideology of the myth of the dying and rising god was not appropriated in Israelite theology. These texts, in indicating what Israel accepted and what she rejected in Canaanite culture, serve to emphasize the peculiar ethos of that peculiar people.

The Baal-myth by its very bulk in the Ras Shamra texts suggests that the Canaanites were preoccupied with ritual and myth to predispose Providence in nature to supply their material needs, and that is the impression we gain from the Old Testament. There are other indications in passages and fragments that there were other, social, aspects of Canaanite religion, which, not lending themselves to expression in myth, have been all but lost.

Though Canaan was the immediate source of influence in Hebrew religion in seasonal rituals of the fertility-cult, which Israel was to adapt to express her own historic faith, there are also parallels in Mesopotamian religion which help to a fuller understanding of Israelite religious practice, sometimes by emphasizing essential features which are obscured if we study the religion of Israel in isolation, and usually emphasizing the peculiar ethos of Israel by comparison.

The Mesopotamian variation of the myth of the triumph of the god over the forces of Chaos, in Babylon the victory of Marduk over Tiamat, the sinister deity of the lower deep and her allies, which was an element in the chief seasonal crisis of the Mesopotamian year, the Spring New Year festival, was re-echoed in the Hebrew Psalms and Prophets and in Wisdom literature, though it was rather a conscious literary borrowing comparatively late in the history of Israel. In other liturgical types such as psalms of lamentation, confession (usually negative) in fast-liturgies, and hymns, a feature of which is the invocation of the deity by a number of his titles, or, as in Israelite psalms, by the mention of his exploits, we have not so much a direct borrowing as the expression of the same general nature of the spirit of the common Semitic stock in similar circumstances. Incantations and counter-incantations are familiar in Mesopotamia, where it was believed that the forces of nature might be enlisted for good or evil by magic means. The *ašipu*, or priest potent to use spells, was in great demand, and he employed incantation and rites which neutralized the spell in each particular detail. This is an element in primitive prayer of supplication, and the detailed enumeration of sufferings survives as an essential element in psalms, and in Lamentations, Jeremiah, and Job. A feature of such liturgies is hyperbole and conventional expressions, such as being brought down to death, or being the prey of beasts, and the like. Even to read all such passages in the Old Testament together as one well-defined literary type convinces us that we cannot take all such expressions as literal, and certainly when we find similar accumulation of details in the Mesopotamian texts this view is corroborated.

The Mesopotamian texts also throw an indirect light on Hebrew prophecy in familiarizing us with the *baru* priests, who mediated the direction of the deity by augury and divination by entrails, stars, sacred arrows, or by oil drops in water. The Mari texts and a late Assyrian text from Kalhu contemporary with Isaiah suggest a closer analogy with Hebrew prophecy in referring to the direct interposition of an oracle at a political juncture by *maḫḫe*, or ecstatics. The analogy is rather with the members of the prophetic guilds than with the great prophets, in that the *maḫḫe* limit themselves to oracles *ad hoc*, whereas the great Hebrew prophets, though likewise giving topical oracles, comprehended the whole destiny of Israel in their mediation of the word of God.

The Hebrew conception of covenant too is elucidated by comparison with secular covenants of Hittite kings in the fourteenth and thirteenth centuries, which probably reflected the general practice of the time throughout the Near East. Formal affinities with the Sinai Covenant have been noted, both being imposed by the stronger on the weaker party, after a declaration of the name and status of the suzerain, who enumerates the benefits the vassal has received as a claim to obedience. Then follows the obligations, one of which is exclusive allegiance to the suzerain. Heaven and earth and various natural forces are then called to witness in the Hittite covenants, and the recipients, as in Deut. 27, are laid under the sanction of the curse. The analogy again, however, reveals the distinctive nature of the experience of Israel. The Covenant was indeed a salutary imposition from above, but the very nature of the obligations imposed was a revelation of the nature of Israel's God and an incentive to willing obedience, a revelation which declared God's love and hope for His people rather than His mere power. The vassal-treaties of the Hittite and Assyrian kings did indeed guarantee their vassals protection, but solely in the interests of the suzerain. The fact that the close formal correspondence of the Sinai Covenant is with the Hittite vassal-treaties of the fourteenth and thirteenth centuries has particular point, since the later Assyrian vassal-treaties, though corresponding in substance, do not show such close *formal* correspondence. This indicates the antiquity of the tradition of the Covenant in Israel, which by all appearances antedates the Monarchy, though the literary sources in which it is transmitted are from the early Monarchy.

(vi) ARCHAEOLOGY AND THE LITERATURE OF THE BIBLE

Ancient literature and various literary types and their forms, conventions, diction, and themes in their relation to their place in the life of the people is in itself a notable contribution by archaeology to the rediscovery of the Bible. In the light of Babylonian and Canaanite myths relating to the epiphany of God as King much that is implicit in the Psalms and Prophets is made explicit. Mesopotamian penitential psalms and even magical counter-incantations help us to understand essential features in psalms of lamentation, and incidentally emphasize by contrast the distinctively Hebrew ethos. The legends of Gilgamesh from Mesopotamia and of Aqhat and Keret and the epic style of the Baal-myth from Ras Shamra show us the features of saga-style and help in the literary analysis and thus in the appraisal of the content of Hebrew narrative.

Such texts also, and particularly the Ras Shamra texts, have helped in the restoration of the Hebrew text where it is doubtful. Many words in the Old Testament, suspect as *hapax legomena* and for that reason discarded in favour of a conjectural emendation, generally much more prosaic, are now attested in the Ras Shamra texts in so many contexts and in parallelism with words so well known that the meaning is beyond all doubt. Though the Ras Shamra texts in such instances support the Massoretic text, however, there are other cases where they suggest emendation, usually where the Massoretic text is hopelessly corrupt. In a special investigation of such cases, however, we have found that instances where the Ras Shamra texts support the Massoretic text are notably more numerous than those which suggest emendation.

Finally the most recent and striking archaeological discovery, the MSS. from Qumran and its vicinity, elucidates the period from Maccabaean times to the fall of Jerusalem in A.D. 70, particularly on the subject of an important Jewish sect, in our opinion Essenes, their ethics, eschatology, their interpretation of Scripture, and their whole theology as distinct from Rabbinic orthodoxy in the days of our Lord and the Apostles on whose authority the Gospel rests. The significance of these discoveries for Old Testament scholarship lies in the

Biblical fragments and scrolls in Hebrew, which carry the textual tradition back at least 300 years before the Greek Codices Sinaiticus and Vaticanus. If certain of these support the Massoretic text in the main, others by supporting variants from the Massoretic text in the Septuagint and, in the case of papyri from the Wadi Murabbaʿat, even peculiarities in the later recension of Lucian of Antioch (†. A.D. 312), take us back to Hebrew texts underlying the Greek translations. These indicate that the text was still fluid, though already tending towards standardization, so strongly in fact that no major doctrine based on Scripture is affected by any of the Qumran variants.

(vii) ARCHAEOLOGY AND THE TEXT OF THE NEW TESTAMENT

From the end of the eighteenth century to the present day the dry soil of Egypt has been a particularly rich source of papyrus fragments, which are of direct and indirect value for Bible study.

Some papyri contain texts of canonical Scripture of varying length, among which the most noteworthy are the fragments of John's Gospel ($18^{31-33.\ 37.\ 38}$) from the first half of the second century A.D. and the earliest papyrus fragment of the Greek Old Testament, containing Deut. 23^{24}–24^{3}, 25^{1-3}, $26^{12.\ 17-19}$, 28^{31-33}, dated *c.* 150 B.C., both in the John Rylands Library in Manchester, where they were discovered. Of equal note are eleven codices dating from the second to the fourth century A.D., and containing besides parts of nine books of the Old Testament, parts of fifteen of the New and the apocryphal Book of Enoch. These codices were for the most part acquired by Sir Alfred Chester Beatty in 1931, and are known by his name, though some are the property of the University of Michigan. They include the epistles of Paul, excluding those to individuals, but including "Hebrews," coming after "Romans," arranged according to length. There are also portions of the Gospels, Acts, and Revelation. These date from *c.* A.D. 200 and are the oldest MSS. of the Epistles. With the Bodmer Papyri, at present being published, from about the same date and including Luke, John, and 1 Peter, these challenge a reinvestigation of the authority of the Codices Sinaiticus and Vaticanus, and the modern critical text based on these.

Other papyri are para-Scriptural, such as the famous "sayings of Jesus," familiar since their discovery by Grenfell and Hunt at Oxyrhynchus in 1896, and dated in the third century A.D. Many of these sayings are Scriptural; others reflections, expansions, and adaptations of Scriptural dicta; and others again quite out of character with the sayings of

Jesus in the Gospels. The fact, however, that Luke (Acts 20^{35}) cites a saying of Jesus unrecorded in any of the four Gospels indicates caution in the rejection of such matter. These may attest either less accurate oral tradition of our Lord's teaching or the tradition of His teaching fostered by popular homilies in Egypt in the second and third centuries, though the question must remain open as to the extent to which they are based upon the " sayings " source Q, which is generally admitted to have been used in the Gospels of Matthew and Luke. In general it may be said that, with certain exceptions, they are sufficiently faithful to the spirit of the canonical Gospels to be strong enough proof of the reliability and antiquity of that tradition.

Other papyri are of secular import, personal letters, not always from Christians, correspondence of local administrators, receipts on papyrus scraps or potsherds, but all are of value as illustrating the Graeco-Roman provincial world to which the Gospel was taken, and the language and idiom of the common Greek which Paul used in his missionary letters. These, however much dogmatic theology has capitalized on them, are—Hebrews and part of Romans excepted—the practical correspondence of an active field missionary.

Non-canonical, or apocryphal, Gospels too are known since the discovery in 1885 of the Gospel and Apocalypse of Peter. Most of these are late and add nothing of material worth to the canonical Gospels which bears the obvious stamp of authenticity. They are generally held to go back to second century archetypes, however, and one discovered in 1934 is dated *c.* A.D. 150. This again must be treated with respect before rejection in view of Luke's statement in the prologue to his Gospel (Luke 1^1) that many had undertaken the account of Jesus' ministry.

The find by natives of forty-four writings on papyrus wrapped in leather at Chenoboskion near Nag Hammadi in Upper Egypt almost simultaneously with the Qumran discovery is of interest rather for early Church history. These include three works known as the *Gospel of Truth*, the *Gospel of Philip*, and the *Gospel of Thomas*. They have little in common with the canonical Gospels, being not biographical but collections of more or less esoteric sayings ascribed to Jesus. From the fourth century at the earliest, they are Coptic versions of Greek originals which are thought by experts to date to the second century, but on what evidence one fails to understand. In any case, they are the earliest Gnostic writings extant in the Christian period and inspired by Christianity, but their value for New Testament study is decidedly limited. This much can be said, however, that the *Gospel of Truth* shows a knowledge of, and dependence on, the four canonical Gospels, the Pauline Epistles including the pastoral letters, Hebrews, the Epistles of Peter and John, and Revelation. Thus, bearing in mind its duration in Coptic and in the Greek original, it attests the early date of the New Testament canon. Moreover, in view of the theory that the Gospel of John has a Gnostic background, these indicate clearly that Gnostic features such as the Fourth Gospel reflects are sober in comparison. John's Gospel was a reply to a different kind of Gnosticism, which we know from the Manual of Discipline and the Hymns of the Qumran community to have been specifically Jewish and controlled by the Old Testament.

BIBLIOGRAPHY

H. W. Saggs, *The Glory that was Babylon*, 1962.
Seton Lloyd, *Foundations in the Dust*, 1947.
J. A. Wilson, *The Burden of Egypt*, 1951.
H. Frankfort, *Kingship and the Gods*, 1948.
M. Burrows, *What Mean these Stones ?*, 1941.
W. F. Albright, *The Archaeology of Palestine*, 1949.
G. E. Wright, *Biblical Archaeology*, 1957.
K. M. Kenyon, *Archaeology in the Holy Land*, 1960.
N. Glueck, *The Other Side of the Jordan*, 1940.
H. H. Rowley, *The Rediscovery of the Old Testament*, 1946.
J. Gray, *Archaeology and the Old Testament World*, 1962.
J. B. Pritchard (ed.), *Ancient Near Eastern Texts relating to the Old Testament*, 2nd ed., 1955.
J. B. Pritchard, *The Ancient Near East in Pictures*, 1954.
D. W. Thomas (ed.), *Documents from Old Testament Times*, 1958.
G. R. Driver, *Canaanite Myths and Legends*, 1956.
C. H. Gordon, *Ugaritic Literature*, 1949.
J. Gray, *The Legacy of Canaan*, 1957.
M. Burrows, *The Dead Sea Scrolls*, 1955.
M. Burrows, *More Light on the Dead Sea Scrolls*, 1958.
J. M. Allegro, *The Dead Sea Scrolls*, 1956.
T. H. Gaster, *The Scriptures of the Dead Sea Sect*, 1957.
J. T. Milik, *Ten Years of Discovery in the Wilderness of Judah*, 1957.
M. Black, *The Scrolls and Christian Origins*, 1961.
A. Dupont-Sommer, *The Essene Writings from Qumran*, 1961.
A. Barrois, *Manuel d'Archéologie Biblique*, 2 vols., 1939, 1953.

XI. THE HISTORY OF ISRAEL

By P. R. Ackroyd

There has been some discussion in recent years as to what precisely is meant by the term "Israel," the history of which is the subject of this chapter. The term is used with a variety of meanings within the Old Testament—as the name of the ancestor (Jacob), as an indication of the group of tribes often now referred to as the amphictyony, as the name of the northern kingdom, as the term suitable for describing the people of God conceived of as being both ideal and actually realized in the post-exilic community, and in the phrase "new Israel" of the Church. The extension in time into the New Testament period of the term, as well as the purpose of this volume, makes it proper to carry over the story to the second Jewish revolt of A.D. 132–5. The Jewish religious community, for which the term Israel was then appropriate, did in fact continue beyond that point, so that it is not a real terminus. At the same time, the "new Israel," the Church, which claims descent from the old, had come into being, and by that date the writings of the New Testament were in being and the earliest stages of the formation of the Church were past. The detail of this aspect has, however, not been treated here. At the other end, it may be appropriately argued that until the tribes came together in a recognizably united form, the term Israel is unrealistic. Yet the Old Testament itself claims continuity with what preceded the period of united Israel, and saw in the traditions which it preserved about the earliest periods the evidence for a divine purpose which had ultimately issued in their possession of the land in which their full unity was developed. For this earliest period, historical reconstruction in detail is not possible, but the traditions can be seen to be meaningful against the background of the events and life of the second millennium B.C.*

(i) BEFORE THE EXODUS

1. *The General Background.* The early centuries of the second millennium B.C. were marked by considerable movements of peoples and changes of rule within the area of

* It is clearly impossible in so short a survey to discuss the evidence for precise dating. The dates which are cited are for the most part the conventional ones, and the reader is referred to the fuller discussions of chronology for the detail.

Mesopotamia and Palestine. The Sumerians in Mesopotamia were succeeded by various powers, notably those of Amorite (Semitic) origin, and by the end of the eighteenth century, Amorite rulers were to be found in a number of great centres. Assyria in the north, earlier important under Akkadian rulers who extended their influence well into Asia Minor, came under Amorite rule. So too did the important centre of Mari which has yielded rich information about the political and social situation of the time. The most powerful of all was to be Babylon, under Hammurabi (around 1700 B.C.), whose reign brought a great cultural development of which the promulgation of his law-code was but a part. To this period belong Amorite movements into Palestine.

Egypt, which had enjoyed relative peace during the first centuries of the millennium, was now thrown into confusion with the invasion of the Hyksos rulers, a name which denotes foreigners and probably indicates invaders connected with the Amorite stock. They mastered the whole of Egypt, while at the same time controlling Palestine. Eventually, in the middle of the sixteenth century, they were expelled by a new, native dynasty.

During the Hyksos period, new elements forced their way into Mesopotamia and Palestine, and appear as Hurrians in a variety of places, including Palestine where they are referred to in the Old Testament as Horites. They controlled a large part of northern Mesopotamia as the kingdom of Mitanni, under Indo-Aryan rulers who were part of a companion movement which also probably brought Indo-Aryan population into the regions of Persia and India. Light on Hurrian life has come abundantly from the excavations at Nuzu and from elsewhere. Pressure was also felt from Asia Minor, where the growth in power of the Hittites hastened the downfall of Amorite power in Babylon.

The second half of the millennium saw a further series of like changes. Under Thutmosis I. and the even more powerful Thutmosis III., the Egyptians overran Palestine and advanced north-eastwards, to be halted only by the kingdom of Mitanni in northern Mesopotamia with which they then remained in peaceful association. Egypt's control weakened in the fourteenth century under Akhenaton, a religious reformer representative perhaps of a party resenting the power of the priests of Amon. The Amarna letters from Syrian and Palestinian dependent rulers belong to this period and reveal how security was being reduced in the little states of the area. Hittite revival brought a further threat, and it was only with a new Egyptian dynasty that it was halted by a treaty between the two powers, Assyrian pressure into Mitanni on the eastern side probably contributing to the Hittite willingness to negotiate. Egyptian domination of Palestine continued under Rameses II. and Merneptah, but the Egyptian power then declined at the end of the thirteenth century, and with the Hittite empire falling, and the Assyrians soon also weakening, Palestine was for the next two centuries and more to be free of threats from great powers from outside. It was open however to invasion, and it is in this context that both the settlement of the Philistines—part of the " Sea People " movement of the early twelfth century—and the development of Israel are to be seen.

2. *The Hebrew Patriarchs.* It is against this wider background that the stories of the patriarchs are to be set, with, however, considerable uncertainty as to precisely in what relation they stand to it. The assessment of these problems depends partly upon the examination of the internal evidence of the traditions themselves, and partly upon the consideration of the actual conditions in Palestine and elsewhere during the period. The difficulty is increased by the uncertainties which attach to the immediately succeeding period, that of the Exodus and conquest. The difficulty of giving a precise date to the Exodus, the uncertainty as to what tribes were involved in its events, the consideration of the nature of the occupation of Palestine by the tribes, are all points which complicate the discussion of the patriarchal narratives. Without a precise date, the later limit of the patriarchal period cannot be accurately determined. If only some tribes were in Egypt, the possibility of prior settlement in Palestine and continued occupation of certain areas can be envisaged. Similarly, if the account of the conquest conceals some indications of continuity in settlement and of peaceful infiltration, it is possible that some part of this belongs to the patriarchal rather than to the conquest period.

The patriarchal narratives themselves depict a pastoral people—" shepherds, as our fathers were " (Gen. 47^{3})—which nevertheless does not exclude the probability that, like modern bedouin, they were able to cultivate quickly grown cereal crops. This is indicated, for example, by Abraham's offer to his heavenly visitors of cakes of fine meal (Gen. 18), since it is more likely that he had grown the grain himself than bartered it with more settled people. They were thus not nomads, or even semi-nomads, but wandering shepherds, keeping within the area in which there was sufficient rainfall for there to be food for their flocks, but wandering within that area relatively far. Joseph went from the Hebron region to Dothan searching for his brothers with their flocks. The narratives reveal little contact with the cities of Palestine, but hardly allow us to determine whether the political organization was that of the earlier part of the millennium, when the land was relatively meagrely populated and cities appear to have been of little importance, or that of the later centuries, marked by city-states whose rulers exerted control over surrounding areas. The wandering shepherd's interest in such centres is, in any case, limited; he might go to the markets of Hebron and Beersheba, cities most mentioned in the traditions; he might purchase a piece of land for burial purposes, as Abraham did; but he lived apart, and intermarriage or any other real connexion was unlikely.

The narratives and the confessional statement of Josh. 24 trace the origins of the people back to the area "Beyond the River," which in this context means the region north-east of the Euphrates, the region of Paddan-aram, and specifically Haran. Another statement, that of Deut. 26, describes the people's ancestor as "a wandering Aramaean" or "one about to perish." This immediately suggests the possibility that some link may be traced between general movements of peoples and the migration of Abraham and his family into the Palestinian area. Such a movement has been noted in the Amorite period, connected also in some way with the rise of the Hyksos rulers to dominance over Egypt and Palestine. At a later period, another movement can be discerned in that of the Aramaean peoples, to be seen in the emergence to the north-east, east and south-east of Palestine of the various groups of Aramaeans, Moabites, Ammonites, and Edomites.

Association of the emergence of Israel with one or other of these movements has been suggested. In favour of the former is the evidence of the names of the patriarchs themselves, which find close parallels among the Amorites, and in the laws and customs of Amorites and Hurrians, seen in the Mari and Nuzu material, which correspond at many points closely with what is presupposed in the patriarchal narratives. It must, of course, be made clear that the Israelites can then be thought of only as coming within that wave of invasion, since, unlike its leaders and unlike the Hyksos, they show no interest in the occupation and building of the cities or in the large-scale conquests and other military activities which the main Amorite invasion reveals. Nor is the evidence of the laws and customs entirely unequivocal, since Amorite and Hurrian settlers in Palestine would presumably have made familiar there just those practices which appear in the patriarchal narratives, and the possibility cannot be excluded that those narratives owe something to the absorption of local elements or that they represent the grafting of Amorite elements on to Israel's own ancestral traditions. The tradition which describes the people's ancestor as a " wandering Aramaean " would seem rather to suggest links with the other Aramaean peoples which came to settle in the Palestinian area in about the fourteenth century B.C. Israel claimed close kinship with these other peoples, describing Edom (Esau) as full brother to Jacob, and recognizing family links with the Aramaeans of the north-east in the figure of Laban. The association with Paddan-aram fits well into this context. The similarities which exist between the evolution of the north-eastern Aramaeans, the Moabites, Ammonites, and Edomites from tribal groups into organized monarchies and the rather more complex development of Israel suggest close affinities of origin and custom.

There is other evidence which, without solving these problems, helps to fill in the picture. In a variety of ancient records, from Mesopotamia, Syria and Egypt, there is reference made to people called Habiru—variously spelt—which may reasonably be equated with the term Hebrew. The term normally appears to have a pejorative sense, and is applied particularly to various groups of trouble-makers, bandits, aliens, tribes difficult to control, and the like. In the Old Testament " Hebrew " is also often used in a pejorative sense, though its origin is traced to an ancestor Eber. Simple identification is obviously impossible. But it seems not unreasonable to suggest that to the inhabitants of settled communities, the inroads of rather unruly elements could be described by the use of this convenient term and that the activities of the ancestors of Israel might well look very much like what may be seen of the Habiru in the Nuzu texts, in Egyptian records and elsewhere.

The stories of the patriarchs have now been grouped into cycles, associated with great figures of tradition. No historical account can be derived from these cycles of tradition, because it is clear that material originally separate in origin has been grouped together and arranged to form a clear genealogy. In the process the figure of Isaac has been much subordinated to the greater figures of Abraham and Jacob. But the tenacity of tradition is such that behind these narratives we may discern personalities and groups. The names themselves, the genealogical information, the kind of stories told, reflect the realities of a situation which cannot be described in a series of concrete statements. Later Israel knew that her ancestors had come from the north-east ; she knew that they had been shepherds, moving from place to place with their flocks though associated with particular areas. Not unnaturally in the course of time they had become associated with particular sacred places, some of which were undoubtedly much more ancient in origin, but which, by means of these stories, were now claimed to belong both to the religious life of her forefathers and to be genuinely her own, as at a later point Canaanite shrines became Israelite sanctuaries. The richness of the material defies complete analysis ; but it provides us with deep insights into Israel's understanding of herself and her place in the world.

(ii) THE EXODUS AND CONQUEST

(a) *Egypt and the Exodus.*

1. *Into Egypt.* The Old Testament has more than one record of a temporary settlement in Egypt because of famine in Palestine. Such a stay is recorded of Abraham (Gen. 12), and a similar story of Isaac relates that he was divinely forbidden to go to Egypt, but rather to go to Gerar (Gen. 26). It is evident that to the wandering shepherds, Egypt represented a place secure from the disadvantages of a land dependent upon rainfall, enjoying as it did the blessing of the annual flooding of the Nile. From the Egyptian side too, such a movement is intelligible, and there are indications of the place which such settlers could occupy in the border country as a protection to Egypt against the inroads of desert bandits and other invaders.

It is therefore entirely intelligible that the tradition should tell of a settlement of Israel in Egypt in the time of Jacob's old age, in a story interwoven with elements of popular tale some of which find parallels elsewhere, in part in Egypt itself. It is much less clear whether it can ever be determined at what period the settlement took place or who was involved in it. From the point of view of later Israel, to whom the deliverance from Egypt was a vital landmark in their historic experience and in the formation of their faith in God, it was natural to suppose that all Israel had been involved. It is also natural to find that various attempts are made within the narratives to identify the moment at which the events took place. Such points have to be investigated along with the non-biblical evidence for the period—some part of which has already been outlined—and the whole complex tradition considered. This, the most crucial period from the point of view of Israel's faith, has not surprisingly gathered to itself a tremendous wealth of narrative, as well as a great deal of legal and other material which does not belong to the original outline of the events. No suggested outline of the events or explanation of the problems of date and place can be adequate unless it takes into account the whole mass of the Old Testament tradition and accounts for all its many elements. It is clear that such a completely satisfactory account is unlikely to be possible.

If the ancestors of Israel were associated with the Amorites, they may have gone to Egypt during the period of Hyksos rule and have been welcomed there by the rulers who were, if only remotely, related to them. Such a view fits some elements of the material, but it must be admitted that there is nothing in it to suggest that such kinship was envisaged. Neither Joseph, the slave who rises to high office, nor the whole family of Jacob coming to settle in Goshen, appears to have any idea that the Egyptian rulers are anything other than aliens. Furthermore, while the Old Testament gives no clear indication of the length of the stay—the evidence is not consistent—there is little to suggest that the period was sufficient to cover the time from Hyksos period down to the thirteenth century in which occupation of Palestinian cities by Israelites appears likely.

The troubles in Palestine in the Amarna period of the fourteenth century coincide with the period at which various peoples were on the move. A period of Egyptian weakness is more likely to be one in which frontier settlers are welcomed than a period of strength such as had existed in the previous century. A settlement in Egypt during this later period would allow time for the change of dynasty which appears to be indicated in the narrative—to a king who knew not Joseph (Ex. 1[8]). But it must be acknowledged that there is no precise evidence to fix this.

Nor is it easy to determine just what tribes went into Egypt and came out. There is some evidence to suggest that Asher and Zebulun were already settled as tribal groups in Palestine at the end of the fourteenth century. The central area around Shechem, the subject of a tribal legend in Gen. 34, appears not to have been conquered or occupied by the Israelites on their entry into Palestine after the Exodus, which suggests that related groups may have been there already. Josh. 24 appears to indicate an acceptance of the experience of Israel's deliverance from Egypt by groups which had not previously shared it, and thus to indicate a grafting into the Israelite tribal association of some who had never been through that experience historically. Such points as these make it probable that the Egyptian sojourn was experienced by only some of those who were to be the ancestors of the Israelite tribal amphictyony. It is thus improbable that either the date or the extent of the settlement can be determined precisely.

2. *The Oppression and Exodus*. The references in Egyptian sources to the employment of ʻAperu (equivalent to Habiru) as slave labour on building projects provide the background to the Biblical tradition that this was the fortune of the Israelites who had settled there. According to Ex. 1[11], they built the cities of Pithom and Raamses; this fits well with

the supposition that the XIXth Dynasty marks the period of oppression, and in particular that Rameses II. was the Pharaoh most involved. The names of these two cities appear to enshrine a piece of concrete evidence which cannot be lightly set aside. At the same time, it must be remembered that the experience of the Israelite settlers in Egypt is unlikely to have been unique, and there is no reason to believe that similar experiences may not have been known to earlier groups. As the story now stands, it is overlaid with a wealth of pictorial detail, vivid indications of divine judgment upon Egypt and its ruler. The plagues stories, in most cases genuine impressions of the strangeness of Egyptian conditions, heightened into enormous disasters, are part of the building up of the whole narrative into a conflict between God and the power of Pharaoh in which it is made clear that however much Pharaoh seems able to resist the divine purpose, he is in fact all the time subject to it. The series culminates in the killing of the first-born which may best be understood as a historification in terms of judgment of the ancient practice of dedicating—and even sacrificing—the first-born to the deity, one of the elements which underlies the Passover celebration as it is later known.

The actual escape from Egypt may be seen, in the light of what has already been said about the nature of the Israelites' position there, as a not unnatural return to the independence of shepherd life of a group which had for a time enjoyed Egyptian protection but had also had to submit to Egyptian dominance. No trace remains in Egyptian records of the event, nor is this surprising. Such movements are likely to have been frequent enough. The attempt at preventing their escape would be made by frontier troops, and the Egyptian disaster on which the Biblical record lays such emphasis was a minor incident. The relative historical importance of the event, however, does not affect the significance of Israel's own interpretation of it as a divine deliverance. The change in the fortunes of the people as they returned to their independent way of life was marked, as the tradition makes clear, by experiences which impressed upon their minds the reality of divine power. When in their subsequent history they were again delivered, or anticipated deliverance, it was with the memory of these events that they spoke. The faith of the Exodus impressed itself upon their interpretation of later experience.

The route which they followed as they left Egypt is indicated by a series of place-names no longer identifiable with any certainty. Various theories have been proposed. The coastal road might have led them along one of the arms of land which allow a passage between the waters of the Mediterranean and the inland lagoons; the disaster to the Egyptians would be intelligible there. A route farther south would perhaps have brought them between stretches of water—the exact location of such lakes in ancient times cannot now be determined—in which a similar explanation is possible. The "reed sea" is unlikely to have been the Gulf of Suez, though it is understandable that they were later thought to be identifiable. The later stages of the route will have been determined by the need to move from one water supply to another.

3. *Israel in the Wilderness.* We meet again with divergent traditions concerning the period spent by the Israelite tribes in the wilderness, and it seems very probable that quite independent traditions have been brought together so as to give a unified impression of the place which this period occupied in later thought. On the one hand, there are clear indications of the importance of a period spent in the neighbourhood of the waters of Kadesh. On the other hand, prominence is given to the events associated with the mountain of God, named both as Sinai and as Horeb. The identification of Kadesh is sufficiently clear; that of the mountain very uncertain. The relationship between these traditions is difficult to determine. The more radical approach is to make a sharp separation between them, and to associate the experiences of Kadesh with one group of tribes, and the experiences of Sinai (Horeb) with another; the unification of the traditions would then be due to the eventual incorporation into one tribal association of those groups which had undergone the different experiences. The Exodus events may be supposed to belong with only one group, but eventually the combined traditions were seen as part of the experience of the whole people.

Such a taking over of experience as part of a religious faith is intelligible, and in view of the divergences within the Biblical material, it would appear most probable that some such explanation is necessary. It must, however, be recognized that the point at which the various traditions came together is early, and that any reconstruction of the historical sequence on the basis of such an analysis is inevitably hazardous. To some extent it is further dependent upon the interpretation of the evidence concerning the occupation of Palestine; the possibility that separate entries may be discerned, perhaps widely apart in time, would link to the associating of one group with the Kadesh traditions and another with Sinai (Horeb). To which of these the Exodus itself belonged is again impossible to determine with certainty, for while in some ways the experience of divine revelation associated with the sacred mountain might be appropriately regarded as an alternative experience to that of the divine action in deliverance at the sea, it is also possible that the sojourn of some tribes in the Kadesh area might be connected with the southern invasion of Palestine indicated in some parts of the material, while another series of events would trace the fortunes of tribes from Egypt via Sinai to the east and thence into Palestine at the Jordan ford near Jericho.

What is abundantly clear is the significance which Israel attached to this period in the wilderness. The giving of the covenant relationship is linked both to the act of deliverance at the sea and to the giving of the law by divine revelation at the mountain. The delay which the narrative indicates in the entry into the promised land is made the occasion for revealing the underlying pattern of disobedience and of divine grace which marks so much of the Old Testament interpretation of history. The stress which is so marked in the Psalms on the divine guiding of Israel and the divine action in deliverance is written into every part of the narrative, so that historical uncertainty is overshadowed by theological significance.

4. *The Personality of Moses.* Another unifying factor in the present form of the tradition rests in the personality of Moses as the leader and interpreter of events. Here too there must inevitably be uncertainties of historical reconstruction. The Biblical record is not concerned to provide a biography of Moses, and at the same time it is clear that there are elements within the story which are quite evidently legendary, being of the kind which attaches to every great historical personality. The borderline between legend and history is impossible to define with exactness. Legend in any case sheds light on the understanding of the historical personality as it appeared to subsequent generations, and testifies to the recognition of his importance in the events. Without such a personality the events are themselves unintelligible, for the interpretation of them in such a way as to make their lasting significance evident to succeeding generations demands the presence of one who could mediate between divine action and human understanding—performing a function comparable to that of later charismatic leaders and prophets.

The picture of a deliverer born into the enslaved people and ironically protected from destruction by a member of the hostile Egyptian royal house is a vivid statement of the conviction of divine providence in the events. Such dramatic irony is common to many accounts of deliverance. The murder by Moses of an Egyptian taskmaster and his subsequent flight testifies to a vigorous personality, and expresses the reality of his concern with the evil fortunes of his own people. The experience of the revelation of God in the burning bush and of his commissioning to act as deliverer sets out, in terms comparable to those used for the description of later deliverers and prophets, the reality of the divine purpose and the overruling power of the divine call. This call is set in the wilderness, in Horeb the mountain of God. It is marked by the revealing of a new name of God, though some of the traditions of the patriarchal period use this name already. Since the call occurs during the period of Moses' association with the Kenites, a group who appear to have been smiths and who subsequently appear in close association with Israel, it has seemed not unreasonable to trace some connexion between the new name and the religion of the Kenites. Moses' father-in-law appears subsequently as his adviser and as a priest. Possible as this view is—and its full discussion would be out of place here—it is clear that what subsequently happened to the Israelite group under Moses gave them a new and deeper understanding of the nature of the God who, they believed, had called Moses and promised deliverance. In this subsequent complex series of events, Moses is depicted as mediator between God and Israel, as prophet of the divine judgment on Egypt, and as proclaimer of the kind of obedience demanded from his people.

If, as has been suggested above, a distinction is to be made within the series of events and some are to be assigned to one tribal group and some to another, with a possible time diversion between them too, then it is clear that Moses cannot have been associated with the whole series. But it is again entirely intelligible that all the narratives should have been focussed on him, and that the whole series of events, together with the whole body of Israel's law, should have gathered around this one great personality. The same process can be observed in the figure of Joshua in the conquest, and with such figures as David and Solomon. To this extent, the historical Moses is now concealed behind the wealth of tradition, and there is no completely satisfactory method of disentangling his personality from what it has gathered in the course of time.

(b) *The Entry into Canaan.*

1. *Canaan and Its Life.* The Amarna letters give a clear impression of the organization of the land into city-states, ruled by petty princes who, while nominally subject to Egyptian control, engaged in intrigues among themselves and were always watchful for a chance at gaining advantage for themselves. The letters also indicate Habiru activities, though since the appeals for help to the Pharaoh look for only modest assistance, it would seem that the threats were not in most cases of any very great moment. The troubles were mainly in

north and south, though Shechem in the centre fell to these Habiru. It is clear that these troubles are not the invasion of the Israelites ; but it is not impossible that the occupation of the Shechem area could account for the absence of any reference to its conquest by the Israelites simply because it was already in the hands of related people. The narrative of Gen. 34 may be linked with this. In the years following the Amarna period, the city-states became more numerous and hence smaller and weaker. In the latter part of the thirteenth century, Egyptian protection was becoming decreasingly effective, and the destructions of cities attested by archaeology for this period may represent the Israelite occupation.

2. *The Biblical Evidence for the Conquest.* The first impression is of a march by all Israel east of the Dead Sea, avoiding Edom and Moab, engaging in conflict with the rulers of the territory east of the Jordan, and arriving just prior to the death of Moses at the threshold of the promised land. The campaign under Joshua began with the crossing of the Jordan, the taking of Jericho, and an advance into the hill-country to Ai and Bethel. A series of swift campaigns to south and to north brought the land into subjection. Elsewhere there is other evidence. A report of an unsuccessful attempt from the south in the book of Numbers finds a certain sequel in the indications of an advance from the south in which Judah and related tribes were involved. The latter part of the book of Joshua and the opening of Judges indicate substantial areas of territory not occupied. At a much later date, there were still certain strong cities, including Jerusalem, which remained in hostile hands.

The lack of cohesion between north and south which appears again at a later period, together with these indications of different conquest traditions and the probability of diverse origin and experience in the earlier period by those tribes which ultimately made up Israel, suggests that in fact the conquest was not the result of a single series of swift campaigns, but of a much more piecemeal occupation. Archaeological evidence is in a number of cases confusing or incomplete ; the capture of Jericho cannot be confirmed, the destruction of Ai appears to lie right outside the period. There is every probability that earlier stories of conquest in Canaan came to be integrated in the Israelite story. But there is sufficient evidence of a change of occupation in some of the cities excavated to make it most probable that the Israelites, while no doubt as wandering shepherds more concerned in making use of the land which would provide pasturage for their flocks and so infiltrating the hill-country, were also able to take control of some of the cities and hence of valley areas. The rebuilding of these cities in a simpler style, with less elaborate fortifications and houses, would suggest their occupation by a community not yet accustomed to the more complex city life of Canaan.

3. *Conquest and Infiltration.* The wandering shepherds of the patriarchal time had gone to and fro in the land with apparently little contact with the city life. Their descendants were to come more and more into that life. Partly no doubt this was due to a change in the social life of the land itself; there were many more cities, and it may be supposed that movement was less easy for the wandering shepherds. The urge to the greater security of agricultural life, with crops which demanded more settled conditions than were available to the shepherd communities, is itself natural. It is reasonable also to suppose that there was a higher degree of tribal organisation and a greater coherence of life which made possible a move towards conquest. Such a purposeful conquest is now a central element in the tradition. Words of promise to the patriarchs, perhaps originally much more limited in their scope, were seen to be relevant to the new situation, and offered a purpose which now, under divine aegis, was seen to be coming to fruition. The coherence brought about by a great religious experience in the events of the Exodus and the interpretation of that and of the subsequent events in terms of a new divine revelation gave to the invaders a vitality which made them able to meet and overcome the better equipped forces of the Canaanite cities and to tackle the cities themselves. To them the campaign was of the nature of a "holy war," God and people together fighting against their enemies.

But not everything was achieved by conquest. The period of the conquest passed imperceptibly into that of the "judges," in which one element is that of consolidation in the land. At an early point, we find representatives of the Gibeonites managing by a stratagem to gain protection for themselves and so to gain a place within the Israelite group. There is considerable evidence of intermarriage, and in the statements made about the various tribes in Judg. 1, there is much that indicates peaceful life side by side of Israelite and Canaanite groups. What in the Biblical narrative has, for theological reasons, been compressed into a series of campaigns, is better understood as spread over a much longer period. Within that period there were vital moments and battles, the overcoming of crucial cities and the establishment of useful alliances, and it is these more outstanding moments which give to the tradition its present character. But Israel was for a long time precariously situated and could not really claim to possess the land.

(c) *Israel in Canaan.*

1. *The Movements of Other Peoples.* Around the turn of the thirteenth to twelfth century, a substantial movement of "Sea Peoples" in the eastern Mediterranean area brought great turmoil. Traces of their occupation have been found in Cyprus; Egypt recorded a great victory over them. But it is evident that their pressure was great enough to enable some of them to settle within the Palestinian area which nominally belonged to Egypt, and here, as the Philistines who were in the later Roman period to give their name to the whole land, they occupied the coastal area, particularly of the five cities which were their centres, and probably also parts at least of the central plain. At the moment of their greatest threat, they were to be a factor in leading Israel into the acceptance of the monarchical system. Earlier indications of their pressure are to be found in the vicissitudes of the tribe of Dan and the stories of the hero Samson.

Other pressures were exerted on the Israelites. Such organised kingdoms as that of Moab pressed across the Jordan into Benjaminite territory. The camel raiders of Midian swept through the land even as far as Gaza. Israelite settlers found themselves subjected to the same kind of insecurity as they themselves had brought to the settled communities of Canaan. Many of the "judge" stories are concerned with this kind of situation.

2. *The Tribal Amphictyony.* Josh. 24 indicates an assembly of tribal representatives entering upon a solemn covenant and accepting as their God the one who had brought them out of Egypt and into the land. It is not unreasonable to suppose that this may represent two things. It may indicate a repeated celebration in which the obligations of the covenant were renewed. It may also indicate a ceremonial by which groups which had not previously formed a part of Israel could come within it. It shows furthermore the meeting together of tribal representatives for a religious purpose. From other passages, for example, the Song of Deborah (Judg. 5) and the account of the campaign of Gideon against the Midianites (Judg. 7), it is clear that action against their enemies was undertaken by the tribes in the name of their God, Yahweh.

To describe the kind of association which was formed by the tribes, it has become customary in recent years to use the term amphictyony, taken from the description of the Greek states in their association together for the sacred Games. The Israelite tribes appear as independent groups, each of which has a history of its own and in large measure had to carve out its own place in the land of Canaan. Traces can be seen of tribes which were once strong and which subsequently disappeared or were absorbed into other groups. The historic experiences of the tribes before the settlement were not identical. But partly through common experience in the Exodus, partly through sharing of other parts of the pre-settlement life, they had been drawn together and in particular had come to be dominated by the idea of a special relationship or covenant between the deity Yahweh and themselves. There is furthermore an evident possibility that the association did not always consist of the same tribes, and that the southern tribes, eventually incorporated largely in Judah, may have formed a separate association. Such a union was not merely political, it was religious, and there are indications of a shrine where the sacred Ark was kept, though this was not always at the same place. For their domestic concerns, the tribes appear to have operated independently, and there are indications of conflict between them. But there was a religious bond which held them together and which was expressed in the kind of ceremonial which is seen in Josh. 24. At times it seems to have been possible for the whole group to take disciplinary action against one member, as in the story concerning Benjamin in Judg. 19–21. It is probable that the collections of tribal blessings in Gen. 49 and Deut. 33—though not perhaps now in their original form—express the association and in some measure reflect upon the members of it.

A shrine would involve personnel. At the end of the period of the judges, just before the monarchy came into being, a clearer picture emerges of this organization. Eli at Shiloh, as priest of the shrine of the Ark, and his successor Samuel are the chief officials. Their predecessors are more nebulous, but the so-called " minor judges " of Judg. 10 and 12 who do not effect military deliverance as do the charismatic leaders of other narratives, have some signs of exalted position and have been thought to be such officials. Whether this is so or not, it is clear that a line must be traced from Moses, the mediator of the covenant, through Joshua who is thus depicted in Josh. 24, through other officials to Eli and Samuel, and thence to the kings and priests of the monarchical period. The succession of faith, needing to be maintained in the settlement period with all the pressure of Canaanite religion to be resisted if Israel was to remain in any way distinctive, is transmitted through them. Towards the end of this period, uncertainty about the future of the tribes grew; the Philistine threat became more intense, and, not inappropriately, the compiler of the book of Judges, who emphasized throughout that the life of the Israelite tribes depended upon their obedience to their God, painted a gloomy picture of the conditions which he saw belonging to the time before the monarchy was established.

(iii) THE MONARCHY (*c.* 1050–586 B.C.)

(a) *The Origins of the Monarchy.*

1. *Kingship in Canaan and in the Surrounding Countries.* In the narratives of the Israelite wanderings and of the conquest of Canaan, there is frequent mention of kings of different areas or cities. Gen. 36[31ff.] has a list of Edomite kings of the period before there was a king in Israel. Other areas, such as Moab and Ammon, also had monarchies. It is probably to these monarchies, established over peoples which were very closely kin to Israel both by blood and in organization, that we should look for the nearest parallels to the evolution of the monarchy in Israel. Canaanite kingship was rule over a city-state, an urban centre with its immediate dependencies, rather than rule over various tribal groups, linked by kinship and drawn together by common concerns. But Canaanite kingship also has its importance, as may be seen when the development of the monarchy under David and particularly under Solomon is considered. Without making an artificial contrast between two types of kingship, we may nevertheless usefully recognize the type which emerged in tribal society as being what we may term more " democratic " and see that in some respects this tradition is more clearly perpetuated in the northern kingdom of Israel. The hereditary monarchy of Judah, with what appear to be its much greater religious associations, expressed in the language of the Psalms, is in some respects closer to that of Canaan. But the tension between the two types, as well as the tension between monarchical ideas and ideas more deeply rooted in Israel's ancient traditions, resulted in the development of a form of monarchy which must be considered for itself and not rigidly described in terms of similar organizations.

2. *Earlier Moves towards Monarchy.* There are two recorded instances in the stories of the judges of attempts at establishing a king. They shed light on different aspects of the matter. In Judg. 8, hereditary kingship is offered to Gideon and his family after his successful campaign against the Midianites. This expresses the kind of pressure which came as a result of the acknowledged skill of leadership of a particular individual ; the case of Jephthah (Judg. 11) is in some ways similar. Here Jephthah imposes as a condition of his acting as leader the demand that if he is successful he should be acknowledged as head over Gilead. It is uncertain whether Gideon refused the offer of kingship or declared his kingship to be the expression of divine rule. It is not surprising to find one who was so obviously a traditionalist in his thinking either rejecting or so defining a new and alien practice. His son Abimelech,

half-Canaanite, had no such hesitation. He appears to have established himself as a king very much on the Canaanite pattern—and the ridiculing of his pretensions in Jotham's fable (Judg. 9^{7-21}) reveals an appropriate Israelite reaction to him.

A critical attitude towards the idea of kingship, whether because of its Canaanite associations or because it represented a break away from older traditional patterns, was not, however, the only one. In the last chapters of the Book of Judges, various ancient traditions are preserved which stress the idea of the king as the guarantor of law and order. The picture is of unsatisfactory social and political organization. "Every man did what was right in his own eyes"; there was no king to maintain order and uphold law. Against this background has been set the story of the first real establishment of a king.

3. *Samuel and Saul:* The contrast between hostility to the idea of monarchy and acceptance of it as a divinely ordained blessing is amply expressed in the complex narratives which describe the actual establishment of the first king, Saul. The background is prepared in the story of the downfall of Shiloh and the Eli priesthood. In battle with the Philistines, now the most serious rival to Israel for the control of Palestine, the Ark was lost, and Shiloh itself must have been destroyed shortly after, in the latter half of the eleventh century. No statement is made of this in the narrative, but it is clearly indicated by Jeremiah and confirmed by the excavations on the site.

The Philistine threat provides a background to the movement towards monarchy, and is the underlying motif of the story which tells of the divine choice of Saul by the agency of Samuel when Saul is led to him in the course of his search for his father's lost asses (1 Sam. 9–10^{16}). What appears to be an alternative story tells of Saul's divinely inspired leadership against the Ammonites who had besieged Jabesh-gilead and his acclamation as king by the people (1 Sam. 11). Both of these accept kingship as divinely ordained. A different type of tradition is also present. A great victory over the Philistines by Samuel (1 Sam. 7) would seem to have made kingship unnecessary, so that the subsequent narrative, linked to the failure of Samuel's sons and to the desire of Israel to be "like all the nations," reads as a description of rebellion against God, who nevertheless, with due warning of the consequences, appoints a king chosen by lot (1 Sam. 8, 10^{17-27}). These stories are now closely interwoven so as to form a literary unity. The idea of hostility to the monarchy is continued in the warning speech of Samuel in 1 Sam. 12, and in the rejection stories of Saul in 13 and 15, whereas 14 contains more positive assessment of the achievements of Saul's family and at the same time indications of the weakness of his position. But the interweaving of motifs is evident. Some element of conflict between the older type of leadership expressed in the judge-prophet-priest figure of Samuel and the new charismatic kingship of Saul is also present. But the idea of kingship is also accepted in the story of the divine choice of David as successor, long before the point is reached at which he actually becomes king.

Saul is the type of the charismatic leader. Like Gideon, he was evidently able to extend the sphere of his control beyond the immediate tribe to which he belonged, and the Philistine threat was the most potent factor in encouraging more general acceptance of him. Like Jephthah he was given a leadership which ceased only with his life, though there was more than this to it in that as the anointed of Yahweh he was regarded with respect and honour and as having a special sanctity. Like Samson he experienced the loss of the divine power, and the picture of him is the rather pathetic one of a man struggling to do the right thing and failing where his successor David is depicted as blessed in his endeavours.

Saul's royal establishment at Gibeah and his organization were evidently modest. Against the Philistines, whose power pressed so hardly on Israel, with a control of iron which made the military balance unfavourable, he was unable to take much more than local action against their garrisons, though this provides stories of notable exploits. When at Mount Gilboa he came up against the larger Philistine forces, he was inevitably defeated.

(b) *The United Monarchy.*

I. *The General Political Situation.* The latter part of the eleventh century and the main part of the tenth was a period during which political developments in Palestine were unhindered by the pressure of great powers outside. We have already noted that the power of Egypt was in decline after the great period of Rameses II. and Merneptah. At the time of the successful repelling of the "Sea Peoples" early in the twelfth century she was not able to prevent their settlement in Palestine. In Mesopotamia no new power had yet arisen to take the place of the ancient empires, and the Hittites in Asia Minor had also declined. There were numerous small kingdoms in the area of Syria and Palestine, and the possibility was open for the dominance of the area by one of them. For Israel, the most urgent problem remained the Philistine menace which was the serious barrier to the development of her own life. At the death of Saul, the Philistines not only controlled the coastal areas and the plain of Esdraelon right through to Beth-shan where they exposed the king's body, but Saul's son Eshbaal could be established as king only in the Transjordan area, with his centre at Mahanaim, though he exercised some control in the areas of Ephraim and Benjamin. David, the vassal of Achish of Gath, with his centre at Ziklag, was also nominally at least under Philistine control. But he was soon to show his military ability against his masters.

2. *David's Rise to Power.* There are two stages distinguished in the early career of David. During the reign of Saul he is depicted as a popular and successful military leader, a skilled musician introduced to the court of Saul where he assuaged Saul's melancholia, and a youthful hero recommended to Saul by his killing of the Philistine giant. He was able to establish close relationship with the royal family, both in friendship with Jonathan and in marriage with Saul's daughter Michal. But already in the latter the jealousy of Saul appeared, since a task was laid upon him which was clearly designed to cost him his life. When the relationship with Saul worsened, David became an outlaw, leader of a band of malcontents in the Wilderness of Judah. Saul's attempts at suppressing him were unsuccessful and must have cost energy and time which were needed for other tasks. The story is told from the viewpoint of one who saw in David the divinely chosen king who was to found the dynasty of the kingdom of Judah ; it shows little sympathy for the difficulties of Saul, who remains a rather pathetic figure, struggling against the adversities of fortune. David became a vassal of the Philistine, Achish of Gath, but this left him considerable independence of action, and he was able to benefit on the one hand from Philistine protection and from gaining knowledge of Philistine military methods, and on the other hand from skilful manoeuvres by which he commended himself to the clans of Judah and allied himself with them in a number of cases by marriage.

With the death of Saul, therefore, David was already in a strong position in the south of the country, and while Saul's general Abner placed Eshbaal on the throne in Mahanaim, David was anointed king over the house of Judah in Hebron. The Philistines appear to have been quite content to see the rivalry between the two rulers, whose troops engaged in intermittent warfare for some years. A quarrel between Abner and Eshbaal brought the former to David to negotiate, and although Abner was murdered by David's own general Joab, David was the obvious candidate for the kingship of the other tribal groups when Eshbaal was assassinated. In all this, David showed skill in taking advantage of each situation as it occurred, protesting against any complicity in the events which were to his advantage while accepting them as divinely indicated marks of favour to him.

Thus David became king of two kingdoms, combining them in his personal rule. The Philistines could clearly not allow such development of his power, but he was able to defeat them in two great battles in the valley of Rephaim to the west of Jerusalem. Subsequently, with the conquest of the Jebusite city of Jerusalem he became king there and established it as his capital, on neutral territory not belonging to either tribal group. With his conquests farther afield, he extended his rule, establishing garrisons in some areas whereas apparently in Ammon he became successor to the royal line. The kingdom extended into the Aramaean regions to Damascus and beyond, and southwards through Edomite territory to the Red Sea.

The development of such power brought David also into contact with other surrounding countries at the diplomatic level, and notably with Hiram of Tyre. It necessitated the development of a more elaborate government organization, as is indicated in the lists of officials and the importance of the royal bodyguard of foreign mercenary troops. But though David's personal rule over Judah and Israel drew the two parts of the country together, the internal situation was never entirely stable. Rebellion against the rule of David came from Benjamin, the tribe to which Saul belonged, and also from David's own son Absalom who was able to gain considerable support when he raised the standard of revolt at Hebron and forced David to abandon Jerusalem. The vivid picture of the family of David in the latter half of 2 Samuel indicates the problem of the succession to the throne and the gradual elimination of possible claimants. With the decline of David's strength, a quarrel ensued, in which the eldest surviving son Adonijah was unable to maintain himself against the younger Solomon who had the support of the royal bodyguard and of Nathan the prophet and Zadok the priest. In these struggles there can be seen the pressures at work against the new kind of dynastic rule which was being established by David in Jerusalem in succession to the line of Jebusite kings, and to the importance of the royal shrine there with its priesthood over against the older priestly line represented by Abiathar who lost his position in his support of Adonijah. By bringing the Ark into Jerusalem David appropriated to his kingdom the symbol of the ancient tribal association. The establishment of the capital there paved the way for the greater degree of organization and centralization which followed with Solomon.

3. *Solomon.* The intrigues which led to the accession of Solomon and his ruthless action against opponents are seen by the compiler of the narratives as overruled by the divine purpose. The son of the marriage between David and the wife of the murdered Uriah the Hittite was to be the builder

of the Jerusalem Temple and a king around whom a wealth of legend was to gather. In the Old Testament narratives many indications appear of the degree to which political organization developed under Solomon, and archaeology has confirmed the impression of his energy in building. The relationship with Tyre developed into a full-scale trading contract for building materials, and also made possible the building and equipping of an Israelite fleet on the Red Sea for trade farther afield. Trade with Arabia indicated by the visit of the queen of Sheba, copper and iron mining, and smelting at Ezion-geber, and the position of Solomon as middleman in the horse and chariot trade brought further accession of wealth.

The building programme, in which pride of place in the narrative is given to the Jerusalem Temple, was concerned primarily with military strength—in the building of chariot and fortified cities in strategic positions, as at Megiddo and Hazor—and with the development of royal power—as in the palace and shrine at Jerusalem. The support of the central organization necessitated heavy taxation in kind, and the building programme demanded the development of the forced labour system already known under David. Control of the different areas of the kingdom was placed in the hands of officers. It is not clear whether these areas included or excluded Judah, though it seems most probable that they followed the old tribal areas and that Judah did in fact make its own contribution. When complaint was made at Solomon's oppressive policy, no mention appears of Judah's exemption. With Solomon too a much closer welding together of the various population elements appears, Canaanite and Israelite together being involved in the closer integration of the country's life. As befitted the ruler of such an empire, Solomon had an even more elaborate harem than his father David, expressing in part his relationships with surrounding countries, including Egypt. The reputation for wisdom which Solomon acquired, expressed both in vivid story and in a note of his compositions, perhaps indicates the degree to which the development of the monarchy was accompanied by literary developments. The rise to national power would naturally carry with it the desire to express in literary form the process by which it had been achieved, and wisdom material, so evidently international in character, may have been given added impetus by contacts with other countries.

National security was not, however, complete. Solomon lacked David's military genius ; there were troubles in Edom, and Aram was lost to the kingdom to become an independent state centred in Damascus. Internal discontent was expressed in the person of Jeroboam, one of the royal officers, supported by Ahijah, a prophet of Shiloh. The old traditions were not dead.

(c) *The Divided Monarchy.*

1. *The Disruption.* Solomon's death precipitated the crisis. The recognition of Rehoboam as successor in Judah was followed by a ceremonial at Shechem, where the representatives of the northern kingdom laid down conditions for their acceptance of him as king. Clearly there was a continued readiness to acknowledge a ruler of the Davidic line, but equally clearly there was widespread resentment at the effects of Solomon's policy, and protest against both taxation and forced labour. The refusal of Rehoboam to accept the conditions provided the opportunity for Jeroboam, unsuccessful rebel of the reign of Solomon, to return from Egyptian protection and become king of an independent northern kingdom, perhaps with Egyptian support. The forced labour officer was stoned to death, and Rehoboam escaped to Jerusalem. Jeroboam organized an independent kingdom with royal shrines at Bethel and Dan, though it is clear that this did not represent a departure from traditional Yahwistic belief. The use of calf symbols did not in itself indicate idolatry. Warfare between the two kingdoms—no doubt in part for the control of the border territory of Benjamin—continued intermittently, but the situation was also aggravated by Egyptian intervention under Shishak who marched swiftly through the northern kingdom, presumably claiming it as under his protection, and made threats and attacks in the south, carrying off gold treasures from palace and shrine. The division thus appears as the result of several forces. The old spirit of independence of the northern tribes combined with resentment at oppressive policy made a difficult internal situation; it may well be that this was exploited by an Egyptian ruler who was strong enough to look beyond his own borders. The area unified under David disintegrated into a number of smaller states.

2. *The Two Kingdoms in the Ninth Century.* Warfare between the kingdoms continued under succeeding rulers. Judah maintained reasonable stability under the Davidic line, and was able at times by judicious alliances to gain border advantage. Israel's kings were not so stable and a repeated pattern of prophetic judgment and change of dynasty is to be observed. In the rebellions, and in particular in the complex series of events by which Omri came to the throne, we may detect the important part played by military power within the kingdom. Personal ambition and military control made successful rebellion possible. But this is accompanied by

indications of divine sanction which suggest the continuance of the tradition of a charismatic rule and an unwillingness to accept a hereditary kingship which involved a departure from older Israelite traditions.

Such a protest becomes clearest in the period of Omri's dynasty, when the pressure of the Aramaean kingdom of Damascus necessitated the forming of a close alliance with Phoenicia, and this brought in its train religious influences. The protest of Elijah against alien religion and against alien ideas of kingship and morality represents a revival of the older religious traditions, and this continues in his successor Elisha. Yet it is clear that politically Omri and his successor Ahab were able rulers. Omri's building of a new capital at Samaria was a shrewd move and gave the kingdom a very strong centre. Ahab's contribution to the military forces which met the Assyrians at Qarqar in 853 B.C. and for the moment halted the advance of this new power in the east, shows the strength of the kingdom. The pressure of the Aramaeans continued intensively, and the Assyrians forced the submission of the founder of the next dynasty, Jehu. But by the end of the century the Aramaeans were weakened by the Assyrian conquest of Damascus in 802 B.C., so that when the Assyrians became occupied further east, a resurgence of Israelite power was possible.

The change of dynasty itself was assisted by prophetic action, instigated by Elisha who appears also to have been involved in a similar change of dynasty in Damascus. It was supported by conservative groups within the northern kingdom, and resulted in a ruthless campaign against the survivors of the house of Ahab and against the supporters of alien religious practice.

In the kingdom of Judah, a similar situation had developed. The hostility between the two kingdoms had subsided, with Israel the dominant partner in an alliance sealed by marriage. Jehu's rebellion in the north, in which the king of Judah was also killed, gave the opportunity for Athaliah the queen mother, daughter of Ahab and Jezebel, to seize power and suppress the other members of the royal house with the exception of a boy who was subsequently put on the throne by the priests, representatives here of the old tradition. The extirpation of the usurpers and of alien religious practice followed a similar pattern and the dynasty of David continued to rule for the remainder of the kingdom's existence.

3. *Prosperity and Collapse in the Eighth Century.* The period of Assyrian withdrawal from the west coincided largely with the reigns of Jeroboam II. in the north and Azariah (Uzziah) in the south, both of whom occupied their thrones for

a long period. The renaissance of power and prosperity can be traced in the historical and prophetic material. On the one hand, both kingdoms were able to extend their power abroad. Israel renewed its pressure against the Aramaeans and recovered the areas beyond Jordan which had earlier been lost. The later history of the Chronicler indicates that Uzziah recovered Elath (Ezion-geber) on the Red Sea, which presumably marks a restoration of some degree of control over Edom and a revival of industry there. On the other hand, the internal prosperity of certain classes of the population is clearly depicted in the prophetic judgments of Amos and Hosea for the north, and of Isaiah and Micah for the south. The wealth which expressed itself in summer houses and winter houses, in ivory inlays as decoration (the work of foreign craftsmen, of which examples have been discovered from various periods, as far back as the reign of Ahab) and in large-scale religious festivities and banquetings, is matched by pictures of the oppression of the poor, the stark situation of the unprotected, the loss of freedom by the impoverished peasant. The standards of justice, upheld in the village communities by the independent members of them, were now lost in the pressures which the wealthier members could exert over the poorer.

The situation, seen by the prophets as a departure from the ancient standards of just dealing and as a denial of Israel's true allegiance to her God expressed both in alien worship and in a wrong understanding of the nature of obedience, was in fact overshadowed by the prospect of Assyrian revival. Soon after the middle of the century, as the reigns of the two kings came to an end, the pressure of Assyria began to be felt again in the west with the campaigns of Tiglath-pileser III. (745–727 B.C.). Israel was clearly involved since Menahem accepted Assyrian protection and paid heavy tribute. Probably his position as king, replacing Shallum who had murdered Jeroboam II.'s son and successor, was due to Assyrian influence. His son was replaced by Pekah, the army commander and anti-Assyrian in policy, who led a campaign together with Rezon of Damascus to force Ahaz of Judah into an alliance against the Assyrians. The plan was to replace Ahaz on the throne by a sympathetic personage, and there can be little doubt that within Judah there would have been support for such a move. The existence in both kingdoms of pro-Assyrian and anti-Assyrian groups is readily intelligible. The attempt failed, but Ahaz had called in Assyrian help which necessitated his recognition of Assyrian suzerainty, and he was summoned to Damascus, which the Assyrians had conquered, to make his submission. The subordinate position of Judah was expressed in the acceptance of Assyrian influence in the Jerusalem

Temple. The northern kingdom was shorn of its northern and eastern sections which came under direct Assyrian control, and a rebel named Hoshea was confirmed as king. When subsequently he too was tempted to seek Egyptian support and rebel, the central part of the kingdom was overrun and Samaria itself captured in 721 B.C. Many were deported and Assyrian colonists were placed in the area, and the kingdom ceased to exist, being replaced by the Assyrian province of Samaria.

(d) *The Kingdom of Judah Alone.*

1. *Judah and Assyria.* The kingdom of Judah was not directly involved, though it is possible that its loyalty was rewarded with some part of the border territory so often coveted. Under the next ruler Hezekiah, however, rebellion was attempted, probably in 713–711 B.C., though speedy submission evidently prevented the consequences which might otherwise have followed. A definite act of rebellion at the accession of the Assyrian Sennacherib (705–681 B.C.) was made in conjunction with rebellion in Babylonia and with promises of Egyptian help. Hezekiah was deeply involved and there are indications of his strengthening of the defences of Jerusalem and securing of its water-supply in anticipation of Assyrian action, as well as carrying out reforms which suggest the repudiation of Assyrian overlordship. The course of the Assyrian campaigns is not entirely clear, nor even whether the Biblical account covers one campaign in duplicate or indicates two separate campaigns, though the former seems the more probable. The promised Egyptian help proved of little value. Lachish was besieged and captured; many of the fortified cities of Judah were overrun. Jerusalem alone escaped the consequences of siege and capture. If this appeared as a great act of deliverance and was hence elaborated in later story, it was in fact only one moment in the continuing dependence of Judah on Assyria which was to last for another eighty years. Prominent in the political situation was the prophet Isaiah, at times foretelling utter disaster, at other times pointing to a glimpse of hope, but always passing judgment upon the inner significance of the situation as demanding renewed obedience and faith on the part of Judah.

The subservient position of Judah continued during the long reign of Manasseh, in a period of great Assyrian power. This is reflected in the Old Testament in the condemnation of Manasseh's evil ways, since it would seem likely that some of the abuses, such as the astral cult, later remedied by Josiah, were introduced under Assyrian influence and in recognition of Assyrian overlordship. The Assyrian conquest of Egypt reached its climax in the destruction of Thebes in 663 B.C., though immediately after under a new ruler, Psammetichus I., Egypt's power began again to increase. Pressure from the north and east began to make the Assyrian position less secure, and in the middle of the century rebellion in Babylon and disturbances in the west, probably encouraged by Egypt, may even have involved Judah, if we may interpret the rather muddled story in 2 Chron. $33^{10ff.}$ as indicating that Manasseh was taken captive to Babylon to answer for his involvement before the Assyrian ruler. It is appropriate to remember in this that Manasseh's subservience and his acceptance of Assyrian religious practice were not necessarily so much to his taste as the Old Testament narrative suggests, but were dictated by Assyrian power.

2. *Independence under Josiah.* Anti-Assyrian feeling certainly continued strongly, and after a complex series of events at the death of Manasseh—his son Amon assassinated by one court party, and the assassins themselves removed by the "people of the land"—the young king Josiah was placed on the throne. This was done by the same "people of the land" (*'am hā'āreṣ*), who appear to be what we might term the "country landowners," representative of a conservative religious tradition and nationalistic in outlook. This happened in 639 B.C., while the Assyrian Ashurbanipal was still on the throne. It suggests that signs of Assyrian weakening were beginning to be noticed, and its consequences are to be seen some years later when, roughly at the time that an independent kingdom was established in Babylon by Nabopolassar, Josiah began "repairs to the Temple" which are likely to indicate a throwing off by him of the Assyrian yoke. No indication appears of Assyrian intervention, not even when subsequently he engaged in full-scale religious reform, aimed at both centralization and purification of the cult, and carried this reform into the area belonging to the old northern kingdom, as far as Bethel and Samaria. The Assyrian governor there was presumably unable to prevent this; perhaps he adopted a sympathetic attitude to save his own position. It is significant that Jeremiah began his prophetic activity in this same period, threatening judgment from the north, and we may speculate as to whether, if he was intending to identify the hostile power, he anticipated an Assyrian revival to bring doom on the corruptions which he saw, for such a revival had been experienced in earlier times.

The reform of Josiah, beginning in Temple repairs and carried further in measures based on the law-book then discovered, was a religious and national movement. Centralization of the cult at Jerusalem with the abolition of the local centres of worship may be seen at one and the same time as a move for consolidating royal power and as an endeavour to suppress alien religious practice offered in the name of Yahweh. The removal of elements from the cultus in Jerusalem which were associated with foreign power is clearly tied up with the move to independence. The extension of control into the area of the old northern kingdom shows an expansionist policy suggesting that Josiah was aiming at re-establishing the kingdom of David, and so too does his presence at Megiddo at the end of his life, for this was the administrative centre of the north-westerly Assyrian province. From recent discoveries, it appears probable too that he controlled part at least of the coastal plain.

The moment was opportune. The power of Assyria waned rapidly under the pressure of Babylonians and Medes. Nineveh fell to them in 612 B.C. For the moment none of these eastern powers could be concerned with Palestine. Egypt's power was increasing, but no indication appears of intervention until after the fall of Nineveh, and so for a decade or so Josiah could rule an independent kingdom, and there was no doubt a considerable upsurge of national feeling. The end came when Josiah attempted to resist the passage of Pharaoh Necho's army, marching to support the last remnants of the Assyrian empire with a view to establishing a buffer state between himself and the Babylonians. Josiah met his death in 609 B.C., probably in battle, as the Chronicler clearly indicates. The "people of the land" made a valiant attempt to retain independence by putting Jehoahaz (Shallum) on the throne, but Egypt intervened and took him to die a prisoner in Egypt, placing Jehoiakim (Eliakim) on the throne, and exacting tribute.

3. *The Last Years of the Kingdom of Judah.* The defeat of Necho by Nebuchadrezzar, son of Nabopolassar, at Carchemish in 605 B.C., must have seemed to offer the chance of independence to Judah again. But Nebuchadrezzar, succeeding to the throne immediately after the battle, showed his energy, and the kings of Syria and Palestine submitted in 604 B.C., Jehoiakim presumably among them. Egypt was not, however, finished, and when the Babylonian army marched west in 601 B.C., it met with a decisive set-back. Jehoiakim, probably with the promise of Egyptian support, withheld tribute, but in 598 B.C. retribution came and, Jehoiakim having died at the end of the year, his son Jehoiachin was forced to submit under the pressure of the Babylonian siege in March 597 B.C. The Babylonian record of the capture of the city is now available to attest the date of this event.

Babylonian policy was relatively lenient. The king and

court, the leaders and craftsmen, were taken into exile. A regent was appointed, another son of Josiah named Zedekiah (Mattaniah), though it appears that the captive Jehoiachin was still recognized as being the legitimate king. Zedekiah proved a weak and vacillating ruler, unable to decide between the various policies open to him. Secretly he seems to have respected Jeremiah's counsel to be loyal to Babylon, but he succumbed to the pressure of courtiers who urged resistance. In about 594 B.C. he was apparently summoned to Babylon, perhaps to allay suspicions as to his loyalty, for just at this time there were prophets active both in Babylon and in Jerusalem proclaiming the imminent deliverance from Babylonian power. He evidently cleared his name, but it was not long before Egyptian offers of help provoked new moves to rebellion, and the Babylonians came to besiege Jerusalem again in 588 B.C. The siege was severe and famine in the city was rife. The approach of an Egyptian army created a lull, but pressure was soon resumed. The remainder of Judah fell into Babylonian hands and a vivid glimpse of the uncertainties can be seen in the Lachish letters, part of a military correspondence during these years. Finally the wall was breached and the city fell. The king's attempt at escape was frustrated, and he was brought before Nebuchadrezzar at his headquarters at Riblah. His sons were killed and he was blinded and taken to prison in Babylon. More of the leaders were exiled, and systematic destruction of city and temple and walls was carried out by the Babylonians.

The kingdom of Judah was at an end. The hopes raised by Josiah's reign were shattered, and the attempts at restoring that situation had proved vain. Disaster had come, as the prophets had said it would. Yet politically the situation was never a simple one, and the indications of Egyptian power in the last years reveal that the attempts at rebellion against Babylon were not so completely without reasonable hope as to be absurd. Egypt had nearly shattered Nebuchadrezzar in 601 B.C. Assyria which had once been so menacing had fallen. Independence had for a time been enjoyed. All this must have made it seem a risk worth taking, and its failure all the more shattering because hopes were so high. The apparent defeatism of Jeremiah and of the Uriah who prophesied in like words and was put to death by Jehoiakim, must have seemed very much like treason to those who were attempting to keep up the national morale. To many of their contemporaries their gloomy prognostications must have seemed very much less attractive than the fair hopes offered by Hananiah and his like. But Babylon was too strong, and Egypt in the end an unreliable ally. Disaster overtook Judah.

(iv) EXILE AND RESTORATION (586–333 B.C.)

The marking of a break in the history at the year 586 B.C. has certain obvious disadvantages, for it suggests that there is no continuity of life across the gulf created by the downfall of the kingdom of Judah and the exiling of some part of its population. Life did continue in Palestine, and an attempt was made at creating a new community there. But the break is nevertheless of great significance. The end of the kingdom, even though it had been a subject state for virtually a century and a half, marks the end of an era, and in particular marks the accomplishment in historical terms of those judgments upon the life of Israel which had been made by the prophets from the eighth century onwards. The anticipation of disaster, however certain, could not be the same as the disaster itself. A reorientation of thinking, for better or for worse, was necessitated by the events themselves.

(a) *The Exilic Age.*

1. *General Background.* The reign of Nebuchadrezzar of Babylon continued until 562 B.C. He was involved in a thirteen-year siege of Tyre from 585 B.C. onwards, and made a third deportation from Judah in 582 B.C. (Jer. 52[30]). Josephus (*Ant.* x. ix. 7 [181 f.]) has a very garbled account of a campaign in Coele-Syria, Moab and Ammon in that year, followed by a campaign in Egypt. Subsequently, in 568 B.C., Nebuchadrezzar intervened after Apries (Hophra) of Egypt had been succeeded by a rebel Amasis in 570 B.C.

Nebuchadrezzar was succeeded by his son, Amel-marduk (Evil-merodach) (562–560 B.C.) who released Jehoiachin from prison (2 Kings 25[27-30]). Nergal-shar-usur (Neriglissar) reigned from 560–556 B.C., but his young son was then ousted from the succession by a rebellion in which the leader Nabunaid (Nabonidus) became the new ruler and in fact the last ruler of the Babylonian empire (556–539 B.C.). Opinions differ as to his ability and policy. He alienated the population of Babylon itself, where the conqueror Cyrus was to be welcomed as the restorer of the deity Marduk. But from the fact that he was already middle-aged when he came to the throne, that he carried through some reorganization of religious life, with particular devotion to the moon-god Sin, and that he was apparently able to continue to rule from Tema in northern Arabia—to which he went probably for commercial reasons—it seems likely that he was a man of considerable ability. The growing threats to the empire and the already unstable internal political situation might well have toppled a less able ruler. It appears also that his reputation lived on among the Jews, as may be judged from the fragmentary "Prayer of Nabonidus" from Qumran, and this suggests that the basis of some of the stories in the Book of Daniel may be found in his political and religious activities.

The end of the empire came with the rise to power of Cyrus of Persia, a vassal of the Median empire. He was at first supported in rebellion by Nabonidus, but the latter soon found himself faced with the threat of a Median empire under Cyrus' control. Alliance between Babylonia, Egypt and Lydia was met with tremendous energy by Cyrus, who first overthrew Lydia and gained control of Asia Minor and then, probably after campaigns in the east, conquered Babylonia. The city of Babylon was occupied without a struggle by Cyrus' general Gobryas, and Cyrus himself entered the city shortly after.

2. *The Situation in Palestine.* With the capture and destruction of Jerusalem in 586 B.C., a reorganization of the political situation in Judah became necessary. The area was placed under a governor. The appointment of Gedaliah, of a well-known Judaean family and possibly an important official under Zedekiah, shows an unexpected leniency on the part of the conquerors. The prophet Jeremiah elected to remain with him, and the attempt was made at building up new life and restoring confidence. Those who had scattered during the war returned (Jer. $40^{11f.}$) and joined Gedaliah at Mizpah, his centre of administration. The situation in the area was not so bad that harvests could not be gathered.

To ardent nationalists, Gedaliah's attempted co-operation with the Babylonians no doubt seemed treasonable, but though his close associates warned him of the danger, he refused to allow action to be taken against one Ishmael of the royal family who, with the support of the Ammonites, assassinated him after probably only a short period of office. The associates of Gedaliah, after rescuing those who had been taken captive by Ishmael though failing to catch Ishmael himself, resolved to escape to Egypt, fearing Babylonian reprisals. Jeremiah's advice was sought, but though he warned them against flight to Egypt and assured them of God's blessing in Palestine, they disregarded his advice and took him with them.

This information, meagre as it is, provides some clues to the state of affairs in Palestine. The archaeological evidence indicates with fair clarity the extent of the devastation and destruction of the cities of Judah, though conclusive evidence is not available in every case. But the possibility of continued life was not entirely lacking. While it is uncertain what the population of Judah was before the war, and calculation of the casualties and the number of the exiles is inevitably impossible, the analogy of other such wars—for example, the Jewish War of A.D. 66–70—would indicate that many of the country folk would succeed in escaping to the caves and other refuges of the Wilderness of Judaea, and would soon return. Pressure from surrounding areas probably made the situation more difficult.

A changed social situation was to be found. What the Old Testament describes as the *dallath hā'āreṣ* (the poor of the land) in contrast to the *'am hā'āreṣ* (the landowning men of standing), came to occupy positions of prominence. The exiling of many of the leaders would seem to have led to a situation in which their place was taken by propertyless persons, presumably coming to occupy their lands and perhaps also to become tenants of the old royal lands now in the control of the Babylonian authorities.

Religious life too continued, for it is unthinkable that it should not. A story is told of a group of men from Shechem, Shiloh, and Samaria who came to make offerings at the Temple of Yahweh at the time of Gedaliah's assassination. Arriving at Mizpah, they found themselves involved in the aftermath of this event, and most of them lost their lives. It seems that they were going via Mizpah to Jerusalem as would be reasonable in view of the places from which they were coming, and it would be natural for them to pay their respects to the governor—perhaps even obtain his sanction for their journey. It is true that the suggestion has been made that a shrine—temporary or more permanent—may have been established at Mizpah or in its vicinity, but it is much more likely that the Jerusalem shrine, destroyed as it was, retained its sanctity and was soon sufficiently cleared for some measure of religious observance. The places from which the pilgrims came indicate the degree to which Jerusalem had become the central shrine even for those who lived outside the actual area of Judah, perhaps partly as a result of the extensive reforming activities of Josiah.

Guesses may be hazarded, but without certainty, as to what parts of the Old Testament took on their final or nearly final form in Palestine during the Exile. In particular this has been thought to be true of the Deuteronomic History, extending from Deuteronomy to 2 Kings. The work takes little account of the exiles themselves, though it looks at the very end to the release of Jehoiachin. If it was produced in Palestine, it witnesses to the existence there of a circle of theological thinking of great profundity and influence. But its rather disparaging comment on the *dallath hā'āreṣ* (2 Kings 25[12]) hardly suggests that it saw in the Palestinian community any real hope for the future.

3. *The Exiles.* The main body of exiles was in Babylonia,

in various settlements (Ezek. 3^{15}, Ezra 2^{59}=Neh. 7^{61}). If we may judge from Jeremiah's letter sent during the reign of Zedekiah (Jer. 29^{4-23}) and assume that conditions after 586 B.C. were much the same, the exiles enjoyed considerable freedom to organize their own life, to build houses for their own occupation and to cultivate land for their own support. The tablets from Babylon, belonging to the same period and indicating the allowances made to the captive king Jehoiachin and to others, give no precise indication of conditions, though they do not conflict with the other evidence. No doubt the king and his entourage were subject to greater restriction than the other people. The mention of craftsmen of various nationalities in these tablets (cf. 2 Kings 24^{14}, Jer. 29^{2}) suggests the probability that such skilled labour was employed in the building works of Babylon itself, while other exiles lived in settlements farther afield. The indications in the book of Ezekiel reflect similar freedom of association (8^{1}, 14^{1}, 33^{30-33}). The release of Johoiachin in 561 B.C. presumably gave rise to speculation about the future of the Davidic line, but no precise allusion to it appears except in the narrative of 2 Kings (25^{27-30}).

The possibility has been mentioned that during the reign of Nabonidus conditions deteriorated and that the later traditions of religious oppression owe something to his policy. Certainly Babylon became a figure typifying the hostile power *par excellence*, as may be seen from later writings (*e.g.* Rev. 14^{8}, etc.). But some part of this view of Babylon must derive simply from the fact that Babylon was the conqueror, the destroyer of Jerusalem and its Temple. The uncleanness of the land of Babylonia from the point of view of the Jews (cf. Ezek. 4^{13}) must have made adjustment to the new situation difficult. The complaint of the psalm ($137^{5f.}$) of the impossibility of singing the songs of Yahweh in a strange land, and the violence of the hostility expressed (vv. $^{8-9}$), indicate a not unintelligible reaction to the continued power of the conqueror, and the desire for Babylon's overthrow is expressed in a number of prophecies (cf. Isa. 13–14, Jer. 50–51).

Yet the loss of the Temple at Jerusalem evidently did not mean a complete end to cultic practice. The evidence from Egypt, which we shall see in a moment, points to a less stringent attitude than has sometimes been thought to belong to the Deuteronomic legislation, suggesting that the intention was not an exclusion of places of worship outside Palestine—if indeed such a question was at all in view—but simply the centralization and unification of worship within the area of the kingdom. Ezra 8^{17-18} tells of Ezra sending for " sons of Levi " from the " place Casiphia," and this curious method of reference to a locality strongly suggests that the word " place " is here equivalent to " sanctuary " as frequently in the Old Testament. This evidence is from a considerably later date, but the possibility cannot be excluded that during the actual period of the Exile such developments had taken place, alongside other development of forms of worship more connected with the exposition of law and tradition which is so clearly reflected in such works as the Deuteronomic History and the Holiness and Priestly Codes, as well as in the prophetic exhortations of Jeremiah, Ezekiel and Deutero-Isaiah. This latter point provides some clue to the evolution of the synagogue—an institution for which evidence is directly available only at a much later date. But while it would be improper to speak of " synagogues " in the exilic age, the evidence, again from the period of Ezra (cf. Neh. 8), of an evidently well-established practice of reading and expounding the law from a wooden pulpit, suggests that we may not unreasonably see in the necessities of the exilic period, and perhaps earlier still in the situation created by religious centralization, the impetus towards the development of forms of worship which did not involve sacrifices but which did represent a proper retention of traditional forms and patterns.

There were other exiles too. Of the group who took Jeremiah to Egypt little more is known. They are found—some of them at least—abandoning their ancestral faith to the extent of reverting to the worship of the Queen of Heaven, regarding their neglect of that worship as the explanation of the disasters which had come upon them (Jer. 44). Jeremiah had prophesied no escape for these exiles (Jer. $42^{16ff.}$) and had foretold Babylonian conquest for Egypt (Jer. 43^{8-13}). That Jeremiah's gloomiest forebodings were not entirely fulfilled must be seen from the fact that the record of his words in this period was preserved. Perhaps some of his associates subsequently returned to Palestine, but of this we have no direct knowledge.

At a later date, in the fifth century B.C., we can trace from contemporary documents something of the life of a Jewish military colony at Elephantine, at the first Nile cataract. This community possessed its own temple, and claimed that it went back at least to the time of Cambyses (529–522 B.C.). When this was destroyed, an appeal was made to the authorities in Jerusalem and in Samaria, and it does not appear that any charge of illegitimacy was levelled against the sanctuary. The origin of the colony—presumably a garrison of Jewish mercenary troops with their families—is not known, but not improbably it went back to the Babylonian period, or even to an earlier date. The documents reflect an interesting syncretistic form of the religion of Yahweh (appearing here as Yahu).

4. *The Significance of the Exile.* The disruption of life in Judah and the fact that the religious community, which had formerly consisted virtually entirely of those living within the area of the two kingdoms, now numbered among its members some who lived very remote from the centre, demanded a good deal of rethinking. The reassessment of earlier prophetic teaching was necessitated by the fulfilment of the words of doom. In a very real sense, the Day of the Lord might be said to have become a reality in history, as the prophets had proclaimed. Reliance upon the monarchy and upon the Temple was seen to be insufficient, while the value of these two institutions remained impressed upon men's minds, to issue in new hopes for a rebuilt Temple, especially in Ezekiel, and for a perfect Davidic kingship, as expressed in a whole series of prophetic sayings and eventually in Messianic hopes. The lessons of the past and its reinterpretation for the future were set out by various historians and theologians, by the great exilic prophets Ezekiel and Deutero-Isaiah on the one hand, and by the writers of the Deuteronomic History and of the Priestly work on the other. Over into the following centuries, the impulse to new life seems often to have come from Babylonian Jewry, and this suggests that considerable literary activity was undertaken there. The reconstitution of the religious community in Palestine evidently owes much to such rethinking and replanning.

(b) *The Restoration.*

1. *Reconstructing the Historical Events.* Cyrus' conquest of the Babylonian empire marks the turning point anticipated by Deutero-Isaiah and seen by the later historian, the Chronicler, as the fulfilment of prophecy (2 Chron. 36^{22}=Ezra 1^{1}). The latter records an edict of Cyrus in his first year (538 B.C.) authorizing the rebuilding of the Temple and the return to Jerusalem of those who had been exiled, supported with gifts from the people of the places in which they lived (Ezra 1^{2-4}). The edict is quoted again (in Aramaic) in a different form (Ezra 6^{3-5}), with no reference to such a full-scale return. The commissioner appointed for the work of rebuilding was one Sheshbazzar, prince of Judah—evidently not of the royal family, but a man of standing. No description is available of what he actually undertook in Jerusalem, for the story continues with a report about the activities of Zerubbabel, of the Davidic family, and Jeshua the priest. Since in the books of Haggai and Zechariah, which describe the activities of the opening years of the reign of Darius I. (522–486 B.C.), these two persons are evidently in authority and are actively engaged in the rebuilding, with no mention of earlier work, it has

seemed very probable that the Chronicler has conflated two different periods, no doubt with the desire of stressing the significance of the new period and the importance of the restoration of the Temple. But although this may be the case, there is every reason to believe that the essential content of Cyrus' edict is historical. It corresponds very closely both with the statements of the Cyrus cylinder in which the authority of Marduk is claimed for his conquest of Babylon and the restoration of the gods to their own places is indicated, and also to the known policy of the Persians in regard to the religious life of their subject peoples. The Jews at Elephantine were later to be given similar consideration.

Cyrus himself does not appear to have campaigned in the west, and only under his successor Cambyses (529–522 B.C.) does it appear to have been brought really under Persian control. The task of Sheshbazzar must be seen against this background. He would be dependent for its success on the co-operation of the local authorities, and presumably of the governor in Samaria who appears to have had control over the Judaean area after the assassination of Gedaliah. If, as seems likely, the Persians had not replaced the governor there and submission to Persia had been very much a formality, Sheshbazzar might well have met with considerable reluctance to allow him to proceed. Sanballat in a similar position a century later was able to cause some difficulties to Nehemiah, the royal favourite and nominee. Perhaps some measure of repair to the Temple was achieved—as is suggested by the report in Ezra 5—but it is likely that Sheshbazzar was unable to fulfil his commission. Economic problems may have been a further factor. That a relatively small number of exiles returned seems to be indicated both by the evident delay in restoration and by the subsequent need to urge the Jews in Babylonia to escape (cf. Zech. 2[6f.]). Even Ezra found no very great enthusiasm for return (cf. Ezra 8), and indeed conditions in Palestine can hardly have been very attractive to those Jews who had been able to settle down and establish themselves in Babylonia.

Cyrus' successor Cambyses campaigned in the west and in Egypt. Judah as an important point on the route to Egypt may have caused him some concern, and it is possible that Zerubbabel was appointed by him. Darius I. who succeeded him had at first to contend with a great deal of unrest and rival claimants to the throne. These uncertainties raised speculation in the minds of Jews in Palestine, but the prophets Haggai and Zechariah stressed that it was not in political events but in divine action that hope lay, and so urged the Jewish community and its leaders to rebuild the Temple.

From the lists in Neh. 12 it appears that a quite considerable group of exiles returned with Zerubbabel and Jeshua, and it is not improbable that the two prophets were of this party. If, as seems probable, Zechariah had already been active as a prophet in Babylonia before his return, then the background to the appointment of a Davidite, Zerubbabel, as new commissioner for Judah may be a movement towards restoration among zealous Jews who saw with regret that the promises of Deutero-Isaiah were not yet fulfilled.

2. *The Rebuilding of the Temple.* The real impetus to rebuild the Temple came in the second year of Darius I. from the two prophets Haggai and Zechariah. The difficulties of the economic situation, and distress caused by poor harvests, were not allowed to stand in the way of this central duty. It was indeed a vital task, for the life of the post-exilic community was to centre in the Temple, and Jews in more outlying places looked towards Jerusalem and its Temple in spirit. But the task was not to be completed without opposition. Here again the Chronicler's account gives rise to difficulties. He has two different accounts of opposition, one of which (Ezra 4^{1-5}) is connected by him with the long delay between the first years of Cyrus and the actual time of rebuilding. The other represents a more official enquiry into the undertaking by Tattenai, governor of the province " Beyond the River " —the official title given to the area within which Judah was situated. This latter enquiry appears to have been sympathetic, for work on the Temple was not halted while a letter was sent to Darius with a report and the original edict of Cyrus was looked up in the archives. The edict was confirmed with the assurance of further support, and the officials involved are said to have carried out the royal command. The account of opposition placed earlier may, in fact, refer to the same situation, and indicate the cause of the official enquiry. The opposition is there attributed to descendants of colonists placed in Palestine in the reign of the Assyrian king Esarhaddon who claimed to be worshippers of Yahweh and demanded a share in the work. It is possible that this refers to the descendants of those settled at the time of the fall of Samaria, who may well have been regarded as unfit by the zealous Jews or who may simply have been engineering difficulties for the builders.

With Persian support the rebuilding was completed in the sixth year of Darius, and the Temple was rededicated. Zerubbabel is not mentioned in this context, though the two prophets are. There has been speculation as to whether he was removed by the Persians for rebellious activities, but at the time of Darius I.'s campaign in Egypt in 518 B.C. there is no indication of any intervention, and the fact that the rebuilding of the Temple continued peacefully suggests that Zechariah was right when he claimed that it was Zerubbabel who would complete the Temple (4^9).

(c) *The Period of Nehemiah and Ezra.*

1. *The General Background.* The history of the next century is little known so far as the Jews are concerned. Darius I. was succeeded by Xerxes (486–465 B.C.), but there is no passage in the Old Testament which clearly reflects his reign, nor the momentous wars with Greece which belonged to it. Under his successor, Artaxerxes I. (465–424 B.C.) there is information about a frustrated attempt at rebuilding the walls of Jerusalem (Ezra 4^{7-23}—placed out of chronological order by the Chronicler, perhaps so as to bring together various indications of difficulty ; 4^6 contains a brief reference to problems of the reign of Xerxes). It is perhaps against the background of this frustration that a report reached a Jew in Susa, one of the capitals of the Persian empire, telling of the distresses of Jerusalem. This Jew, Nehemiah, was cupbearer to the king and appears to have enjoyed the royal favour. He was commissioned to go to Jerusalem to rebuild the walls. To the period of Artaxerxes I. is also attributed the activity of Ezra, but the chronological difficulties are considerable and must be discussed separately.

For the remainder of the Persian period, little is known directly of the affairs of the Jews apart from the records of Nehemiah and Ezra. The later rulers were much concerned with Egypt, which rebelled and became independent soon after 400 B.C. There were internal troubles too, and a gradual weakening of Persian authority which led eventually to the fall of the empire to the energetic conquests of Alexander the Great in 333 to 330 B.C. These conquests mark another decisive change in the political situation, and appropriately begin a new section. In these last years of Persian rule, the Jewish community enjoyed, in fact, considerable autonomy in its own affairs, able to issue its own coinage and governed in all probability by its high priests.

2. *The Sequence of Events.* The Chronicler dovetails the activities of Ezra and Nehemiah, so that as the material now stands some part of the work of Ezra, beginning in the seventh year of Artaxerxes, precedes the main part of that of Nehemiah, beginning in the twentieth. The account of Ezra's reading of the law (Neh. 8) follows, and subsequently there is a report of the second period of the governorship of Nehemiah (Neh. 13). But the two men do not really satisfactorily overlap, and the present order suggests that the primary task for which Ezra

was sent, the promulgation of the law, took place some thirteen years after his commissioning.

The chronological setting of Nehemiah may be established with reasonable certainty, for he is described as the contemporary of Sanballat of Samaria who appears in the Elephantine letters of a generation later as the father of two men to whom an appeal was sent by the Jews there. This letter is clearly dated to the year 410 B.C. (the fourteenth year of Darius II. (423–404 B.C.). In about 445 B.C., therefore, he was presumably in his prime, and from this letter we know that he was governor. In Neh. 3^1, Eliashib is mentioned as the high priest contemporary with Nehemiah. In Ezra 10^6 reference is made to Jehohanan the son of Eliashib, and the high priest Johanan appears in the Elephantine letter just mentioned. In the priestly list in Neh. 12^{10}, the order of the priests is given as Eliashib, Joiada, Jonathan. These, and certain other indications, do not add up to a completely assured picture, but they strongly suggest that Ezra came after Nehemiah, and probably as much as a generation later. If the dating of Ezra in the seventh year of Artaxerxes is correct, then this will refer to Artaxerxes II. (404–358 B.C.). Some scholars place Ezra between the two periods of Nehemiah's activity; others place him in the thirty-seventh year of Artaxerxes I. (*i.e. c.* 428 B.C.), but neither of these fits the Biblical evidence so well. In view of the Chronicler's very considerable rearrangements of chronology elsewhere, we may suppose that he deliberately placed the material in its present order to give priority to Ezra. It is also possible that the Nehemiah material was only subsequently inserted, and that the present confusion is due to its having been inserted at the wrong point.

3. *The Achievement of Nehemiah.* As cup-bearer to Artaxerxes I., Nehemiah was able to gain a favourable hearing for his petition on behalf of Jerusalem, the centre of his people's life which he loved though almost certainly he had never visited it. With royal support, and a commission fixing a period for his activity, he went to Jerusalem and undertook first the repair of the city walls. Recognizing that there would be internal opposition, he reviewed the project in secret by night, and then gained general support by a skilful speech. The work was carefully organized and rapidly completed, in spite of the opposition which it met from Sanballat, the governor at Samaria, and also of two other notables, named as Tobiah the Ammonite slave, and Geshem the Arab. It is uncertain who these were or what authority they had. The repair of the walls was not Nehemiah's only measure for the restoring of Jerusalem's prestige. An increase was made in

the population by bringing in a proportion of the inhabitants of the countryside. Nehemiah also led the way in economic measures to relieve the distress of the impoverished members of the community. After a twelve-year period of office, he returned to the Persian court, but was subsequently sent again and carried the work of reformation further. In his absence, Tobiah, through the help of the high priest Eliashib, had gained a foothold in the Temple buildings. We also learn that Eliashib was connected by marriage with Sanballat. Measures to exclude non-Jewish practices by forbidding foreign marriages were evidently designed to introduce a stricter atmosphere. The same is true of the measures to enforce the Sabbath laws and to deal with various cultic and priestly matters.

Nehemiah's achievement must be measured in terms of the consolidation of the Jewish community and the securer establishment of it under Persian rule. This represents a further working out of the problems created by the exilic situation, and indicates a deepened understanding of the nature of a religious community, separating itself because of its religious tradition, but forced to live peaceably under the control of a world empire. What he did may also be seen intelligibly against the background of Persian affairs. However much may be owing to the whim of a Persian ruler who may grant unexpected favours to one of his servants, the policy underlying this action was undoubtedly dictated by wider considerations of security within the western part of the empire. The satrap of "Beyond the River" had rebelled in about 449 B.C.—perhaps it was at this moment that the attempt to rebuild the walls was halted so abruptly as rebellious—and the earlier years of Artaxerxes' reign had been marked by difficulties with both Egypt and the Greeks. A strong, loyal Judah would be a not unimportant asset.

4. *The Achievement of Ezra*. The same motive of security may well have motivated the Persian commissioning of Ezra who is likely to have been a Jewish official at the Persian court. The Egyptian problem was acute in about 400 B.C., and Josephus indicates that there were internal difficulties in Judah where there was conflict between Bagoas the governor and Johanan the priest. Ezra's commission was directed primarily towards the consolidating of the Jewish community by the imposition of a uniform legal standard. This was to include not only the population of the Judaean area, but also all those who accepted this standard throughout the province "Beyond the River." Along with this, Ezra is shown as enforcing even more rigidly than Nehemiah the policy of excluding foreign marriages. As the narrative now stands,

this precedes the reading of the law, but it may well be that the events have been rearranged by the Chronicler so as to stress that the great celebration was made only by those who were acceptable members of the community. More naturally the action against foreign marriages follows on the reading of the law and the acceptance of its obligations.

Nehemiah's consolidation of Jerusalem as the capital of the community as a subject people is here taken a stage further. The community is no longer seen in geographical terms, but incorporates all those within a wider area who accept its obligations. The complexities of the later situation, under Greek and Roman rule, can only be understood against this background. To be a Jew is being defined in terms of acceptance of the law, and the problem of the Jew who lives in an alien environment is already recognized in the commission given to Ezra.

5. *The Samaritan Schism.* It was probably at about this time that a breach occurred which resulted in the establishment of a separate religious community later to be known as the Samaritans. Nehemiah's conflicts with Sanballat do not seem to have raised religious issues at all, and from the names of his sons Delaiah and Shelemiah we know that Sanballat was a worshipper of Yahweh. The Chronicler's history, while making no direct reference to the Samaritan community, appears to be in part a polemic against it and an appeal for a new unity in the religious community. The tradition is that a separate temple at Gerizim, the Samaritan centre, dates from the time of Alexander the Great. The difficulty in discovering the truth lies in the later antagonism, perhaps intensified by the military action of John Hyrcanus in the second century B.C., which results in both parties giving prejudiced accounts. The fact that the Samaritans possessed the Law, the Pentateuch, and that they regarded Gerizim as sacred rather than Jerusalem, which had only been in Israelite hands since the time of David, suggests that they cannot have been in origin the alien religious group descended from the mixture of Assyrian colonists of 722 B.C. and surviving Israelite population. But it may well be that they attracted some of these descendants, as well as others from the old northern tribes which made easy the application to them of reproaches based on passages such as 2 Kings 17. It is also possible that something of the political antagonism between Samaria and Jerusalem was absorbed by the new religious group, and that the situation was exacerbated by this.

6. *The Chronicler's History of Israel.* In many ways the most vivid expression of the life of the community in the fifth and fourth centuries is provided indirectly by the Chronicler.

Writing perhaps about the middle of the fourth century he was able to look back on the work of Ezra and see in this the culmination of the ancient promises for Israel. Through his history, he surveyed the divine process by which an acceptable religious community was created in spite of the repeated failure of men. To him the Exile marked an essential stage, expressive of both judgment and grace: the hope of his own day derived from it. The unity of the people in the time of David which coincided with the establishment of Jerusalem—a point probably of polemic against the Samaritans to justify the divine choice of this place instead of any older sanctuary—was seen by the Chronicler to have been re-created in the reformed community of Ezra's day. The political problems of loss of nationhood have been met; the community has been reconstituted on a religious and legal basis; it is in this prepared for the serious challenges to its life in the centuries of Greek rule. This lay ahead of the Chronicler's understanding of his people's life, but his appreciation of its essential nature is deeper than that of the militant nationalists who in the later centuries tried to recreate the political entity in a situation which would no longer admit it.

(v) THE GREEK AND ROMAN PERIODS (335 B.C.–135 A.D.)

(a) *The Period of Greek Rule.*

1. *Alexander the Great and His Successors.* The stupendously rapid series of campaigns by which Alexander the Great not only took over the area of the then Persian empire, but also extended his domain to include Egypt as well as compaigning far to the east to India, brought to the areas in which Jews were living more than a simple change of master. The unification of Greece, begun by his father Philip, was followed by the conquest of Asia Minor, and then, with the defeat of Darius III. in 333 B.C., Syria and Palestine fell into his hands. Taking Tyre after a seven-month siege, he entered Egypt leaving to his subordinates such other operations as were necessary in Palestine. From Egypt he proceeded to Mesopotamia, where he inflicted final defeat on the Persians, and thence to Susa, Persepolis, and India. In 323 B.C. he was dead, leaving his empire as legacy to struggles between his commanders. But short as the period of his conquest had been, it had brought with it tremendous change. The transplantation of Greek colonists, the establishment of many Greek cities—for example at Alexandria and Samaria—the policy of spreading the Greek culture so beloved by Alexander and by some of his successors, brought a greater impact than appears to have been felt from any of the preceding empires. In near proximity to Jewish areas, there were now established centres of Greek life, and if

the Greek culture which spread was rather more popular and less exalted than the heights reached in Greece itself and often accommodated itself to already existing ideas and traditions, it nevertheless had a profound effect. Greek language did not in Palestine displace Aramaic as the *lingua franca*, but it came to be widely used and as the horizon westwards opened up, it became the essential medium of communication.

The details of the struggles of the successors, the Diadochi, are complex, but the essential from the point of view of the Jewish population in its main centres was that under the successors of Ptolemy, governor of Egypt, a kingdom with Greek culture and ideals was established which during the third century dominated Palestine. Rival to it was the Seleucid state to the north-east, under Seleucus and his successors, dominating Babylonia and Syria.

2. *The Jews under the Ptolemies.* Little is known of the internal history in Palestine during the third century; from the subsequent period, with the predominance of the High Priest as a political figure, it may be surmised that this was developing during the Ptolemaic period. Very important for the development and influence of the Jews was the existence of a settlement in the new Greek city of Alexandria, where the Jewish population became a significant element. The close contact there with the Greek-speaking colonists led to the adoption of this language by the Jewish community, and, with the gradual loss of Hebrew as an actively spoken language, the necessity for Greek translations of the sacred Scriptures expressed itself in the production of the law in Greek. The story of its making and of its subsequent history is obscure, but of its importance both for the Jewish community, and subsequently for the Christian, there is no doubt. It was significant too for the non-Jewish population, for while exaggerated statements may be discounted, there is no lack of evidence of the impact which it had on cultured Greek-speaking people. The story told in the letter of Aristeas is a pious legend, but it is the repository of considerable elements of truth concerning the reverence for the ancient Jewish writings which was felt in many circles.

The attraction which the Jewish Scriptures and faith exercised upon non-Jews was to be seen in the influx of proselytes and others who accepted the Jewish way of life to a greater or less degree. But the exclusivism of the Jews and the difference in their way of life also attracted hostility, and there are indications of anti-Jewish feeling in Alexandria at various times. At the same time, willingly or unwillingly, the Jews themselves absorbed elements of the Greek culture with which they came in contact, and even in Palestine, where the

Jewish communities were less closely in contact with Greek population, there was sufficient influence to begin to create difficulties. The more whole-hearted acceptance of Hellenism which was favoured by some contrasted sharply with the refusal to compromise of the strictly orthodox, though even here a measure of Greek influence may be reasonably assumed. Under the Ptolemies, however, this contrast remained relatively unimportant, and only with a changed political situation did the internal differences come sharply to the surface.

3. *Seleucid Rule. Antiochus* IV. *Epiphanes.* The change came with the eventual success of the Seleucid Antiochus the Great (III.) in gaining Palestine from the Ptolemies at the beginning of the second century B.C. The Jews appear to have regarded this change with sufficient favour to have gained considerable concessions from their new rulers, according to a decree of Antiochus recorded by Josephus. But it is possible to discern an undercurrent of tension between rival parties within the Jewish community, and this was soon to break out into open attempts at manoeuvring the Seleucid rulers into support for claimants for the high priesthood.

With the accession of Antiochus IV. Epiphanes, these internal problems were aggravated by the policy of the ruler himself, a policy not easy to trace in detail, though there is ample evidence to show that he was both an ardent supporter of Hellenistic culture and also a ruler with increasingly clear notions of the nature of his own position. The legitimate High Priest Onias III. was ousted by a rival who offered a bribe to the king, and this rival, Jason, appears to have favoured a thoroughgoing Hellenizing policy. In part, this and similar actions were encouraged by the economic difficulties of the Seleucid rulers. Sanctuary treasures were a ready source of revenue, and another claimant to the high priesthood, Menelaus, made use of these treasures in furthering his claims.

The situation is one in which a great many different motives are involved. On the one hand, there were personal and family rivalries within the Jewish community, centring in the office of High Priest. These rivalries overlapped with party interests in fostering a greater degree of Hellenization or in resisting it. The emergence of clearly defined Jewish parties from this period onwards—their later descriptions as Pharisees, Sadducees, Essenes probably does less than justice to their variety—shows how with the embittering of the situation the rivalries could become hardened into strongly opposed groups. On the other hand, the policy of Antiochus represented both an encouragement to Hellenism, and a desire to maintain his own position on the throne—from this point on rivalries within the Seleucid house were very marked—and also what appears to have been a growing sense of his own place as representative of the gods, and indeed as a manifestation of the divine, as his cognomen Epiphanes indicates. The evidence of his coinage confirms his conviction that he was the embodiment of Zeus and his viceregent on earth. The acceptance of his rule would therefore inevitably involve the acceptance of his pretensions, and it was among the Jews that this met with resistance.

After a victorious campaign in Egypt in 169 B.C., he returned via Jerusalem, and with Menelaus' connivance, he violated and pillaged the sanctuary. A year later, he met with Roman opposition in Egypt, and a false report of his death seems to have reached Jerusalem. Jason attempted to regain his position, and Antiochus on his return took much more violent action against the city. Subsequently a fortress occupied by a Seleucid garrison and Hellenistically inclined Jews—the Akra—was established in the city, and this was followed by an outright attack on Jewish religion, no doubt because of the intransigeance which Antiochus found in certain members of the community. The characteristic practices of Judaism were forbidden, and the sanctuary was desecrated by the establishment of the cult of Zeus Olympios there.

4. *The Maccabaean War*. While there were Jews who submitted to the pressure of Antiochus' policy and to the persuasiveness of those who favoured increased Hellenization, there were others who resisted passively or who took refuge in the hills and caves. Active opposition was provoked by the members of a priestly family at Modein. This family, called Hasmonaean after a recent ancestor, appears prominently in the probably late priestly lists in 1 Chron. 24[7] and its members had perhaps withdrawn to the family property in the country because of the political situation in Jerusalem. When a Seleucid official required sacrifice, the head of the family, Mattathias, refused to comply and killed a renegade Jew and the royal official. He and his family, together with other supporters, fled to the hills to begin armed resistance. Mattathias' death left the leadership in the hands of his third son Judas, nicknamed the Maccabee (possibly "The Hammer"), and it is this nickname which has given its name to the rising which proved to be militarily so successful during the years that followed.

The story of the campaigns, vividly told in the books of Maccabees, is one of heroic resistance and guerilla warfare, fought out in the hills and narrow valleys of Judaea. The Seleucid commanders, like the Romans later, were sometimes tempted to regard the troubles as unimportant but were soon to discover that the rapidly moving Jewish soldiers, familiar with the land, were more than a match for the more cumbersome armies sent against them, provided a pitched battle could be avoided. The result was a series of minor successes for Judas, and by the end of 164 B.C. it was possible for him to advance to Jerusalem, to contain the hostile troops of the Akra and to restore the sanctuary which was rededicated in December of that year. Further campaigns were undertaken to protect Jews who lived in more outlying areas, and, assisted by the dissensions within the Seleucid state after the death of Antiochus IV. in the spring of 163 B.C., the Jews were able to win official recognition of their religious freedom.

The book of Daniel, written in this period, reflects the underlying hopes and fears of orthodox Jews in a time which appeared to some to mark the winding up of history and the moment for the establishment of God's final kingdom. It also reflects something of the internal dissensions which were soon to come to the surface. The devout Jews who welcomed the relief brought by the military successes of Judas found themselves allied with others whose policy was by no means purely religious. The exact relationship between the Hasmonaean family and other party groups within Judaism is impossible to trace, but it is clear that as political aims became clearer in that family and its supporters, the strictly orthodox became less convinced that they were acting under divine guidance. The appointment of a new High Priest, Alcimus, of proper family standing, designed to conciliate the orthodox and to establish peace within the community, seems to have satisfied some but not others. These withdrew from the armed conflict, but probably still resented the idea that the High Priest had been appointed with royal Seleucid support. The aims of Judas and his party were more far-reaching, and war again broke out in which, after initial successes, Judas was defeated and killed.

Leadership passed to his youngest brother Jonathan and he proved to be most skilful in utilizing Seleucid dissensions to his own advantage. Playing off one claimant to the throne against another, he engineered advance for himself and his appointment as High Priest, though his family was not of the proper standing. The years which followed were a period of gradual consolidating of the Jewish position. When Jonathan was caught up in his own intrigues and lost his life, his place was taken by an elder brother Simon who became more and more an independent ruler. He subdued the Akra and enlarged the area of the Judaean province. His son John Hyrcanus (I.) went even further in gaining political independence, and the weakening of the Seleucids in the latter part of the second century made possible virtual independence by about 128 B.C.

(b) *The Hasmonaean Rulers.*

1. *The Establishment of the Monarchy.* John Hyrcanus, using mercenary troops, campaigned to extend the area under Jewish control—east of Jordan, into Samaria where he destroyed the Samaritan temple, and into Idumaea (Edom) where the inhabitants were compulsorily brought within membership of the Jewish religious community. After his death in 104 B.C., his son, Aristobulus, was in power for a year and assumed the title of king. Intrigue within the Hasmonaean family saw the appearance of a notable woman, Salome Alexandra, who was wife first of Aristobulus and then of his brother Alexander Jannaeus. Subsequently, after Jannaeus' death, she took over the government herself. Jannaeus was engaged in a series of military campaigns, endeavouring to extend his control over the surrounding areas, while at the same time involved in considerable internal troubles. He did in fact control an area fairly close to that of the ancient monarchy of David and Solomon.

Salome Alexandra herself took the throne on his death in 76 B.C., appointing her elder son Hyrcanus (II.) as High Priest, but when she died, after fairly effectively keeping the kingdom together and winning support from the Pharisees who had opposed her husband, a struggle between Hyrcanus II. and his younger and more energetic brother Aristobulus II. was to lead before long to the downfall of the family.

2. *Internal Conditions under the Hasmonaeans.* The policy of the earlier members of the Maccabaean family did not, as we have seen, entirely commend itself to the stricter members of the Jewish religious community. Political manoeuvring around the high priesthood and the pursuing of political aims by intrigue, and the acceptance by Jonathan of the high priesthood for himself and for his family after him, provoked considerable resentment. The situation worsened under the Hasmonaean rulers. The unpopularity which they provoked in certain circles is indicated both by their reliance on mercenary troops for their campaigns and by the lack of support and even active opposition which they met with at home. Reprisals against their opponents, such as were taken by Alexander Jannaeus, exacerbated an already difficult situation.

It is against this background that the gradual evolution of various parties and groups within Judaism is to be set. The main detailed evidence comes from Josephus' history, and is probably oversimplified since Josephus was writing in part at least for a non-Jewish audience. The discovery of the Qumran documents has revealed rich evidence of the variety of thought in the inter-testamental period. The name Hasidaeans (Hasidim) is used in 1 Maccabees to describe the more quietistic orthodox group. The names of other groups—Pharisees, Sadducees, and Essenes—are known to us from their later form, but the precise history of their evolution is by no means clear, and while the Qumran community has many points of affinity with the Essenes, the exact relationship is not in fact clear.

In all probability it should be recognized that during the period of external pressure on Jewish religion under Antiochus IV. Epiphanes, there were various groups claiming adherence to the tenets of the ancient faith and reacting both against Hellenism and its supporters and against the political aspirations and religious pretensions of the Maccabaean family. As time went on, these groups may well have subdivided and realigned themselves, with the result that the hints which the Qumran documents provide of the history of that particular group do not entirely fit into what we know of Sadducee and Pharisee reactions to the Hasmonaeans. If the name Sadducee indicates supporters of the Zadokite priesthood, to which the Hasmonaeans did not belong, the precise nature of their apparent support of the Hasmonaeans is difficult to determine. Alexandra Salome appears to have gained the support of the Pharisees, and this may suggest that there are much more complex patterns behind the too simple statements which are sometimes made about the parties. The attitudes and behaviour of Sadducees and Pharisees indicated in the rather limited material of the New Testament provides, as we know in the case of the latter group, only a partial picture, and while it is probable that the Sadducees were politically minded, it seems rather unlikely that they were less than orthodox in their religious pretensions; their conservatism over against the Pharisees accords ill with the idea that they were really Hellenizers at heart.

It may be hoped that the complexities of the internal situation will be further illuminated as the Qumran discoveries come into proper perspective. But already the impression is given of a great richness of religious thought, ranging from the quietism of those described as Hasidaeans in I Maccabees to the militant nationalism of those whose successors were to become active as the Zealots in the first Christian century. If Josephus is right in indicating the Essenes as passivist and monastic rather than activist, we may nevertheless recognize that the Qumran community, closely related to them as it seems to be, is in many respects strongly nationalistic and not averse to more violent activity. The literature—apocalyptic, Biblical commentary, hymns, and legislation—reveals a wealth of activity and speculation, as well as indicating many endeavours at reform and reorganization in a period of great political tension and unease.

(c) *Roman Rule of Palestine.*

1. *The Roman Intervention.* The development of the various groups just indicated runs over into the period of Roman rule. The presence of Roman forces under Pompey in Asia Minor and his intervention in the affairs of the Seleucid state, provided an opportunity to the Hasmonaean rivals Hyrcanus II. and Aristobulus II., both of whom offered a bribe to Pompey's legate in Damascus. The intervention which followed was to lead to considerable diplomatic acrobatics by Jewish leaders and others in the Palestinian area as the changing fortunes of Roman commanders dictated changes of support in those who were anxious for their protection. A further complicating factor, so far as the Jews were concerned, was the increasing influence of Antipater, son of the governor of Idumaea under Jannaeus and Salome. He gave his support to Hyrcanus and appears also to have brought Aretas, king of the Nabataean Arabs, to give assistance. Wars with these Nabataeans had concerned Jannaeus, and they represented an important force on the eastern side of Palestine.

Pompey intervened in 63 B.C., and Aristobulus found himself besieged in the fortified Temple area in Jerusalem. Pompey defeated him and entered the Holy of Holies, which outraged the pious members of the community, but subsequently he carried out skilful reorganization of Palestine and Syria, taking careful account of many of the problems of the area. The Hasmonaean kingdom was broken up, but those areas which were occupied mainly by Jews—Galilee and Peraea—remained under the control of Jerusalem, as did also Idumaea. The Jerusalem religious community under the high priest Hyrcanus was re-established; side by side with it was the independent area of Samaria with recognition accorded to its religious life.

The pattern set by Pompey was followed by later Roman commanders, but their efforts at solving the problems of Palestine were frustrated. Internal dissensions were still very strong, and the intrigues of the members of the Hasmonaean family continued. Antipater and his sons Phasael and Herod were also involved. The changing fortunes of Roman commanders—Pompey, Julius Caesar, Mark Antony, and Octavian—made for uncertainty, and there were also Romans like Crassus who in 54 B.C. plundered the Temple treasury. Roman difficulties were increased by the threats of Parthian invasion from the east.

The result was a period of unrest and struggle in which power came eventually into the hands of Herod. The attempts made by the Jews at preventing the rise of the family of Antipater were unsuccessful, and the last members of the

Hasmonaean family were eventually set aside when the Roman Senate resolved in 40 B.C. to appoint Herod king of Judaea. Within three years he had fully established himself with Roman help, and sought by alliance in marriage with the Hasmonaean family to overcome the reluctance of the Jews to accept him.

2. *The Rule of Herod the Great* (37–4 B.C.). The unpopularity of Herod among the Jews is understandable enough. He was appointed by the Romans and responsible directly to the central government. It is probable—though not in fact absolutely certain—that he was an Idumaean by descent, though he certainly claimed to be of the Jewish faith. His religious adherence, however, was hardly of a kind to satisfy the stricter Jews, for his building of temples dedicated to Augustus and his support of such alien institutions as the games were not counterbalanced by his outstanding work in Jerusalem in the rebuilding and glorification of the Temple there. His cruelty reveals him as a tyrant when policy seemed to dictate the necessity of ruthless action.

Yet his achievement in maintaining reasonable order and peace for over thirty years, and the undoubted prosperity which is expressed in the multiplicity of his building activities, could not have been possible without a man of real ability in so difficult a period. He showed himself skilful in retaining the confidence first of Antony and then of Octavian, and from the latter he was able to regain the coastal areas which Antony had granted to the ambitious Cleopatra and also to extend the area of his rule to the north and east. He honoured Octavian by renaming the rebuilt city of Samaria as Sebaste (from *sebastos*, Greek equivalent of Augustus), and his new seaport of Caesarea also commemorated the Roman ruler. The work on the Temple at Jerusalem was only part of the extensive rebuilding of the city which he undertook. Elsewhere he built or rebuilt fortresses such as that at Masada by the Dead Sea, a stupendous feat.

Probably not without good reason Herod was continually suspicious of intrigue within his own family, and the execution of his Hasmonaean wife Mariamne typifies his reaction to it. Not surprisingly his own death left an unstable position, with his kingdom divided between three of his sons, while leaders of the Jewish community pressed for independence of this hated family. Augustus made Archaelaus ethnarch of Judaea, Idumaea and Samaria, Antipas became tetrarch of Galilee and Peraea, and Philip of Trachonitis and other areas to the north. While the two latter continued to rule, the former till A.D. 39, when he was deposed and exiled, the latter till his death in A.D. 34, Archaelaus was so hated that he was deposed and banished in A.D. 6, and in his place a series of Roman procurators governed the territories which had been his. Antipas was responsible for the death of John the Baptist, imprisoned, so Josephus relates, in the fortress of Machaerus, east of Jordan.

3. *The Period of the Procurators.* Apart from one short period, Judaea and Jerusalem were under the rule of Roman procurators until the time of the Jewish War of A.D. 66–73. Not a great deal is known of them, and in the face of a growing undercurrent of discontent and desire for freedom, they do not always seem to have behaved with very great wisdom. The situation was such, however, that it may be doubted whether any procurator could have done much to allay the dissatisfaction with alien rule and ultimate alien control of the religious office of the High Priest. The best known, Pontius Pilate, in office from A.D. 26–36 made himself unpopular eventually with both Jews and Samaritans and was removed. His part in the death of Jesus is to be seen against the background of the continual fears of insurrection in so unstable an area and of his own willingness to conciliate Jewish leaders when this might be to his own advantage.

For three years, A.D. 41–4, the line of procurators was broken by the rule of Herod Agrippa (I.) whose appointment with royal rank by Caligula to the tetrarchy of Galilee and Peraea in A.D. 39 was followed at Caligula's death by his appointment over Judaea and the areas associated with it. Like his grandfather Herod, he combined a nominal adherence to Judaism in Jerusalem with quite alien activities elsewhere. At his death in A.D. 44, the line of procurators continued, controlling the larger area which Agrippa had ruled.

4. *The Jewish War.* At various moments, notably in the time of Caligula, the pressure of the religious ideas connected with the imperial power had made itself felt and had provoked violent hostility in Jerusalem. The Zealot party had been in existence since the beginning of procuratorial rule, engaging in small incidents against the Roman power and creating an atmosphere of unrest. From A.D. 50 onwards, the control of the high priesthood had been granted by Rome to the younger Agrippa (II.) son of Herod Agrippa (I.), but although he made some endeavours to conciliate the stricter Jews, he was unsuccessful as a ruler and in his personal life unacceptable. It was he who, with his sister Bernice, was present at Caesarea for one of the hearings of Paul before Festus (Acts 25–26). Increased unrest under procurators, some of whom were very much hated for corruption and tyrannical behaviour, led in A.D. 66 to an outbreak of hostilities provoked by particularly inconsiderate actions by the procurator and his troops. Efforts by Agrippa and the more moderate Jewish leaders were unavailing.

Jerusalem was in the control of the extremists. The fortress of Masada was occupied, and in Galilee Josephus the historian, as a more moderate rebel leader, faced the extremist John of Gischala as well as the Romans.

Josephus' own account of the war is a vivid commentary on the ready success which was won by the rebels with their mobile forces. It also reveals the weaknesses which stemmed from the sharp personal and party differences among the Jews themselves. In Jerusalem these greatly weakened the defenders and the Romans could afford to wait rather than make too costly assaults on the city. The situation in Rome itself complicated the position, for Nero died in A.D. 68, and it was Vespasian, commander in Palestine who, after a period of rival claimants and assassinations in Rome, became emperor in A.D. 70, leaving his son Titus to complete the campaign. Jerusalem fell after a fearful siege, with looting and carnage among the ruins. Captives and spoils were carried to Rome for Titus' triumphal procession and to be recorded on his triumphal arch. Other strongholds, including Masada, held out, eventually to fall into Roman hands so that the campaign was completed in A.D. 73.

5. *The Last Years*. The Temple was destroyed and no possibility now existed of rebuilding it. Jewish religious life, however, continued under Roman protection, and Jewish and Jewish Christian groups settled again in the devastated centres. A rethinking of Judaism—and to some extent also of Christianity—was necessitated by the end of the Temple worship. Greater importance still came to belong to the Jews in the Dispersion, and the predominantly Gentile character of the Christian church became increasingly clear. At first the centre of Jewish life was at Jamnia, where preoccupation with the position and authority of the sacred Scriptures marked an important stage in the evolution of the Old Testament text and canon. The interpretation of Scripture in the light of the changed situation of the Jewish community fills the pages of the literature produced in this period and subsequently.

A last attempt at restoring an independent national organization was made in the reign of the emperor Hadrian (A.D. 117–38). Simon bar Koseba was its leader, nicknamed, perhaps by his most famous supporter the Rabbi Akiba, " bar Cochba "—" son of the star." The rebellion, breaking out in A.D. 132, gained immediate success, but in time the Roman power made itself felt, and by A.D. 135 all was at an end. Recent discoveries in caves in the region between En-gedi and Masada by the Dead Sea have shed new light on some of the refugees trapped there by the Roman forces, including documents issuing from the rebel leader himself. Jerusalem was refounded as Colonia Aelia Capitolina, a Roman city with temples and public buildings, and Jews were excluded from it. Israel had ceased to exist as a political entity in the land which had seen its history ; its continued life was to lie in the Jewish and Christian communities, scattered throughout the Mediterranean world, which were its successors and the inheritors of its life.

BIBLIOGRAPHY

J. Bright, *A History of Israel*, 1960.
M. Noth, *The History of Israel*, 2nd English ed., 1960.
The former is more conservative, the latter radical but very penetrating ; they provide a stimulating contrast.
W. O. E. Oesterley and T. H. Robinson, *A History of Israel*, 2 vols., 1932.
A. Lods, *Israel, from its beginnings to the middle of the 8th century*, Eng. trans., 1932.
A. Lods, *The Prophets and the rise of Judaism*, Eng. trans., 1937.
Although older and to some extent outdated, these still contain valuable material.
H. H. Rowley, *From Joseph to Joshua*, 1950. Indispensable for the Exodus period.
Shorter but useful are :
W. F. Albright, *The Biblical Period*, 1952.
H. M. Orlinsky, *Ancient Israel*, 2nd ed., 1960.
E. Ehrlich, *A Concise History of Israel*, Eng. trans., 1962.
B. W. Anderson, *The Living World of the Old Testament*, 1958.
Cf. also the Atlases of the Bible, and collections of documents in :
J. B. Pritchard, *Ancient Near Eastern Texts*, 1955.
D. Winton Thomas, *Documents from Old Testament Times*, 1958.
C. K. Barrett, *The New Testament Background : Selected Documents*, 1957.

PART III

THE RELIGION OF THE BIBLE

XII. THE RELIGION OF ISRAEL

By Walter Harrelson

The origins of Israelite faith lie in north-west Mesopotamia, the traditional homeland of Abraham (Gen. 11[31]). Numerous connexions between customs and legal practices of this general area and the patriarchal narratives have been disclosed by studies of the literature unearthed at several north-west Mesopotamian cities (particularly at Nuzu on the upper Tigris and Mari on the upper Euphrates). The general cosmological orientation of the early Israelites, the remnants of mythological materials found in the Old Testament, and the bodies of law and custom of early Old Testament literature all reflect a close relation between the life and religion of early Israel and the culture and religion of Mesopotamia. Yet the distinctive faith of the Israelite community is radically different from the religious orientation of the Mesopotamian cultures. The numerous connexions between the religion of Israel and that of her neighbours only serve to reveal the great gulf which separates Israelite faith, at its centre, from the religions of the surrounding peoples. The process of borrowing religious motifs, ideas, and practices from other peoples continued within Israel from earliest times to the time of final canonization of Israelite Scripture (A.D. 90–100). The materials borrowed, however, were radically transformed and caused to conform with the fundamental assertions of Israelite faith. This remarkable process has greatly enriched Israel's religious thought and life and has enabled the religious community to meet numerous threats to its existence and yet to survive. It has also prepared the way for Israelite faith to become that extraordinary reality which has contributed so significantly to the life and thought of mankind throughout the earth.

(i) PATRIARCHAL RELIGION

The stories of Abraham, Isaac, and Jacob found in the Book of Genesis have been preserved to us through the great narrative traditions of the Pentateuch, J, E, and P (see above pp. 27 ff.). It is extremely difficult to determine which of the stories or incidents (if any) carry us back to the actual religious ideas and practices of the patriarchs. Generally speaking, however, it seems probable that two fundamental features of patriarchal religion can be discerned within the later narrative traditions. The first is the portrayal of the deity, frequently called the " God of the Fathers " (Gen. 26^{24}, 28^{13}, 31$^{5. 29. 42. 53}$, 32^{9}, 46^{13}, 48^{15}, 49$^{24-25}$, 50^{17}), as closely related to the head of the tribe. The deity is almost a member of the family, the actual head of the tribe, closely bound to the life of the people, serving as their guide and protector, concerned with the daily events of their lives. The God of the Fathers is occasionally designated by terms that indicate his close connexion with the three patriarchs. He is the " Shield " of Abraham (*māghēn,* 15^{1}), the " Fear " or " Kinsman " of Isaac (*paḥadh,* 31^{42}), the " Bull " or " Strong One " of Jacob (*'ābhîr,* 49^{24}). This religion of the patriarchs is later to be viewed with suspicion by the tribes who enter the land of Canaan under Joshua (see Josh. 24^{15}). Elements of polytheism there may have been within it, but it seems doubtful that the epithets for the deity just referred to represent the names of distinct deities. Albrecht Alt (*Der Gott der Väter,* 1930) has brought to light the meaning of the worship of the God of the forefathers and has indicated the distinctiveness of this form of worship in the ancient Near Eastern world. The intimate relation between God and people here affirmed is to continue to characterize Israelite faith throughout the centuries.

The second feature is closely related to the first. The God of the patriarchs accompanies the tribes in their wanderings. He is bound to no specific cult site, no temple or place of special revelation. The patriarchs build altars and call upon the name of the deity (at Shechem, Bethel, Hebron, etc.) but the worship of the deity is not centralized at the places of his appearing. He accompanies the wanderers in their wanderings, directs them toward some goal that yet lies ahead.

The life of the tribes corresponds well with these features of patriarchal religion. The patriarchal tribes seem to have been a part of the movement of peoples in the early and middle parts of the second millennium B.C., which is revealed by the spread of cities and culture throughout Mesopotamia, Asia Minor, and the area of Syria, Palestine, and Phoenicia. They probably were closely related to the population centres in north-west Mesopotamia, from which place they moved into the central hill country of Palestine. In the Palestinian area they appear as half-nomads—that is, as a group of tribes dependent upon both their flocks and their modest agricultural pursuits. In the planting season they would settle in the more arable areas, plant and tend their crops, only to depart for the pasturelands after the crops had been harvested. Such a people is regularly on the march. They were not wilderness nomads, but neither were they agriculturists. The deity would lead them in their move out into the wilderness with their flocks, provide the necessary grassland and the water. He would then lead them back into the settled land. Perhaps this kind of existence led by the patriarchs accounts for the apparently aimless wanderings of the tribes as revealed in the Book of Genesis. But of course the cultural conditions alone do not account for the faith of Israel. Many semi-nomads were to be found in the ancient Near Eastern world. Why should this group alone have come to worship the deity and understand His purpose in the distinctive way characteristic of later Israel?

The answer to this question lies later in the history of the tribes. Yet there is more to be said about the characteristic features of patriarchal religion. In addition to the understanding of the deity as the head of the tribe who directed it on its travels and led the people forward towards some goal yet to be realized, the patriarchal tribes also understood the deity to be related to the culture in which they had settled. Various cult sites came to occupy particular importance for the half-nomads in their wanderings and settlements: Shechem, Bethel, Hebron, Beersheba, Kadesh. At these sites the local population worshipped the gods of the land, those who provided its fertility, who maintained the cosmos and cared for their worshippers. The high god of the Canaanite-Phoenician pantheon was El, the "Father of Years"—as he is called in the Ugaritic literature. But the active deity was Baal, the lord of fertility and giver of life to man, beast and soil. The patriarchs, however, seem to have held themselves apart from the worship of Baal. The name of El, the less active deity in Canaanite religion, rather finds its place in their designation of their cult sites. The God of the fathers is identified as *El Bethel* (31^{13}, 35^{7}), *El 'ôlām* at Beersheba (21^{33}), *El ro'î* at or near Kadesh (16^{13}), and *El 'elyôn* at Jerusalem ($14^{18-19, 22}$).

It would appear that the patriarchs in this way were adapting their religious life and practices to those of the Canaanite setting, while at the same time avoiding any connexion with the worship of the fertility deity Baal. We do not know just how far such adaptation may have gone. No indication appears, at any rate, that the worship of El at the local sites in Canaan and on the fringes of the land was accompanied by any elaborate sacrificial acts or that any priesthood developed to care for the sites or to serve as intermediary between the worshippers and the deity. The chief emphasis continued to lie with the family relationship to the deity and to his actual guidance of the people in their movements throughout the land and to their pasturelands. The deity of the patriarchs was more closely connected with specific cult sites than he formerly had been, but he was not the deity of a particular land. His fundamental relationship was to the wandering tribes.

In Palestine during patriarchal times the tribes were augmented, in all probability, by groups and individuals who withdrew from the established culture of the land, separating themselves from the legal ties binding them to the kings and institutions of the local city-states. This withdrawal from the dominant power within Canaanite society may have contributed very significantly both to the social and cultural institutions of the tribes and to their religious views and practices. Some interpreters, in fact, hold that the term " Hebrew " meant primarily the " outsider "—the person who had broken with the prevailing social institutions and no longer enjoyed their protection or was subject to their benefits. If this be the case, the patriarchal tribes were less closely related to the life of semi-nomads than has been suggested above (see G. E. Mendenhall, " The Hebrew Conquest of Palestine," *The Biblical Archaeologist,* xxv. (Sept. 1962), pp. 66–87).

(ii) MOSES AND ISRAELITE FAITH

The Genesis narratives relate the movement of the tribes into the Delta region of Egypt where the high position of Joseph in the Pharaoh's court enabled them to thrive while the land of Palestine was plagued by a severe famine. While this story has been stylized by the later traditionists, there seems to be no reason to doubt that a considerable number of the tribal groups associated with the names of the patriarchs (and especially with the names of Jacob and his sons) had made their way into Egypt. In the Sinai wilderness the fundamental faith of the Israelite community now emerges—a faith inseparably related to the life and work of Moses.

The contributions of Moses to Israelite religion are also difficult to determine with any precision. Again we must reckon with the fact that the traditions relating this connexion are from a later time than the events related. It would be unwarranted and unnecessary scepticism, however, to maintain that the contributions of Moses to Israelite religion are entirely beyond recovery. Three elements in this contribution stand out above all others : (1) Moses' connexion with the appearance of the divine name " Yahweh " ; (2) Moses' role as the leader and guide of the Israelite people ; and (3) the covenant at Sinai.

In Ex. 3 is related the encounter of Moses with the God of the forefathers and the revelation of the name " Yahweh." The old Yahwistic narrative (J) has simply used the name " Yahweh " for the deity in patriarchal times and earlier (see already Gen. 4[26]). The Elohistic tradition (E) has normally avoided the name until this particular time, apparently under the conviction that the name "Yahweh" began to be used for the deity only as a result of Moses' experience on the holy mountain. The Priestly tradition (P) explicitly states that the deity was known in earlier times by the designation *El Shaddai* (Ex. $6^{2ff.}$), a name which may be another of the ancient epithets for the deity of patriarchal times ("El of the Mountains," from the Akkadian *šadū*, "mountain").

One widely maintained explanation of the appearance of the name Yahweh to Moses is the view (associated with the name of Karl Budde in particular) that the Kenites (or Midianites) worshipped the deity under the name "Yahweh" and that Moses thus learned the name from his father-in-law, Jethro, priest of Midian. Such a view seems to us too simple to fit the complex associations of the name with the early traditions. It is apparent, nonetheless, that Moses' sojourn among the Midianites was of great importance for the reshaping of Israelite faith. The name "Yahweh" was probably the name or epithet for the God of the Fathers worshipped by one or more of the tribal groups in patriarchal times. The fierce zeal for Yahweh shown by the tribe of Levi leads us to think of this tribe (see Ex. 32^{25-29}). The early history of the tribe is obscure, but it is apparent that some disaster befell Simeon and Levi in the period prior to Moses (Gen. 49^{5-7}), probably connected with their attack upon the men of Shechem (Gen. 34). Simeon later appears as a clan within the tribe of Judah and the tribe of Levi is associated (rightly or wrongly) with the priestly class within Judah, the Levites. The secular tribe of Levi may therefore have worshipped the deity under the name "Yahweh." Its removal to the southern area (along with Simeon) perhaps resulted in a meeting of the Levites with the Kenite tribe of the Midianites, probably around the sacred site of Kadesh. Moses, himself from the tribe of Levi, thus may have been introduced to specific traditions of his own tribe through the mediation of the Kenites in the Sinai peninsula as the latter moved from place to place with their flocks. The connexion of the name "Yahweh" with the earlier patriarchal traditions which is taken for granted in the Yahwistic tradition (J) becomes understandable on the basis of this hypothesis, while the tradition that the name "Yahweh" was introduced to the Israelites in Egypt as a result of Moses' encounter with the deity on the sacred mountain is also understandable.

The specific meaning of the name "Yahweh" is difficult if not impossible to discern, either from Ex. 3 or from other references. In the nearly 7,000 occurrences of the name in the Old Testament, no clear etymology is to be found. The expression "I am who I am," or "I will be who I will be"

(Ex. 3^{14}) is most probably to be understood as the refusal of the deity (in Moses' encounter) to explain the interior meaning of the name. To know the name of a person or thing is to have power over that person or thing. Moses is not to exercise authority over Yahweh ; the deity remains free—the sovereign Lord of the one to whom He reveals Himself. Moses is given the name of God, but he is not given an explanation of its meaning which would enable him to force the hand of the deity. " I will be who (what) I will be, " therefore, lays stress upon Yahweh's revelation of His nature through what He does with and among His people. Such a meaning corresponds well with the new emphasis upon Yahweh's active intervention in human affairs, even on the international scene. In Ex. 33^{19} the same explanation of the name, or rather the activity, of Yahweh is given. Moses asks to see Yahweh's glory. He is told that he cannot see Yahweh's glory but that the " goodness " of Yahweh will pass by. As Yahweh passes by Moses, who is in a cleft of the rock, Yahweh Himself pronounces His name. But the meaning assigned to the name is " I will be gracious to whom I will be gracious, and will show mercy to whom I will show mercy." The prohibition of the misuse of the divine name found in the Ten Commandments (Ex. 20^{7}, Deut. 5^{11}) has the same end in view. Man must not suppose that in the power of the divine name he is at liberty to pronounce curses upon someone or otherwise to act as though the power inherent in the name of the deity were at his disposal.

Moses' life and education in Egypt may also have contributed significantly to the understanding of Yahwistic faith associated with him and his work. His concern for the oppressed and humiliated people to whom he belonged broke out into violence as he slew an Egyptian who was flogging a Hebrew (Ex. 2^{11-12}). His zeal for righteous conduct appears also in his effort to settle a dispute between two of his people (2^{13-15}), in his championing of the women at the well who were being mistreated by the shepherds (2^{17}), and in the remarkable body of legislation associated with his name. We cannot determine whether these features of the man's character are all to be attributed to the later narrators. It may well be the case that the importance of right order, of justice, in Egyptian society helped to shape the ethical concern of Moses. Yet it must be granted that the notions of justice and righteousness in Yahwistic convenant faith are remarkably different from the rather static idea of the just society such as is revealed in the literature of ancient Egypt.

In the encounter of Moses with Yahweh on the sacred mountain, Israel's future leader is presented with a deity who is actively concerned for the plight of the oppressed slaves in

Egypt. Yahweh has seen their sufferings, has heard their outcry, and has determined to intervene in their behalf. Moses has been selected as the leader of the people, but Yahweh is the real deliverer. Mosaic faith thus adds two features of decisive importance to Israelite religion of patriarchal times: Yahweh's active intervention in the affairs of men and nations, and his zeal for the righting of wrongs done to the weak and helpless by the arrogant and powerful rulers of the earth. Yahweh's interest is centred in the people whom He has called to be His own. Yet the pervasive concern for active righteousness which characterizes Israelite faith and provides the basis of much of the prophetic polemic against the Israelite community itself in later times can hardly be entirely unrelated to the faith of Moses himself.

Yahweh demonstrates His power to deliver His people from the Egyptian world power. The forces of the Egyptians are destroyed at the Sea of Reeds while the Israelite slaves pass out to freedom. Moses' role in that act of deliverance is portrayed vividly by the old traditions: he calls upon the people to "stand firm and see the salvation of Yahweh, which he will work for you today" (Ex. 14^{13}). The deed of deliverance is the work of Yahweh alone. In a hopeless situation the tribes are redeemed by the mighty hand of Yahweh. This deed of salvation is celebrated in the Song of Miriam, probably contemporary with the event: "Sing ye to Yahweh for he has triumphed gloriously; the horse and his rider he has hurled into the sea" (Ex. 15^{21}, see 15^{1}). The entire drama of Israel's redemption from Egyptian bondage is celebrated in subsequent centuries at the spring festival of Passover. The acts of celebration, indeed, may have contributed significantly to the development of the narrative tradition as now found in the Book of Exodus. The elaboration of the tradition and the introduction of numerous legendary elements can easily be understood, as the tradition continues to occupy a central place in the community's worship throughout the centuries.

The community makes its way to the sacred mountain. There the faith of the community is given its institutional form and the people delivered from Egyptian bondage are organized for the next stage in their history: the march into the land of the promise. The traditions relating the covenant act at Mt. Sinai are later than the event itself. It is impossible to recover the specific acts of the community as the covenant between Yahweh and Israel was consummated. From other Old Testament texts, however, and by analogy with the form of ancient Near Eastern treaties and covenants now available for comparison, it has been possible to reconstruct at least the chief features of the Sinai covenant and to understand more clearly the relationship between the act of covenant making and the giving of the covenant law. The chief elements in the covenant ceremony appear to have been the following:

1. The assembling of the tribes, or their representatives, at the holy place.

2. The recitation of the historical background of the covenant act, consisting of a summary of Yahweh's deeds of salvation in behalf of His people.

3. Call to the people to respond to the saving work of God by their decision to serve and obey Him.

4. The covenant act itself, probably consisting of a sacrifice and a sacred meal sealing the relations between God and people.

5. The giving of the law of the covenant. This law governs the relations between the covenant partners and consists fundamentally in a set of policies dictated by the deity which the people are pledged to obey scrupulously.

6. A ceremony of blessings and cursings which warns of the consequences of disobedience to the covenant stipulations and declares the positive results of covenant faithfulness.

7. The dismissal of the people.

Other elements appear in the treaty forms of the Hittites, which provide the closest parallels to the form of the Israelite covenant with Yahweh. It is not certain that Moses himself introduced this covenant form into Israelite religion. The covenant between God and people was regularly reaffirmed in subsequent times (see especially Josh. 24) and the more complete form of the covenant act may have entered the community at some later time. Yet it seems highly probable that Moses presided over an act of covenant making similar in form to that outlined above. The Ten Commandments (in their original, short form) are similar in form to the categorical requirements laid down by a sovereign for his subjects to obey without deviation—requirements that have certain parallels in the treaties of the ancient world. In content, however, they correspond remarkably well with the features of Israelite faith that have been suggested as characteristic of the religious outlook of Moses. The deity who summons Israel to accept these unconditional obligations is the God who delivered the people from Egypt. He will tolerate no rivals to His sovereign authority. He will permit no images of Himself to be made, images whose existence might suggest that the worshipper can command obedience from the deity whom they represent. He will not allow the use of His name for the purpose of pronouncing maledictions upon the enemies of the people. The life of the community is to be safeguarded by the prohibitions against murder, adultery, theft, the bearing of false witness, and covetousness. The health of the community is to be maintained by a day of rest. Family life is to be maintained by the honour shown to parents by (adult) children.

Other legislation from early Israel also is associated with the Sinai covenant. The Covenant Code (Ex. 20^{23}–23^{33}) contains a body of legislation closely related to ancient Near Eastern collections of positive law. The Israelite version of ancient Near Eastern law represented in this collection, however, demonstrates a striking concern on the part of the Israelite community for the life of man in society. Property values tended to predominate over human values in the civilizations of the ancient world. This was not the case in Israel. Again we meet the strong ethical dimension of Israelite faith, impressed upon this ancient collection of Israelite law. The collection is not earlier than the time of the Judges, in all probability, but it bears the distinctive mark of Mosaic religious faith.

The contributions of Moses to the religious practices of Israel are even more difficult to determine than is his part in the shaping of religious thought. The Passover rite, a pastoral festival celebrated in the spring, is almost certainly older than the time of Moses. Some early form of the festival of Unleavened Bread may also be as old as the time of Moses or even more ancient. These two festivals may have marked the beginning of the agricultural year of the semi-nomads of patriarchal times and the close of the pastoral year—that is, the festival of the barley harvest may have been the first cultic act in the settled land, while the Passover rite may have concluded the annual sojourn in the wilderness area. The connexion of the two festivals could easily have occurred in later times, when the people under the leadership of Joshua had occupied the land of Canaan and had begun the new mode of existence appropriate to their changed cultural circumstances. The Deuteronomic calendar, however, is the first to represent Passover and Unleavened Bread as a single festival commemorative of the departure of the Israelites from Egypt (Deut. 16^{1-8}).

The origin of the sabbath is also associated with Moses by tradition (Ex. 16^{22-30}). It is probable that the sabbath developed in connexion with a festival of seven days' duration in the spring and in the autumn. Yet the interpretation given to the sabbath is remarkably non-cultic. It is a day of rest for man and beast, a time for refreshment of the spirit of man rather than a day appointed for specific religious duties. The seventh day of the week is marked by a cessation of the daily routines of life, quite irrespective of when the natural rhythms of life on the soil might normally call for a pause or for festivities. Just as the sabbath year was connected with a special act of reaffirmation of the covenant Law (Deut. 31^{9-13}), so also each sabbath provided a means for the regular recognition that the land and people belonged to the covenant God. The sabbath was a sabbath " to Yahweh " (Ex. 20^{10}, Deut. 5^{14}). The tradition that Moses introduced this order into Israelite society may be correct, since the sabbath as a sign of Yahweh's claim upon the entire life of the covenant people corresponds remarkably well with the basic features of the covenant law referred to above.

The cult objects and cultic institutions of the community in the wilderness are described in full detail by the later Priestly tradition (Ex. 25–31 and 35–40). Much of this priestly lore belongs to a considerably later period of time and depicts acts and institutions of the later community. The cult objects of the wilderness period were in all probability associated with the life of the semi-nomads who moved back and forth between the settled land and the wilderness. A place of encampment for the tribes would presumably have been arranged according to a fixed order. The description of the tabernacle in the wilderness may contain some original features of the tribal encampment. Two cult objects of decisive importance are referred to: the tent of meeting (*'ōhel mô'ēdh*) and the Ark (*'ᵃrōn*). The ancient tradition in Ex. 33 (vss.$^{7-11}$) portrays the tent of meeting as the central cult object of the tribes, the place where the people would enquire of Yahweh and where Moses spoke with Yahweh " as a man speaks to his friend." No reference whatever is made to the Ark of the covenant in this tradition; the tent and the Ark appear to be quite distinct cult objects. The " Song of the Ark " (Num. 10^{35-36}) indicates that the Ark symbolized the active presence of Yahweh in time of battle. It is later understood to be the throne-seat of the invisible deity of the covenant, and may indeed have been so understood in the wilderness period. The Ark is closely connected with the central sanctuary of the tribes in the days of Joshua and subsequently and may have been originally a cult object associated especially with the tribe of Joseph. The tent of meeting in all probability, then, was originally a wilderness cult object related to the southern tribes, perhaps Judah and Levi in particular. It is not impossible, however, that in the wilderness period the Ark was housed in a tent, so that the separate cult objects of the northern and southern tribes were both connected historically with the period of Israelite wanderings in the wilderness.

The central features of the work of Moses thus stand out quite clearly. He led the Israelite slaves from Egypt into the wilderness at the direction of Yahweh who broke the hold of the great monarch upon them and set them free. Yahweh is thenceforth to be recognized as the God Who exercises authority in the world of men and nations, intensely jealous over the life and safety of His covenant people, ready to come to their aid in every time of peril. Yahweh is also recognized to be jealous over the loyalty of His people to Him. The Sinai covenant specifies the relationship that is to obtain between God and people. Israel's responsibility to obey the covenant stipulation is summed up in the categorical law of the covenant —the Ten Commandments. Yahweh will lead His people in battle, guide them into the land promised to the forefathers. But He will exact grim retribution against all who violate the requirements of the covenant. In this connexion it is important to note that the tradition records the violation of the covenant at the very time when the covenant law is being revealed (Ex. 32). Israelite faith is too realistic to suggest that the community perfectly embodied the requirements of the covenant God. Moreover, Moses himself is not a perfect representative of the covenant faith. The sin of Moses is recorded (Num. 20^{11-12}) but this tradition is less important than the portrayal of Moses' readiness to lose heart over the extraordinary burden that he is required to bear (Num. 11, etc.). Yet the most remarkable feature of Moses' place in Israelite religion is the unanimous testimony of the tradition that Moses died outside the land of the Promise and was buried in a grave the location of which was known only to Yahweh. The hero who wrought Israel's redemption dies before seeing the fulfilment of the work which he had begun. He had been the mediator of the covenant between Yahweh and the tribes, had interceded in behalf of the people when they sinned (Ex. 32^{30-34}), had carried them in his bosom (Num. 11^{12}), providing for their every need. Yet his reward was to see the land from afar—and to be buried by Yahweh (Deut. 34). The very centre of Israelite faith thus portrays unmistakably the character and future of that faith to be no success story. The covenant faith of Israel is by no means the story of Israel's glorification among the nations as the favourite people of Yahweh among the nations. It is the story of a pilgrimage of faith, of a community called by Yahweh to demonstrate before the nations what it means to be Yahweh's covenant people, and thus to provide blessing to " all the families of the earth " (Gen. 12^3).

(iii) THE TRIBAL LEAGUE

The conquest of portions of the land of Canaan under the leadership of Joshua and the settlement of the tribes in their respective territories within the new land brought a number of changes into Israelite religious thought and practice. The relationship of Yahweh to the soil and its fertility was probably the most pressing religious issue confronted by the tribes. Later confessional texts, used on the occasions of the great festivals, enable us to discern how the tribes came to understand Yahweh's Lordship over the natural processes of an agricultural existence. The land of Canaan was understood to be a direct gift of Yahweh to the covenant people ; He had provided this rich land to His people. They had not won it by their own might nor prepared it by their own labours (Josh. 24^{2-13}, Deut. 26^{5-11}).

Such a confession of faith, however, required religious and cultic support and implementation. It seems evident that the tribal league quickly adopted from the local population numerous religious rites. The three major agricultural festivals—Unleavened Bread (the festival of the barley harvest in the early spring), Weeks or Pentecost (the festival of the wheat harvest about fifty days later), and Tabernacles or Booths (the festival of the fruit harvest in the early autumn)—were adopted from the Canaanites, although as noted above the semi-nomads may already have observed some form of agricultural rites in connexion with their moves back and forth between the wilderness and the settled land. Of decisive importance, however, was the relating of these festivals to the saving work of Yahweh Who had brought the forefathers from Mesopotamia, delivered them from Egyptian bondage, and provided this goodly land as their inheritance. The natural festivals were "historicized," given their place in the continuing story of Yahweh's historical guidance of His people. The relating of the three festivals to specific epochs in Yahweh's saving work was accomplished only later in the history of Israel, but the celebration of Yahweh's saving work in behalf of His people was probably a part of the proceedings at each of the three festivals.

In the days of Joshua one festival stood out as the most important for the tribal league : the autumn festival observed at the central sanctuary of the tribes. On the occasion of the harvest of the fruits, the new year was inaugurated (see Ex. 34^{22}, 23^{16}) with a solemn ratification of the covenant between Yahweh and the tribes. The ceremony depicted in Josh. 24 almost certainly represents an annual festival of covenant renewal. The tribes (or their representatives) assembled at the central sanctuary, first at Shechem and later at other cult centres (Bethel, Shiloh, perhaps Gilgal). The covenant representative would recite the story of Yahweh's saving deeds, the people would pledge their allegiance to the God of the covenant, the covenant ceremony would be performed, and the covenant law recited.

This festival in all probability did much to cement relations among the twelve tribes, jealous of their separate life and traditions. On this occasion, moreover, the possibility was open for the incorporation of additional regions and peoples into the covenant community. The ceremony thus provided significantly for the growth of the Israelite community within the land. A ceremony of abjuration of the worship of the gods of Mesopotamia or of Canaan apparently was a fixed part of the ritual of the autumn festival (see Josh. 24[15. 23], Gen. 35[1-4]). The ranks of the community were swelled not alone by the conquest of the peoples of Canaan; perhaps of greater importance was the making of covenant with the local population (Josh. 9) and the annual adoption of additional peoples and areas into the community of Israel and their assignment to one or other of the twelve tribes.

Very little is known of the importance of the other two agricultural festivals at this time. Passover continued to be celebrated as a family rite, perhaps until the time of Josiah (2 Kings 23[21-23]). Yet there can be no doubt that, with all the precautions which may have been taken, the community more and more adopted the forms of Canaanite worship and much of the meaning associated with such worship. It is indeed remarkable that the Mosaic faith should have survived at all, given the extraordinary attractiveness and meaningfulness of the religion of Canaan, so admirably suited to the needs of an agricultural society. It seems evident that the ceremony of covenant reaffirmation with its strong emphasis upon the guidance of Yahweh in Israel's historical pilgrimage and the repeated reaffirmation of the specific claims of the covenant God upon the totality of Israelite life offered the best defence against the fertility religion of Canaan. If the Sabbath were already a fixed part of the community's life, this day of rest also would have contributed significantly to the community's reflection upon Yahweh's guidance of the people in their pilgrimage and would have marked their religious practices off from those of their neighbours—as the observance of the Sabbath clearly did in the period of Babylonian exile.

It is also possible that the tribes in the land of Canaan continued to maintain their connexion with the desert traditions. The site of Kadesh probably continued to be of great religious importance for the southern tribes. Gilgal may have been the setting for a festival which commemorated the crossing of the Jordan under Joshua. The location of the Ark at the central sanctuary and the preservation of the tent of meeting also served to keep alive the wilderness traditions and the religious practices associated with the period of Moses. But the sources available to us do not allow us to recover such elements of the worship of the early community in Palestine.

The new life in the land of the Promise brought many changes to the community's worship beyond those connected with the major festivals. Much of the sacrificial practice of the community appears to have been adopted directly from Canaanite practice. The sacrificial acts recorded in the Book of Judges are not identical with those specified in the priestly legislation of the Pentateuch. The worshipper himself made his offering to the deity, not necessarily at some special cult site. The deity received the offering. Several sacrificial acts in this period are closely connected with the appearance of the deity in time of national danger. It may be, therefore, that the sacrificial system in Israel was understood to be particularly related to Yahweh's continuing guidance of the people in their historical existence, rather than simply a means for maintaining wholesome relations with the deity. In any event, the traditions place greater emphasis upon Yahweh's active intervention in Israelite affairs than upon the maintenance of the sacrificial system. The ancient "Blessing of Moses" (Deut. 33[8-11]), which belongs to the period prior to the Kingship, assigns to Levi, the priestly tribe, responsibility for the receipt of oracles from Yahweh, for the teaching of Torah, and places the offering of sacrifices in a subordinate position behind these two basic responsibilities. It is not to be denied that the sacrificial acts were of great religious importance. Yet it seems unlikely that such acts ranked in importance with the seeking of the guidance of Yahweh in the continuing life of the tribal league.

Three kinds of sacrifice can be roughly distinguished in Israelite religion during the early period. The first was a whole burnt offering (animal or vegetable) placed entirely at the deity's disposal. The second was an offering by means of which communion between the worshipper and the deity was symbolized; portions of the animal or the grain were offered to the deity alone, while the remainder of the sacrifice was eaten by the worshipper "before Yahweh." The third type was a gift to the deity, perhaps offered in payment of a vow, perhaps a free-will offering. Such offerings were shared by the priesthood at the local sanctuary, as were the communion meals also. The meaning of the act of sacrifice is not easily stated. A sacrifice is at one and the same time a gift to the deity, a means of creating or releasing holy power, and an act which establishes or strengthens communion between the worshipper and the deity. Fundamentally, sacrifices enable the community to enter more fully into the life and presence of the deity. They are designed to overcome the distance between God and people, to heal the breach created by man's sin and guilt, to bring the worshipper into the circle of the deity's presence, power, and purpose. It is not too much to say, therefore, that reconciliation or atonement is the fundamental element in sacrificial worship (see J. Pedersen, *Israel, Its Life and Culture,* iii.-iv., 1940, p. 359). The various forms of Israelite sacrifices should not, therefore, be sharply distinguished from one another.

Thus we may conclude that the Israelite community in the new land quickly adopted a number of the religious practices of the Canaanites and at the same time preserved its distinctive faith. The cultural changes incident to Israel's settling down in the land of Canaan were of great religious consequence. But the remembrance and continuing experience of the active leadership of Yahweh in their daily life prevented the simple adoption of the nature religion of Baal. The God of the forefathers was still leading the Israelites forward toward the realization of a great purpose. The covenant between Yahweh and Israel required that Israel relate all religious powers in the land to the sovereign power of Yahweh. Thus Yahweh came to be the giver of rain and of fertility to the soil as well as the deliverer in time of oppression. It is clearly the case, however, that the traditions of the Book of Judges lay much more weight upon Yahweh's historical guidance and deliverance of His people from oppression and danger than they do upon the Lordship of Yahweh over the processes of an agricultural existence. The battle with Baalism is joined in this period, but the actual conflict becomes critical in a considerably later period.

The role of the " Judges " in early Israel is difficult to determine. Apparently there were two distinct types of community leaders : those individuals singled out in time of peril to lead the people in battle against the enemy (the " charismatic leaders " of Israel), who were endowed with Yahweh's Spirit ; and those regular " judges " of Israel who functioned as representatives of the tribal league throughout the years. The latter group probably continued the role of Moses and Joshua as the " mediators " of the covenant " (as they have been recently designated). At the tribal centre they would adjudicate inter-tribal disputes, see to the designation of a leader of the tribes in time of danger, officiate at the ceremony of covenant reaffirmation, and above all things see to the maintenance of the categorical law of the covenant in the life of the tribes. The figure of Samuel probably best represents this office of the covenant mediator. He officiates at the central sanctuary, seeks to maintain fidelity to Yahweh in a time of lax religious practice, is the designator of Israel's deliverer from the Philistines, and judges all Israel in his regular circuit throughout the land (1 Sam. 3–12).

(iv) THE KINGSHIP

The tribal league functioned, quite imperfectly, for about two hundred years. Gideon may have instituted a form of kingship in central Palestine, despite his refusal of the invitation to rule over the people (Judg. 8[22-23]), but if he did so that institution was not destined to survive. The appearance of the Philistines required a modification of Israelite political life and introduced important changes in the religious beliefs and practices of the community. Samuel was the immediate initiator of these changes, although they may have been prepared for by previous practices and changes in political thought. Saul's tragic career as Israel's first king is marked by a profound effort both on his part and on that of Samuel to hold faithfully to the religious traditions of the tribal league, as new measures are being introduced. But changes of a radical nature were inevitable. Begun under Saul, they reached full flower under David.

Of greatest significance was the alteration of the meaning of the covenant between Yahweh and Israel. It now became a covenant between Yahweh and David, although of course the king was understood to be the representative of the whole people. In all probability, however, the ratification of the covenant between Yahweh and Israel quickly came to mean primarily the renewal of loyalty to the reigning king on the part of the people. The development of the tradition that Yahweh had promised to maintain David's dynasty in perpetuity, a tradition associated with the prophet Nathan (2 Sam. 7), served to stabilize the Davidic dynasty in Judah and thus brought positive gains to the Judaean state. At the same time, this tradition threatened the covenant faith of Israel at its root. Yahweh had delivered a people, had led them into the land of the Promise, had raised up deliverers in time of danger, and had required fidelity to the covenant requirements from all members of the twelve tribes. The tribes declared their allegiance directly to the God who had revealed Himself to them in the daily events of their historical existence. Political authority was vested in the leaders of the people chosen by Yahweh as occasion required. Now, however, a single family had been established as the ruling dynasty in Jerusalem. Yahweh has delegated His authority to the house of David.

This change brought others in its path. The sacrificial system and the worship of the community were now closely related to state affairs in the capital city. The sons of David are appointed as priests in Jerusalem (2 Sam. 8[18]) and David himself officiates as priest on some occasions (2 Sam. 6[12-15]).

The priesthood of Abiathar which had continued the Levitical priestly tradition within David's kingship (1 Sam. 22^{20-23}) was soon suppressed by the priestly authority of Zadok, a priest who almost certainly represented religious traditions from the Jebusite cult centre in Jerusalem. Worship in Jerusalem comes more and more to be directed toward the maintenance of Yahweh's favour and blessing upon David and his kingship. Important additions to the religious life and thought of the community were thus introduced, but the danger was grave that these innovations would compromise the authority of the covenant God over all aspects of Israelite life and worship.

A third change in Israelite religion occurred which was also to be of great significance. Yahweh's past guidance of Israel came to be understood to have aimed at the day now at hand. Israel's borders had been extended, her enemies defeated, her glory among the nations made evident. The sense of destiny within the community, expressed in the old traditions, could thus be fully secularized and come to mean the rule of the kingdom of David over the other kingdoms and peoples of the surrounding lands. Yahweh's fulfilment of His purpose for the nations, therefore, quite easily could be understood to be identical with Israel's conquest of her enemies.

Yet the old covenant traditions did not lose their force as these radical changes occurred. David himself was eager to indicate the continuity between the tribal system and the new kingdom. The city of Jerusalem was made into the central cult site of the tribal league by the removal of the Ark of the covenant into the city (2 Sam. 6). David's selection as king was understood to have occurred at Yahweh's choice, and the great Samuel anointed him as king. Yahweh's choice of David was demonstrated by the gift of the divine Spirit and was ratified by the elders of the twelve tribes.

The early traditions were maintained with even more rigour by the prophetic spokesmen. Nathan could denounce Israel's great king for his sin in the Bathsheba affair (2 Sam. 11–12). Ahijah could undermine the kingdom of Rehoboam by the designation of Jeroboam as the leader of the northern tribes (1 Kings 11^{29-39}). And in the northern kingdom at a later time the prophets Elijah and Elisha introduced a prophetic movement that was to challenge the innovations that were threatening to destroy the covenant faith of that kingdom.

In the period of the early kingship the spokesmen for the covenant faith provided other and more important safeguards for the fundamental motifs of Israel's religion. The Yahwist (J) produced his magnificent narrative of the beginnings of mankind and of Israel during the tenth century, in all probability. Here was summarized the story of the election of Israel to be a blessing to all peoples, the sublime faith of Abraham, the fidelity of Moses to the covenant God and his continued intercessions with Yahweh for a sinful and rebellious people, the continuing mercy of Yahweh toward sinful man, the Lordship of Yahweh over all the nations of the earth, and the very beginnings of life on the earth. The Yahwistic narrative provided (or should have provided) a strong deterrent to the view that the destiny of Israel lay in the conquest of the enemy peoples and the glorification of Israelite life at the cult centre in Jerusalem.

The remarkable traditions in the Books of Samuel relating the rise of David's kingship and the story of the struggle for the succession to his throne also indicate the strength of the covenant faith within the new cultural situation of the kingship. No effort is made to interpret the appearance of the kingship as the ultimate fulfilment of Yahweh's purpose for Israel. The favour of Yahweh rested upon David in his struggle with Saul, yet the measures taken by David to establish himself as king are not glossed over or made to appear more pure than they were. The city of Jerusalem is represented to be a former Jebusite city, captured by David by stealth. The glorious beginnings of the capital cities of the ancient Near Eastern world have no counterpart in the traditions of Jerusalem's beginnings. A sober honesty, an interest in the actual happenings within the life of the state, a remarkable portrayal of the weaknesses and strengths of the persons associated with David and Saul in their governments distinguish these annals of Israel's first kings. The motive behind such historical writing must be sought in the covenant faith of Israel. Yahweh's activity within the community is to be traced in the actual happenings as these occur. The traditions reveal that the unknown authors of these narratives neither glorify the marvellous and miraculous works of Yahweh in their midst nor idealize their political and religious leaders. It is difficult to overestimate the positive value of such a portrayal of the beginnings of Israel's life and institutions in the community's later life. Such a portrayal probably did much to prepare the community to give heed to its prophets of a later time, who attack with merciless rigour all elements of Israelite society that disclose the apostasy of the people and its leaders from the covenant God.

The division of the kingdom in the early years of Rehoboam's reign also reflects to some degree the continuing vitality of the old covenant traditions. The revolt of North Israel under Jeroboam no doubt had a number of motives. One of these, it would appear, was basic dissatisfaction with the changes in Israelite life and religion introduced by Solomon and reaffirmed by his son Rehoboam. Jeroboam's reform of the worship of North Israel was probably intended to purify the worship of the community, yet the unhappy choice of the two bulls, placed at Bethel and at Dan, only accelerated the introduction of fertility motifs into the religion of the northern kingdom. The bulls probably were understood as pedestals upon which the invisible Yahweh took his stand in the cult centre (as the Ark was understood to be the throne-seat of the deity in Jerusalem). The priesthood at Bethel was hardly less legitimate than that in Jerusalem. Yet the religious developments in North Israel were destined to lead the community farther and farther from the faith of Moses and Joshua. Only the remarkable flowering of the prophetic movement in North Israel, and developments growing out of that flowering, enabled Israelite faith in the unstable kingdom of the north to survive at all. In Jerusalem, the stability of the Davidic dynasty and subsequent interpretations of the meaning of Yahweh's promise made to David (especially by Isaiah of Jerusalem) provided for a more stable development of religious thought and practice in Judah than in North Israel. It must be granted, however, that the perils of religious and political life in the northern kingdom often led to more exciting and important disclosures of the meaning of Israel's life under Yahweh's guidance than appeared in the more stable situation of the south.

(V) THE GREAT PROPHETS

Prophecy has at least two distinct sources as it develops within the Israelite community. The ancient Near Eastern cultures had their prophetic spokesmen and it has become all the more clear in recent years that the prophetic movement in Israel owes much to the corresponding movements in Mesopotamian and Syrian-Palestinian society. The prophets spoke directly in the name of the deity, conveying oracles from the deity in the form of messages such as were sent by the kings to their authorities throughout their realm. Prophets often accompanied the kings in battle, received omens and messages which were influential in the decisions taken by the kings. Some prophetic texts from Mari also contain explicit or implicit reproaches against the kings in the name of the deity. The prophets of the ancient world were intermediaries between the deity and the people, provided counsel for king and people in times of crisis, interpreted the future by various means, and were an established part of ancient Near Eastern society and religious life. The oracles or counsel from the deity might be received in a number of ways. The visions and dreams of the prophets were of particular importance, and their messages often were received in the throes of an ecstatic seizure. The ecstatic prophets of the time of Saul and David (1 Sam. 10, 19) represent, in all probability, the adoption of the ancient Near Eastern type of ecstatic prophecy (perhaps in its Canaanite-Syrian form) into the Israelite community. Israelite prophecy was much more closely related to the regular Israelite cult than has sometimes been supposed, despite the frequent assaults upon the sacrificial system by the prophets of Israel.

The other source for Israel's prophetic movement is of great importance, although it is difficult to trace its influence upon the words and deeds of the prophets. The covenant community from the days of Moses forward depended upon the interpretation of the divine will for the Israelite community. Yahweh was understood to be actively at work within Israel to guide His people in the path of truth and fidelity to the covenant. Moses is viewed as the interpreter of the divine will for the entire community. He is called a prophet by the later tradition (Deut. 18^{15}, 34^{10}). It has been pointed out that the maintenance of the tribal league in Palestine required the leadership of a person appointed to continue the work of Moses and Joshua. The "judges" of Israel included, we suggested, some who exercised this function. The task of this "mediator of the covenant" resembled that of the ancient Near Eastern prophets in some respects (he received oracles from the deity, interpreted the will of Yahweh in time of battle or danger, etc.), but the basic task was that of discerning the will of Yahweh for this particular covenant people in their daily lives. He was to officiate at the gathering of the tribes for the renewal of the covenant, and was no doubt charged in particular with the interpretation of the meaning of the covenant law.

When the kingship was established in Israel, much of the responsibility of the former covenant representative was assumed by the kings. The rise of the prophets, clearly related historically to the establishment of the kingship, almost certainly is to be traced to the community's determination to preserve the freedom of Yahweh to declare His will for all Israel in the new situation. The king was not permitted to become the official spokesman for the deity, despite his unquestioned importance as Yahweh's adopted son, Yahweh's chosen representative for all Israel. The kingship was too dangerous an institution to stand unchecked by the tenets of the covenant faith. David is not permitted to build a house for Yahweh in Jerusalem (2 Sam. 7), although the same text which preserves this limitation upon the king's plans and desires also contains the promise of an eternal dynasty to David. Thus we may conclude that the former functions of the covenant representative or mediator in ancient Israel were divided between the king and the new prophetic spokesmen for Yahweh. The prophetic challenges of the king's authority appear as soon as the institution of kingship is established (see already 1 Sam. 13^{13-14}).

The individual prophets of Israel interpret the will of Yahweh in ways quite distinct and various. The prophet's own intellectual, literary, and spiritual gifts find expression in the form and content of his words. Changing political, cultural, and religious circumstances also are reflected in the variety of the prophetic judgments and promises. Yet there are certain main features of the prophetic message discernible in the midst of the large body of prophetic literature.

Israelite prophecy is sharply distinguished from the prophetic movements known from the surrounding peoples by the radical seriousness with which the divine Word is taken by Israel's prophets. Yahweh's Word comes to the prophet as a word of judgment, guidance or promise for the entire people, not alone for the king. The prophets speak of issues of life or death. They call upon all Israel to face the most severe judgment of Yahweh upon them for their sin and apostasy. In the message of Elijah this radical call to fidelity to Yahweh is clearly apparent: "If Yahweh be God, follow Him; but if Baal, then follow him" (1 Kings 18^{21}). The people cannot continue to "go limping with two different opinions." This text has often been used to indicate the monotheism or monotheistic tendency of Elijah's message to Israel. But the question of Israelite monotheism is less important than that of the claim of Yahweh to Israel's full and unqualified allegiance. Yahweh will tolerate no other gods alongside of Him (Ex. 20^{3}); other gods may exist, but they exercise no authority whatever in the life and world of the covenant people. When the people turn to Baal or to other gods they are forsaking the deity who alone deserves to be worshipped and obeyed for those who have no claim whatever upon Israel's life or allegiance.

It is this exclusive loyalty to the God of the covenant which stands behind the prophets' denunciation of Israel's sin. Yahweh will not stand idly by while His people forsake Him and spurn His guidance. He will execute the judgment of wrath implicit in the covenant agreement against the violator of the covenant (see Jer. 34^{18}). The prophets do not often refer explicitly to the covenant between Yahweh and Israel, probably because of the connexion between Yahweh and the king in the covenant acts. But the reality of the covenant faith lies behind virtually all that they say and do.

The attacks by the prophets upon the social iniquities of Israel derive from the demands of Yahweh for Israel's total allegiance. Amos denounces North Israel for the oppression of the poor, for the indolent and luxurious life of its higher class, for the rapacious desire for profit in business, the corruption of justice in the courts, the breakdown of family and public morality. Such signs of infidelity to the God of covenant faith cannot be covered up by pious religious devotion or the multiplication of sacrifices and offerings. Hosea attacks North Israel for the corruption of the covenant faith (see Hos. 4^{1-6}); "knowledge of God" has virtually disappeared in the land. The adoption of elements of the fertility religion only illustrates the departure of the people from their true "lover" Yahweh (2^{8} [Heb. 2^{10}]). The assaults upon a false and faithless political policy are a part of the same demand for total allegiance to Yahweh. Egypt and Assyria cannot help Israel; only Yahweh her God can provide peace and security in the troubled times sketched by the prophets.

The positive side of the prophetic message to Israel is easily discernible through their judgments upon the people. Justice (*mishpāṭ*) and righteousness (*ṣᵉdhāḳāh*) should characterize their total existence before Yahweh. In public and private life the covenant community should display its obedience to Yahweh, its fidelity to the covenant law. This law of the covenant means life and peace and blessing to Israel, while departure from it means nothing less than death, annihilation. We do not know in detail the contents of the covenant law in terms of which the prophets denounced the community. It seems highly probable that they appealed primarily to the contents and implications of the policy legislation of the Mosaic covenant: the Ten Commandments and the body of law derivable from these categorical statements of the divine law. The law collections of the ancient Near Eastern world gave great place to the preservation of the property rights of citizens. Israelite law, while not insensitive to the importance of property, lays its fundamental weight upon the maintenance of man's communal life. Human values outrank property values. Over and again the prophetic tradition upholds and deepens this understanding of the primacy of human life in community. Yahweh wills that His people live a full and rich life on the land which has been given to them, practising justice in business and in family relations, speaking the truth, caring for the poor and the weak, maintaining a wholesome and peaceful life in community.

The remarkable legislation contained in Deuteronomy (especially in chaps. 12–26) is one of the great fruits of the prophetic tradition, although it does not derive directly from the prophetic circles. In North Israel from early times the Levitical priests and teachers appear to have addressed themselves to the practical requirements of the covenant faith in the towns and villages outside of the great centres of political and religious life. In their preaching and teaching, these spokesmen for the ancient faith prepared the way for the great reform movements in Israelite society, in particular those associated with the Judaean kings Hezekiah and Josiah. Some of the prophets may have arisen from the circles that produced this Deuteronomic legislation. In any event, the positive message of the prophets for Israelite life is well summed up in the admonitions and laws of the Book of Deuteronomy.

The sweeping judgment of the prophets upon Israelite society comes at a time when Israel is threatened by the rise of the great kingdom of Assyria. Yet the prophetic denunciation of Israel rests not primarily upon the recognition that the political situation is perilous. It seems evident that Amos, Hosea, Isaiah, and Micah understood Israel's situation in terms that transcended the political perils of the day. In their judgment, Yahweh was about to initiate a new and decisive epoch in the life of the people. The faithlessness of Israel had gone so far that little hope could be held out for a reform of Israelite life and faith. Yahweh himself was bringing an enemy to sweep away His people. The end of Israel's existence was at hand. No moderate chastisement of the people would suffice; only utter ruin could adequately express Yahweh's wrath with His people. It seems unlikely that any prophets of the ancient Near Eastern world outside Israel would ever have threatened complete destruction of the people to whom they prophesied. The prophets named above, however, excepted nothing from the coming catastrophe: the kingship, the Temple, the priesthood, the prophetic officials, the sacrificial system, the land of the Promise, the elect peoples of Yahweh itself—all were to be swept away in the divine wrath.

The words of hope in the literature of the pre-Exilic prophets include some later additions designed to soften the judgment of the prophets. Other words of hope, however, are original with the prophets who have pronounced unalterable doom upon Israel. The judgment of Yahweh upon the faithless people was always understood to lie within Yahweh's power to execute as He chose. The possibility always remained that Yahweh might choose to be gracious to "the remnant of Joseph" (Am. 5^{15}). Nor was Yahweh's purpose for Israel and the nations abandoned. Amos implies that Yahweh could call another people to carry on that purpose (Am. 9^{7}), while Hosea, Isaiah, and Micah seem never to have abandoned the conviction that beyond the dreadful judgment lay the prospect for a fresh start with Israel. Hosea speaks of a new period of guidance in the wilderness and re-entry into the Promised Land (2^{14-23}

[Heb. 2^{16-25}]), Isaiah of the transformation of the formerly faithless Zion into the centre of the earth, from which God's teaching will be imparted to the nations. Strife and warfare will cease and the purpose of Yahweh will be fulfilled for all the nations (Isa. 2^{2-4}, cf. Mic. 4^{1-4}). The same prophet also portrays the rise of a royal figure whom Yahweh will use in the fulfilment of His purpose for Israel and the nations (9^{1-7} [Heb. 8^{23}–9^{6}], 11^{1}). The prophet Micah, despite his prophecy of the coming destruction of Zion (3^{12}), also forecasts the rise of a " ruler " from Bethlehem who will be used to fulfil Yahweh's world-wide purpose (5^{1-5a} [Heb. 4^{14}–5^{4a}]).

The prophetic hope centres upon three distinct realities in Israel's life. Some of the pictures of the future fulfilment of the divine purpose single out Zion the city of God as the centre of the work of Yahweh at the Last Day. Others focus attention upon the dynasty of David, portraying the rise of a royal figure whom Yahweh will use in the establishment of His kingly rule over Israel and the nations. Still other passages concentrate upon the election of Israel, the deliverance from Egypt, the guidance of Yahweh in the wilderness, and the entrance of a chastened and faithful people into a transformed land of Promise. All three of these features of the prophetic hope, however, are closely related. In the worship of the community they have been fused into a magnificent portrayal of confidence in Yahweh, Who will not let His purpose for Israel and the nations finally be thwarted—not even by the apostasy of His chosen people. North Israel and Judah may have to be devastated in order that they may learn obedience and faithfulness to Yahweh, but the purpose of the divine judgment is the refashioning of a people through whom His purpose for all the nations will be realized.

This message of the prophets is not alien to the ancient covenant faith. Yet it has radically new features. These prophets lived in intimate relationship to God, drew their strength and insight from His presence in their own lives. The lives of the prophets thus reveal a new dimension of Israelite religion which is of incalculable importance. Yahweh wishes to live in close relationship with every son of Israel, indeed, with all men. The relationship to which Israel is called by the prophets is that quality of communion with the living God which characterizes the lives of those to whom Yahweh revealed His Word. The covenant faith is thus made more intimate, more personal. Yahweh still deals with Israel as a people ; the life of the individual can flourish only in community. But within a faithful community of God's people the individual finds himself in closest relationship with the source of all life and blessing. The prophets called all Israel—

the community and each of its members—to live in that depth of communion between God and man out of which all authentic faith and all true obedience flow.

Such a relationship to the source of life is not without its costs. The prophets of Israel paid a high price for their interior faith in God. Such faith took precedence over loyalty to tradition, to the state, to the form and the content of the religious tradition. Amos was driven from the sanctuary at Bethel and probably from the land of Israel (7^{12-13}). Hosea was called a fool and a madman (9^{7}), and Isaiah was probably driven into temporary retirement by Ahaz (chaps. 7–8). Other prophets laid down their lives in Yahweh's service (see Jer. 26^{20-23}). Moses had been required to intercede in behalf of a rebellious people often ready to take his life. Fidelity to the will of Yahweh became doubly difficult when the prophets spoke a message that branded them as traitors to their land, haters of their own people. We do not know how many prophets may have been led by the enormity of their task to forsake the Word received from Yahweh and choose the easier path of speaking smooth things, prophesying what the people wanted to hear. The words of such men, in any case, were not to be remembered—except as the words of false prophets. In various ways the community was able to recognize the true prophet when he spoke (a testimony to the residual health of the community attacked by the prophets). Such words were remembered even when they were not heeded. Preserved by a small circle of disciples of the prophet (Isa. 8^{16-20}), they eventually were acknowledged by the entire community to be Yahweh's own Word to Israel. In fact, it seems highly probable that the words of the prophets were used in the regular worship of the community, just as the prophets drew upon the vocabulary, imagery, and traditions of the worshipping community in the shaping of their message.

After the fall of the northern kingdom in 721 B.C. the situation of the Judaean state became more and more perilous. Ahaz maintained the kingdom by becoming subservient to Assyria. Hezekiah carried through a limited reform of Israelite worship and rebelled against the authority of Assyria, only to find his land quickly plundered and Jerusalem itself encircled. Isaiah's call to depend upon Yahweh alone and not to seek aid either from Egypt or from Assyria went unheeded in Hezekiah's later years. Yet Jerusalem was spared destruction, an event interpreted by Isaiah to be the direct work of Yahweh. Under Manasseh the kingdom survived by docile acceptance of the rule of Assyria and by the silencing of prophetic calls to faithfulness to the covenant demands. In the late seventh century, however, prophecy came afresh to life in the words and works of Zephaniah, Habakkuk, Nahum, and Jeremiah.

Jeremiah's message is closely analogous to that of Hosea and Isaiah. He summons the people of Judah to the same quality of covenant devotion found in the appeals of Isaiah. He attacks the unrighteous for their sins with the same directness as his predecessors. His most characteristic words, however, come in connexion with the rise of the Babylonian state which had brought the Assyrian empire to its final end at the battle of Carchemish in 605 B.C. Jeremiah not only viewed the coming of Babylonia as Yahweh's judgment upon a sinful people, the "rod of Yahweh's anger" (Isa. 10^{5}). He called for submission to the power of Babylonia, encouraged the exiles of 597 B.C. to adjust their lives to the new situation, even told them to pray for the welfare of the land in which they were captives (Jer. 29). The exile itself was to provide, in his view, the setting for a new and glorious work of Yahweh. After seventy years (25^{12}, 29^{10}) the exiles would be led back into the homeland, Yahweh would make a new covenant with His entire people (31^{31-34}), and Yahweh Himself would be known and served by all His people. A new and decisive stage in the relations between God and people would be ushered in by the return from exile.

The people could not accept Jeremiah's promises. Zedekiah the puppet king in Judah was prevailed upon to rebel against Nebuchadrezzar. The end of the Judaean state came quickly. Jerusalem was besieged and destroyed, thousands of captives were taken into exile, and the glorious promises for the glorification of Jerusalem and the rule of the Davidic prince over the nations of the earth must have seemed to be a mocking word of Yahweh in the ears of those who had held to such hopes.

In Jeremiah's struggle with the men of Judah and his combat with Yahweh, however, additional preparation had been made for the faith of Israel to survive even this disaster. Jeremiah's prayers to Yahweh for vengeance, his appeals to Yahweh for the removal of the burden of prophesying a message that seemed not to be destined for fulfilment, his attacks upon Yahweh for having deceived him (see esp. Jer. 15^{15-21}, 18^{19-23}, 20^{7-18}) mark an intensification of the life of prayer in the Israelite community, a deepening of the communion between the deity and the individual worshipper, a readiness to overstep the bounds of propriety in the earnestness of prayer and petition. Jeremiah's life of communion with God, despite all the suffering entailed in his prophetic ministry, sustained him in every trial. He displayed to the Judaean community the quality of faith that was to support the exiles, after the loss of land and Temple and the shattering of their fondest hopes for the future of God's people.

Ezekiel spoke from Babylonian exile a message similar in many respects to that of Jeremiah. He denounced the Judaeans for their continuing apostasy from the covenant faith, using the most bitter and uncompromising language and imagery. His picture of the corruption of religion in Jerusalem, in the Temple itself (chap. 8), is probably exaggerated, and the tone of his denunciations hardly reflects the profound compassion of Jeremiah for the people against whom his words were directed. After the fall of Jerusalem in 586 B.C., however, Ezekiel's message becomes a word of hope and encouragement for the exiles. Yahweh's appearance to him by the river Chebar (a canal in the vicinity of the city of Babylon, 1^1) is of particular importance for Israelite faith. Yahweh is seen not to be bound to the Temple in Jerusalem. He comes to His people far from the holy land, displaying His majesty and splendour to those who have eyes to see in a manner not at all inferior to His appearances in the cult centre of Jerusalem. Ezekiel also maintains, with Jeremiah, that the exile will not endure for ever. Yahweh will restore His people to their land, will Himself transform Temple, land, and people and fit them for the life of fidelity to Yahweh for which they had been called. The "dead bones" will be given new life, the "whole house of Israel" will rise from death to a new and glorious life in Yahweh's presence on the transfigured land (chap. 37 and chaps. 40–48).

Prophecy came to its zenith in Babylonian exile with the message of an anonymous prophet called Second Isaiah (the author of Isa. 40–55). This prophet looked back over the entire scope of Israel's life under God's guidance, back to the creation itself. He saw the day of culmination of Yahweh's work in all history to be near at hand. Israel was summoned, in matchless words and subtle imagery, to prepare for the day of fulfilment. The people had no need to doubt either the power or the determination of Yahweh to deliver them and to fulfil His work among the nations. Was not Yahweh the creator of the ends of the earth? Had He not long before and repeatedly demonstrated His mercy and love for Israel? Moreover, could Israel not see that Yahweh was already at work to accomplish His saving work for Israel and the nations? Was Cyrus not Yahweh's anointed agent (44^{28}, 45^1), appointed to bring liberation to His people? Over and again the exilic prophet restated the imminence of Yahweh's salvation.

But it was not through Cyrus that Yahweh's most glorious and strangest work would be accomplished. The Servant of Yahweh would mediate God's salvation to the ends of the earth, would provide forgiveness of sins and newness of life. His faithfulness to death, his innocent suffering in behalf of "many" would bring God's salvation to the foreign nations, to the ends of the earth. The enigmatic figure of the Servant of Yahweh in four passages of Second Isaiah's prophecies (42^{1-4}, 49^{1-6}, 50^{4-9}, 52^{13}–53^{12}) seems to represent Israel, God's people. Yet the personal features of the Servant are clearly depicted and his mission also involves a mission to Israel (49^{5-6}). The Servant probably is to be understood as a representative of Israel in the manner of the ancient covenant mediators or representatives. The Servant is at once a prophet "like Moses" (Deut. 18^{15}), an anointed royal figure who is glorified and stands before the kings of the earth (52^{13-15}) and whose sacrificial death is portrayed in the priestly language of the Israelite cult (chap. 53). We suspect that Second Isaiah has reunited the tasks and function of the covenant mediator, which since the time of the kingship had been divided among the royal, prophetic, and priestly officials. The Servant as here portrayed thus lays before the exilic community the basic calling of the people of God: to be a people faithful and obedient to death, to hold before the nations the light of Yahweh's saving purpose for the universe, and to greet with joy the new work of Yahweh which would enable Israel to be the people that she had been called to be.

The message of Second Isaiah is clearly dominated by the conviction that Yahweh is about to do new, glorious things. Yahweh's Word will accomplish its purpose; nothing can stay the imminent deliverance of Israel or the new life which awaits both Israel and the nations (chap. 55). The exilic prophet's indomitable hope is to continue to keep the eyes of many within Israel fixed upon the future, upon the day of consummation which lies ahead. The ways of portraying that day will continue to vary, the imagery in some Israelite groups growing more bizarre and the hope marked by a fanatical zeal. Few if any direct references to the figure of the mysterious Servant of Yahweh are discernible in the literature until New Testament times. The very fact that the prophecies of Second Isaiah were preserved and that a large body of additional prophetic material was connected with his prophecies (probably by his disciples in the post-Exilic community), including some oracles of extraordinary literary power and religious insight (chaps. 56–66; see esp. chaps. 59–62), testifies to the continuing vitality of the prophet's message within the later community.

Prophetic voices continued to be heard in the post-Exilic community. It may appear that the prophets Haggai, Zechariah, Malachi, Joel, and Obadiah speak with less power and eloquence of the central realities of covenant faith than had their predecessors. Yet it is the nature of the prophetic movement to frame its affirmations and judgments in terms appropriate to the times and to the issues confronted by the community. Zechariah's strange visions (chaps. 1–6) bear testimony to the prophet's profound faith in the power of Yahweh to bring His work to fruition in a day of " small things " (Zech. 4^{10}). These prophets and their followers have not at all lost the vision of the coming triumph of Yahweh's purpose for Israel and the nations. Joel speaks of the pouring out of the divine Spirit upon " all flesh " (2^{28-29} [Heb. 3^{1-2}]), a disciple of Zechariah portrays the king who comes to Zion to establish Yahweh's worldwide dominion and usher in peace for all the nations (Zech. 9^{9-10}). The appearance of the Book of Jonah at this time with its remarkable picture of Yahweh's readiness to heed the repentance of the most hated city in the ancient world also indicates the continuing vitality of the prophetic tradition. Nor should it be forgotten that as the line of prophets seems to diminish, the prophetic testimony left by Yahweh's spokesmen from the days of Elijah forward has now become material over which the community labours. The words of the prophets were studied in synagogue and around the feet of the teachers of the community, were carefully preserved by the faithful at the risk of their lives, and also continued to be heard in connexion with the worship of the community. Prophecy has not died so long as the witness of Amos, Hosea, Isaiah, Jeremiah, Ezekiel, and Second Isaiah continues to be heard.

(vi) ISRAELITE WORSHIP*

The religion of a people is as much a matter of things done as of things said or believed. We have spoken above of the importance of the major festivals and have referred to the sacrifices and other elements in Israelite worship. Now we shall attempt to sketch the chief features of the community's worship more comprehensively, although it must be granted that the sources do not permit us to recover the actual proceedings of Israelite worship.

In the period prior to the establishment of the kingship, the historical dimension of Israelite faith had already modified the character of the community's worship. This modification took at the least the form of confessions of faith in the God Who had brought Israel from Egypt, led her in the wilderness, and provided the good land for her. One element in the community's worship, then, was praise to the God who had demonstrated His power and mercy in specific acts of deliverance and guidance.

* See also below, pp. 523 ff.

As enemies continued to threaten the life of the community in the Promised Land, and as new agents of deliverance were raised up by Yahweh, renewed acts of praise found their place in the community's worship and continued the story of Yahweh's guidance of His people in their historical pilgrimage.

Along with the hymns of praise to Yahweh for His saving help, however, rose those cries for help which fill the Psalter and appear throughout other parts of Old Testament literature. Worship consists essentially of praise and petition (Claus Westermann, *Das Loben Gottes in den Psalmen*, 2nd ed., 1961). Israel was not reluctant to turn to Yahweh for aid. Yahweh was understood to be actively involved in the daily affairs of Israelite life ; He was the living God, not a deity who appeared only occasionally on the historical scene, and not one whose powers had to be revived in connexion with the rhythms of life and death in the natural order.

Israelite worship is marked by an extraordinary candour in prayer. The insistence that Yahweh alone governed the universe, that no other powers beneficent or malevolent functioned beyond the range of His rule, brought particular spiritual problems to the community in its life and worship. Quite obviously Yahweh did not always come to the aid of His people. How was His refusal to act in their behalf to be understood ? It was granted that Yahweh (like Chemosh of the Moabites ; see the Mesha monument) was sometimes angry with His people and refused to come to their aid. On some occasions, however, the community would insist that it was relatively free of guilt ; why should Yahweh be angry ? The Psalter is full of the most candid complaints laid before Yahweh, complaints that are marked by painful honesty, by a stubborn refusal simply to submit to the divine will in a spirit of resignation. Israel expected Yahweh to help and would not be put off in its petitions by abstract notions of the wise providence of Yahweh or pious words that hid the anxiety and bitterness of the heart.

The seriousness of the community's wrestlings with Yahweh for a blessing is one of the most prominent features of Israelite spirituality. The community seems to have assumed that when Yahweh withheld His favour He did so for reasons that had to do with Israelite daily life. The works of Yahweh were not capricious, although they often were mysterious. His will could normally be known by men. No conflicts or jealousies in the divine realm could account for the deity's displeasure, as was frequently understood to be the case in Mesopotamian and Canaanite-Syrian religion. In fact, Israelite worship shows the same concentration upon the earthly realm, the world of man's daily experience, that we have observed in the community's religious thought.

The establishment of the Temple in Jerusalem brought considerable change into the worship of Israel. Worship at the local shrines and high places was not abandoned, but the norm for worship in its fulness very probably was provided by the practices in the Jerusalem Temple. The old festival calendars specified that the community was to appear before Yahweh three times in the year (Ex. 23^{14-17}, 34^{22-23}). The three great festivals of the agricultural year probably were celebrated in the Jerusalem Temple, representatives from each of the tribes taking part in the celebration. Yet it is clear that one of these festivals—the autumn festival at the beginning of the new year—was of decisive importance.

We have noted above that this festival had become the occasion for the renewal of the covenant between Yahweh and Israel. The establishment of the kingship, however, placed the king in the position of the covenant representative; Yahweh's covenant was now with David and his house. The autumn festival thus became an act of worship dominated by the king. In all probability the ancient Near Eastern New Year's Day festivities exercised considerable influence upon the procedures and the significance of the autumn festival in Israel. The king was re-invested with Yahweh's authority. Prayers for the life of the king were uttered. The covenant between Yahweh and the king was ratified, the allegiance of the people to Yahweh consisting fundamentally of a pledge of loyalty to the earthly king. The king was understood to be Yahweh's adopted son (Ps. 2^{6-9}), designated to rule at Yahweh's pleasure and direction. Mythological elements in the ancient Near Eastern religious traditions concerning kingship almost certainly were adopted into the Jerusalem cult. Yet it is doubtful that the kings of Israel were considered to be " divine " in the way in which the kings of Egypt were understood to be gods incarnate, or even in the more limited view of " divine kingship " held by the various Mesopotamian states. The traditions relating the establishment of kingship in Israel prevented any such development, as indicated above.

The bringing of the Ark of the covenant into Jerusalem by David is not identified as an act associated with one of the major festivals. Solomon's consecration of the Temple, however, is placed in the month of Ethanim, the seventh month (the beginning of the religious year). If, as seems probable, the autumn festival involved the bringing of the Ark into Jerusalem and its being placed anew in the Holy of Holies of the Temple (see Ps. 132), this festival was thereby related to the most sacred cult object of ancient times and enabled the community to discern the continuity of worship in the city of Jerusalem with the older ceremony of covenant renewal at the central sanctuaries of the twelve tribes.

In Jerusalem it also became necessary to maintain a regular ritual of worship. In the early days the fixed elements of daily worship apparently consisted of morning and evening prayers accompanied by sacrificial acts. A festival of the New Moon is attested in the days of Saul (1 Sam. 20^{5}). We do not know what form this festival may have taken in the Jerusalem Temple. Nor are we informed as to the significance of Sabbath observance in the Jerusalem Temple. The Passover rite probably continued to be a family festival for some centuries, as noted above. As the ritual acts of the Jerusalem Temple multiplied throughout the centuries the autumn festival continued to be the most central religious act of the community.

The worship of the community not only gave increasing prominence to the king who ruled in Jerusalem. The cult centre itself, Zion, the city of Yahweh, came more and more to be understood as the centre of the world, the meeting place of God and man. Mythological imagery from the surrounding religious traditions made its way into Israel's portrayals of the importance of Zion. Several passages reveal that the ancient myth of the first city, set upon a high mountain, was modified and related to Yahweh's establishment of Zion (see especially Pss. 46 and 48 and Isa. 2^{2-4}, Mic. 4^{1-4}). Yet once more the old traditions clearly indicate that Zion was not the "first city" but a former Jebusite town conquered by David. The Temple was not built in primordial time but was established by Solomon, after David had been refused permission to build it. The community in its worship referred to the future the glories that were to be showered upon Zion. Its present glory was as nothing compared with what Yahweh would do for Zion at the Last Day. Thus the Temple and the holy city were not permitted to become guarantees for the unfailing presence and blessing of Yahweh, nor were the traditions and practices in the Temple cult given divine sanction in such a way as to prevent their being challenged or changed.

The worship of Israel in the Temple also provided ample place for families and individuals to make their prayers to Yahweh and seek His aid. We do not know a great deal about the private acts of devotion at the Temple or elsewhere, but it is clear from occasional references that the individual on numerous occasions would beseech the help of Yahweh (1 Sam. 1^{9-18}), sing His praises and give thanks for benefits received, and make vows to Yahweh. At the Temple such acts of individual worship were almost certainly to be found. The emphasis probably lay upon the worshipper's desire for

Yahweh's aid in the concreteness of his daily life. Yet joy and delight in God's presence appear in many of the psalms. Yahweh was worshipped not alone for bestowal of blessing upon the individual or the community. Simply to be in God's presence at the holy place was itself a joy, just as separation from the Temple was a major disaster (Pss. 84, 137).

On occasion, the worshipper would spend the night in the Temple precincts in prayer. It has been suggested that this practice represented an ordeal, a test of the righteousness of the worshipper. Accused of wrongdoing by his enemies, the worshipper would submit his case to Yahweh. If Yahweh did not bring judgment upon him during the night, he was by that fact shown to be innocent of the charge laid against him. Such a practice probably was common in Israel. Yet many worshippers probably spent the night in the Temple area in order quite simply to engage in prayer to Yahweh. The innocence or guilt of the one accused, moreover, would probably have been indicated not alone by his surviving a night spent in the Temple. The importance of the priestly pronouncement of guilt or innocence must not be overlooked.

The range of subjects and moods reflected in the Psalter is sufficient indication of the breadth and depth of Israelite spirituality. Frequently the worshippers would recount the saving works of God, both as evidence of God's goodness and mercy and as the basis for a fresh appeal for aid. The contrast was frequently drawn between Yahweh's past deeds of mercy and His present refusal to come to the help of His people (see especially Ps. 44). In times of despair such remembrance of past mercies also served to focus the eye of the worshipper upon the future. What did Yahweh have in store for His people in the coming days ? How long would Israel's present plight endure ? How did the present distress relate to the coming triumph of Yahweh's grace ? Thus in the community's worship, and not alone in the thought of the prophets and seers, Israelite eschatology took shape. The worldwide dominion of Yahweh, believed to lie ahead, provided both direction for the life of the worshipper and strength with which to bear present adversity. The fact that Israel had no hope in the resurrection of the individual from the grave gave particular strength and poignancy to the community's hope in the coming triumph of Yahweh's grace and purpose. Simply to live in Yahweh's presence in the midst of trials and adversity, however, and to know that Yahweh shared the plight of the worshipper was perhaps the greatest support to the worshipper in his time of trials (see Ps. 73).

The reform of Israelite worship carried through by Josiah in 621 B.C. (2 Kings 22–23) gave to the Temple service even more importance than it had formerly had. Josiah abolished the worship of Yahweh at local cult sites and shrines, making Jerusalem the exclusive centre of worship under royal and priestly supervision. The Book of Deuteronomy, parts of which provided the basis for Josiah's reform, bears witness to a long flowering of Israelite spirituality outside of Jerusalem, under the Levites who guided the people of the towns and villages into the meaning of the covenant faith. The centralization of worship in Jerusalem brought to the community at its centre the product of the work of these teaching and preaching Levites, thus greatly enriching Israelite worship and piety. During the Exile, still further developments occurred that were to prove to be immensely enriching for the community's worship. The Psalms were collected and used by the exiles in their worship in home and in local gatherings (Ps. 137). Deprived of the Temple, the sacrificial system, and the guardians of public worship, the community was required to live on those resources of faith and worship which they had brought from the homeland—or to develop other resources. The sacred Scripture took shape during the Exile. Much of the Old Testament in its present form was brought together during the Babylonian exile, in all probability. The process of collecting, studying, editing, and preserving the story of Israel's past must have had its influence upon the community's worship as well as upon its religious thought. The importance of the sabbath should not be overlooked in this connexion. The sabbath helped to distinguish the Israelite community in the foreign land, as did circumcision. It also provided the time and opportunity for acts of religious devotion, for the study of the Scripture, and for continuing preoccupation with the question of the community's future in the purpose of Yahweh.

The beginnings of the synagogue may lie in the period of the Exile. Such gatherings as those reported in the Book of Ezekiel (8^1, 14^1, 33^{30-33}) and implied by Ps. 137 must have contributed to the rise of the synagogue, as did the task of collecting, editing, and studying the sacred traditions during the time of the Exile. The rebuilding of the Temple in post-Exilic times restored much of the former significance to the Temple in Israelite worship. Yet it is doubtful that the Temple was ever to be of the decisive importance to the community that it once had been. The king no longer ruled in Jerusalem. The glories of the Temple had formerly been connected with the glory of the Judaean state. Neither Temple nor state any longer existed in their former splendour. Israelite religion was thenceforth to flourish in the local communities just as significantly as at the cult centre in Jerusalem. The synagogue, originally a place for the study of the Law and for instruction in the duties of the covenant faith, came more and more to occupy the practical centre of Israelite religious life. The prayers and blessings, the regular reading of Scripture, the instruction in the requirements of the Law, and the preservation and elaboration of the unwritten requirements of the Law which developed in the synagogue did not reduce the Temple worship to an inconsequential status. But these religious acts provided a highly significant expansion of Israelite religious life and worship, making it possible for the life and worship of Israel to survive when the Temple was finally destroyed in the Roman war of A.D. 66–70.

(vii) THE WISDOM TRADITION

The means by which the peoples of the ancient world came to understand their world and the place of man in the world were quite varied. Two rather distinct intellectual efforts, however, stand out in the cultures of the ancient Near East. The first is the more influential : the development of a cosmology, a world-view, on the basis of which man's place in the world could be comprehended and explained. Fundamental to these world-views was the explanation of the relationship between the life of the gods and the life of man. The actions, purposes and plans of the gods in heaven provided " archetypes " for the life of man on earth. The religious and intellectual leaders of the various societies sought to work out the specific means by which man's life on earth conformed with the will of the gods. All the powers and instruments of religion were devoted to this fundamental task. Myths, rituals, prayers, and the lore of the religious leaders provided the basic products of the world-view of ancient peoples. We have noted above that the Israelite community drew heavily upon such religious resources but transformed its borrowings in the light of its understanding of Yahweh's revelation of His purpose in the concrete events of Israel's historical experience.

The other approach to an understanding of the world depends to a considerable degree upon the fruits of the first approach. But the second way of coming to terms with man's world is more earthy, more practical, more closely related to man's critical evaluation of his daily experiences. The second approach is the search for wisdom and the production of a body of critically evaluated experiences on the basis of which a people may find orientation and guidance for daily life. The cultures of Mesopotamia, Egypt, and the Palestinian area all had their wise men and produced their bodies of wisdom. The wisdom thus produced was maintained in the form of pungent sayings, often marked by sharp contrasts, drawn from all areas of the life of man. The experiences of family life, commerce and business, political action, and the realm of nature all appear in the wisdom tradition. Moreover, the wisdom traditions of the ancient world were remarkably similar ; wisdom is by nature supra-national. In the various cultures of the ancient world, wise men and their disciples sought to sum up the experiences of their world in large bodies of quite unrelated sayings and observations. These were available to the entire people, could be drawn from at will as guides for the young, for the leaders of state, for the religious leaders.

The first approach leads to a systematized world-view ; the second leads to a rich collection of human experience in daily life, critically evaluated and presented in the form of pithy sayings, easily remembered, suitable for guidance of the individual or the community at all critical points in their lives. We have one large body of such sayings in the Old Testament : the Book of Proverbs. But the influence of the wisdom tradition appears throughout the Old Testament and is particularly observable in certain psalms (Pss. 1, 37, 119, etc.). The Apocrypha contain two additional wisdom collections : the Wisdom of Solomon and Ecclesiasticus (Ben Sira, Sirach).

Within the wisdom tradition of the ancient world, two types of collections are found. The first, like the Book of Proverbs, is marked by a positive and indeed optimistic outlook upon life. Man's life is beset by many perils, but the pursuit of wisdom and the scrupulous regard for its precepts will carry the wise man to his goal, even in the most perilous times. The second type, however, is profoundly sceptical in its view of the possibilities open to man in his earthly pilgrimage. It seems evident that the first view produces the second, as certain spokesmen for the wisdom tradition become dissatisfied with the answers to life's meaning provided by the tradition which they themselves have maintained. Yet these sceptical wisdom documents are still a part of the wisdom tradition. The language and imagery of the wisdom school are employed in an attack upon the traditional answers to life's meaning. The critical evaluation of human experience which had produced the practical and positive wisdom tradition is subjected to an even more critical and searching evaluation. The result is sometimes resignation before the meaninglessness of life, sometimes positive submission to the deity whose ways cannot clearly be known by man, and occasionally a new vision of the glory and majesty of the deity, whose knowledge, power and wisdom far outstrip man's puny efforts to comprehend His ways (*e.g.* the Book of Job).

Because the wisdom tradition is by nature international, Israel's wisdom writers appear not to stand in very close relationship to the covenant faith affirmed in other portions of the Old Testament. In two respects, however, even the Book of Proverbs is brought within the framework of Israelite faith in Yahweh the God of the covenant. The source of all wisdom is God Himself—the God Who created the heavens and the earth and Who sees to the needs of His people. God created wisdom as the first of His acts of creation (Prov. 8^{22-31}). He provided wisdom to man as one of his most precious treasures, so that man's life on earth might prosper and flourish. Moreover, the heart and centre of all wisdom is the "fear of God" (Prov. 1^{7}); to know and to obey God—this is wisdom. All other fruits of wisdom derive from the knowledge of the being and purpose of God.

In the second place, the wisdom tradition in Israel contributes greatly to the guidance of the community in obedience to the covenant. The Ten Commandments specify, for example, that the Israelite is not to commit adultery. The author of Prov. 7 provides a marvellous picture of the attractions of the loose woman, enabling the community to recognize with all clarity the seductions and temptations to adultery, while grimly portraying the ruin that will befall those who yield to this temptation. Ancient Near Eastern wisdom in general serves this function, yet the graphic imagery of the Book of Proverbs almost certainly derives in part from the covenant tradition, with its uncompromising insistence upon fidelity to the will of Yahweh.

Moreover, the sceptical wisdom collections (Job and Ecclesiastes) are of even greater service to Israel's covenant faith. The author of the poems of Job lays before the community the most central question of Israelite faith in Yahweh's just guidance of the life of man: is it really possible to love and to serve God freely, without reward? When all the supports of faith are removed, can man still believe in the righteousness and mercy of God? Is there such a thing as faith in God which is not marked finally by self-interest? The poet portrays Job's struggle with God, his refusal to accept the easy answers of the religious tradition, his insistence upon the injustice of God's condemnation, his final confrontation with God Himself which turns all his violent words into repentance and praise. This poet, who probably writes from Judah after the fall of Jerusalem in 586 B.C., thus says that if such a thing as authentic faith in God exists, it can only be the product of an honest and relentless search for God, for the true God, through all the forms of religion and piety, through and underneath all the easy answers to life's meaning which his friends are eager to supply. When true faith appears, it appears as man stands in communion with God, sees the holy

God in all His mystery, power, justice, and mercy. The man of true faith does prosper, does benefit from his faith. But the basic reward of faith is precisely to be in God's presence, to be " held by his right hand," as a wisdom psalm from about the same date declares (Ps. 73²³).

(viii) THE SECOND TEMPLE

Israelite religion takes on a considerably altered form when the Babylonian exiles make their way back to the land of the Promise. In the restored community those forms and supports of the religious life of the exiles continue to flourish. The observance of the sabbath is no less important than it had come to be during the Exile (see Isa. 56). The stricture against defilement by idolatry or by intermarriage which had done much to preserve the community during the Exile continues to be a feature of religious life and teaching within the restored community (Neh. 13, Ezra 10). The importance of the priests and teachers of the Law is all the greater in the post-Exilic community, since the governor of the land is now appointed by the Persian government. During the time of the prophets Haggai and Zechariah, great hopes were placed in the role of Zerubbabel, who was from the line of David (Hag. 2^{20-23}, Zech. 4^{6-10a}). These hopes were not to be realized. More and more the authority of the religious community was vested in the leading priest, and strict obedience to the Law of God came to be the test of fidelity to the divine will.

This development within the post-Exilic community is easily misunderstood. We have noted that the Law of the covenant had been closely associated with the saving work of Yahweh in Israel's history and that in connexion with the reaffirmation of the covenant the Law was recited and placed anew upon the community. During the period of the kingship, the Law continued to be the community's guide under the leadership of kings, priests, and prophets. The kings of Israel are never credited with having promulgated laws on their own account; all legislation is traced to the work of Moses in the wilderness. Now, however, the community has no king. The prophets who interpreted the direct meaning of Yahweh's guidance of His people seem to be less numerous and less influential. The established religion of the community is maintained largely by those whose own personal interests are bound up with the maintenance of the religious heritage as they themselves understand and promulgate it. True faith in Yahweh thus could easily be reduced to strict adherence to the letter of the Law. A narrow and sterile legalism might easily develop, largely in consequence of the political and cultural changes which had occurred.

The widely held view that a disastrous decline in Israelite religion occurred in the post-exilic period cannot be accepted without great qualifications. Obedience to the Law is marked also by profound delight in Yahweh for His having provided this path on which Israel is to walk (see Pss. 1, 119). More importantly, the Law of the post-exilic community is not a set of regulations alone. " Torah " is the name for the entire Pentateuch, including the matchless story of Yahweh's guidance of His people in their pilgrimage, the narratives of the patriarchs, the account of the Creation, the Flood, the Tower of Babel, the story of Israel's redemption from Egyptian bondage and Yahweh's guidance in the wilderness. The term " Torah " means not Law but " guidance," " instruction." To obey the Torah means to submit one's life to the guidance of God in history, to live by faith in His active presence, to hope in His coming triumph, to trust His power to save, to submit to His chastening and His judgments.

The importance of Torah for the life of the Jewish community can hardly be overestimated. It is wrong, nonetheless, to suppose that " legalism " is the only possible result of this devotion to Yahweh's guidance and teaching. In the great collection of the oral law now found in the Mishnah and the Gemara (which together make up the Talmud) we find abundant evidence of the freedom of the Jewish community to interpret the meaning of the Torah. Repeatedly we hear of debates among the rabbis as to the meaning of a particular passage or phrase or word. The opinions of the rabbis are often left unreconciled, the community being free to follow one interpretation or another. Such debates could, of course, become trivial, could draw the leaders of the community away from the fundamental issues of faith in Yahweh and obedience to His will. And indeed, the devotion to Torah could result in the development of a legalistic attitude towards religion, could produce the notion that man's own obedience to the Torah was indispensable in Yahweh's fulfilment of His purpose for Israel and the nations. Religion, in short, could stand in the way of authentic faith in the love and mercy of God, readiness to depend upon God alone for redemption from sin and fulfilment of life. But these temptations are clearly no less present in the Christian community than they were in the post-exilic Jewish community. Men are always able to transform the free mercy and love of God into a system of religious duties which, properly observed, assures the divine favour.

The community, or some of its members, did come to hold the view that Yahweh had already prepared the Torah in heaven and that it was existent at the creation of the earth, or was one of the first of God's creations. The giving of the

Torah at Mt. Sinai is thus the imparting of that which Yahweh had already prepared for mankind's guidance. And it is affirmed that Yahweh looked among the nations for one people who would receive and hallow His Torah. Israel was found and the Torah was given to her. This is the chief distinguishing mark of Israel among the nations: she has been entrusted with the Torah of God. None the less, the Torah was God's gift to Israel in behalf of all men. Should Israel for one day keep the requirements of Torah, the Kingdom of God would come on earth—and the nations would share in the benefits of the Messianic age.

Reference must also be made to another significant development within the post-exilic community: the appearance of what is called apocalyptic literature and an apocalyptic world-view. The worship of Yahweh had led, as noted above, to the attribution of all authority to the one Lord of the universe. Israelite monotheism was not without its difficulties in the interpretation of the events and processes of the community's life. Yahweh must not be made responsible for the appearance of evil in the world, for the sin of man, for the dark and malevolent powers that threatened man's existence and the fulfilment of God's purpose. Man's freedom to obey or to disobey God must be preserved. At the end of the Babylonian exile and in the subsequent two centuries the Israelite community lived in close relation to the Persian religion centred in the work and teaching of the great Zoroaster (Zarathustra). The popular religion of Zoroaster made great use of the imagery of cosmic conflict within the created world-order: the forces of light and good under the leadership of Ahura Mazda did constant battle against the forces of darkness and evil led by the prince of evil, Ahriman. The ultimate outcome of the conflict was to be the triumph of Ahura Mazda. In the meantime, however, the world was the battle ground of these spiritual forces of good and evil, and the battle also raged within the life of each individual. In the last and decisive conflict between light and darkness the earth itself would undergo convulsions, the entire cosmos being affected by this struggle. Yet those who placed their allegiance in the ruler of the forces of light could face that cosmic catastrophe with confidence that the victory of the truth and the right was assured.

This popular Persian world-view, modified by various other religious movements and streams of thought, probably prepared the way for the development of Israelite apocalyptic literature, such as the Book of Daniel, Isa. 24–27, Ezek. 38–39, and the intertestamental apocalypses of Enoch, the Book of Jubilees, some of the Dea Sea Scrolls (especially the Wars Document) and the still later Apocalypse of Baruch (2 Baruch) and 4 Ezra (2 Esdras). Once more, however, it is clear that the Israelite community modified the religious imagery and thought which was borrowed from its neighbours. The Book of Daniel was written during the Maccabaean period (*c.* 165 B.C.) and reflects the orientation of apocalyptic thought in many respects. The kingdoms of the world are seeking to overthrow the authority of Yahweh. The time of the last struggle of the forces of evil against the authority of God is close at hand. But the triumph of God over the kingdoms of earth is assured. The " Son of Man " (Dan. 7^{13-14}) is not some heavenly figure who destroys the forces of evil by the terrible weapons which he wields (as he is portrayed in other apocalyptic literature, especially in the Book of Enoch and in 4 Ezra). This " Son of Man " in Daniel is a figure stripped of its mythological trimmings and is none other than God's people Israel, the " saints of the Most High " ($7^{18.\ 27}$).

The community is summoned by the author of the Book of Daniel to wait in confidence in Yahweh until the end comes (12^{12}). This waiting is to be marked by no passive resignation before the forces of evil. Each member of the community is to hold firmly to faith in God. The stories of the fidelity of Daniel and the three friends in the court of the kingdoms of the east (chaps. 1–6) no doubt represent the author's counsel to Israel in the time of the oppression of Antiochus IV. Epiphanes. The author of Daniel calls for a quality of faith that might well issue in martyrdom. The stories of the Jewish martyrs found in the apocryphal book of 2 Maccabees probably illustrate the faith of the author of the Book of Daniel.

The apocalyptic outlook could easily contribute to the view that Israel was destined to triumph over all the nations of the earth, that Jerusalem was to be enriched and glorified at the nations' expense (Isa. 60^{4-22}, 61^{5-7}, etc.). In the post-exilic community, however, are found spokesmen for quite the opposite view. In the latter days the blessings of Yahweh will flow out to all the nations. Israel will have no privileged position among the nations, for Yahweh's kingly rule will be acknowledged by all the peoples of earth. One remarkable addition to the Isaiah tradition (19^{19-25}) speaks of Egypt and Assyria as standing upon the same level as Israel before Yahweh. Yahweh blesses Egypt and Assyria as His people, the work of His hands. The prophet Zechariah, or a later writer (8^{20-23}) describes how each Jew will be the means for the redemption of ten foreigners, who will lay hold upon his cloak because they know that Yahweh is with him. The Isaiah tradition also contains a late reference to Yahweh's choosing some priests and Levites from the foreign nations to serve Him (Isa. 66^{18-21}, the apparent meaning of this remarkable text). These magnificent instances of the faith of some members of the post-exilic community in the coming triumph of Yahweh's purpose for all the nations should not be overlooked when the religion of this period is described. Tendencies towards universalism are just as real as tendencies towards an exclusive nationalism. Strict obedience to the Torah could issue in a narrow legalism or in a profound faith in the covenant God who had provided so freely for the needs of man.

The struggle of the Jewish community to maintain itself under the pressure of foreign powers becomes more acute in the reign of Antiochus IV. Epiphanes (175–164 B.C.). The relative independence from Syrian domination won by the Maccabaean brothers and maintained by their successors with varying success still left the community under the necessity to adapt its religious life and thought to the new religious, cultural, and political situation resulting from Alexander's conquest of the West Asian states. From various ancient sources it is possible to distinguish four major groups within the Jewish community of these days, each of which offered a particular solution to the problems of life and faith in the changed political, cultural, and religious setting. The various groups should not be contrasted with one another too sharply, nor should we make the mistake of supposing that the entire community was divided into these four groups.

The Sadducees were conservative in their religious-theological orientation and liberal in their attitude towards the new cultural situation. They held firmly to the written requirements of Torah but refused to acknowledge the authority of the oral tradition. Religious ideas and practices not clearly prescribed by the Torah were rejected (such as the belief in the resurrection of the individual from the dead). Yet the Sadducees found it possible to make their way in the political world, often rising to the highest positions in the state, both during the period of the Maccabaean and Hasmonaean kingdom and during the time of Roman domination (63 B.C. and following).

The most important group was the Pharisees, whose origins are obscure but who apparently chose a middle path between the position of the Sadducees and the other two groups. The Pharisees gave themselves zealously to the interpretation of the Torah for contemporary Jewish life. Their collections of the oral traditions explaining and elaborating the meaning of Torah came later to be accepted as an authoritative part of the Mosaic Law. Their approach to the problems of existence under the new situation was marked by firm adherence to the essential elements of Mosaic faith and at the same time by a readiness to adapt and make more practical the tenets of the ancient faith. They were Israel's teachers, Israel's guides on the path of obedience to Torah. They resisted both the temptation to a narrow religious orthodoxy and to a cynical compromise with the governing authorities in order to maintain their position of religious leadership.

Certain movements within Judaism led to the designation of the representatives of such movements by the title "Zealots." It seems doubtful that there was a distinct party of Zealots. But at various times the longing of the community to be free from the rule of the heathen led to outright political rebellion. The action and successes of the Maccabees no doubt encouraged such rebellions. They were based upon profound religious convictions, in all probability. Yahweh had not intended that His people should indefinitely suffer under the weight of foreign oppression and domination. The promise of the prophets for Israel's glorification at the Last Day fed the flames of rebellion. Until Israel had regained her freedom, how could the promises made to the forefathers be fulfilled? Were not the signs of the times pointing towards the divine liberation of Israel? Thus the activity of these Zealots may well have had as deep religious roots as did the other movements within Judaism. Among the disciples of Jesus there probably were Zealots. The great rebellions of the years A.D. 66–70 and 132–135 were inspired by this movement within Judaism. But the future of the Jewish people did not lie along the path laid out and followed by the Zealots.

The other distinct group was called by several ancient sources by the name Essenes. The community which produced the Dead Sea Scrolls seems almost certainly to have been an Essene community. The Essenes were no less zealous for the triumph of Yahweh's historical purposes than were the Zealots. But the demonstration of their zeal took quite a different direction. The Essenes understood the times to require a devotion to the Torah more rigorous than that demonstrated by any members of the community. Such devotion called for the separation of the faithful from the ordinary life of the community. The community which produced the Dead Sea Scrolls gave strict attention to the make-up of its membership, requiring a lengthy period of probation, tests of the fidelity of the membership and a series of stages through which the probationer had to pass before he became a full member of the community. This Essene group gave itself with equal zeal to the study of Scripture, to the interpretation of the meaning of Torah and Prophets for the community of the Last Day, and sought in every possible way to prepare itself for the final fulfilment of the divine purpose on earth. The prayers and hymns of the community that have been unearthed disclose a profound quality of religious insight and devotion. The influence of this community upon the establishment of Christian faith has been variously estimated; it seems evident that such influence was very considerable.

This brief sketch of the chief groups and movements within Judaism prior to the first Christian century indicates the variety of ways by which the community sought to be faithful to the demands of covenant faith and to prepare itself for the coming fulfilment of God's kingly rule. In the area of eschatological expectation and Messianism a very considerable variety is also observable. The Pharisees looked for the appearance of the Messiah from the line of David, a royal figure who would be God's agent in the triumph of the divine purpose for Israel and the nations. The Essenes clearly anticipated the rise of a messianic figure from the tribe of Judah and another from the tribe of Levi. The priestly (Levitical) figure was to exercise authority above that of the Davidic Messiah. The community also placed great hope in the rise of a prophet of the Last Day, probably a prophet "like Moses." The Zealots understood the leaders of the movements for freedom to be "messianic" at least in the general sense that Yahweh had raised up these men to prosecute the battle for the restoration of the Judaean state and the overthrow of the enemy. Yet in one essential respect the hopes of the entire Jewish community were united: Yahweh was bringing His purpose for Israel and the nations to fulfilment. The means for that fulfilment were interpreted in a number of ways, but the expectancy and the indomitable faith of the Jewish community are testified to in all of the literature available for examination. The rule of the Romans over the covenant people was not what Yahweh purposed for His people. The triumph of paganism in the tolerant Roman religious system was not to endure. A new work of God lay ahead.

(ix) ISRAELITE RELIGION AND CHRISTIAN FAITH

Christian faith is the heir of Israelite faith. The Christian community saw in the work of God centred in Jesus of Nazareth the triumph of the divine purpose for which the Israelite community had longed. Yet the Jewish community was to continue as a separate testimony to the purpose of God for the covenant people and for the nations. It is by no means easy to draw the lines of distinction between Judaism and Christianity without doing injustice to one or both of these religious traditions. In the polemical situation of New Testament times it is not surprising that the entire Jewish community should be attacked in the New Testament literature for its refusal to recognize the messianic authority of Jesus and for its part in the crucifixion of Jesus. Yet the same New Testament literature clearly testifies to the inseparable relation between Israelite and Christian faith, clearly indicates that Jesus' mission was to the Jewish people and His disciples drawn from the ranks of the Jewish community. Thus it cannot be said that "Judaism" rejected the work of God accomplished in the life, work, death and resurrection of Jesus. The majority of the membership of the Jewish community did not accept Jesus of Nazareth as the fulfilment of the promises of God to Israel, while a minority did accept Him. The Jewish and Christian communities continued for some time to live side by side, the Christian group constituting a "sect" within Judaism similar in many ways to the Essene community known more fully through the discovery of the Dead Sea Scrolls. The Christian missionary activity among the non-Jewish peoples, the destruction of Jerusalem in A.D. 66–70 and the abolition of the Temple worship and the sacrificial system, the later dominance of the Pharisaic party within Judaism, plus the critically important theological developments within the Christian community led to ever further separation between the Jewish and the Christian communities. The Church saw in the life and work, the suffering, death, resurrection and ascension of Jesus of Nazareth the fulfilment of the Israelite Law, the fulfilment of God's demand for perfect obedience in the perfect life and atoning death of Jesus, the fulfilment of the sacrificial system in Christ's sacrifice on the Cross, and the fulfilment both of the promise to the forefathers and the needs and hopes of mankind in the new community created by Christ. Yet this new community did not abandon the Scripture of the Jews. The "Apostle to the Gentiles" regularly addressed the Gospel to the Jewish community in Gentile lands before turning to the Gentiles, and the message presented to the Gentiles was itself shaped by the life, witness and Scripture of the Jewish community.

It is necessary, therefore, to insist that Israelite religion has culminated in the appearance of two distinct communities whose life and faith are strangely intertwined. As each bears its particular witness to the God of covenant faith, the creator, supporter, judge and redeemer of all mankind, the glory and mystery of covenant faith need not be dissipated but may be enriched by their separate testimonies—until the time when the one God worshipped by both draws them together, along with the entire human family.

BIBLIOGRAPHY

William F. Albright, *From the Stone Age to Christianity*, 2nd ed., 1957.

Walther Eichrodt, *Theology of the Old Testament*, vol. i., Eng. trans., 1961.

A. S. Herbert, *Worship in Ancient Israel*, 1959.

Yehezkel Kaufmann, *The Religion of Israel, from its beginnings to the Babylonian Exile*, Eng. trans., 1960.

Hans-Joachim Kraus, *Gottesdienst in Israel, Grundriss einer alttestamentlichen Kultgeschichte*, 2nd ed., 1962.

George E. Mendenhall, *Law and Covenant in Israel and the Ancient Near East*, 1955.

Sigmund Mowinckel, *He That Cometh*, Eng. trans., 1956.

James Muilenburg, "The History of the Religion of Israel," *The Interpreter's Bible*, I, 1952, pp. 292–348.

Johannes Pedersen, *Israel, Its Life and Culture*, I–II, III–IV, 1926, 1940.

Gerhard von Rad, *Old Testament Theology*, vol. i., Eng. trans., 1962.

H. Wheeler Robinson, *Inspiration and Revelation in the Old Testament*, 1946.

H. H. Rowley, *The Faith of Israel, Aspects of Old Testament Thought*, 1956.

Roland de Vaux, *Ancient Israel, Its Life and Institutions*, 1961.

XIII. JUDAISM: ITS FAITH AND WORSHIP

By Marcel Simon

When we speak of Judaism, we must bear in mind that, although primarily a religion, it always has been and still is to a large extent linked up with an ethnical or national group, the Jewish people. Today, of course, it is possible still to be a Jew without being a practising one. The very concept of Jew, in the State of Israel as well as outside, has become partly secularized; Jewry and Judaism are no longer synonymous. At the beginning of the Christian era, the situation was very different. It was indeed impossible to draw the distinction which to a modern mind appears as a natural one between religion and nationality. To be a member of the people of Israel and to practise Judaism was one and the same thing. As the religious Law of Moses was the national law of Israel, regulating both the life of the community and the conduct of the individual, all political and social problems were posed and solved in terms of religion. Even at a time when Israel had lost its independence, its foreign rulers had to take this fact into account. Whether Palestine was, in its totality or in part, administered, under the Roman protectorate, by the dynasty of Herod the Great or was organized as a Roman province under the direct administration of the procurators, there existed beside the political head of the country a religious authority—High Priest and Sanhedrin—which was to many Jews the symbol of independence lost but some day to be regained. The country still was Holy Land, and its people always considered Yahweh as their only legitimate sovereign Lord. Thus, even under the Roman procurators, Israel can still be described as a theocracy. At least it thought of theocracy as an ideal and never gave up the hope of making it actual.

But only part of the Jews lived in Palestine. Certainly a much larger proportion—exactly how many, we cannot know—had settled outside its borders, owing to various causes, in the course of the previous centuries. We must not draw too sharp a dividing line between the Palestinian Jews and those of the Diaspora or Dispersion. All of them followed the same Law. To all Jerusalem was the divinely chosen centre of Jewish religious life. We know from Josephus, one of our most important sources on the subject, that a number of Diaspora Jews considered it a duty as well as a privilege to take part in a pilgrimage to the Holy City at least once in their life. These pilgrimages, of which we have a striking illustration in Acts 2, took place at the great annual festivals of the Jewish calendar. It none the less did make a considerable difference whether one was able, living in Jerusalem or in the immediate neighbourhood, to attend regularly the stately worship of the Temple, or whether one could do so only once or twice in a lifetime or even, if one could not afford the cost of the journey, never at all. The religious life of the Diaspora Jews was, by necessity, built on a basis completely different from that of the Palestinians.

They were, moreover, settled among the Gentiles and, though usually very eager to keep their originality and not to be merged in their heathen *milieu*, at least, unlike their Palestinian brethren, they would not feel the presence of the Gentiles as an offence to God and to His people. As they were granted special privileges by the emperors and also, in some cases, on the municipal level, they had no reason, since they lived outside their own country, to nurture systematic hostility towards their neighbours. Hostility, when it arose here, usually sprang from the heathen rather than from the Jews, precisely because the mob and sometimes even the more cultured elements of the population and those in authority were impatient of a minority group which enjoyed a privileged status and still insisted on its not being like its neighbours. Anti-semitism was not unknown in the Graeco-Roman world. But its violent outbursts were rather exceptional. A *modus vivendi*, which included mutual tolerance and could even lead to friendly intercourse, seems to have obtained in many cases between the two communities.

This situation certainly made an impact on the religious life of the Diaspora. It can safely be admitted that the more nationalistic features of Judaism were less salient here than in Palestine. Sure enough, there existed a strong solidarity between the two elements. It did not, however, go so far as to make the whole Diaspora revolt against the Romans whenever Palestine was involved in heavy trouble. As far as we know, the Diaspora remained completely unaffected by the events of A.D. 66–70. It could of course be argued that a revolt in Rome, Antioch, or even Alexandria would have been hopeless. But so it was also in Palestine. And, on the other hand, a revolt did indeed take place in Egypt and Cyrenaica some time later, owing to the fact that some fiercely nationalistic Zealots who had fled from Palestine succeeded in stirring up the local Jewry against the godless. This was by no means a natural reaction of the Diaspora Jews who, generally speaking, seem to have been rather lukewarm regarding too precise messianic hopes and very reluctant to hasten by violent means the coming of the Kingdom.

Moreover, the Diaspora, however suspicious about every aspect of Graeco-Roman life and culture, could not avoid its influence altogether. To the rank and file, this did not go very far beyond using the language, whether Greek or Latin, commonly spoken in their environment, and perhaps adopting those uses and habits which, from a religious point of view, appeared harmless. We know from archaeological finds, in Rome and elsewhere, that even some themes of pagan art, mainly but not exclusively funereal, found access into Jewish communities. It has even been maintained that this iconography, far from being purely decorative, is to be interpreted symbolically, which would mean that the pagan influence on those Jews who used these monuments was not merely formal, but affected very deeply their religious outlook. This poses a difficult problem, which I can only mention here without discussing it at length, that of the possible influence on Judaism of pagan thought, and on Diaspora Judaism as a whole of Judaeo-Alexandrian thought, as exemplified chiefly by Philo.

There is indeed no doubt that the writings of Philo, a contemporary of Jesus, represent a deliberate and systematic attempt to reconcile and combine Biblical revelation and pagan philosophy. We shall come back to it later on. Let it suffice here to note that there existed, at least in Alexandria, a Jewish intelligentsia which was very eager to make the largest possible use, primarily for apologetical and missionary purposes, but also because this met their own intellectual demands, of Greek cultural tradition at its best. In the hearts and minds of these people there was certainly no room for either hatred or contempt towards their pagan fellow-citizens. The relationship Bible versus philosophy was interpreted not in terms of radical opposition, but as providing two different but complementary ways of approaching the truth. It was none the less taken for granted that the divinely inspired Scripture provided the more perfect way and that the Greek philosophers were, consciously or not, dependent on it. This means that Philo and his Judaeo-Alexandrian forerunners were fully aware of the privilege imparted to Israel. In this respect as well as by their careful observance of the Law they remained Jews to the core. They had no intention to debase Judaism by putting it on the same level as Greek philosophy, but were anxious to make it understandable and acceptable to those, whether Jews or heathen, who had been educated according to the methods of Greek *paideia*. The same tendency appears already in the

Greek translation of the Bible, the Septuagint, which had become the official Bible of Alexandrian Judaism. It obviously aims at attenuating those features of Biblical thought and language which were repugnant to the mind of a cultured Greek. It is intended both for the internal use of the Greek speaking congregations and for circulation *in partibus infidelium*. The Alexandrian interpretation of Judaism, founded on the Septuagint, favoured a universalist outlook and would normally imply religious propaganda ; the Jewish religion was intended not only for Israel, but for the whole of mankind.

In fact, some quarters of the Diaspora developed a very active and often successful missionary effort. A good number of Gentiles either joined the Synagogue and, having accepted the whole Law, and in particular circumcision, were recognized as full-fledged Jews. Probably a larger proportion stopped half-way and, without accepting the full Jewish status, became what we usually call semi-proselytes or God fearing people (*metuentes*). They gave up the worship of idols, practised the moral Law written down in the Decalogue and observed that minimum of ritual Law known as the Noachic commandments (Gen. 9[4]) which is, after all likeness, to be recognized in the so-called Apostolic Decree (Acts 15), codified by the Jerusalem Church for non-Jewish converts to Christianity. Jewish proselytism in its various forms undoubtedly prepared the way for the early Christian mission, because it had already made the teaching of the Old Testament and the idea of monotheism familiar to pagan minds.

This was not, however, the concern of the Diaspora only. Judging from the Gospels and a number of Rabbinic texts, there existed also in some Palestinian circles a feeling or conviction that Judaism, though primarily the religion of Israel, was intended also, in God's own design, to become " a light to lighten the Gentiles." Many Roman soldiers, tradesmen or civil servants, settled in Palestine, who felt attracted by the teaching and practices of Judaism, far from being spurned by the Jews, were given a hearty welcome among God's chosen people. In fact, Judaism was far from unanimous on this issue. It displayed that same opposition of two conflicting tendencies which seems to have existed in the early Jewish-Christian Church and which expresses itself in the Gospel in the contradictory injunctions on the one hand to preach the message to every creature, and on the other to bring it only to the lost sheep of the house of Israel.

(i) FUNDAMENTAL BELIEFS

This is but one point among many on which the Jews disagreed among themselves. Judaism was by no means a monochrome religion. The picture is, on the contrary, complex and many-shaded. Even in Palestine there existed a considerable variety of beliefs and opinions, in matters which would appear to us fundamental. Not only were there, as in every religion, important differences of approach and outlook, in religious matters, between the cultured *élite* and the masses, between the Doctors of the Law and the so-called *'ammê-hā-'āreṣ*, the people of the land; but even among those who had received a thorough religious education there existed deep divergencies and oppositions. It must be strongly emphasized that Judaism never had, and still lacks, an elaborate system of doctrine, to which it would be every Jew's duty to subscribe. There is nothing here to be compared with the various Christian catechisms or Confessions or even with the Nicene Creed. For Judaism is not primarily a set of doctrines. It is a way of life, or, as scholars usually put it, an orthopraxy rather than an orthodoxy.

The essentials of Jewish belief and theology are to be found in the Old Testament, which is anything but a systematic exposition of the faith. God does not appear in the Bible as a subject of theological or philosophical speculation. He is God in action, in the universe and in human history, especially the history of Israel. There is no need to prove His existence: He is there. Those Jews—and there were certainly a good number of them—who felt inclined to speculate and demonstrate, could not be content to read their Bible, where many questions remained without an answer, or were completely ignored. They had to go beyond the written text and to make it more explicit, with the help of other means than the text itself. They had to turn to the Gentiles and more or less willingly and consciously to listen to what foreign teachers, Greek, Egyptian or Persian, had to say on such topics as the problem of evil, the relationship between God and the material universe, human destiny, the hereafter. They could thus be led to take up into their teaching elements which did not belong to the inspired Scripture. But then there was no unanimously admitted authority able to put its seal upon these accretions, and to impose them upon all the faithful. Consequently, all this remained a matter of personal choice, and gradually led to the constitution of what is usually described as the Jewish sects, which will be briefly analysed later on. It is very important, when we speak of Jewish beliefs and even practices, clearly to distinguish between the essentials, without which there is no Judaism, and those optional beliefs and observances which gradually enlarged this primitive nucleus and, though they eventually became an integral part of the teaching of some group or other, never were accepted, during the period we have to consider, as really binding by the whole company of those who professed to be Jews.

The fundamental belief—and in this case at least one could almost speak of a dogma—is the belief in the existence and oneness of God. By the time of Jesus no traces were left of the Canaanite cults which, during the first centuries after the settlement in Palestine, had made it somewhat difficult for Yahweh to impose His exclusive and all-embracing sovereignty and had, sometimes, led the Israelites either to forget their own God and to worship idols, or to indulge in some sort of syncretism. All these deviations had gradually disappeared, with the possible exception of some small marginal sects. The strong centralization of Israelite worship in Jerusalem in a unique sanctuary and its very strict codification had eradicated them. To the outsider, to be a Jew was essentially to profess monotheism. The solemn declaration of Deut. 6^4, the so-called *sh^ema'*, which every practising Jew still utters in his daily prayers and which represents, as it were, the creed of the Synagogue, was, in all likelihood, already part of the Jewish liturgy: "Hear, O Israel, the Lord our God, is the Only Lord." It is quoted by Jesus as constituting the essentials of true religion (Mark 12^{29}).

This God, though being transcendent, can none the less be apprehended. Being the creator of the universe, He has revealed Himself in His works: "The heavens declare the glory of God" (Ps. 19^1). The Letter of Aristeas, a document of Alexandrian Judaism, puts it as follows: "In the first place, Moses taught that God is One, and that His power is made manifest through all things, every place being filled with His sovereignty." He is personal and almighty. These attributes are emphasized on every page of the Old Testament. It has sometimes described them in terms of a rather crude anthropomorphism, which the Judaeo-Alexandrian thinkers as well as the Palestinian doctors were eager to rule out or to explain away. God is also a terrible and jealous God, who "visits the sins of the fathers upon the children unto the third and fourth generation of them that hate Him." He is therefore to be feared: "The fear of the Lord is the beginning of wisdom." His name, Yahweh, is not to be pronounced. Whenever it occurs in the Bible, "Adonai," "our Lord," is to be read instead. But God is at the same time a God of mercy and love, who wants and deserves to be loved: "Thou shalt love the Lord thy God with all thy heart and with all thy soul and with all thy might." The love of God goes along with the mutual love of men: "Thou shalt love thy neighbour as thyself" (Deut. 6^5, Lev. 19^{18}). What the Jews understood by neighbour is not always absolutely clear. Some would probably restrict the extension of the word to those who shared their faith, to the children of Israel and the proselytes. But as the universalist ideal became more and more firmly rooted in some quarters of Palestinian Judaism as well as in the Dispersion, an increasing number of Jews would consider every man as their neighbour. Philanthropy went hand in hand with proselytism : " Love the creatures and bring them to the Law " is the commandment given by Rabbi Hillel to his disciples.

This did not, however, alter the conviction that Israel stood in a privileged relationship to God. It had been chosen, by a free act of divine will, as God's own people. The Creator of the universe, Lord of all mankind, was also, in a very special way, God of the Fathers. The election of Israel can be considered as the second dogma of the Jewish creed. It needs no demonstration, but is made evident on every page of Holy Scripture. This election is materialized, as it were, in the Covenant concluded between God and Israel on Mt. Sinai, and written down in the prescriptions of Mosaic Law. To be a Jew is not only to believe in one God (some sort of monotheism appears also, by that time, among the enlightened heathen). It is also, and even more, to keep God's commandments. Judaism—I have already emphasized it—is orthopraxy as well as, and even more than, orthodoxy.

(ii) WORSHIP : THE TEMPLE AND PRIESTHOOD*

Orthopraxy is the service of God, as He Himself has ordered it, in public as well as in private life. The rites of the Israelite-Jewish cult were codified in detail by the Law. They culminated in the very elaborate functions of the Jerusalem Temple, which was the only officially recognized place of worship. It had taken the place, when Israel settled in Palestine, of the mobile Tabernacle of the desert. Its unicity expressed that of God Himself. Only in this sanctuary was it legitimate to offer sacrifices. This rule suffered no exception by the time of Jesus. Of course, the Samaritans had their own place of worship and sacrifices, on Mt. Gerizim. But though being a schismatic branch of Judaism, they were not considered as Jews by the Jews themselves, who abhorred them, all the more as they did not accept the Jewish Canon of the Bible : they considered as Holy Scripture only the Pentateuch. The schismatic temple of Onias at Leontopolis in Egypt, built at the beginning of the second century B.C., closed by the Romans in A.D. 73, after the first Palestinian war, and of which we know very little, was intended by its

* See also below, pp. 523 ff.

founder to meet the religious needs of the Jews who lived in this part of the world. The enterprise was not very successful. Not only was the new sanctuary looked at askance by the Palestinian Jews, and never recognized by them as a legitimate place of worship, but even the Alexandrian Jews were hardly attracted by it. Philo does not mention it, and makes it clear that only the Jerusalem sanctuary, which he describes as the Temple of his fathers, deserved consideration and respect. It was, in fact, the centre of Jewish national as well as religious life.

The first Temple, built by Solomon, was destroyed by the Babylonian army after the fall of Jerusalem in 586 B.C. The rebuilding was completed on the same site, after the Exile, at the end of the sixth century B.C. This second Temple was given its final shape by Herod the Great, who spent an enormous amount of money in renovating and enlarging the sacred buildings. His piety was rather dubious, but he wanted to increase his popularity among his subjects, who never forgot that he was an Idumaean, an alien, and a very tyrannic ruler at that. The sanctuary rose in the middle of the holy city and every Jew, when he looked at, or thought of, it felt proud of this unique and, so we are told, wonderful piece of architecture.

If we trust Josephus, about twenty thousand people were involved, somehow or other, in the service of the Temple. In fact, the total number was much larger still, for the whole population of Palestine was divided into twenty-four classes, which had to take part, each in its turn, in the daily services. Of course, not all of them did it actually. But it seems that a delegation, including men from Jerusalem as well as from the immediate neighbourhood, went up to the Temple every day. Their presence signified that here was really the sanctuary of the whole Jewish nation. The link between Temple and people was materialized also by the cult tax, the so-called didrachmon which every Jew had to pay and which was collected in all the Jewish congregations throughout the world. As far as the Palestinians were concerned they were expected to provide also the necessary stuff, whether animals or products of the field, for the public sacrifices and oblations. And the pious Jew was always prepared to offer, for his own sake and at his own expense, a private sacrifice of petition, atonement, or thanksgiving.

But however important the part played by the laity, the organization of the Temple was fundamentally clerical. The priesthood constituted a caste, recruited among those Jews who could prove that they were of the lineage of Aaron. Although the Levites, members of the tribe of Levi, did not partake of the priestly dignity, they none the less assumed important functions in public worship, particularly as regards instrumental music and psalm singing. The supreme office was that of the High Priest, who was the recognized religious leader of Judaism and possibly also, in the eyes of a number of Jews, the revered head of the nation. In a past which was not very remote, a family of priests, that of the Hasmonaeans, had become the last of the native dynasties to reign over an independent Israel. But since the Roman intervention in and occupation of Palestine, the high priesthood was no longer hereditary. It was conferred first by Herod then by the procurators upon men whom they felt they could trust, and usually for a short time. It thus appeared as a pale shadow of its own previous splendour. The High Priest none the less enjoyed considerable prestige. To him alone it was permitted, once a year, on the Day of Atonement, to enter the most sacred part of the sanctuary, the Holy of Holies, and there to intercede, before the invisible divine Presence, for the sins of the people. When he presented himself, on the high festivals, in the splendour of his pontifical vestments, before the crowd of the faithful gathered in the precincts of the Temple and gave them his blessing, he might indeed appear as a reflection of God's own majesty. He was, moreover, *ex officio*, the president of the Supreme Court of Justice, the Great Sanhedrin, which was competent in all cases in which religious questions were involved. As the Law of Moses was *the* law to every Jew, there were indeed very few cases which did not fall under the jurisdiction of the Sanhedrin. Whether or not it still had the power, under Roman occupation, to inflict capital punishment has been for a long time a vexed question. It is now generally admitted that it had.

If we trust our sources, the Sanhedrin had 70 or 71 members. How they were chosen we do not know. The majority belonged to the priestly families, representing the Jewish aristocracy. But Josephus as well as the New Testament mention also, in relation with the Sanhedrin, Scribes, Elders, and Doctors of the Law. This is very important, because it shows in what direction Judaism was evolving. In the light of its subsequent developments, we are entitled to say that, whereas the High Priest and the priestly aristocracy represented the past, the other, obviously still subordinate, elements represented the future. In this respect, the composition of the Sanhedrin faithfully reflects the situation of Judaism as a whole during the Roman period.

(iii) WORSHIP: THE SYNAGOGUE

The strong centralization of the cult, initiated by Solomon and achieved after the Exile, was intended to eradicate every possible deviation from monotheism. It could meet the religious needs of a small population, concentrated on a small territory. Even thus, it was not very easy for those living in the more remote parts of the country, in Galilee for instance, frequently to attend the services of the Temple. Thus, under the pressure of circumstances, the religious life of the Jews was gradually reshaped and became, so to speak, bifocal. Side by side with the cult of the Temple another type of worship appeared and spread out wherever there was a Jewish congregation: that of the Synagogue.

As far as we can see, two main factors account for its development. First, it was necessary to give those Jews who lived outside Jerusalem an opportunity of worshipping together and to provide them with a place adapted to this purpose. There could be no question, for reasons both religious and financial, of building new Temples, in the precise meaning of the word. The offering of sacrifices in any place but Jerusalem was explicitly forbidden. And probably no single congregation, however large and wealthy, could afford to build anything resembling, even on a much smaller scale, the Jerusalem sanctuary. Second, Judaism was essentially the religion of the Book, in which God had revealed Himself and His will. The prescriptions and commandments of divine Law applied to the individual as well as to the nation as a whole. Now, observance of the Law implied, of necessity, knowledge and understanding of the Law, of its precise meaning and various implications. It needed interpretation of the text. But not every Jew was able by himself to achieve this task. The humble, less cultured and sometimes illiterate needed the help of some expert who would explain to them the divine ordinances and lead them along this way of life. Originally it was for the priests to do this job. Theoretically they still did it until the destruction of Jerusalem. But in fact, they seem to have been so much involved in their ritual duties and so exclusively concerned with those parts of the Law which were related to the cult, in some cases perhaps also so mundane, that they gradually ceased to be the spiritual leaders of the people. Moreover, the existence and growth of the Diaspora made it impossible for them to play this part *vis-à-vis* all the Jews. They could do it only through ordinances of a general character, concerning for instance the calendar, which were sent out throughout the Diaspora. But even in the Sanhedrin, either acting as supreme religious court of justice for the whole Jewish world or dealing with the individual problems of some Jerusalemite Jew, the priesthood lost more and more of its influence. The Scribes and Doctors of the Law, being present not only in Jerusalem but also in every Jewish congregation, gradually came to constitute the very backbone of Judaism. The synagogal type of worship is intimately related to the growing importance of the Scribes—those who could write and also interpret the sacred text—and of the doctors or rabbis.

The Greek word *synagōgē*, exactly like the word *ekklēsia* in the ancient Christian use, applies to both the place of worship and the congregation which meets there. The first synagogues probably date from the Exile. At any rate, the roots of the institution are to be found in the Diaspora. But by the time of Jesus every Palestinian village had its synagogue too. And we know that a large number of them existed in Jerusalem itself. This clearly indicates that the Synagogue was first intended to be a complement or an *Ersatz* to the Temple, rather than a rival institution. Synagogues could probably not have been created in the Holy City without the assent of the priesthood. But as the latent tension between priests and doctors gradually developed, as we shall see, into open hostility between two religious parties, the mutual relationship of Temple and Synagogue tended to evolve from co-operation to opposition. It is certainly excessive to consider "*Kultfrömmigkeit*" and "*Frömmigkeit des Gesetzes*" as more or less exclusive of one another, for, after all, the Temple cult was also part of the Law. The Jews of the time could hardly feel the opposition as strongly as a modern Liberal Protestant scholar like Bousset, to whom sacrificial worship appears as utterly repulsive. Perhaps the majority were not at all conscious of any opposition. There is none the less something in this view. And the historian must indeed notice that the destruction of the Temple in A.D. 70, though resented by the Jews as a national and religious catastrophe, did not alter fundamentally the conditions under which they practised their religion, precisely because the synagogal system was there already, omnipresent, and could assume the role until then played by the Temple. To the vast majority of the Jews, living far from Jerusalem, the Temple never had been much more than a symbol. It is the synagogal system which ensured the survival of Judaism until today.

The originality of a synagogue consists in the fact that it is both a place of worship and a place of learning. In Yiddish speaking congregations it is still commonly called the school. Study of the Law was to the faithful Jew a fundamental duty. Consequently, the synagogal worship combined prayers to God, reading of Holy Scripture and commenting on it. This type of religious service compares in a certain measure with the Protestant type, with its strong emphasis on the ministry of the word, while the stately and very elaborate services of the Temple, performed by the priesthood, might be compared, *mutatis mutandis,* to the solemnity of a Catholic Pontifical High Mass, with its emphasis on the idea of a sacrifice. Of course, the comparison must not be pressed too far. The Free Church type of service makes a large use of extempore prayers. Though these were certainly not unknown among the Jews, we have good reasons to believe that the present synagogal pattern of a fixed liturgy can be traced back to an early date and gradually prevailed everywhere, however with a number of local variations, strong enough always to prevent absolute uniformity.

The Synagogue has no institutional clergy. As the service is focused on reading and interpretation of Holy Scripture, the central part is played by those who have been trained for this purpose, Scribes, Doctors, or Rabbis (the word Rabbi means "teacher" or "master"). As they have a thorough knowledge of the Law and the other canonical books, they are able to explain them to their brethren. Some sort of ordination qualified the professional rabbi, but it seems to have been of an academic as well as of a religious nature, combining, as it were, the conferment of a degree and the laying on of hands. In fact, interpreting the Bible to the congregation was no exclusive privilege of the rabbis. Whosoever, resident member or visitor, thought he had something to say was entitled to do so. We have a striking illustration of this use in the Gospels, where we see Jesus, who was not a rabbi in the technical meaning of the term, being admitted to speak in the synagogues and explaining passages of the Bible.

In the synagogues of the Diaspora, services were usually conducted in Greek. But our information here is very scanty. As regards Palestine, where the Aramaic vernacular combined with the Scriptural Hebrew, we have to rely mostly, and almost exclusively, on later sources, Mishnah and Talmud. But it can be assumed that no fundamental change took place between the period under consideration and the Talmudic period. Such elements of synagogal worship as the *shᵉmaʿ*, the *shᵉmōneh ʿeśrēh* or Eighteen Benedictions (also called *Tᵉphillāh,* the prayer *par excellence*)—these perhaps not exactly in their present shape—and the singing of psalms were already in use. Services were held not only on the great festivals, New Year, Day of Atonement, Passover, Pentecost, and the like, but every week on the sabbath, whose strict observance, excluding every kind of work or profane activity, was one of the most striking features of Jewish religious life. The sabbath, being the day of the Lord, who hallowed it by His own rest, at the end of creation, was set apart for His praise and service. It was spent in meditation of the Law and in prayer, for which the whole congregation assembled. But in addition meetings took place, in a number of synagogues, on all other days of the week, the only condition being that a minimum of ten male people—the so-called *minyān*—could be gathered together. And the building probably remained open, in many places, most of the time, for private prayer and meditation.

Thus the life of the synagogue, with its observance of the official calendar and its daily services, tended to shape itself exactly on the life of the Temple, despite the completely different emphasis. Even as the Temple was the centre of religious life to the whole people of Israel and in particular to those living in Jerusalem, so was the synagogue to the local congregation. But people would normally go to the synagogue even for more secular purposes, to meet friends, to discuss everyday problems, or to ask for the arbitration of the local teacher in some dispute between two neighbours, all the more as there was no clear-cut division, in the Jewish perspective, between what was religious and what was mundane. Religion was present at every moment, almost in every gesture, and made the synagogue play a role not unlike that of the forum in Roman cities, as the very heart of the community in all its various activities.

Interpreting the Law was not limited to the moments of public worship. It was to every pious Jew a permanent duty. It is at least likely that, already in the time of Jesus, provisions were made for the religious education of the young, at least in the larger cities of Palestine and of the Diaspora. The local rabbis and their staff of learned men were probably by that time, as during the Talmudic period, schoolmasters to the children as well as religious leaders to the grown up. Philo repeatedly emphasizes the capital importance of education, by which he means essentially religious education, among his co-religionists. The Bible was the book in which all young Jews, at least all boys, learned to read. Differences in education tended to be more important than social differences. Those who had attended a synagogal school regularly were fully aware of their representing the true aristocracy, over against the uncultured *'ammê-hā-'āreṣ*. To be able to read the sacred text and to know the usual prayers by heart was the touchstone of elementary education. Women and girls, though being in a definitely subordinate situation, and even the slaves, were expected to know at least the *Tᵉphillāh* and Grace. As they did not attend school, it was for the father to teach them.

Indeed, the family was, in every respect, the fundamental religious institution. There the daily prayers were said, the high festivals as well as the sabbath were celebrated with great fervour ; circumcision, weddings, funeral rites constituted the landmarks in the life of the family as well as of the individual. Meals were religious functions, with their own ritual and liturgy, where the father was officiating. He was invested with a sort of priesthood, as revered and effective, in his own sphere, as that of the rabbis at the synagogue level. All through the day, even the most humble acts were hallowed by appropriate words of prayer or thanksgiving. Wherever there was a Jewish congregation or family, one would expect this synagogal and domestic liturgy to be celebrated. It represented, along with the common basic beliefs, the very foundations of Judaism, and the immediately perceptible sign of its unity.

(iv) JEWISH SECTS: SADDUCEES, PHARISEES, ZEALOTS

Unity is not, however, to be identified with uniformity. Even as regards worship, and quite apart from the fundamental distinction between Temple and Synagogue, there existed probably more or less important differences from one country or city to another. In matters of belief they were still more striking. Not only was the Jewish faith extensible, so to speak: new articles could be and indeed were added, in some quarters, to the very plain creed accepted by all. There also appeared some strong discrepancies and even oppositions about doctrines which, at least from our point of view, could hardly be considered as secondary.

Judaism must not be judged by usual Christian standards. It would probably be wrong to describe it as more tolerant than Christianity. For these *de facto* differences were by no means officially recognized as legitimate. Jewish history in the Hellenistic and Roman period shows that whenever one given religious party succeeded in mastering the situation, it was prone to persecute those who held opposite views. But it so happened that no single party was ever strong enough to enforce its own views once for all, everywhere and in an exclusive way. All had to come to terms with each other and, without attempting to find a more precise common platform than that provided by the *sh^ema^‘* and the observance of the Torah, to accept, be it unwillingly, a wide diversity of opinion. Even the Sanhedrin, which, theoretically, was entitled to arbitrate conflicts in matters of religion, was, as we shall see, a house divided against itself, and therefore unable to play the part which should have been its. In fact, there existed no unanimously recognized authority in doctrinal matters. Every rabbi enjoyed a considerable amount of freedom in his interpretation of the faith. This accounts for the existence of what are commonly called the Jewish sects.

The term sect applies, in its more usual acceptance, to Christian groups which have organized themselves independently from and in opposition to the more important denominations, and claim to know the only possible way to salvation. It generally has a more or less disparaging nuance, unless one agrees to describe as sects, in contradistinction to the Churches, numerically small groups, the difference then being only quantitative. But it is difficult in this case to draw the dividing line and to decide what figures are requested for a sect to be promoted to the rank and dignity of a Church. In fact, no Christian would probably accept the description of himself as a member of a sect. The term is generally applied to other groups than one's own. And even thus, its use and meaning vary considerably according to one's personal outlook. But, however difficult its precise definition, one feature at least is characteristic of a Christian sect : it is, from the dispassionate point of view of a historian or sociologist, a body separated not only from the Catholic Communion, but also from those denominations which represent the main traditions of Reformed Christianity.

If we turn from the Christian realities of today to early Judaism, the situation appears completely different. There were indeed groups which either had deliberately seceded from or had been excommunicated by what we may call official Judaism, that which was organized around the Temple and synagogues and accepted the authority of the Sanhedrin. The classical example is that of the already mentioned Samaritans, who were indeed completely cut off from Judaism. There certainly existed other such sects, most of them very small, mainly on the desert outskirts of Palestine, along the Jordan or beyond. What we know about them—very little indeed—comes chiefly from the writings of some Church Fathers, whose testimony is not always very reliable. But however poor our information, there can be no doubt about their reality, and some of them may have played a fairly important part in the origins and growth of ancient Christian heterodox groups, into which they were eventually absorbed.

What we are concerned with and what must be briefly described here is something very different. By Jewish sects in the usual acceptance of the word we mean the fundamental interpretations of Judaism which coexisted, more or less friendly, by the time of Jesus. They were in theory exclusive of each other. But their mutual opposition expressed itself within the limits of what may, *cum grano salis,* be called the Jewish Establishment. Indeed the most adequate term of comparison is provided not by the Christian sects, but by the various "schools of thought" of the Anglican Communion, which having agreed to disagree, still remain an integral part of their mother Church and all claim to represent its authentic tradition. Just as Anglicanism is comprehensive enough to include its schools of thought, thus did Judaism include its various "sects." We know them mainly from the Gospels, which have made us familiar with Pharisees and Sadducees, and from the Jewish historian Josephus who, in addition to these two, describes two more sects, the Essenes and the Zealots. A distinction must be made between the first two and the two others. Pharisees and Sadducees represented the fundamental aspects of Palestinian official Judaism. Essenes and Zealots were on the fringe and are more akin to a Christian sect, without, however, constituting the exact equivalent. It is to be noted in this respect that Josephus, although his sympathies are on the side of the Pharisees and Essenes and although he has very little sympathy with the Zealots and hardly more with the Sadducees, abstains from uttering excommunication against either of these two groups, which he obviously considers as branches of one and the same tree.

The name of the Sadducees is probably related to that of Zadok, who held the office of a High Priest in the time of Solomon. This etymology emphasizes the main characteristic of the Sadducees: they are closely linked up with the priesthood and the Temple. They are recruited chiefly among the priestly aristocracy, and have little influence, if any, on the mass of the people. Once the Temple had been destroyed, the sect of the Sadducees disappeared *ipso facto*. Even before A.D. 70 they seem to be on the decline. They are no longer the undiscussed leaders of the Sanhedrin, where Scribes and Doctors, most of them probably Pharisees, sit by their side. Even in their traditional stronghold, the Temple, worship, if we trust Josephus, had come to be conducted according to Pharisaic regulations. And though not all the synagogues were of one and the same persuasion, the synagogal institution itself hardly supported the Sadducean conception of religion, which was fundamentally conservative and stubbornly attached to the past. Sadducees were distrustful of new ideas and even more so of whatever had a messianic flavour or could lead to some political upheaval and consequently entail difficulties with the Roman authority. They seem to have whole-heartedly supported the Romans in ensuring public order. Their only rule of religious, moral and social life was the Law of Moses, as written down in the Bible. They took the commandments literally, and felt apparently no need to interpret and adapt them. According to some ancient Christian writers, they even refused to consider as canonical writing anything but the Pentateuch, which would mean that their position was the same in these matters as that of the Samaritans. This is rather doubtful. But it can at least be taken for granted that these well-to-do people had little understanding of the message of the Prophets, with its precise social implications.

Their position in matters of belief, too, was fundamentally conservative. It is difficult to trust Josephus when he asserts that they believed neither in the influence of Destiny—by which he probably means divine Providence—nor in the intervention of God in the world and in human history. How could any faithful Jew hold views diametrically opposed to those developed all along the pages of the Bible ? It can be assumed that Josephus, who compares the Sadducees to the Epicureans, in order to make himself better understood by his Gentile readers, has overdone the analogies and given a somewhat distorted view of the Sadducean position. He also maintains that, according to the Sadducees, the souls die with the bodies, and that the sect consequently denies " the rewards and punishments of Hades." This would imply the complete negation of an afterlife, which is not absolutely unbelievable, all the more as the Old Testament doctrine on this question is not very precise. The Sadducean view, however, is probably more faithfully expressed by the New Testament statement that they do not believe in the resurrection (Matt. 22²³, Acts 23⁸), which in fact represented a fairly recent addition to the primitive faith of Israel. We thus have here a striking example of the religious conservatism of the Sadducees. Another point of their creed is to be interpreted along the same line : " they did not believe in angels and spirits " (Acts 23⁸). By spirits the writer probably means bad spirits, devils. This again might well be an oversimplified view, since angels are indeed mentioned in the Bible, the Pentateuch included. The statement is probably to be understood as meaning that the Sadducees rejected those very elaborate speculations about angelology and demonology which had, by that time, become very popular in some quarters of Judaism and were favoured by the Pharisees.

In fact, on almost every point, the Sadducean position represents the exact opposite of that of the Pharisees, who can be described as the progressive wing of Judaism. The meaning of their name is pretty sure : the Hebrew *pᵉrûshîm* means the separated ones. This leads us back to a time when the Pharisees, still a minority group, had seceded from official Judaism, probably by way of protest against the position taken by the then leading element. It is commonly admitted that this happened in connexion with the attempt made by Antiochus Epiphanes, with the help of some Jews, drastically to hellenize Palestine and its people. The result was the Maccabean revolt, backed by those Jews who wanted to safeguard their religious traditions and to uphold the Law against the ungodly. They called themselves *Hasidim*, the pious ones. These are, almost certainly, the ancestors of the Pharisees who, in the meantime, had become a powerful party, spread their influence all over the country and succeeded in outweighing the priestly caste of the Sadducees. T. W. Manson has proposed another etymology, more attractive however than really convincing: Pharisees, he says, means those who imitate the Persians, and is a nickname by which their opponents used to call these people. This explanation is, almost certainly, not the right one. There is none the less something in it. It emphasizes one of the most characteristic features of the Pharisees, namely the fact that their faith bears the stamp of foreign influences, especially Persian, but also Greek.

This may appear somewhat contradictory. How can people who had revolted against hellenization hold beliefs taken over from the Gentile world? To this objection there are two answers. First, those who accepted these influences may not have fully realized what was at stake. There certainly was no carefully worked out plan on their part for introducing foreign conceptions into the faith of the fathers. But, as this faith provided no answer to certain questions, those who pondered over them had, of necessity, to look for a solution elsewhere. Secondly, we must make a very precise distinction between practice and belief. What the Maccabees and the Hasidim had so fiercely opposed was an acute hellenization of the original ways and manners of Israel. Since religion permeated and shaped the whole life of both society and individuals, this meant the eradication of the Law and the ruling out of any difference in behaviour between Jews and heathen. Violating the Law in matters of practice naturally included or entailed giving up the fundamental beliefs of Judaism. Antiochus Epiphanes took a very logical line when he asked those Jews who "had made themselves uncircumcised" to transform the Temple into a pagan shrine. But as long as the holy Covenant stood and was observed, making it impossible for the Jews to be mixed up with and merged into the mass of the Gentiles, the monotheist faith was in no danger, even if its primitive simplicity came to be enriched with various speculations. Indeed, uncompromising rigorism in matters of religious observance and a certain amount of openmindedness in matters of doctrine and beliefs are not necessarily contradictory attitudes. They may sometimes become complementary. At least, the first one is the necessary condition, as far as Judaism is concerned, of the second. Their combination appears inherent in Pharisaism.

The primary concern of the Pharisees was observance. According to Josephus, " they constitute an order which outweighs all other Jews by its piety and by a more careful interpretation of the Law " (*B.J.* I. v. 2 [110]). Their religious life is centred on the meditation and the practice of Torah. There exists, in this respect, a very close connexion between the Pharisees and the synagogal institution, which provides the means for this almost permanent study of God's commandments. But, as the Mosaic Law has not made and could not make provisions for every possible situation, it is for the doctors or Rabbis and their pupils to complement it and to decide, in the light of the sacred text, how to behave in each case. Casuistry is an integral part of Pharisaic teaching. The Pharisees are thus led, quite naturally, to go beyond the written text and to make the general principles which it codifies more explicit. Beside Torah, they appeal to Tradition : " They have transmitted to the people certain uses which came from the traditions of the fathers, but which are not written down in the Law of Moses " (Josephus, *Ant.* XIII. x. 6 [297]). Tradition is, in their eyes, the normal extension of Torah. It goes back, just as Torah, as far as Moses, to whom it was revealed together with the written Law, and it was subsequently handed down from generation to generation. Thus there exists an unbroken continuity between the Legislator and the Rabbis. This tradition was eventually written down, in its turn, in the Mishnah and Talmud, and became for the subsequent generations matter of exegesis, just as the Torah. But during the period under consideration, this process had not yet been initiated : the rabbinic tradition, which includes the teaching of the various Pharisaic teachers, is transmitted and discussed orally in the schools. It is being unceasingly revised, adapted and completed, and admits of a great diversity of points of view, according to the personal outlook of the Rabbis. There are those who incline, in every case, to the more rigid of several possible interpretations of one given commandment, and there are those who take a more lax view. To put it in a simple and somewhat schematic way, some would consider that whatsoever is not explicitly forbidden is *ipso facto* permissible, and others that whatsoever is not explicitly permitted is to be forbidden. Hillel is the best known representative of the milder tendency and Shammai of the more rigid one. But however different their positions and conclusions, the Pharisees are all convinced that the written text of the Law must be vivified, as it were, by careful and continuous rethinking, to make it fit in as exactly as possible with the needs of daily life. Here lies the fundamental opposition between them and the Sadducees. The idea of tradition, as they understand it, has undoubtedly been a factor of development and, up to a point, of progress, in the religious life of Israel.

This may sound paradoxical to one who has become acquainted with the Pharisees through the picture drawn of them by the Gospels. Here they are indeed described as mere hypocrites, as people who waste their time in futile and sometimes grotesque discussions and distinctions, and enforce on the Jews the burden of innumerable observances, going far beyond what is actually required by divine commandment. They keep the letter without grasping the spirit. They seem utterly unable to distinguish between what is essential and what is of minor importance, and in particular between the commandments of the moral Law, which admit of no exception or compromise, and the ritual ordinances. There is of course a certain amount of truth in this, and the New Testament view of Pharisaism cannot be dismissed as a mere caricature. The Pharisaic method of discussion implied a perpetual risk of running into sheer formalism and of becoming an end in itself instead of providing the instrument for a more perfect understanding and observance of the Law. And some Pharisees may well have nourished undisguised contempt towards the ignorant and sinful, as exemplified by the Publican in the Gospel Parable.

But if we attempt to draw from all our sources and to take as complete and balanced a view as possible, we shall come to the conclusion that the early Christian picture of the Pharisees is at least onesided. It reflects the acute controversy which opposed the primitive Church, mainly after Paul's appearance on the stage, and the Pharisaic rabbis, who were the leaders of Jewish resistance against Christianity. It retains only those features of Pharisaism which Jesus Himself denounced, which are repugnant to the Christian ideal and indeed difficult to accept to anyone who is not a Pharisee or a Jew himself. It ignores the positive elements which an unbiased enquiry will be able to detect.

The casuistry of the Pharisees was intimately related to everyday life. Since they considered the Law as a whole, it was just impossible for them to make any difference between the moral and the ritual commandments which, all alike, expressed the will of God. We certainly must not judge them by Christian standards. If we are inclined to deny Pharisaism any positive value, then we must do so with Judaism at large, for ever since A.D. 70 Judaism and Pharisaism are one and the same thing. If these originally self-segregated few have succeeded in shaping after their own pattern the religious life of a whole people and in thus ensuring the survival of Judaism for centuries, there must be very definite spiritual values in what they had to offer. We ought not to forget that the dry juridical formulations of the Talmud spring from the same source as the Synagogal liturgy, which breathes deep and intense piety, beautifully expressed.

Already at the beginning of our era, the Pharisees were the religious leaders of their nation. In spite of some sectarian features, they certainly were well prepared to assume this task because, being laymen and not members of a priestly caste and belonging, moreover, from a social point of view, to what could be described as a sort of middle class, they were in much closer contact with the mass than the haughty aristocracy of the Sadducees. Their influence has been diffused through the synagogues all over Palestine. The Diaspora, too, seems to a large extent to live according to Pharisaic rules and patterns.

The Pharisaic ideal is adequately expressed by a saying in the rabbinic treatise *Pirke Aboth* : " Build ye a fence around the Torah." This fence is made of the multiplicity of commandments which spring from interpretation of the written Law. This multiplicity was by no means felt as an intolerable yoke. It was both sign and source of divine blessing. The fence was intended, to begin with, as a wall of separation from the impure *gôyîm* and the secularly minded Jews. As the Pharisaic way of life became more and more commonly accepted in Israel, the fence tended to include the whole nation. And in some quarters of rabbinic opinion, even the heathen were considered as being called by divine election. They, too, could be invited to join God's people on the inner side of the fence. It was the Pharisees who initiated proselytism among the Gentiles, as is made clear, *e.g.* by Matt. 23^{15}. We have every reason to believe that the Pharisaic message attracted a number of truth-seeking Gentiles, and that proselytism remained active and successful even after the national catastrophies of A.D. 70 and 135.

In matters of belief as well as of observance, the Pharisees felt they could go beyond the written text. They are not philosophers and metaphysicians, as Josephus, who assimilates them to the Stoics, would have us believe. Perhaps the only point the two sects had in common was an equally predominant concern for conduct. But the motivations were, of course, totally different. The basic beliefs of the Pharisees are all more or less connected with this practical outlook. They seem, for instance, to have attempted a synthesis between the idea of universal divine Providence and that of human free will. What Josephus says on this point is confirmed by a sentence which the *Pirke Aboth* attribute to Rabbi Akiba : " All is foreseen, but freedom is granted to man." They also had developed views concerning the hereafter for which the

Bible provided little or no support. According to Josephus, they believe in the immortality of the soul and in *post mortem* rewards and punishments. Only the souls of the righteous pass into another body, while those of the wicked are punished by everlasting torments. At first sight, this could be taken as meaning that, as regards the righteous, the Pharisees taught metempsychosis. But this is certainly not the case. What Josephus means by another body is the resurrection body. Consequently, resurrection is a privilege granted to the righteous only. In fact we know, from rabbinic sources, that there was no unanimity on this point among the doctors. By the time of Josephus, only a minority taught the final resurrection of all men, as a prelude to the great assizes of the Last Judgment. Anyhow, whether particular or general, the resurrection was one of the fundamental tenets of Pharisaic belief. This is repeatedly emphasized in the New Testament as being a bone of contention between the two major Jewish sects (Acts 23[8]), in the same way as the existence of good and evil spirits. Speculations about angelology were indeed very common among the Pharisees. They were more and more widely accepted and eventually became common stock of Judaism as a whole, a fact which illustrates the all-pervading influence of Pharisaism. We shall therefore come back to this point later on. Belief in the resurrection and angelology both bear the stamp of foreign speculations, mainly Iranian.

Josephus, who is himself, being pro-Roman, little interested in the subject, does not speak of the messianic beliefs of the Pharisees. We have good reasons to think that they looked forward to the coming of the Messiah and the inauguration of the Kingdom. But most of them considered that this would be achieved in God's good time, and the only way in which they could hasten these eagerly expected events was to pray fervently, to practise the Law as best they could and to encourage their fellow-Jews to imitate them. For the Kingdom would be, to a large extent, the fruit of the merits accumulated by Israel through the centuries.

On this point they were in complete disagreement with another of the sects mentioned by Josephus, namely the Zealots. For them he has no sympathy whatever. Moreover, what he says of them is somewhat contradictory. He maintains, on the one hand, that they have absolutely nothing in common with the rest of the Jews, and on the other that they agree on every point with the Pharisees. This means probably that, while they were as strictly legalistic as the Pharisees, they differed from them and from all other sections of Jewish opinion by their violent nationalism. Josephus traces their origin back to Judah the Galilean who in A.D. 6–7, when

Judaea was organized as a province, revolted against the Romans and was rapidly defeated. He describes the Zealots as another philosophical school, and Judah as a very clever sophist. It is doubtful that these are the adequate terms. We have probably here just another example, and a particularly striking one, of Josephus' tendency to hellenize even the most unhellenistic aspects of Jewish life. The Zealots, he says, have a passionate love of freedom, do not recognize any other lord than God, and are always ready to face torture and even death rather than accept any human authority. They thus appear as religious anarchists or, better still, since human authority in Palestine is, by that time, foreign authority, uncompromising nationalists. They represent a typically Jewish attitude, in so far as the religious and the national element are intimately bound together and even confounded in their ideology and behaviour. Their political and religious ideal is that effective theocracy for which every Jew is then longing. But they consider it their duty to take an active part in its carrying out. Latent hostility towards the Gentile rulers of the land was present in many sections of Jewish opinion. With the Zealots it turns into open hatred. The zeal after which they are called expresses itself in terrorist action. They are also known as *sicarii*, those who make use of a dagger. Some of them are accustomed to organize ambushes against the Romans and also against those Jews who are too prone to compromise with them. They are to a large extent responsible for fostering in Palestine that atmosphere of chronic agitation which eventually led to the great revolt of A.D. 66 and the final catastrophe of A.D. 70. Social and economic factors most probably contributed in bringing about the Zealot movement, which seems to have drawn its followers mainly from the more miserable rural proletariate of Roman Palestine. That they were both patriots and religiously minded people can hardly be doubted, and it is quite possible that Josephus has drawn too gloomy a picture of a sect which, being fundamentally anti-Roman, was in complete opposition to his own views. But on the other hand, it is certainly excessive to describe the Zealot movement, as a recent book has done, as the noblest expression of Israelite patriotism and the authentic lineage of the Maccabees. For the Romans, however unsympathetic and contemptuous, never made themselves guilty of such an aggressive policy of paganizing as that of Antiochus Epiphanes, which called forth the Maccabaean revolt. Judaism under the Romans enjoyed an official status of *religio licita*. To the Zealots, the very presence of the Gentiles, even without any sign of intolerance, was a sufficient reason for revolting. Their revolt was, of course, religiously motivated. But with them, religion was inseparable from fanaticism.

(v) THE ESSENES

The Essenes represent, as far as we can see, the most original interpretation of Judaism. At first sight they have hardly anything in common with the three sects just described. They seem to live completely outside the compass of official Judaism. Their headquarters is not located in Jerusalem, but near the Dead Sea, in the wilderness. Their organization and community life very closely resemble those of a religious order. They have deliberately segregated, like the Pharisees at the beginning of the movement, from the mass of the Jews, whom they consider as almost as impure as the Gentiles. Unlike the Pharisees, they remain in this position until their final disappearance, and consider themselves as the only true Israel, the small flock of the elect. Their teaching is esoteric. Here we have, it would seem, a sect in the most precise and modern meaning of the word. And still Josephus, who speaks of them in a highly appreciative way, obviously considers them as genuine representatives of Judaism, as authentic as the Pharisees and Sadducees, and certainly more so than the Zealots. This strikingly illustrates the suppleness and fluidity of Judaism, and the absence of any clear-cut dividing line between orthodoxy and heterodoxy.

Moreover, a more thorough enquiry into their peculiarities reveals some precise connexions with all the three other sects. They have in common with the Pharisees a hyper-legalistic conception of religion, a fundamental concern for ritual cleanness, for the minutiae of observance, for an unceasing study of the Law: Essenism has sometimes been described as the superlative of Pharisaism. But on the other hand, their whole organization displays a very definite priestly character. It is based on the conviction that they alone represent the authentic priesthood. While this claim is obviously directed against the Jerusalem priestly caste and the Sadducees, the very idea that priesthood is fundamental none the less establishes a link between the two sects: the conclusions are radically divergent, but the premiss is the same. Josephus describes them as pacifists and conscientious objectors, who unreservedly condemn the use and even the making of weapons. Essenes and Zealots would thus appear to be poles apart. But Josephus' assertions on this point can perhaps be questioned. It is not established beyond doubt that all the Essenes have always remained unswervingly faithful to this ideal of non-violence. There might have existed at certain moments contacts and alliances between them and the Zealots. More generally speaking, the testimony of Josephus has to be critically reconsidered in the light of a recent discovery, that of the Dead Sea Scrolls.

There is no room here to enter into a complete discussion of this fascinating subject. It has raised storms among the scholars, and the bibliography of the question is enormous. I must limit myself to a rapid survey, leaving it to the reader to look for further information in more specialized publications. We are concerned here neither with the circumstances of the discovery, nor with the precise description of the Scrolls, or the detailed history of the Dead Sea community. What interests us is to know who this people were, what they believed and how they lived, what place they held within first-century Judaism. Let it be noted that the initial, rather disquieting, divergencies between the scholars have been gradually reduced and that an increasing measure of agreement is being achieved on a number of points. That the Dead Sea community is in some way related to the Essenes is hardly to be questioned. The vast majority of scholars today accept either complete identity or very close affinity. What Pliny says of the geographical location of the Essenes, on the West shore of the Dead Sea, at some distance to the North from the city of Engedi is so well adapted to the site of Qumran, where the Scrolls have been found and important remains of "conventual" buildings dug out, that identity seems to me by far the more plausible of the two hypotheses (this is only one among a number of arguments). And the divergences, in some cases important, which exist between the picture drawn by Josephus and that which we get from the Scrolls can be explained by assuming either that Josephus' account is not absolutely accurate or that there existed various branches within the Essene sect, or again that Essenism has undergone notable changes as years passed away.

Neither the etymology of the name Essenes nor the origins of the sect are absolutely clear. It is, however, commonly admitted that the beginnings of Essenism are closely related to the Maccabaean revolt. The Hasidim of that time might well be the ancestors of both Pharisees and Essenes. The Dead Sea Scrolls use the title "sons of Zadok," amongst others, to describe the Qumran sect. This name comes very close to that of the Sadducees, which means that both sects probably considered themselves as the authentic lineage of the high priest Zadok. The first nucleus of what was to become the Essene sect was perhaps constituted of members of the old priestly families who had sided with the Maccabees at the time of the insurrection, but went into the opposition once these had made the high priesthood hereditary in their own family and later on associated it with the royal function. The Hasmonaean dynasty alternatively favoured the Sadducees and the Pharisees. While these gradually gained ground even in official quarters, the Essenes seem to have been in a rather uncomfortable position for some time. There are allusions, in some of the Qumran texts, to persecutions suffered by the sect and especially by the revered, and to us mysterious, figure of the "Teacher of Righteousness," whom it is very difficult to date and probably impossible to identify. The group remained more or less on the fringe of Judaism until its final disappearance. Archaeological evidence has made it clear that the Qumran monastery was destroyed during the Jewish war of A.D. 66–70. It is not impossible that some at least of the Essenes took an active part in the national insurrection. Their settling on the inhospitable shores of the Dead Sea certainly expresses their opposition to the Jerusalem hierarchy and their ideal of a secluded ascetic life. It might also reflect a concern about their own safety, as against possible outbursts of intolerance. But by the time of Jesus they apparently enjoyed a fair amount of popularity, not only among cultured people like Josephus, but also, judging from the influence they seem to have exerted on large sections of Judaism, among the rank and file. They were not all concentrated on one single spot. Small Essene colonies seem to have existed in various Palestinian towns or villages. Whether these lived exactly after the same rule as in Qumran, or represented a milder brand, remains an open question. This is one of the points on which our various sources are not in complete agreement with each other. The fundamental features, however, appear with sufficient clearness.

The most striking one is the very peculiar organization of the Essenes, which has often been compared with that of a Christian monastic order. They had all things in common and lived in cenobitic communities : the buildings of Qumran are obviously intended for this purpose. Celibacy was compulsory, at least in the main branch of the order, which is described by Pliny as *gens in qua nemo nascitur*. We do not know if women were admitted there, under the same condition, as was the case among the Therapeutai, another Jewish monastic order, established in Egypt, which Philo has described with great precision, and which, though being strictly contemplative, might be in some way connected with the Palestinian Essenes.

The whole life of the Essenes was regulated by precise and severe rules. The majority among them were probably laymen, but the priests assumed a leading role, not only in religious and cultic matters, but also in the administration of the community. They are described in the Qumran texts as sons of Aaron or of Zadok, whereas the community as a whole constitutes "the people" or "the children of Israel," and is, on some occasions, invested with judicial powers. Severe punishments, including temporary or final exclusion and even the death penalty, could be inflicted by this court of justice upon those who had transgressed the rule of the order.

Whosoever wanted to join it had to go through a probationary period and a novitiate, which lasted three years altogether, after which the neophyte was officially received as a regular member. He had already been clad in the white linen clothes which were the distinctive uniform of the community. He was admitted to the ritual baths and finally to the sacred meal, in which no outsider was ever allowed to participate. But before that he had to pronounce his vows. He solemnly pledged his word to observe the Law in every detail, to practise the virtues prescribed by the rule of the order, to transmit faithfully to his brethren and never to reveal to anybody else, even under the threat of death, the teaching he had received. The esoteric character of Essene doctrine appears here very clearly.

Daily life is divided between manual work and spiritual activities. The Essenes get up before dawn, and begin with morning prayer, which they say facing the rising sun. Then they go to work, according to the instructions given by the leaders of the community, which is self-sufficing and provides itself for all its needs. They meet at midday for a common meal. The evening is devoted to religious meetings, including prayer, reading of and commenting on the Law and other sacred texts. All secular activities are interrupted on the sabbath, which is exclusively dedicated to the praise of God and the meditation of His revealed ordinances.

The rites of the Essenes were fundamentally the same as those of average Jewish religious life, whether synagogal or domestic. But it can safely be assumed that they were given here a significance of their own. In addition to the great annual festivals, the Essenes probably held a few others. And their calendar was different from the one used in Jerusalem; it was perhaps that which had formerly been observed in the Temple, in which case the giving of it up by the official priesthood may have been one of the reasons of the Essene schism. The position of the Essenes towards the Temple is not absolutely clear. According to Josephus, they do send oblations to the Sanctuary, but abstain from attending its services, and offer their own sacrifices among themselves. Whether this last sentence is to be taken literally, or means that the Essenes considered their own rites as equivalent to the sacrifices or even superseding them, cannot be decided with certainty. It can however be assumed, at the very least, that they held the Temple and its sacrifices in low esteem, either because they repudiated them on principle, or perhaps rather because in their eyes the whole system of worship centred on Jerusalem was spoilt and deprived of its efficacy by an unworthy priesthood. Their own pattern of religious life and in particular their ablutions and sacred meals are probably best understood as a deliberate transposition of and substitute for the liturgies of the Temple.

Of their peculiar beliefs we knew very little before the discovery of the Dead Sea Scrolls. Philo insists on their concern for ethics. Josephus provides some information regarding their doctrine on the soul and the hereafter. But here again he uses the language of Greek philosophy. The human soul is by nature immortal. It has been imprisoned in the body and is delivered by death from this bondage. The souls of the righteous then migrate "beyond the Ocean" and dwell in the Isles of the Blessed, while the souls of the wicked are tormented in a dark cave, which our writer calls Hades. This is Hellenistic phrasing—Josephus assimilates the Essenes to the Pythagoreans—and must be completed or corrected by what we know from other sources. The Christian writer Hippolytus, though dependent on Josephus, adds that the Essenes believed in the final resurrection and judgment and in a universal conflagration. The Qumran texts have made the picture considerably more precise. They show that the Essenes have indeed, consciously or not, drawn from foreign sources in order to enrich their doctrine. Greek influences are at least likely. And it seems hardly possible to explain for instance the so-called Instruction on the Two Spirits without taking into account definite Mazdean influences. It describes the struggle between the Prince of Light and the Angel of Darkness, who both attempt to hold dominion over the individual soul and over the whole creation. The underlying dualism is, of course, toned down and brought into accord with Jewish fundamental monotheism. God Himself has created both the good and the evil Spirit. But whereas Biblical thought and official Judaism consider the sovereignty of Almighty God as being already actual, this text very strongly emphasizes the dramatic tension between Good and Evil which is to last until the end of time.

The Essene code of ethics, with its sharp opposition of virtues and vices and its severe asceticism, based on contempt of the flesh, reflects the same dualistic tendency as the Instruction on the two Spirits. The organization of the community aims at mobilizing its members for God's service and the final triumph of His cause. Isolated from all defiling contacts, it constitutes the remnant of Israel, ready for the impending battle against Satan's hosts. It is against this background that other aspects of Essene doctrine, in particular angelology and eschatology, are to be understood. But the Essene views in these matters seem gradually to have gained ground even outside the community itself. Of course, the various sects were all very small minority groups. According to Josephus, the Pharisees numbered in his time about six thousand, and the Essenes four thousand. As regards the Sadducees, he just says that they were very few. This means that the overwhelming majority of the Jews did not belong to any of the sects. But the importance of the sects in the religious life of Judaism is not to be measured by figures only. They were in fact, each in its own way, the active element and the leaven, so to speak, of Judaism. With the only exception of the Sadducees, they extended their influence far beyond the limits of their own conventicles. Pharisaism gradually became coextensive with Judaism. Many in Palestine had at least some sympathy for the views of the Zealots. As for the Essenes, it is quite sure that the esoteric character of their teaching and their secluded life did not prevent them from playing an important part in the evolution of Judaism as a whole. To what extent they may have exerted an influence on early Christianity remains a vexed question. But some of the beliefs which eventually tended to become common good among the Jews seem to originate in the Essene community, whose influence was diffused throughout Palestine by its local branches.

Of the various works which constituted the Qumran library some have undoubtedly been written by the community itself, for its own use. This applies, amongst others, to the so-called Manual of Discipline, which is the rule of the sect. But the Scrolls have also brought us copies or fragments not only of nearly all the books of the Old Testament, but of writings like the Book of Jubilees, Enoch, Testaments akin to the Testaments of the Twelve Patriarchs, which were already known to us and belong to the non-canonical writings, Apocrypha or Pseudepigrapha, of the Jewish Bible. The fact that these were found at Qumran is no sufficient proof that they have been composed on the spot and are consequently to be labelled Essene writings. One thing, however, can be safely assumed : the Qumran library was completely different from a modern research library. It is most unlikely that the Essenes should have collected and read documents which expressed views and doctrines conflicting with their own and, which, from their point of view, were heretical. What they used to read was intended for specifically religious and not merely scholarly purposes. Whether these Apocryphal writings are of Essene origin or not, they certainly express the views of large sections of Judaism in the New Testament period. Their presence at Qumran bears witness to the fact that the people who lived there kept in touch with the main stream of Jewish religious thought, possibly by borrowing from it and certainly also by nourishing it.

(vi) ANGELOLOGY AND DEMONOLOGY; PHILONIC SPECULATION

In their Essene setting, angelology and demonology on the one hand, eschatology on the other are very closely linked together. The angelic hosts, divided into various categories, are the protagonists in that cosmic drama in which men too are expected to take an active part. It is therefore essential to know as precisely as possible who and what they are, and especially their names, in order to establish close and active co-operation with the heavenly spirits and effectively to fight the evil ones who are busy tormenting mankind by way of demonic possession and the like. But angelology is also connected with astrology, since the heavenly spirits are more or less nearly related to, or even identified with, the stars and planets. Astrology in its turn is the twin sister of magic. We know from a number of documents that Judaism was not entirely successful, at the level of popular practices, in avoiding that religious syncretism which it uncompromisingly condemned in matters of doctrine. The so-called magical papyri make an abundant use of names of angels and devils, borrowed from Jewish, mainly non-canonical writings. The Jews had the reputation, in some Gentile circles, of being clever magicians and of worshipping the angels. This is hardly consonant with the fundamentally monotheistic position of official Judaism. But it is quite possible that in some popular quarters the basic distinction between the Creator and His heavenly creatures was somewhat confused. Angelology could occasionally lead to some sort of polytheism, all the more as the names of the best known among the angels or archangels, Michael, Gabriel, Raphael, included the generic Semitic name of the godhead, El. It is to be noted that on the magical papyri the various Biblical names of God, Adonai, Elohim, and even the sacred Tetragrammaton, written in Greek or Latin letters, are used along with those of the angels, and that distinction is not always clearly made between the two. Now, most of these documents are of pagan origin and more or less tinged with Gnosticism. But it is not to be excluded altogether that individual Jews or marginal Jewish conventicles should have indulged in this kind of speculation and practice. It is, moreover, commonly admitted that the main roots of Jewish angelology and demonology are to be found on foreign, *i.e.* pagan ground, chiefly Persian.

In official orthodox Judaism, however, speculations about angels and devils did not affect the rigorous monotheistic doctrine. Here, angels are considered as constituting the heavenly court of God, and their task is to serve and worship Him in everlasting adoration. They are also His messengers, who on special occasions come down on earth to make divine decisions or ordinances known unto men. To the more theologically minded, angelology helped to solve the problem of the relationship between God and creation. It provided the possibility of explaining, at least in part, the anthropomorphisms of the Bible and the theophanies, which some cultured Jews deemed incompatible with the nature of the Deity. Whenever God was said to appear or to behave like a human being, the answer could be that this applied to one of the angels and not to God Himself. The existence of a hierarchy of intermediate beings, active throughout the universe as God's delegates and factotums, helped to fill the gap between the transcendent majesty of an invisible and spiritual God and the material world. Conversely, the conception of the demons as fallen angels who had revolted against their Lord provided a clue to the problem of evil, material and moral. Sin and disease were often considered as closely related to each other and imputed to possession by evil spirits ; healing could then be achieved by appropriate exorcisms.

The metaphysical and theological problems here involved were systematically tackled by Philo who, applying the methods of Greek philosophy, attempted to make the best possible use of the Biblical data. There is no room here for a complete analysis of his thought, based on the Platonic opposition between the sensible and the intelligible world, between matter and spirit, and on allegorical exegesis of the Bible. This method aims at discovering, behind the immediately perceptible and obvious meaning of the sacred text, which must not be neglected and which, as far as the Law is concerned, is indeed binding, a deeper and, in the last resort, more important sense which, though unattainable by the vulgar, is the very essence of revelation, intended not for Jews only, but for all mankind. Philo deals at great length with intermediate heavenly beings which he calls *logoi* or *dynameis* and which are more or less clearly and consistently identified with the angels on the one hand, with the Platonic Ideas on the other. They are divided into various categories, according to the traditional Jewish subdivisions of the heavenly host. At the highest level are the five major *Dynameis* or Powers, and higher still is the

Logos. He is at the same time the most exalted of the individual *logoi* and also a sort of collective being, from which all other beings have emanated, and which is principle and instrument of the whole creation. Though inferior to God, the Logos partakes of the divine nature, and the spiritual element in man partakes of him. It is therefore through him that the liberation of the soul from the bondage of the flesh and its return to God can be achieved.

This of course is Judaism dressed in the Greek fashion, and can hardly be considered as a common type of Jewish theology, whether in Palestine or even in the Diaspora. In fact, the importance of Philo in the history of religions is on the side of Christianity rather than Judaism. But though this type of speculation of which he is the classical representative flourished chiefly in Alexandria, something of it found access even in Palestinian rabbinic thought. The rabbinic *Memra* is like a shadow of the Philonic *Logos*. Divine Wisdom, the Spirit of the Lord, His Glory, His *Shekinah* or indwelling (in the Temple) are both verbal substitutes for the unutterable divine names and also more or less clearly individualized divine attributes, hypostases. Thus angelology and hypostatic speculation, which are, in Philo's thought, closely linked together, serve the same purpose: they bring something of God's majesty nearer to men, while at the same time safeguarding divine transcendence.

(vii) MESSIANIC BELIEFS AND ESCHATOLOGY

It is doubtful, however, whether these speculations ever became very popular outside the rabbinic circles. The interest of the rank and file was mostly attracted in another direction: they looked for the Messianic Kingdom, for "the world to come" and for life eternal. The apocalyptic literature which flourished by that time, and of which our canonical Book of Revelation is the most widely known example, provides us with a fairly clear and precise picture of what the Jews believed in these matters. It seems likely that these beliefs belonged to the common stock of early Judaism. People were not all concerned to the same degree, and there were considerable nuances and differences from one quarter to another. But no Jew, with the only probable exception of the Sadducees, remained utterly indifferent to the problems of the future, which were of fundamental importance for the nation as well as for the religious life of Israel.

Ever since Palestine had fallen under foreign rule, the Jews were looking back with deep nostalgia upon the time of independence, and particularly upon the most brilliant period in their history, that of the undivided Israelite kingdom, under

David and Solomon. On the other hand, pagan occupation of the Holy Land was only one sign among many others that the universe was to a large extent held in bondage by the powers of evil. The original divine order had been corrupted and must of necessity be restored. God would not always tolerate the present state of things. The day would come when His kingdom, the Kingdom of Heaven, would be established on earth. The majority of the Jews were waiting for this day, the Day of the Lord, which had been announced by the prophets and was commonly believed to be near at hand. The accumulated calamities of the recent past and of the present were nothing but the necessary and very clear prelude to that glorious event. Whether national or cosmic, these catastrophes would probably become more numerous and more terrible still, until the fulfilment of time. Of what would happen then there was no unanimously admitted picture. Elements borrowed from the Prophets and chiefly from post-exilic writings, and also from non-Jewish sources, were variously combined and enriched by the Apocalyptists. To some, the rule of Yahweh would be essentially, or even only, an effective and unlimited domination over Israel. According to some others it would embrace the whole earth. Some would consider the Day of the Lord as a day of liberation and of revenge for Israel, and a day of divine wrath only with regard to the Gentiles. Others would think that God's verdict was to punish Gentiles and Jews alike in so far as all were sinners, and that only a small remnant of Israel would survive. Despite this wide diversity of opinions, at least the main features of that final drama were pretty clear: extermination of the wicked, turning back to Palestine of the truly faithful Jews of the Dispersion and of their proselytes, enduring prosperity and happiness, renewed splendour of the Holy City and of its Temple, as the basis of a new covenant, peace and justice. This blessed period is usually described by modern scholars as the Messianic age. The phrase also appears in Jewish sources. But it must be noted that the Messianic beliefs have undergone considerable changes throughout the centuries of Israelite and Jewish Biblical and post-biblical history, and that complete uniformity was never achieved in these matters.

The hope in a future which would restore both Israel's national pride and the paradisiac bliss of the origins of human history seems to have been cherished by almost all Jews. According to some of them, God alone would be at work in the final process. In the opinion of an increasing number, however, especially during the period under consideration, the Almighty was to appoint as it were a vice-king, in the person of His Anointed, or Messiah, who would be the effective instrument in the inauguration of the Kingdom. Here again, as regards the person of the Messiah, there was a certain amount of variety of opinion. He was most commonly regarded as a merely human ruler, of royal Davidic lineage. But the Qumran sect seems to have expected two Messianic figures, the so-called Messiah of Israel, and an eschatological High Priest.

This duality emphasizes the separation of royalty and priesthood, as it existed at the time of David and Solomon, and which the Essenes apparently considered as essential, thus showing their disapproval of the policy of the Hasmonaeans, who had concentrated in their own hands both the temporal and the spiritual power. Whether the expected High Priest can accurately be described as a Messiah and whether the mysterious Teacher of Righteousness was in any way related to this figure and was expected by the Qumran sect to reappear in this capacity at the end of time, remains a vexed question. If the Teacher of Righteousness was really considered by his followers as Messiah designate and if moreover, as some scholars think, he died a martyr, this would mean that the idea of a suffering Messiah was not so completely repugnant to Jewish thought as is commonly admitted. But our texts are too obscure and too vague on this point, as on many others, to allow any definite conclusion. And while we should be prepared to accept that even supposedly specific Christian features could already be present in some quarters of Judaism, we must also be careful not to read Christianity into the writings of Jewish apocalyptists or sectarians. One point at least is sure in matters of Messianic beliefs: to the overwhelming majority of the Jews, the earthly career of Jesus, culminating in His infamous death, was completely discrepant from the traditional picture of a triumphant Messiah, who was to fight and win battles against the foes of God and of His people, and to reign in glory over the Holy Land and the whole earth.

But there was no unanimous agreement concerning his origin and nature. Some Jews, mainly during the two last centuries B.C. and probably under the influence of Persian ideas, came to the conviction that the expected Messiah must be more than an ordinary human creature: he was of heavenly origin, and pre-existent. This conception is closely related to the speculations about the Son of Man. This term, which meant nothing more, in its original acceptation, than just "man," assumes a completely different meaning in some Biblical and non-canonical writings. The first instance appears in Dan. 7^{13}, which describes "one like a son of man" coming down with the clouds of heaven. Obviously this figure, though looking like a man, is a superhuman personality. He is to exert everlasting dominion over all the nations of the earth.

In what relation he stands to "the saints of the Most High," mentioned in the immediate context, who, too, will possess the kingdom for ever, is not absolutely clear. The most plausible interpretation is that the Son of Man is a figure both individual and collective. He is, in a way, like the Suffering Servant of Isa. 53, the symbol and personification of the Chosen People, which is called to rule the Gentiles; but he seems to be also a real sovereign, come down from heaven in order to lead Israel to its glorious destinies, identifying himself with it, but still transcending it. However Daniel is to be interpreted, in the Similitudes of Enoch, where the mysterious Son of Man reappears, he is undoubtedly an individual figure. He stands, as it were, midway between man and God. He existed before the creation of the world, is superior even to the angels, partakes of divine wisdom and righteousness and stands in as close a relationship to God as could be admitted within the limits of Jewish monotheism.

The Son of Man is sometimes thought of as exerting an everlasting dominion over a completely renewed and transformed universe. His kingdom thus represents the last stage in the development of the divine plan. This was not, however, the most common view. It did not agree with the fundamentally theocentric tendency of Jewish thought. The Jews usually made a distinction between the Messianic kingdom, which was to last a limited time—a thousand years according to a fairly common reckoning—and the more precisely eschatological or final period, when God would be the only actor and, as St. Paul puts it, "all in all." At the end of the Messianic age the whole universe would be completely transformed, a really new creation would bring forth a new earth and new heavens. The resurrection would then take place, in relation to the great assize of the Last Judgment. As already noted, some rabbis taught a general resurrection of all the dead, some a resurrection of the righteous only. In the first case, the resurrection would precede the judgment, which was to achieve the final division between those called to everlasting felicity and those condemned to everlasting torment. In the second case, the fate of the individuals was already sealed before the resurrection, which was thus considered not as the necessary step towards the ultimate discrimination, but as being in itself part of the reward of the blessed.

The question necessarily arose of what happened to the departed between their physical death and the final events. Here again there was a considerable amount of variety of opinion. The old Biblical idea of *Sheol*, where good and wicked men alike either were asleep or survived as mere shadows, had not completely died out. In this perspective, both categories would awake again to real life at the end of the present world, but the wicked would then remain and suffer eternally in the darkness of the underworld while the righteous would rise to the light and enjoy eternal felicity. But whereas in the *Sheol* conception the intermediate state of the departed was undifferentiated, the idea gained ground more and more that it already implied either bliss or torment, following on an individual judgment which was pronounced immediately after death. Thus the idea of *Sheol* was gradually replaced by that of Heaven or Paradise and Hell, thought of as two different places, where the dead were located. This conception is clearly expressed in the New Testament parable of Lazarus and Dives (Luke 16^{19-31}). It could easily be related to the idea of immortality as the Greeks understood it. Indeed, some quarters of Jewish opinion seem to have come very close to it. But to most of the Jews the idea of a soul completely deprived of its body did not make much sense, and some sort of body was necessary to life, even beyond the grave. This possibly explains why the idea of a general resurrection of both righteous and wicked eventually became the commonly accepted belief of Judaism, combined with a belief in the intermediate state, which could be diversely pictured.

Once these various trends of Jewish belief and worship have been rapidly analysed, there still remains untouched one very important aspect of the picture : I mean the religious life of the " humble and meek " who, though possibly influenced by one or other school of thought, did not formally adhere to any of them. This is very difficult to seize, because it has not expressed itself in written documents. There certainly existed among those people, who represented the overwhelming majority in Israel, a certain amount of religious indifference or at least lukewarmness. The fact that the *'ammê-hā-'āreṣ*, in Galilee or elsewhere, were looked upon with contempt by priests and rabbis alike is no sufficient reason for us to assume that they, and not their despisers, treasured up the most genuine forms of Jewish piety. But we are not bound, either, to admit that the official norms, whether Sadducean or Pharisaic, or those of the marginal sects, were the only standards by which Jewish religious life is to be judged. Humble submission to, and unswerving trust in God, unobtrusive practice of the Law, true piety and charity, plain and sincere devotion could be found in many Jewish homes, in every class of society, outside the sects as well as within. Of all this we have at least an echo in such texts as the Canticles in Luke's Gospel, which breathe the authentic spirit of common Jewish piety. It is against this background that the rise of Christianity is to be understood.

BIBLIOGRAPHY

W. Bousset and H. Gressmann, *Die Religion des Judentums in späthellenistischen Zeitalter*, 3rd ed., 1926.

J. Bonsirven, *Le Judaïsme Palestinien au temps de Jésus-Christ*, 2 vols., 1931.

A. Dupont-Sommer, *The Essene Writings from Qumran*, Eng. trans., 1961.

M. J. Lagrange, *Le Judaïsme avant Jésus-Christ*, 1931.

G. F. Moore, *Judaism in the First Centuries of the Christian Era*, 3 vols., 1927–30.

W. O. E. Oesterley, *The Jews and Judaism during the Greek Period*, 1941.

H. H. Rowley, *The Faith of Israel*, 1956.

E. Schürer, *Geschichte des jüdischen Volkes im Zeitalter Jesu Christi*, 3 vols., 4th ed., 1901–9.

M. Simon, *Les Sectes Juives au temps de Jésus*, 1960.

H. A. Wolfson, *Philo*, 2 vols., 1947–8.

XIV. BIBLICAL ETHICS

By A. S. Herbert

The Bible is not a code of ethics, any more than it is a textbook of theology; yet both Jews and Christians have found here not only a standard of moral conduct but also a kind of compulsion to seek its fulfilment. It is also true that any attempt to reduce the Biblical teaching on morality to a carefully articulated code of conduct can produce quite unlovely results. This has happened both in Judaism and in Christianity; the Pharisaism which is so vigorously denounced in the Gospels has had its counterparts in the Christian Church. It would appear that to make moral perfection the chief end of man can have disastrous consequences. It leads to what the New Testament describes as hypocrisy; that is to say, not merely conscious dissembling, but the perverting of human life to an end other than that for which man was created, which is to glorify God and enjoy Him for ever. It is true that the Bible speaks of "the Law of the Lord" (Ps. 19^{7}, $119^{1, 174}$), and "the Law of Christ" (1 Cor. 9^{21}, Gal. 6^{2}). But both the word "Law" and the context in which it is used need to be understood. The English word "Law," like the Greek *nomos*, represents the Hebrew *tôrāh*, and this means the direction or instruction which God gives. This came by priest and prophet, and stands for the whole content of revelation. The first five books of the Old Testament are called the Law, and they include the Book of Genesis and the account of God's coming to the help of the oppressed Israelites in Egypt in Exodus. In fact less than half of the Torah consists of ordinances, precepts, etc. Of course such a self-disclosure demands a response from those to whom He has come; but the response is to a Person, and is basically one of reverence and gratitude. For the Person is He Who rescued His people from slavery (Ex. 20^{2}), Who saves His people from their sins (Matt. 1^{21}). Explicitly or implicitly the ethical demands of the Bible are made within the context of the divine work of salvation. Moral endeavour is not the way to salvation but (like faith and worship) the product of salvation. Augustine's "give what thou commandest and command what thou wilt" goes to the heart of the matter.

It is not likely to be disputed that the Bible, taken as a whole, sets before mankind a lofty standard of morality. It is true that there are passages, notably in the Old Testament, which appear to advocate or approve conduct bordering on immorality (*e.g.* Gen. 38^{26}, Est. 9). It is also true that the Bible seems to be indifferent to certain moral issues that properly concern twentieth century man, *e.g.* racial prejudice and war. These and other difficulties may not be disregarded. Some of our difficulties arise from the nature of the Biblical material. There is, for example, a greater consistency within the New Testament than within the Old. But the former is the product almost wholly of one lifetime, while the latter is the deposit of a thousand years ; and that is a factor of fundamental importance for an understanding of Biblical ethics as it is of Biblical theology in general. Yet this points to the real difficulty of the subject. For if Ethics be defined as the normative science of morals, then we shall look in vain for any such systematic articulation in the Bible. Certain summary statements occur, *e.g.* Ex. 20^{2-17}, Deut. 12–28, Lev. 19, the Sermon on the Mount and various injunctions in the Epistles. But these contain much that is not of a specifically ethical character. Frequently, and this is notably true of the Old Testament prophets and the teaching of Jesus, there is penetrating criticism of contemporary human conduct, but again this is rarely expressed in systematic form. Ethics, as an autonomous science of human conduct, is alien to the spirit of the Bible. It is more characteristic to ask " What does the Lord require of thee ? ", than to ask, " What is man's highest good ? ", although the latter may be included in the former.

It is appropriate and illuminating to begin with the question addressed by a lawyer (*i.e.* a careful student of the Torah) to Jesus : " Master, what must I do to inherit eternal life ? " (Luke 10^{25}). This was a test question, but there is no need to doubt the sincerity of the questioner. The lawyer was referred to what he would recognize as the ultimate authority, the Torah, and quotes, with our Lord's approval, passages from Deut. 6^{5} and Lev. 19^{18}. The incident is given, with slight variations in Matt. 22^{35-40} and Mark 12^{28-34}. A similar incident is reported in Mark 10^{17-22} and parallels. The teaching of the Bible comes to a focus here. Obviously it was a matter of primary importance to the lawyer and his contemporaries. Furthermore, the fact that the incident was reported with variations suggests that the question and answer were of importance to the Christian community. The Jew might add that the answer came from the Torah which long ante-dated Jesus. The Christian might wish to say that what is meant by loving one's neighbour must be understood in the light of John 13^{34}, 15^{12}. Clearly, if love for man is to be defined in terms of Christ's love for His disciples as He gave Himself for them, the commandment is not easily to be associated with eudaemonism or utilitarian ethics, and seems to breathe a freer air than Kant's categorical imperative. This is not to deny that the conduct required might result in a special kind of "happiness," or that it might lead to the greater "happiness" of mankind. It might even be said, in terms of perfectionist ethics, to lead to the fullest development of human potentialities, and could hardly fail to generate the "good will." But none of these could be regarded as the real goal of human conduct according to Biblical teaching.

That goal is "to inherit eternal life" or "to enter the Kingdom of God." Now if this be taken out of its Biblical context, and in particular out of the context of Jesus' teaching, it could be made to sound like a reward for good conduct; even worse it could sound like "pie in the sky when you die." This in fact is precisely how the Marxist understands Christian teaching. The misunderstanding arises from giving non-biblical meanings to Biblical phrases. What Jesus and His hearers understood is clear. The Kingdom of God is God's victorious rule over all that is evil and death-dealing. God is the living God from whom all life derives. Life, and in particular eternal life, is what a man in fact receives and enjoys now in fellowship with God. Manifestly the full enjoyment of eternal life can only be known in conditions beyond the limitations of space and time; but in the words of a later New Testament writer, "we know that we have passed out of death into life because we love the brethren" (1 John 3^{14}; cf. Rom. $6^{4, 23}$, 1 Tim. 6^{12}). The New Testament has in fact taken up the saying of Hab. 2^{4}, "The righteous shall live by his faithfulness" and given it new depth of meaning in the light of the Resurrection of Jesus and the gift of the Holy Spirit (cf. Rom. 1^{17}, Gal. 3^{11}, Heb. 10^{38}).

The question, "What shall I do?" is an ethical question. The answer is not so obviously an answer in terms of ethics. The first quotation describes an attitude towards God which many outside the Biblical tradition would regard as irrelevant to the ethical enquiry. The second also describes an attitude of mind rather than a course of conduct, and seems at first to narrow the sphere of life ("the neighbour") in which that attitude of mind should operate. However, the development of the teaching makes it clear that this attitude of mind has direct bearing on conduct. It has often been noted that the lawyer's question, "Who is my neighbour?" is not really answered. Perhaps this was because it could so easily lead to a nice discussion about degrees of relationship. Jesus turned the issue into a concrete illustration of neighbourly love. Where there is need, love-in-action must be shown without consideration for personal convenience or religious orthodoxy.

On more than one occasion Jesus called in question the "rightness" of an orthodoxy which in any way inhibited love in action; cf. Mark 3^{1-5}. So, what generates motive and conduct in relation to the neighbour is to be found in the love relationship with God. Moreover, this relationship with God must issue in neighbourly love. In other words, there can be no true understanding or effective practice of morality without religion; while a religion which does not lead to vigorous ethical endeavour, is not worthy of the name. This lies at the heart of Biblical Ethics. There is, in the midst of His people, One Whose very presence compels men to call in question the accepted canons of law and human behaviour, creating the desire and the energy to become like Him Who is holy, perfect, and merciful. Biblical ethics is the product of Biblical religion. Just as the religion of the Bible is alive and growing, so men's ethical insights become deeper and more sensitive as they come to know the Holy in the midst. If then we recognize a unity of revelation and life in the Bible, we must also recognize growth and development; for we do not find a systematic statement of morals any more than we find an articulated theology. Instead, we find a people within whose life the creative energy of God was at work. It was necessary for them to meet the challenges of ever new situations and thus to grow to maturity. The work of Jesus in this field was not to abrogate the Law and the Prophets, but to bring to its proper fulfilment what God had given to His people.

The Old Testament is an immensely varied body of literature and we can recognize certain "critical" situations in which it came into being (see above, pp. 27 ff.). In the Old Testament itself, the Exodus series of events is regarded as of cardinal importance. There, an enslaved people, without hope in man or God, were freed from oppression by Yahweh's mighty acts, and bound to Him in the covenant relationship. This totally unexpected and undeserved act of God lies at the heart of Israel's life. Within this covenant relationship, Yahweh assured the people of His guidance, protection, and help; if they are to live as His people, they must respond in loyalty, faith, and obedience. Where we should look for moral injunctions, Israel was commanded to "hearken attentively to His voice and do all that he says." In other words, the primary question for Israel was, not "What is the good?", but "What does Yahweh require of me?" This Covenant is neither a bargain nor a legal contract, but a personal relationship, brought into being by Yahweh and received by Israel. Clearly it requires a response from Israel, the recipient of this gracious act of Yahweh (*ḥesedh*), but Israel did not make the Covenant. She may reject or ignore, but only Yahweh could make and maintain it. It is this which gives its special quality to Israel's understanding of morality. What Yahweh requires is based on what He has given. However that may need to be further defined and made more specific, it is received by Israel with gratitude and a response of loyalty to Him Who has given all. This is apparent in the earliest statement of Israel's obligations in the Covenant relationship, Ex. 20^{1-17}, and this Decalogue, at least in its prohibitions and commands, may reasonably be associated with the Mosaic period. The profoundly ethical character of these Ten Words is obvious enough, and is the more remarkable when it is recognized that they appear in a society which was, by our standards, primitive. There is little need to comment on the moral obligations of the Decalogue; but we may note that v.^{12} does not refer primarily to children in the household, but to adults in relation to their aged parents; that v.^{16} has a particular reference to a legal trial; that v.^{17}, while it refers to the inner life, includes also the expression in action whereby a man seeks to gain control over his fellow-member of the community. But it is especially important to notice that the Decalogue is firmly anchored in the Salvation-event, v^{2}. To quote the Decalogue without these opening words is wholly to distort its meaning. These injunctions are laid upon Yahweh's people because they are His, and because of the kind of God that He is. Their conduct is a matter of interest to Him as well as to them. The ethical demands are not simply such as will maintain a healthy society; they define the way of life for a people who belong to Yahweh and have been saved by Him. Moreover, whatever be the content of meaning in the name of Israel's God, He has been defined for Israel as the One who "has seen the affliction of my people, heard their cry, known their sufferings" and acted to deliver (Ex. $3^{7f.}$). Further, their relationship with Him has been defined, not only in terms of Ruler and subject, but in terms of Father and son (Ex. $4^{22f.}$).

The Book of the Covenant (Ex. 20^{22}–23^{33}) appears to be a collection of such laws as governed the life of Israel during the period of the Monarchy, and has parallels in other parts of the Semitic world. The society is still at a humble level, consisting in the main of peasant farmers. It is not the function of law to inculcate ethics, but the laws that govern a people's life will reflect their ethical insights. There is a deep concern for justice, which may not be perverted (23^{6}), and for the needs of the weak and defenceless ($22^{21-24.\ 25-27}$, 25^{9}). Oppression of any kind is sternly forbidden—Israel had its beginning in a divine rescue from oppression. Therefore the wrath of Yahweh burns fiercely against any kind of cruelty or exploitation. Profound social changes occurred in the life of

Israel as, beginning with David, the transition took place from semi-nomadic life and from the conditions of the city-state to that of a kingdom. Kingship as known in the ancient world was despotic in character, with a class of nobles and officials who used their position to exploit the peasant farmers. The remarkable thing is, not that this happened in Israel at least under Solomon, but that it is strongly condemned, and condemned by the man of God (cf. I Sam. 8^{10-18}, I Kings 12^{1-24}). Elijah's indictment of Ahab over the judicial murder of a peasant farmer is of the same character (I Kings 21). It is evident from the story that Elijah is not enunciating some new principle, but setting the crime in its true context. It is evil in the sight of Yahweh (21^{20}). Apparently Ahab knew that already (21^{4}), though the Phoenician princess did not; the gods of Sidon were not greatly concerned with ethical conduct.

In the eighth century B.C., the evils in this social revolution reached full expression with the acquisition of new sources of wealth. This was particularly apparent in the Northern Kingdom though present also in Judah. The strong government of Jeroboam II. was able effectively to police the great trade route of the maritime plain and suppress brigandage; and for this security the traders willingly paid. The influx of wealth benefited the few and they used their riches for selfish and ostentatious luxury. The poor were exploited either by taking advantage of their poverty or by the perversion of justice. The rich lived in luxury, displaying their wealth in magnificent houses, fine clothes and jewels and sumptuous banquets, while their fellow-members of the covenant community were sold into slavery or starved. The desire to get richer led to all sorts of commercial trickery and a callous disregard for human suffering. The Rechabites condemned the new factors that had entered the Israelite society and the social revolution that had ensued: the only cure was a return to the fine simplicities of the nomadic life. The prophets, Amos, Hosea, Isaiah, Micah, with deeper insight recognized that the new social conditions, perhaps because they were not covered by ancient Israelite law and custom, simply provided the soil in which human greed, lust for power, selfish pride, disregard for the sanctity of human life, as well as the more obvious sins of gluttony and sexual immorality, could flourish. What was needed was not to turn back to the simpler forms of society, but a serious concern for the divine requirements of righteousness, justice, and mercy within the context of a humble walking with God (Mic. 6^{8}). But they spoke, not as moralists or social reformers, but as men called of God (Am. 7^{15}, Isa. $6^{8f.}$, Mic. 3^{8}). They knew that the ancient Covenant relationship was as necessary and as relevant in the new social and political situation as it had been in the desert or at the entry into Canaan. It was the only factor which could control human selfishness and conduce to the life and well-being of Yahweh's people. This prophetic insistence on Justice, Righteousness, and Mercy needs some explication. The Hebrew words are not abstract nouns or exclusively ethical qualities. They are all construed with the verb "to do." Justice is not only a judge's decision; it includes the action consequent on that decision whereby the accused, if innocent, is restored to his rightful place in society, and the guilty appropriately punished. Deliverers like Gideon and Jephthah were called judges. Righteousness is the effective removal of evil and oppression. R.S.V. at Judg. 5^{11} rightly interprets the word as "triumphs"—guerilla fighters on the eve of a battle which threatens their extermination are not primarily concerned with abstract qualities of the divine personality. Mercy corresponds to a Hebrew word which defies adequate translation into English; it may be understood as that Covenant love and loyalty, resolute to promote the welfare of the Covenant people. These terms characterize the divine activity; therefore they must be prized and practised by Yahweh's people. (For a fuller discussion of these words cf. N. H. Snaith, *The Distinctive Ideas of the Old Testament*, pp. 68–130.) The fact that the Old Testament prophets appear to exalt morality above ritual must be seen in the total context of the historical and religious situation. There was no need to plead for the sacrificial system, though, through the considerable infusion of Canaanite rituals, contemporary practices were gravely imperilling the sacramental character of Israel's sacrifices. The real danger was that Israel should substitute ritual for moral conduct. Again, there was urgent need for an exposure of contemporary moral conduct. Moreover, the prophets were not liturgiologists any more than they were social reformers. But the effect of their words was to promote both a liturgical and a social reform.

There are many echoes of the prophetic teaching, particularly that of Hosea and Amos, in the Book of Deuteronomy which appears to have been the basis of Josiah's reform in 621 B.C. It is probable that this book is the result of a gathering together of material from more than one (Northern?) shrine and has been influenced by the eighth century prophets' teaching which history had so terribly vindicated. Certainly it contains much traditional material, however much that may have been modified. Within it we can recognize the patient instruction given by faithful priests and Levites who were loyal to the Yahweh tradition. The ritual act is important, but the book sets forth with singular eloquence how Israel should walk " in the way of Yahweh " (Deut. 10^{12}, etc.). Here are enumerated both the motives, without which ethical conduct becomes self-centred and moralistic, and a number of practical examples. The motives are reverence (" fear," though a correct translation, is misleading ; fear and love frequently appear together in Deuteronomy ; cf. 10^{12}) and love for God which allow no rival, and the pursuit of righteousness (cf. 16^{20} literally " Righteousness, righteousness shalt thou pursue ! "). Since Yahweh is righteous and just (Deut. 32^{4}), His people must exalt righteousness and justice, in the law courts (16^{18}) and in commerce (25^{15}). Particular attention is paid to the sojourner, the fatherless and the widow, *i.e.* those who in any society are least able to defend themselves and most vulnerable to acts of oppression, and it is positively commanded that every help must be given to them (14^{29}, $16^{11.\ 14}$, 24^{19-21}, 26^{12-13}). The reason is given that just as Yahweh came to Israel's aid when they were in need, so they must help the needy (16^{12}, 24^{22}). Generosity is a sacred obligation for a people who have experienced the divine generosity. The emphasis on liberality is a notable feature of this book, as is a fine sensitiveness for the feelings of others. Even the commandment affecting the sabbath is given here in a form which insists on the rights of the slave ($5^{14f.}$).

Another collection, Lev. 17–26, is often called the Holiness Code because of its frequently recurring phrase, " You shall be holy, for I, Yahweh, am holy." This may well have been a book of priestly instruction belonging to the Jerusalem Temple. Although it is mainly concerned with matters affecting ritual, it, too, is concerned with moral conduct, especially in Lev. $19^{9-17.\ 32-36}$. Again we find, together with the normal pattern of moral requirements, a consideration for the poor ($19^{9f.}$), the hired servant (v.^{13}), a respect for the aged (v.^{32}), and a notable command to love both the neighbour and the resident alien (vv.$^{17f.\ 33f.}$). All this belongs to the " holy " life. But this needs some explication. Holy is a word that properly belongs, not to human conduct, but to the divine activity. It indicates the mysterious, fearful, and incalculable otherness that distinguishes the gods from men. Men and objects claimed for the divine use are holy, in that they are set apart from common usage. Obviously everything depends on the kind of god who is known as the Holy. In Canaanite religion, as elsewhere in the world outside the Mosaic tradition, there were women attached to the shrines for the purposes of religious prostitution and these were called " holy women " (cf. the hierodules or temple slaves of Greek religion). The practice was vigorously condemned in Israel, although it continued as late as the time of Josiah (2 Kings 23^{7}). But it is one of the most remarkable features of Israelite morality that so " sacred " an institution was repudiated. The reason lies in the revealed character of Yahweh. His holiness included and was manifested in moral purity and righteousness (cf. Isa. 5^{16}). To say, therefore, " ye shall be holy " is to say, " the religious life of the people of Yahweh necessarily includes moral purity."

In the Psalter and the book of Proverbs we find much material for an estimate of the good life as expounded by the official teachers of Israel. Many of the Psalms must, at least in their original form, have come from the monarchy period and prescribe the manner of the king's rule. Similarly, much of the material in Proverbs, however late the final compilation, derives from the same period and represents a distillation of the " wisdom " of the ancient world as taught by the wise men in Jerusalem, apparently at the court or in the Temple. In the " royal psalms," the king is responsible for the maintenance of righteousness in the life of the nation (Ps $72^{1-3,\ 12-14}$). The ethical demands made upon the true worshipper of Yahweh are briefly described in Ps. $24^{3f.}$, and in greater detail in Ps. 15; while in Ps. 101 we have a negative confession or a formula of self-examination before coming into Yahweh's presence (perhaps leading to the General Confession of Ps. 51). The familiar virtues are exalted and vices condemned; but we note the emphasis on speaking the truth, fulfilling a promise at whatever cost, and on the evils of slander, repetition of evil gossip and exploitation of the needy.

The ethical teaching contained in Proverbs and to some extent also in Ecclesiasticus gives the impression of being merely prudential and utilitarian in character. This is probably an unjust estimate. Wisdom, in Egypt as well as in Israel, was essentially practical rather than speculative, and was very much concerned with right and wrong conduct. Experience and reflection had taught men how to live the good life and the consequences of so living, or by contrast the disastrous consequences of evil living. But the living context of Wisdom in Israel was the " knowledge of God." While in the Wisdom writers generally there is an absence of reference to the Covenant terminology, wisdom is defined in religious terms: " Wisdom's beginning is to fear Yahweh, and to know the Holy is understanding " (Prov. 9^{10}). So wisdom is essentially a characteristic of God (cf. Job 28) and is received by the man who lives in reverent fellowship with God. In the light of this, the sages give their minds to the practical matters of human living. There was no thought of life after death until we come to the Wisdom of Solomon (*c.* 100 B.C.), and if at times we feel that they are over-confident in their doctrine of rewards and punishments we should recall that from these circles also came

Job and Ecclesiastes with their disturbing and bold questions. The virtues commended include self-control, benevolence, forgiveness, humility, truthfulness, industry, and honesty. The vices condemned are pride, laziness, scandal-mongering, lying, covetousness, sexual impurity, hatred, gluttony, and drunkenness. A very high estimate is placed on the maintenance of the family and on good citizenship. Perhaps the finest expression of Israel's moral insights is to be found in Job 31.

The ethical insights of the Old Testament are the product of an exclusive loyalty to, and reverence for, Yahweh, the Saviour and Covenant-maker; He is the Holy in the midst. In this context, Israel grew to maturity, and so we find a continual deepening of ethical teaching in the Law and the Prophets. The great aim is to maintain the society, and within that, the family, which Yahweh has made. Conduct or speech, and the thoughts that produce them, which impair or threaten to impair this integrity are condemned. Jeremiah especially is acutely aware of the fact that the source of conduct in thought, imagination and will must be set right. Man is a unity, and to devise or plan is to release those living energies from the soul that will issue in speech or conduct. "Evil men do not understand justice, but those who seek Yahweh understand it completely" (Prov. 28^5); and to understand is not only to have an intellectual apprehension, but to engage in appropriate activity. Moreover, Israel's teachers were well aware of the fallibility of human judgment, and knew that the inner motives of life lay open before God (Prov. 16^2, Jer 17^{10}). What we call ethics was, for the men of Israel, that conduct which has its constant point of reference to the divine King who exercises perfect justice among His people and continually sustains their life; to the divine Father who maintains, as He brought into being, the family of Israel. Moral conduct is the "natural" outcome of a personal relationship with God and with one's fellow-members of the divine community. It is the aim of the Law to set before the people of God that direction which life with Him will take; of the Prophets, to recall Israel to the covenant which they have forgotten or from which they have (ignorantly or deliberately) departed; of Israel's sages to depict the life which Wisdom, begotten of God, will produce and to expose the disastrous consequences of folly.

It does not fall within the scope of this article to consider in detail the ethical teaching of the Jewish Rabbis in the time of Jesus, except as it relates to His teaching and that of His apostles. Before we presume to criticize we must, with sympathy, seek to understand their aims and acknowledge the passionate zeal and sincerity with which they sought to interpret the Law and to practise its precepts. We know that Jewish ethical teaching attracted the admiration of many sensitive Gentiles of the period. The Law was holy, and the commandment holy and just and good (cf. Rom. 7^{12}). Therefore nothing in it could be repealed. Yet there were many areas of life in first-century Palestine (an occupied country) or in the cities of the Gentile world in which the majority of the Jews lived (the Diaspora), to which the Law was not obviously relevant. So there had grown up around the Law, and associated with it, a considerable body of oral tradition. The Rabbis had devised rules of interpretation whereby the precepts of the Law were integrated and related to contemporary conditions. Inevitably this resulted in an ever more subtle definition of the terminology of the Law and the growth of a formidable body of casuistry in which relatively trivial matters ("tithing mint and cummin") became no less important than doing justly and loving mercy. Yet tithing is part of the Law; those who daily recited the *Sh^e^ma*ʻ (Deut. 6^{4-9}, 11^{13-21}, Num. 15^{37-41}) were taking upon themselves the yoke of the Kingdom, and this included the keeping of the Law in all its parts. So the Rabbis were acting logically and with great sincerity in thus rigorously applying the Law. That this can lead to a distortion of the Law is obvious enough. It would, however, be a mistake to accuse the Rabbis as a whole of this kind of distortion, or to suggest that this and nothing else gives a true picture of rabbinical teaching. Alongside this scrupulosity we must set such a saying as, "By three things is the world (*i.e.* human society) sustained, by the Law, by worship and by deeds of loving-kindness" (*Pirke Aboth* 1^2). Yet such an attitude all too easily led to legalism. It may be possible to deduce the whole Law from the two great commandments, but in the process love itself may wither. For Jesus the two great commandments were primary not in the logical sense but as regulative even of the Law and its interpretation.

The ethical teaching of Jesus must not be separated from the religious context in which it was given; it was in fact Law in the Old Testament sense of the word. He came proclaiming the Good News of the Kingdom which He summoned His hearers to receive. This kingdom is a personal relationship with God as King into which men are called to enter. Then, and only then, can they know the ethos of the kingdom. Men do not gain the Kingdom as a reward for good living. It is God's gift which, when received, produces a certain quality of life. This is what is illustrated in the Sermon on the Mount. We observe first that it is addressed to the disciples (His apprentices in the art of living); it is not a public manifesto. Then it begins with a series of Beatitudes. These are not blessings invoked upon those who behave in certain ways; they are statements of fact. The word translated "Blessed," occurs again in 1 Pet. 3^{14}, 4^{14}, where it is rendered "happy." It corresponds to the word in Deut. 33^{29}, Job 5^{17}, Ps. 144^{15}. It is a word of congratulation to those who have entered the Kingdom. The converse, "woe," is not a curse, but a cry of distress over those who have rejected the life which Jesus came to give. The remainder of Matt. 5 describes the manner of life of those who belong to the Kingdom. This is the Torah of Jesus which does not abrogate but brings to its complete expression the Mosaic Torah. It is, for example, all too human to say, "Thou shalt not kill but need'st not strive Officiously to keep alive." But the disciple will understand the command as repudiating hatred or any kind of bad relationship with another. Adultery consists not only in the act, but in any kind of attitude to a woman that treats her as less than personal and a member of the holy community (cf. Job 31^{1}). Perjury is not simply a legal offence; it is any kind of speech which lacks sincerity. The *lex talionis* (Matt. 5^{38}), formerly a restraint on unlimited revenge, now becomes an eager desire to help those who have done one an injury. The Mosaic Torah had taught the Israelite to love his neighbour; Jesus would see no limitation to the word "neighbour." The clue to this manner of life is to be found in the closing words of the chapter. The disciples of Jesus who have received the Kingdom know themselves to be claimed by God as His children. They will therefore display the family likeness, "Be ye perfect as your heavenly Father is perfect" (Matt. 5^{48}; or in the Lukan form "Be ye merciful . . ." Luke 6^{36}). The ethos of the Kingdom is the *imitatio Dei*. But God is not remote, nor the unseen guardian of men's loftiest ideals. He is in life as the present and active King and Father, and Jesus is the living evidence of that. To be a disciple is not merely to be a learner of new truths; it is to be a sharer in a new relationship and to become skilled in the art of living. This he will do, not by zealously observing many rules and precepts (the righteousness of the scribes and Pharisees), but by being with Jesus (Mark 3^{14}). The teaching of Jesus is in fact the expression of His own life. It is given to His disciples and so made available to those whom "the Lord added to their number." The new relationship with God finds expression in a new relationship with men who are seen as belonging to His kingdom and as members of his family. Many of the parables of Jesus, though not primarily given for purposes of ethical instruction have the same moral implications. In Luke 15^{11-32}, the elder brother had every moral justification in speaking of the returned prodigal as a good-for-nothing wastrel. Was there not in fact a real danger that the father's welcome might seem like condoning evil conduct? Yet every pious Jew who had read Hos. 11^{1-9} (cf. also 2^{14-20}), knew that he was the recipient of just such a love. The elder brother had in fact succumbed to the corrupting sins of self-righteous pride and uncharitableness. Again the parable of the good Samaritan in Luke 10^{29-37} makes the point that the sight of need and suffering compels action to help. Doubtless the priest and Levite had their reasons for not responding; but no reader of the Torah (and this applied to Jew and Samaritan) could forget that it was at the point of Israel's deepest need that God had acted to save (Ex. $3^{7f.}$). Thence arises the inescapable obligation to go and do likewise. That is what is meant by seeking first God's kingdom and righteousness. That is what is involved in being the people of God and members of His family.

It is sometimes said that the distinctive quality of love in Jesus' teaching is indicated by the use of the particular Greek noun and verb (*agapē* and *agapaō*), words that emphasize will and action rather than emotion. This may well be true when the Gospels were written in Greek as it was when the Old Testament was translated and the Epistles were written. For the commonly used words in Greek were either inadequate or inappropriate to the love of which the Bible speaks. But this can hardly be applied to the teaching that Jesus was giving to His hearers, since He was hardly likely to have spoken to Palestinian Jews in Greek. In fact there was only one word available, and it is precisely that love which is seen between husband and wife, parents and children and in the deepest of human friendships, that the disciple must foster in his relationships with others (cf. Mark 3^{31-35}, $10^{29f.}$). Indeed this command to love becomes a possibility as men learn from Him to think of their fellows in terms of God's family. Similarly the command "As ye would that men should do to you, do ye also to them likewise" (Luke 6^{31}), expressed in this positive form, not only sets a high ethical standard, but requires the exercise of creative imagination in the fulfilment of moral obligation. Clearly for the followers of Jesus there could be no room for self-interest, pride or self-satisfaction, nor for possessiveness, malice, deceit, or jealousy. There could be no limit to forgiveness or to the effort required to heal the breach of fellowship, even when the hostile acts were done by the other. All this is expressed in the vivid language of going the extra mile, visiting the prisons, regarding one's self as of no importance whatever, which is what self-denial really means.

Jesus appears to have given His disciples little in the way of precise ethical instruction. In part this is due to the impossibility of reducing the law of love to a system of rules and regulations; in part also to the well-known fact that contemporary Judaism already accepted a standard of conduct that needed no further development; in part no doubt too, to His obvious respect, the product of love, for human personality, which must leave a freedom of response to situations and circumstances as they will arise. Ethical maturity can only come about when there is this freedom. So His specific injunctions are given in response to actual situations as they arise. This is well illustrated in His treatment of the man/woman relationship. His high estimate of this relationship would preclude any possibility of sexual immorality in any form. But two comments may be made. First He makes the point that lust is not merely what we usually call a sin of the flesh, but of the inner self; it is lustful thought no less than immoral act that is condemned (Matt. 5^{28}). It is a sin against love. In sexual immorality most especially, either or both of the parties is dealing with the other impersonally, as a means to self-gratification and with indifference to others who are more or less directly involved. Secondly, we note His profound respect for women. In this He was undoubtedly in advance of contemporary thought, even in Judaism; yet He insists that in this He is recalling men to the profound insights of the Torah (Matt. 19^{4}; cf. Gen. 1^{27}, $2^{23f.}$). The exact meaning of His teaching on divorce may be disputed; but there can be no misunderstanding about His teaching on marriage. This is a relationship whose significance goes far beyond compact or contract; it can only be understood as a union which God has made. Divorce may be *lawful* because of the hardness of men's hearts, itself sinful, but it is manifestly contrary to the divine will and to the very nature of man as created by God. Again, Jesus says nothing explicitly about the monogamous nature of marriage, yet it is difficult to see how polygamy could have any place in a way of life which sees marriage as "the two shall become one flesh." Perhaps here we may see most clearly the nature of His ethical teaching. For sexual morality must always be a crucial test, because it necessarily involves persons in the most intimate of relationships; and any lowering of standards in this sphere involves a depreciation or denial of personality. Yet this sanctity of personality lies, not in man, but in the purpose of "your heavenly Father."

Many of the issues that challenge the moral conscience of the modern man receive no specific mention in the teaching of Jesus because the society in which He moved already had a high ethical standard. The situation was very different when the Church moved out into the Graeco-Roman world, whose standards were, except for such as the Stoics, at a much lower level. The apostolic writers must address themselves to a world that knew nothing of Moses, and needed guidance in matters of conduct as well as of faith. Yet here too we find that the Apostles do not give an articulated system of ethics, but deal with specific matters as they arise. But again we must note the context in which ethical instruction is given. With the possible exception of James, all the writers first set before the readers the saving work of God in Christ ; in the light of this men will see what ought and what ought not to be done. Further, throughout the letters, there are frequent allusions to the two dominical sacraments, whereby the believer is united with Christ and participates in the life of Christ. It is in this context that the writers give moral guidance to the Church.

The Epistle of James is almost wholly concerned with moral instruction. We know nothing about its destination apart from what may be inferred from the letter itself. Eusebius described it as an epistle for the whole Church, but the contents suggest that originally it was addressed to a local congregation. Whether or not the James was the Lord's brother, his Epistle is full of allusions to the teaching of Jesus, as though this was very well known to the readers. Read by itself, the Epistle may leave the impression of being over-moralistic in tone and insufficiently aware of the real nature of faith and worship. But the contents suggest that it was written to a group of Christians who were making pietistic religiosity a substitute for vigorous faith and religion. It gave a kindly but firm reminder that they must confront the world with good works and so enable men to recognize the judgment of God on a secular society and the urgent need for salvation. It is something more than moralism that calls for endurance of trial as the way of happiness (James 1^{2-12}) ; that speaks of a certain privilege in poverty, not for its own sake but because it enables a man more readily to recognize the help of God ; that firmly calls to account the rich man who is in mortal peril lest his riches make him callous to human need and insensitive to his own need of God (1^{9-11}, $2^{5-7.\ 15-17}$, 5^{1-6}). Neither can we dismiss as trivial the vigorous exposure of the evils of bitter and malicious speech (3^{3-12}). The concern of the Epistle is for the cultivation of those virtues that promote and strengthen the health of the brotherhood ($3^{17f.}$). It condemns therefore jealousy, censoriousness, ambition and covetousness, for these destroy the fellowship (3^{14-16}, $4^{1-3.\ 11-12}$). It insists that the relief of poverty (1^{27}) and fair treatment of employees (5^{41}) are necessary products of a right relationship with God. It is a high morality that expresses a concern for the sinner and seeks to restore him to the brotherhood (5^{19-20}).

In the view of many scholars 1 Peter is closely related to

the sacrament of Baptism, and if this is so then the ethical teaching contained here has a peculiar significance. It contains the basic instruction given to those who have come from the pagan world into the new relationship with God in Christ. The Christian life is an *imitatio Dei*, quite in the manner of the Old Testament and the teaching of Jesus (1 Pet. $1^{15f.}$). Similarly again, the maintenance of the fellowship is the special responsibility of each member of the society ($1^{22f.}$). Malice, deceit, insincerity, jealousy, and resentment have no place in the Christian life (2^{1}). Detailed application of Christian ethical insights by contrast with the earlier self-regarding mode of life (lusts of the flesh, 2^{11}) are given in 2^{11}–3^{12}. Christians have a God-given responsibility to fulfil their obligations as citizens (2^{13-17}). The Christian society is not to provide men with an excuse to escape from political responsibility. The state belongs to God, even though its rulers do not acknowledge His rule. The earthly ruler, even a Nero or Domitian, must be honoured. Slaves—and this meant most Christians in the first century—must willingly fulfil the demands of their masters (2^{15-18}). There was, of course, no attempt to initiate a slave revolt or to abolish slavery. But in fact, the real evil of slavery is destroyed when the slave was given what the institution had destroyed, namely responsibility and an inner sense of obligation. The instruction to wives and husbands (3^{1-7}) must also be seen in the light of contemporary thought. But once it is accepted that men and women are equally partakers in the grace of God, unworthy conceptions of marriage are doomed. The controlling thought in all human relationships is fellowship, mutual respect, courtesy, and genuine humility (3^{8}).

Much of this is repeated and expanded in the letters of Paul in which he expresses his pastoral concern for his fellow-Christians in a variety of circumstances. Paul himself had been educated in the Jewish faith and had given himself fully to the realization of its ethical insights. But he also knew and appreciated the ethical teaching of contemporary philosophy. Much in his teaching would have commended itself to the moral philosopher of the ancient world. Yet fundamentally his teaching derives from Jesus. It had to take on new forms to meet the needs of people very different from those in the Palestinian society. But in effect he is saying in all his teaching : put to death what belonged to your old manner of life and put on Christ (cf. Col. 3^{5-12}). Here too we find that the ground of all his ethical teaching is the saving work of God in Christ whereby the Christian has been brought into a new relationship with God and man. That is the significance of his " therefore " in Rom. 12^{1}, Eph. 4^{1}, Phil. 2^{12}, Col. 3^{5}. He does not portray an ideal world, but speaks as a pastor to men and women as he found them in the Graeco-Roman world. Many of the immoralities he refers to would excite little comment in that society except perhaps an aristocratic disdain from the philosopher. What could you expect from slaves and the riff-raff of society? There was a widespread loss of confidence in the old religions and therefore in the sanctions they had imposed on conduct. Slavery, with its denial of responsibility and worth to the slave, and its tendency to encourage irresponsibility in the master, was a widespread social phenomenon. The Roman Empire, by the very effectiveness of its rule, tended to rob the individual life of meaning. On the other hand, the elements of which it was compounded were so diverse that there was little sense of community, except that of language (Greek was the *lingua franca*) and of obedience to Roman law. It was to people drawn from such an environment that the Apostle addressed his words.

The heart of the Apostle's ethical teaching is to be found in the words faith, hope and love, of which love is the greatest. Faith is the complete trust in and dependence on Christ, the Redeemer and Reconciler, who has transferred alienated, godless and sinful men into the kingdom of His Father. Hope is the profound confidence in the consummation of the divine purpose in the individual and the world. Love is that great energy by which God in Christ met men in their dire need and saved them, which then becomes the compelling power in their life. It is love which actuates all human conduct (Col. 3^{14}), for the new society is rooted and grounded in love. The noble hymn of 1 Cor. 13 is at the centre of all Paul's teaching both for individual and social ethics. It is perhaps this which explains his apparent inconsistency in his treatment of the Law. He knows its value as setting forth the ethical requirements of God—it is holy and just and good; but he knows also the perennial temptation of man to turn this into a sytem, the observance of which might secure God's favour, and it is this legalism which is death-dealing (2 Cor. 3^{6}). He knows also, as did the Roman poet, that he can approve the higher way and practise the lower (Rom. $7^{21ff.}$), and at this most critical point the Law cannot help; but "God's love has been poured into our hearts through the Holy Spirit" (Rom. 5^{5}), and life has a new compulsion, the self-giving love of Christ crucified (2 Cor. 5^{14}). Paul condemns those actions and inner thoughts which would deny or corrupt the fellowship because they are a denial of love. Such evils are described in Gal. 5^{19-21} and it is to be noted that not only sexual immorality, greed, drunkenness and angry passion but also party intrigue, contentiousness and hatred are called the works of the flesh (cf. also 1 Cor., 2^{3},

$6^{9f.}$, 2 Cor. 12^{20}, Col. 3^{5-9}). Love as Paul understands it will exclude all that corrupts the life of the individual or destroys the health of the community, " for ye are the Body of Christ and severally members thereof." In love, Christians will seek to be " pleasing to God," an activity open to children no less than to adults (Col. 3^{20}, Eph. 5^{10}). Finally we should observe that Paul is not merely summoning men to heroic moral endeavour. He is not writing about some ideal world, but about a world that includes the people of Corinth. The life of moral attainment is not so much an ideal towards which men must struggle, as a way in which men are led and invigorated by the Spirit which enables men to say with humble confidence " Abba, Father." Those who walk this way will need and will receive the divine energy of the Holy Spirit (1 Cor. $6^{19f.}$, Gal. 5^{22-25}).

If, as Jesus and the Apostles taught, we find the heart of Biblical ethics in love, then " we love because He first loved us " (1 John 4^{19}). This must issue in love of the brethren (1 John 4^{7-12}). The new commandment is that men love one another as Christ has loved them. Biblical ethics is not so much a system which can be compared with Confucian, Buddhist or Aristotelian ethics, although in its requirements it has much in common with all these. It is rather a life in fellowship with God so that it meets, with creative energy, ever new situations and releases into the life of men the power to respond in thought and action. It is for the individual as a member of a community whose life is the Spirit, whose head is Christ.

BIBLIOGRAPHY

C. Ryder Smith, *The Bible Doctrine of Society*, 1920.
C. Ryder Smith, *The Bible Doctrine of Man*, 1951.
N. W. Porteous, " The Basis of the Ethical Teaching of the Prophets " (in *Studies in Old Testament Prophecy*, ed. by H. H. Rowley), 1950.
W. A. L. Emslie, " Ethics " (in *Record and Revelation*, ed. by H. Wheeler Robinson), 1938.
C. A. Anderson Scott, *New Testament Ethics*, 1930.
T. W. Manson, *Ethics and the Gospel*, 1960.
W. Lillie, *New Testament Ethics*, 1961.
C. H. Dodd, *Gospel and Law*, 1951.
J. Muilenburg, *The Way of Israel*, 1961.
W. F. Lofthouse, " Biblical Ethics " (in *A Companion to the Bible*, ed. by T. W. Manson), 1939.

XV. THE LIFE AND TEACHING OF JESUS CHRIST

By H. E. W. Turner

(i) SOURCES OF INFORMATION

The evidence for the life and teaching of Jesus Christ is almost entirely confined to the New Testament. There is a reference in the letters of the Younger Pliny (early second century) based on Christian information which speaks of the sect as "singing hymns to Christ as to a god" (Ep. x. 96). His contemporary Tacitus in his account of the persecution of the Christians under Nero speaks of Christ as the founder of the sect and as having been put to death under Pontius Pilate (*Ann.* xv. 44). The source of his information is unknown but may well have been independent of the Christian community. Suetonius (*Life of Claudius*, 25) in a reference to the expulsion of the Jews from Rome, possibly in A.D. 49 or 50 (cf. Acts 18²¹) has a further allusion in which either by mistake or deliberate intention he gets the name Christ slightly wrong. In any case he wrongly implies that He was present at Rome and the direct cause of disturbances in the Roman ghetto. The references to Jesus in the Romanized Jewish historian Josephus (*Ant.* XVIII. iii. 3 [63 f.]) raises greater problems. Some scholars regard the whole passage as an interpolation but more probably it has been slightly touched up in the course of transmission. In any case his reference to James the Just as "the brother of Jesus called the Christ" (*Ant.* XX. ix. 1 [200]) is clearly authentic. There are a number of references to Jesus (naturally hostile) in the Talmud. It is unlikely that they represent an independent historical tradition but are valuable indications of the kind of reply made by Jewish apologetic to certain features of the life of Jesus. This evidence is sufficient to exclude the improbable theory of the Christ-Myth but indicates that the life and ministry of Jesus passed virtually unnoticed in secular history. This is hardly surprising since from the point of view of the Roman government Jesus was an unprivileged provincial from a third-rate province and enjoyed no protection before Roman Law. Pilate had every inducement not to bring the case to the notice of the authorities at Rome.

The New Testament evidence is largely confined to the Gospels which are both our primary sources for the life and teaching of Jesus and documents of the Christian Church written by believers for the needs of the Church either for apologetic or domestic reasons. Paul can record at need two detailed passages, the Institution of the Eucharist (1 Cor. 11^{23-26}) and a list of Post-Resurrection Appearances (1 Cor. 15^{3-8}) in a manner which indicates that Gospel material in a relatively developed form was available to him some years before the compilation of our present Gospels. A standard outline of the principal events in the life of Jesus has been deduced with great probability from the early sermons in Acts. While some scholars consider this to be a Lucan construction, it is more probable that the underlying form goes back to the earliest stage of the history of the Church.

The Gospels themselves represent compilations from earlier material. Indications of the period of oral transmission can be traced in the form in which both sayings and incidents are recorded. The term "Form Criticism" is applied to this branch of study and some of its results are attended by a high degree of probability. But the value of the inferences drawn from this study still divides scholars. The legitimacy of arguing directly from formal criteria to historical judgments on the material is open to serious question. Some light is certainly cast by this approach on the Christian motives for the preservation of Gospel material and the uses to which it may have been put. But it is as well to remember that we are not perfectly informed about the life of the Church in the Apostolic Age and that the Gospels were primarily intended to give us information about Jesus Himself. The material has a double setting, within the life of Jesus and within the activity of the Primitive Church. Thus two questions which are related but not identical can be asked of the Gospel material and an answer to the one does not enable us to exclude the other.

It is now almost universally agreed that the earliest Gospel preserved to us is that of Mark (*c.* A.D. 65–70). The first part of the Gospel seems to be arranged topically rather than chronologically (groups of parables, miracles, controversy stories, and the like). Clearly nothing depended upon the precise order of the material at this stage of the narrative. These groupings may well represent units in the oral tradition or possibly fly-sheets written for catechetical purposes. The second half of the Gospel bears greater traces of historical integration beginning with the Confession at Caesarea Philippi and reaching its climax in the fast-moving and closely-knit Passion Narrative. It is probable that the Passion Narrative in a fairly complete form was in circulation as an independent unit even before the Marcan Gospel was written. The authentic text of the Gospel ends at 16^{8}. Despite strong argument to the contrary it still appears probable that a brief ending (now lost) completed the book.

Both Matthew and Luke used Mark's Gospel but combine it with other material. Some is special to each Gospel but a sizeable block chiefly devoted to teaching is common to both Gospels. The theory of a written source (Q) behind this material has recently come under heavy fire but still remains the most economical hypothesis. The common material has a strongly Palestinian flavour and there are some indications of a distinctive theological emphasis. Matthew can best be described as an enlarged edition of Mark, but there are some indications that Luke may have used Mark as a supplementary source after the bulk of his Gospel was at least in draft form. As far as we can tell however this "Proto-Luke" does not appear to have been current as a complete Gospel.

Recent scholarship has become less interested in the sources of the Gospels, whether written or oral, and turned its attention to the theological purpose of the Evangelists, their interpretations of the Person and Work of Jesus and the principles of construction which underlie their Gospels. That the Evangelists were men of faith interpreting as well as recording the sources at their disposal can hardly be disputed. It is however questionable whether the complex patterns which some detect behind the Gospels are more than figments of the scholarly imagination. The interpretations of Jesus offered in the Gospels fall within two limits represented by Mark and John. Part at least of the purpose of Mark is to align the reader with the first disciples in the vicissitudes of their discipleship of Jesus. This marks a "historicizing" of the earlier tradition and the Gospel is sufficiently early in date to enable the attempt to be made with a reasonable degree of success. On the other hand, John appears to represent an interpretation of Jesus in the form of a rehandling of the historical tradition. While valuable historical traditions may be contained in the Fourth Gospel, its value does not lie primarily as a factual supplement to the Synoptic tradition but as an interpretation of the meaning of Jesus not only in His earthly life but also in the experience of the Church. The difference, however, remains one of degree rather than of kind. If reliable factual traditions are preserved in John, interpretative elements are not absent from Mark.

(ii) CHRONOLOGY

It is disappointing to have to record that there is no agreement among scholars as to the absolute chronology of the life of Jesus. The Birth Narratives give certain indications that His birth fell between 9 and 7 B.C. though some authorities prefer a slightly earlier date. A firm date for the opening of the public ministry of John the Baptist is given by Luke as A.D. 28/9. The length of the public ministry of Jesus is variously estimated between eighteen months and three years. The Marcan record seems to imply two years (Mark 6^{39} and the later springtide of the final Passover), but allowance must be made for some overlap in the ministries of Jesus and John the Baptist and a possible foreshortening in Mark of the events preceding and even during the Passion. The Fourth Gospel indicates a three-year ministry. The date of the Crucifixion is bound up with the question whether the Last Supper was strictly speaking a Passover or whether the Crucifixion took place as John implies on the eve of the Festival. Astronomical calculations for the years which fell within the procuratorship of Pilate leave open A.D. 27 for the first possibility and A.D. 30 and 33 for the second. The hypothesis which seems most satisfactory is the latest of three dates A.D. 33. Some authorities however prefer a slightly earlier date.

(iii) THE LIFE OF JESUS

Matthew and Luke alone record the Virgin Birth or, more accurately, the Virginal Conception of Jesus. A few other passages in the New Testament might however be interpreted as consenting allusions (Mark 6^3 Son of Mary, John 1^{13} which uses a curiously cumbersome form of expression for the New Birth of Christians and, less probably, Gal. 4^4). John 8^{41} seems to anticipate the reply of Jewish apologetic to the Virgin Birth contained in some later passages in the Talmud. Both Evangelists clearly accept it as a historical fact though they use different supporting traditions and handle it in different ways. While the Matthaean Infancy Narratives are an integral part of his Gospel, there are some indications that the Lucan account forms a kind of appendix to his Gospel though clearly by his own hand. The Genealogy of Jesus, for example, occurs after the first mention of His name in chap. 3 (Luke 3^{23}) instead of in its natural place earlier in the Gospel and the elaborate date at the beginning of the chapter might well have been intended as the opening of the Gospel. Matthew accentuates the theme of the fulfilment of prophecy and his use of Old Testament texts is generally reminiscent of the Qumran texts. The incidents which he records are however probably independent of the prophecies which he attaches to them. The Lucan narrative bears a greater impression of verisimilitude. It breathes a thoroughly Old Testament spirit and the milieu of the families of John the Baptist and Jesus is that of a group of apocalyptic pietists strikingly unlike that of Luke himself. Here the Virgin Birth is recorded in its context with great delicacy and reserve and in its Lucan form the tradition may well go back to the Virgin Mother herself (Luke 2^{51}). The tradition of the Davidic descent of Jesus does not depend solely on the Virgin Birth narratives (Rom. 1^{3}, 2 Tim. 2^{8}, Rev. 5^{5}; cf. Mark $10^{47f.}$ and possibly 12^{35-37}).

Though born, it seems, at Bethlehem, Jesus was brought up at Nazareth in Galilee in an artisan home (Mark 6^{3}). We read of sisters and four brothers of whom at least one (James the Just) was closely connected with the Church in Jerusalem despite initial disbelief (Acts 12^{17}, 15^{13}, 1 Cor. 15^{7}). Galilee itself was a district of mixed cultural and religious heritage, early lost to Israel (Isa. 9^{1}) but forcibly rejudaized by Alexander Jannaeus. Religiously it seems to represent a somewhat more open type of Judaism than the capital. While the Pharisees certainly had followers in Galilee, the main types of Judaism were either a non-sectarian pietism (the Hasidim) or nationalists of the Zealot type. Judging by the Gospels the hopes nourished by the apocalyptic movement seem to have made some considerable impact and it is possible (though by no means proven) that the piety of the Qumran community was not without its influence here. Jesus Himself appears as a practising Jew who observed at least on occasion the pilgrimage feasts at Jerusalem. Luke records a sermon in the synagogue at Nazareth where He was invited to expound the Scriptures. It is clear that He sat very loosely to the Halakah or the expanded oral tradition of the Pharisees. His own approach bore a greater resemblance to the prophetic than the legal tradition. The influence of apocalyptic, a movement which was in some respects the residuary legatee of prophecy, although couched in a different idiom and set against a wider canvas, is unmistakable. His directness of approach and authoritative impact on those who heard were certainly all His own. That His normal dialect was Aramaic is proved by phrases recorded in their original form by Mark. Recent research has made it probable that an Aramaic original often lies not far behind the Greek of the Gospels. It is probable that He knew classical Hebrew. Scholars are divided on the question whether He was acquainted with Greek and if so, to what extent. There is no evidence for any knowledge of the third language current in the Palestine of His day, Latin, and the probability is small.

All the Gospels agree that the immediate background of the ministry of Jesus was the mission of John the Baptist. John is represented as a prophetic figure of the type of Elijah or Amos. His message of repentance (personal renewal) was however connected with the eschatological expectation of one who was to come described in terms drawn from the reaper or the harvester. His functions are Messianic although the title itself is not used in the Synoptic accounts of John's teaching. As a preparation he performed a rite of Baptism. This is a natural piece of prophetic symbolism but its immediate background is not clear. It may have some connexion with proselyte baptism, part of the procedure by which Gentiles became full Jews. If some problems about dating could be resolved this connexion would give added point to his rejection of racial privilege (Matt. 3^{9}, Luke 3^{8}). While some connexion between John the Baptist and the Qumran sect is possible, there are more points of contrast than of similarity between his use of Baptism and their own. The Baptism of John was eschatological, preparative to the coming of the Reaper-Messiah ; the Qumran rite is rather a ritual purification. John's ethical teaching as recorded by Luke (3^{9-13}) seems strangely commonplace and down to earth for one whose manner of life was strongly ascetic (Mark 2^{18-20}).

In the course of John's ministry Jesus presented Himself for baptism and a voice from heaven acclaimed Him in terms drawn from Ps. 2^{7} (the coronation of the Son) and Isa. 42^{1} (the ordination of the Servant). Whether His experience is to be described as subjective or objective it is probably idle to speculate. The Baptism clearly represented a decisive moment in the life of Jesus, the call to a public ministry. The Gospels indicate that at this point also John recognized in Jesus the Coming One to whom his ministry was directed though they also record a time of hesitation and enquiry after his arrest and imprisonment. It is possible that Jesus and John worked in parallel for a time (John $3^{22f.}$, 4^{1}). If according to the Fourth Gospel the first disciples had already been caught up in the Baptist's movement, we learn from elsewhere in the New Testament that the disciples of John continued to form an independent group (Luke 11^{1}, Acts 19^{1-7}).

The Temptations of Jesus, simply noted as a fact by Mark, are more fully recorded in a passage derived from Q in Matthew and Luke. Nothing short of a strong element of personal reminiscence can adequately explain them. The rebuke to Simon Peter (Mark 8^{33}) may imply a knowledge of them on the part of Peter. If an elliptical expression may be permitted, they are rather Temptations of the Christ officially than of Jesus personally. They arise directly out of His call to a public ministry as at once Messiah and Servant. The rejected Temptations represent three false ways of fulfilling His mission, an economic Messiah satisfying the obviously urgent needs of the people, a sign-giving Messiah who would thereby convince and silence ecclesiastical opposition, and a political Messiah who would equate world dominion with the Kingdom of God and replace the *Pax Romana* with a *Pax Christiana* of the wrong type.

The early chapters of Mark organize the material under different heads. A series of controversy stories illustrate the beginnings of a division between Jesus and the Pharisees, the dominant religious party of the day. There are some indications that they belong to the earlier part of the ministry while the Pharisees were engaged in making up their minds about the new teacher. Jesus plainly cared little for the precisions imported into the Law by the Oral Tradition (halakah) and sketches in outline the basis of His later and more bitter polemic against the Pharisees. A correct order of priorities and devotion to true religious principles mattered more than scrupulous obedience to a multitude of legal precepts. A selection of Parables is given in chap. 4. This method of teaching is not quite unique to Jesus but His material is always drawn from actual or possible experiences in daily life and indicates a remarkable directness in His approach as a teacher. Usually (though not quite universally) one point alone is meant to be drawn from the parable. Their aim is to illustrate the key concept of the Kingdom of God though the precise application is normally left to the hearer. The section on the meaning of parables in Mark 4^{10-12} is still much debated among scholars. It seems to suggest that the purpose of parables was to conceal rather than to reveal truth. Its meaning may however be closely similar to the catchword " He that hath ears to hear let him hear " and embody the principle that Jesus demands the response of faith and understanding from His hearers. There is a similar seeming ambiguity about the miracles of Jesus of which a selection is given in the next chapter of Mark. There can be no doubt that these were intended as outgoing acts of love rather than as inward-looking demonstrations of power. If Jesus always condemned the Jewish demand for signs presumably as an attempt to contract out of the risks and demands of discipleship (Matt. 12^{38-39}, 16^{1-4}, Mark 8^{11-12}, Luke $11^{16, 29-32}$), He nevertheless interpreted His exorcisms as the rout of the demonic powers and as evidence of the presence of the Kingdom of God (Matt. 12^{22-30}, Mark 3^{22-27}, Luke 11^{14-26}). Miracles also play a major part in the confirmatory message sent to John in prison (Matt. 11^{2-6}, Luke 7^{19-23}). Mark freely includes injunctions to secrecy both to demoniacs and with other forms of healing. Combined with the difficult section on the purpose of parables this fact has been built into a theory of the Messianic Secret and credited to Mark rather than to Jesus Himself. This view which claims that the Evangelist thought of the Messiahship of Jesus as a secret known to the demons but closely guarded from human beings until its revelation to Simon Peter at Caesarea Philippi will call for fuller discussion later. So far as the miracles are concerned the evidence suggests that Jesus regarded them as signs of the coming Kingdom but only for those with eyes to see and not external substitutes for the adventure of faith. The words " He that hath eyes to see let him see " might be the sub-title of the Marcan miracles. While John still retains traces of the Synoptic perspective (John 4^{48}, 6^{30}) he is more prepared than Mark to stress the miracles as " signs " or " works " of Jesus revealing His person and glory.

The call of twelve disciples " that they might be with him and that he might send them forth " (Mark 3^{14-18}) established an inner core of followers. The term Apostle derives from their function as missionary agents of the coming Kingdom. Among them, Peter, James and John formed a kind of inner group who alone attend Jesus on a number of occasions (Mark 5^{37}, 9^{2}, 14^{33}). The number is significant as representing the Twelve Tribes and foreshadows the description of the Christian Church by Paul as the Israel of God (Gal. 6^{16}). It is more deeply embedded in the tradition even than their names. At least one (Simon the Cananaean or Zealot), and probably another (Judas Iscariot or better the *sicarius*), seem to belong to the nationalist wing of Judaism. But political or national hopes were probably present in the minds of other disciples as well (Mark 10^{35-40}) and contributed to their misunderstanding of the nature of the coming Kingdom.

The main centre of the early part of the ministry appears to be the shores of the Sea of Galilee (Capernaum, Bethsaida, Chorazin, but not apparently Tiberias), although the Johannine tradition of visits to Jerusalem need not be altogether excluded. Despite the critical attitude of the religious authorities the common people heard Him gladly. There are indications of hostility on the part of Herod Antipas, the tetrarch or ruler of Galilee (Mark 6^{14-16}; cf. Luke 13^{31-33} where the informants of Jesus are surprisingly Pharisees). This may be due, as Mark indicates, to the former close association of Jesus with John the Baptist, but fear of the growing popular support which His ministry was receiving was probably no less important. A note significantly attached to the Johannine account of the Feeding of the Five Thousand speaks of a popular attempt to make Him a king or to turn His ministry into a Messianic movement of the political or insurrectionary kind. The evidence suggests that such popular pressure might have found support even among His own disciples. This is the probable background of the Northern journeys implied in such passages as Mark $7^{24.\ 31}$, $8^{22.\ 27}$ and 9^{30}. It is clear that Galilee is being avoided but whether this is due to the hostility of Herod or the popular but shallow support of the crowd, or more probably both, is not easy to determine. At least Jesus takes the opportunity to continue the spiritual education of the Twelve. At Caesarea Philippi, a place where Jewish currents of thought were not strong, Jesus questions the Twelve on popular interpretations of His person and work and leads on their own understanding of Him. Peter replies significantly "Thou art the Messiah." The injunction to secrecy which follows is probably based upon popular misunderstanding of the Messianic vocation. A new note now appears in the Marcan record of the teaching of Jesus that the Son of Man must suffer. Peter's rebuke of Jesus shows how far short the disciples still fell in their understanding of Jesus and the need for further teaching on the new mark of Messiahship. The paradox of a suffering Messiah would pursue the Church as a burning problem in the missionary conditions of the Apostolic Age (1 Cor. 1^{23}).

Of late years the Transfiguration has become the subject of considerable debate. Some scholars regard it as post-Resurrection appearance misplaced in the Gospel records, others transpose the Transfiguration and the Confession at Caesarea Philippi, others again maintain that either the Baptism or the Transfiguration are significant but not both. No valid objection either to the Marcan order or significance has been adduced. It appears as the seal of God both on the new insight of the disciples and the new stage in the self-disclosure of Jesus which it evoked. The voice from heaven is closely similar to that recorded at the Baptism but the new note of suffering in the teaching of Jesus makes a fresh divine validation anything but superfluous. The mention of Moses and Elijah may be merely as representatives of the Law and the Prophets bearing witness to Jesus but it is doubtful whether this exhausts their significance. Both figures were associated with suffering (Elijah plainly in the Old Testament narrative, Moses in Acts 7^{22-39} and Heb. 11^{23-27}). Mystery surrounded the death of both men, Moses whose sepulchre no man knoweth unto this day (Deut. 34^{6}) and Elijah translated to heaven in a chariot of fire (2 Kings 2^{11}).

At this point in the narrative Jesus turned south to go up to Jerusalem. That this was not His first visit to the capital is suggested by a Q passage (Matt. 23^{37}, Luke 13^{34}) as well as the traditions contained in the Fourth Gospel. His route cannot be plotted with certainty. Mark implies a Peraean journey (on the other side of Jordan, Mark 10^{1}) with a halt at Jericho on the way up to Jerusalem (Mark 10^{46-52}). Luke, on the other hand, in the course of a somewhat miscellaneous central section (Luke 9^{51}–18^{34}) contains some indications of a journey through Samaria using the main route from Galilee to Jerusalem through the Central Highlands (Luke 17^{11-19}). No satisfactory solution of the difficulty has been found though it has been suggested that Mark has a tendency to telescope events or shorten his perspective. The suggestion that we are entitled to disregard notes of place and time in the Gospels seems a veritable counsel of despair which makes it difficult to understand why anything so puzzling should have been placed on record.

Whatever its route the journey to Jerusalem was made in an atmosphere heavy with expectation. The acceptance by Jesus of Peter's acclamation despite the repeated prediction of the Passion naturally raised in the disciples' minds the expectation of an earthly Messianic Kingdom. It is against this background that the attempt of James and John to secure for themselves places of prominence in the coming Kingdom is to be seen. This attempt would gain in force if Jesus had made certain promises to Peter as the man of faith on which the Church (the Messianic community) would be built. The passage is not however beyond critical doubt. For Jesus Himself the journey probably represented a final bid for the soul of the nation though the prospect of death was plainly before His mind.

The Triumphal Entry is normally (and probably rightly) interpreted as a Messianic ovation. There is evidence of careful preparation in the arrangement of a password and the supply of an ass. The rumour of a promising Messianic movement from Galilee may also have had its part to play. The welcoming crowd appear to be either fellow-Galileans up for the Festival or Jerusalem sympathizers or possibly a combination of both. As it stands in the Gospel record it is connected closely with the final Passover but the mention of palm branches suggests the ceremonial of Tabernacles and a case might be made out for a date in the previous autumn. This would certainly allow more time for the development of events instead of the tightly packed narrative and hurried climax of the Marcan record as it stands at present. The theory however implies a drastic foreshortening of the Marcan perspective and remains no more than an attractive possibility. The point of the story lies in the conscious fulfilment by Jesus of the prophecy of Zech. 9[9] —the peaceable Messiah. The appended saying in Luke 19[39-40] may amount to a recognition by Jesus that the very stones of Jerusalem are so impregnated with political expectation that a favourable outcome to His mission there could hardly be expected.

The Cleansing of the Temple is a further prophetic action revealing the Messiahship of Jesus. The Temple was the dwelling-place of God in His Kingdom but the concerns of Mammon had penetrated the sanctuary of God. It was the focus of ecclesiastical Judaism, the rallying point of the forces ranged against Him. Its outer precincts had become a place of merchandise though no doubt the business was closely related to the cultus and primarily intended for the convenience of worshippers. If the suggestion that it was the Court of the Gentiles which was so cleansed is correct, the action of Jesus would have the further intention of vindicating against Jewish encroachment their rights in the only part of the Temple to which they had access. The gauntlet had been thrown down and the Jewish authorities were not slow to take up the challenge (Mark 11^{18}). The garbled evidence given by the false witnesses at the Trial indicates the importance of the attitude of Jesus to the Temple in deciding the Jewish authorities to take action against Him (Mark 14^{58}, 15^{29}, John 2^{19}).

The controversies which follow in Mark seem to be the direct outcome of these two incidents and breathe a different spirit from the earlier sighting shots of the Pharisees in Galilee. The latter were concerned to test the attitude of the new teacher to current legal practice while the present group are more conscious attempts to trap Him in His words. The question on authority was directly raised by the Cleansing of the Temple while the question on the Tribute Money sought to clarify the attitude of Jesus to the secular arm. The dilemma which the Pharisees and Herodians (though it is curious to find them in Jerusalem) wished to impose was that Jesus was either a political Messiah (and therefore capable of being denounced as a rebel to the Roman authorities) or an unpatriotic Jew and therefore undeserving of popular support. The question on the Resurrection raised in a paradoxical form one main issue between the leading parties of the day. The Sadducees were particularly strong in Jerusalem.

The Passion narrative proper begins with Mark 14. The Passover is about to begin, and it is significant that this Festival was linked not only with the classical deliverance of the Old Testament but also with the expectation of the future restoration by God of His people. The presence of Pilate in the capital suggests that the potential threat to public security which it presented did not go unnoticed by the Roman authorities. Coming at such a time the challenge of Jesus to the Jewish authorities seemed doubly dangerous. An open clash which might rally many to His side, no doubt for wrong reasons, was at all cost to be avoided. By contrast the Anointing at Bethany, probably intended by the woman as a sign of royal dignity (a point obscured by Luke and John), is reinterpreted by Jesus in terms of His approaching death. He is clearly thinking not in terms of a speedy victory but of impending suffering. The final saying suggests that His aim was to embrace the Gentile world and not to overthrow the domination of Gentile rulers. After this incident, it seems, Judas decided to betray Jesus to His enemies. If the fact is certain, the motive remains unclear but no suggestion is more probable than disappointment. Jesus was throwing away good chances of bringing in the Kingdom in the only way in which Judas could understand it.

Mark now passes in his narrative to the Last Supper. Here an important problem of dating arises. The chronology of the Passion recorded in the Fourth Gospel implies that Jesus died on the Cross at the time when the Paschal lambs were slain in the Temple courts. The official Passover would therefore begin on the Friday evening. But the date given in Mark 14[12] appears to equate the Last Supper held on the previous day with the Passover, though much of the detail in the Marcan Passion narrative is difficult to reconcile with this dating. Older attempts to harmonize the two accounts by suggesting that two alternative calendars were current have been revived by the discoveries at Qumran, but it is most unlikely that the Temple authorities would grant facilities for a use other than their own. Conditions at Qumran and in Jerusalem were widely different. The absence of any mention of a Lamb at the Last Supper, although an argument from silence, is extremely strong. Attempts to identify the Last Supper with some rite other than the Passover known to contemporary Judaism seem to raise more problems than they solve. Yet whatever Jesus did on the night on which He was betrayed was shot through and through with Paschal significance. Elaborate arrangements for eating the Passover in Jerusalem had already been made. The Upper Room is described as furnished and ready and it was there rather than in Bethany where Jesus and His disciples were lodged that the Last Supper took place. It could reasonably be described as an anticipatory Passover lacking only the Lamb. But it also clearly pointed to the very event which led Jesus to anticipate as far as might be the official festival. We have already noted that the Passover looked not only back to the deliverance of the Exodus but also forward to a time of national restoration which many interpreted in political rather than in eschatological terms. The Last Supper (whatever its relation to the Passover) looked forward to a greater deliverance to be accomplished by Jesus Himself on the Cross. In this sense at least the Lamb was not simply absent for, as with Abraham of old, God would provide a Lamb for sacrifice. In the course of the meal Jesus took bread and brake and gave to His disciples with the words " This is my body " and wine saying " This is my blood of the covenant which is shed for many." An eschatological meaning is given to the whole rite in a closing saying which spoke of drinking wine new with the disciples in the Kingdom of God. Expanded forms of the words of administration are given by Paul in 1 Corinthians and by Luke and probably derive from a different form of the tradition. Which form is the earlier is much disputed. Possibly the simpler form in Mark stands closer to the original tradition. The root meaning is "This is I myself, my life enriched and made available through my death" and is best understood in the light of the dynamic categories of the prophetic symbolism of the Old Testament. Later Christian doctrine has all too frequently divorced the two aspects of realism and symbolism which the Gospels unite. The command to repeat is only explicitly recorded by Paul and Luke. It is not however excluded in the Marcan tradition in view of the obvious fact that the Eucharist was held in the Church for which the Gospel was written. Its probable purpose to align its readers with the original disciples of Jesus in His earthly ministry may also be relevant here. The precise reference of the phrase of the words "in remembrance of me" is not wholly certain. Biblical usage could support either a memorial before God or before men. Possibly both may be in mind here. The interpretation "that God may remember me" is unlikely.

After the completion of the Supper Jesus and His disciples leave the Old City and begin their journey back to Bethany. In the garden of Gethsemane at the foot of the ascent to the Mount of Olives Jesus takes the inner group of the disciples apart and prays in an agony of spirit that the cup of suffering may pass from Him. Judas leads a party, possibly of Temple police, possibly a hastily gathered band of irregulars, to make the arrest. It is difficult to fit all the material relating to the trials of Jesus recorded in the four Gospels into the time available. The Marcan record opens with a night trial before the High Priest of which the findings were confirmed at a short meeting on the following morning (Mark 15[1]). There are evident signs both of haste and illegality in the original hearing. A trial by night, the continuance of proceedings after the court had heard discordant testimony, and the adjuration of the prisoner to give evidence in his own case all fell short of the best legal standards of Judaism. The evidence of the false witnesses at least indicates the place which the Cleansing of the Temple occupied in determining the action of the chief priests. The High Priest's question to the prisoner brings the Messiahship of Jesus plainly into the picture. The reply of Jesus is differently recorded in the Synoptic Gospels but an affirmative answer is the most probable. The action of the

High Priest is tantamount to the charge of blasphemy. The confession of Messiahship can hardly be regarded as blasphemous in itself. This would stultify the whole expectation. The point is rather that such a confession on the lips of Jesus was regarded in this light. He was the wrong kind of Messiah and completely unaccredited in Jewish eyes. Strictly in Jewish law blasphemy involved the open use of the Divine Name. Unless the reply of Jesus " I am " was considered in this light something less than full blasphemy was involved. The legal status of these proceedings before the Sanhedrin is doubtful. This depends upon the question whether the supreme Jewish court possessed the power of passing capital sentences under Roman rule. There are arguments on both sides, but the balance of probability suggests that its jurisdiction was limited. There is however some evidence that in certain cases which touched Jewish susceptibilities closely the Roman procurator's court would be likely to rubber stamp Jewish decisions. Almost certainly offences against the Temple would fall within this class. In that case the importance of the discordant testimony becomes clear. Its failure meant that another line of approach must be tried. After a formal ratification of the night proceedings Jesus is hurried away before Pilate. The charge is now altered to one of high treason against Rome, presumably based upon the equation of Messiahship with political Messiahship, the very identification which Jesus had steadfastly refused to make. Pilate recognizes that Jesus is not the type of Messianic insurgent with which the Roman government in Palestine was becoming familiar and exerts himself to release Him. Luke speaks of an abortive attempt to shift the responsibility to Herod Antipas on the ground presumably that as a Galilean Jesus was not under Pilate's jurisdiction but " that fox " (Luke 13[32]), though no doubt flattered by Pilate's unexpected observance of protocol, was not to be trapped in this way. Pilate tries to secure a special release of the prisoner by means of a Passover exchange with Barabbas. There is no supporting evidence for this custom but the tradition need not be disputed on these grounds. The local attempt of an unpopular procurator to ingratiate himself with the province might leave no further trace on the records, especially as it was in evident conflict with the best traditions of Roman justice. Popular pressure amounting in the Fourth Gospel to scarcely concealed blackmail overbore Pilate's reluctance and the sentence of death by crucifixion was pronounced. The two facts of Jewish initiative and execution by Roman methods are quite indisputable. The scene of the mockery placed by Mark after the Roman sentence is also attached to other incidents in the other Gospels. There is nothing inherently improbable about horseplay at the prisoner's expense at various stages of his Passion progress. The scourging was a normal part of death by crucifixion. Luke less correctly treats it as a further attempt by Pilate to save Jesus from the extreme penalty. The prisoner usually carried the heavy crossbar (*patibulum*) to the place of execution but a rough mercy on the part of the under-officer in charge of the execution squad permitted the impress of a passer-by, Simon of Cyrene, probably a Paschal pilgrim, to discharge this duty. A personal note appended in Mark suggests that his sons were well-known members of the Church for whom his Gospel was written. The kindly action of a guild of ladies in Jerusalem provided a drugged potion for prisoners executed by this means. This Jesus refused to drink. He would meet His death "for the many" with an undimmed consciousness. Two "robbers" (probably insurrectionaries) shared His crucifixion. Christians have always seen in the two companion crosses part of the problem to which the death of Jesus provided the answer. The mysterious cry preserved by Mark in an Aramaic form is derived from Ps. 22^1. Although this Psalm of a Righteous Sufferer ends with a note of confidence and even triumph the traditional interpretation of a Cry of Dereliction remains more probable. Why otherwise should the despairing opening words have been handed down instead of the final words of confidence? Christians believe that the burden of sin which Jesus carried blotted out at that moment even the face of God. By contrast Mark's note about the rending of the veil of the Temple is to be interpreted as the removal of all that hides God from His people.

The death of Jesus left His followers cowed and beaten. It was left to a highly placed Jerusalem sympathizer to beg the body of Jesus from the procurator and to save it from a criminal's grave. The women performed as much of the final rites as time allowed before the Passover began.

The Resurrection itself is never described in the canonical Gospels. An apocryphal Gospel, the Gospel of Peter, later broke the seal of reverence and tried to offer a description of the Act. It is clear that this was the last event which the women expected as they hurried to the Tomb at first light on the Sunday morning to complete the burial rites of their dead Master. The last authentic section of the Marcan Gospel speaks of the Empty Tomb, the angelic messenger which serves as a provisional Christophany and the women's fear. Many scholars believe that this forms the natural ending of the Gospel but it seems more probable that a short ending resolving the mingled fear and disbelief of the women and an appearance of the Risen Lord to Peter confirming his position as a disciple despite his denial was either intended or originally current. This might have been combined with a confession of Jesus as the Son of God which is absent in the Marcan account of Caesarea Philippi. A conclusion of this type is therefore suggested by the Gospel itself. A list of post-Resurrection appearances is contained in 1 Cor. 15^{3-8} which antedates the written Gospels and contains items not recorded in the canonical tradition. The appearance to James, for example, is almost demanded by his later position in the Church at Jerusalem. No note of time or place is attached to this list, possibly because it was irrelevant to the particular purpose which Paul has in mind here. No mention of the Empty Tomb is made, again probably because it was irrelevant to the theological question of the resurrection body of Christians which was under discussion. Two traditions of the locale of the post-Resurrection appearances are current in the Gospels. Matthew and (by inference) Mark place them in Galilee, Luke only in Jerusalem. With a fair measure of historical probability the Fourth Gospel combines both traditions. Neither need be regarded as historically suspect if the historical circumstances of the disciples is taken into account. The future was far from clear. Their homes and livelihood lay in Galilee and they could not be chargeable to the generosity of Jerusalemite sympathizers indefinitely. While normally the Jerusalem appearances were evidential and the Galilean appearances vocational, it is unlikely that the notes of place mean no more than this. The whole period of the appearances may be justly regarded as a time of accommodation to the needs of the disciples, a transition from the previous fellowship of sight and touch to the new impact of the Risen Christ through the Spirit. The Ascension, deliberately recorded by Luke both at the end of the Gospel and the beginning of the Acts of the Apostles, marks the final watershed between the earthly life of the Incarnate Lord and the new phase of His fellowship with His people.

(iv) THE KINGDOM OF GOD IN THE TEACHING OF JESUS

It is difficult to consider the Kingdom of God in the Gospels without a simultaneous discussion of the self-designation of Jesus, but for the sake of clarity a somewhat artificial distinction of treatment must be attempted here. The close relationship between the two will become apparent as our discussion proceeds.

The term " The Kingdom of God " is rendered in Matthew as " the Kingdom of Heaven." This slight modification is in line with Rabbinic usage and recalls the Jewish custom of employing reverential reserve in using the name of God to avoid any breach, however unintentional, of the third commandment. In its root meaning of the sovereignty or rule of God it is a leading theme of the Old Testament. "The Lord God omnipotent reigneth," "The Lord is King" and the "Kingdom of God" are correlatives. Naturally enough the rule of God implied a realm in which it was exercised. The Old Testament found no difficulty in asserting both the universal kingship of God and its actualization in the Chosen People. In the prophetic period this was particularly associated with the royal house of David though in the apocalyptic era the concept (never formally detached from national aspirations) was deepened and widened in the light of the new horizons of the Jewish Faith. The balance of expectation became reversed in the later period, though its ingredients remained broadly the same. If an eschatological significance is already assigned to the political fortunes of the house of David in the eighth century prophets, this expectation becomes even more pronounced in the apocalyptic writings, though, if circumstances appeared favourable, it could easily be applied to the resurgence of national hopes. The faith that God was the Sovereign King of the Universe, and particularly over His Chosen People, and that He would assert His Kingly Rule over every adverse power was the basic principle behind the concept; the hope that in a given political situation this would be realized through the appropriate human agencies was a persistent but more fluid part of the expectation.

The concept is clearly central to the teaching of Jesus. The meaning "the kingly rule of God" remains fundamental though in a few passages the rule is interpreted in the light of the realm which is its logical implicate and natural corollary. In the teaching of Jesus it is the eschatological and not the political aspect of the Kingdom which is clearly fundamental.

There has been much debate among scholars on the question whether Jesus believed that the Kingdom of God was already in some sense "realized" in His earthly ministry or whether His teaching pointed solely or merely to the future and, if so, how far into the future His foresight extended. The issue partly depends upon the precise shade of meaning of the Greek words used in two passages "The kingdom of God is at hand" (Mark 1^{15}) and "The kingdom of God is come upon you" (Matt. 12^{28}, Luke 11^{20}). In the first passage the literal meaning of the Greek is "has drawn near." This leaves open two interpretations, either "has drawn near and therefore at the door or on the threshold" or "has drawn near and therefore already here." In the second text the question is whether the note of anticipation which attached to the word in classical Greek still persisted in New Testament language. Examples both of the strict and looser usage can be quoted from Biblical Greek. A further passage in which the precise shade of meaning is disputed is Mark 9[1] " Verily I say unto you, There be some here of them that stand by, which shall in no wise taste of death, till they see the kingdom of God come with power." In translation this sounds easier than it actually is. The words " until they see " plainly point to the future, but the participle with which it is combined in the Greek as in the perfect tense, which expresses an act in the past with consequences continuing in the present. The most satisfactory interpretation of the text is probably of a decisive act in the future with consequences which will persist.

There are certainly a number of passages in the Gospels which appear to point plainly to the future. What may be called the Futurist school of interpretation regards these as the most reliable guide to the teaching of Jesus and they are certainly in keeping with some aspects of Jewish thought widely current at the time. Others however claim that here we find the hand of the Church approximating the teaching of Jesus to its own expectation and it may possibly be significant that this note is more prominent in a later Gospel like Matthew than in the earliest presumed Gospel source (Q). They would admit that there were traces of a genuine prophetic foresight extending to the destruction of Jerusalem in the Gospels but claim that the apocalyptic expectation with which it is combined is a reflection of the hope of the Parousia or Second Coming of Christ which was vividly held in New Testament times. But the habit of seeing impending historical events in an eschatological context is to be found even in the prophetic period of Old Testament religion and it would be wholly natural if the same idiom of thought, partly historical and partly eschatological, was also characteristic of Jesus Himself. The sharp distinction between historical prediction and eschatalogical hope is a modern invention which is not calculated to get the best of the Gospel evidence. What tells most heavily against the exclusive adequacy of the futurist interpretation is the presence (chiefly in the Q source) of a number of passages which plainly imply that for Jesus the Kingdom was in some way already present in His words and works.

Others are inclined to make a sharp division in the teaching of Jesus at the Confession at Caesarea Philippi and to argue that before this turning point in the Gospels Jesus spoke of the Kingdom of God as future but that later He increasingly emphasized its close connexion with His own person. Henceforward His teaching on the Kingdom of God was reinterpreted in terms of discipleship. This might work well enough for Mark, but it is difficult to apply satisfactorily to the material believed to derive from Q, where the proportion of incident to saying is much lower. There is no evidence that Q contained any narrative corresponding to Peter's Confession.

The probability is that the teaching of Jesus on the subject of the Kingdom was more rich and many-sided than most of the current theories are prepared to admit. While some scholars claim that the Church imported its own conception into the Gospel record, it is more likely that later New Testament teaching represents a simplification of the doctrine of the Kingdom given by Jesus Himself or the isolation of one element at the expense of the rest. It will be argued here that there are really three aspects of the Kingdom in the teaching of Jesus, each linked with successive phases of His own person and work.

For the earlier part of the Ministry (particularly as evidenced by the Q source) we have an anticipated eschatology of the Kingdom. It is already present as it were by anticipation in the mighty works of Jesus. This is expressly stated with regard to the expulsion of demons by the finger (Luke), or the spirit (Matt.), of God (Matt. 12^{28}, Luke 11^{20}). A similar appeal to miracles is made in the message to John the Baptist in prison (Matt. 11^{2-6}, Luke 7^{18-23}). They are the natural confirmation of his faith in Jesus as the Coming One designed to impel rather than to compel belief because they are evidence of the coming Kingdom. Another Q passage speaks of " something greater than Solomon " (neuter, not masculine) which is already present with Jesus Himself (Matt. 12^{41-42}, Luke 11^{30-31}). What is present is the Kingdom of God, a greater sovereignty than that of Solomon, the son and successor of King David. In another passage of similar origin (Matt. 13^{16-17}, Luke 10^{23-24}) the disciples are accounted blessed because they see and hear what prophets, saints, and kings of old desired in vain. Jesus then is no mere eschatological prophet peering into the future ; the Kingdom is already in some sense present already in His mighty acts.

There is a difficult but significant passage, probably of Q origin but recorded in notably different form in Matthew and Luke (Matt. 11^{12-13}, Luke 16^{16}). It refers explicitly to the Kingdom of God and marks John the Baptist as the end of a dispensation. " The law and the prophets were until John, after that the kingdom of God. . . ." Luke characteristically reads " The kingdom of God is preached " (cf. his interpretation of the sign of Jonah in Luke 11^{32}), and the violence with which it is associated represents the multitudes clamouring for admission as the result of its proclamation. The Matthaean version is more difficult and therefore more likely to be original. " The kingdom of God is forced (or exerts its own force) and men of violence take it by storm." The verb here might be either middle (vaguely reflexive) or passive. Much here depends on the further question whether the men of violence in this form of the saying are to be understood in a good sense (as in Luke) or as an allusion to the enemies of the Kingdom of God, whether as open opponents or as those who try to turn the mission and message of Jesus to their own lesser ends. The middle voice of the verb gives an attractive sense "The kingdom of God exerts its own force" (much as a thunderstorm exerts its own pressure before it finally breaks) "and forceful men (men of like temper) take it by storm." The alternative rendering would be "The kingdom of God suffers violence and forcible men take it by storm" (in a bad sense in both halves of the passage). In either case and in both forms of the saying the Kingdom is interpreted as a new dispensation marked off from the old order by the coming of Jesus Himself.

A similar theme is found in certain parables relating to seed or leaven. Although modern evolutionary ideas of growth were unknown in New Testament times (1 Cor. 15^{36} speaks of the death of the seed and the birth of the plant), the contrast between small beginnings and the final result is plainly made. Parables of this type include the Mustard Seed (Mark 4^{30-32}, Matt. 13^{31-32}, Luke 13^{18-19}), the Seed growing secretly (Mark 4^{26-29}) and the Leaven (Matt. 13^{33}, Luke $13^{20f.}$ (Q)). Something is already present but not in its full effects or at its full power. We might almost describe the picture of the Kingdom given in these parables as present germinally or potentially.

This evidence suggests that in the earthly ministry of Jesus before the Passion the Kingdom of God is already at work in a way in which it was not present before but which does not exhaust its full range of possibilities. This aspect of the teaching of Jesus on the Kingdom of God has come to be known as "realized eschatology"; it might be more correctly described in the light of the evidence as "anticipated eschatology" in the sense indicated above.

One criticism which might relevantly be raised against the description of the Kingdom of God in the earthly ministry of Jesus as realized eschatology is that it seems to blur the decisive significance of the Passion, Cross, and Resurrection of Jesus. It is suggested that together they form a Messianic moment of such significance as to justify separate classification as "inaugurated eschatology." It is difficult to regard such incidents as the Entry into Jerusalem, the Cleansing of the Temple, the Last Supper, Cross, and Resurrection as of less relevance to the Kingdom of God than the miracle stories of the earlier part of the Gospel. They certainly belong to the same pattern of salvation history as the mighty works and the expected Parousia. A major problem is certainly the almost complete absence of any direct correlation of these events with the Kingdom of God in the teaching of Jesus himself. But the difficulty may largely be met by the fact that at this point in particular in His ministry He was confronted by the political reference given to the Kingdom by His contemporaries and particularly by His opponents. The cry of Bartimaeus "Jesus thou Son of David" (Mark 10^{47}), the acclamation at the Triumphal Entry "Blessed is the kingdom that cometh, the kingdom of our father David" (Mark 11^{10}), the arrest and execution of Jesus as a Messianic pretender (the King of the Jews), all point plainly to a situation in which open teaching on these lines would appear to be dangerously misleading. But the point is plainly made at the Last Supper "until I drink it new with you in the kingdom of God" (Mark 14^{25}, Matt. 26^{29}, Luke 22^{18}), the dialogue with the penitent thief on the Cross "Jesus remember me when thou comest into thy kingdom" (Luke 23^{42}) and again in the Fourth Gospel before Pilate "My kingdom is not of this world" (John 18^{36-37}).

It remains to consider the evidence for a third phase in the coming of the Kingdom, futurist or consummated eschatology. Here some scholars find the heart of the teaching of Jesus on the Kingdom while others are more inclined to suspect the hand of the Church modifying it in the light of current expectation. Two questions are really involved here. Did Jesus look beyond His death and Resurrection to a future in which the Kingdom by an act which transcended history should fully come? and how far did He associate such a coming with His own person? On the first question the evidence seems difficult to dispute. In both versions of the Lord's Prayer the petition "Thy kingdom come" occurs (Matt. 6^{10}, Luke 11^{2}). It might possibly be argued that this clause is identical with the succeeding words "Thy will be done." But other clauses such as "Lead us not into temptation" (the Messianic woes) and possibly "Give us this day our daily bread," where an unusual word is translated "daily" (the Messianic Banquet) appear to have eschatological overtones. Again in Mark 9^{1} (cited above) a futurist reference seems unmistakable. Attempts to interpret it either of the Transfiguration considered as a post-Resurrection appearance or of Pentecost fail to convince. The word "power" is used in an eschatological context elsewhere in the New Testament (*e.g.* 1 Cor. 15^{43}). Even more clear-cut is a saying linked with the Last Supper in all three Synoptic Gospels "I shall no more drink of the fruit of the vine until I drink it new with you in the Kingdom of God." Mark followed by Matthew places it after the Supper, Luke (doubtless to avoid the suggestion that Jesus Himself partook of the Eucharist) reverses the order. This seems to point forward to the Messianic Banquet which is the subject of a Q saying (Matt. 8^{11}, Luke 13^{29}). Critically unassailable sayings which refer to the " days of the Son of Man " or " that day " seen in the light of Old Testament expectation clearly point in the same direction. Parables of watchfulness and judgment again imply a future consummation, if they are read in their present context. Even allowing for the need of watchfulness under the conditions of present discipleship of Jesus and the fact that judgment was already implicit in His words and works, it is difficult to believe that this exhausts the full range of His meaning. Crucial event (whether in the present or the future) rather than general principle was characteristic of His teaching. The evidence therefore strongly suggests that the teaching of Jesus on the Kingdom of God included the expectation of a future consummation.

The range of the foresight of Jesus into the future and the time-span of the interval before the consummation are among the most difficult problems which confront the student of the Gospels. Three sayings (all introduced by the solemn formula of asseveration which some believe to be an important mark of authenticity) appear to predict a consummation within a generation of His own lifetime (Mark 9^{1}, Matt. 16^{28}, Luke 9^{27}; Mark 13^{30}, Matt. 24^{34}, Luke 21^{32}; Matt. 10^{23}). Yet there are other indications in the Gospels which blunt the force of this suggestion. While the Marcan Apocalypse (Mark 13) is difficult to expound as a whole with any degree of confidence, it contains material which points in other directions. Thus Mark 13^{32} " Of that day and hour knoweth no man, not even the Son but the Father " is a plain statement of ignorance on the matter of a kind most unlikely to be attributed to Jesus by the Church. Other indications of activity leading up to the End are wholly independent of considerations of time-span. Such are persecution and confession before rulers (Mark 13^{9}), the preaching of the Gospel (Mark 13^{10}) and (if we are entitled to appeal to Paul) the celebration of the Eucharist (1 Cor. 11^{26} " till he come "). It is noteworthy that all these marks of the end are independently evidenced elsewhere in the Gospels.

It is impossible to construct a fully consistent picture either of the signs leading up to the end or of the consummation itself from the recorded teaching of Jesus. Much of the material contained in the Gospels is obviously traditional within Judaism and it must be remembered that the eschatology of the period was in a highly fluid state. Symbolic and pictorial language is the sole idiom appropriate to such themes and it is not at all surprising that it is difficult to construct a single coherent account which covers all aspects of His teaching. The time factor involved can hardly be regarded as a matter of salvation. What is of obligation is the duty of watchfulness and belief in the consummation of the Kingdom both in mercy and judgment. Perhaps the most difficult part of the evidence, the sayings which seem to point to the consummation as within the lifetime of a single generation, may be due to a kind of prophetic foreshortening in which the spiritually urgent was interpreted in terms which suggest the chronologically imminent.

In other aspects of His teaching on the Kingdom Jesus plainly associated the various aspects of its coming with His own person and work. But did He regard its consummation as similarly associated with Himself? It would no doubt be theoretically possible to believe that at this point He simply repeated current Jewish expectation without bringing it into any closer relation to Himself and some scholars are prepared to believe that this was the case. The question largely turns on the interpretation of the Son of Man passages which will concern us later. Parity of reasoning creates at least the strong presumption that here (as elsewhere) the concept of the Kingdom has been revalued by its close association with Himself. In their natural sense the parables of the absent householder (Matt. 21^{33-41}) or landlord (Mark 12^{1-9}, Luke 20^{9-19}), the returning king (Matt. 22^{2-13}; cf. Luke 14^{16-24}) and the delaying bridegroom (Matt. 25^{1-13}) suggest a recognizable strain in the teaching of Jesus of which an expectation centred in His own person is the natural explanation. In each case it is a coming or returning figure who is involved. There is no convincing reason to assume the invention or adaptation of this material by the Church. A Lucan saying which is only loosely attached to the preceding parable and which bears all the marks of an authentic logion runs as follows "Howbeit when the Son of Man cometh, shall he find faith on the earth?" (Luke 18^{8}).

The key passages for the centrality of Jesus in the consummated Kingdom (the doctrine of the Parousia or Second Coming) derive from Mark. The first is the reply of Jesus to the question of the High Priest, where in answer to the question "Art thou the Christ, the Son of the Blessed," Jesus affirms "I am, and ye shall see the Son of Man sitting on the right hand of the Power and coming in the clouds of heaven" (Mark 14^{62}). The reference here is plainly to Daniel 7. Some scholars believe that a single process of divine vindication is described here in a twofold manner, first statically (sitting on the right hand of the Power) and then dynamically (coming in the clouds of heaven). The difficulty here lies in the order of the clauses which seems to give an unnatural climax. The alternative and more attractive explanation is to find in these clauses a double movement, the one of exaltation and the other of return in judgment. The second passage " For whosoever shall be ashamed of me and my words in this adulterous and sinful generation, the Son of Man shall also be ashamed of him when he cometh in the glory of his Father with the holy angels " (Mark 8^{38}) appears even more explicit and anchors the expectation in the person of Jesus Himself. Attempts to shake its force have been made by the quotation of a Q saying which is closely parallel but which speaks only of confession and denial before the angels of God (Matt. 10^{32-33}, Luke 12^{8-9}). This is claimed to be the original form of the saying which has been adapted to include a reference to the Parousia in its Marcan form. Neither Matthew nor Luke seems to have noticed any discrepancy for they record both forms of the saying in their Gospels. No doubt the function of the returning Son of Man differs in the two sayings. In Mark he is regarded as the Judge, in Q as the Advocate. But these are two roles of the returning Christ which are united somewhat paradoxically elsewhere in the New Testament (cf. the Johannine literature). It is altogether more probable that both forms of the saying go back to Jesus Himself, each emphasizing a different aspect of His function at the Parousia.

The teaching of Jesus on the Kingdom of God starts from the eschatology current in His own day but passes beyond it at every point by associating it with His own person and work. The eschatological framework of contemporary Judaism was already shattered beyond repair when Jesus claimed that the Kingdom was already proleptically present in His own words and deeds. The great moment of its inauguration (if our interpretation is correct) through His own Passion, Death, and Resurrection carries us still further from the accepted pattern, while a new character and definition was given to the expectation of a divine visitation in judgment, for which many circles in Judaism were looking, by the provision of a new focus in His own person. Yet Jesus was no mere eschatological prophet like John the Baptist nor did He come the first time merely to proclaim a Second Coming in glory to judge both the quick and the dead. At every stage Jesus and the Kingdom of God involve each other. In the words of Origen He is the Kingdom itself (*autobasileia*) and He is this precisely because He is the King Himself.

(v) THE TITLES OF JESUS USED IN THE GOSPELS

We have seen that the concept of the Kingdom of God in the teaching of Jesus cannot be divorced from the titles used about Him in the Gospels. Conversely a discussion of the titles, Messiah, Son of Man and Suffering Servant will throw light not only upon the person and work of Jesus but also upon the content of the Kingdom of God. The same process of revaluation which we found in our discussion of the Kingdom may also be expected to apply here.

(a) *The Messiah* (*Christ*). The cardinal doctrine of the Old Testament was that "the Lord is King." Some expectations of the Kingdom were quite independent of any figure in which the hope might be said to be embodied. Yet just as in the earlier period the Kingdom of God was, as it were, incarnated in the kingdom of the house of David, so it became natural for later forms of the expectation to be associated with a particular figure. The word "Messiah" means anointed and this left open the question whether He was to be conceived primarily as a priestly or a regal figure. Indeed the restored community after the Exile seems at one time to have possessed two heads, Joshua the son of Jozadak and Zerubbabel, representing the ecclesiastical and secular arms respectively. Variations in the political and ecclesiastical fortunes of the Jewish community in post-exilic times were not without some influence on the interpretation of the figure of the Messiah. While the political hopes associated with the house of David were never formally abandoned and remained below the surface ready at any moment to be revived, the Hasmonaean ascendancy gave currency to the belief that the Messiah should be of Aaronic stock. The Qumran documents seem to speak of two Messiahs of Aaron and of Israel while the influential Psalms of Solomon revived the hope of a Davidic Messiah described in markedly political terms. In some documents such as Daniel the Messianic figure, the Son of Man, is a community figure transposing into an apocalyptic idiom the corporate conception of the Servant of God in Second Isaiah. While the Sovereignty of God was a firmly established doctrine in Judaism, Messianism was a matter of speculation widely held but equally widely interpreted.

There is cumulative evidence that in the time of Jesus there was a popular crystallization in terms of a political expectation or possibly it might be more correct to say that political aspirations were tending to rise to the surface. The evidence of Josephus proves that in the period between the establishment of Roman rule in A.D. 6 and the Fall of Jerusalem in A.D. 70 Messianism in this form was a potent factor in Jewish life. A number of Messianic outbreaks occurred and were as promptly suppressed. The rise of the Zealots or *Sicarii* as a political and religious force is clearly noted despite the fact that Josephus himself for apologetic reasons is concerned to play down their significance.

A general background of Messianic hope underlies the early traditions contained in the first two chapters of Luke. The Benedictus speaks of "the horn of salvation in the house of his servant David" (Luke 1^{69}), Simeon is described as "righteous and devout and looking for the consolation of Israel" (Luke 2^{25}), while Anna spoke of the babe to "all those who were looking for the redemption of Jerusalem" (Luke 2^{38}). The angelic message to Mary is of special importance for it links the title "Son of God" with "the throne of his father David" (Luke 1^{32}). The circle here depicted seems to be marked by an apocalyptic pietism but it is easy to see how these and similar phrases could assume a political significance.

Echoes later in the Ministry are not wanting. The cry of Bartimaeus and the acclamation of the crowd at the Triumphal Entry are indications of a link in the popular mind of Jesus Himself with Messianic expectations. Even the disciples are not free from the temptation to interpret the mission of Jesus in political terms (Mark 10^{35-40}). The Fourth Gospel even provides a valuable clue in the attempt to make Jesus a king which led at least in the Evangelist's mind to the departure of Jesus from Galilee at the height of His success. The arrest and examination of Jesus as a Messianic pretender alone serves to reconcile the alteration of the charge against Him between the Jewish and the Roman trials. The words "robber" and "malefactor" used of Barabbas and the two companions of Jesus on Calvary probably have a similar background (Mark $15^{7, 27}$).

Following the clue provided by Luke 1^{32}, it seems probable that the title "Son of God" must be taken in close connexion with Messiahship in cases where it occurs on the lips of others. The identification is certain in the case of the High Priest in Mark 14^{62} and is the most likely interpretation with demoniacs (Mark 3^{11}, 5^{7}). We have no means of knowing the background of the centurion's confession at the Cross (Mark 15^{39}). In view of the content of the Temptations as three false ways of fulfilling the Messianic vocation a similar exegesis of the Q narrative of the Temptations is probable. The title "Son of God" in such cases is therefore probably an honorific title for one who is believed to be Messiah. It is in sharp contrast to the use made by Jesus of the correlatives "The Son . . . the Father," which contain a marked overplus of significance.

The conservatism in the Marcan usage of the title is noteworthy. Apart from passages which plainly reflect the faith of the Church (Mark 1^{1} and probably 9^{41}), or where it is used in a purely general sense (Mark 13^{21}), it is found on the lips of Peter at Caesarea Philippi (Mark 8^{29}), the High Priest (Mark 14^{61}) and the chief priests in mockery at the Cross

(Mark 15^{32}). The title "Son of God" (used in a quasi-Messianic sense) is restricted to demoniacs and the High Priest. There is no instance in Mark in which Jesus directly applies the title to Himself although He accepts it either explicitly (Peter, the High Priest) or implicitly (demoniacs) when it is referred to Him. In the two former cases He immediately tries to reinterpret it. The question, significantly raised by Jesus Himself, "How say the scribes that the Christ is the Son of David?" (Mark 12^{35}) is not to be explained as a denial of Davidic Sonship (Messiahship in the context) but as an assertion of something more (David's Lord) and therefore as a question mark placed against the crystallization of Messiahship as a political Messiahship. Although there is an increase in the editorial introduction of the title in Matthew and Luke the main characteristics of Marcan usage are retained. The sparing use of the term in the Synoptic Gospels is in striking contrast to its unstinted use in the rest of the New Testament.

The Marcan record then discloses a curious indirectness in the evidence relating to the Messiahship of Jesus. Various explanations have been proposed to explain the facts. One widely held hypothesis appeals to the injunctions to secrecy which extend to the mighty works, the supernatural knowledge of the demoniacs, the "mystery of the Kingdom of God" to which reference is made in the Marcan interpretation of the Parables and the statement that flesh and blood has not revealed the truth of the Messiahship to Peter at Caesarea Philippi (Matt. 16^{17}). This is built into a theory of a Messianic Secret withheld from men until its revelation to Peter and only openly revealed through and after the Resurrection. Its source is normally held to be Mark rather than Jesus Himself. Despite the wide acceptance which this view has received it is difficult not to suspect a good measure of over-interpretation. Others again prefer to describe the ministry of Jesus as unmessianic and to deny that it was ever interpreted in Messianic categories at all by Him. This however represents an opposite extreme and leaves out of account the fact that Jesus appears to accept the term when used of Him by others. The facts prove that in any case the ministry was inevitably caught up in a welter of Messianic speculation. It would be surprising if Jesus had no definite attitude to an interpretation which on this hypothesis was a palpable mistake. Others with greater justification speak of a Messianic veiledness on the part of Jesus.

But the historical situation behind the material is probably an indirectness of approach on the part of Jesus Himself to the question, arising from a cross-purpose on the implications of the title between His contemporaries and Himself. Evidence for such a view is not far to seek. The puzzle about David's Son and David's Lord represents a question mark placed against current misconceptions. The mighty works are signs but only for those who have eyes to see. The acclamation by Peter is accepted but immediately revalued in terms of suffering. The question of the High Priest was most probably answered in the affirmative but immediately diverted into other channels. It is no accident that Jesus used other titles by preference such as Son of Man which left more living space for His own understanding of His person and work. The evidence is consistent with the view that Jesus was all the Messiah there was, all the Messiah that there was going to be but with such an overplus of meaning as to leave no " joy in the telling " in the unguarded use of the term in the contemporary setting. There seems little need to elaborate a theory of the Messianic Secret and then to attribute it to the Evangelist.

(b) *The Son of Man.* Of even greater importance is the title " Son of Man " which is freely used in the Gospels as a self-designation of Jesus. Its Old Testament background is rich and puzzling. Three passages in the Psalms (Ps. 8^{4}, 144^{3}, and 80^{17}) plainly indicate that there is no difference grammatically between " Son of Man " and " Man " though the last passage possibly contains a reference to a particular figure, either the community messianically interpreted or an individual of Messianic or similar status. In Ezekiel the term is freely used as a generalized form of address to the prophet himself. The evidence does not however warrant the theory of a special prophetic or psalmic application of the title. Here the Son of Man is almost exclusively used as a mere stylistic equivalent of Man.

An extension of the title occurs in Dan. 7. Apocalyptic literature showed a special fondness for allusive titles such as the Coming One, the Righteous One or the Elect and a similar use of " the Son of Man " or " the Man " would be wholly in keeping. In the passage where it occurs in Daniel " the Son of Man " is interpreted as " the saints of the Most High " (Dan. $7^{13-14, 27}$). The title therefore bears a corporate conception, the righteous remnant of Israel as exemplified by the Maccabaean resistance movement. Paradoxically enough the term speaks of the divine mission and destiny of the Remnant in view of the simple code by which the kingdoms of men are described as beasts and Israel correspondingly upgraded as Son of Man. The note of suffering is introduced in vv.$^{7, 21}$ and is plainly indicated in the first six chapters of the book, though here it is not closely integrated with the title Son of Man. The vision seems to speak of vindication after suffering, but never approaches the theme of exaltation through suffering.

It is a prelude to vindication but not apparently part of a single redemptive process to which both are integral. Combined with an allusion to an Enthronement Psalm (Ps. 110^1) Daniel 7 provides the background to the reply of Jesus to the High Priest.

A marked development of the concept took place in the later apocalyptic literature. In the Similitudes of Enoch (1 Enoch 37–71) the Son of Man has become an individual and exalted figure whose identity is at present concealed but who will be revealed at the coming of the Kingdom of God. The theory that the Son of Man represents Enoch himself falls short of demonstration. Scholarly opinion is still divided on the question whether 1 Enoch was known to Jesus Himself. The Gospels provide no direct evidence on the point and the best that can be said is that some passages in the Gospels would gain in significance if a knowledge of 1 Enoch could be assumed. The uncanonical status of the book might go some distance to explain the absence of direct quotations in the Gospels. The question remains open but the probabilities are rather against than for the view that Jesus was acquainted with 1 Enoch. Little is added to the picture of the Son of Man in 4 Ezra 13 where political conceptions may have been added to the concept found in 1 Enoch. The probability is that in these documents the Son of Man who is certainly a superhuman figure has a quasi-Messianic status and that the contrast in 1 Enoch with a political Son of David Messiah is conscious and deliberate.

It is clear at the outset that for the Evangelists the Son of Man is identical with Jesus Himself. This is proved by variant forms of a single saying in which Son of Man in one Gospel is replaced by " I " or " me." This equation gains in force when it is realized that the title played a surprisingly restricted part in the Christology of the Apostolic Age. The only passages in the rest of the New Testament where the term Son of Man explicitly occurs are Acts 7^{56}, where the fate of the protomartyr is specifically linked with the Passion of his Lord with the significant difference that here the Son of Man is represented as standing rather than sitting, and two allusions in the Apocalypse (Rev. 1^{13}, 14^{14}), where apart from the identification of the Son of Man with the Exalted Christ nothing goes beyond the content of Jewish expectation.

The passages in which the title is found in the Synoptic Gospels fall into three main groups. The first group which has been described as " Present usage " is a somewhat loosely knit collection of sayings. The two sayings in Mark which occur before the Confession at Caesarea Philippi are the sole cases in the Gospels where the generalized meaning found in the

Psalms might conceivably be applied, " The Son of Man hath power on earth to forgive sins " (Mark 2^{10}) and " The Son of Man is Lord also of the Sabbath (Mark 2^{28}). In the first example this interpretation is most unlikely. Judaism has never possessed the notion of a mediatorial priesthood. It was difficult enough for the claim of Jesus to forgive sins to be received; it would have been impossible for Jesus even to make a generalized statement covering humanity at large. The second example is added as a consequential clause to the statement " The Sabbath was made for man and not man for the Sabbath " for which partial parallels can be quoted from the Rabbis. It is probably best interpreted as an *a fortiori* application by Jesus of the general principle enunciated in the previous verse, but it may possibly be a Christian gloss making plain the application of this principle in a Christian context.

Three passages from Q are included in this group. " The Son of Man hath not where to lay his head " (Matt. 8^{20}, Luke 9^{58}). This obviously refers to Jesus Himself in the conditions of His ministry. It might even be the nearest to a Passion saying in the Q material. The title also occurs in two passages which point a contrast. The first expresses the characteristic difference between Jesus and John the Baptist. In contrast to the asceticism of John " the Son of Man came (or 'is come') eating and drinking " (Matt. 11^{19}, Luke 7^{34}). A much more difficult saying contrasts speaking against the Son of Man and against the Holy Spirit—" Whosoever shall speak a word against the Son of Man it shall be forgiven him but unto him who blasphemes against the Holy Spirit it shall not be forgiven " (Matt. 12^{32}, Luke 12^{10}). The passage is clearly related to Mark 3^{28-29}, where the title Son of Man does not occur though the unusual phrase " sons of men " is employed. One further passage is found in the material special to Luke " The Son of Man is come to seek and to save that which is lost " (Luke 19^{10}) which plainly refers to the objectives of the earthly ministry.

This is clearly a very miscellaneous group of passages. The Marcan passages indicate the authority of Jesus. Two passages (from Q and Luke respectively) apply the term to the lowly conditions of His ministry while in two passages from Q the title is used in a pair of contrasts. If anything can be deduced from so disparate a collection the combination of authority and humility may be regarded as noteworthy.

The second group of passages relate to the Passion, Death, and Resurrection of Jesus. They are virtually confined to Mark and are only introduced after the confession at Caesarea Philippi (Mark 8^{31}, 9^{13}, 9^{31}, 10^{45}, ; cf. $14^{21.\ 41}$). The first five are contained in predictions of the Passion, the last two in the Passion narrative itself. The absence of Q material may readily be explained in view of the probable absence of a Passion narrative in this source. Two instances from Matthew (26^2) and Luke (22^{22}) may be editorial. That the Marcan material indicates a new stage in the teaching of Jesus seems wholly probable. Some details in this group of sayings may be prophecies after the event but to disperse all the material in this way goes beyond any reasonable probability. It is no valid argument against their authenticity that the disciples failed to comprehend their meaning. That Jesus should have foreseen His fate and tried to share its meaning with His disciples remains wholly probable. The close connexion between the title and suffering is noteworthy and goes far beyond the probable sources. This again is wholly probable and arises directly from Jesus Himself.

The third group of future usage passages refer to an exalted and glorified Son of Man. These occur in all the sources with a slight preponderance (as might be expected) in the material special to Matthew. Here the teaching of Jesus is at its most traditional and (apart from the obvious connexion with Jesus Himself) call for no special comment.

Radical criticism accepts the third group of sayings as authentic but not as a self-designation of Jesus Himself, dismisses the second group as a piece of Marcan theologizing and is prepared to find a genuine nucleus (though without the title) in the first group. The arguments behind these opinions is, however, too doctrinaire to be convincing. After due allowance has been made for editorial revision and assimilation there remains an impressive body of evidence that Jesus used the title Son of Man and in more than one context.

We have seen that the Evangelists clearly interpreted the Son of Man sayings as self-designations. This is certainly the case with present usage passages and with the group which refer to the Passion. By inference and for reasons already discussed in connexion with the concept of the Kingdom of God, this is most probably true of future usage passages as well. Two sayings have however been interpreted in the opposite sense. " Whosoever is ashamed of me and of my words, of him shall the Son of Man be ashamed when he comes in glory with the holy angels " (Mark 8^{38}) and the reply to the High Priest " I am and ye shall see the Son of Man sitting at the right hand of the power and coming on the clouds of heaven " (Mark 14^{62}). Both passages might be regarded as contrasts between Jesus and a coming Son of Man. In neither case however is this conclusion compulsory. We have already noted that the title Son of Man can refer both to the Passion and to the Exaltation of the Son of Man and it is more probable that in both cases a similar contrast is being drawn between Jesus as He is under the conditions of His earthly ministry and as He will be in His future exaltation. Naturally although the title is used in both senses it could hardly be used significantly on both sides of the contrast in a single saying. Another and even more significant interpretation of the second saying is however admissible. The opening words " I am " may be more than a simple affirmative answer. In line with Old Testament usage they can be regarded as a solemn self-affirmation amounting to a claim to divinity. This would serve to explain the shocked action of the High Priest which is otherwise left hanging in the air.

Some have claimed that the title Son of Man had a definite and restricted usage at the time of Jesus with the meaning of Messiah designate. This lacks any worthwhile support. While the term was no doubt loosely associated with expectations of a Messianic type it is impossible to draw such a tightly constructed picture of the Jewish Messianic hope to justify this interpretation. Indeed it may reasonably be claimed that it was precisely the absence of any premature crystallization of ideas round the title which made it particularly suitable for the use to which it was put by Jesus Himself. What is most distinctive in its content is derived not from its sources but from the person and work of Jesus Himself.

Others have claimed that the title in the Gospels still retains the corporate intention which can plainly be seen in Dan. 7. It therefore belongs to a complete sequence of concepts which include the Remnant, the Servant and the Body of Christ both Head and members. Whether suffering or glorified the Son of Man would therefore include both Jesus and His disciples under a single common denominator. This suggestion has received a fair measure of support but it is difficult to regard it as completely satisfactory. No passage unambiguously demands this explanation and it would be difficult to account for the existence of a separate group of discipleship sayings on this hypothesis. If the phrase " the Son of Man must suffer many things " includes both Jesus and His own, a separate group of sayings on crossbearing and discipleship might seem superfluous. It is particularly difficult to apply this interpretation to two sayings. In Luke the reply to Judas in the Garden reads " Betrayest thou the Son of Man with a kiss ? " (Luke 22[48]). This is less easy to interpret to mean " You are letting down the fellowship " than as a reproachful denunciation of an act of treachery to Jesus Himself. The alternative is singularly jejune. The second saying occurs in Matthew with a remote parallel in Luke which lacks the title Son of Man. " Verily, verily I say unto you, my followers, at the regeneration when the Son of Man shall sit on the throne of his glory, you also shall sit upon twelve thrones judging the twelve tribes of Israel" (Matt. 19^{28}). Here the terms of the contrast expressly exclude the corporate conception.

The evidence then suggests that Jesus used a title drawn from apocalyptic literature (probably directly from Dan. 7) as a vehicle into which to pour His own conception of His person and work. He could do this with the greater confidence because (unlike other titles) it retained a greater measure of flexibility. The Synoptic Gospels give no indication of the response which it evoked in those who heard it. Probably the future usage was familiar to many though the new contexts in which it was employed would be altogether strange. The puzzled question of the multitude in the Fourth Gospel "Who is this Son of Man?" in a verse which brings Messiah and Son of Man together (John 12^{34}) and underlines the contrast between current expectation and present fulfilment in the person and work of Jesus may well reflect the historical situation.

(c) *The Servant of God.* A group of four passages in the unknown prophet Second Isaiah (Isa. 42^{1-4}, 49^{1-6}, 50^{4-9}, 52^{13}–53^{12}) speak of the Servant of Yahweh. The concept, which differs somewhat from passage to passage, probably has a corporate significance analogous to the Remnant of Isaiah son of Amoz. The concluding passage speaks of the suffering and vindication of the Servant. The theme of suffering recurs in the Psalms of the Righteous Sufferer (especially Pss. 22 and 69) and similar passages are to be found in Trito-Isaiah (Isa. 56–66) and in the figure of the lowly King of Zech. 9^{9}. It is possible that the note of suffering enters as a subordinate theme into the picture of the Son of Man in Dan. 7 while fugitive traces of the Servant Songs though not, it seems, of the Suffering Servant passage are to be found in 1 Enoch.

The concept then was not without a wider influence on later literature but it is a striking fact that the figure of the Servant never overflowed into, still less dominated, the concept of the Messiah. Whether in some circles such as the Qumran community an esoteric connexion between the two was ever traced still remains doubtful.

For anything like a genuine integration we must await the New Testament, though even here the evidence is hotly disputed by some critical scholars. It is not in doubt that in some parts of the New Testament a Servant Christology can be found though it is not evenly distributed throughout the documents. It is most conspicuous in the early chapters of the Acts of the Apostles (particularly in the sermons of Peter and the encounter of the Ethiopian eunuch with Philip

(Acts 8^{26-40}) which contains a long citation of Isa. 53^{7-8}. The concept clearly underlies Phil. 2^{5-11}, which is probably a pre-Pauline hymn though it exercises little or no influence on Pauline thought as a whole. In the rest of the New Testament 1 Peter alone can be said to be deeply indebted to the theme of the Suffering Servant. A partial explanation of the gaps in the evidence can be found in the disparity between the Semitic and Greek understanding of the idea of servanthood and slavery.

Explicit quotations of the Suffering Servant passage in the Gospels are confined to three passages (Matt. 8^{17}–Isa. 53^{4}, Matt. 12^{17}–Isa. 42^{1-4}, Luke 22^{37}–Isa. 53^{12}). The first two are obviously editorial though a strong case can be made out for the view that the Lucan passage is an authentic quotation by Jesus Himself.

But the influence of the theme is not confined to deliberate quotations. The Voice from Heaven at the Baptism (Mark 1^{11}, Matt. 3^{17}) certainly echoes Isa. 42^{1} probably in combination with Ps. 2^{7}. An attractive case can be made out for the view that the initial call of Jesus to Messiahship was already mediated through the Servant theme. The Passion Sayings of Jesus in Mark which combine the themes of suffering and the Son of Man must also be taken into account here. The blending of the two far exceeds the proportions observable in Dan. 7. While some verbal echoes of the Suffering Servant passage are to be found in other members of this group (*e.g.* Mark 9^{12}–Isa. 53^{3} set at nought), the most noteworthy is Mark 10^{45} "The Son of Man is come not to be ministered unto but to minister and to give his life a ransom for many." The source of the root ideas appears unmistakable although the verbal equivalents are somewhat free and do not correspond at all closely to the Septuagint version. It would be difficult to deny the influence of the concept on the Words of Institution at the Last Supper ("covenant," "for many"). The silence of Jesus in many of the Trial scenes (Mark 15^{5}, Luke 23^{9}, John 19^{9}), while no doubt an authentic part of the tradition, also recalls Isa. 53^{7}. The reserves and silences imposed upon Jesus by His interpretation of His mission bear a strong similarity to the portrait of the Servant.

If it is permissible to fill in the picture from passages closely related to the Servant theme in the Old Testament, the case is even stronger. From Trito-Isaiah is drawn the text of the Sermon at Nazareth recorded by Luke (Luke 4^{16-30}–Isa. 61^{1-2} and 58^{6}). Part of this material recurs in the answer of Jesus to John the Baptist in prison derived from Q (Matt. 11^{2-6}, Luke 7^{18-23}–Isa. 61^{1}). The narrative of the Triumphal Entry clearly turns upon Zech. 9^{9} which is a closely associated proof-text. The Cry of Dereliction from the

Cross (Ps. 22^{1}) is a basic element in the Passion Narrative and other echoes not only of this Psalm but also of Ps. 69 lie at a level deeper than direct quotation in this part of the Gospel. There seems no reason (despite radical opinion to the contrary) to doubt the evidence that Jesus foresaw His own impending Passion. Indeed sayings with a Passional import occur at many points in the Gospel narrative, though there is a marked crescendo after the Confession at Caesarea Philippi. That Jesus saw His Passion as invested not only with a certain historical inevitability but also with a theological significance is plainly indicated by Mark and cannot be satisfactorily regarded as a piece of early Christian theology. While the influence of other Old Testament passages is by no means excluded by the evidence, the figure of the Servant obviously took pride of place in Old Testament treatments of the theme. It is as difficult as it is unnecessary to maintain that it was not present to the mind of Jesus Himself. In the remainder of the New Testament the concept appears in material which is either early or based on early sources. The restraint with which it is introduced in the Gospels is noteworthy. It has been well compared to the transposition of other themes into a minor key. The concept of the Servant is not as it were added as a third figure to the Messiah and the Son of Man and the resultant amalgam applied by Jesus to Himself. Rather the other titles are interpreted in terms which reach their apex in the Old Testament in Isaiah 53.

(d) *The Son of God*. We have noted the immediacy and authoritativeness of the impact of Jesus which is in decided contrast to the religious idioms historically current within Judaism. The oracles of the prophet were prefaced by "Thus saith the Lord." The visions of the apocalyptist were attributed to the leading figures of the past. The debates of the Rabbis were guided by precedent and based on the Mosaic Law. The teaching of Jesus, though related in some ways to all three strands rests on a different basis, a first-hand and underivative insight into the purpose and character of God. Functions like forgiveness and judgment which are appropriate to God are performed by Him without consciousness of stepping outside His proper framework of reference. The existence of a hinterland of significance behind His person and work is difficult to dispute on a careful reading of the evidence as a whole. It remains to discuss whether in His recorded teaching there is evidence of any particular concept or title associated with or expressing this fact.

In the Old Testament sources the title "Son of God" is somewhat widely used. It could be used of Israel (Hos. 11^{1}, Ex. $4^{22f.}$) and of individuals such as David or Solomon (Ps. 89^{26},

2 Sam. 7^{14}). In Wis. 2^{18} (cf. Ecclus. 4^{10}) it is used in a diluted sense of a righteous man. In the light of Ps. 2^{7} it seems probable that it could be applied to the Messiah in an honorific sense and this seems to be confirmed by the evidence of the Gospels.

In the Gospels the title is never used by Jesus of Himself but only by others about Him. In Mark it is used by demoniacs (Mark 3^{11}), by the High Priest obviously as identical in meaning with the Messiah (Mark 14^{61}) and by the centurion at the Cross in an unspecified sense (Mark 15^{39}). Not even at Caesarea Philippi is it used by the disciples themselves. It is an attractive suggestion that for Mark the High Priest represents the sample rejecter of the Jewish world, the Centurion the sample confessor of the Gentile world. In other Synoptic Gospels the Devil in the Temptation narratives (Q) urges "if thou be the Son of God," while Matthew introduces the term in his account of the Confession at Caesarea Philippi. This reserve in the use of the title on the part of the Synoptic Gospels is all the more striking in view of its place in the faith of the Apostolic Church.

It seems therefore that Jesus, while using "Son of Man" as a self-designation, avoids the title "Son of God" no less than that of "Messiah." This is probably due to the fact that the term was in contemporary usage bound up with current forms of Messianic expectation. Paradoxically it may have been avoided because it said not more but less than what Jesus knew to be true of Himself. The preferred title "Son of Man," despite its linguistic history, did not mean humanity as contrasted with divinity but was always applied in apocalyptic literature to figures whether corporate (as in Dan. 7) or individual (as probably in 1 Enoch) closely related to divine purposes. If however the concept of the Servant who should not cry nor lift up his voice played an important part in moulding the vocation of Jesus, His reserve at this point would be even more readily explicable.

The evidence in the Gospels for a divine hinterland to the person of Jesus does not depend exclusively on the use of the title Son of God but upon hints of a unique Father-Son relationship less directly expressed. Thus in the prayer formula retained in the original Aramaic not only by Mark but also by Paul Jesus uses the more intimate form of address "Abba" rather than the more formal "Abbi" used by the ordinary Jew. In Q passages followed closely by Luke and even more frequent in Matthew God is described as "My Father" and "Your Father" but never (except in a prayer given for the use of disciples) "Our Father." This difference at first sight trivial seems to denote a special relationship to God. The standard Johannine contrast between the Father and the Son occurs sparingly in the earlier Gospels but a dovetail into the Synoptic tradition is provided by two passages in Mark and Q. Thus Mark 13^{32}, " But of that day and hour knoweth no one, not even the angels in heaven nor the Son but the Father," seems plainly authentic in view of the fact that the mind of the Church would hardly have ascribed ignorance to the Son on so important a matter as the date of the Parousia. The cry of thanksgiving (Matt. 11^{25-27}, Luke 10^{22}), a Q passage, reads " All things have been delivered to me by my Father, and no man knoweth the Son except the Father nor the Father except the Son and he to whomsoever the Son willeth to reveal him." This has been described as the Johannine thunderbolt owing to its close relationship with the teaching of the Fourth Gospel. It is therefore not surprising that it has been subjected to critical fire. Yet the text in Matthew and Luke is almost identical and such variants as occur in the manuscripts are hardly significant. Patristic quotations display greater variation either by reducing the three clauses to two or by omitting one or other of the clauses. This is more likely to be due to faulty memory than to a genuine difference of text. It is in any case a passage which is difficult to memorize exactly, partly because of the unusual order of the clauses and partly because of its three-member structure where Johannine usage leads us to expect two clauses and no more. It has been claimed that the passage is a Christological hymn produced in a Hellenistic environment. But the term " knowledge " is no proof of a Gnostic or mystical environment. The background of a prophetic knowledge carried to an incomparably deeper level remains more probable. A further objection that the genuineness of the passage would imply an open claim to divinity on the part of Jesus and would therefore be incompatible with the reserves attendant upon the use of the title Son of God elsewhere cannot stand in view of the form of the passage which is couched in the form of a prayer of thanksgiving. Here as often the Fourth Gospel appears to deepen and extend a Synoptic usage.

The concept of a unique Filial consciousness on the part of Jesus Himself is confirmed by other passages in the Gospels. The voice from heaven at the Baptism, repeated at the Transfiguration, reads " Thou art (or ' This is ') my beloved Son." On both occasions Luke records a different version. At the Baptism he simply copies Ps. 2^{7} while at the Transfiguration he substitutes " The Chosen " (a Servant title) for the phrase. The term " beloved " both in classical usage (Aristotle) and in the Septuagint (of Isaac, Gen. 22^{16}; of Jephthah's daughter, Judg. 11^{34} some MSS) can bear the meaning of " unique " or " only." The word recurs in the same sense in the Parable of the Wicked Husbandmen (Mark 12^6). On this occasion it is retained in Luke (20^{13}), though omitted by Matthew. The authenticity of the parable, though sometimes disputed, can be satisfactorily defended. The sharp distinction between genuine parable and allegory, beloved by scholarship of the older type, is too sharply drawn to be sustained and the siting of the parable in the Passion narrative is wholly natural.

A further possibility which goes even further concerns the interpretation of the words "I am" in certain Marcan passages. In the Fourth Gospel the words introduce a series of far-reaching affirmations. Especially noteworthy is the phrase "Before Abraham was I am" (John 8^{58}) which provoked an attempt to stone Jesus (in Jewish usage the appropriate punishment for blasphemy). In Mark 13^6 false Christs make the claim "I am." In the Marcan narrative of the Stilling of the Storm (Mark 6^{50}) Jesus says "Be of good cheer, I am, be not afraid" while, in answer to the High Priest's question "Art thou the Christ, the Son of the Blessed?" Jesus replies "I am, and ye shall see the Son of Man sitting on the right hand of the power and coming with the clouds of heaven." The reaction of the High Priest, "Ye have heard the blasphemy," accompanied by the symbolic action of rending his clothes can best be understood if the words "I am" are not a simple affirmative but a self-designation of a particularly exalted type.

The evidence therefore points to the conclusion that behind the earthly ministry of Jesus there lies the consciousness of a unique Sonship of God, of which the Church's faith in a spiritual and even a metaphysical solidarity with God is merely the appropriate expression of the facts of the Gospels.

(vi) THE ETHICAL TEACHING OF JESUS

The ethical teaching of Jesus is an integral part of His whole life and teaching. It cannot therefore be regarded, as much nineteenth century thought was inclined to do, as an independent strand which can be readily detached as a self-standing unit. It represents life under the rule of God and would frankly make nonsense on any other premises. It can be described as theocentric since it is based upon His insight into the character and purpose of God and upon the absolute worth of the individual in the sight of God and man. To expect the ethical teaching of Jesus to survive the erosion or abandonment of His teaching in other respects would be an idle hope.

This organic relationship can be illustrated by two facts which have often been noticed but which are capable of being misapplied or misunderstood. If the ethics of Jesus are related to His teaching as a whole they are clearly related to His eschatology. Here however due caution must be observed. Some scholars hold that they represent an ethic of the interval and explain their apparently extreme demands by denying that Jesus was concerned in the least with their practical character. Since the New Age was coming quickly men should henceforth live as citizens of the coming Kingdom without regard to the claims and demands of the existing world order.

It is however difficult to be satisfied with this theory as it stands. The leading motive of the ethics of Jesus is not

" Passing soon and little worth
Are the things that tempt on earth,"

but " Be ye therefore perfect as your Father in Heaven is perfect." It is normally true to say that passages in the Gospels where the ethical teaching of Jesus is rich and distinctive do not possess any notably eschatological character while passages which are chiefly devoted to eschatology do not contain the most distinctive ethical insights of Jesus. Eschatology speaks primarily of judgment and watchfulness, both of which no doubt have obvious ethical implications since the God of Ethics and of Eschatology is one in character and operation, but it is not to passages of this type that we should normally turn for the deepest ethical insights of Jesus. Nor is it by any means uniformly true that the ethical teaching of the apocalyptic literature with which this part of the teaching of Jesus is most closely related displays any notable tendency towards ethical rigorism.

Yet, more widely interpreted, the connexion between the ethics and eschatology of Jesus is just. In a formal sense all ethics until the final consummation are " ethics of the interval " but this fact cannot be regarded as particularly illuminating. As we have seen, the eschatology of Jesus has other strands besides belief in a future consummation of the Kingdom and it is at these points that His teaching on the subject becomes most distinctive. The assumption of a strictly futurist eschatology to the exclusion of any other view does less than justice to the complexity of His teaching on the Kingdom of God. But even in the passages where the future coming of the Kingdom is most plainly stressed the expectation that the interval will be of short duration does not represent the full extent of the evidence. It would therefore be precarious to accept this explanation of His ethics as it stands without careful qualification. What is crucial to the eschatology of Jesus is not that He believed that the Kingdom was shortly to be consummated but the urgent reality and immediate pressure of the rule of God both as a present reality in His own person and work and as a final consummation. It is the active presence of the rule of God both here and hereafter which is at once the background of His ethical teaching and the heart of His eschatology.

A similar attempt to explain the character of the ethical teaching of Jesus tries to save their practicality by restricting their range. It is claimed that they are ethics for disciples on the assumption that discipleship of Jesus could be equated with membership of small, self-sufficient pietistic communities. Once again there are mingled elements of truth and falsehood in such a view. It is certainly true that the whole teaching of Jesus depends upon His person. He is no teacher of a system of propositions which stands or falls independently of the character of the person who taught them. His teaching was not given merely for information or even illumination. Acceptance of His teaching and discipleship of His person are closely bound together. That is why the imperatives of Jesus often transcend the limits of ethical teaching and pass into the region of spiritual demands. It can again be maintained with good reason that the perspective of the Gospel does not directly envisage a situation in which the disciples of Jesus would have to provide ethically for the maintenance of the existing world order. The political horizons of Jesus and His disciples were necessarily limited. His steadfast refusal to interpret the Kingdom of God in political terms necessarily meant that He was unlikely to be greatly concerned with the ethical issues involved in government. A request to intervene in the matter of a disputed inheritance received the answer " Who made me a judge or divider over you ? " (Luke 12[14]). If he refused to arbitrate in a private matter of this kind we should hardly expect to find any traces of a developed sociology. The precept " Render unto Caesar the things that are Caesar's and unto God the things that are God's " (Mark 12[17], Matt. 22[21], Luke 20[25]) appears to accept by implication the rights as well as the duties of Caesar. Taken in its original controversial setting, the attempt to embroil Jesus with the Roman authorities on the question of tribute money, it is far from the character of a principle of political philosophy.

The restrictive element in this interpretation lies in the assumption that the practicality of the teaching of Jesus can be saved by restricting the circle to which it applies to small groups of dedicated disciples virtually sealed off from the public life of the world. Its starting point that ethics and discipleship are closely related is clearly sound, the deduction drawn from this principle that the range to which discipleship can extend is necessarily limited is inadequate. This will become even clearer when we turn to consider the teaching of Jesus with regard to the Gentiles and the Church.

While then the ethical teaching of Jesus is certainly related to His eschatology and even more closely to the demands of discipleship, the answer to the problem of its character does not lie in the limit of the time-span of the interval or in the restriction of its range to small groups of devout pietists.

The answer appears rather to lie in the character of the teaching itself. In contrast to the Judaism of His day the ethics of Jesus represent not an ethic of law but an ethic of insight. The objectives of Jewish legalism were to provide a code of rules readily applicable to any situation. The observant Jew was to be left in no doubt where his duty lay if only he was willing to obey it. This led to a detailed casuistry of conduct, some aspects of which are mercilessly pilloried in the Woes against the Pharisees (Matt. 23, Luke 11[37-52]). Doubtless not all Jewish ethical teaching was equally exposed to this critique, but the method employed was always liable to produce this result. A permanent difficulty about an ethic of law is that it tends to become obsolete as conditions change. With changing circumstances new problems arise which cannot easily be brought under the older rubrics of proof.

By contrast the ethics of Jesus represent an ethic of insight. To the question "What ought I to do?" Jesus seems to reply with the counter question "What sort of person are you?" The Parable of the Good Samaritan (Luke 10[29-37]) is recorded in answer to the question "And who is my neighbour?" The scope of Lev. 19[18], "thou shalt love thy neighbour as thyself," could no doubt be debated and might be interpreted merely as an injunction to do good to fellow-Jews. Jesus reverses the question in the parable by making the Samaritan the donor and not the recipient of neighbourly love. But he goes even further by depicting a pattern of conduct of such kind as to make the original question inappropriate. The deepest ethical teaching of Jesus resembles the Parables of the Kingdom, the vivid sketching of a situation to which the appropriate reply is not "Now I know what to do" but "Now I see the kind of person I ought to be or to become." The application to particular moral dilemmas is left to the recipient to draw for himself but is never made explicit by Jesus Himself. It is as if the ethical teaching of Jesus like the parables of the Kingdom could be rubricated "Go and work it out for yourself." This means that the ethical insights of Jesus are ageless but that each succeeding age must come to grips for itself with their application to the ethical problems of their own times. On the other hand an ethic of case law offers a predigested application which can become obsolescent in the course of time. Thus the principle "Thou shalt love thy neighbour as thyself" implies a sociology although no Gospel sociology is provided in the teaching of Jesus. The saying " Render unto Caesar the things that are Caesar's but to God the things that are God's " governs any Christian approach to the relation of Church and State. It does not, however, draw any precise line of demarcation for our guidance in the relations between the two. The necessity for the application of the teaching of Jesus to contemporary conditions is obvious enough ; indeed there are some indications in the Gospels that the process had already begun in the first century. This duty is not excluded by the teaching of Jesus but equally it was not attempted by Jesus Himself.

Two examples of this approach may serve as illustrations.

(a) *The use of force and non-resistance to evil.* Outside the Sermon on the Mount four passages come under discussion. The first " I came not to send peace but a sword " (Matt. 10^{34}) is virtually irrelevant. It is a reminder that discipleship must always be at cost. So far from being a facile instrument of unification it challenges men to take sides, to make decisions and is therefore liable to provoke conflict and opposition. The metaphor drawn from peace and war is purely illustrative of the main theme. Again in the Johannine narrative of the cleansing of the Temple mention is made of a " scourge of cords " (John 2^{15}), perhaps a whip or a clutch of rope ends is in mind here. The silence of the Synoptists on the point may be noted but does not necessarily imply that one was not used. But the significant part of the incident is not the weapon which Jesus may have wielded but the selfless wrath of the angry Christ which was a more potent weapon than anything which He carried in His hand. There is also a difficult passage in Luke 22^{35-38} where Jesus contrasts the earlier welcome experienced by His disciples in Galilee when they could go without scrip or purse and be sure of a welcome and the stormclouds now gathering round His person as the Passion approaches. Now is the time to sell purse, wallet, or cloak and to buy a sword. The disciples produce two swords and Jesus replies " It is enough." The interpretation is, however, uncertain. Does it mean " Two swords are enough," and, if so, enough for what ? In the event they proved unavailing and Jesus in fact rebuked the attempt to use them. Or is the phrase to be rendered " enough of this, you have misunderstood my meaning ? " In any case the point is rather the contrasted moods of the crowds than in swords considered as weapons of offence and defence. Finally, in the Matthaean account of the Passion, Peter (possibly misunderstanding the last passage) uses his sword and is rebuked by Jesus, " those who take the sword shall perish by the sword " (Matt. 26^{52}). This may be a proverbial saying like " Violent come, violent go " applied to the particular circumstances of the Passion. In any case the concept of the Suffering Servant of God extends over the whole Passion narrative.

In the Sermon on the Mount a series of illustrations covering a general principle are set out. The disciple is to turn the other cheek. The detail of the passage indicates rather an insulting flick on the cheek designed to suggest that the victim is not worthy of the use of force rather than a blow intended to do as much physical damage as possible. For an Oriental this would be the more deadly insult. At law the disciple must surrender not only his outer cloak but also his tunic as well. When the corvée or duty of forced labour is imposed by an occupying power, the disciple must not only perform his allotted span but an extra mile as well. The general rubric is " Resist not evil " and it makes little difference whether we take " evil " as masculine or neuter. The principle underlying this set of illustrations is an unstinted generosity of spirit which reflects the sovereignty of God the Unconditioned Giver. The picture of a Christian disciple is clearly exemplified, the sort of person he is intended to be set out in three different situations, personal relations, legal proceedings, and political relations. Its application in international relations must be made in the light of each new situation. Neither the doctrine of the just war nor the policy of nuclear disarmament are plainly contained in the teaching of Jesus.

(b) *Marriage and Divorce.* Here the situation differs slightly and there is good reason to suspect the intervention of one of the Evangelists (Matthew). Many would, however, regard the teaching of Jesus as containing both the insight and its application. In full harmony with Old Testament teaching Jesus regarded marriage as a natural and God-given provision for the life of man (Mark 10^{6-8}). Even in Old Testament times He regarded divorce as a later and possibly a temporary concession to human weakness (Deut. 24^{1}), " For the hardness of your hearts Moses gave you this precept." The reply of Jesus to the question of the Sadducees reveals that Jesus (in line here with much contemporary teaching) believed that at least in its physical aspects marriage played no part in the life to come (Mark 12^{18-27}). Family obligation remains sacrosanct provided that it does not conflict with the prior claims of discipleship. Even the institution of Corban (a religious vow devoting property either in whole or in part to the service of God) must be set aside as false piety if it is made an excuse for failure to meet the needs of parents (Mark 7^{11}). Here again Jesus is fully in accord with the best traditions of the Judaism of his day.

For Jesus Himself the claims of family yielded pride of

place to the concerns of the Kingdom of God. In an incident placed by Mark after the Beelzebub controversy a family deputation waited upon him. His reply is significant : " Who is my mother and my brethren ? . . . Whoever does the will of God, he is to me brother and sister and mother " (Mark 3^{31-35}). Similar passages with regard to his mother occur in later Gospels (Luke 11^{27-28}, John 2^{4}). So for others the claims of family life cannot be pleaded as an excuse for not following Him. At the call of James and John their father Zebedee is left in the boat with the hired servants (Mark 1^{20}). To the apparently reasonable request of a would-be disciple " Suffer me first to go and bury my father " (Matt. 8^{21-22}, Luke 9^{59-60}) Jesus replies " Let the dead bury their dead." The precise nature of the request may be slightly obscure, the general meaning could not be more plain. Discipleship may even introduce division into the family circle (Matt. 10^{35-36}, Luke 12^{52-53}). The King's business requires urgency and nothing can be allowed to stand in its way.

Two sayings of Jesus on the subject of divorce are recorded in the Gospels. The first occurs in Mark 10^{11}, with a parallel in Matthew (Matt. 19^{9}) but not in Luke. The section in which it occurs keeps divorce firmly in the context of marriage. The second (derived from Q) is recorded as a free-standing saying (Matt. 5^{31-32}, Luke 16^{18}). Neither the Marcan passage nor the Lucan form of the Q saying appears to permit divorce but in his version of both sayings Matthew adds an exceptatory clause permitting divorce on grounds of adultery. Attempts to harmonize the two interpretations have been made with a notable lack of success. It seems clear that Matthew offers a self-consistent interpretation of his own. In the Matthaean parallel to the Marcan passage the case is stated precisely as it would appear to the Rabbinic schools of the day. " Is it lawful for a man to put away his wife for every cause ? " The reply of Jesus favours the stricter ruling of Shammai rather than the looser casuistry of Hillel. It looks as if Matthew with the Rabbinic debates in mind is here playing the part of an incipient Christian casuist applying the teaching of Jesus to contemporary conditions within the Church. A similar tendency can be found in Matt. 18^{15-17} with its graded procedures of dealing with a refractory brother as compared with the sharper outlines of Luke 17^{3} which is probably the original Q nucleus of the passage. The exceptatory clause is worthy of every respect as a first-century interpretation of the teaching of Jesus but His own teaching seems to follow quite different lines. His teaching on divorce forms part of his ethic of insight. " In the light of the nature of marriage divorce is unthinkable." On the other hand Matthew probably tries to apply this insight to a situation in which broken homes are all too possible.

The ethic of Jesus is given in a series of insights. It depends entirely upon the concept of the Kingdom of God and the paramount claims of discipleship of Himself by which the Kingdom is implemented on earth. The principles on which it rests are absolute just because the rule of God itself is absolute. The Sermon on the Mount in which much of his ethical teaching is embodied is organized as a vignette of life within the Kingdom. The first attempts to apply the teaching of Jesus to conditions within the Church are found in Matthew, and the process necessarily goes on as the Christian community grows and becomes involved in tasks and problems which the Evangelists themselves never envisaged.

(vii) JESUS AND THE CHURCH

Older liberal scholarship made a sharp distinction between Jesus and the Church and almost by instinct doubted whether the idea of the Church could have played any part in His teaching. The word itself (whatever its Aramaic equivalent) only occurs twice in the Gospels, both in the material special to Matthew and neither passage has escaped unscathed at the hands of the critics. It occurs in the promise to Peter, a Matthaean supplement to the Marcan account of the Confession at Caesarea Philippi (Matt. 16^{18}). The Semitic background of the passage is, however, clear and the saying is at least capable of reasonable defence. Its interpretation is, of course, another question. The second passage to which attention has already been called is probably a supplement to a Q saying which Luke records in a more original form (Matt. 18^{15-18}, Luke 17^{3}). It forms part of a crescendo of disciplinary treatments in which the hand of the Evangelist may well be detected.

But the question of the Church in the teaching of Jesus cannot be decided on the basis of these two passages alone. It would be antecedently improbable that a teacher cradled within Judaism should detach himself completely from all thoughts of a religious community. While the concept of the Kingdom of God which forms the central theme of His teaching primarily means the kingship or rule of God, it certainly implies a realm in which it is exercised. A social reference cannot therefore be excluded. While this becomes explicit in the Parables of the Wheat and the Tares (Matt. 13^{24-30}) and the Dragnet (Matt. 13^{47-50}), both peculiar to Matthew, it is also implied in the phrase " to enter the Kingdom " which has a wider extension in the Gospels (Mark 9^{47} absent from the Matthaean parallel; Matt. 7^{21} absent from the Lucan parallel–Q; Matt. 23^{13}, Luke 11^{52}–Q). Although an individual significance in the Gospels is more probable than a corporate meaning, the background of the title Son of Man is certainly corporate in the principal Old Testament source. In any case the link between Jesus the Son of Man and the content which He gave to discipleship of Himself is not far to seek. In suffering and service as is the Son of Man so shall His disciple be. The term " covenant," which is found in all three accounts of the Last Supper, in the light of Old Testament usage has a societary reference. The point is reinforced when it is seen as a foretaste of the Messianic Banquet (Mark 14^{25}, Matt. 26^{29}, Luke 22^{18}), an expectation to which reference is also made in other passages (Matt. 8^{11}, Luke 13^{29}–Q; cf. Matt. 22$^{1-10}$, Luke 14$^{15-24}$).

Old Testament images with a corporate intention are frequently used in the Gospels. The image of the shepherd with his flock occurs in a saying which is certainly authentic and which also echoes the idea of the Remnant, " Fear not, little flock, it is your Father's good pleasure to give you the Kingdom " (Luke 12^{32}). Two Marcan passages bear similar implications. In the incident of the feeding of the five thousand Jesus is described as having compassion on the multitude " because they were as sheep not having a shepherd " (Mark 6^{34}). They are leaderless men lacking a sense of religious solidarity. Matthew retains the mention of the compassion of Jesus but gives the Marcan reason elsewhere (Matt. 9^{36}). In a series of sayings connected with the Passion Jesus refers to Zech. 13^{7} " I will smite the shepherd and the sheep shall be scattered " (Mark 14^{27}, Matt. 26^{31}). The Q Parable of the Lost Sheep is another application of the same image (Matt. 18$^{12-14}$, Luke 15$^{3-7}$) and naturally develops into the Johannine allegory (John 10$^{1-16}$). Again in the light of Old Testament precedents parables depicting growing things such as the Mustard Seed (Mark 4$^{30-32}$, Matt. 13$^{31-32}$, Luke 13$^{18-19}$), the Vineyard (Mark 12$^{1-9}$, Matt. 21$^{33-41}$, Luke 20$^{9-16}$), and the Withered Fig-tree (Mark 11$^{13-14. 20}$, Matt. 21$^{18-20}$; cf. Luke 13$^{6-9}$) plainly bear a corporate reference. The last example is particularly instructive since, whether it be parable or miracle or possibly even both, it refers to Judaism in terms drawn from the life of a tree.

The plainest evidence for the place of the Church in the teaching still remains to be mentioned. The call of the Twelve is deeply embedded in the historical tradition. The number is no mere historical accident and the allusion to the twelve tribes of Israel is proved by a passage in which they are entrusted with the role of assessors in the Day of Judgment (Matt. 19^{28}; cf. Luke 22$^{29-30}$– ? Q). It is implicit in the Gospels that before the Great Day they are to be regarded as the nucleus of the New Israel. They are usually described as the disciples and as such they are roughly parallel to the disciples of the rabbis or the followers of John the Baptist (Mark 2^{18}; Matt. 11^{2}, Luke 7^{18}–Q; John $1^{35, 37}$, 3^{25}). The term "apostle" occurs in Matthew only at the head of the list of their names (Matt. 10^{2}) and in Mark only at the close of his account of their missionary journey (Mark 6^{30}). Luke uses the term somewhat more freely, possibly in the light of post-Resurrection usage (Luke 6^{13}, 9^{10}, 17^{5}, 22^{14}). The reason assigned by Mark for their choice " that they might be with them and that he might send them forth " combines the root ideas both of disciple and apostle. They are directly associated with and commissioned by Jesus Himself. To receive or to hear them is to receive or to hear their Master (Matt. 10^{40}; cf. Luke 10^{16}). Comparison with the *shālîaḥ* concept in Judaism whereby one man is designated as the personal and accredited representative of another is tempting but should be used with caution. The double role of the Twelve as both the Church and the Ministry in the Gospels must be kept steadily in mind in evaluating their significance. They are at once the Remnant and the nucleus of the new people of God. They have both present and future functions. They are authorized to cast out demons (though others can do this as well—Mark 9^{38-41}, Luke 11^{49-50} and even more widely Matt. 12^{27}, Luke 11^{20}–Q), to heal the sick and to go on missionary journeys (Mark 3^{14-15}, 6^{7}) as well as their promised role as assessors in the final Judgment.

It seems then beyond dispute that the intention of Jesus implied a community and no less certain that He called a body of disciples who companied with Him and shared His authority to some extent, although they notably failed to understand the close relationship between authority, service, and suffering which lay at the heart of His own mission and message.

The extent to which Jesus made detailed provision for the life of this community in the Apostolic and subsequent ages is a separate question. It certainly included one prayer for disciples to use (Matt. 6^{9-13}, Luke 11^{2-4}–Q). The request of the disciples with which the Lucan account is introduced mentions a pattern prayer given by John the Baptist to his disciples. No further information on the subject is available but this does not entitle us to question the fact. Whether Jesus or His disciples practised Baptism during the early ministry is uncertain and depends largely on the relationship between Jesus and John the Baptist. Here Matthew and Mark give a uniform and consistent picture. The public ministry of Jesus does not begin until after the arrest of John the Baptist (Mark 1^{14-15}, Matt. 4^{12}). Matthew reinforces the point in his introduction to the question asked of Jesus by the disciples of

John, though Luke is silent on the point (Matt. 11^{2-6}, Luke 7^{18-23}–Q). Matthew includes the command to baptize in his account of the post-Resurrection appearances though the form in which he gives it may well have been influenced by later usage (Matt. 28^{18-20}). Although Luke makes no mention of the arrest of John the Baptist in his parallels to either passage (Luke 4^{14}, 7^{18-23}) and omits the long account in Mark 4 altogether, there is no indication of a different perspective. An important saying of Jesus recorded only by Luke " I have a baptism to be baptized with : and how am I straitened till it be accomplished " bears more directly on the Passion than on the practice of baptism (Luke 12^{50}). The Fourth Gospel on the other hand gives a different account on both heads, though there are clear indications that the author is also familiar with the Synoptic tradition (John 3^{24}, 4^{1-2}). Not only does he recall that some of the disciples of Jesus had previously followed John but he also claims that for a time before the arrest of John the two ministries went on in parallel (John 4^{1-3} ; cf. 3^{22-30}). This temporary phase is confined to Judaea and may well represent a historical tradition. In harmony with this account, teaching about Baptism as the sacrament of New Birth is given in John 3 (the discourse to Nicodemus). This anticipation of an important theme may be compared with the combination of teaching on the Eucharist with the account of the feeding of the five thousand. It appears that the Evangelist wishes to put the reader in possession of the sacramental clues to the understanding of Jesus as early as possible in his account of the Ministry. Whatever the solution of these problems the Synoptic record clearly implies that Baptism played no part in the independent public ministry of Jesus in Galilee. Yet the record in Acts clearly indicates that Baptism formed part of the Christian movement from the day of Pentecost and the Pauline discussion in Rom. 6 is excellent evidence that it was closely connected with the death and resurrection of Jesus. It is highly unlikely that the Church would have invented a new rite with dominical warrant either implicit or explicit. Probably the Matthaean passage represents the explication of what was already understood to be implicit in the intention of Jesus although the Baptismal Formula which it records seems to bear traces of a development between the Pauline theology of Baptism and the writing of the First Gospel.

The evidence for the institution of the Eucharist (though not without its problems) can be more clearly traced. It must not be forgotten that the Gospels were written in Churches where the Eucharist (no less than Baptism) was in common use. The Marcan account contains no command to repeat, though this may be explained by the intention of the Evangelist to align the reader deliberately with the historical situation of the first disciples. It is perhaps more surprising that this is not included in the Matthaean narrative, especially since in certain minor particulars (such as the placing of the words of Jesus before the reception of the Cup by the disciples) the author, good Churchman as he was, tidies up the rubrics. This may be a case where fidelity to his source took precedence over the introduction of new material.

On the other hand Luke (supported by the earliest record of the Last Supper in 1 Cor. 11^{23-25}) attaches the command both to the bread and the cup. The Lucan narrative however is more complex. It opens with the mention of a cup which the disciples are bidden to distribute among themselves accompanied by the words "For I say to you that I will no more henceforward drink of the fruit of the vine until the Kingdom of God comes" (Luke 22^{17-18}). The saying appears at the end of the Last Supper narrative in Matthew and Mark. Luke's transposition here may be due to the desire to indicate that Jesus did not take part in the Last Supper Himself and the first cup may simply be a substitution for or explanation of the Marcan phrase "and while they were eating." In other words it seems probable that it does not belong to the rite instituted at the Last Supper. Several manuscripts offer a shortened text in which the command to repeat attached to the mention of the second cup disappears. In no case is the command itself the sole omission. The most complete and satisfactory explanation of the difficulty is the suggestion that the scribes of some manuscripts (either using their own initiative or copying early manuscripts in which the alteration already occurred) were trying to assimilate the narrative to the Marcan text on the mistaken assumption that the first cup belonged to the rite. On this view the longer Lucan text is the more difficult reading from which all later variants can be explained. A less satisfactory explanation regards the shorter versions as primary and accounts for the longer text as an assimilation of the Pauline account to the Marcan through the introduction of the second cup in the wrong place. While it is certainly the less liturgical reading and therefore possibly the harder text, it affords a less comprehensive explanation of all the variants. In any case the command to repeat rests firmly on the evidence of our earliest witness, Paul.

The evidence suggests that the sum-total of the provision of Jesus for his Church consisted in the Lord's Prayer, the Eucharist, and at least by implication Baptism. This might seem scanty enough but in the light of His method of teaching both in Parable and in ethical insight we probably ought not to expect more. It was never His intention either to offer a predigested systematization of His teaching or to do for His disciples what they ought to do for themselves. Twelve men, a veritable job-lot of humanity of whom one betrayed, another denied and the rest forsook Him and fled, assured by the Resurrection of His continuing presence and using as sacraments the rites which He enjoined, proved equal to anything, even the organization and expansion of the Christian Church.

(viii) JESUS AND THE JEWISH LAW

We have called attention to the fact that the number of the original disciples contains more than a hint that Jesus regarded His Church as in some sense a new Israel. It is therefore important to determine as far as possible His attitude to the Jewish Law. Is He to be regarded merely as a religious teacher who sat rather loosely to the Law or as a root and branch reformer or as something between the two ?

Jewish legalism in the time of Jesus had already started on the road which led to the full development of Rabbinic Judaism after the destruction of the Temple. The attempt to make the Torah relevant and applicable to contemporary conditions was not in itself wrong. Indeed the spiritual earnestness which underlay Pharisaic Judaism is beyond dispute. The " tradition of the elders " so far as it concerned legal precept was called " halakah " while narrative expansions with a didactic as well as an imaginative purpose such as we find in the Book of Jubilees bore the name of " haggadah." It is with the former that we are concerned here. Controversies over the Sabbath Law recorded in the Gospels indicate that Jesus dealt trenchantly with some of these provisions. Nothing forbade " work " on the Sabbath Day which was needed to save human life but the healing of the man with a withered hand could not be brought under this rubric (Mark 3^{1-6}, Matt. 12^{9-14}, Luke 6^{6-11}). Nevertheless for Jesus the inbreaking of the Kingdom of God displayed in a healing miracle overrode the strict Sabbath law. The action of the disciples in plucking the ears of corn was technically " reaping " and therefore an act forbidden on the Sabbath (Mark 2^{23-28}, Matt. 12^{1-8}, Luke 6^{1-5}). Matthew alone describes the disciples as hungry possibly in order to lend point to the Old Testament parallel cited by Jesus. We might perhaps interpret their action as the kind of instinctive conduct natural to people passing through cornfields and therefore expect Jesus to point out that some actions fall below the level of legal enactment. Instead He quotes the precedent of David (1 Sam. 21^{2-7}) and in Matthew the " work done " by the priests on the Sabbath Day (Matt. 12^{5-7}). The discourse on the " tradition of the elders " is not without its difficulties but it clearly sets out the chief danger to which an enhanced legalism is always exposed, forgetfulness of the inward through undue engrossment with the outward. The comment of the Evangelist " making all meats clean," which grammatically is only loosely attached to the remainder of the sentence, points to a conclusion, the abolition of the food laws which Jesus apparently never drew Himself (Mark 7^{1-23}, Matt. 15^{1-20}). The earliest sources (Mark and Q) both record denunciations of the Pharisees (Mark 12^{38-40}; Matt. 23^{1-36}, Luke 11^{37}–12^{1}–Q). The extent to which Pharisaism as a whole had fallen into these pitfalls may be open to question. There is no doubt that the main defects to which legalism is liable are plainly indicated—indifference to the needs of others, ostentation, a restrictive approach to religion, scrupulosity and the drawing of fine casuistical distinctions, as well as the neglect of the inward through an undue concern with the outward. The question of the Great Commandment or the premises from which the whole Law could be deduced was a standing problem in Rabbinic circles related to, but not identical with, the distinction between light and heavy precepts (Mark 12^{28-34}, Matt. 22^{34-40}, Luke 10^{25-28}). For Jesus it is no mere matter of systematic theology, the apex on which the Law rested, but a reaffirmation of spiritual priorities.

At many points in the Gospels parallels can be found to concepts or methods of argument found in the Rabbinic literature. Caution is needed here particularly in the dating of Rabbinic material. In many cases parallelism is a more likely explanation than indebtedness. While it is probable that Jesus had some familiarity with Rabbinic trends in the Judaism of His day and could turn His knowledge to good effect in controversy by meeting His critics on their own ground and with their own weapons, He certainly possessed no formal Rabbinic training and would not be regarded by the rabbis as one of their number. The real roots of His religion lay rather in the prophetic and apocalyptic movements. As elsewhere in His teaching He cuts directly to the heart of the matter, testing the legalism of His day by His primary insight into the purpose and character of God.

In some matters of controversy the best Rabbinic teaching would have supported Jesus. His denunciation of the misuse of Corban harmonizes with much contemporary teaching (Mark 7^{11-13}). The legality of raising an animal which had fallen into a pit on the Sabbath Day remained an open question for some time to come (Matt. 12^{11}, Luke 14^{5}–Q). For Jesus humanitarian claims outweigh legal considerations.

The approach of Jesus to the Law as a whole as distinct from current tendencies and particular provisions needs somewhat careful qualification and discloses a double attitude of acceptance and rejection. It is very similar to the approach of Paul in the Epistle to the Romans. To consider him either as a liberal Rabbi critical of some recent provisions or as a root and branch reformer with distinct antinomian tendencies would be equally wide of the mark.

In His own conduct Jesus is depicted as an observant Jew. This is emphasized so far as His family circle is concerned in the Lucan Infancy narratives (Luke $2^{24.\ 27-28}$). The Fourth Gospel records a number of occasions on which He observed the Pilgrimage Feasts. The Rich Young Ruler (to use the traditional composite description) is reminded of the commandments and in Matthew bidden to keep them (Mark $12^{28f.}$, Matt. 19^{17-19}, Luke 18^{20}). The question about the Great Commandment is answered out of the Law itself (Deut. 6^{5}, Lev. 19^{18}). It is treated as a genuine question, and no criticism of the Law is either stated or implied. The cleansed leper is bidden to show himself to the priest and to make the traditional offering (Mark 1^{44}, Matt. 8^{4}, Luke 5^{14}). If Jesus had a special mission to those who had cut themselves off from the Law, the tax-collectors and open sinners, He never condones their disobedience. Zacchaeus is prompted to make restitution by the action of Jesus (Luke 19^{1-10}) and in an incident of the Synoptic type in the Fourth Gospel the Woman taken in adultery is told " Go and sin no more " (John 8^{11}). Relief is promised to those weighed down by the yoke of the Law, they are not thereby released from the duty of obedience (Matt. 11^{28-29} ; cf. Matt. 23^{4}, Luke 11^{46}–Q).

Two passages suggest that Jesus might have gone even further, though neither is beyond the range of legitimate doubt. Both occur in the material special to Matthew who discloses a heightened interest in the problem. The first occurs at the beginning of the Matthaean discourse against the Pharisees and seems out of harmony with the remainder. " The scribes and Pharisees sit in Moses' seat. All things therefore whatsoever they bid you, do and observe, but do not ye after their works, for they say and do not " (Matt. 23^{2-3}). This may represent a conservative stream of Jewish Christianity ; it would have been impossible even to frame if the attitude of Jesus Himself had been one of deliberate and calculated disobedience. With this may be compared a more extended passage in much the same sense. " Think not that I came to destroy the law and the prophets : I came not to destroy but to fulfil. For verily I say unto you, Till heaven and earth pass away, one jot or one tittle shall in no wise pass away from the law, till all things be accomplished. Whoever therefore shall break one of these least commandments, and shall teach men so, shall be called least in the Kingdom of heaven, but whosoever shall do and teach them, he shall be called great in the Kingdom of heaven" (Matt. 5^{17-20}). If these verses are to be taken with uncompromising literalism they can only be ascribed to the same circle. An authentic nucleus is however probable and vv.$^{18-20}$ may represent a Jewish Christian gloss on v.^{17}. Some find an allusion to Paul in v.^{18} and this remains probable but not certain. While the section might conceivably be defended as a strong rejection of antinomianism it remains difficult to reconcile with other aspects of the teaching of Jesus on the subject.

No serious objection can, however, be raised to v.^{17}, "Think not that I am come to destroy the law: I came not to destroy but to fulfil." It appears to represent the double approach to the Law which seems to be confirmed by other evidence outside the passage. But the meaning of "fulfil" still requires examination. It has recently been suggested that the argument of the legal sections of the Sermon on the Mount, "Ye have heard that it was said by them of old time . . . but I say unto you" is based upon Rabbinic formulae of controversy. The literal interpretation of a passage was introduced by the formula "I might understand," the preferred exegesis by the phrase "But thou must say." The aim of this substitution of a false exegesis by a truer interpretation was to uphold the Law. It is claimed that differences between Jesus and the Rabbinic schools can be exaggerated and that their aim was the same. But the differences here are profound. "Thou must say" is not identical with "I say unto you," particularly in the light of the important and characteristic "Amen I say unto you" group of sayings. The inference that the intention of Jesus in these contrasts was to uphold the Law in the Rabbinic sense and the further explanation of "fulfil" in this sense falls a good deal short of demonstration.

The alternative is to take "fulfil" in a wider and less technical sense, "to fill full of meaning" or "to reveal its true meaning and significance." For Jesus the claims and demands of discipleship go beyond the provisions of legal obedience. Thus the questioner in Mark 12^{34} despite his obedience to the Law is "not far from the Kingdom of God." The Rich Young Ruler must bring his legal obedience to fulfilment by discipleship of Jesus Himself (Mark 10^{21}, Matt. 19^{21}, Luke 18^{22}). The Law and the Prophets represent an epoch which has come to an end with John the Baptist as a means adequate to provide man's salvation (Matt. 11^{12}; Luke 16^{16} blurs the point in the interests of his Jewish legalism). The new obedience on which man's eternal destiny depends is now bound up with the acceptance of Jesus and His teaching

(Matt. 10^{32}, Luke 12^{8-9}–Q). The Love of God is summed up in the presence of the Kingdom of God through Jesus Himself and the love of neighbour in the life of service and sacrifice which discipleship involves. Similarly legal observance is subsumed under the new obedience of those who enter the Kingdom of God. Moral duty remains of obligation but it is fulfilled in the claims of discipleship. The double purpose of the Law for religion and ethics is thus fulfilled without the evacuation of its meaning or the abolition of its obedience.

(ix) JESUS AND THE GENTILES

The relation between the mission of Jesus and the Gentiles raises a problem similar to one which we have already considered in connexion with consummated eschatology. In the one case the question has been raised whether the range of the foresight of Jesus extended beyond the time-span of a single generation after His Resurrection, here the problem is whether the range of the intention of Jesus though virtually restricted to Jews during His earthly ministry envisaged the inclusion of Gentiles at least in principle at some further stage. While in both fields there is some evidence which appears to support the view of a more limited compass this conclusion is not upheld by a study of all the available data.

The evidence of the Apostolic Age does not all point in the same direction. There is no doubt that the Evangelists accepted the legitimacy of the mission to the Gentiles though it is possible that they might have maintained this with varying degrees of conviction and justified it on somewhat different grounds. Indeed one of their number, Luke, was himself, it seems, a product of the Gentile mission. On the other hand, the Acts of the Apostles records a serious cleavage of view on the subject in the Apostolic Church at the Council of Jerusalem (Acts 15) at which no evidence of the Gospel type is adduced and which Luke interprets as the urgent pressure of the Holy Spirit outwards from Jerusalem and Judaea to the ends of the earth.

It is clear that the earthly ministry was virtually confined to Judaism. The historical and geographical circumstances of the ministry of Jesus are no doubt quite sufficient to account for this fact. There are, however, two significant exceptions, the healings of the daughter of the Syrophoenician woman (Mark 7^{24-30}, Matt. 15^{21-28}, no Lucan parallel) and of the Centurion's Servant (Matt. 8^{5-13}, Luke 7^{1-10}–Q). Both are healings from a distance and in both cases the faith of the suppliant is specially recorded. The Marcan account of the former miracle emphasizes that the children must first be filled (Mark 7^{27}), whereas in Matthew the dialogue is introduced by the emphatic statement "I was not sent but to the lost sheep of the house of Israel" (Matt. 15^{24}; cf. Matt. 10^{6}, discussed below). In both accounts the faith of the woman is commended but a slight, though significant, difference of emphasis between the two accounts can be detected. What is for Mark an illustration of an order of priorities becomes for Matthew an exceptional case which raises in itself no question of principle. The omission of the incident by Luke is probably to be explained by the fact that for a whole-hearted believer in the Gentile Mission the description of the Gentiles as dogs would hardly make an appeal. In both accounts of the former miracle the contrast between the faith of the centurion and the unbelief of Israel is drawn and Matthew appends a saying which Luke records elsewhere in a somewhat heightened form (Matt. 8^{11-12}; cf. Luke 13^{28-30}). This refers to the presence of "many from the east and from the west" at the Messianic Banquet and contrasts the exclusion of the sons of the Kingdom. Whatever differences of emphasis there may be between the Evangelists, it is clear that for Jesus Himself the miracle represents a kind of overflow activity in a mission devoted to His own people.

The evidence which points to a wider range in the intention of Jesus is cumulative in character. The description of disciples as the salt of the earth or the light of the world contains nothing which must of necessity be restricted to Jews (Matt. 5^{13-14}; cf. Mark 9^{50}, Luke 14^{34}). The eschatology of Jesus is entirely free from the idea of vengeance against the Gentiles in marked contrast to the use made of some Old Testament passages in Judaism. Thus in the sermon at Nazareth (a scene which modern Jewish authorities regard as a thoroughly reliable picture of synagogue worship) the quotation of Isa. 61^{2} stops short of the words "a day of vengeance of our God" (Luke 4^{19}). The same phenomenon can be observed in the passage quoted in answer to the question of John the Baptist (Matt. 11^{5-6}, Luke 7^{22}–Q). If Jesus still retained the distinction between Jew and Gentile, there is a complete absence of any traces of hatred either towards Romans or Samaritans. Indeed on two occasions a Samaritan is held up as an example of neighbourly love (Luke 10^{25-37}) and of gratitude (Luke 17^{16}). The account of an outrage perpetrated against Galileans by the Romans is made the occasion not for an outburst of hatred against Rome but for a summons to Israel to repent (Luke 13^{1-3}). Further evidence of a similar type can be drawn from three Q passages in which Gentiles like the Queen of Sheba, the men of Nineveh and even cities like Tyre and Sidon are favourably contrasted with "this generation" (Matt. 10^{15}, Luke 10^{12}; Matt. 11^{21-22}, Luke 10^{13-14}; Matt. 12^{41}, Luke 11^{31-32}). The Old Testament precedents of Elisha in the healing of Naaman and of Elijah in the case of the widow of Zarephath are cited at the conclusion of the sermon at Nazareth (Luke 4^{25-27}) and reinforce the mention of Jonah in the Q passage (Matt. 12^{39-41}, Luke 11^{29-32}).

So far the positive evidence points to a complete absence of bitterness to other religious and racial groups and at the very least a theological justification of overflow activity by the citation of the appropriate Old Testament precedents.

It is noticeable how indications of a Gentile mission tend to gather round the Passion and Resurrection narrative. The Marcan account of the Cleansing of the Temple (though not the other Synoptic parallels) speaks of " the house of prayer for all nations " (Mark 11^{15-18}, Matt. 21^{12-13}, Luke 19^{45-46}). The words form part of a composite quotation from the Old Testament (Isa. 56^{7} and Jer. 7^{11}). The omission of the crucial words in Matthew can be readily explained but the failure of Luke to continue the quotation is less intelligible. Possibly He regarded them as wholly inapplicable to the Jewish Temple. If the area cleansed was the Court of the Gentiles from encroaching Jewish traffic and barter the action of Jesus would be even more significant. But this explanation is not entirely beyond dispute. In the account of the Last Supper the words of institution over the cup speak of the blood of the covenant which is shed " for many " (Mark 14^{24}, Matt. 26^{28}; Luke misses the point of the Semitism and renders " for you "). In Semitic usage " the many" would bear an inclusive and not a restrictive sense. The double character of the Last Supper as proleptic to the Cross and as the foretaste of the Messianic Banquet is relevant here. Whatever its basis in history the rending of the veil of the Temple (the curtain between the Holy Place and the Holy of Holies) reveals part of the significance of the death of Jesus to the Evangelist, the removal of all barriers which previously existed between God and man here typified by Jewish particularism. For Mark the veil of the Temple plays the part of the " middle wall of partition " in the Pauline letters. Finally the post-Resurrection commission to the disciples recorded by Matthew, " Go ye therefore into all the world and make disciples of all nations," not only proclaims the belief of the Evangelist that the Gentile mission was according to the mind of the Risen Lord but plainly associates the extension of the mission of Jesus into the Gentile world with the crowning event of the series which have been described here as inaugurated eschatology (Matt. 28^{19}).

Some evidence to the contrary must be briefly reviewed. Three passages, all derived from the material special to Matthew, are in question here. The stern judgment passed by

Jesus on the quest for converts on the part of the Pharisees is dubiously relevant. While two views were held in Judaism on the desirability of converts (" compassing sea and land to make one proselyte "), the charge made by Jesus really turns on the character of the end-product (" twofold more a son of Gehenna than yourselves, Matt. 23^{15}). More relevant are two Matthaean additions to the Marcan mission charge to the Twelve, " Go not to the Gentiles and enter not the province of Samaria but go rather to the lost sheep of the house of Israel " (Matt. 10^{5-6}). This may either be a temporary restriction confining the Twelve to the limits imposed by Jesus on Himself for the duration of their journey or a piece of narrowly Jewish-Christian propaganda incorporated by the Evangelist into his source. The second saying is more difficult. " Verily I say unto you, 'Ye shall not have gone through the cities of Israel till the Son of Man be come' " (Matt. 10^{23}). Its genuineness is not beyond dispute but the contrast word " go rather " is to be noted and may be connected with the statement of priorities on the part of Jesus. Its connexion with the context is uncertain and it may well be a floating saying attached to other material. Alternatively both sayings may derive from a narrow and particularist school of Jewish Christianity.

We have seen that the miracles of Jesus performed on non-Jews probably represented the kind of overflow activity appropriate to anticipated eschatology and that evidence for an extension of the intention of Jesus to the Gentiles is connected with inaugurated eschatology. It remains to consider the place of Gentiles in a consummated eschatology. The chief evidence here is derived from the Q saying which refers to the Messianic Banquet, " Many will come from the east and from the west and shall sit down with Abraham, Isaac and Jacob in the kingdom of heaven " (Matt. 8^{11}, Luke 13^{28-29}–Q). No explanation of their presence, still less of the means by which it is attained, is given in the saying. It would indeed be unreasonable to expect as much in a brief saying which makes a single point. Two passages where Mark is followed by Matthew may however provide a clue. The incident of the anointing at Bethany is concluded by an Amen saying, " Verily I say unto you, wherever the Gospel is preached throughout the whole world that also which this woman hath done shall be spoken of for a memorial of her " (Mark 14^{9}, Matt. 26^{13}). Indications of an Aramaic original make it unlikely that this is an intrusion designed to support the Gentile Christian mission. There is a similar reference to Gospel preaching as a sign of the end in the Marcan apocalypse (Mark 13^{10}, Matt. 24^{14}). Recently both passages have been explained in the light of the " eternal Gospel " proclaimed by " another angel " in the Apocalypse

(Rev. 14^6) but it is the purest speculation to interpret the Gospels (even in their most apocalyptic moments) by the Revelation. The allusion in the first passage to "wherever the Gospel is preached" rather suggests a gradual process of Gospel proclamation by the Church than an eschatological event closely connected with the consummation itself.

If this interpretation of the evidence of the Gospels is accepted it will be readily seen that both the Pauline words "To the Jew first but also to the Greek" (Rom 1^{16}) and the Johannine saying "I if I be lifted up will draw all men unto me" (John 12^{32}) have a dovetail into the historical tradition.

(x) CONCLUSION

Any consideration of the Life and Teaching of Jesus inevitably raises for the reader as for the first disciples the question "What manner of man is this?" Nothing strikes the student of the Gospels more forcibly that His sureness of touch in the things of the spirit, the authority which He displays rather than argues. He speaks with authority and not as the scribes, as though (under God) the springs of thought and action lie wholly within Himself. He reveals the character of God by being Himself and His reactions to situations are those of God Himself. Divine functions such as forgiveness and judgment are already exercised by Him. This solidarity with God in word and deed forms part of the evidence which lies behind the acclamation of the modern disciple "Truly this man was the Son of God." But we also see in His ministry a complete realism in His approach to men. There is no trace of sentimentalism in His dealings with sinners or His training of the Twelve. He is under no illusions about the fickle, shallow response of the crowd, the entrenched position of ecclesiastical Judaism or the malleable rectitude of Roman justice. Yet neither ill-grounded enthusiasm nor unyielding opposition made Him falter in His purpose or weaken His challenge. "He knew what was in man" and possessed a solidarity with man no less striking than His solidarity with God.

But this note of authority was (humanly speaking) vulnerable. It could never be established by any external criteria. If many Old Testament anticipations met in His person and work, there was no uniform "blueprint" hope which He fulfilled in every particular. If He performed mighty works, He refused to give a sign which would establish His position as it were externally and beyond doubt. Challenge and demand are words which come naturally to mind in describing His teaching. The appropriate response to Him lay in a discipleship within which His authority was felt and His words and deeds became luminous. Its conditions still remain unchanged.

The Resurrection and the living witness of the Church prove that Jesus is still our contemporary, " Jesus Christ, the same yesterday, today, and for ever " and (like Thomas of old) the modern believer greets Him in faith and love as " My Lord and my God."

BIBLIOGRAPHY

G. Bornkamm, *Jesus of Nazareth*, 1960.
C. H. Dodd, *The Parables of the Kingdom*, 1935.
R. Newton Flew, *Jesus and His Church*, 1938.
J. Jeremias, *Jesus' Promise to the Nations*, 1958.
T. W. Manson, *The Teaching of Jesus*, 1931.
T. W. Manson, *The Servant-Messiah*, 1953.
W. Manson, *Jesus the Messiah*, 1943.
E. Stauffer, *Jesus and His Story*, 1960.
Vincent Taylor, *The Life and Ministry of Jesus*, 1954.
H. E. W. Turner, *Jesus, Master and Lord*, 1953.

XVI. THE HISTORY AND DOCTRINE OF THE APOSTOLIC AGE

By F. F. Bruce

(A) APOSTOLIC HISTORY

(i) THE BEGINNINGS OF "THE WAY"

THE small band of disciples who remained with Jesus almost to the end, but took to flight when He was arrested, came together again after His resurrection and, a few weeks later, were able to present a united front to the inhabitants and rulers of Jerusalem. The radical change which they underwent in less than two months demands for its explanation revolutionary experiences of the kind which the New Testament narrative associates with the first Christian Easter and Pentecost. In consequence, so confidently and effectively did they maintain that the crucified Jesus had been raised from the dead and was accordingly the man marked out by God as Israel's Messiah, so convincingly did their whole demeanour and way of life attest the genuineness of their claims, that great numbers of the people of Jerusalem joined their ranks. Attempts were made by the chief priests and Temple authorities to check the growth of this new movement, but it was so popular that they could make little headway against it. Jesus might have been accused of using language which portended the downfall of the Temple and all that it stood for, but no such charge could be brought against the apostles, who attended the Temple services and conducted themselves as pious and observant Jews.

Inherent in the very existence of the apostles, however, was a claim which must in the long run present a challenge to the establishment in Judaea. The care which they took to fill the vacancy in their number caused by the defection of Judas Iscariot, and so to maintain their strength at twelve, suggests that they were not unconscious of their status as the leaders of a new Israel—the faithful Israel to be called out from the nation as a whole, in response to the exhortation: "Save yourselves from this crooked generation" (Acts 2^{40}). But the attempt to form a gathered community of volunteers for holiness was no innovation in the religious history of Israel, and neither by speech nor by action did the apostles break the law. They had sympathizers in the most unlikely quarters, even among the Temple police, if not in the Sanhedrin itself.

At an early stage, however, the new movement—" The Way," as its adherents called it—attracted the allegiance of a considerable body of Hellenists. Just who these Hellenists were is a debatable question, but they appear to have been Jews whose family ties were with the Diaspora of the Eastern Mediterranean lands rather than with Palestine, even if for longer or shorter periods they were resident in Palestine. The Hellenists who attached themselves to the apostles took a much more critical attitude to the Temple order and all that it stood for than the apostles themselves did. To them the Temple order was an obstacle in the path of true religion; it had outlived such usefulness as it ever had. It was the activity of these Hellenists that first provided the authorities in Jerusalem with an opportunity of taking effective action against the new movement.

The leading spokesman of the believing Hellenists, Stephen, expressed their point of view so eloquently and vigorously that he was accused before the Sanhedrin of blasphemy, and on conviction was duly executed by stoning. The sequel was a campaign of repression in which the believing Hellenists appear to have been the principal target of attack. The apostles, the leaders of the " Hebrew " wing of the movement, were unmolested. Evidently they continued to enjoy the good will of the Jerusalem populace, unlike the Hellenists, whose opposition to the Temple made them as unpopular as Jeremiah had been in his day for much the same reason. The Hellenists belonging to the Way found it impossible to remain in Jerusalem or Judaea; they scattered accordingly in all directions. But wherever they went, they visited the Jewish communities and spread their message; in the event their persecution and dispersal brought about an increase in the number of those who acknowledged Jesus as Lord and Messiah, instead of checking their growth.

One of the leaders of these Hellenists, Philip, went to Samaria and began to evangelize part of that region where, some years previously, John the Baptist and Jesus Himself had been active for a short time (John 3^{23}, $4^{38ff.}$). Philip's Samaritan mission was extraordinarily successful, although its aftermath does not belong to the main stream of Christian development. A notable incident in his mission was the adherence to him of Simon Magus—followed almost immediately by the secession of Simon and his personal disciples from the apostolic fellowship. Those early Christian writers who trace to Simon and his entourage the beginnings of what later developed into Christian Gnosticism had probably a sound historical basis for their account of the matter.

(ii) THE GENTILE MISSION

Other Hellenists were even more adventurous than Philip ; such were the men who came to Antioch on the Orontes, the third largest city in the world at that time, and began to propagate their teaching there. At first, like their fellow-Hellenists elsewhere, they propagated it within the local Jewish community, which was an exceptionally large one. But some of them conceived the idea of evangelizing the Greeks of Antioch, and found a prompt and widespread response. They quickly realized that they had started something which they could not check, even had they wished to do so. Their Gentile hearers recognized in the news of a Saviour which these Hellenists brought them something that spoke directly to their condition. Before long the followers of Jesus in Antioch included more Gentiles than people of Jewish birth ; practically from its inception the Church of Antioch was predominantly Gentile, and it was there that the designation "Christians"—a thoroughly Gentile designation—was first given to the followers of Jesus.

The apostles in Jerusalem, who endeavoured to keep the expansion of Christianity within their control, sent a leader of the Jerusalem Church, one in whom they had confidence, to undertake the supervision and direction of this forward movement at Antioch. This was the generous-hearted Barnabas, who found the task with which the apostles entrusted him a highly congenial one. And it must be recognized that the apostles displayed greater liberal-mindedness than they are sometimes credited with when they chose a man like Barnabas as their commissioner on this occasion. What might have happened if they had sent as their commissioner someone who shared the viewpoint of the men who later visited Antioch and tried to impose circumcision on the Church there (Acts 15^1) may well be imagined. Barnabas soon found his task, congenial as it was, too much for one man to discharge, and associated a colleague with himself in the work.

This colleague was a man from Tarsus, a Jew of that city, and a Roman citizen to boot, a Pharisee by family tradition and personal education, and now a Christian by conviction. As befitted a member of the tribe of Benjamin, he bore the family name of Saul ; as a Roman citizen, he was known by the cognomen Paullus—Paul. Paul had actually been the leader of the campaign of repression which followed the death of Stephen ; but, while pursuing Christian refugees beyond the frontiers of Judaea to bring them back for trial to Jerusalem, was converted at Damascus to the faith which he had tried to uproot, and from then on became its most energetic champion and propagator.

At Antioch (if not indeed earlier) Paul found his life-work —the evangelization of Gentiles. Thanks to the prominence in the New Testament of Paul's correspondence and the record of his apostolic activity in Acts, we are much better informed about him than about other early preachers of the Gospel. Our sources concentrate on the progress of Christianity along the road leading from Jerusalem via Antioch to Rome; but it progressed along other roads at the same time. Within a few years of A.D. 30, Christianity was established probably in Egyptian Alexandria, and certainly in Rome—having reached the capital by some other route than that which led by Antioch. The Christian community in Rome suffered a setback in A.D. 49, when the Emperor Claudius expelled the Jewish colony from the city, for in its first phase the Christian group in Rome appears to have been entirely Jewish in origin and not yet completely dissociated from the synagogue. When, after some years, the Church of Rome was reconstituted, it contained a considerable Gentile element (as is plain from Rom. 11[13], written early in A.D. 57), and was firmly established and justly renowned for its faith and works years before any apostle is certainly known to have visited Rome.

The Church of Antioch speedily became a base for more advanced missionary operations. About A.D. 48 Barnabas and Paul were released by the Church for an extensive journey through Cyprus and South Galatia (on the Anatolian mainland), where they planted churches of the same general character as the Gentile-Christian community of Antioch.

This rapid increase in the strength of Gentile Christianity caused misgivings among the Christians of Jerusalem. Many of the more conservative Jewish believers there maintained that Christian converts from paganism should be required to observe circumcision and other provisions of the Jewish law. So strongly did they feel about this that some of them made it their business to visit the Gentile churches of Antioch and the other cities more recently evangelized, to press upon them the necessity of conformity to the law. As they saw it, the same kind of requirements should be imposed on these converts as were normally imposed on Gentile proselytes to Judaism.

It was necessary that this question should be discussed and settled "at the highest level." At a council held in Jerusalem between the leaders of the mother-church and delegates from Antioch it was agreed that no requirements should be imposed on Gentile converts apart from confession of faith in Jesus as Lord (with which baptism in His name and the reception of the Spirit were inseparably associated). It was, in addition, represented to them in quite emphatic terms that they should abstain from practices which were in any way tainted with idolatry, and that they should observe the same food-laws and code of sexual relations as the Jews did. These last provisions were designed, very reasonably, to ease the practical tensions in the new situation in which Jews and Gentiles, as fellow-members of the Church, had to learn to live together and eat together.

There was, however, a strong body of opinion in the Church of Jerusalem which would have liked to see further conditions imposed on Gentile converts; circumcision they regarded as the absolute minimum. In their eyes Paul, above all others, was a traitor to Israel's holy heritage for his inflexible opposition to the imposing of any such requirements on the Gentile churches. They refused to admit that he was an apostle at all, although their leaders at Jerusalem acknowledged that he and Barnabas were as truly apostles to the Gentile world as they themselves were to the Jewish people. In the course of Paul's subsequent apostolic career his steps were continually dogged by these opponents of his; they visited the cities where he had preached the Gospel and planted churches, insisting that circumcision and various other requirements of the Jewish law were necessary if the fullness of salvation in Christ was to be enjoyed, and trying to undermine Paul's apostolic authority in his converts' eyes.

(iii) THE GOSPEL IN THE ROMAN EMPIRE

It is to Paul that the evangelization of Western Asia Minor and the Balkan Peninsula was due. Making his headquarters for shorter or longer periods at centres such as Corinth (A.D. 50–52 and again 56–57) and Ephesus (A.D. 52–55), he established churches along the main roads and in the principal cities of these territories. In A.D. 47 there were no churches in the provinces of Galatia, Asia, Macedonia, or Achaia. By A.D. 57 Paul had done his missionary work so thoroughly in them, as far west as the frontier areas of Illyricum, that he considered his task in that part of the world finished. He looked farther afield to Spain, hoping to repeat in the Western Mediterranean the achievement he had brought to completion in the east.

Nor was Paul the only apostle to be active in the Eastern Mediterranean in those years. From the middle of the century onwards the original Jerusalem apostles appear to have embarked on a more extended ministry than they had undertaken thus far. They are heard of no more at Jerusalem, but their activities elsewhere are almost entirely unchronicled.

About A.D. 54 we hear of a "Peter party" in the Church of Corinth, although it does not follow from that that Peter had paid a personal visit to Corinth. At a later date there is evidence that he visited Rome. The only detail of his association with Rome of which we can be reasonably certain is the last act, his martyrdom, which was an incident in Nero's persecution of the Christians of the capital which broke out in A.D. 64. In his later journeys Peter was accompanied by John Mark of Jerusalem as his interpreter and general aide-de-camp; according to Papias and other second-century writers Peter's preaching formed the basis of Mark's written Gospel.

The Christian mission throughout the Eastern Roman Empire, especially the Pauline mission, was considerably facilitated in the fifties of the first century by the benevolent neutrality of the representatives of Roman law. Attempts were indeed made to convict Paul and his associates of spreading seditious propaganda. For example, at Thessalonica in A.D. 50 he was accused before the city magistrates of belonging to a subversive movement which fomented agitation in the interests of a revolutionary Jewish "messianism" and proclaimed Jesus as a rival emperor to Claudius. But the magistrates dealt with the charge calmly, stipulating only that Paul's friends in Thessalonica should give security for his good behaviour, which meant in effect his quiet departure from the city. Echoes of this experience, which caused Paul considerable concern, may be heard in his two letters to the Thessalonians sent from Corinth a few months later. In the attempts to silence him he discerned the activity of anarchic forces endeavouring to prevent the advance of the Gospel in the Roman world. One day, he believed, they would break out in all their fury and malignity, but he hoped that by that time Christianity would be securely enough established to meet and overcome their attack, and for its secure establishment he exerted himself unsparingly. Meanwhile he recognized in the supremacy of imperial law and order a power which held the forces of anarchy in check and thus afforded protection to the propagation of the Gospel, while he knew very well that he and his fellow-missionaries could not count on this protection indefinitely.

In Corinth a more serious attempt was made to bring him into conflict with the authorities. There the leaders of the Jewish community lodged a complaint against him before the Roman proconsul of Achaia, Lucius Junius Gallio, shortly after he entered upon his office in the summer of A.D. 51. They accused Paul of propagating an illegal religion—for they refused to acknowledge Paul's message as a legitimate interpretation of Judaism (which enjoyed the express sanction of Roman law). Roman law, as was well known, looked with no favour on new and unauthorized cults. Gallio, however, decided quickly that the dispute concerned rival interpretations of Judaism, and refused to take up the matter. His decision, negative as it was, implied that, so long as the law was not violated and public order not disturbed, Paul and his colleagues were entitled to share in the protection which Rome extended to the practice of the Jewish religion. It would inevitably be followed as a precedent by other governors and magistrates, not only because of the distinction of Gallio's proconsulship but also because of his influential family connexions (he was a younger brother of Seneca, who was at this time tutor to the future Emperor Nero).

Thanks to this helpful ruling, Paul was able to continue his apostolic activity for ten more years. His appreciation of the impartiality of Roman law finds expression in his language about "the powers that be" (the civil magistrates) in Rom. 13^{1-7} (written early in A.D. 57); it was probably his happy experience of Roman justice that moved him so confidently to exercise his citizen-rights and appeal to Caesar two years later, when he had reason to fear that the procurator of Judaea, who held him in custody on a charge of infringing the sanctity of the Jerusalem Temple, might yield to the pressure of his accusers in that province. While he awaited his hearing before the supreme court in Rome, he was kept under house-arrest as a Roman citizen, free to receive visitors and continue his ministry without any attempt being made to prevent him.

(iv) THE CHURCH OUTLAWED

But the conditions of the fifties could not go on unaltered into the sixties. Paul's own missionary activity had done as much as anything to change the picture; as a result of his planting of Christianity in so many of the eastern Roman provinces there were now many more Gentiles than Jews in the Church. It became a sheer impossibility for Christians, the majority of whom were plainly Gentiles, to continue to enjoy legal privileges which were intended strictly for Jews. The Jewish communities themselves would take steps to dissociate themselves from the Christians; they had done so before, but in the sixties they could do it with greater hope of success, not only because the Gentile character of Christianity now spoke for itself, but also because they had a powerful supporter at court. Poppaea Sabina, whom Nero married in A.D. 62, was a good friend to the Jews, and may have been a "God-fearer" or near-proselyte.

It may be, indeed, that Paul, realizing this new situation, hoped to gain from the emperor or his representatives legal sanction for the practice of Christianity (if not, as some have thought, to win them outright for Christianity). But if he did cherish any such hope, it was doomed to disappointment.

Deprived of the protection it had formerly shared, Christianity was now exposed to whatever hostile measures the authorities might at any time decide to take against it. The Christians, moreover, because of their refusal to join in most social activities (on account of idolatrous or immoral features in them which forbade their participation), were disliked as " haters of the human race " and suspected of anti-social vices. They would serve as convenient scapegoats against whom the wrath of society could be diverted whenever the occasion so required. Such an occasion came with the Great Fire of Rome in A.D. 64, which Nero was popularly (though perhaps unjustly) blamed for starting.

The Christians of the capital were rounded up and accused of arson. Although this charge broke down, many of them were put to death by way of public entertainment as enemies of society. Either at this time or within the next three years the apostles Peter and Paul were executed at Rome. From then on until the establishment of religious toleration under Constantine two and a half centuries later, Christians, whether in Rome or in the provinces, were always liable to coercion at the hands of the magistrates, although only on rare occasions was the repression more than local and temporary.

The fortunes of Christianity under the Flavian emperors, Vespasian and his two sons (A.D. 69–96), are scantily documented. While no wholesale attack on the Church, such as that which broke out in Rome under Nero, is recorded, the official attitude to it was consistently hostile, and from time to time there were outbursts of active persecution, both in Rome and in the provinces. Domitian, the third and last ruler of the Flavian dynasty, has been traditionally depicted as a persecutor of Christians, though the specific evidence on this point relates to punitive measures taken against members of the Roman nobility and of his own family. Some, but by no means all, of the victims of these measures were apparently Christians. Even so, the indications are that by A.D. 95 Christianity was making its way into the upper strata of Roman society, and even into the imperial house itself.

The changed attitude of the Roman state to Christianity brought about a changed attitude on the part of many (but not all) Christians towards the state. A marked contrast to Paul's language about " the powers that be " in Rom. 13^{1-7} is found in the book of Revelation, which belongs to the Flavian period. In it the city of Rome is portrayed as a scarlet-robed harlot, " drunk with the blood of the saints and the blood of the martyrs of Jesus," while the empire appears as a seven-headed beast (a new manifestation of the Old Testament Leviathan) on which she sits enthroned (Rev. 17). The seven heads of the beast symbolize both the seven hills of Rome and seven successive emperors, of whom the sixth (Vespasian, probably) is now reigning. After all seven have run their course, one of them will return to life as the last imperial Antichrist (probably *Nero redivivus*), and his assault on the followers of Christ will be the deadliest of all, but it is he and not they who will be overthrown in the end. Rome herself will be attacked and destroyed by powers which were previously allied to her, and her place as the world's capital will be taken in the new creation by the Jerusalem that is to come, the metropolis of the saints. But it is not only Rome that is to be replaced by the new Jerusalem; she also takes the place of the old Jerusalem, destroyed with its temple in A.D. 70.

(V) PALESTINIAN CHRISTIANITY

The Church of Jerusalem, which lost most of its Hellenists at an early stage in its history, became in consequence much more conservative in its Jewishness than it might otherwise have been. Under the leadership of James the Just and his fellow-elders it became very strong numerically, but in spite of the *modus vivendi* agreed upon at the Council of Jerusalem in A.D. 49 it never became completely reconciled to the way in which the Gentile mission was conducted. Even Peter and his fellow-apostles were too liberal in their outlook for many members of the Jerusalem Church, while Paul was regarded as practically an apostate. When Paul visited Jerusalem in A.D. 57 with delegates from several Gentile churches who brought gifts to relieve the poverty of their Jerusalem brethren, he and his companions received a friendly welcome from James and the other elders, but were warned of the suspicion with which Paul was looked upon by thousands of the believers in Jerusalem, " zealots for the law " as they were. In the event, however, there was little opportunity for Paul to meet the rank and file of the Jerusalem Church on this occasion, for he was arrested and held on the charge of sacrilege only a few days after his arrival.

The judicial murder of James at the instance of the High Priest Annas II. in A.D. 62 was a heavy blow to the Jerusalem Church. When the Jewish revolt against Rome broke out in A.D. 66, the whole community left the city and went into dispersion. According to Eusebius (*Hist. Eccl.* III. v, 3), they received an oracle some time before the fighting began charging them to leave Jerusalem and migrate to Pella, one of the cities of the Decapolis. That some Christians did settle in Pella in due course is certain: from one of them, the second-century Ariston of Pella (author of a Christian apology against the Jews), Eusebius may have acquired this information. But that refugees from Jerusalem settled in Pella immediately on their flight in A.D. 66 has been questioned, in view of the anti-Jewish riots which raged there and in other Gentile cities of Syria and the Decapolis at the beginning of the war. They may well have sought refuge to begin with in the less frequented parts of Transjordan ; indeed, the flight of the mother-church to the wilderness and her preservation there seems to be reflected in the language of Rev. 12^{14}. Egypt could also have provided a haven for some refugees ; indeed, Egypt and Transjordan appear to have been in later generations the principal centres of Ebionite Christianity (which derives from one phase of Jerusalem Christianity, perhaps in conjunction with Samaritan or Essene tradition).

There is evidence of another Christian migration—to the province of Asia, where a number of "great luminaries" of the early Judaean Church spent their last days and slept their last sleep. Some of these migrants disapproved of the laxity of Christian practice in proconsular Asia : the severe words about the Nicolaitans and others in the Letters to the Seven Churches in the Apocalypse reflect the attitude of those who held fast by the provisions of the Council of Jerusalem towards those Christians who felt that these restrictions were no longer binding. "John the disciple of the Lord" was outstanding among those Christians who migrated to Asia, as were also Philip and his daughters. If, as seems probable, this Philip is "Philip the evangelist" of Acts 21^{8} (rather than "Philip, one of the twelve apostles," with whom Polycrates of Ephesus identified him *c.* A.D. 190), then part of the Church of Caesarea evidently joined in this migration. Certainly Caesarea cannot have been a comfortable place for Christians of Jewish birth to remain in when the Jewish war broke out. Generally speaking the Palestinian migrants to Asia represented a much less Judaistic understanding of Christianity than the migrants to Transjordan and Egypt.

With the end of the Temple order in A.D. 70 the Church and the Synagogue went their separate ways. The Church saw in the events of A.D. 70 the judgment of God on the old Israel and the confirmation of her own status as the new "Israel of God." The Synagogue for its part, by introducing into its liturgy the *birkath ham-mînîm*, a malediction on apostates which disciples of Jesus could not utter because that term included them, effectively debarred all "Nazarenes" from its fellowship.

* * * * *

A sympathetic observer in the middle forties of the first century might have concluded that the new movement inaugurated by Jesus and now led by His apostles had come to stay. By surviving the death of Jesus it had overcome the greatest setback it was likely to meet. He might even have contemplated the possibility of its spreading until it attained a dominating position in the Jewish world. By the middle fifties he would have seen, to his surprise, that it was spreading swiftly through the Graeco-Roman world and was being eagerly accepted by Gentiles. In the middle sixties, however, he would have viewed with grave misgivings the hostile attention which it was attracting from the imperial authorities, and might well have regretted that it had not been content to remain as a leavening influence within Judaism. But the events of the later sixties and early seventies showed on the one hand that its dissociation from Judaism was timely and on the other hand that it had not succumbed to the first imperial attack upon it. These years decided that, though the struggle might be long, Christianity was not to be crushed out of existence. By the very fact of surviving the first round of the conflict with the Roman state, its ultimate triumph was assured.

XVI. THE HISTORY AND DOCTRINE OF THE APOSTOLIC AGE

(B) APOSTOLIC DOCTRINE

(i) THE PRIMITIVE PREACHING

THE theology of the Apostolic Church, for all the diversity that can be traced between one teacher or school and another, is based on the conviction and affirmation that Jesus of Nazareth, repudiated and crucified by men, has been highly exalted by God, and thus vindicated as Messiah, Lord, Son of God. Humiliation and exaltation form a recurring Biblical pattern, exemplified in the Servant of the Lord of Isa. 42–53, in the one like a son of man in Dan. $7^{13f.}$, in the righteous sufferer of the Psalms (cf. Ps. 22^{24}), and in Israel's national history: " The stone which the builders rejected has become the head of the corner " (Ps. 118^{22}). At a very early point in New Testament times it was claimed that this pattern had reproduced itself, and indeed fulfilled itself, in Jesus. A sample of the most primitive Christian theology is Peter's address in the Temple court in Acts 3^{12-26}, which makes the announcement: " The God of Abraham, of Isaac and of Jacob, the God of our fathers, glorified his servant Jesus, whom you delivered up and denied . . ." (v.[13]). The hymn in Phil. 2^{6-11}, widely believed nowadays to be of pre-Pauline origin (although Paul incorporates it in his letter in order to set Jesus before the Christians of Philippi as the supreme example of humility and self-effacement), reveals the same pattern: " Christ Jesus . . . humbled himself and became obedient unto death, even death on a cross. Therefore God has highly exalted him. . . ."

But the early disciples of Jesus would not have thought of finding this pattern fulfilled in Him if something had not happened to assure them that His humiliation, of which they were well aware, was followed by His vindication and exaltation by the hand of God. This " something " was His resurrection from the dead, of which they were equally well aware, for He had appeared to them " alive after his passion " in circumstances which left them in no doubt that He had conquered death, and that God had reversed the death-sentence passed on Him by His human judges. Their claim to be eyewitnesses of Jesus in resurrection found a central place from the start in the apostolic preaching; without it, in fact, there would have been no apostolic preaching.

The outline of the message first proclaimed by the apostles may be reconstructed with a high degree of certainty from allusions and fragments scattered throughout the New Testament—in the Epistles (both Pauline and non-Pauline), in the reports of early Christian preaching in the first half of Acts, and in the framework on which much of the material in the Gospels is built up. No attempt to reconstruct or summarize it should be made without an acknowledgment of indebtedness to Professor C. H. Dodd, whose pioneer work in this field from 1932 onwards has been unsurpassed in its value and influence.

The following features are fairly constant in the apostolic preaching:

1. God has fulfilled His promises recorded in the writings of the prophets, and has visited and redeemed His people by sending the long-expected Saviour.

2. The Saviour came as Jesus of Nazareth, born (as the Scriptures foretold) of Israel's race, of Judah's tribe, of David's royal house.

3. In accordance with these same Scriptures He suffered death (accepting it willingly as a means of atonement for His people's sins) and was buried.

4. Also in accordance with the Scriptures, He was raised from the dead on the third day and appeared to many witnesses.

5. In His name God now offered remission of sins to all who repented and believed in Jesus as Saviour and Lord.

6. Those who believed were baptized in the name of Jesus, received the Holy Spirit (whose outpouring on all flesh at the end-time was likewise foretold in the prophetic writings), and became members of a new community, the "congregation" (*ekklēsia*) of God.

7. This same Jesus, now exalted at the right hand of God, would be universally manifested as judge of the living and the dead. (It should be borne in mind that Christians of the first century were no more, and no less, likely than those of the twentieth to envisage "the right hand of God" in a literal sense; they derived it from the oracular language of enthronement in Ps. 110[1].)

One of our earliest and most important sources for such an outline of the apostolic preaching is 1 Cor. 15[3-11], where Paul reminds the Christians of Corinth of the Gospel which they heard from his lips when first he visited their city. He emphasizes that the message which he "delivered" to them was one which he himself had "received." The part which Peter and James play in Paul's list of those to whom the risen Christ presented Himself strongly suggests that it was from them that Paul "received" the main details of his account; we know, moreover, that when he visited Jerusalem in the third year after his conversion he spent two weeks with Peter and also met " James the Lord's brother " (Gal. $1^{18f.}$). Whatever differences there might be between Paul and others in their interpretation and presentation of the message, he and the Jerusalem apostles were evidently in agreement on the basic facts : " Whether then it was I or they," he says, " so we preach and so you believed " (1 Cor. 15^{11}).

This passage in 1 Cor. 15 is one of several instances of an early Christian " tradition " referred to in the New Testament Epistles. This " tradition "—which is indicated not only by the appropriate substantive *paradosis* but also by the verbs for " receiving " and " delivering," *paralambanō* and *paradidōmi* —is not peculiar to any one apostle or preacher ; it is shared by them all. It goes back to Jesus and is invested with His authority. The tradition might be variously interpreted and applied, but the interpretations and applications could not carry the same authority as the tradition itself carried. Paul's information about the saving events might have been derived in part from Peter and James, but they are not his authorities for the tradition ; the authority is derived from Christ, by Whom Paul was called to be an apostle as directly (albeit belatedly) as Peter and his colleagues. Similarly it is not of the first importance to Paul or his readers who his immediate informant was about what Jesus said and did " on the night when he was betrayed " ; Paul records the tradition of His words and actions as carrying Jesus' own authority. " I received from the Lord what I also delivered to you," he says to the Corinthians when reminding them of the institution of the Lord's Supper (1 Cor. $11^{23ff.}$).

(ii) LIVING BETWEEN THE TIMES

Another phase of the apostolic tradition can be recognized in the ethical teaching of the primitive Church. Jewish believers already had the " form " of knowledge and truth in the law (Rom. 2^{20})—although even that " form " had now to be understood in the light of the words of Jesus and not in accordance with the interpretations current in the various rabbinical schools. But converts to Christianity from paganism required to be taught the rudiments of ethical behaviour, and especially of sexual behaviour. For it was in this last area that there was the widest divergence between current pagan practice and the standards which, restated by Jesus in uncompromising terms, the Church took over from its Hebrew background. All Christians, in fact, whether Jewish or Gentile in origin, had to learn and obey what Paul calls " the law of Christ " (1 Cor. 9^{21}, Gal. 6^{2}) or, as it is called in the Epistle of James, " the perfect law, the law of liberty . . . the royal law" (Jas. 1^{25}, $2^{8, 12}$). This law is clearly recognizable as the ethical teaching which Jesus gave His disciples. A comparison of Paul's practical instruction in Rom 12^{1}–13^{10} with the Sermon on the Mount in Matt. 5–7 is eloquent enough in this regard; it is the principles of Jesus that Paul applies throughout, and repeatedly the very words of Jesus are echoed.

A comparative study of the ethical teaching in several New Testament Epistles, irrespective of their authorship, has led to the conclusion that this teaching was arranged quite early in catechetical form, classified under short captions so as to be the more easily taught and memorized as the number of converts increased. Such captions are "Put off," introducing a list of unworthy and unregenerate practices to which Christians must bid a decisive farewell, and "Put on," introducing a list of graces by which their lives must henceforth be marked; "Be subject," inculcating a mutual willingness to subordinate their own desires and interests to those of others (not least within the Christian household, where husbands and wives, parents and children, masters and servants had to carry out the law of Christ in their relations with one another), and "Watch and pray," enjoining a constant attitude of moral alertness.

Sometimes the abandonment of pagan vices and the cultivation of Christian virtues are expressed even more concisely in terms of "putting off the old man" and "putting on the new man." This last concept, startlingly enough, is occasionally expressed in terms of "putting on Christ." This means, at the lowest, exhibiting the graces that characterized the life of Christ—and it is plain that the qualities which, in the Epistles, Christians are urged to cultivate are those which, in the Gospels, mark the character of Christ as well as being the material of His teaching. Not only submission to the law of Christ, but the imitation of His character and conduct, are urgently recommended to His followers.

The way in which this language is used, moreover, indicates the tension in Christian living between the ideal and the reality, between the indicative and the imperative, between what God has done for them and what He will yet do in them. If, in Gal. 3^{27}, Paul says that all who have been baptized into Christ "have put on Christ," in Rom. 13^{14} he urges his readers to "put on the Lord Jesus Christ." If, in Col. $3^{9f.}$, Christians are reminded that they "have put off the old man" and "have put on the new man," in Eph. 4^{22-24} they are exhorted to "put away the old man" and "put on the new man." "Be what you are" is a recurring note in the ethical teaching of the New Testament; that is, be in practical life what your baptism proclaims you to have become; be in daily reality what you are in God's purpose.

It has been said that in this oscillation between the radical change as something already accomplished and as something yet to be realized the New Testament writers, and especially Paul, are guilty of inconsistency because they are trying to fit the stubborn facts of life to the Procrustean bed of an abstract theological theory. But this is not so; the difficulty arises from the inevitable tension of Christian life in the environment of this world. As Paul and others saw, the Christian, both in fact and in his conscious experience, lives on two planes, or in two ages, so long as his present mortal life lasts. He belongs already to the age to come while he is still involved in the age that now is. As Paul puts it, he is spiritually united to Christ at the right hand of God while temporally he lives on earth. The new life imparted by Christ and received by faith does not immediately annihilate the "old Adam" which is his inheritance by natural birth; so long as he lives in this age the "flesh"—his inherited nature—persists as a dormant force which may awake and assert itself at the most unexpected moments.

This doctrine of the two ages permeates New Testament thinking. It is, of course, a thoroughly Jewish doctrine, but for the early Christians it had been radically reinterpreted by the fact of Christ. With the coming of Christ, and especially with His triumph over sin and death, the new age arrived, yet not so as to terminate the old age conclusively. It is true that "if any one is in Christ, he is a new creation; the old has passed away, behold, the new has come" (2 Cor. 5^{17}). But within and around him there is abundant evidence of the continuance of the old order. At present, between Christ's first coming and His parousia, there is an overlapping phase in which the two orders coexist concurrently. One day the old order will be done away with altogether, but for the present the believer lives between the times, in "the last days." The eschatology of the apostolic age is both realized and unrealized—realized, because Christ has come and triumphed; unrealized, because He is yet to come and manifest the universal fruits of His triumph. At present the believer enjoys by anticipation the heritage of glory which will then be his in its fullness; he is enabled to do this in substantial and effective fashion by the gift and activity of the Spirit.

(iii) THE TEACHING OF PAUL

The function of the Spirit in enabling Christians to live here and now the life of the age to come is not a doctrine peculiar to the Pauline writings. The gift of the Spirit was long since expected to be a feature of the end-time and the new age, and since Christ came, as His forerunner announced, to baptize with the Holy Spirit, the belief that the age of the Spirit has dawned is naturally common to most strata of primitive Christianity. But the implications of this belief for Christian life are brought out with special clarity in Paul's writings.

For Paul the age of the Torah, which was the period of infancy and tutelage, has been replaced by the age of the Spirit, in which believers in Christ come of age and enjoy their liberty as responsible sons of God. The Spirit is the guarantee of their inheritance, the firstfruits of that fullness of resurrection life to be received at Christ's parousia. It is by the Spirit that they are "baptized into one body," whatever their previous status may have been—Jewish, Gentile, or whatnot. This one body is "the body of Christ"; that is to say, His people are brought by the Spirit into one common life which is nothing other than a sharing in Christ's risen life. The life which they now live, "by faith in the Son of God," differs in degree but not in kind from the life which they will live hereafter. The "body of flesh" which they wear at present is mortal, and will one day be replaced by a "body of glory" after the fashion of Christ's resurrection body; but the indwelling Spirit is preparing them already for that new "house not made with hands, eternal in the heavens" (2 Cor. 5^{1}).

The common life in the body of Christ which believers experience is concisely expressed by the characteristically Pauline phrases "in Christ," "in the Lord." They are "in Christ" because they have been baptized "into Christ" and are incorporated into His risen life; conversely each of them can say, like Paul, "Christ . . . lives in me" (Gal. 2^{20}), because by His Spirit He indwells them individually, and this present indwelling of Christ in His people is their hope of glory (Col. 1^{27}).

This hope of glory will be realized at the parousia of Christ, which is at the same time the hour of judgment: "we must all appear before the judgment seat of Christ" (2 Cor. 5^{10}; cf. Rom. 14^{10}). But if men are to be judged by the record of their own deeds, no one can expect anything but condemnation, for all have fallen short. Jews will be judged by the Torah, which was specially entrusted to them, while Gentiles will be judged by such knowledge of right and wrong as they possess in the inner law of conscience; but Jews and Gentiles alike have sinned and must plead guilty at the bar of God's righteousness. But at the moment when all hope must be abandoned, new hope is given. While none can claim acquittal on the basis of personal merit or achievement, those who acknowledge their bankruptcy may be put in the right before God by the gift of His grace. This "righteousness from God" is based on the redemptive death of Christ, Whom God has provided as an all-sufficient atonement for sin. Nor need men wait until the parousia of Christ before they hear God's verdict of Not Guilty and receive His "righteousness"; it is theirs here and now through faith in Christ. This gracious act of God is affirmed and reaffirmed by Paul, sometimes in paradoxical language, as when he speaks of God as "justifying the ungodly" (Rom. 4^{5}) —as doing that which the Torah says God will not do (Ex. 23^{7}).

To Paul himself the experience of the justifying grace of God brought a sense of pardon and release, joy and hope, such as his painstaking conformity to the written and oral Torah had never brought him. His ambition henceforth was to "gain Christ and be found in him, not having a righteousness of my own, based on law, but that which is through faith in Christ, the righteousness from God that depends on faith" (Phil. $3^{8f.}$).

The twofold sense of "righteousness" found in Paul's writings—God's personal righteousness and the righteous status which He bestows on believers—may be recognized also in the Qumran texts, notably in the *Hymn of the Initiants* which concludes the *Rule of the Community*. The hymn-writer who says, "I will call God 'my righteousness,'" would have been acknowledged by Paul to have the root of the matter in him, even if Paul would have thought it necessary to teach him the way of the Lord more perfectly.

This sentence of acquittal was pronounced at the beginning of a man's life "in Christ," not at the end of it. It was not based on any works which he had performed up to that time, but carried with it the impartation of power to perform good works in the future. Those who are justified by faith are "created in Christ Jesus for good works, which God prepared beforehand, that we should walk in them" (Eph. 2^{10}). Moreover, those who are justified by faith enjoy peace with God; whereas they were formerly estranged from Him, and even rebels against Him, He has now reconciled them to Himself by Jesus Christ (Rom. $5^{10f.}$, 2 Cor. $5^{18f.}$). Christ, in the totality of His redemptive and reconciling work, is His people's life, peace, and hope.

Paul has been criticized for analysing the divine forgiveness into justification and reconciliation, especially by those who deprecate the expression of divine forgiveness in judicial terms at all. But Paul, inheriting the Old Testament conception of God as judge of all the earth, had little choice in the matter. Jesus Himself, while He spoke of God as Father, evidently saw no inconsistency in speaking of Him also as judge; he reminded his hearers about the day of judgment and told them what would secure their acquittal on that day and what would ensure their condemnation. Indeed, the distinction between justification and reconciliation, with logical priority given to justification, is rooted in the insight that there is no peace worthy of the name which is not founded on righteousness. If men are to be conscious of peace with God, they must have the assurance that He Who " will by no means clear the guilty " (Ex. 34[7]) has nevertheless pardoned and accepted them, sinners though they are.

The reconciliation which men may enjoy through Christ, first with God and then with one another, is for Paul but the first stage in a wider reconciliation, which will ultimately embrace within its scope " all things, whether on earth or in heaven " (Col. 1[20]). The Church, God's masterpiece of reconciliation, is the blueprint for the cosmic reconciliation of the future when God unites the universe under Christ as its true head (Eph. 1[9f.]). For this consummation Paul depicts the whole creation as eagerly waiting ; at present it is out of joint, but when the sons of God are manifested in glory, then " the creation itself will be set free from its bondage to decay and obtain the glorious liberty of the children of God " (Rom. 8[21]).

(iv) CHRISTIAN APOLOGETIC

On the morrow of the death and resurrection of Christ the Church found itself faced with an urgent apologetic task. His followers might well appear to have begun their work under an almost impossible handicap—the acknowledged fact that He in whose name they spoke and acted had been crucified by the sentence of a Roman judge. Far from trying to conceal this fact they placed it in the forefront of their propaganda ; but their doing so made it all the more necessary to accompany their recital of the circumstances of Jesus' death with some explanation of why He died thus, and how (despite appearances to the contrary) His cross was the token of His victory, not of His shameful defeat.

This apologetic task was threefold, according as they had to do with Jews, Greeks, or Romans (in practice all three aspects had to be borne in mind simultaneously). The Jew recalled the statement of the Torah, " a hanged man is accursed by God " (Deut. 21[23]), and argued that for this reason, apart from any other, it was impossible that Jesus should be the Messiah (which His disciples proclaimed Him to be). The Messiah, almost by definition, was one on whom God's blessing rested in a unique degree ; to claim the messianic dignity for one whose death declared him to be under God's curse (whether he deserved that death or not) was blasphemy. The Greek, more generally, argued that a man who had neither the wisdom nor the power to save himself from so disreputable and agonizing a form of death could not be seriously considered as a saviour of others or a guide for their lives; the claim that he was so was sheer folly. To the Roman, the fact that Jesus was executed after condemnation in a Roman court meant that He was a convicted criminal, and the movement which claimed Him as its founder must rightly be suspected of complicity in the sedition for which He was sentenced to crucifixion.

So far as the approach to Roman authorities is concerned, the lines which early Christian apologetic followed are specially clear in Luke-Acts. The conviction and execution of Jesus are presented as a miscarriage of justice, and officials great and small are recorded as bearing repeated witness to the innocence of His followers in relation to Roman law. As for the scandal of the cross in the eyes of Greek wisdom, the apostle of the Gentiles points out that, while the preaching of the cross did seem utterly foolish by the standards of that wisdom, it accomplished the moral and spiritual regeneration of men and women as Greek wisdom had signally failed to do. The "wisdom of the world" thus stood revealed as foolishness in God's sight, while Christ crucified was vindicated as the demonstration of divine power and wisdom.

The answer to Jewish objections, however, was more positively theological in character, and it was to a large extent in the elaboration of this answer that the foundations of early Christian doctrine were laid.

The first answer to the charge that the manner of Jesus' death proved Him to be accursed by God was given in the claim that God had raised Him from the dead. In the earliest apostolic witness the contrast is pressed between men's treatment of Him and God's reversal of their action. "*You* killed him," said the apostles to the Sanhedrin, "by hanging him on a tree; *God* exalted him at his right hand as Leader and Saviour" (Acts 5[30f.]). The verdict and sentence of the earthly court had been set aside by the judgment of the heavenly court.

In addition, it was emphasized that Jesus' death took place in accordance with the Hebrew Scriptures. Those who put Him to death were all unwittingly carrying out "the definite plan and foreknowledge of God" (Acts 2[23]). In what is recognizably a primitive outline of the apostolic preaching Peter says to the people of Jerusalem: "I know that you acted in ignorance, as did also your rulers. But what God foretold by the mouth of all the prophets, that his Christ should suffer, he thus fulfilled" (Acts 3[17f.]). The belief that the death of Christ fulfilled Old Testament prophecy did not originate with the apostles; it goes back to their Master, who (according to the oldest Synoptic narrative) submitted to arrest in Gethsemane with the words: "let the scriptures be fulfilled" (Mark 14^{49}).

But what Scriptures were believed to have been thus fulfilled? One which we can be sure was present in Jesus' mind on the evening of his arrest was Zech. 13^{7}, "Strike the shepherd, that the sheep may be scattered" (cf. Mark 14^{27}). Again, Peter's speech in Acts 3 begins, as we have seen, by echoing the opening words of the fourth Isaianic Servant Song, which was increasingly recognized in the Church as a prophecy of "the sufferings of Christ and the subsequent glory" (1 Pet. 1^{11}). If, then, the death of Christ was foretold and foreordained by God in the prophetic oracles, it followed that its explanation in terms of the divine curse was too superficial; the Scriptures which predicted His death showed that God had a greater purpose to accomplish by its means, in which the curse was turned into blessing. Those Scriptures, or others, also foretold the resurrection and exaltation of Christ, and the way in which they had been fulfilled in this respect proved Jesus to be both Lord and Messiah.

(v) TYPOLOGICAL EXEGESIS

In addition to the apologetic use of the Old Testament, with which its use in the proclamation of the saving message to Jewish and God-fearing audiences was closely associated, it was used also to make the Christian community aware of its own existence, character, and purpose.

Whole areas of Old Testament literature were found to reveal patterns of divine action and human response which reproduced themselves definitively in the coming of Christ and its aftermath. The very word "gospel" (*euangelion*) became the most generally accepted term for the Christian message because of the repeated occurrence of the word itself or its cognates in Isa. 40–66. The proclamation of "good tidings to Zion" (Isa. 40^{9}), announcing the end of its desolation and the restoration of its exiles (cf. Isa. 52^{7}, 60^{6}), becomes transmuted into the proclamation of the new redemption accomplished by Christ. As Jesus, in Luke $4^{16ff.}$, points to His own ministry as the fulfilment of Isa. $61^{1f.}$, where an unnamed speaker is anointed to proclaim good news to the poor, so in the apostolic writings passage after passage in these twenty-seven chapters is interpreted of the Gospel events, from John the Baptist's mission onwards, or of the worldwide announcement of these events. The preachers are the men with the "beautiful feet" in Isa. 52^{7} who bring glad tidings of good things (cf. Rom. 10^{15}), and if they find that their proclamation is not as eagerly welcomed as they hoped (especially when it is made to Jewish hearers), they express their astonishment in the Septuagint version of Isa. 53^{1}: "Lord, who has believed our message?" (cf. Rom. 10^{16}, John 12^{38}).

But the deliverance from Babylonian exile, foretold and celebrated in Isa. $40^{1ff.}$, is itself presented there as a recurrence of the pattern earlier displayed in Yahweh's bringing his people out of Egypt. So too in the New Testament the pattern of Christian redemption is seen as a recurrence and fulfilment of the Exodus from Egypt as well as of the return from Babylon. The death of Christ is called His "exodus" (Luke 9^{31}); He is the true passover, sacrificed for His people (1 Cor. 5^{7}), "a lamb without blemish or spot" (1 Pet. 1^{19}). His people, like Israel after the Exodus, are "the church in the wilderness" (Acts 7^{38}); their baptism into Christ is the antitype of Israel's passage through the Red Sea; their sacramental feeding on Him by faith is the antitype of Israel's nourishment with bread from heaven and water from the rock; Christ, the living Rock, is His people's guide as He guided the earlier Israel through the wilderness (1 Cor. $10^{1ff.}$). The heavenly rest which lies before them is the counterpart of the earthly Canaan, to which many members of the old Israel did not attain because of unbelief (Heb. $3^{7ff.}$).

The practical implications of this typology are pressed upon Christians by various New Testament writers, in a manner that suggests that the typology belongs to the common stock of primitive Christian teaching. Paul tells the Corinthians that the record of Israel's rebellion and punishment has been preserved for their admonition, lest they should imitate their disobedience and be overtaken by comparable judgment; the writer to the Hebrews seems to envisage a forty years' probation following on the death of Christ foreshadowed by Israel's forty years of testing in the wilderness, and warns his readers not to forfeit the saints' everlasting rest by cherishing "an evil, unbelieving heart"; Jude draws similar lessons from the fact that "Jesus, having saved a people out of the land of Egypt, afterward destroyed those who did not believe." (The reading "Jesus" probably preserves the original text of Jude ^{5}, and points to an understanding of the recurring pattern which goes beyond ordinary typology.)

The early Christian interpretation of the Old Testament thus supplied material not only for the defence and propagation of the Gospel, but also for a more comprehensive theology of Christian faith and life.

(vi) TEMPLE AND PRIESTHOOD

A distinctive strand of Hellenistic Christianity is recognizable in two New Testament documents—Stephen's apologia in Acts 7 and the Epistle to the Hebrews. Both emphasize the "pilgrim" character of the people of God, like Israel in the wilderness with their movable sanctuary, always ready to pull up their tent-stakes and march forward at God's bidding. There are, however, differences between the two. Stephen expresses a negative attitude towards the Temple at a time when the apostles were still frequenting its services, and argues that a shrine fixed to one place was always unsuitable for a pilgrim people and inculcated false religious notions. The writer to the Hebrews, on the other hand, regards the Temple order as instituted for a temporary purpose which the coming of Christ has rendered obsolete; to him its deficiency lies in the fact that it symbolized a heavenly reality to be manifested in the future, and served no good purpose when once that reality was manifested.

Hebrews is specially important in that it presents the one systematic exposition in the New Testament of the priestly aspect of Jesus' messiahship. Obviously the expectation of a priest of the new age, descended from Aaron or Zadok, could not be fulfilled in Jesus, who belonged to the non-priestly tribe of Judah. This author, however, recognized in Ps. 110 (whose opening words served as a primitive *testimonium* of Jesus' exaltation) a firm basis for the belief in Jesus' messianic priesthood. In Ps. 110^4 the king already invited by God to sit at His right hand is hailed by Him as a perpetual priest after Melchizedek's order. Historically it is probable that after David's capture of Jerusalem he and his heirs succeeded to the ancient dynasty of priest-kings to which Melchizedek belonged, so that Ps. 110^4 could properly be interpreted of the Davidic Messiah. Our author does not appeal to history, but he does find in Ps. 110^4 the divine ordination of a new and permanent priesthood which was to replace the Aaronic order. This priesthood is now exercised by Jesus in the heavenly temple of which the earthly sanctuary was a copy, by virtue of the unique, unrepeatable and infinitely acceptable sacrifice of Himself. The heavenly temple is that eternal order of reality in which men have access to God and fellowship with Him and with one another.

A similar concept appears in Eph. $2^{20ff.}$ where the united community of believers is described as a holy temple for God's abode, with Christ Himself as the chief corner-stone. The concept is amplified in 1 Pet. $2^{4ff.}$ where the individual believers are not only living stones in the temple, bonded together by Christ, but also members of the royal priesthood which ministers in the temple, offering "spiritual sacrifices acceptable to God through Jesus Christ" and proclaiming their great Redeemer's praise. The Apocalypse too shares this picture of the people of God as his dwelling-place. Meanwhile the worship of the Church " militant here in earth " is the echo of the worship presented in His heavenly temple, but when the new creation is consummated and the heavenly city is established on earth, God's tabernacle appears among men, for His people are then coterminous with mankind.

(vii) THE HOPE OF GLORY

The apostles' experience of the resurrection of Jesus and their reception of His Spirit enabled them to put a practical interpretation on His words about the impending coming of the kingdom of God " with power " (Mark 9^{1}), for they themselves had seen it. True, the parousia of the Son of Man, with their entrance into the glory which was their heritage in association with Him, lay in the future ; but the Spirit was present with them as the firstfruits of that fullness of glory. Their consciousness of the continuing ministry of Jesus now exercised through their own, and the clear evidence that " the powers of the age to come " were operating in their midst, sufficed to convince them that the promise of His parousia was not in vain.

At an early stage (Acts 3^{19-21}) there seems to have been an expectation that, if only Israel as a whole came to recognize and welcome Jesus as the true Servant and Prophet of God, He would return to them speedily in messianic power and usher in the " times of refreshing from the presence of the Lord " which would complete the fulfilment of all that the prophets had spoken. The same essential hope reappears in Paul, who envisages the ultimate conversion of all Israel, to which he looks forward, as bound up with the emergence of the Deliverer from Zion (interpreted by him, surely, as the heavenly Zion) foretold in Isa. 59^{20} (Rom. 11^{26}).

It soon became evident, however, that Israel was not going to embrace the Gospel in the foreseeable future ; if Paul persevered in the hope that she would do so one day this was because of a special revelation granted to him (the " mystery " of Rom. 11^{25}).

No doubt Israel's non-acceptance of the Gospel modified the apostles' eschatological perspective. Our fullest information about Christian eschatology in the apostolic age comes from Paul, who in this as in other matters probably shared the basic outlook of the other apostles, although he developed it along lines of his own. His earliest eschatological work appears in the two Thessalonian Epistles, written in A.D. 50 against a background of eschatological excitement. In the first Epistle he reassures his readers that their Christian friends who have died before the parousia will be raised and reunited with them when Christ appears; the general impression is that the intervening period will not be long. But a few weeks later, in the second Epistle, he adds that, while the parousia is certain, it will not come immediately. Other things must happen first; in particular, the restraint now exercised on the forces of anarchy by the Roman administration will be withdrawn, and anarchy incarnate will dominate the situation with God-defying arrogance, until it is annihilated by Christ at his parousia. In the mind of Paul, and of other Christians at that time, the memory would still be alive of the Emperor Gaius's attempt to set up his image in the Jerusalem Temple ten years previously—an attempt in which some were probably disposed to recognize "the abomination of desolation standing where he ought not" (Mark 13[14]). Gaius had failed, but another would succeed in establishing himself in the temple of God and claiming supreme divine honours for himself.

While the eschatological note in the Thessalonian Epistles (especially in the second Epistle) is more markedly apocalyptic than anywhere else in the Pauline corpus, his emphasis even so is essentially ethical. The unveiling of the future is intended not to gratify curiosity but to stimulate holy living.

Four years later we find in 1 Corinthians substantially the same eschatological teaching as in 1 Thessalonians, but the apocalyptic terminology has largely been abandoned. The resurrection of believers "at the last trumpet" is assured; the surrender of this hope would undermine the Gospel. But the resurrection of believers is the corollary of Christ's resurrection; it is a feature of the new creation whose head is Christ, the last Adam, the counterpart of the first Adam whose mortality involves in death the old creation of which *he* is head. The conception of Christ as the last Adam represents Paul's distinctive recasting of the "Son of Man" theme.

At his parousia Christ will execute judgment and His people will share His royal and judicial authority. Paul directs his life in the light of that coming day of review, and cares but little for temporary human judgments passed on his conduct. He associates himself now with those who will survive to see the parousia—"we shall be changed" (1 Cor. 15[51f.])—and now with those who will be raised from the dead then (1 Cor. 6[14]). So too in Philippians he says that "we" wait for a Saviour from heaven (Phil. 3[20f.]), but he is equally prepared for life or death at any time; and if his portion must be death, the interval between death and resurrection implies no hiatus in his fellowship with Christ (Phil. 1[21ff.]).

In 2 Corinthians Paul associates himself with those who will be raised from death at the parousia (2 Cor. 4[14]), but finds the resurrection principle already at work in the servants of

God ; the spiritual body of the resurrection is even now being formed as the inner man experiences daily renewal, and death will mean the immediate putting on of that " heavenly dwelling " which is prepared in advance (2 Cor. $5^{2f.}$). Similarly in Romans the believer, who rejoices in " hope of sharing the glory of God " (5^{2}), has the assurance of resurrection and immortality implanted within him by the life-giving Spirit : " if the Spirit of him who raised Jesus from the dead dwells in you, he who raised Christ Jesus from the dead will give life to your mortal bodies also through his Spirit which dwells in you " (Rom. 8^{11}).

What is to take place at the parousia is thus not something entirely new ; it is but the full flowering of that life in the Spirit which is a present reality for believers. And when the full flowering is displayed in them, it will mean the renovation of the created universe, transformed throughout by the radiance of the divine glory.

In the apostolic teaching, then, as in the words of Jesus, we find an eschatology " in process of realization." This note is specially dominant in the fourth Gospel. This Gospel does not jettison the idea of resurrection and judgment " at the last day " (cf. John 6^{40}, 12^{48}) ; but it lays chief weight on resurrection and judgment here and now. " Now," says Jesus, " is the judgment of this world " (John 12^{31}). Men pass judgment on themselves by their choice between light and darkness (John 3^{19}). The hour has come " when the dead will hear the voice of the Son of God, and those who hear will live " (John 5^{25}). Since He is the resurrection and the life, those who are united to Him by faith live in Him for ever even if they pass through physical death (John $11^{25f.}$). Already they possess eternal life, the life of the age to come, and need fear no condemnation ; whereas those who reject Him are " condemned already " (John 5^{24}, 3^{18}).

No two books are more dissimilar in outward appearance than the fourth Gospel and the Apocalypse, which was written under the Flavian emperors (A.D. 69–96) to encourage the churches (primarily those in the province of Asia) to stand firm and not lose heart in face of persecution. Yet the apocalyptic symbolism of the latter book has received a new meaning in terms of the fact of Christ. This Christian Apocalypse is distinguished from Jewish apocalypses in its insistence that the decisive action has already taken place. Christ has triumphed ; the " Lion of the tribe of Judah " has prevailed ; His followers are " overcomers " through their faith in Him. For all the differences between the Apocalypse and the fourth Gospel, in both documents we hear one who is called " The Word of God " saying to His disciples : " In the world you have tribulation; but be of good cheer, I have overcome the world" (John 16[33]). What lies ahead, the final abolition of evil from the universe and the creation of new heavens and a new earth, is but the "V-Day" which, in Oscar Cullmann's language, must follow the "D-Day" that is already past. In the Apocalypse, as elsewhere in the New Testament, eschatology is inaugurated, but not yet consummated.

* * * * *

The theology of the apostolic age, whose written deposit we have in the New Testament documents, is Christocentric from first to last. Christ is the Logos of God, the Alpha and Omega, through Whom and for Whom all creation exists. He is the fulfiller of God's age-long purpose to bring the universe, with all its rebellious forces, into reconciliation with Himself. But this cosmic Christ is presented, with no sense of incongruity, as identical with Jesus of Nazareth. In Him the divine Logos became real man; His ministry reveals the truth of God; His death on a terribly real cross just outside the wall of Jerusalem, by sentence of a Roman governor in A.D. 30, is set forth not only as the crisis of world history but as the turning-point in individual human lives, when it is made real to them in effective contemporaneity by the power of His Spirit. By the power of His Spirit men may live in God and God in them; by that same power His people are united in an eternal blood-brotherhood, which is the firstfruits of the coming consummation when all mankind, and all creation, will be united in the love of God.

The New Testament theologians, in their varying imagery and terminology, bear this consentient witness, and in so doing testify to the impact which Jesus made on the world into which He came. For here, they all agree, is the way of eternal truth and life: to "know thee, the only true God, and Jesus Christ whom thou hast sent" (John 17[3]).

BIBLIOGRAPHY

C. K. Barrett, *From First Adam to Last*, 1962.

S. G. F. Brandon, *The Fall of Jerusalem and the Christian Church*, 2nd ed., 1957.

R. Bultmann, *Theology of the New Testament*, Eng. trans., 2 vols., 1952, 1955.

G. B. Caird, *The Apostolic Age*, 1955.

O. Cullmann, *Christ and Time*, Eng. trans., 1951.

O. Cullmann, *The Early Church*, Eng. trans., 1956.

O. Cullmann, *The Christology of the New Testament*, Eng. trans., 1959.

C. H. Dodd, *The Apostolic Preaching and its Developments*, 1936.
C. H. Dodd, *Gospel and Law*, 1951.
C. H. Dodd, *According to the Scriptures*, 1952.
C. H. Dodd, *New Testament Studies*, 1953.
A. M. Hunter, *Paul and his Predecessors*, 2nd ed., 1961.
B. Lindars, *New Testament Apologetic*, 1961.
T. W. Manson, *Studies in the Gospels and Epistles*, 1962.
C. F. D. Moule, *The Birth of the New Testament*, 1962.
J. Munck, *Paul and the Salvation of Mankind*, Eng. trans., 1959.
A. Richardson, *Introduction to the Theology of the New Testament*, 1958.
A. Schlatter, *The Church in the New Testament Period*, Eng. trans., 1955.
H. J. Schoeps, *Paul*, Eng. trans., 1961.
C. A. A. Scott, *Christianity according to St. Paul*, 1927.
E. Stauffer, *New Testament Theology*, Eng. trans., 1955.

XVII. WORSHIP IN THE OLD TESTAMENT*

By N. H. Snaith

Once a holy site, always a holy site. It may be that a different deity is worshipped, but the shrine is the same, more often than not on a hill-top. Also, customs and rites live long and die hard. Particularly is this the case with religious customs and rites. The tendency is for all worshippers of whatever deity to do the same things in worship: a different deity, sometimes but by no means always differing words, but generally speaking the same motions and movements, closely similar rites. There would appear to be a common pool of religious customs and rites, and each religion chooses out of that pool. To express this in another way: man reacts in substantially the same way all the world over to whatever gods there be. What ultimately matters is not what is done (for this is much the same everywhere), but why it is done, and what is the nature and the character of the deity in whose name it is done. For instance, in more than one religion worshippers turn towards the east. Presumably this was originally a turning towards the rising sun. The rite is observed by Muslims and some Christians, but new explanations are provided and it is in the service of a different God.

It is therefore necessary at the outset in any study of Israelite worship to emphasize the unique nature and character of the God of Israel. The Israelites may have worshipped their God with rites similar to those of the nations, and probably in many celebrations they did this. It may well be that at some shrines, and perhaps in some periods at all shrines, they intended by their rites much of what the nations intended. Perhaps many of the worshippers did not know what was intended or exactly what the priests were doing. Maybe the priests themselves were not always wholly clear. All this, however, is not "Worship in the Old Testament." Worship in the Old Testament is worship of the God of Israel, this God who was known to be different, so that the Israelite could say, "Who is like unto thee, O Yahweh, among the gods?" (Ex. 15^{11}).

There are two major things to be said concerning the God of Israel and his worship (cf. A. S. Herbert, *Worship in Ancient Israel*, 1959, pp. 5–9). The most important thing is that

* See also above, pp. 363 ff., 387 ff.

Yahweh is the Saviour of Israel. He is " the Lord thy God, which brought thee out of the land of Egypt, out of the house of bondmen." When Israelite worship is at its truest, this is the God that is worshipped. He was their Saviour out of Egypt ; He was the Saviour and Guide of the patriarchs : He is their Saviour now : He is the same yesterday, today and forever. Whatever rite may have been taken over by the Israelites, we must be prepared for the influence of this main theme (cf. von Rad, *Old Testament Theology*, Eng. trans., i., 1962, p. vi). The second thing is that this God is " the Holy One of Israel." Yahweh is *ḳādhôsh*, a word which emphasizes His Otherness, not only the " numinous," that *mysterium tremendum* of which Rudolf Otto writes (*The Idea of the Holy*, Eng. trans., 1924) with its elements of awefulness, overpoweringness and urgency, but much more importantly manifesting itself in justice and in a righteousness which tends to belong to the vocabulary of salvation rather than to that of ethics. Combined with this is the firm conviction that Yahweh is God alone, so that *ḳādhôsh* is that which pertains to Yahweh alone, this God of Israel who is Israel's Saviour. It is a commonplace in these days that the Bible is *Heilsgeschichte* (holy history) ; it is indeed this : but it is *ḳādhôsh*-history, because it is the story of the mighty deeds of salvation which the one and only God wrought for Israel. This theme was read into the story of the ancient shrines, the ancient sacrifices, the ancient rites and customs. All these traditions and rites, however ancient and whatever their original association and significance, were swept into the Yahweh sphere and used to reveal this God Who chose Israel as slaves in Egypt and made a covenant with them alone out of all the families of the earth.

(i) THE AGE OF THE PATRIARCHS

We deal with this period first, because in those days the patriarchs were almost wholly nomadic, and rites were very different from afterwards when the Israelites settled in Canaan. For the picture of these times we are dependent upon the patriarchal traditions in Genesis. There we see Abraham, Isaac and Jacob moving to and fro from place to place in Palestine, building altars, sacrificing whole-offerings (*'ôlôth*) and " calling upon the name of Yahweh " : Abraham at Shechem (12^{7}–J, at the sacred tree at Moreh), between Bethel and Ai (12^{8} and 13^{3}–J), at Hebron (13^{18}–J, at the sacred tree of Mamre) : Isaac at Beersheba (26^{25}–J), and Jacob at Bethel (28^{10-22}–JE and 35^{1-7}–E). The first impression is that the patriarch builds an altar on every arrival at an encampment, but doubtless the intention of the narrator is to tell how and when the place became a holy place, in his mind for the first time ever, but more likely for the first time as a Yahweh shrine. In some cases the intention of the narrator is clear : a pillar (*maṣṣēbhāh*) is erected, oil is poured on to it (28^{18}, 35^{14}–JE) and a drink-offering (*nesekh*) is poured out, (35^{14}–E). All these are concerned with the inauguration of Bethel as a shrine by Jacob. Beersheba is said to have become a sacred site when Abraham plants a tree there (*'ēshel*, 21^{33}–JE). Other references to worship are : Cain brings a tribute-offering (*minḥâh*) of the produce of the soil, and Abel brings firstlings (*bᵉkhôrôth*) from the flock ($4^{3f.}$–J) ; Yahweh worship began in the time of Enosh son of Seth (4^{26}). Noah built an altar after the flood had subsided and offered whole-offerings unto Yahweh of every clean animal and bird (8^{20}–J), " and Yahweh smelled the sweet savour " (*rêaḥ han-nîḥōaḥ*). No altar is mentioned when " sacrifices " (*zebhaḥ*) are made, either after the oath-taking ceremony of 31^{54} (JE) by Israel at Beersheba on his way down to Egypt (46^{1})—which is correct, since the *zebhaḥ* was essentially a sacred meal eaten by the worshippers, and even in the latest time when the altar was involved, only the blood and the fat went to the altar, as always, whatever the animal offering.

There are many divine names in Genesis, though never (whether by accident or design) in association with an altar, and once only (31^{13} : El-bethel) in connexion with a pillar (*maṣṣēbhāh*). The names are El-'Elyon (14^{22}), El-Ro'i (16^{33}), El-Shaddai (17^{1}), Yahweh El-'Olam (21^{33}), " The God of my father, the God of Abraham and *Paḥadh* (Fear, Kinsman ?) of Isaac " (31^{42}), " the God of his father Isaac " at Beersheba (46^{1}). It is said also that Rachel stole the teraphim which belonged to her brother Laban (31^{19} : they are called " gods " in verse 30), and presumably we are intended to understand that these are the " foreign gods " which Jacob collected from his household and buried with the ear-rings under the sacred tree in Shechem ($35^{2, 4}$–JE). Here the name El-Bethel occurs, as in 31^{13}. All this gives a picture of simple, straightforward primitive religion ; the High-God, El, worshipped locally with different appellations, but always the one High-God, and at the same time a cult of low-gods, in this case, the teraphim, the household deities. We find no fertility cult, because here we have the nomad life and virtually no agriculture : it is only whilst Adam was still in Eden or Isaac settled for a while in the Philistine country (26^{12}) that we get any agriculture. This is the general pattern of early man : a High-God and low-gods, since nowhere is there any actual evidence of either of a High-God without low-gods, or of low-gods without a High-God, though sometimes there may be a High-God but dimly remembered (even otiose). This is not monotheism, nor is it strictly henotheism. Actually neither ever existed in earlier times, since always we find also the existence of low-gods. The patriarchs were El-worshippers and they had their household deities: there was the one High God and the lowly near-by gods. To what extent the wandering patriarchs were influenced by the gods and cults of Canaan, it is impossible to say. There is no evidence. The editors of the ancient traditions identify El and all his local appellations with Yahweh, the God of Israel.

(ii) THE POST-MOSAIC PERIOD

With the entry into Canaan the whole pattern changed. With the story of Sinai the whole complex of worship is altered. We find it convenient, not to deal with the pattern as a whole, but with differing elements as they develop from the Exodus onwards.

1. *Sacrifices.* The clearest picture, and indeed the only place where developed details are to be found is given in Leviticus. Here presumably we have the regulations of the Second Temple with the sacrificial ritual fully developed and carefully described.

(*a*) The *'ôlāh* (whole-offering: EVV "burnt offering"). Another term is *kālîl* (EVV "whole burnt offering"), a word which describes the completeness of the offering. This sacrifice was at all times a living creature (young bull, sheep, goat, bird) wholly burnt on the altar (Lev. 1). If an animal, it had to be a male without blemish. EVV have "bullock," a word which in the seventeenth century meant a "young bull," but today refers always everywhere in the country to a castrated animal, so that this is therefore now a wrong translation. The animal, whether "of the herd" or "of the flock" was presented at "the door of the tent of meeting": in the Second Temple, this meant the Gate of Nicanor (after the time of Judas Maccabaeus). The priest laid his hand on the animal "and it was accepted to make atonement" for the offerer. The blood was drawn off into a bowl and then flung "round about" the altar. The "round about" meant flinging the blood at the north-east corner and then at the south-west corner so as to cover all four sides. The animal was then flayed, dismembered, and all of it laid in proper order on the altar—the joints, the head and the fat, together with the entrails and the legs after they had been washed. The animal was thus a "whole offering." It was called an *'ôlāh* because it "went up" in smoke; it was called a *kālîl* because it was wholly burnt; it was called an *'ishshāh* (offering by fire) because it was burnt with fire. The blood and the fat are mentioned separately. The blood is flung against the altar, because it is blood. Similarly the fat was burnt on the altar, because it was fat. Always, whatever type of animal sacrifice is concerned, both the fat and the blood are for the Lord ($3^{16f.}$), the fat equally with the blood (3^{17}). It is " God's food " (3^{11} ; cf. 7^{22-25} and $7^{26f.}$). The same ritual is followed if the whole-offering is " of the herd " (1^{10-14}), and, so far as the blood is concerned, for a bird (1^{14-17}).

The purpose of the whole-offering according to P (Lev. $1^{3f.}$) is " to make expiation " (EVV " atonement ") for the man. Originally the whole-offering was a complete gift to God and it was a living creature. It was offered in order to please God, an ancient offering originally a " sweet savour," *rêaḥ nîḥōaḥ* (lit. " a soothing odour ") unto the Lord ; cf. the Babylonian flood-story, lines 160 ff, " The gods smell the savour, The gods smell the goodly savour, The gods gathered like flies over the sacrifice." This is the purpose of the earliest *'ôlāh,* whole-offering ; by the time of the Priestly Code the whole-offering is connected with the removal of sin, as was the whole sacrificial system.

(*b*) The *zebhaḥ* (EVV " sacrifice ") involves the slaughter of an animal. Originally the word meant " slaughter " and it had reference to all slaughter of animals, whether for general eating or for sacrifice. It was wrong for the people to slay sheep and oxen " on the ground " and " with the blood." In order to put matters right Saul had to slaughter the animals on a great stone, which was now a *mizbēaḥ* (lit. " a place of slaughter "), *i.e.* an altar, the first which Saul built unto the Lord (1 Sam. 14^{35}). The blood was poured out over the stone. So it was properly for all beasts slaughtered for food. There was ordinary slaughter for food and there were special sacred meals, *e.g.* 1 Sam. 20^{6} (EVV " a yearly sacrifice," but AV margin has " feast " which is correct, because it was an annual *zebhaḥ,* a Sacred Meal at which all the family was expected to be present and which they were all supposed to partake). With the establishment of the law of the single sanctuary following Josiah's reformation, a distinction had to be made between ordinary slaughter for food and the sacred meal at the central shrine. The law concerning this is Deut. $12^{15f.}$. Always when a beast was slaughtered for food, the blood was poured out on the ground, but the *zebhaḥ* proper as a sacrifice was essentially a sacred meal. It is usually stated that it is " the common and most ancient sacrifice, whose essential rite was eating the flesh of the victim at a feast in which the god of the clan shared by receiving the blood and the fat pieces." This is the generally accepted view, and it is based on W. Robertson Smith's totemic theory of the origin of religion : the god of the clan eats with the clan and this union-fellowship and suchlike is promoted. This last is presumably the reason for calling it " the most ancient sacrifice." It is not accurate to say that the *zebhaḥ* is the most ancient sacrifice. It is certainly primitive, but both it and the whole-offering go back to the most ancient times. The fact that the blood and the fat of the *zebhaḥ* both go to the altar is not significant for the meaning and intention of the *zebhaḥ*. These always went to the altar whatever the animal, whether whole-offering (*'ôlāh*), sacred meal (*zebhaḥ*, so-called " sacrifice ") or even sin-offering. It is said of the sin-offering (Lev. 4^{31}), " and all the fat shall be taken away, as the fat is taken away from off the sacrifice of peace-offerings " (*zebhaḥ sh^elāmîm*). Nobody would be foolish enough to say therefore that the sin-offering was a meal shared with the Deity.

There were three types of *zebhaḥ*, all of which (certainly so far as the sacred meal is concerned) were called *zebhaḥ sh^elāmîm*. We would translate *sh^elāmîm*, not by " peace " but by " health." They were sacred meals in which the worshipper ate the holy-food (the God-stuff) and received thereby new life and vigour. The three types were *tôdhāh* (thank-offering), the *n^edhēbhāh* (freewill offering), and the *nedher* (offering brought in fulfilment of a vow). In all cases, the " wave offering " (*t^enûphāh* : it was the breast) went to the priests as a whole (Lev. 7^{30}), and the " heave-offering " (*t^erûmāh* : it was the right thigh) went to the actual priest who performed the ceremony (Lev. 7^{33}). How far back these regulations as to the share of the priests went back, it is impossible to say. In earlier times the priests did not receive so much, and things were certainly different in the time of Eli and his sons (1 Sam. 2^{12-17}).

The translations " heave " and " wave " are difficult and by no means self-explanatory. *T^erûmāh* probably means simply " that which is lifted off," and the portion may have been lifted at arm's height in the air as a sign that this portion of the offering was for God. Or the word may mean " removal," cf. Bab. Talmud, *Yoma* 22a, where the word is used for the removal of the ashes from the altar. G. R. Driver (*Journal of Jewish Studies*, i., 100–105) takes *t^erûmāh* to mean " levy " ; cf. Akkadian *tarāmu*, " to levy," *tarimtu*, " offering." The EVV " wave-offering " for *t^enûphāh* assumes a derivation from the root *nûph* I (" wave "), but it may well be derived from the root *nûph* II (" be high," " overtop "), in which case both terms mean " that which is lifted off " the offering, the one for the Lord and the other for the priests. We judge that *t^enûphāh* became a technical term for that which was taken away as the share for the priests, so that when Num. 8^{19} says that the Levites are a *t^enûphāh*, the meaning is that they were a gift allocated to the priesthood as a whole. G. R. Driver also thinks of the root *nûph* II ; cf. Akkadian *nuptu*, " additional payment," and New Babylonian " gift," " bonus," " special payment."

All these variations in the type of *zebhaḥ* were concerned with the thank-offering. This had to be accompanied with unleavened cakes and leavened bread (Lev. $7^{12f.}$), one of each was a "heave-offering" for the officiating priest. Also the flesh of the thank-offering had to be eaten on the day it was killed, but that of the other two types could be eaten on the second day also, but definitely not on the third day (Lev. $7^{15f.}$).

(*c*) The *minḥāh* (A.V. "meat-offering," R.V. "meal-offering"). The root means "lend," "give a gift" and the noun in earliest times means "gift," "present," "tribute" (Gen. 32^{13}, etc., and Judg. 3^{15}, etc.). In earlier times, before the exile, the word was used on occasion in a general way to denote an offering to God (1 Sam. 2^{17}, etc.), but only once with any reference to a flesh-offering (Gen. 4^4, where Abel's sacrifice is first called "firstling" *beḵhôrôth*). In post-exilic times the word refers to the offering of cereals (grain in the ear, "grits," barley meal), and mainly to the cereal-offering which had to be brought with every *'ôlāh* ("whole-offering"; Lev. 14^{31}), but also to all kinds of cereal-offerings. It is difficult to see how the *minḥāh* of post-exilic times could invariably have been a cereal-offering, unless it had always been a cereal-offering. Indeed the reference in Gen. 4^4 suggests this rather than otherwise. Cain's offering is "from the ground" and it is certainly a *minḥāh*. Abel's offering is "from the flock." Either his *minḥāh* was separate from his animal-offering (the Hebrew could mean this) or his animal-offering was comparable to his brother's because it was a firstlings offering, just as his brother's was a firstfruits offering. In post-exilic times the *minḥāh* went wholly to the priests, except for a token handful (EVV "memorial") which was taken by the priest and placed on the altar. It is most probable that the allocation of this *minḥāh* to the priests was a later development, due to the growing power, growing needs, and growing number of the priesthood.

(*d*) *Ḥaṭṭâth* (EVV "sin-offering"). It is misleading to call this a sacrifice, since nothing of it (except as usual the blood and the fat) was given to Yahweh. It is particularly misleading to call it an offering. The word itself means "sin." The same word means both "sin" (strictly in the sense of error, unwittingly) and also the animal which is part of the sin removal ritual (Lev 4–5). The animal may be a young bull (4^{1-21}), a goat (male for a ruler 4^{22-26}, female for ordinary person 4^{27-31}), or a lamb. If the individual is too poor for this, then a pair of pigeons was accepted (5^{7-10}), but if too poor even for that, a tenth of an ephah (an ephah is about seventy pints) of flour without oil. This last was treated as an ordinary *minḥāh* (meal-offering), a token on the altar and the rest to the priest. When the animal was brought forward the individual who brought it placed his hand on the head of the animal, thus transferring the Sin. The animal thus became the *ḥaṭṭâth*, the Sin. The blood was poured (*shāphakh*, not *zāraḳ*, flung) at the base of the altar. The blood, being taboo because it is the "life," could have no other destiny than to be handed over to the god. It could not be flung against the sides of the altar, because that ceremony was the survival of the god eating the life-stuff, and this blood, as part of the Sin, was unclean. It was nevertheless taboo, as was all blood, and so it was poured out at the foot of the altar. The fat, as always, was placed on the altar, not because it was the Sin (which Heaven forbid!), but because, as in the case of the *zebhaḥ* (sacred meal), it was taboo (Lev. $3^{9f.}$, 3^{11}, $7^{22ff.}$). The rest of the Sin had to be disposed of, taken away, removed, destroyed, so that it no longer existed. Normally, the Sin was disposed of by the priests, who ate it in the holy place (6^{26} [Heb. 6^{19}]), but if the blood had been taken inside "the tent of meeting" (6^{30})—*i.e.* if the Sin was on behalf of a priest ($4^{6f.}$)—then the carcase had to be destroyed by fire. This was presumably because a priest could not eat his own Sin. The whole ceremony was therefore not in any sense a sacrifice to God. It was a sacrifice (Lat. *sacrificium*) only in the sense that it was within the realm of the holy (*sacer*). The Sin was not an offering to God, but an offering only in the sense that it was provided by the suppliant.

There were variations in the rite, depending upon whether the Sin was a young bull, a goat or a lamb, and so forth, but one common feature was that before the priest poured out the blood at the foot of the altar, he dipped his finger in the blood and put some of the blood on the horns (*i.e.* the holiest part) of the altar. This rite is parallel to that of de-sinning the altar (Ex. 29): the actual word is the pi'el of *ḥāṭā'*, the regular word for "sin." We are here in the strange and confusing world of taboo, a realm in which what is good for one can be bad for another, what is life for one can be death for another.

(*f*) *'āshām* (EVV "guilt-offering"). This was a special type of Sin (EVV "sin-offering"; Lev. 5^{14-26} and 7^{1-7}) and it was applicable to cases where a *ma'al* (trespass) had been committed against the Lord. This could be either in the matter of "holy things" (*ḳodhāshîm*) unwittingly (5^{17}) or in a or a group of offences detailed in Lev. 6^{1-7} (Heb. 5^{20-26}). These are indeed deliberate offences, but the only deliberate offences with which the sacrificial laws could deal. They are all cases in which nobody else knows, false dealing in pledges or deposits or robbery when a relation is involved (*'āmîth*, not *rē'eh*), and stealing by finding. They are either offences within the family or a group of offences of which nobody would know anything unless the offender talked. This whole class includes cases where the damage done can be assessed: the value of the "holy thing" is not what it ought to be, or the value of the pledge is involved. In these cases restitution has to be made in cash (silver shekels) and one-fifth has to be added. If the trespass was in respect of a "holy thing," then the one-fifth went to the priest, but if against an associate (relation) to the wronged one. Thus everything went where it ought to have gone originally, because "holy things" were the perquisite of the priests in any case. The "sacrifice" was a ram without blemish and the priests ate it in the holy place (7^7); in this respect there was one law common to the "sin-offering" and the "guilt-offering." The idea of compensation, substitution is dominant in the *'āshām* ("guilt-offering"), and this is the original meaning of the word before it became a temple-term; cf. Num. $5^{7, 8}$ and especially Isa. 53^{10}, where the context makes plain that the Servant's suffering is substituted for the deserved suffering of others. The last development of the "guilt-offering" was the "suspended guilt-offering" (*'āshām tālûy*). This developed out of Lev. 5^{18}, and in the last days of the Second Temple the ultra-devout would bring this "suspended guilt-offering" every morning in case unwittingly they had committed any offence.

(*g*) There are two general names for gifts brought to the Temple; *ḳorbān* (A.V. "offering," R.V. "oblation") and *ḳᵒdhāshîm* (EVV "holy things"). The word *ḳorbān* can be used generally of anything that is "brought near" (Lev. 1^2, etc.), but its stricter use is referring to that which is presented and used for the maintenance of the Temple and its services. The *ḳᵒdhāshîm* ("holy things") go to the priests and are for their maintenance. This is why in the case of the trespass (*'āshām*, "guilt") offering, the one-fifth went to the priest. It was the priest who had suffered the loss in the first place.

(*h*) There remains the Passover (*pesaḥ*). This was originally an apotropaic rite, *i.e.* for the turning away of evil spirits, but it became in Israel the sign of the great Deliverance from Egypt, when the Angel of Death "passed over" (literally "limped," "hopped") the houses of the Israelites. It was essentially a home ceremony, and until the Law of the Single Sanctuary (Josiah's time) the passover was celebrated at home immediately before the pilgrimage of *maṣṣôth* (Unleavened Bread). But the law of the Single Sanctuary involved the faithful in celebrating the Passover in Jerusalem, where they had to establish a temporary "home." In the last days the Passover lamb was slain in the Temple, and the blood poured out at the altar, but the carcase was taken home, and all had to disappear (either eaten or burnt) by the morning. The

Passover lamb was in no sense a gift to God. It never went anywhere near the altar. It was the sign of the Lord's salvation of Israel.

There is evidence that human sacrifice was a feature of Canaanite religion, and it was, to some extent at least, practised by the Israelites. The sacrifice of Jephthah's daughter (Judg. 11^{34-40}) was in fulfilment of a vow; Hiel the Bethelite buried his firstborn as a foundation-offering in the rebuilding of Jericho (1 Kings 16^{34}). Other instances concern the "passing through fire" of children to a god whose name is given as Molech (2 Kings 23^{10}, etc.). This is a pious vocalization of the name Melek, and we may assume that this fire-rite is a survival or a recrudescence of ancient Canaanite practice (cf. A. S. Herbert, *op. cit.*, p. 19). The story of the binding of Isaac (Gen. 22) tells of the substitution of animal sacrifice for human sacrifice, and the early laws concerning the redemption of the firstborn suggest that once in oldest Israel the firstborn was actually sacrificed as a whole-offering to God. But there are two passages which show that the sacrifice of the firstborn as the ultimate offering in a time of utmost urgency was legitimate even as late as the eighth century. The first is Mic. 6^7, a passage which speaks for itself. The second is 2 Kings 3^{27}, which tells how the king of Moab as the last act of despair sacrificed his eldest son as a whole-offering on the wall of his beleaguered city, with the result that "there was great wrath against Israel: and they departed from him, and returned to their own land." The efficacy of such a sacrifice is admitted by writer and editor, and there is no reproof.

2. *Temple Personnel.* In patriarchal times, the head of the family offered the sacrifices, and even in the time of Eli (1 Sam. 1), although Eli and his two sons were priests at Shiloh, it was Elkanah who "sacrificed" the sacred meal and gave portions to his family. Samuel offers a whole-offering (*'ôlāh, kālîl*) and makes his prayer for victory (1 Sam. 7^9). There was a sacred meal where Samuel was (1 Sam. $9^{13f.}$) at the high place, but it could not be eaten till Samuel had blessed it, and Saul was given what later was the priest's portion (EVV "the thigh"). Apart from the case of Jethro, priest of Midian (Exod. 18^{12}) who made whole-offerings to God and was involved in the sacred meal (*zebhaḥ*), the only reference to the priests (here Levites) offering whole-offerings (*'ôlôth*) on the altar and sending up smoke (*ḳeṭôreth*) is Deut. 33^{10}. Originally their function was to instruct the people and cast the sacred lot by Thummim and Urim (Deut. 33^8). The probability is that they were also responsible for the whole-offerings (which were a gift to God), but not to the same extent for the *zebhaḥ* (which was the shared meal, sacred meal, and did not go to

the altar). The priests were intermediaries, declaring the ways of God to man, and seeing to it that man's approach to God was correct and according to precedent.

Apparently originally any man could be a priest, so that when Micah built a shrine with " a graven image and a molten image " in it, he " filled the hand " (this was the inauguration ceremony, ? making his first offering) of one of his sons (Judg. 17[5]). He may have been deputizing for the head of the family, just as David later made two of his sons priests at Jerusalem. But as soon as a wandering Levite came, Micah installed him as priest. It was evidently better to have a Levite as priest. This young man later went off with the Danites, set up a shrine at Dan in the far north using Micah's image, and his descendants were priests at Dan as long as there was a shrine at Shiloh (Judg. 18[31]). This Levite was from Bethlehem-judah, and the Levites mentioned in the latter part of Judges all seem to have associations with Bethlehem-judah. The priests of the Ark at Shiloh were of the family of Eli and they had been priests of the Ark since Egypt (1 Sam. 2[27]). These priests were later at Nob, presumably after the destruction of Shiloh by the Philistines, and were massacred by Doeg the Edomite acting under Saul's orders. Abiathar alone escaped and he followed David in all his wanderings. When David captured Jerusalem the priests there were Zadok and Abiathar. Zadok probably belonged to the original Jebusite priesthood. At the accession of Solomon, Abiathar supported Adonijah and lost his place as priest. Henceforth the priests at Jerusalem were all Zadokites, and this continued down to the exile when they were carried away to Babylonia. After the exile the priests are called " the sons of Aaron," but one-third of them were Aaronite, descended from Ithamar, Aaron's younger surviving son, and two-thirds of them were Zadokite, who now claimed descent from Aaron through Eleazar, the father of Phinehas and Aaron's elder surviving son. This is doubtless a post-exilic compromise, the Aaronites having moved in during the exile and the returning exiles not being able to oust them. Kennett (*Cambridge Biblical Essays*, p. 102) believed the Aaronites came in from Bethel and occupied the site at Jerusalem whilst the Zadokites were away. This may well be so. We certainly know that the returning Zadokite, Jeshua, was not admitted without a struggle to the high-priesthood. He was arrayed in filthy garments, having come from an unclean land, and was finally declared pure (Zech. 3). The pre-exilic picture is : non-Levites at northern shrines, with descendants of Moses through Gershom at Dan and descendants of Aaron through Phinehas at Bethel ; Levite priests at Judaean shrines, but Zadokites only at Jerusalem. After the exile: no priests anywhere except at Jerusalem, where eight of the twenty-four courses were Aaronites through Ithamar and the other sixteen courses were Zadokites, who now traced their descent from Aaron through Eleazar and Phinehas. The final settlement was not without its problems. In Josiah's time with the institution of the Single Sanctuary the phrase was "the priests, the Levites," and so also in Deuteronomy. But the Zadokite priests of Jerusalem did not admit the provincial (southern) Levite priests to their own status (2 Kings 23^{9}), with the result that the Levites had to be content with minor Temple duties and offices. It was not until the reign of Herod Agrippa II. that they were permitted (*c.* A.D. 60) to wear the white robes of the priesthood (Josephus, *Ant.* xx. ix. 6 [216 ff.]). Just as Ezekiel 40–48 is strongly pro-Zadokite, so Chronicles is strongly pro-Levite, but the Chronicler did not manage to advance the status of the Levites, even though he told many and marvellous stories of their singing prowess.

The origin of the Levites is a matter of obscurity. The evidence for Levi as a tribe is small, but it is there in Gen. 49^{5-7}, where Simeon and Levi are mentioned together as violent and fierce, and scattered and divided. They are the second and third sons of Leah (Gen. $29^{33f.}$) and they shared in a treacherous and murderous assault on Shechem (Gen. 34^{25-31}), for which Jacob feared reprisals. Later we meet with wandering Levites, usually connected with Judah (Judg. 17^{7}, 19^{1}), and we know that cities allocated to Simeon in Josh. 19^{2-7} are allocated to Judah in Josh. 19^{2-7}. This is stated definitely in Josh. 19^{1}, and Judg. 1^{3} confirms this. Further, whilst both Simeon and Levi are tribes in Gen. 49, Simeon is not listed in Deut. 33, and Levi is there only as a priestly caste. Jewish tradition therefore is firm that both Simeon and Levi were originally tribes, that Simeon was absorbed into Judah and that Levi was scattered mostly also in Judah but became a priestly tribe (southern). In the days of the Judges and of the united kingdom cultic acts were by no means confined to Levites, but Samuel the Ephraimite is reckoned a Levite in 1 Chron. 6^{28}, and Obed-Edom the Gittite is a Levite (a Korahite) according to 1 Chron. 15^{24}, 26^{1-4}. Evidently by the Chronicler's time "levite" was a cultic term, as it was in the Minaean colony at *el-'Ôla*, some 400 miles south of Jerusalem at an uncertain date, given variously between 1500 B.C. and sixth century B.C. Possibly the word "levite" as a cultic official has a wholly cultic origin, and Levi was truly a tribe in ancient Israel, but because of the accidents of history and the similarity of the name the scattered tribe became a cultic group, especially since the great Moses himself was a Levite. We do not know enough to be sure of the details, but Haldar (*Associations of Cult Prophets among the ancient Semites,* 1945, pp. 98 f.) is quite sure that the Levites were priests from the first, though they had no monopoly, and that the name means " consecrated ones."

We turn to the problem of the " cult prophets " and their possible association with the " literary prophets " (*i.e.* Amos, Isaiah, Jeremiah, and the like). Most scholars agree that the prophets were originally a cultic order, and it is agreed also that there were prophets throughout the ancient east. Their function was to mediate inspired words of God to king or chief or enquirer generally, though probably in earliest times the association between ruler and shrine was such that the official at the shrine gave oracles to the ruler (chief, king) on behalf of the community as a whole. For Haldar, all the prophets, early and late, were associated with the shrines and " like Isaiah and Ezekiel, Jeremiah obviously belongs to the temple staff " (*op. cit.*, p. 121). The contrary view is of " an official body of prophets, attached to the court, practising rituals and a technique similar to those in use in neighbouring states ; and on the other hand, single prophets, opposed to the official prophets, independent of court patronage, and giving a message based on direct experience " (Hooke, *Prophets and Priests,* pp. 18 f.). According to A. R. Johnson (*The Cultic Prophet in Ancient Israel,* 1944, 2nd edn., 1962) the cult-prophets ultimately became the Temple-singers at Jerusalem, and came to be reckoned as Levites when this title came to be used of all Temple personnel except the sacrificing (Aaronic) priests. There seems to be little actual evidence to connect the literary prophets with the cultic prophets of the local shrines, those whom they unmercifully criticized together with the priests at the shrines. Haldar, like many moderns, sees cultic officials, cultic ceremonies everywhere, and almost every passage of psalm and many passages of Scriptures speak " plainly " and " obviously " of these things.

But, certainly at particular periods, we must regard the king as being the chief cult personage. David took the lead in the celebrations which accompanied the bringing up of the Ark to Mount Zion. He set up the altar (2 Sam. 24^{25}) ; he controlled the ceremony, stopped the Ark at the house of Obed-edom, and had the journey restarted later (2 Sam. 6). David sacrificed an ox and a fatling every six paces (2 Sam. 6^{13}), and himself led the dance clad in a linen ephod (vv.$^{14,\ 20}$). Although Zadok and Abiathar were the hereditary priests, yet David appointed two of his sons priests (2 Sam. 8^{18} ; R.V.m. and A.V. assimilate to 1 Chron. 18^{19} " chief about the king ") and Ira the Jairite is said to be priest to David (2 Sam. 20^{26}). It is difficult to see how this could be unless David himself as king was priest equally with Zadok and Abiathar and could himself appoint his own deputies. Solomon offered sacrifices, uttered the prayer and blessed the people (2 Kings 8). Ahaz modified the ritual (2 Kings 16^{10-18}) and so did Manasseh (2 Kings 21^{3-7}) ; so also did the reforming kings, Asa, and especially Hezekiah and Josiah. The later story (2 Chron. 26^{16-21}) claims that King Uzziah offered incense in the pride of his heart, when it was well known that only the priests had this right, but that the king fulfilled all sacredotal functions in the early times of the kingdoms (at least) is certain. Possibly the time of Uzziah was the time when the crisis came between the king and the rising power of the priests.

In recent years much has been written concerning the role of the king in the cult, seeing in Israel similar rites to those which have been found in Mesopotamian cults. The Mesopotamian tablets on which many of these studies are based are much more fragmentary than many realize. It has been alleged that there was in Israel an annual New Year Festival celebrated at the turn of the year (autumn) and at this festival Yahweh was ritually installed as King, the life of the nation was renewed, and many cultic acts parallel to those of Babylonia were repeated. It is said that there was a sacred marriage, a ritual combat, a ritual drama of the dying and rising god, the king taking the role of the god. We find no evidence anywhere in Israel of any of this, though some seem to find the references "obvious." What is certain is that at all the three great Feasts of pre-exilic days, the rescue from Egypt and the whole story of the Exodus and the Settlement in Canaan were emphasized ; the Covenant was renewed. Whether there were any of these other elements in the cultus in pre-exilic times must remain a matter of conjecture. If there were any traces in the ancient traditions, these elements have been most successfully expunged. From Mowinckel onwards, scholars have seen in Psalms 47, 93, 96–99 the nucleus of the apparatus of a great New Year Feast in which by some ritual act Yahweh was established as king. It has been supposed that the king took the leading part in these dramas. Also it is suggested that just as the Babylonian creation epic (*enuma elish*) was used in the New Year liturgy, so also in Israel Gen. 1 and 2 f. were used. It is also suggested that the numerous references to the fight between Yahweh and the sea-monster of the primaeval deep indicate their use at the shrines, as a legacy of Canaanite religion (see A. S. Herbert, *op. cit.*, p. 25) : Job 9^{13}, 26^{12}, Isa. 26^{1}, $51^{9f.}$, etc. Mowinckel's theories have been developed far beyond the stage to which he himself would allow; cf. in particular *Myth and Ritual* (ed. S. H. Hooke, 1933), and Ivan Engnell, *Studies in Divine Kingship in the Ancient Near East,* 1943. A more moderate position in regard to the functions of the king in Israel is put forward by A. R. Johnson, *Sacral Kingship in Ancient Israel,* 1955. The original theme appears again in *Myth, Ritual, and Kingship* (ed. S. H. Hooke, 1958) with modifications to meet the criticisms of the intervening years. These criticisms have been made by N. H. Snaith (*The Jewish New Year Festival,* 1947), Henri Frankfort (*Kingship and the Gods,* 1948, and especially *The Problem of Similarity in Ancient Near Eastern Religions,* 1951), by S. G. F. Brandon, " The Myth and Ritual Position Critically Considered " in *Myth, Ritual, and Kingship* (1958), and most recently by R. de Vaux, *Ancient Israel,* Eng. trans. 1961, pp. 504 f. That the king took a part of paramount importance in the pre-exilic New Year ritual is certain, and it is also plain that the welfare of the nation was bound up with the welfare of the king. There were certainly processions in those days, and Ps. 24 belongs to a procession in which the Ark was carried into Mt. Zion into the Temple. But how much of the Mesopotamian ritual and the general cult-pattern is to be read into the Old Testament is an open question. What is plain is that the ancient Canaanite harvest festivals, Unleavened Bread, Weeks, Ingathering, were taken over by the invading Hebrews with doubtless a varying extent of the assimilation of ideas also. The official religion as shown in the Old Testament gave all these feasts a historical significance. The eating of unleavened bread became the remembrance of the Exodus from Egypt (Ex. 13^{8}–J, 12^{34}), commemorating the haste with which they departed. The feast of Weeks which was originally the wheat harvest festival but became the general firstfruits festival, was the occasion for remembering not only that the firstfruits belong to Yahweh, but that it was Yahweh who brought them out of Egypt and gave them this good land (Deut. 26^{5-10}). The feast of Ingathering was the vintage feast. This was the autumnal feast about which so much has been written as the Coronation Feast of Yahweh together with all the myth-ritual details. There is nothing of this in the Pentateuch. Whatever there may have been in earlier times, the emphasis in Lev. 23^{43} is on the journey through the desert when their fathers lodged in booths. Thus the rituals of the festivals became interlocked with the history of the mighty saving deeds of Yahweh on behalf of His people Israel. (See von Rad, *Old Testament Theology,* Eng. trans., i., 1962, *passim.*) All this runs parallel with the early creeds of Israel, the credos which were to be recited. These included, in addition to Deut. 28^{5-10}, Deut. 6^{20-25}, and Josh. 24^{2-13}. This is all bound up with ideas of Yahweh's special choice of Israel (election) and of the Covenant (cf. John Bright, *A History of Israel*, 1960, pp. 132 f.).

Later festivals in Israel divide into two groups. The first concerns the festivals of Tishri, the seventh month of the post-exilic calendar with its Spring New Year. These changes were necessitated by the adoption of the Babylonian calendar with its Spring New Year and the months beginning with the new moon. The major part of the festivities and rites of the Autumnal Feast of Ingathering, including the all-night opening, torch dances, etc., clung to the autumnal full moon (the Harvest Moon) and thus began with 15 Tishri. The blowing of trumpets went to 1 Tishri, and the major part of the penitential rites gravitated to 10 Tishri (the Old New Year's Day; cf. Twelfth Night) and became the Day of Atonement (*Yôm Kippûr*). The new feasts consisted of the Feast of Hanukkah (Dedication) which was inaugurated to celebrate the restoration of the altar of Judas Maccabaeus, 25 Kislev, 164 B.C., after its profanation three years before by Antiochus Epiphanes. Some have seen pagan influences here, associations with the feast of the *Sol Invictus*, but 1 Macc. 4^{36-59} is clear concerning the Maccabaean origin. Josephus called the festival the Feast of Lights (*Ant.* XII. vii. 7 [325]), but the Greek name is Encaenia. A second late festival is the Feast of Purim, held on 14 and 15 Adar, to commemorate the revenge upon their enemies of the Jews who lived under the Persian régime. In latter years Purim has attracted to itself all kinds of games and jollifications, Purim plays, games for children, and so forth. It appears to have originated in Persia, possibly modelled in part on the Persian New Year ceremonies, and travelled via Babylon to Palestine, possibly in the first century B.C.

3. *The Temple.* In the time of the patriarchs we have simple sacrifices at sacred sites, indicated by sacred trees (Moreh, Mamre, Shechem) or by sacred wells (Beersheba), but after the settlement in Canaan we have shrines on hill-tops (high places), much as in South India today, not built so that the worshipper may get nearer heaven, but because (certainly in Palestine) they are models of the Holy Mountain away in the north, where the true Palace (*hēkhāl*) of God (the gods) is situated. Solomon's Temple consisted of a porch with two pillars in front of it but separate from it, a *hēkhāl* (Sumerian *e-gal*, great house) sixty feet long by thirty and forty-five feet high, and behind it the *d^ebhîr* (*i.e.* " behind "), a windowless room, a thirty-foot cube, the dark place in which Yahweh dwelt. The newly excavated temple at Hazor is on the same plan, and evidently this was the general pattern of Palestinian temples. The Phoenician builders whom Solomon employed,

knew how a temple should be built, and in this fashion they built it. Much confusion has been caused because of the way in which a later writer has approximated the description of Solomon's Temple in 1 Kings 8 with the Second Temple which he knew well. There was, for instance, no Most-Holy-Place (Holy of Holies) in Solomon's Temple. In the Second Temple there was the court where the worshippers stood, but within that a Holy Place, and within that again, the Most-Holy-Place.

We have very little actual detailed information about the worship in the Temple at any period. The fullest details are to be found in Ecclus. 50^{5-21}, a description of the conclusion of a service in the time of the high-priesthood of Simon son of Onias. It is clear that there were the three annual pilgrimages, and that these were observed in Canaan before and after the Israelite occupation. They were all three harvest celebrations, *Maṣṣôth* (Unleavened Bread), *Sh^{e}bhû'ôth* (Weeks) and *'Asîph* (Ingathering), the first of these beginning with the spring full-moon, the second seven weeks later, and the last with the autumn full-moon. Each feast lasted for seven days, though in later years an eighth day was added. This was an *'^{a}ṣereth* ("closing," "closure"; EVV "solemn assembly"). It is most probable that in the days of local shrines, there were various local celebrations there, perhaps connected with new-month-days and sabbaths, both of which in pre-exilic times were monthly festivals. It is probable that when the law of the Single Central Sanctuary was enforced in Josiah's time, the local shrines continued as meeting-places, and it is possible that here we have the first beginnings of the synagogue, with its non-sacrificial services but with instruction and guidance and so forth.

We know that every day in the Second Temple the *Tāmîdh* (continual sacrifice) was offered, both in the morning and "between the two evenings." This last phrase has caused considerable discussion, but probably it originally meant between sunset and dark, which in those latitudes embraces no great period of time. The *Tāmîdh* consisted of an *'ôlāh* (whole-offering) with its appropriate *minḥāh* (cereal-offering) and *nesekh* (drink-offering); cf. Ex. 29^{38-41}. There was an additional offering made on the Sabbath (Num. 28^{9}), and other offerings on other occasions according to rule.

It is generally agreed that the Psalter was in some sense the hymn-book of the Second Temple. How the psalms were used and when, we do not know with precision. We know the proper psalms for the days of the week in the latest period, according to the Mishnah—24 for the first day, 47, 82, 94, 81, 93 and, for the Sabbath, 92. At this time the psalms were sung in three sections, with intervals during which the priests blew with their trumpets. Probably these intervals are marked with "selah," which may mean musical interlude; cf. a cadenza, although very much shorter. The psalm was sung whilst the drink-offering was being poured out; as the Rabbis said, "There is no song except over wine." The first part of the Psalter (1–89) is composed in the main of four separate psalters, two Davidic (2–41 and 51–71 plus 72), and two Levitical psalters, Asaph (50 and 73–83) and Korahite (42–49), together with a miscellaneous supplement (84–89). The rest of the Psalter is composed of liturgical groups, 90–99 (ancient Sabbath psalms), 100 (the regular daily psalm), and various other groups, thanksgiving, praise, including the fifteen step-psalms (120–134) which were sung on the first night of the feast of Tabernacles by the Temple choirs as they stood in the Gate of Nicanor during the all-night dancing in the court below. The presumption is that all the psalms had their place in the post-exilic Temple, whatever may have happened in earlier years. There are some details of the services for special occasions during the last period of the Temple to be found in the Mishnah and in the Tosephtas, and much of the available material has been collected by Edersheim in *The Temple, its Ministry and Services in the Time of Jesus Christ*. For details of the Temple buildings, both before and after the exile, see A. Parrot, *The Temple of Jerusalem*, Eng. trans., 1957.

The chief of the Temple furnishings of pre-exilic days was the Ark of the Covenant. The most recent discussion as to the origin and significance of this important cult object is by R. de Vaux, *Ancient Israel*, Eng. trans., 1961, pp. 297–302. It stood in the Debir, the dark cube farthest from the entrance. This Ark was the palladium of the nation, originally of the great Joseph tribes, and it symbolized the Presence of Yahweh in the midst of His chosen people. The tradition is that above the covering (lid) of the Ark were two cherubim, wooden figures plated with gold, kneeling facing towards each other, with wings outstretched but forwards, almost touching, wing to wing. Yahweh dwelt "between the cherubim" so that in some sense the Ark and the cherubim were His throne. The name *k^{e}rûbh* is apparently of Akkadian origin, where the word refers to the genie who was the intercessor for the righteous and the adviser of the god. But there seems also to have been another tradition concerning the cherubim in the Debir, according to which there were two gigantic figures, facing outwards towards the main body of the building, reaching half-way to the ceiling, and their wings touching in the middle, and reaching the outer walls of the Debir. These are guardian spirits, comparable with those who guarded the gate of the Garden of Eden. The Ark contained the two tables of stone, and possibly Aaron's rod that budded, and the pot of manna. In the later tradition, the Ark was a small box made to hold the two tablets on which the Ten Commandments were written (Deut. 10^{1-5}). In any case, the Ark disappeared at the exile and was probably destroyed with the Temple in 586 B.C., though there is a tradition (2 Macc. $2^{4f.}$) that the prophet Jeremiah hid the Ark and the Tent of Meeting and the altar of Incense in a cave on Mt. Pisgah.

There was an incense altar in the Second Temple, though not in Solomon's Temple, since there is no evidence of incense being used in the Temple until after the exile. In Solomon's Temple the altar of burnt-offerings was in the outer court. In the Second Temple it was immediately in front of the Holy of Holies, and the worshippers, standing in the Court of the Women, could look up through the Gate of Nicanor, and through the rising smoke of the sacrifices they could see the huge golden vine (with clusters of grapes as large as a man) which covered the front of the porch of the Holy of Holies. The whole account of the altars in 1 Kings 6–9 is confused because of the later editor who knew only the Second Temple.

According to 1 Chron. $6^{12f.}$ there was a platform, on which the king stood. This is late evidence, but the finding of a stele at Ras Shamra suggests that perhaps the platform is an ancient institution. This stele portrays a king standing on a small platform with his back to the god and his right hand raised. There was in Solomon's Temple a huge bronze basin, supported by four groups of three bulls, facing the four points of the compass. In later times the priests used the water in the basin in their ablutions (2 Chron. 4^{6}), but originally the " brazen sea " was a representation of the primeval ocean, the *apsu*, which is found in some temples of Mesopotamia. There is in the Louvre a large circular limestone basin nearly seven feet in diameter, found in Cyprus, with four " handles " carved on the edge each embodying the figure of a bull. Other Temple furniture included ten bowls set on wheeled stands, six feet square and about four and a half feet high. The bronze stands were decorated with symbolic beasts and palm-trees. Bowls similar to these have been found in Cyprus, at Larnaka and Enkomi. In addition to these, there were various utensils needed in the sacrificial and cleansing rites ; spoons and basins and pots and shovels. There was a table for the shew-bread, on which twelve small loaves were placed, in two rows, sprinkled with frankincense and renewed every Sabbath. There were also ten candlesticks, according to 1 Kings 7^{49}, arranged five on each side of the Debir, but there is no record of these in the post-exilic Temple. In later days there was the great golden seven-branched candelabra, carried off with other

Temple furniture by Antiochus Epiphanes, replaced by Judas Maccabaeus three years later in 164 B.C., and finally carried off by the Romans under Titus and exhibited as a trophy in his triumph at Rome, still to be seen depicted on the Arch of Titus in Rome.

There were three Hebrew Temples on Mt. Zion. That built by Solomon was a hundred feet long (1 Kings 6^{2}), and this was the length of the Second Temple, but the proposals in Ezek. 40 ff. envisaged a length of a hundred cubits (a little more than a hundred and fifty feet) and this was the length of Herod's Temple. It is probable that the Second Temple was no larger than Solomon's and certainly it was not as splendid (Ezra $3^{12f.}$, Hag. 2^{3}). Herod the Great began the extension of the Temple in 20–19 B.C., his eighteenth year. The main changes were complete in ten years, but building was still going on after forty-six years (John 2^{20}) and the work was not complete until 64 B.C., six years only before it fell in the final Roman assault.

4. *Cultic Objects*. There is frequent mention of stone pillars (*maṣṣēbhôth*). There were three types of these. First, there was the pillar at Bethel which Jacob set up (Gen. 28^{10-12}). In this way Bethel became God's dwelling-place. Such pillars are probably connected with the age-old veneration of strange and special stones and trees as the abode of the Deity. This is probably the significance of the pillar set up to witness to the covenant between Laban and Jacob and to see to it that each party kept his word (Gen. $31^{44f.}$). A stone pillar is mentioned favourably in Isa. 19^{19}, and Hos. 3^{4} mentioned the lack of king, prince, sacrifice, pillar, and so forth as though this was a deprivation. It would appear that at one time there was no objection in the worship of Yahweh to such pillars as these, but the association of similar pillars with Baal worship ensured in course of time a prohibition of all such in the worship of Yahweh (Lev. 26^{1}). A second type of pillar is that instanced in the finds of Gezer, where there was a number of stone pillars with hollows on the top of them, as though they had been used for altars. A third type involved the association of the stone pillar and the wooden pole (*'ashērāh*). The two found together close by an altar stood for the male and female deities of the fertility cult, the one being a local manifestation of the great god Baal, the rain and fertility god of Canaan, and the other a local manifestation of Astarte or Asherah, the consort of Baal, there being confusion and a certain amount of transference of function between the two goddesses. Such truly Canaanite cult-objects were ruthlessly destroyed by all reforming Yahweh worshippers.

References are also found to the teraphim. These were

household deities, possibly Canaanite in origin, but more likely Amorite or Near-East in general. They were acceptable in early times, Rachel stole her father's teraphim (Gen. 31[19. 34f.]), though, as we have already pointed out, these may be the " strange (foreign) gods " which Jacob buried under the sacred tree of Shechem (Gen. 33[4]). There were teraphim in Micah's shrine (Judg. 18[14]), and they were used in divination (Ezek. 21[21]) and even as late as Zech. 10[2]. Michal saved David's life by putting the teraphim in the bed, covering the head of it with a rug made of goat's hair (1 Sam. 19[13]) ; from which we may conclude that a teraphim could be big enough to be mistaken for a man's body, though in what may have been a bad light. The teraphim were spoken against as early as 1 Sam. 15[23], and finally were prohibited and destroyed by reforming kings.

The ephod was closely associated with the teraphim, and the two are frequently mentioned together. It has been thought that an ephod was some kind of image, but this is doubtful. See S. R. Driver, *Exodus* (Camb. Bible), pp. 312 ff. There was certainly the linen ephod, worn by the priest, a pair of drawers sufficient to cover only the private parts (2 Sam. 6[14. 20]). There was also an ephod which was used in divination, and when Abiathar managed to escape from the massacre at Nob he was able to bring the ephod with him. He was bidden by David to " bring hither the ephod " whenever the will of God was to be sought (1 Sam. 23[6. 9]). This ephod was big enough to have Goliath's sword placed behind it (1 Sam. 21[9]), though this does not mean that the ephod hid the sword from sight. We know that later the sacred lots, Urim and Thummim, were kept in pouches in the high-priestly ephod. This ephod was highly decorated and had an embroidered waistband and shoulder-straps. Some have thought the ephod at Nob and that in Micah's shrine (Judg. 17[5]) to have been an image, but the cognate *'ᵃphuddāh* was a gold casing of an image (Isa. 30[22]). We conclude that the ephod was not an image but a garment, and that there were two such priestly garments, one the ordinary linen ephod and the other a somewhat ornate kind of tunic possibly stiff with gold and precious stones, and the post-exilic high-priestly ephod was a development of this.

Urim and Thummim were the sacred stones (?) with which divination was performed. They were housed in pockets in the ephod, and were thrown in some way like dice. They may well have been two discs, one side one colour and the other side another colour. In any case three answers were possible, Yes, No, and neutral (no answer). Possibly Urim means No (? curses) and Thummim means Yes (perfect ?).

There is division of opinion as to whether the young bulls

at Bethel were images of Yahweh. Formerly it was held that these were actually images of Yahweh, as the Bible itself implies (1 Kings 12^{28}), just as the Golden Calf of the desert was held to be a god (Ex. 32^{5}), the cry being in both cases, "These be thy gods, O Israel, which brought thee up out of the land of Egypt." This view would seem to be confirmed by the regular recurrence of the title "the bull El" (*tr 'el*) in the Ugarit tablets. Most modern scholars deny this and regard the animals as a throne, so that just as the Ark with the cherubim above it formed the throne of Yahweh, and as He rode upon the cherubim, so also He rode upon the bull. This will be similar to the statues of horses in the outskirts of south Indian villages, on which the gods ride round the village by night in order to protect it. It is held that in the primitive religions of the Near-East the sacred animal embodies the god's attributes, is a throne or footstool for the god but not the god himself.

There was also the bronze serpent which Hezekiah destroyed (2 Kings 18^{4}). This was associated with the "brazen serpent that Moses made," but Hezekiah destroyed it because it was worshipped, and it is probable that, just as Zadok belonged to the old Jebusite priesthood, so Nehushtan the serpent was the original Jebusite fetish (Rowley, *Journal of Biblical Literature*, lviii., 1939, pp. 113 f.).

5. *The Synagogue.** Probably no institution of Judaism has exercised a greater influence on mankind than the synagogue. From it much of Christian worship has developed (W. O. E. Oesterley, *The Jewish Background of the Christian Liturgy*, 1925), and Islam also owes a great deal to it. There is a tradition (Philo, *Vita Mosis*, ii., 27; Josephus, *Cont. Ap.*, ii., 17 [175]) which ascribes the origin to Moses, but the origin is doubtless to be found in the Babylonian exile. It is possible that ruins at Elath are of a synagogue from *c.* 500 B.C. (see *BASOR*, 84, pp. 4 f.; 82, pp. 11 f.). There is a possibility that the first beginnings are to be found in the local shrines when they had ceased to be sacrificing centres under the reforming influence of King Josiah. It is unlikely that even that king's strong hand could prevent devout men and women meeting together in worship. Certainly by the beginning of the Christian era the synagogue had become such an institution in the life of the Jew that such houses of prayer were to be found wherever Jews were, and Judaism survived through the synagogues when the Temple was destroyed. St. Paul found them everywhere. It is said (Bab. Talmud, *Keth.* 105a) that when the Temple was destroyed there were 394 synagogues in Jerusalem alone: the Jerusalem Talmud (*Meg.* 73d) says there

* See also above, pp. 389 ff.

were 480. There was a synagogue within the Temple precincts (Mishnah, *Yoma* 7^{1}; *Sotah* $7^{7, 8}$; Tosephta, *Sukkah* 4^{5}). In course of time in the synagogues certain passages from the Law, and later from the Prophets also, were read at the festivals to ensure the proper observance of them, and gradually this was extended to the four Special Sabbaths and finally to every Sabbath and to cover the entire Pentateuch. In Palestine, possibly in the time of Christ, the whole Pentateuch was arranged for a three-year lectionary, though in Babylonia the portions were arranged for an annual system. In course of time a fixed Haftarah ("closure," a short selection from the Prophets) was added to each Seder of the Law, and it is possible that the Psalter was also used in similar fashion. Ultimately the Babylonian system triumphed, but not for many hundreds of years.

After the exile the common people ceased to be able to understand Hebrew, so that the reading from the Law was followed by an Aramaic rendering. This had not to be "translating with strict literalness" nor "making additions to it" (Tosephta, *Meg.* iv., 41). By the time of Jesus a homily had become the custom if there was anyone present who was competent. In New Testament times, the synagogue service consisted of an invitation to prayer, the prayer itself, a reading from the Law, a reading from the Prophets each with translation, and a homily based on the Scripture. The invitation to Prayer consisted of a Blessing and then the *sh^ema'*, which originally consisted of Deut. 6^{4-9} (beginning with "hear ye, O Israel . . ."), and later with the additions of Deut. 11^{13-21} and Num. 15^{37-41}. There was also singing since we know that the two songs of Moses, Deut. 32 and Ex. 15, have been Sabbath Canticles from a very early date. Also, since in the early Christian services there were "psalms and hymns and spiritual songs" (Eph. 5^{19}, Col. 3^{16}), we may presume that this custom, with much else, came from the synagogues.

BIBLIOGRAPHY

A. Edersheim, *The Temple, its Ministry and Services*, 1874.
G. B. Gray, *Sacrifice in the Old Testament*, 1925.
W. O. E. Oesterley, *Sacrifices in Ancient Israel*, 1937.
A. R. Johnson, *Sacral Kingship in Ancient Israel*, 1955.
A. S. Herbert, *Worship in Ancient Israel*, 1959.
R. de Vaux, *Ancient Israel : its Life and Institutions*, 1961.

XVIII. THE ORGANIZATION AND WORSHIP OF THE PRIMITIVE CHURCH

By C. W. Dugmore

(i) THE NATURE OF THE CHURCH

For any proper understanding of the organization or the worship of the primitive Church, it is vitally important to remember that the Church was founded within Judaism and that the first Christians were all Jews. Whether we put the founding of the Church at the call of Abraham, or Christ's call of His first disciples, or the confession of Peter at Caesarea Philippi, or the inauguration of the New Covenant at the Last Supper, or the event fulfilled through Easter and Pentecost, the *milieu* was the same. Acts records how Gentile converts very soon began to join the Church, but the Church was already in existence before that. Therefore, we may expect to find that her organization and her worship grow out of contemporary Jewish practice, even if other factors also influence their development.

The Christian *ecclesia*, or Church, as its name implies, is the assembly or congregation (or people) of God. In the LXX the word *ekklēsia* had been used to translate the Hebrew *ḳāhāl*, the assembly of the congregation of Israel. In the New Testament it is employed to denote an assembly of people (Acts 19[32. 39. 41]), but more usually to denote the whole body of Christians (Acts 5[11], 12[5], Col. 1[18. 24], Eph. 1[22-23], Gal. 1[13]). Perhaps from the moment of the inauguration of the New Covenant at the Last Supper, or even from the incident at Caesarea Philippi recorded in Matt. 16[13ff.], and certainly after the resurrection, the disciples believed themselves to be the Messianic community, the true Israel of God. (For the subsequent working out of this theme in Christian apologetic and polemic, down to A.D. 425, see Marcel Simon, *Verus Israel*, 1948.)

The etymology of the word *ecclesia* as used in the New Testament, has been much debated. As long ago as 1888–9, in a series of lectures (published as *The Christian Ecclesia*, 1897), F. J. A. Hort noted that the Christian *ecclesia* is not to be identified with the Kingdom of God (*op. cit.*, p. 19), and that the word itself is not derived from the verb *ekkalein* (adj. *ekklētos*) so that it means a community "called *out of the world* " by God (*ibid.*, pp. 5 ff.). K. L. Schmidt (*The Church*, Eng. Trans. " Bible Key Words " from Kittel's *Theologisches Wörterbuch zum Neuen Testament* (1938), 1950, p. 58) asserts that that is precisely what it does mean, but this has been denied by G. Johnston (*The Doctrine of the Church in the New Testament*, 1943, p. 35). Similarly Alan Richardson (*An Introduction to the Theology of the New Testament*, 1958, p. 287) regards K. L. Schmidt and others as mistaken in thinking that Ephesians and Colossians must be non-Pauline because they develop the conception of the *ecclesia* as a " mystery," the consummation of God's purpose of the ages (Eph. 3^{9-11}, 5^{32}), the body and bride of Christ (Eph. 1^{22}, 5^{23-32}, Col. $1^{18.\ 24}$). Richardson rightly points out that the references to the Church in Ephesians-Colossians develop ideas which have all along been present in Paul's conception of the body of Christ, even though he has not used the word *ecclesia* in this connexion.

Paul undoubtedly thinks of the Church as " Christ's Body " and he was, indeed, the first to use the expression " Body " or " Body of Christ " to convey the unity of Christians effected through their sharing in the partaking of the Body of Christ in the Eucharist (1 Cor. $10^{16.\ 17}$, 12^{27}, Rom. $12^{4.\ 5}$), and " to be identified with Christ's Body meant, in Hebrew usage, to be identified with Christ Himself" (*A Catholic Dictionary of Theology*, i., 1962, p. 284; cf. L. Cerfaux, *The Church in the Theology of St. Paul*, Eng. Trans. 1959, p. 265). Thus, already in 1 Cor. $12^{12ff.}$, Paul used the analogy of the one body with many members as a description of Christ Himself—" so also is Christ " (12^{12})—and went on to speak of the one Spirit in which all the members of the one Body are baptized, " whether Jews or Greeks, whether bond or free." If one member suffers, all suffer; if one member is honoured, all rejoice together. Finally, addressing the Christians at Corinth, Paul declared, " ye are the body of Christ and severally members thereof " (12^{27}). It is in this context that we hear of the different functions of some of the members—how " God hath set some in the church, first apostles, secondly prophets, thirdly teachers," and so on—but there are several further aspects of the nature of the primitive *ecclesia* which must be mentioned before we shall be in a position to try to evaluate its organization.

First, other metaphors than that of the Body are used in the New Testament to describe the Church. In the fullness of time God sent forth His Son, " born of a woman, born under the law, that we might receive the adoption of sons " (Gal. 4^{4-5}), for what the law could not do, God did, " sending His own Son in the likeness of sinful flesh . . . that the ordinance of the law might be fulfilled in us, who walk not after the flesh, but after the Spirit " (Rom. 8^{3-4}). Paul, however, insists that none of us liveth to himself and none dieth to himself (Rom. 14^{7}): God's people are brethren (1 Cor. 1^{10}), God's fellow-workers (1 Cor. 3^{9}), having their citizenship in heaven (Phil. 3^{20}). Jesus is Himself the head corner-stone (Matt. 21^{42}) and His Church is described by the author of Ephesians as a great building in course of erection, " being built upon the foundation of the apostles and prophets, Christ Jesus himself being the chief corner-stone ; in whom each several building, fitly framed together, groweth into a holy temple in the Lord ; in whom ye also are builded together for a habitation of God in the Spirit " (Eph. 2^{20-22}). But the Church, whether described as the Body of Christ or a " holy temple " is not a mere fellowship of men who worship Christ. As K. L. Schmidt has said, " What goes on in the communion of Christ and the *ecclesia* is something conceived by God, created by God, maintained by God " (*op. cit.*, p. 16).

Thus, although the word *ecclesia* only occurs twice in the Gospels (Matt. 16^{18}, 18^{17}), according to John $10^{7ff.}$ Christ spoke of Himself as the Good Shepherd and the door of the sheep-fold ; He described His disciples as His " little flock " (Luke 12^{32}), and His parables of the Wheat and the Tares and of the Drag Net are interpreted to mean that an admixture of good and bad will have to be tolerated in the Kingdom of the Son of Man until " the end of the age." *Ecclesia* does not occur at all in 2 Timothy, Titus, 1 Peter, 2 Peter, 1 John, 2 John, or Jude. There are parallel expressions, however, especially in 1 Peter, which aptly describe the nature of the *ecclesia* : " a spiritual house " (2^{5}) ; " an elect race, a royal priesthood, a holy nation, a people for God's own possession " (2^{9}) ; " the people of God " (2^{10}).

Secondly, alongside the passages already cited, in which the term *ecclesia* is used of the whole body of Christians, we find other passages where the same word is used of a local congregation, *e.g.* " the church in Jerusalem " (Acts 8^{1}) ; " the church in Antioch " (Acts 13^{1} ; cf. 14^{27}, 15^{3}) ; " the church at Cenchreae " (Rom. 16^{1}) ; " at Corinth " (1 Cor. 1^{2}, 2 Cor. 1^{1}) ; " of the Thessalonians " (1 Thess. 1^{1}, 2 Thess. 1^{1}) ; and even " in the house of " Prisca and Aquila (Rom. 16^{5}, 1 Cor. 16^{19}) ; Moreover, the word frequently occurs in the plural (*ecclesiai*). Thus, Acts records that Paul " went through Syria and Cilicia confirming the churches " (Acts 15^{41}), and Paul himself speaks of " the churches of the Gentiles " (Rom. 16^{4}) ; " all the churches of Christ " (Rom. 16^{16}), or " all the churches of the saints " (1 Cor. 14^{33}) ; " the churches of Asia " (1 Cor. 16^{19}) ; while John sends greeting to " the seven churches which are in Asia " (Rev. 1^{4}—they are named in Rev. 1^{11}).

Are we to suppose that the organization and the worship

were the same in all these "local" churches from the beginning? And what was the precise relation between the Church and the "local" churches in the minds of the first Christians? As long ago as 1892 Rudolph Sohm argued that "there is but one *Ecclesia,* the assembly of all Christendom; though this one Church has innumerable manifestations" (*Kirchenrecht,* i., p. 21), and in 1897 F. J. A. Hort declared that "the One Ecclesia includes all members of all partial Ecclesiae. . . . There is no indication that St. Paul regarded the conditions of membership in the universal Ecclesia as differing from the conditions of membership in the partial local Ecclesiae" (*The Christian Ecclesia,* p. 168). These statements by eminent German Protestant and Anglican scholars seem to give the lie to the tendentious statement of K. L. Schmidt (*op. cit.*, pp. 1–2) that "the question is generally decided on denominational rather than scientific grounds. . . . The orthodox Protestant puts the universal first, the liberal the local, a certain confusion being due perhaps to reaction against the hierarchy." As we have already pointed out, the New Testament knows nothing of separate organized communities of Christians living only to themselves: on the contrary, it uses the same word *ecclesia* for the whole Christian Church, the "Body of Christ," and for the churches in each city or locality which together constituted the "Body." It does not follow that the local communities of Christians were everywhere organized in precisely the same manner. Was the church "in the house of" Prisca and Aquila as fully organized as the church in Rome or the mother church of Jerusalem? We cannot tell from the evidence that is available, but it would seem to be unlikely. Were there several such house-churches in Rome or Corinth or Ephesus? Did they celebrate as many eucharists as there were house-churches, or one eucharist, in each town? What are we to make of the statement that the earliest Christians in Jerusalem were regular in attendance at the Temple and that they broke bread at home (Acts 2^{46})? Was the latter a Christian Sabbath meal, or an Agape or a Eucharist? Was it observed in each household or in one particular house, or at each house in turn? and who presided? We simply do not know.

However, we are not left entirely in ignorance concerning the general and local ministries in the primitive Church and scholars have made various attempts to evaluate the meagre evidence of the New Testament and the sub-apostolic writings which have come down to us. To these we now turn.

(ii) ORGANIZATION OF THE PRIMITIVE CHURCH

The Dissertation on "The Christian Ministry" by J. B. Lightfoot (*St. Paul's Epistle to the Philippians,* 1868, pp. 179–267) is acknowledged to be a standard classic on the evolution of Church Order in the New Testament and the Early Fathers of the Church. After remarking that, as individuals, all Christians are priests alike (1 Pet. $2^{5, 9}$, Rev. 1^{6}), he noted that as members of the Christian society they have several and distinct offices and that Paul gives two summaries of those offices. In the earlier one (1 Cor. 12^{28}) he enumerates "first apostles, secondly prophets, thirdly teachers, then powers, then gifts of healing, helps, governments, kinds of tongues." In the second, which Lightfoot regarded as written by Paul (Eph. 4^{11}), we have: "some apostles, and some prophets, and some evangelists, and some pastors and teachers." He shrewdly observed that these lists are not exhaustive and that they come from a period when the work of converting unbelievers and founding congregations was in the foreground, while the permanent government and instruction of the churches was kept in the background. But the permanent ministry must be alluded to in the phrases "teachers, helps, governments" and "pastors and teachers," and as the Church assumed a more settled form and the higher but temporary offices, such as the apostolate, fell away, this permanent ministry gradually emerged from the subordinate place which it occupied in the notices of Paul. It is generally accepted that by the middle of the second century each church had its three orders of ministers: its bishop, its presbyters, and its deacons. Scholars have differed, however, in their attempts to explain how and when these three orders arose, and particularly in regard to the origin of the episcopate.

Lightfoot asserted that "the establishment of the diaconate came first," accepting the unanimous tradition which goes back to Irenaeus (*Adv. Haer.*, III. xii. 10) that the seven men appointed to "serve tables" (Acts 6^{2}) were deacons and so represent the later diaconate. This has been disputed, as J. Armitage Robinson pointed out* and, as indeed, Lightfoot himself noted in his own day (*op. cit.*, p. 186). The order of deacons was well established by the time of Ignatius, in the early second century, but there are only two references to such an order in the New Testament (1 Tim. 3^{8-13}, Phil. 1^{1}). The Seven are never called "deacons" (*diakonoi*): nevertheless, on the strength of Acts 6^{1-6}, Lightfoot concluded that "the Apostles suggested the creation of this new office, but the persons were chosen by popular election and afterwards ordained by the Twelve with imposition of hands" (*op. cit.*, p. 185). The office thus created was entirely new and was

* See his essay "The Christian Ministry in the Apostolic and Sub-Apostolic Periods" in H. B. Swete (ed.), *Essays on the Early History of the Church and the Ministry*, 1918, p. 81.

not derived from the Synagogue. A woman deacon of the church at Cenchreae, Phoebe, may be referred to in Rom. 16¹, but there is no mention of an order of deaconesses in the New Testament.* The deacons were regarded as of apostolic appointment before the close of the first century (1 Clem. 42⁴), and as fellow-servants with the bishop by Ignatius (Smyrn. 12², Philad. 4). As time went on and the work of the bishop increased, they tended to usurp more and more of the liturgical and other functions of the bishop. Indeed, at the beginning of the third century, as T. W. Manson observed (*The Church's Ministry*, 1948, p. 69) : " The deacon in the *Apostolic Tradition* is firmly put in his place. It is emphasised that he is no more than the bishop's adjutant. He has no place in the council made up by bishops and presbyters."

Lightfoot held that, while the diaconate was an entirely new creation, the institution of presbyters, or elders, was taken over from the normal government of the Synagogue, which was everywhere directed by a body of *zᵉḳēnîm*, or elders. Thus the *presbuteroi* (presbyters, or elders) of the church in Jerusalem are linked with the Apostles in Acts (11³⁰, 15²· ⁴· ⁶· ²²· ²³, 16⁴). On his last visit to Jerusalem, Paul is received by " James and all the elders " (Acts 21¹⁸). In the Gentile world Paul and Barnabas themselves appointed elders in every church on their first missionary journey (Acts 14²³), so that the office was not confined to the Jewish-Christian church in Jerusalem. There is general agreement that Lightfoot was correct in his derivation of the presbyterate. But what were the functions of the presbyter ? and what is to be said of the term " bishop " (*episkopos*) ? " In the apostolic writings," said Lightfoot, " the two are only different designations of one and the same office " (*op. cit.*, p. 191), though he noted that it was in the Gentile churches alone that the terms were interchangeable—*e.g.* at Philippi (Phil. 1¹), in Asia (Acts 20²⁸), and in Crete (Tit. 1⁷). It is now recognized that while all bishops were presbyters, not all presbyters were bishops, or, to put the matter in another way, that the term " presbyter " connotes a function shared with the other members of the college of presbyters, whereas the term " bishop " (*episkopos*) connotes a personal function of oversight, superintendence (*episkopē*) exercised by one of the presbyters in a church. By the middle of the second century such an arrangement, known as " monepiscopacy " was universal. How did it arise ?

Lightfoot held that the office of bishop in this later and Catholic sense was not a continuation of the apostolate. " The

* For the latest discussion of the whole subject see J. G. Davies, " Deacons, Deaconesses and the Minor Orders in the Patristic Period " in *JEH*, xiv. (April 1963).

episcopate was formed," he believed, " not out of the apostolic order by localisation but out of the presbyteral by elevation: and the title, which originally was common to all, came at length to be appropriated to the chief among them " (*op. cit.*, p. 194). But, as has been already noted, it is now recognized that the title *episkopos* was not, in fact, " common to all " the presbyteral order.

The discovery and publication by Bryennios in 1883 of a short early Christian Church Manual entitled *The Didache*, or *The Teaching of the Twelve Apostles*, caused something of a sensation in academic circles and, among others, the German church historian, Adolf Harnack, believed that it shed new light upon the problem of the development of the early Christian Ministry. His theory, first set out in the Prolegomena to his edition of the *Didache* in 1884 and repeated with slight modifications in his *The Constitution and Law of the Church in the first two centuries* (Eng. trans., 1910), was that there existed in this period side by side a universal and a local ministry. The former was a " charismatic " teaching ministry, consisting of Apostles, Prophets and Teachers, which was revealed in the *Didache* as being on the point of handing on its original supreme authority, derived directly from the Holy Spirit, to the local administrative ministry of Presbyter-Bishops and Deacons, appointed by popular election in particular local churches and having no status outside those churches. The theory of a threefold ministry of Apostles, Prophets, and Teachers whom " God hath set in the Church " (1 Cor. 12^{28}; cf. Eph. 4^{11}) seemed at first sight to square with both the Pauline teaching and the situation revealed by *Did.* 10–13. Harnack was, however, severely criticized by C. H. Turner in an article entitled " The Early Christian Ministry and the Didache " (*CQR*, April 1887—reprinted in his *Studies in Early Church History*, 1912, pp. 1–32), who pointed out that the bishop " is connected simultaneously and equally, with two lines of ancestry, with the presbyteral office of the primitive episcopos and with the apostolic and prophetic office, which combined together to realise the bishop " (*op. cit.*, p. 28). J. Armitage Robinson (*Essays on the Early History of the Church and the Ministry*, 1918, pp. 67, 72 ff.) also attacked the new theory on the grounds that Harnack's triad of Apostles, Prophets, and Teachers " appears nowhere except in 1 Cor. 12^{28} " and that to regard this triad as representing a " charismatic " ministry involves a misuse of the term " charisma " which, in Paul's language, stands for any " gift of grace " that " enables any member of the Church to fulfil his appropriate function, however exalted or however humble that function may be " (*ibid.*, pp. 78–9).

Armitage Robinson was a conservative and cautious scholar, but one who was deeply versed in the literature of the patristic age. Like Turner he realized that Harnack and his followers had seized upon the *Didache* as the only clue to the solution of all problems concerning the organization of the early Church and had been beguiled into imagining that in the earliest period a ministry of enthusiasm stood over against the ministry of office which eventually superseded it. His own view was that " when a more careful study of the 'prophet' of the New Testament has set aside the notion that Apostles, Prophets, and Teachers formed a triad of ruling officers in the early Church, we shall not any longer be disposed to question Lightfoot's view that authority rested with the Twelve and St. Paul on the ground of a commission held directly from the Lord; that at Jerusalem the position of St. James practically anticipated the form of the later episcopate and was not without influence in promoting its universal extension . . . while for Asia Minor the tradition may be accepted which connects the appointment of bishops with the Apostle St. John " (*op. cit.*, p. 88).

The " careful study of the 'prophet' " was embarked upon with considerable zest and much learning by B. H. Streeter in *The Primitive Church* (1929). He rejected Harnack's theory of a universal and a local ministry as an abstract and systematic way of looking at a concrete and ever-changing situation which did not take sufficient account of the original diversity of organization in the different churches nor the evolution of church order in response to urgent local needs. Streeter stressed the importance of James as the leader of a kind of Christian Sanhedrin at Jerusalem, the equivalent of the later " mon-episcopos ": the constitution of the church at Antioch, he believed, was definitely *not* modelled on that of Jerusalem—Acts (13^1) spoke of " prophets and teachers " and the *Didache* suggested that, at least in some districts of Syria, " there were still churches at the end of the first century where Prophets and Teachers existed, but in which there were as yet no Episcopoi or Deacons " (*op. cit.*, p. 76). Even in the Gentile church of Corinth, founded by Paul, " the terms Prophet and Teacher represent the two most important offices in what may be called the normal ministry of a local church (1 Cor. 12^{28}; cf. Rom. 12^{6-8})." But, already in the early epistles of St. Paul, Streeter recognized that a growing importance was assigned to the bishops (*episkopoi*) and deacons (*e.g.* Phil. 1^1), and he believed that the Johannine Epistles provided conclusive evidence of the development of a " mon-episcopal " system of church government in at least one of the churches of Asia. " In this church," says Streeter, " Diotrephes held the office of Bishop, in the full monarchical sense " (*op. cit.*, p. 85)—he is described in 3 John [9] as " he who loveth to have the pre-eminence "—but T. W. Manson, with greater caution, remarks " *If* Diotrephes was a monarchical bishop, the Presbyter *may* have been a kind of archbishop ; but it is not certain that Diotrephes was a bishop : he may only have been a successful ecclesiastical demagogue " (*The Church's Ministry*, p. 61 ; cf. C. H. Dodd, *The Johannine Epistles*, pp. 155–68). Even Streeter was forced to admit that at Rome the prophet was definitely subordinated to the regular ministry (*op. cit.*, p. 219), but he believed that mon-episcopacy was not established there until after the arrival of Ignatius, *c.* A.D. 115. Perhaps the chief value of Streeter's study was his insistence upon the original diversity of organization in the various churches in the apostolic and sub-apostolic ages, its rapid evolution and its later standardization upon a uniform model.

The next important study of the subject in English was a series of essays by ten scholars edited by K. E. Kirk (Bishop of Oxford) under the title *The Apostolic Ministry* (1946). To this Bishop Kirk himself contributed the first essay, on " The Apostolic Ministry," and the book as a whole aroused keen controversy both within and outside the Anglican fold. He, together with the other contributors, stood in the Tractarian tradition and accepted the particular theory of apostolic succession restated by Newman : " The Lord Jesus Christ gave His Spirit to His Apostles ; they in turn laid their hands on those who should succeed them ; and these again on others ; and so the sacred gift has been handed down to our present Bishops, who have appointed us as their assistants, and in some sense representatives " (*Tracts for the Times*, i., No. 1 (9th Sept., 1833), 1834, p. 2). Thus Kirk distinguished between the Essential Ministry and the Dependent Ministry : " where we speak of an Essential Ministry, however, the earliest Christians thought of one which was ' apostolic ' " (*op. cit.*, p. 9). Thus, he believed that in the New Testament the earliest " orders " were those of the apostles and the elders : the words " deacon " and " bishop " refer to functions, not orders —a bishop (*episkopos*) is one who has oversight (*episkopē*) over others ; a deacon or " liturgist " is one who does service to God or man or both. " So," he said, " an apostle can have a ' deaconship ' (Rom. 11^{13}, 1 Cor. 3^{5}, 2 Cor. 3^{6}, 4^{1}) or ' liturgy ' (Rom. 15^{16}), whilst an elder can be a ' bishop ' (Acts 20^{28}). It is purely a question of the varying use of words " (*ibid.*). But the apostle he regarded as the plenipotentiary (*shālîaḥ*) of his Master, the accredited representative of the ascended Lord, the guardian of the faith, the source of teaching, the minister of the sacraments, while the elder, derived from Jewish synagogue organization, was the executive or administrative officer of the local church (cf. Harnack). The rest of this learned book of 550 pages—which it is impossible even to summarize here—is but commentary on and elaboration of this thesis. Kirk's essay was followed by others by Dr. L. S. Thornton on "The Body of Christ in the New Testament," by Dr. A. M. Farrer on "The Ministry in the New Testament" and by Dom Gregory Dix on "The Ministry in the Early Church." Of Dr. Thornton's typological approach to the New Testament, Bishop Stephen Neill wrote "some of this typological interpretation seems to me unintelligible except on the assumption of the verbal inspiration of the Septuagint" (*The Ministry of the Church*, Neill and others, 1947, p. 9) and A. E. J. Rawlinson (Bishop of Derby) remarked "I am afraid I cannot resist the impression that in Dr. Thornton's excursions into the realm of mystical exegesis there is not a little which is fanciful" (*Christian Initiation*, 1947, pp. 23–4). Of Dr. Farrer's chapter, Professor C. F. D. Moule said: "it is a difficult essay to follow, and its four sections do not form any very obviously logical sequence. . . . It is profoundly distressing to find a revered theologian persuading himself that they [the New Testament writers] indulged in such wild flights of fancy as meet our astonished eyes in these pages" (*The Ministry of the Church*, p. 46).

Perhaps the most important essay printed in *The Apostolic Ministry* was that by Dom Gregory Dix, on "The Ministry in the Early Church, *c.* A.D. 90–410" (pp. 185–303), in which he argued that the Greek *apostolos* is the equivalent, or rather the mere translation of the Jewish *shālîaḥ*, "the friend or slave 'sent' as a plenipotentiary not only 'in the name' but 'in the person' of his principal, so that the envoy's action unalterably committed the principal" (*op. cit.*, p. 228). He maintained that our Lord made use of this well-known Jewish institution in the foundation of His Church. "As Jesus, 'the Apostle and High-priest of our confession' (Heb. 3^1), is the *shaliach* or plenipotentiary of God, so after His Ascension the Twelve are His plenipotentiaries, empowered like Him by the Messianic Spirit to fulfil and continue His own Messianic mission. Henceforward "the Apostles" replace "the Twelve," and as the Church extends, others outside their original company are included in the term" (*ibid.*, p. 230). Thus the apostolic succession of bishops in the Church from our Lord's commission of the Twelve until the present day, in the sense in which Newman used the term, is guaranteed by the occurrence in the Talmud "no less than nine times" of an adage, which Dom Dix repeated considerably more than nine times: "'A man's *shaliach* is as it were himself' (or 'like himself')."

There is no doubt that there were Jewish " apostles " (*shelûḥîm*) of the High Priest and Sanhedrin, who were ordained by laying on of hands and that a Jewish congregation or even a private individual could appoint a *shālîaḥ* to represent them or him. Unfortunately for Dix's thesis there is no instance in Rabbinic literature of a *shālîaḥ* transmitting his commission to another: when he ceased to exercise it, his authority reverted to the principal; moreover, the term *shālîaḥ* was not one of office but of function, and it was always exercised within Jewry and did not connote any missionary or proselytizing activity. With his customary meticulous scholarship and his deep knowledge of the Rabbinic sources, T. W. Manson examined this theory in some detail (*The Church's Ministry*, 1948, pp. 31–52). He frankly admitted that " the *apostolos* in the New Testament, like the *shaliach* in Judaism, is sent and commissioned by someone for some purpose. . . . As in Judaism so in Christianity the *apostolos* can be the representative of a community (2 Cor. 8^{23} and Phil. 2^{25}) " (*op. cit.*, p. 44), but he contended that " the result of apostolic work is a local congregation; and the local congregation, as part of the Body of Christ, itself enters into the Apostolic Ministry. . . . To the task of the *kerygma* (preaching) is added the responsibility of *didache* (teaching) " (*ibid.*, pp. 54–5). This, however, still leaves us with the question of the relation between the " apostolic " and " local " ministries. Were the local *episkopoi* the direct successors of the Apostles by " devolution," or were they evolved " upwards " from the ranks of the presbyters, as Lightfoot and Streeter believed?

We may never know the answer to this question. The evidence in the New Testament and in the writings of the sub-apostolic age is inconclusive: scholars of repute in the Roman Catholic, Anglican, and Protestant churches have sifted it time and again and have deduced from it contrary conclusions. Looking at their arguments and counter-arguments, after the passage of some years, what seems to emerge as being beyond dispute is that by *c.* A.D. 150 the three-fold ministry of bishops, priests, and deacons was everywhere the norm. It is possible, and indeed probable, that the episcopate developed at different dates in different churches. As T. W. Manson remarked (*op. cit.*, p. 64) " we have good reason to think that when a new local church was founded by an Apostle, its first office-bearers were set apart by him, its first baptisms and eucharists were conducted by him. But we have no reason to think that all subsequent ordinations were held by him, any more than all subsequent baptisms and eucharists. Moreover, we do not know that all local churches were founded by Apostles. Who founded the Church at Colossae, for example? " We know that there were Christians at Rome before Paul arrived there (Acts $28^{14. 15}$) and, almost certainly before Peter reached Rome—scholars have argued both for and against a visit by Peter and his martyrdom there, but the balance of opinion is now definitely in favour of this tradition (see O. Cullmann, *Peter : Disciple, Apostle, Martyr*, Eng. trans., 1953). Lightfoot ("The Christian Ministry," in his *Philippians*, pp. 218–21) accepted as authentic the list of Roman bishops going back to Linus, A.D. 68, given by Irenaeus and partially corroborated by Hegesippus (*ap.* Eusebius, *Hist. Eccl.*, iv. 22). Manson (*op. cit.*, p. 63) thought that there was strong evidence that the Roman church was ruled "not by a bishop but by a college of presbyters until well into the second century," but, more recently, Cullmann has accepted this "particularly well-preserved apostolic tradition," while insisting that it is connected only with the foundation of the Roman church and not with the primacy of Peter (*op. cit.*, p. 234).

Moreover, as Einar Molland pointed out ("Irenaeus of Lugdunum and the Apostolic Succession," in *JEH*, i., 1950, p. 23), the series Linus, Anencletus, Clement, etc., does not imply any continuity of ordinations, as Newman somewhat rashly assumed, since the successor was normally not chosen until the predecessor had died, "as was the case when Irenaeus himself succeeded Pothinus in Lugdunum, and as is already presupposed in 1 Clem. 44^{1-3}." According to Molland, the list of Roman bishops is a catalogue of presidents of the presbytery and, from Anicetus onwards, of monarchical bishops (*ibid.*, p. 24, n. 2). The "succession from the Apostles" was not, however, an apostolic authority to ordain, sacramentally transmitted through an uninterrupted series of imposition of hands, but a guarantee of genuine tradition, of the doctrine and teaching of the Apostles, handed on through a verifiable series of men, in contrast to the un-apostolic, heretical teaching of the Gnostics. The hypothesis that Irenaeus was himself consecrated bishop of Lyons during his visit to Rome in A.D. 177 must be abandoned (cf. F. Vernet, in *Dict. de Théol. Cath.*, vii. 2, col. 2395) : he was probably consecrated by his fellow presbyters at Lyons, in the same way as the bishops of Alexandria (Molland, *loc. cit.*, p. 28).

With regard to Alexandria, W. Telfer followed up Molland's argument and demonstrated ("Episcopal Succession in Egypt" in *JEH*, iii., 1952, pp. 1–13) that the custom of electing a new bishop out of one of themselves by the twelve city presbyters obtained until the time of Alexander (A.D. 313–28), the immediate predecessor of Athanasius (A.D. 328–73), and E. W. Kemp, whilst highly critical of some of Dr. Telfer's arguments, was compelled to admit that, though there was a carefully regulated episcopal succession at Alexandria, it was "a succession through a presbyteral college" ("Bishops and Presbyters at Alexandria" in *JEH*, vi., 1955, p. 142).

In the light of the above discussion, it is no longer possible to accept *in toto* the naïve theory of Dom Gregory Dix that the apostolate was instituted by Christ on the model of the Jewish plenipotentiary (*shālîaḥ*); that the primitive local churches were governed by a group of presbyters and that these presbyters, including the early mon-episkopoi, were ordained not by the presbyter-episkopoi of their own local church, but by such "apostolic men" as Timothy and Titus and the *ellogimoi andres* of 1 Clem. 44; and that the true successors by an unbroken series of laying on of hands were the later bishops. We have seen that, at least in some churches, bishops were recruited from the ranks of the presbyterate and, as S. L. Greenslade has shrewdly observed: "You cannot argue backwards to say that (*a*) presbyteral colleges before this were therefore not self-recruiting, nor (*b*) that a self-recruiting apostolate, distinct from presbyters, always existed" (*The Ministry of the Early Church*, ed. Stephen Neill, p. 59).

Recently attempts have been made to invoke the existence of the parallel organization of the Dead Sea community in support of the apostolic origin of episcopacy. These sectarian Jews had "superintendents" or "overseers" (*mᵉbhaḳḳᵉrîm*) whose functions were pastoral and judicial. Theodor H. Gaster roundly declared that "the Hebrew word is the exact equivalent of the Greek *episkopos*, 'bishop.' We thus see the original form of this office, which later assumed sacerdotal functions" (*The Scriptures of the Dead Sea Sect*, Eng. trans. with Introduction and notes, 1957, p. 107; cf. pp. 45, 60). Fr. J. H. Crehan, S.J. (*A Catholic Dictionary of Theology*, i., 1962, p. 273 s.v. Bishop) does not go so far as to say that the Church copied the Dead Sea Sect, but clearly regards the parallel as shedding light on the apostolic origin of episcopacy and refers, apparently with approval, to the article by A. Adam (*Die Religion in Geschichte und Gegenwart*, 3rd edn., s.v. Bischof) who accepts the parallel of Christian bishop and *Mᵉbhaḳḳēr*. G. Johnston remarks more cautiously that a parallel may be found in the "overseer" (*mᵉbhaḳḳēr*) or "inspector" (*pāḳidh*) and *episkopos*, "but the parallel is not exact" (*Peake's Commentary on the Bible*, ed. M. Black and H. H. Rowley, 1962, § 631d). But it is even less likely that *episkopos* = the sectarian *mᵉbhaḳḳēr* than that *apostolos* = the perfectly orthodox *shālîaḥ*. The Church certainly arose in a Jewish *milieu* and there is every likelihood that the first Jewish Christians organized their affairs by means of *presbuteroi* on the model of the regular synagogue officials, the *zᵉḳēnîm* (elders). It does not follow that every other office and function in the Church's organization was slavishly copied from rabbinic or sectarian Judaism. Bo Reicke rightly concludes that " there is little reason to assume that the Church got its episcopal office from the Essenes and their *mebaqqer* " (in *The Scrolls and the New Testament*, ed. K. Stendahl, 1958, p. 154).

Apostles and prophets of the first generation, or the second, were not immortal. Their roles were sometimes interchangeable : their credentials were not always clear. The *Didache* (11^{4-5}) orders : " Let every apostle who comes to you be received as the Lord, but let him not stay more than one day, or if need be also a second, but if he stays three days he is a pseudo-prophet " (*not* a pseudo-apostle). And again, an apostle who asks for money is a pseudo-prophet (*not* a pseudo-apostle) (11^6). Whether the later bishop was the successor of the apostles or the prophets or both, or was elevated from the ranks of the presbyters, it is evident that any body of presbyters governing a local church would need a chairman to preside over their deliberations. Someone would have to guarantee the handing on of the apostolic doctrine, take the lead in combating heresy, represent the local church in dealings with other churches (cf. the letter of Clement on behalf of the church of Rome to the church in Corinth), and preside at the eucharist. By the middle of the second century these functions were exercised usually by the bishop (*episkopos*), but the different local churches may well have reached the common solution by different roads and at different dates, by trial and error, under the guidance of the Holy Spirit.

(iii) WORSHIP IN THE PRIMITIVE CHURCH

The conversion of a household was the natural way of establishing the new cult and the household remained the basis for the meetings of Christians (cf. E. A. Judge, *The Social Pattern of Christian Groups in the First Century*, 1960, p. 36). In the New Testament we find many references to the conversion and baptism of a " household " (1 Cor. 1^{16}, Acts 11^{14}, $16^{15, 33}$, 18^8)—the households of Stephanas, Lydia, the keeper of the prison in Philippi, and of Crispus being specifically mentioned. E. Stauffer investigated the Old Testament occurrences of the formula " He and his (whole) house " (*oikos*) and similar expressions and reached the conclusion (in *Deutsches Pfarrerblatt*, 1949) that the Biblical " *oikos* formula " not only included all adults but had a special reference to children. J. Jeremias (*Infant Baptism in the First Four Centuries*, Eng. trans. 1960) accepted his conclusions and suggested that in the New Testament the " *oikos* formula " was adopted from the Old Testament cultic language, and influenced the primitive Christian rite of baptism. But Kurt Aland (*Did the Early Church Baptize Infants?*, Eng. trans., 1963) has challenged the conclusions of Stauffer and Jeremias. He would even "contest whether we have any right to talk about an '*oikos*-formula' in the New Testament, as Jeremias and Stauffer and many others do at present" (*op. cit.*, p. 91). He asserts that in more than 1600 cases the LXX *oikos* renders the Hebrew *bayith* (house) and that, in comparison with this number, the forty or so passages on which Stauffer builds his thesis of the "ritual formula" are insignificant. In his view, to base a theory of the baptism of children and infants upon the few *oikos* passages in the New Testament is quite unwarranted. Aland himself believes that it can be no accident that "all our information about the existence of infant baptism comes from the period between A.D. 200 and 250. At that time we hear of its observance in Africa, Palestine, and Italy; in each case the way in which it is spoken of conveys the impression that the practice takes its rise at the end of the second century" (*op. cit.*, p. 101). He agrees with Jeremias that "no special rite for child baptism was introduced" and asserts that the ritual of adult baptism was, therefore, transferred to infants, "although from the beginning it necessitated the assistance of a 'sponsor' (*pater*), who answered and spoke up for the infant during the baptism (cf. the *Church Order* of Hippolytus). . . . When the practice of baptizing children immediately after birth was begun, the formula that had hitherto been used for older children was *further* applied" (*op. cit.*, pp. 110–11). This conclusion seems eminently reasonable.

The great majority of scholars since the beginning of this century have been in agreement that Jewish proselyte baptism came into vogue in pre-Christian times. Jeremias pointed out the many similarities between proselyte baptism and primitive Christian baptism in regard to terminology, baptismal instruction and the rite itself. Oscar Cullmann (*Baptism in the New Testament*, Eng. trans., 1950) had already drawn attention to the use of the word *kōleuein* in Acts 8^{36}, 10^{47}, 11^{17}, Matt. 3^{14} and the Gospel of the Ebionites (*ap.* Epiphanius, *Haer.* XXX. xiii. 3), and had concluded that, in the first century, enquiry was made as to whether any hindrance to baptism existed, *i.e.* whether the candidate had fulfilled the conditions demanded (*op. cit.*, pp. 75 ff.). Einar Molland (in *Studia Theologica*, ix., 1955, pp. 1–39) carried the matter further by demonstrating the survival of the *kōleuein* formula in the Jewish Christian *milieux* of the Pseudo-Clementine Homilies. All this would suggest that, as in the case of proselyte baptism so in the case of Christian baptism, some kind of instruction, however brief or elementary, was given before reception into the Church by baptism. In the *Apostolic Tradition* of Hippolytus (*c.* A.D. 215, but probably representing the practice of the second century—though Aland would deny this) instruction of catechumens over a period of three years is laid down (*Ap. Trad.*, xvii). The date of the *Didache* has been much discussed, but it now seems likely that, in the form we have it, it was completed by *c.* A.D. 100 (so J. M. Creed, *JTS*, xxxix., 1938, pp. 370–87; J. Vernon Bartlet, *Church Life and Church Order*, 1943), or even between A.D. 50 and 70 (so J.-P. Audet, *La Didachè*, 1958). *Did.* 7^1 tells us that a course of moral instruction preceded baptism and *Did.* 1–6 (containing the "Two Ways") provides such a course. In the New Testament itself we have evidence of the instruction of catechumens before baptism (Gal. 6^6, Acts 18^{25}, Luke 1^4) and of public profession of "the faith once for all delivered to the saints" (Jude ^{3}) in the presence of the congregation of the local church (Phil. 2^{11}, 1 Tim. 6^{12}, Rom. $10^{9f.}$, 1 Cor. 12^3). Thus the parallel between Jewish proselyte baptism and primitive Christian baptism seems to be reasonably well established in regard to pre-baptismal instruction.

With regard to the administration of baptism, too, there are some striking parallels. Jeremias (*op. cit.*, p. 31) lists baptism by complete immersion (Rom. 6^4, Col. 2^{12}, 1 Cor. 6^{11}, etc., with Rabbinic authorities); the preference for flowing water, though this is not essential (*Did.* 7^{1-3}; cf. passages in Billerbeck i, pp. 108 f.); confession of sins by the person to be baptized (1 Pet. 3^{21}, Aristides *Apol.*, xvii. 4, and, we may add, Hippolytus, *In Dan.*, i. 16 (cf. J. Crehan, *Early Christian Baptism and the Creed*, 1950, p. 141) and Tertullian, *De Bapt.*, xx; cf. Matt. 3^6, Mark 1^5); and, finally, the regulation that before baptism women should let down their hair and take off their ornaments (*Ap. Trad.*, xxi. 5, *Test. Dom.*, ii. 8; cf. Bab. Talmud, *Baba Qama*, 82 a, b).

Some of these parallels from both Christian and Jewish sources are much later than the period of the New Testament. They should not, for that reason, be dismissed as irrelevant for the apostolic and sub-apostolic ages. Tradition is always slow in achieving written record. The fact that the Mishnah was not committed to writing until about A.D. 200 does not vitiate the record of the disputes between the schools of Hillel and Shammai of the early first century. Similarly, early Christian traditions and practices are likely to be reflected in the *Didache*, the *Apostolic Tradition*, and even in Tertullian and Cyprian.

In Judaism male children of Jewish parents were circumcised at eight days old, in accordance with the Law (Gen. 17^{12},

Ex. 12^{48}). When Gentiles adopted the Jewish faith they were first baptized (since Gentiles were regarded as being permanently in a state of ritual impurity), and then, if males, were subsequently circumcised. Boys born after the proselyte baptism of the mother were treated as other Jewish boys and circumcised on the eighth day; boys born before the baptism of the mother were circumcised on the first day. Gentile girls of less than three years and one day at the moment of becoming Jewesses were treated like Jewish girls, and not baptized; if over that age, they went through the baptismal bath. J. Jeremias has argued (*op. cit.*, pp. 38–40) that in the admission of Gentiles to the Church children of every age, including infants, were also baptized. There is just one snag in his argument: he has to admit that "the first direct mention of the baptism of young proselyte children is by Rab Huna (*c.* A.D. 212–297)," and even this is the case of a "proselyte child whose father had died" (*op. cit.*, p. 38). It is dangerous to argue from a single example of Jewish third-century practice to the practice of Christians in the first century, and Cullmann was much more cautious in his conclusion that "in the New Testament it is certainly proved that Baptism is applied to adult Jews and heathen who come over to Christianity. Proof of infant Baptism is at best indirectly demonstrated from observable indications. On the other hand, infant Baptism is in every detail congruous with the *doctrine* of Baptism" (*Baptism in the New Testament*, p. 70). Aland asserts that nobody can prove an actual case of the baptism of an infant before A.D. 200 on the basis of the sources we have at present.

If the Christian Church is the "Israel of God" (Gal. 6^{16}, etc.), then baptism is inevitably to be regarded as the Christian circumcision (Rom. 2^{29}, Phil. 3^{2-3}, Col. 2^{11}), "not through the law" but "through the righteousness of faith" (Rom. 4^{13}). The comparison of baptism with circumcision is frequent in the early Fathers of the Church (*Ep. of Barn.*, ix. 6; Justin, *Dial.*, xxix. 1; Cyril of Jerusalem, *Catech.*, v. 6; Aug., *Ep.*, clxxxvii. 11, 34). In his baptism the Christian dies with Christ, is crucified with Christ (Rom. $6^{6, 8}$, Col. 3^{3}); eschatologically he is already living with Christ in the resurrection life, "dead unto sin" (Rom. 6^{11-14}), "raised together with Him" (Col. 2^{12}). He is a "new creation" (2 Cor. 5^{17}, Gal. 6^{15}). Here there is certainly a close parallel to Jewish conversion theology, which describes the adoption of the Jewish religion as "a passage from death to life" (D. Daube, *The New Testament and Rabbinic Judaism*, 1956, p. 110). Many other metaphors are also employed in the New Testament, *e.g.* "putting on" Christ (Gal. 3^{27}, Rom. 13^{14}) or "the new man" (Col. 3^{9}, Eph. 4^{24}); the "washing away of sin" (Acts 22^{16}, 1 Cor. 6^{11},

Eph. 5^{26}, Heb. 10^{22}) ; " remission of sins " (Acts 2^{38}, 5^{31}, 10^{43}, 13^{38}, 26^{18}, Eph. 1^{7}, Col. 1^{14}) ; and " the seal " (Rom. 4^{11}, 2 Cor. 1^{22}, Eph. 1^{13}, 4^{30}, Rev. 7^{3-8}). G. W. H. Lampe (*The Seal of the Spirit*, 1951, p. 306) concluded, after an exhaustive and critical examination of the evidence, that " there is no foundation in the New Testament, nor any clear testimony in the early Fathers, for the view that in the Christian dispensation God's people are sealed as His own possession by undergoing an outward and visible ceremony, other than Baptism in water, analogous to the external seal of circumcision in the old Covenant and standing in the same relationship to Baptism as circumcision stood to the proselyte-baptism of the Jews."

Laying on of hands *may* be connected with baptism in Heb. 6^{2} (" of the teaching of baptisms, and of laying on of hands ") : it is certainly connected with the gift of the Holy Spirit in Acts 8^{17-19}, 19^{6}, but the gift of the Spirit can occur without it and before baptism (Acts $10^{44ff.}$). Dom Gregory Dix (*Confirmation or the Laying on of Hands?*, 1936, p. 18) suggested that in Acts the laying on of hands was really an ordination of prophets. Lampe (*Seal of the Spirit*, p. 78) would not restrict it to prophets, but would see the ordination as a commissioning for active service in the missionary work of the Church. He concludes that " there is little convincing evidence in the New Testament for the view that Baptism regularly involved or included any other rite than the Baptism in water which was practised from the earliest days of the Church " (*ibid.*, p. 307). Clear references to ordaining or commissioning by the laying on of hands occur in Acts 6^{6}, 13^{3}, 1 Tim. 4^{14}, 2 Tim. 1^{6}. This is probably another instance of the Church's debt to Judaism, since " laying on of hands " (*s*^{e}*mîkhāh*) was employed in the ordination by presbyters (*z*^{e}*ḳēnîm*) to the office of " rabbi." *

It is time to turn to a consideration of how the early Christian, whether of Jewish or Gentile origin, worshipped with the Church, once he had received remission of sins and the seal of the Spirit and had become " a new creature " (Gal. 6^{15}, 2 Cor. 5^{17}). Cullmann has stressed the fact that the Church chose the day of the Resurrection as the " day of the Lord " and the day of worship ; indeed, that the Eucharist is the foundation and the end of all Christian worship (*Le Culte dans l'Église primitive*, pp. 28–9). Nevertheless, there were other occasions besides the Day of the Resurrection on which Christians offered worship to God, and, in point of fact,

* On the whole subject see D. Daube, *The New Testament and Rabbinic Judaism*, 1956, pp. 224–46 ; A. Ehrhardt, " Jewish and Christian Ordination " in *JEH*, v., 1954, pp. 125–38, and *The Apostolic Ministry* (Scottish Journal of Theology Occasional Papers No. 7), 1958.

the first definite mention of regular assemblies for worship on "the day of the Sun" (Sunday) is in Justin (1 *Apol.*, lxvii), about A.D. 150. It is, indeed, remarkable how little evidence there is in the New Testament and in the literature of the sub-apostolic age that Sunday was the most important day in the Christian week, if it was the regular occasion of the supreme act of Christian worship, viz. the Eucharist. The "first day of the week" is mentioned in the Gospels in all the narratives of the Resurrection, but it is noteworthy that the term *kuriakē* (which is the technical term for "Sunday" in the third and fourth centuries) only occurs in the New Testament at Rev. 1^{10}. The present writer has argued elsewhere ("Lord's Day and Easter" in *Neotestamentica et Patristica: eine Freundesgabe, Herrn Professor Dr. Oscar Cullmann zu seinem* 60. *Geburtstag überreicht,* 1962, pp. 272–81) that "the Lord's Day" (*kuriakē*) was originally a technical term for the annual festival of the Resurrection, *i.e.* Easter Day.

The Christian Church certainly inherited from Judaism the ancient festivals of Easter and Pentecost, associated with the Resurrection of the Lord and the outpouring of the Spirit upon the Church. These were annual feasts. The Church, however, also perpetuated the observance of the Jewish seven-day week and Sunday was not substituted for the Sabbath all at once. The observance of the Sabbath was enjoined in the Decalogue and the Decalogue was certainly recited in the primitive Christian weekly services (Pliny, *Ep.*, x. 96; cf. *Did.*, i, ii, Iren., *Adv. Haer.*, IV. xv. 1). It is unlikely, therefore, that the fourth commandment was alone discarded. As late as the fourth century Gregory of Nyssa could write (*De Castig.*, ii), "If you have despised the Sabbath, with what face (*lit.* eyes) will you behold the Lord's Day? . . . They are sisters." Both days have always been kept as feast days in the East, even in Lent, with the exception of Holy Saturday, and the Western Church only introduced fasting on Saturdays at the end of the third century. Even in the time of Augustine Saturday was not a fast day at Milan (Aug., *Ep.*, liv. 3).

Paul exhorted Christians to "pray without ceasing and in everything to give thanks" (1 Thess. $5^{17.\ 18}$). He told the Corinthian church that "God is not a God of confusion, but of peace. . . . Let all things be done decently and in order" (1 Cor. $14^{33.\ 40}$). Reduced to order, such meetings for worship would doubtless be, generally speaking, on the lines of a service in a Jewish synagogue. Those services were held daily at the hours of the ancient Temple sacrifices, namely at dawn and at sunset. So they were in the Christian Church (Hippolytus, *Ap. Trad.*, xxxv. 1, 2, xxxvi. 7; Origen, *Hom. in Gen.*, x. 3, *Hom. in Exod.*, vii. 8). Tertullian, who supports the introduction of prayer at the third, sixth, and ninth hours among the ascetics, says that these times of prayer should be " of course quite apart from (*i.e.* in addition to) the regular prayers which without any reminder are due at the beginning of day and of night " (*De Orat.*, xxv : *ingressu lucis et noctis*). These were the daily times of prayer in the Synagogue. The content of the daily and Sabbath worship of Christians was likewise modelled on that of the Synagogue. In both there were four main elements—prayer, psalmody, scripture lections, and a homily (or *midrash*) upon the portions of Scripture which had been read (see, further, my *The Influence of the Synagogue upon the Divine Office*, 1944). The chief differences between the Christian Sabbath and week-day services were that the sermon, or instruction (*Ap. Trad.*, xxxvi. 1), was not provided on every week-day, and that the Eucharist followed only on Saturdays and Sundays and Station Days.

The origin of the Christian Eucharist is, by common consent, to be found in the Last Supper, at which our Lord inaugurated the New Covenant in His Blood (Matt. 26^{26-28}, Mark 14^{22-24}, Luke 22^{17-20}, 1 Cor. 11^{23-25}). There is no record of the institution in the fourth Gospel but a eucharistic discourse is attached to the feeding of the multitude, when " the passover, the feast of the Jews, was at hand " (John $6^{4\text{ff.}}$), in John 6^{32-58}. The question whether the Last Supper was a Passover Meal or not has been hotly debated and various alternative theories have been propounded. For example, the view that the Last Supper was not a Passover Meal, already adumbrated by Strauss and Renan in their " Lives " of Jesus, was adopted by Spitta, Drews, Box, Burkitt, Goguel, Oesterley, Lietzmann, Montefiore, Gavin, Cirlot, and Dix. The majority of these scholars saw in the institution of the Eucharist either the Jewish ceremony known as *ḳiddūsh*—the sanctification of the Sabbath or a Festival, such as Passover or Pentecost —or in the wholly erroneous theory that a religious association (*Ḥ^abhûrāh*) regularly held common festal meals on the eve of the Sabbath, beginning in broad daylight and continuing until dusk when they were interrupted for the blessing of a cup of wine in honour of the Sabbath (*ḳiddūsh*). A *Ḥ^abhûrāh* was, to use Geiger's phrase, " a purely pious brotherhood " of associates (*ḥ^abhērîm*), who " were pledged to keep themselves pure from ceremonial defilement and to set apart with meticulous exactness the portion of the products of the soil which were by the Law to be given to the Priests (*terūmah gedōlah*) or to the Levites (tithes) " (G. F. Moore, in *The Beginnings of Christianity*, ed. Foakes-Jackson and K. Lake, i, p. 440 ; cf. R. Travers Herford, *The Pharisees*, 1924, p. 31). A period of probation was necessary and formal acceptance of the obligations of membership in the presence of three associates (*ḥ^a^bhērîm*), so, in view of Christ's attitude to tithing (Matt. 23[23]) and his disciples' practice with regard to hand-washing (Mark 7[2]), it is most unlikely that they would ever have been admitted to or recognized as a *Ḥ^a^bhûrāh*. In any case, the purpose of a *Ḥ^a^bhûrāh* was as stated above and not the holding of quasi-religious meals on the eves of Sabbaths. If we say that our Lord and the Twelve formed themselves into a company (*ḥ^a^bhûrāh*), in the non-technical sense, to eat the Last Supper together we add nothing to what was known before.

The *ḳiddūsh*-theory and the *ḥ^a^bhûrāh*-theory, however, were both invoked (especially by W. O. E. Oesterley, *The Jewish Background of the Christian Liturgy*, 1925, followed by F. Gavin, W. H. Frere, and others) in order to attempt to reconcile the different accounts of the Last Supper given in the Synoptic Gospels and in the fourth Gospel. The former regard the Last Supper as a Passover Meal (Mark 14[12. 14. 16] and parallels, Luke 22[15]). The fourth Gospel, however, regards the Crucifixion itself as having taken place before the Feast began (John 19[14. 31]), so that the Last Supper must have been held twenty-four hours before the beginning of Passover and Sabbath, which coincided in that year according to this Gospel (John 19[31]—" the day of that sabbath was a high day "). But already in 1916 F. C. Burkitt had pointed out that there is no evidence for a Passover *ḳiddūsh* twenty-four hours before the Feast and that the ceremony is essentially the ushering in of a Sabbath or Feast (*JTS*, xvii., p. 294 ; cf. T. W. Manson in *Christian Worship*, ed. N. Micklem, 1936, p. 46). " When will that wholly illusory Passover-*Kiddūsh* on the eve of the feast vanish from discussion ? " asks J. Jeremias (*The Eucharistic Words of Jesus*, Eng. trans., 1955, p. 25). Jeremias believes that " the solemnities of the Last Supper cannot be explained by theories about the *Kiddūsh* or the *Habûrāh* " (*ibid.*, p. 26) and he has argued very cogently that the Last Supper *was* a Passover Meal. Taking the tradition enshrined in Mark and Paul (1 Cor.) as the more primitive, he finds traces of a Synoptic dating in the fourth Gospel (*ibid.*, pp. 55 ff.), and most ingeniously disposes of the common objections to the equation Last Supper=Passover (*e.g.* that unleavened bread (*artos*) was used, that there was no lamb, that some of our Lord's followers carried arms (Mark 14[47]), the purchase of linen cloth and the burial (Mark 15[43-45]), the decision of Caiaphas and his party not to put Jesus to death " during the feast " (Mark 14[2]), etc. It is not possible here to examine in detail Jeremias's important book. He has certainly made it much more possible to hold the view that the Last Supper was a Passover Meal, even if some of his arguments are capable of refutation and he has not achieved positive proof. The question is, in fact, still an open one.

Other factors than the Jewish Passover *motif* and the institution of a New Covenant (Mark 14^{24}, 1 Cor. 11^{25}) doubtless entered into the thinking of the primitive Church about the Eucharist in the New Testament period. Our Lord partook of meals with his disciples and friends on many occasions other than the Last Supper (Mark 2^{15}, 14^{3}, Luke 14^{15}, John 2^{1-10}, 12^{2}, etc.). T. W. Manson remarked, " we have a long series of significant common meals, of which the Last Supper is in truth the last " (*Christian Worship*, ed. Micklem, p. 49). But was it the last ? Several appearances of Christ after the resurrection are associated with a meal (Luke $24^{30-35.\ 41-43}$, John 21^{9-13}), and fish is mentioned in some of these passages, as well as bread. It seems, then, that there was a series of Messianic banquets within the Kingdom, which the Eucharist was designed to perpetuate after the Messiah was ascended, " until he come " (1 Cor. 11^{26}).

Following Théo Preiss (in *Theol. Zeitschr.*, iv., (1948), pp. 81 ff.), who distinguished between the theological ideas inseparable from the Passover Meal and the liturgical Passover Meal itself and held that Jesus brought together the Paschal lamb *motif*, the eschatological expectations of the Passover and the expected Messianic feast in the kingdom of God, Bertil Gärtner (*John* 6 *and the Jewish Passover* (Coniectanea Neotestamentica, xvii.), 1959, pp. 45 ff.) has suggested that the Last Supper was a " lambless Passover meal " held on the night of 14 Nisan, *i.e.* the night before the official Passover, such as He had partaken in Galilee during the Passovers on which He did not travel up to Jerusalem. " When Jesus fed the 5,000 by the sea of Galilee," says Gärtner (*ibid.*, p. 49), " it was the Passover season, and John 6 in particular bears witness to the interpretation of the event in close connection with the Passover meal. Could the fish here mentioned be understood as one of the elements in a more freely organised Passover meal ? According to John 21, Jesus eats a meal with His disciples after the Resurrection ; the food mentioned was fish and bread (cf. Luke 24^{42}). Thus fish is found both in Jesus' feeding-miracle, which is connected with the Passover, and in table fellowship with the Risen Lord. . . . That would explain the close connection between fish and the Eucharist."

There is some evidence of the celebration of the Passover without a lamb in the Diaspora and also in Palestine outside Jerusalem. After A.D. 70 it was inevitable. There is also ample evidence from Capernaum ('Ain et-Tabigha) and from the Catacomb of Callistus in Rome that fish and bread are eucharistic symbols. These symbols continued in use in the

West right down to the fifteenth century (cf. R. L. P. Milburn, "Symbolism and Realism in Post-Nicene Representations of the Eucharist" in *JEH*, viii., 1957, pp. 1–16). Milburn asserts that "the paschal lamb, in place of the fish, occurs first perhaps in Italy, in the work of Duccio and his successors of the Sienese School" (*ibid.*, p. 16, n. 1). In Lutheran Scandinavia, and in Germany, the Passover scene, with a lamb on a platter, has formed the usual centre-piece to the reredos since the sixteenth century, but there must be some reason for the earlier persistence of the fish symbolism. There may, then, be some element of truth behind Gärtner's interesting speculations.

From the very beginning it was the custom of Christians to "break bread" together (Acts $2^{42, 46}$, 20^{7}), but this does not necessarily signify a celebration of the Eucharist. Paul certainly had the Eucharist in mind in 1 Cor. 10^{16-22}, 11^{17-34}. The *Didache* (9–10, 14) contains the earliest blessings said over bread and wine. Ignatius (*Smyrn.* 6) speaks of the Eucharist as "the flesh of our saviour Jesus Christ" and exhorts the Christians of Philadelphia: "Be ye careful to observe one Eucharist, for there is one flesh of our Lord Jesus Christ and one cup unto union in his blood; there is one altar, as there is one bishop" (*Philad.* 4). It is not, however, until we come to Justin Martyr (*c.* A.D. 150) that we get any clear description of the Sunday morning service of prayer, psalmody, Scripture lections and a homily—all derived directly from the Synagogue—followed by the Eucharist (1 *Apol.*, lxv.–lxvii.). Justin is describing the procedure at Rome, but we have to wait until Hippolytus's *Apostolic Tradition* (*c.* A.D. 215) for the earliest text of the Liturgy as it was celebrated at Rome—or, indeed, anywhere else. From later evidence from Syria and Egypt it seems that, just as the Church's organization was not evolved on precisely the same pattern in all churches at the same time, so it was with the Church's worship. And, after all, this is what we should expect to find. The Church is the "Body of Christ," which must continually grow "in wisdom and stature": it is a living organism, not a static corporation but a dynamic force. Her organization and her worship must, therefore, be flexible, capable of reformation and reorientation, of renewal and rebirth, for the individual Christian in his baptism dies with Christ (Rom. $6^{6, 8}$) and begins a new life, risen with Christ (Rom. $6^{11, 13}$); and the Church, which comprises all individual baptized Christians, must also "die daily in Christ Jesus" and continually learn to serve Him "in newness of the spirit, and not in oldness of the letter" (Rom. 7^{6}).

BIBLIOGRAPHY

(*in addition to works cited above*)

C. F. D. Moule, *The Birth of the New Testament*, 1962.
W. Telfer, *The Office of a Bishop*, 1962.
W. F. Flemington, *The New Testament Doctrine of Baptism*, 1948.
A. J. B. Higgins, *The Lord's Supper in the New Testament* (Studies in Biblical Theology No. 6), 1952.
A. Jaubert, *La Date de la Cène* (Études bibliques), 1957.
A. A. McArthur, *The Evolution of the Christian Year*, 1953.
G. R. Beasley-Murray, *Baptism in the New Testament*, 1962.

APPENDIX

TIME AND THE CALENDAR

THE simplest unit of time is the day. In the later parts of the Old Testament this ran from sunset to sunset (Gen. 1^{5}), but this was not always so (1 Sam. 28^{8,19}, 1 Kings 17^{6}). Frequently we have in the Bible only rough divisions into daybreak (Josh. 6^{15}, Matt. 28^{1}) or sunrise (Gen. 32^{31}, Mal. 1^{11}), midday (2 Sam. 4^{5}) or "the heat of the day" (Gen. 18^{1}), "the cool of the day" (Gen. 3^{8}), the time when "the day declines" (Judg. 19^{8}), dusk or "between the evenings" (Lev. 23^{5}), evening, night, and midnight (Ex. 11^{4}). The night was divided into three watches (Lam. 2^{19}, Judg. 7^{19}, Ex. 14^{24}). In the New Testament the Roman division into four watches was used (Matt. 14^{25}, Mark 13^{35}), though we also find the three-watch division (Luke 12^{38}). The division of the day into twelve hours (John 11^{9}) was perhaps borrowed from the Babylonians, though there is no trace of it in the Old Testament. In Mishnaic times the time of daylight appears to have been divided into twelve equal periods; hence the length of the hour was not constant. In the New Testament we have references to the third, sixth and ninth hours, and also to the seventh, tenth, and eleventh. In 2 Kings 20^{11} we have a reference to the "dial of Ahaz" as a means of measuring time.

For longer periods of month or year the difficulties arose from the fact that the lunar month is rather more than $29\frac{1}{2}$ days, while the year is rather less than $365\frac{1}{4}$ days. In the Gezer Calendar (see *Documents from Old Testament Times*, ed. by D. Winton Thomas, pp. 201 ff.) the year was divided into twelve according to the agricultural activities proper to them, and the oldest month-names in the Bible (Abib, Ziv, Ethanim, Bul) are probably to be explained agriculturally. Later the Jews adopted the Babylonian names for the months (Nisan, Sivan, Elul, Chislev, Tebeth, Shebat, Adar), though frequently the month is indicated simply by its number. In the Hellenistic period the months of the Macedonian calendar are reflected (Xanthicus, 2 Macc. 11^{30}; Dioscorinthius, 2 Macc. 11^{21}). Now 12 lunar months=354 days, so that the year of 12 lunar months is short of the solar year by $11\frac{1}{4}$ days. This was met by repeating a month from time to time, and so the months were kept in the same season of the year. When an extra month was required, the last month was repeated. The Babylonian names of the months (not all of which are found in the Old Testament) are :

Nisan (= Abib) = March-April.
Iyyar (= Ziv) = April-May.
Sivan = May-June.
Tammuz = June-July.
Ab = July-August.
Elul = August-September.
Tishri (= Ethanim) = September-October.
Marchesvan (= Bul) = October-November.
Chislev = November-December.
Tebeth = December-January.
Shebat = January-February.
Adar = February-March.

In the book of Jubilees and in the Qumran sect this calendar was rejected for one which contained exactly 52 weeks, in which feasts fell on the same day of the week every year, and Mlle. Jaubert has argued that the Last Supper was held on this sectarian date of Passover, and that this explains the difference between the Synoptic Gospels and the fourth Gospel. While this view has had some following, it has been rejected by a number of scholars.

In the Babylonian calendar the year begins in spring, whereas in the old Hebrew calendar the New Year occurred in the autumn. It seems that the division of the year into two parts, with new beginnings in Nisan and Tishri, goes back to the Sumerian origins of the system. At the beginning of the Christian era the Jews observed both days, 1 Nisan being the beginning of the ecclesiastical year and 1 Tishri the beginning of the civil year (Josephus, *Ant.* I. iii. 3 [81]). The later Jewish calendar, still in use, reckons from 1 Tishri.

The week is an artificial unit of time, whose origin still presents problems. The nearest analogy is the Assyrian system of Ashurbanipal, ordaining as days of rest the 7th, 14th, 19th, 21st, and 28th of the month. The 19th day, which was the 49th from the beginning of the previous month, was a kind of *dies nefastus*. Leaving it aside, we have the seven-day week. But the weeks do not go on continuously. There is a break of one or two days at the end of the fourth week, so that the beginning of the next month should coincide with the first day of a new week. In the Biblical system this rule is no longer observed ; the weeks continue in a regular cycle without regard to the new moon, and the first day of the month may fall on any day of the week. Equally the seventh day of the week, the day of rest, may fall on any day of the month. Snaith has argued (*The Jewish Near Year Festival,* 1947, pp. 103 ff.) that the sabbath was originally the day of the new moon, and not a weekly day of rest. It is significant, however, that the Ritual Decalogue, whose antiquity is generally recognized, makes it clear that it fell every seventh day (Ex. 34^{21}).

This rest-day is, along with circumcision, a fundamental observance of Judaism. Its origin presents difficult problems. In Babylonian the 15th of the month is called *shapattu* or *shabattu* ; but it is not a day of rest. In Babylonia there is the interdiction of work on the seventh day, but it is not called sabbath. In the Old Testament the two things have somehow been combined, and the name *shabattu* transferred to the weekly day of rest. How this happened is unknown. It is to be noted that the sabbath is a whole day running from sunset on Friday to sunset on Saturday.

The year is marked by the recurrence of the annual festivals. The Ritual Decalogue says " Three times in the year shall all your males appear before the Lord " (Ex. 34^{23}), and the reference would appear to be to the feast of unleavened bread (v.^{18}) and the feasts of weeks and of ingathering at the year's end (v.^{22}). In addition the feast of passover is mentioned (v^{25}). The latter, which fell on Nisan 14 was later combined with unleavened bread, which ran from Nisan 15 to 21. The festal calendar in Lev. 23 gives the following, in addition to the weekly sabbath : passover, unleavened bread, firstfruits (Pentecost or Weeks), day of remembrance (New Year's Day in the seventh month, or Tishri), the day of atonement, booths (or Tabernacles). At a later date other feasts and fasts were added, so that we get the following calendar (Thackeray, *The Septuagint and Jewish Worship*, p. 137) :

Nisan 1	Ecclesiastical New Year.
,, 14–21	Passover and Unleavened Bread.
Sivan *c.* 6	Weeks (Pentecost).
Tammuz 17	Fast. (Babylonian capture of Jerusalem.)
Ab 9	Fast. (Burning of the Temple.)
Elul 1	New Year for tithes.
Tishri 1	Civil New Year.
,, 3	Fast of Gedaliah.
,, 10	Day of Atonement.
,, 15–22	Tabernacles and eighth day.
Chislev 25 to Tebeth 2	Dedication (Hanukkah).
Tebeth 10	Fast. (Beginning of Babylonian siege of Jerusalem.)
Adar 14–15	Purim.

In addition to the fasts in the calendar further public fasts could be decreed by the authorities in any time of national distress or danger ; and among the Pharisees there grew up the practice of regular private fasts twice a week (on Mondays and Thursdays). Cf. Luke 18^{12}.

The sabbatical year, in which no agricultural work was

permitted and the land lay fallow, was observed every seventh year in the post-exilic period (cf. Lev. 25^{1-7}, 1 Macc. $6^{49, 53}$, Jos. *Ant.* XIV. xvi. 2 [475] (with which cf. Lev. $26^{34ff.}$), Ex. $23^{10ff.}$). The sabbatical year ran from autumn (1 Tishri) to autumn. There is evidence that it was observed in 164–3 B.C., 38–7 B.C., and A.D. 68–9. From these fixed points it is easy to calculate the intervening sabbatical years. The year of jubilee (Lev. 25^{8-55}, 27^{17-25}, Num. 36^{4}) should be observed after every seventh sabbatical year, *i.e.* every fiftieth year. It appears to have been calculated but not observed.

CHRONOLOGY

THE simplest method of dating an event is by placing it before or after another: the prophetic ministry of Amos is dated "two years before the earthquake," and doubtless the earthquake was a well-remembered event when the note of time was written. More convenient points of reference are provided by the regnal years of kings. The chronology of the kings of Israel and Judah is set out in this way: Jehoram became king of Israel in the eighteenth year of Jehoshaphat of Judah and he reigned twelve years (2 Kings 3^{1}); in Jehoram's eleventh year Ahaziah became king of Judah (2 Kings 9^{29}); and so on. From such data as these a relative chronology can be constructed, showing the order of events in the period and the intervals between them. An absolute chronology is obtained when we are able to measure the interval between the present time and these dated events in the past. For this purpose a fixed point is required from which there may be continuous reckoning by years. The oldest system of this kind is the Seleucid era, whose epoch is 1st October 312 B.C. Given a date in the Seleucid era it is a simple matter to reduce it to a date B.C. or A.D. For the earlier times fixed points can be obtained where astronomical events have been recorded, *e.g.* the eclipse of the sun in the reign of Ashur-dan III. of Assyria, which is calculated as having happened on 15th June 763 B.C. With the help of such data it is possible to construct a chronological table, in which some dates may be regarded as fairly certain, others as probably correct within a few years, others as still uncertain. The Biblical data for the period of the divided monarchy are not always easy to reconcile with one another, and there is diversity of view amongst scholars who have examined them. The following table of the more important events can therefore be regarded as only approximate at a number of points.

B.C.	
c. 1250–30.	The Exodus from Egypt.
c. 1225–00.	Israel's entry into Canaan, followed by the period of the Judges.
c. 1180.	Philistine entry into Palestine.
c. 1025.	Saul.
c. 1010.	David.
c. 970.	Solomon.
c. 930.	Break-up of Solomon's kingdom.

[The Old Testament fixes the relative chronology of the subsequent period by giving the length of each king's reign and the year of his accession in terms of the regnal years of his neighbour. Here length of reign is given in brackets after the name and accession year in roman numerals.]

	JUDAH	ISRAEL
	Rehoboam (17).	Jeroboam I (22).
	Abijam (3).	XVIII
	Asa (41).	XX
	II	Nadab (2).
	III	Baasha (24).
	XXVI	Elah (2).
	XXVII	Zimri, Tibni.
c. 885.	XXXI	Omri (12).
c. 874.	XXXVIII	Ahab (22).
	Jehoshaphat (25).	IV
		Prophetic ministry of Elijah and Micaiah ben Imlah.
853.	Battle of Karkar.	
	XVII	Ahaziah (1).
	XVIII (2 Kings 3^1).	Jehoram (12).
c. 850.	Composition of J.	Revolt of Mesha of Moab.
	Jehoram (8).	V
	Ahaziah (1).	XII
		Prophetic ministry of Elisha.
841.	Athaliah (6).	Jehu (by revolution).
		Jehu pays tribute to Assyria.
	Jehoash (40).	VII
	XXIII	Jehoahaz (17).
805.	Damascus subdued by Adad-Nirari III. of Assyria.	
	XXXVII	Jehoash (16).
c. 800–750.		Composition of E.
	Amaziah (29).	II
c. 785.	Azariah (Uzziah) (52).	Jeroboam II. (41).
c. 760.		Prophetic ministry of Amos.
	(Jotham co-regent from *c.* 755.)	
	XXXVIII	Zechariah (½).
	XXXIX	Shallum (1 month), Menahem (10).
c. 740–22.		Prophetic ministry of Hosea.
738.		Menahem pays tribute to Assyria.
	L	Pekahiah (2).
	Prophetic ministry of Isaiah and Micah.	

B.C.	JUDAH	ISRAEL
	LII	Pekah (by revolution).
	Jotham (alone).	
c. 735.	Ahaz.	II
734–3.	Syro-Ephraimite attack on Judah and Assyrian defeat of Damascus and Samaria. Ahaz vassal of Assyria.	
732.	Fall of Damascus.	Hoshea.
727.	Hezekiah (29) (Biblical chronology very confused here).	
724.		Assyrian invasion of Israel and siege of Samaria.
721.	VI	Fall of Samaria. End of northern kingdom.
711.	Rebellion in Philistia. Assyrians capture Ashdod.	
c. 696.	Manasseh (55).	
c. 675.	Manasseh vassal of Assyria.	
c. 640.	Amon (2).	
c. 639.	Josiah (31).	
c. 626.	Prophetic ministry of Zephaniah and (626–c. 586) Jeremiah.	
621.	Josiah's reform.	
614.	Ashur sacked by Medes.	
612.	Fall of Nineveh. Prophecy of Nahum.	
610.	Fall of Harran.	
608.	Battle of Megiddo and death of Josiah.	
	Jehoahaz (three months).	
	Jehoiakim (11).	
605.	Battle of Carchemish.	
c. 600.	Revolt of Jehoiakim.	
597.	Jehoiachin (three months). Jerusalem captured. First deportation.	
	Zedekiah (11).	
593–86.	Prophetic ministry of Ezekiel (Ezek. 1–32).	
	Zedekiah's revolt.	
586.	Fall of Jerusalem. Second deportation.	
c. 584–72.	Ezekiel 33–39. Ezekiel 40–48 after 572.	
581.	Third deportation.	
c. 550.	Deutero-Isaiah.	
539.	Capture of Babylon by Cyrus.	
538–7.	Return of Jewish exiles.	
521–16.	Building of second Temple. Ministry of Haggai (520) and and Zechariah (520–18).	
c. 460.	Malachi.	
c. 445.	Nehemiah's return.	
c. 432.	Nehemiah's second visit to Jerusalem.	
c. 400.	Composition of Job.	
398.	Return of exiles under Ezra (some scholars place in 458).	
397.	Ezra's reading of the Law (some scholars place in 444).	
c. 350.	Samaritan schism.	
334–30.	Alexander's campaigns against Persia.	
332.	Alexander's conquest of Judaea.	
330.	Death of Darius.	
323.	Death of Alexander.	

B.C.

c. 319. Palestine under Egyptian rule (Ptolemy).
312. Seleucus establishes himself at Babylon.
301. Battle of Ipsus.
300. Foundation of Antioch.
c. 300. Composition of Chronicles, Ezra, Nehemiah.
c. 250. Ecclesiastes.
223–187. Antiochus III. (the Great).
217. Battle of Raphia.
c. 200. Palestine passes to Seleucid empire.
176–5. Accession of Antiochus IV. (Epiphanes).
168. Profanation of the Temple.
c. 166. Composition of Daniel.
165. Rededication of the Temple.
160. Death of Judas Maccabaeus.
152. Jonathan appointed High Priest.
143 (end). Death of Jonathan.
142. Jewish autonomy under Simon, High Priest and Ethnarch.
135–4. Death of Simon and accession of John Hyrcanus.
104. Death of John Hyrcanus and accession of Aristobulus I.
103. Alexander Jannaeus, High Priest and King.
76. Alexandra Salome.
67–3. Civil war between Hyrcanus II. and Aristobulus II.
63. Surrender of Jerusalem to Pompey. Judaea under Roman control.
63–40. Hyrcanus II.
40–37. Antigonus Mattathias.
37. Herod captures Jerusalem.
27–A.D. 14. AUGUSTUS.
20–19. Building of Herod's Temple begun.
4. Death of Herod. His kingdom divided between :
Herod Antipas, Tetrarch of Galilee and Peraea, 4 B.C.–A.D. 39.
Herod Philip II., Tetrarch of Batanaea, Trachonitis, etc., 4 B.C.–A.D. 34.
Herod Archelaus, Ethnarch of Judaea, Idumaea and Samaria, 4 B.C.–A.D. 6.

A.D.

14–37. TIBERIUS.
26. Pontius Pilate becomes Procurator of Judaea.
c. 28–9. Beginning of John the Baptist's ministry.
[The date of the Crucifixion presents an unsolved, probably insoluble, problem. The dates chiefly favoured are 29 (C. H. Turner, art. " Chronology " in Hastings' *Dictionary of the Bible*), 30 (H. von Soden (art. " Chronology " in *Encyclopaedia Biblica*), and 33 (J. K. Fotheringham, in *Journal of Theological Studies*, XXXV., 1934, 146–62).]
37–41. GAIUS (Caligula).
37. Herod Agrippa I., ruler of Ituraea and Trachonitis.
40. Herod Agrippa I., ruler of Galilee.
41. Herod Agrippa I., ruler of Judaea and Samaria (died 44).
41–54. CLAUDIUS.
c. 46. Famine in Judaea (Acts 11).
49–50. Paul's arrival in Corinth.
50–100. Herod Agrippa II.
51–2. Gallio Proconsul of Achaea.
52–60(?). Antonius Felix Procurator of Judaea.
54–68. NERO.

A.D.
60(?)–62. Porcius Festus, Procurator of Judaea.
64. Great fire at Rome and Persecution of Christians by Nero.
66. Outbreak of Jewish War.
68–9. Civil wars following death of Nero.
69–79. VESPASIAN.
70. Fall of Jerusalem.
79–81. TITUS.
81–96. DOMITIAN.
c. 96. Persecution of Christians. Letter from Roman Church to Corinthian (1 Clement).
96–98. NERVA.
98–117. TRAJAN.
c. 107. Martyrdom of Symeon of Jerusalem.
112. Persecution of Bithynian Christians by Pliny.
c. 115. Martyrdom of Ignatius.
115–17. Jewish revolt in Cyrene, Cyprus, and Mesopotamia.
117–38. HADRIAN.
132–5. Jewish revolt under Bar Cochba.
135. Jerusalem destroyed and rebult as *Aelia Capitolina.*

WEIGHTS, MEASURES, AND MONEY

Length :

4 Fingerbreadths (*'eṣba'*) (Jer. 52^{21})	= 1 Handbreadth (*ṭōphaḥ*) (Ex. 25^{25}).
3 Handbreadths	= 1 Span (*zereth*) (Ex. 28^{16}).
2 Spans	= 1 Cubit (*'ammāh*) (frequent)
6 Cubits	= 1 Reed (*ḳāneh*) (Ezek. 40^{5}).
2000 Cubits	= 1 Sabbath day's journey.

The cubit is a variable unit. In Babylonia, Egypt and Israel there were two standards, the common cubit and the " royal " or " holy," which is $\frac{1}{6}$ greater than the common. The Babylonian common cubit is reckoned at 49·5 cm. (*c.* 19·5 in.), the Egyptian at 45 cm. (*c.* 17·7 in.) ; the Babylonian " royal " at 55 cm. (*c.* 21·6 in.), the Egyptian at 52·5 cm. (*c.* 20·7 in.).

In Judges 3^{16} the length of Ehud's sword is given as a *gōmedh*, which is not mentioned elsewhere. It is thought to be a short cubit (so EV), but LXX renders by the same word as span.

The " furlong " (Luke 24^{13}) is also variable : the shorter " furlong " 202 to 209 yds., the longer about 228 yds. The (Roman) mile (Matt. 5^{41}) is reckoned at 1478 metres, or *c.* 1617 yds. The fathom (*orguia,* Acts 27^{28}) is slightly more than 6 ft.

Capacity :

(Dry)

6 Kabs (2 Kings 6^{25})	= 1 Seah (2 Kings 7^{1}, R.S.V. " measure ").
3 Seahs	= 1 Ephah (Judges 6^{19}).
10 Ephahs	= 1 Homer (Isa. 5^{10}) or Cor (1 Kings 4^{22}, R.S.V. " measure " ; in Ezek. 45^{14} a liquid measure).

(Liquid)

12 Logs (Lev. 14^{10})	= 1 Hin (Ezek. 45^{24}).
6 Hins	= 1 Bath (Isa. 5^{10}).

The ephah contains *c.* $\frac{5}{8}$ bushel, and the bath *c.* 5 gals. The *'omer* (Ex. 16^{36}) or *'issārôn* (Ex. 29^{40}, R.S.V. " tenth part ") = $\frac{1}{10}$ ephah, and the lethech (Hos. 3^{2} R.S.V.) = $\frac{1}{2}$ homer so (R.V.).

Measures mentioned in the New Testament are the *xestēs* (Mark 7^{4}, R.S.V. " pots ") = *sextarius* = *c.* 0·96 pint ; the *choinix* (Rev. 6^{6}, R.S.V. " quart ") = *c.* 1·92 pints ; the *modios* (Matt. 5^{15}, R.S.V. " bushel ") = *c.* 1·92 gals. ; the *saton* (seah)

(Matt. 13^{33}, Luke 13^{21}, R.S.V. " measure ") = *c.* 2·66 gals. ; the *koros* (Luke 16^{7}, R.S.V. " measure ") = cor = 79·8 gals. ; the *batos* (Luke 16^{6}, R.S.V. " measure ") = bath = *c.* 7·98 gals. ; the *metrētēs* (John 2^{6}, R.S.V. " ten gallons," R.V. " firkin ") = *c.* 8·66 gals.

Weights. The Israelite system in its earliest form is closely allied to the Babylonian, which was sexagesimal :

60 Shekels = 1 Mina.
60 Minas = 1 Talent.

In Israel, however, at a later time 50 shekels went to the mina (Ezek. 45^{12}) and the table became :

20 Gerahs (Ex. 30^{13}) = 1 Shekel.
50 Shekels = 1 Mina (*māneh*) (Ezek. 45^{12}).
60 Minas = 1 Talent (*kikkār*) (Ex. 25^{39}).

The average weight of Israelite shekels which have been found is 11·42 gr. = 0·42 oz. The *beka'* (Gen. 24^{22}) = $\frac{1}{2}$ shekel (so R.S.V.), and the pim (1 Sam. 13^{21} R.S.V.) = $\frac{2}{3}$ shekel. In the New Testament the *litra* = Lat. *libra* (John 12^{3}, 19^{39}, R.S.V. " pound ") = *c.* 11$\frac{1}{2}$ oz.

Money. The oldest Palestinian coins are Persian darics (1 Chron. 29^{7}), which circulated all over the East in the Persian period. The daric was a gold coin of 8·36 gm. or 129 gr. There was a silver coin = $\frac{1}{20}$ daric (Neh. 5^{15}, R.S.V. " shekel of silver," 86·4 gr.). In the Persian period Judah had a provincial silver coinage of its own. To this coinage is assigned the British Museum specimen (*Catalogue*, Plate XIX. No. 29), on which is the word YHD (Judah). Coins of Alexander the Great, the Ptolemies, and the Seleucids also circulated in Palestine, as did the coins of Tyre and Sidon. In 139–8 B.C. Simon Maccabaeus obtained the right to mint his own coinage. Bronze coins of the Hasmonaeans are known, but no silver coins have survived. Jewish silver shekels and half-shekels of the time of the War of A.D. 66–70 are known (weight of shekel 220·18 gr.). A second series of silver shekels and quarter-shekels was struck during the Bar Cochba revolt of A.D. 132–5. For the rest the native coinage was in bronze only.

For the payment of the Temple tax of half a shekel the money had to be of the Phoenician heavy standard (shekel = 224·4 gr.). For ordinary purposes much foreign money was in circulation. The standard Roman coin was the *denarius* (*dēnarion*, Matt. 20^{2}, R.V. " penny," R.S.V. " denarius "), a silver coin of 60 gr. (rather more than $\frac{2}{3}$ of the weight of a shilling). It was a day's wage for an agricultural labourer ; the Roman legionary got $\frac{5}{8}$ denarius per day. The *assarion* (Matt. 10^{29}, Luke 12^{6}, R.V. " penny," R.V. " farthing ") is probably to be reckoned as $\frac{1}{24}$ denarius ; the *lepton* (Mark 12^{42}, Luke 12^{59}, 21^{2}, R.V. " mite," R.S.V. " copper ") is $\frac{1}{24}$ denarius. The *kodrantēs* (Matt. 5^{26}, Mark 12^{42}, R.V. " farthing," R.S.V. " penny ") is the Roman *quadrans* $= \frac{1}{64}$ denarius. It does not seem to have been in circulation in Palestine in New Testament times.

BIBLIOGRAPHY

Calendar and Chronology :

Relevant articles in Encyclopaedias and Bible Dictionaries.

J. K. Fotheringham, " The Calendar," in *Nautical Almanac*, 1935, pp. 754–70.

J. van Goudoever, *Biblical Calendars*, 1959.

A. Jaubert, *La date de la Cène*, 1957.

S. Langdon, *Babylonian Menologies and the Semitic Calendars*, 1933.

J. B. Segal, " Intercalation and the Hebrew Calendar," in *Vetus Testamentum*, vii., 1957, pp. 250–307.

E. R. Thiele, *The Mysterious Numbers of the Hebrew Kings*, 1951.

Weights, Measures, and Money :

Relevant articles in Encyclopaedias and Bible Dictionaries.

A.-G. Barrois, *Manuel d'archéologie biblique*, ii, 1953.

G. F. Hill, *Catalogue of the Greek Coins of Palestine* (British Museum), 1914.

H. Lewy, " Assyro-Babylonian and Israelite Measures of Capacity and Rates of Seeding," in *Journal of American Oriental Society*, lxiv., 1944, 65–73.

F. W. Madden, *Coins of the Jews*, 1881.

A. Reifenberg, *Ancient Jewish Coins*, 2nd ed., 1947.

A. Reifenberg, *Israel's History in Coins from the Maccabees to the Roman Conquest*, 1953.

R. B. Y. Scott, " Weights and Measures of the Bible," in *Biblical Archaeologist*, xxii., 1959, pp. 22–39.

INDEXES

I. SCRIPTURE REFERENCES

(including Apocrypha and Pseudepigrapha)

OLD TESTAMENT

Genesis:

1 . . 28, 536
1^{5} . . . 570
$1^{26f.}$ . . . 29
1^{27} . . . 431
2 . . . 28
2 f. . . . 536
2^{7} . . . 29
2^{8} . . . 29
$2^{19f.}$ . . . 11
$2^{21f.}$ . . . 29
$2^{23f.}$ . . . 431
$3^{1ff.}$ . . . 127
3^{8} . . 29, 570
3^{21} . . . 29
$4^{3f.}$ . . . 525
4^{4} . . . 529
$4^{23f.}$ . . 35, 125
4^{26} . . 338, 525
6^{1-4} . . . 128
6^{11}–8^{22} . . . 128
$6^{19ff.}$ . . . 28
$7^{2f.}$ . . . 28
$7^{8f.}$ . . . 28
7^{12} . . . 28
7^{16} . . . 29
7^{24} . . . 28
8^{20} . . . 525
8^{21} . . . 29
9^{4} . . . 384
9^{24-27} . . . 127
9^{25-27} . . . 35
11 . . . 11
11^{31} . . . 335
12 . . . 286
12^{3} . . . 345
12^{6} . . . 27
12^{7} . . . 524
12^{8} . . . 524
$12^{10ff.}$ . . . 28
13^{3} . . . 524
13^{7} . . . 27
13^{18} . . . 524
14^{13} . . . 11
14^{14} . . . 27
$14^{18f.}$ . . . 337
$14^{19f.}$ . . . 35
14^{22} . . 337, 525
15^{1} . . . 336
15^{2} . . . 28
15^{7} . . . 28
15^{8} . . . 28
15^{18} . . . 34
16^{2} . . . 28
$16^{6ff.}$ . . . 28
16^{13} . . . 337
16^{33} . . . 525
17 . . . 127
17^{1} . . 28, 525
17^{12} . . . 561
18 . . . 283
18^{1} . . . 570
18^{14} . . . 28
19^{13} . . . 28
$19^{30ff.}$ . . . 127
$20^{1ff.}$ . . . 28
20^{3} . . . 29
$21^{10ff.}$ . . 28, 260
21^{17} . . . 30
21^{31} . . . 27
21^{53} . . 337, 525
22 . . . 532
22^{11} . . . 30
22^{16} . . . 472
24^{22} . . . 579
24^{31} . . . 28
24^{60} . . 36, 126
$25^{19ff.}$ . . . 127
25^{23} . . 36, 130
26 . . . 286
26^{12} . . . 525
26^{23-25} . . . 127
26^{24} . . . 336
26^{25} . . . 524
26^{33} . . . 27
27 . . . 31
27^{27-29} . . . 131
$27^{27ff.}$ . . . 36
$27^{39f.}$ . . 36, 131
28^{10-12} . . . 542
28^{10-22} . . 127, 524
28^{12} . . . 29 f.
28^{13} . . 28, 336
28^{18} . . . 525
28^{19} . . . 28
29^{31}–30^{24} . . . 124
$29^{33f.}$ . . . 534
31^{5} . . . 336
31^{11} . . . 30
31^{11-24} . . . 30
31^{13} . . 337, 525
31^{19} . . 525, 543
31^{29} . . . 336
31^{30} . . . 525
31^{32-35} . . . 260
$31^{34f.}$ . . . 543
31^{42} . . 336, 525
$31^{44f.}$ . . . 542
$31^{44ff.}$ . . . 34
31^{44-52} . . . 126
31^{47} . . . 17
31^{49} . . . 126
31^{50} . . . 126
31^{53} . . . 336
31^{54} . . . 525
32^{1} . . . 30
32^{3b-5} . . . 129
32^{9} . . . 336
32^{22-32} . . . 127
32^{28} . . . 28
32^{31} . . . 570
33^{4} . . . 543
34 . . 287, 292, 339
34^{25-31} . . . 534
35^{1-7} . . . 524
35^{1-14} . . . 347
35^{2-4} . . . 525
35^{7} . . . 337
$35^{9ff.}$ . . . 30
35^{10} . . . 28
35^{11} . . . 28
35^{14} . . . 525
35^{15} . . . 28
35^{17} . . . 124
$36^{31ff.}$ . . 27, 296
36^{31-39} . . . 257
37 . . . 128
$37^{5, 9}$ . . . 30
$37^{27, 28b}$ . . . 28
37^{28a} . . . 28
37^{36} . . . 28
39–45 . . . 128
39^{1} . . . 28
39^{7-19} . . . 209
40^{5} . . . 30
40^{15} . . . 11
41^{1} . . . 30
41^{43} . . . 18

GENESIS—(*continued*)
41^{45} . . . 18, 88
46^{1} . . . 525
46^{13} . . . 336
46^{20} . . . 88
47^{3} . . . 283
48 . . . 31
48^{14-16} . . . 131
48^{15} . . . 336
$48^{15f.}$ . . . 36
49 . 36, 83, 295, 534
49^{5-7} . . . 339
49^{7} . . . 36
49^{12} . . . 36
49^{24} . . . 336
$49^{24f.}$ . . . 336
50 . . . 31
50^{17} . . . 336

EXODUS:
1^{11} . . . 287
$2^{11f.}$ . . . 340
2^{13-15} . . . 340
2^{17} . . . 340
3 . . . 338 f.
$3^{7f.}$ . . 422, 430
3^{14} . . . 340
3^{15} . . . 31
$4^{22f.}$ . . 422, 470
$4^{24ff.}$ . . . 127
6 . . . 30
$6^{2f.}$ . . 28, 30
$6^{2ff.}$ . . . 339
11^{4} . . . 570
12^{34} . . . 537
12^{48} . . . 562
13^{8} . . . 537
14^{13} . . . 341
14^{24} . . . 570
15 . . . 545
15^{1} . . . 341
15^{1-18} . . 125, 133
15^{1-19} . . . 36
15^{11} . . . 523
15^{17} . . . 37
15^{21} . 36, 125, 341
16^{22-30} . . . 343
16^{36} . . . 578
17^{16} . . 36, 125
18^{12} . . . 532
19–24 . . . 129
20^{1-17} . . 129, 422
20^{2} . . 418, 422
20^{2-17} . . . 419
20^{3} . . . 355
20^{7} . . . 340
20^{10} . . . 344
20^{12} . . . 422
20^{16} . . . 422
20^{17} . . . 422
20^{23}–23^{33} . 129, 252, 343, 422
20^{24} . . . 29
20^{24-26} . . . 33
21^{1}–22^{16} . . . 129
$21^{2ff.}$ . . . 29
21^{7} . . . 29
$21^{12. 15. 16. 17}$. 129
$22^{21-24. 25-27}$. 422
22^{26} . . . 265
23^{6} . . . 422
23^{7} . . . 512
$23^{10ff.}$ . . . 573
23^{14-17} . . . 365
23^{16} . . . 346
23^{17} . . . 133
25–31 . . 28, 344
25–40 . . . 129
25^{9} . . . 422
25^{10-31} . . . 130
25^{25} . . . 578
25^{39} . . . 579
26^{7-15} . . . 130
26^{29-37} . . . 130
27^{1-8} . . . 130
28^{1} . . . 29
28^{16} . . . 578
29 . . . 530
29^{38-41} . . . 539
29^{40} . . . 578
$30^{11ff.}$ . . . 34
30^{13} . . . 579
32 . . . 345
32^{5} . . . 544
32^{25-29} . . . 339
32^{30-34} . . . 345
33^{7-11} . . 28, 344
33^{19} . . . 340
34^{7} . . . 513
34^{18} . . . 572
34^{21} . . . 572
34^{22} . . 346, 572
$34^{22f.}$ . . . 365
34^{23} . . . 572
34^{25} . . . 572
35–40 . . 28, 344
35^{21-29} . . . 129

LEVITICUS:
1 . . . 526
1–4 . . . 130
1^{2} . . . 531
$1^{3f.}$ . . . 527
1^{10-14} . . . 527
1^{14-17} . . . 527
2^{14} . . . 275
$3^{9f.}$ . . . 530
3^{11} . . 527, 530
$3^{16f.}$ . . . 527
3^{17} . . . 527
$4^{f.}$ . . . 529
4^{1-21} . . . 529
$4^{6f.}$ . . . 530
4^{22-26} . . . 529
4^{27-31} . . . 529
4^{31} . . . 528
5^{7-10} . . . 529
5^{14-26} . . . 530
5^{17} . . . 530
5^{18} . . . 531
6^{1-7} . . . 530
6^{26} . . . 530
6^{30} . . . 530
7^{1-7} . . . 530
7^{7} . . . 530
$7^{12f.}$ . . . 529
$7^{15f.}$ . . . 529
$7^{22ff.}$ . . . 530
7^{22-25} . . . 527
$7^{26f.}$ . . . 527
7^{30} . . . 528
7^{33} . . . 528
10^{16} . . . 146
11^{42} . . . 146
13^{13} . . . 146
14^{10} . . . 578
14^{31} . . . 529
17–26 . 35, 129, 425
19 . . . 419
$19^{9f.}$ . . . 425
19^{9-17} . . . 425
19^{13} . . . 425
$19^{17f.}$ . . . 425
19^{18} . 386, 419, 475, 487
19^{32} . . . 425
19^{32-36} . . . 425
$19^{33f.}$ . . . 425
23 . . . 572
23^{5} . . . 570
23^{36} . . . 29
23^{43} . . . 537
25^{1-7} . . . 573
25^{8-55} . . . 573
26^{1} . . . 542
$26^{34ff.}$ . . . 573
27^{17-25} . . . 573

NUMBERS:
1^{49-53} . . . 29
2 . . . 29
3 f. . . . 29
$5^{7f.}$ . . . 531
$6^{24ff.}$ . . . 36
6^{24-26} . . . 131
8^{19} . . . 528
$10^{35f.}$. 36, 125, 344
11 . . . 345
11^{12} . . . 345
11^{16-30} . . . 29
12^{4} . . . 29
12^{6-8} . . . 36
13 f. . . . 29, 33
13^{21} . . . 29
13^{22} . . . 29
13^{27} . . . 29
13^{29} . . . 257
13^{30} . . . 29

NUMBERS—(*continued*)
$14^{6f.}$ . . . 29
$14^{8f.}$ . . . 29
14^{24} . . . 29
14^{30} . . . 29
15^{37-41} . . . 428, 545
18^{21-33} . . . 54
20^{14-19} . . . 129
21^{14} . . . 125
$21^{14f.}$ . . . 35
$21^{17f.}$ . . . 35, 124
$21^{27ff.}$ . . . 35
21^{27-30} . . . 125
$22^{21ff.}$ . . . 127
23 f. . . . 36
24^{9b} . . . 131
24^{20} . . . 36
$24^{21f.}$ . . . 36
$24^{23f.}$ . . . 36
28^{9} . . . 539
31^{32-47} . . . 129
32 . . . 36
36^{4} . . . 573

DEUTERONOMY:
1–4 . . . 35
1^{1}–4^{43} . . . 129
$1^{24. 36}$ . . . 33
5–11 . . . 35, 129
5^{6-21} . . . 129
5^{11} . . . 340
5^{14} . . . 344
$5^{14f.}$ . . . 425
6^{4} . . . 386
$6^{4ff.}$ . . . 248
6^{4-9} . . . 428, 545
6^{5} . . . 386, 419, 487
6^{20} . . . 127
6^{20-25} . . . 537
10^{1-5} . . . 541
10^{12} . . . 425
$11^{10f.}$ . . . 199
11^{13-21} . . . 428, 545
12–26 . . . 35, 129, 356
12–28 . . . 419
12^{14} . . . 29
$12^{15f.}$ . . . 527
14^{29} . . . 425
15^{12} . . . 29
16^{1-8} . . . 343
16^{11} . . . 425
16^{12} . . . 425
16^{13} . . . 34
16^{14} . . . 425
16^{15} . . . 29
16^{16} . . . 133
16^{18} . . . 425
16^{20} . . . 425
18^{7} . . . 29, 32
18^{15} . . . 354, 362
18^{18} . . . 112
19^{18-21} . . . 78
21^{23} . . . 513
23^{24}–24^{3} . . . 278
24^{1} . . . 478
24^{10-13} . . . 265
24^{18-21} . . . 425
24^{22} . . . 425
25^{1-3} . . . 278
25^{9} . . . 61
25^{15} . . . 425
26 . . . 284
26^{5-10} . . . 537
26^{5-11} . . . 346
26^{12} . . . 278
$26^{12f.}$ . . . 425
26^{17-19} . . . 278
27 . . . 276
27^{15-26} . . . 130
28 . . . 35
28^{1-19} . . . 131
28^{5-10} . . . 537
28^{31-33} . . . 278
31^{9-13} . . . 342
32 . . . 36, 545
32^{4} . . . 425
33 . . . 36, 295, 534
33^{8} . . . 532
33^{8-11} . . . 348
33^{10} . . . 532
33^{29} . . . 429
34 . . . 27, 345
34^{6} . . . 444
34^{10} . . . 354

JOSHUA:
2–7 . . . 39
3^{17} . . . 38
4^{8-20} . . . 38
4^{9} . . . 38
4^{11} . . . 38
$5^{2ff.}$ . . . 127
6^{15} . . . 570
6^{17-19} . . . 258
6^{26} . . . 34
9 . . . 347
9^{15} . . . 129
9^{27} . . . 38
10 . . . 38, 127
10^{13} . . . 34, 38
$10^{26. 37}$ . . . 38
11^{7} . . . 189
13^{4} . . . 257
13^{13} . . . 38
14^{12} . . . 38
15–19 . . . 129
15^{13-19} . . . 38
15^{14} . . . 38
15^{63} . . . 38
16^{10} . . . 38
17^{11} . . . 204
$17^{11-13. 16-18}$ . . . 38
19^{1} . . . 534
19^{2-7} . . . 534
19^{47} . . . 38
23 f. . . . 38
23^{2-16} . . . 128
24 . . . 39, 284, 294 f., 324, 346
$24^{2ff.}$ . . . 127
24^{2-13} . . . 346, 537
24^{2-15} . . . 128
24^{15} . . . 336, 347
24^{23} . . . 347

JUDGES:
1 . . . 38, 293
1^{1}–2^{5} . . . 39
1^{2} . . . 130
1^{3} . . . 534
$1^{9ff.}$ . . . 260
1^{22-26} . . . 128
2^{6}–16^{31} . . . 39
3^{15} . . . 529
3^{15}–16^{31} . . . 127
3^{16} . . . 578
5 . . . 40, 125, 294
5^{11} . . . 424
5^{15b-17} . . . 125
6^{19} . . . 578
$6^{33ff.}$ . . . 190
7 . . . 294
7^{8b} . . . 125
7^{19} . . . 570
7^{20b} . . . 125
$8^{22f.}$ . . . 350
9^{7-15} . . . 126
9^{7-21} . . . 297
10 . . . 295
11 . . . 296
11^{34} . . . 125, 472
11^{34-40} . . . 532
12 . . . 295
12^{6} . . . 13
14^{12-18} . . . 125
14^{14} . . . 133
15^{16} . . . 125
16^{28} . . . 129
17 f. . . . 39
17–21 . . . 39
17^{5} . . . 533, 543
17^{7} . . . 534
18 . . . 38
18^{6} . . . 124
18^{7} . . . 187
18^{14} . . . 543
18^{29} . . . 27
18^{31} . . . 533
19–21 . . . 29, 295
19^{1} . . . 534
19^{8} . . . 570
21^{12} . . . 126

RUTH:
1^{17} . . . 126
2^{4} . . . 124
4^{9} . . . 61
4^{11} . . . 126

1 Samuel:
1^{3} . . . 133
1^{9-18} . . . 366
1^{18} . . . 38
1^{19-27} . . . 42
2^{12-17} . . . 528
2^{17} . . . 529
2^{27} . . . 533
3–12 . . . 349
3^{17} . . . 126
4^{20} . . . 124
7 . . . 297
7^{2-17} . . . 41
7^{9} . . . 532
7^{13} . . . 41
8 . . . 41, 297
8^{10-18} . . . 423
9^{1}–10^{16} . . . 41, 297
$9^{13f.}$ . . . 532
10 . . . 354
10^{11b} . . . 133
10^{17-24} . . . 41
10^{17-27} . . . 297
10^{24} . . . 124
11 . . . 297
11^{1-11} . . . 41
12 . . . 41, 137, 297
12^{1-18} . . . 129
$12^{5f.}$ . . . 126
$12^{7ff.}$ . . . 127
13 . . . 261, 297
$13^{18f.}$ . . . 355
13^{21} . . . 579
14 . . . 297
14^{12} . . . 125
14^{35} . . . 527
14^{39} . . . 125
14^{44} . . . 126
14^{45} . . . 125
15 . . . 297
$15^{2, 13ff.}$ . . . 258
15^{23} . . . 543
16^{14-23} . . . 41
17 . . . 127
17^{44} . . . 125
17^{55}–18^{5} . . . 41
18^{7} . . . 125
19 . . . 354
19^{6} . . . 125
19^{13} . . . 543
20^{3} . . . 125
20^{5} . . . 366
20^{6} . . . 527
20^{12} . . . 126
21^{2-7} . . . 485
21^{9} . . . 543
21^{10-15} . . . 41
22^{20-23} . . . 351
$23^{2, 4}$ . . . 130
$23^{6, 9}$ . . . 543
24 . . . 41
24^{13} . . . 133
25^{34} . . . 125
25^{36} . . . 126
26 . . . 41
27^{2-12} . . . 41
28^{4} . . . 190
28^{8-19} . . . 570
31^{1-7} . . . 41
31^{1-13} . . . 190

2 Samuel:
1^{1-16} . . . 41
1^{18} . . . 34, 125
1^{19-27} . . . 124
1^{20} . . . 42
2^{1} . . . 130
2^{1-10} . . . 42
$3^{33f.}$ . . . 42
3^{35} . . . 126
4^{5} . . . 570
6 . . . 66, 351, 535
6^{12-15} . . . 350
6^{13} . . . 535
6^{14} . . . 535, 543
6^{18} . . . 131
6^{20} . . . 535, 543
7 . . . 350, 354
7^{14} . . . 471
8^{3-8} . . . 258
8^{18} . . . 350, 535
9–20 . . . 41 f., 44, 128
10^{6-19} . . . 258
11 f. . . . 351
11^{11} . . . 126
12^{1-6} . . . 126
20^{1} . . . 125
20^{26} . . . 536
21–24 . . . 42
22 . . . 42, 144
23^{1-7} . . . 42
23^{24-39} . . . 129
24^{25} . . . 535

1 Kings:
1 f. . . . 42, 128
1^{1}–2^{11} . . . 44
$1^{34, 39}$ . . . 124
2^{1-9} . . . 128
3^{4-28} . . . 128
4^{1-19} . . . 128
4^{21} . . . 34
4^{22} . . . 578
$5^{7f.}$ . . . 128
5^{16-23} . . . 129
6–9 . . . 541
6^{1} . . . 40
6^{2} . . . 542
7^{49} . . . 541
8^{2} . . . 275
8^{14-16} . . . 131
8^{22-53} . . . 129
8^{55-61} . . . 131
9^{26} . . . 262
10^{29} . . . 255
11^{29-39} . . . 351
11^{41} . . . 44, 128
12^{16} . . . 125
12^{28} . . . 544
14^{19-29} . . . 128
$14^{25f.}$ . . . 262
15^{16-22} . . . 262
16^{34} . . . 34, 532
17 f. . . . 127
17^{1-6} . . . 127
$17^{2f. 9}$ . . . 130
17^{6} . . . 570
18^{1} . . . 130
18^{21} . . . 355
$19^{9, 13}$ . . . 130
20^{11} . . . 133
21 . . . 423
21^{4} . . . 423
21^{8-10} . . . 129
21^{20} . . . 423

2 Kings:
1^{2-17} . . . 127
2^{1-5} . . . 127
2^{11} . . . 444
3 . . . 258
3^{1} . . . 573 f.
3^{4} . . . 17
3^{27} . . . 532
4^{1-7} . . . 127 f.
4^{11-31} . . . 127
6^{1-7} . . . 127
6^{25} . . . 578
7^{1} . . . 578
8 . . . 536
9 . . . 190
9^{29} . . . 573
11 . . . 66
11^{12} . . . 124
13^{13-19} . . . 130
14^{9} . . . 126
14^{25} . . . 51
15^{29} . . . 263
16^{10-18} . . . 536
17 . . . 320
18^{4} . . . 127, 544
$18^{9ff.}$ . . . 73
18^{13}–20^{19} . . . 144
18^{19-25} . . . 128
18^{26} . . . 11, 16 f.
18^{28-35} . . . 128
20^{11} . . . 570
20^{20} . . . 264
21^{3-7} . . . 536
22 f. . . . 32, 367
23^{3}–25^{30} . . . 144
23^{7} . . . 425
23^{9} . . . 32, 533
23^{10} . . . 532
23^{21-23} . . . 347
24^{8} . . . 265
24^{14} . . . 265, 312
24^{23} . . . 265
25^{12} . . . 311

2 Kings—(*continued*)
25^{27-30} 309, 312
25^{30} 265

1 Chronicles:
1–9 68, 129
3 66
$6^{12f.}$ 541
6^{28} 534
15 66
15^{24} 534
18^{19} 535
24^{7} 324
26^{1-4} 534
29^{7} 68, 129

2 Chronicles:
4^{6} 541
11^{9} 262
20^{5-12} 129
23 66
26^{16-21} 536
32^{18} 11
32^{30} 264
33 77
$33^{10ff.}$ 306
33^{18} 76
36^{22} 314

Ezra:
1^{1} 66, 314
1^{2-4} 129, 314
2^{59} 312
3^{7} 166
$3^{12f.}$ 542
4^{1-5} 316
4^{3} 66
4^{6} 317
4^{7-16} 129
4^{7-23} 317
4^{8}–6^{18} 16, 67
4^{17-22} 129
5 315
6^{2b-12} 129
6^{3-5} 314
7^{1} 66
$7^{12ff.}$ 267
7^{12-26} 16, 67, 129
$8^{17f.}$ 312
9^{9} 67
10 372
10^{6} 318

Nehemiah:
1–7 128
3^{1} 67, 318
5^{15} 579
7^{61} 312
8 34, 313, 317
8^{14-18} 34
10 68
10^{32} 34
10^{34} 34
12 316
12^{10} 318
$12^{11.\ 22}$ 66 f.
12^{31}–13^{31} 128
13 317, 372
13^{23-27} 54
13^{24} 11

Esther:
9 419

Job:
5^{17} 429
9^{13} 536
26^{12} 536
28 58, 134, 426
31 126, 129, 427
31^{1} 429
32–37 58
$40^{4f.}$ 58
40^{6}–41^{34} 58
40^{15}–41^{34} 128

Psalms:
1 55, 370, 373
1–41 54
1–89 540
1^{1-3} 132
1^{6} 123
2 55, 132
2–41 540
2^{6-9} 365
2^{7} 441, 469, 471 f.
2^{7-9} 132
2^{11b} 132
3 132
4 133
5 132
5^{12} 133
$7^{4f.}$ 126
$7^{10f.}$ 133
8 132
8^{3-6} 123
8^{4} 463
9 55
9 f. 54
10 55
11 133
13 132
13^{6} 133
14 54, 144
15 133, 426
15^{1} 123
16 133
18 132, 144
19 132
19^{1} 123, 386
19^{7} 418
20 132
21 132
22 56, 132, 468
22^{22-31} 133
22^{24} 506
23 133
24 133, 537, 539
$24^{3f.}$ 426
30 132
32 132
$32^{1f.}$ 132
33 55
34 132
37 370
40^{1-11} 132
40^{14-18} 54, 144
41 132
41^{1-3} 132
42 f. 54, 132
42–49 540
42–72 54
42–83 55
44 132, 367
45 132
46 132, 366
47 132, 536, 539
48 132, 366
50 540
51 132, 426
51–71 540
52^{10} 133
53 54, 144
54^{6} 133
56 56
56^{12} 133
57^{8-12} 54
60^{7-14} 54
61^{8} 133
62 133
66 132
69 468, 470
70 54, 144
72 132, 540
$72^{1-3.\ 12-14}$ 426
73 367
73–83 540
73–89 54
73^{23} 372
74 132
75 133
76 132
78 127
79 132
$79^{2f.}$ 79
80 132
80^{17} 463
81 539
82 539
84 133, 367
84–89 55, 540
85 133
87 132
$89^{9f.}$ 128
89^{26} 470
90 56
90–99 540
90–106 54
92 132, 539

PSALMS—(*continued*)
93 . 132, 536, 539
93^{1} . 132
94 . 539
96^{10} . 132
96–99 . 132, 536
97^{1} . 132
99^{1} . 132
100 . 540
101 . 132, 426
102 . 132
103 . 132
104 . 132, 209
105 . 127, 132
107–150 . 54
108 . 54
110 . 132, 517
110^{1} . 464, 507
110^{4} . 112, 517
118^{22} . 506
119 . 370, 373
119^{1} . 418
$119^{1f.}$. 132
119^{174} . 418
120–134 . 132, 540
122 . 133
125 . 132
126 . 133
129^{8} . 124
131 . 133
132 . 132, 365
132^{11-18} . 132
136 . 127
137 . 367 f.
$137^{5f.}$. 126, 312
137^{9} . 132
144^{3} . 463
144^{15} . 429
145–150 . 132

PROVERBS:
1–9 . 56, 133
1^{1-6} . 56
1^{6} . 125
1^{7} . 371
1^{10-18} . 134
2^{1-22} . 134
4^{3-9} . 134
7 . 371
7^{6-27} . 134
8 . 56
8^{22-31} . 134, 371
9^{10} . 426
10^{1} . 56
10^{1}–22^{16} . 56 f.
16^{2} . 427
22^{17}–23^{11} . 133, 209
22^{17}–23^{14} . 56 f.
23^{15}–24^{22} . 56
24^{23} . 56 f.
24^{23-34} . 56
25–29 . 56 f.
25^{1} . 56
28^{5} . 427
30^{1} . 56
30^{1-14} . 56
30^{15-33} . 56
31^{1} . 56
31^{1-9} . 56
31^{10-31} . 56

ECCLESIASTES:
3^{16} . 62
4^{1} . 62
4^{13-16} . 62
9^{4b} . 133
10^{16-20} . 62
10^{20} . 62

ISAIAH:
1–39 . 45
1^{1} . 45
1^{10-17} . 130
2^{1} . 45
2^{2-4} . 45, 144, 358, 366
2^{3} . 133
3^{13-15} . 130
4^{7} . 125
5^{1-7} . 126
5^{8-25} . 130
5^{10} . 578
5^{16} . 426
6 . 45
6^{3} . 132
$6^{8f.}$. 423
7 f. . 45, 359
7^{14} . 124
8^{16-20} . 359
9^{1} . 263, 440
9^{1-7} . 358
9^{2-7} . 46
9^{3} . 126
9^{6} . 85
10^{5} . 300
10^{15} . 133
11^{1} . 358
11^{1-9} . 46
11^{10-16} . 46
12 . 46
$12^{1f.}$. 132
13 f. . 312
13–23 . 45
13^{1}–14^{23} . 46
$14^{4ff.}$. 125
14^{4b-23} . 46
14^{12-20} . 128
16^{10} . 126
19^{18} . 11
19^{19} . 542
19^{19-25} . 375
21^{1-10} . 46
$21^{11f.}$. 124
22^{13b} . 124
23^{11} . 257
23^{16} . 124
24–27 . 45 f., 374
26^{1} . 536
26^{8-14} . 132
26^{16-19a} . 132
27^{1} . 128
28–35 . 45
30^{22} . 543
33 . 133
34 f. . 46 f.
36–39 . 45, 144
36^{4-10} . 128
36^{11} . 11
36^{13-20} . 128
37^{22-29} . 125
40–55 . 47, 361
40–66 . 45, 47, 515
$40^{1ff.}$. 516
40^{1-11} . 130
40^{9} . 515
41–66 . 152
41^{1}–42^{4} . 130
41^{8} . 47
41^{8-13} . 130
42–53 . 506
42^{1} . 447, 469
42^{1-4} . 47, 362, 468 f.
42^{10-13} . 132
43^{1-7} . 130
$44^{1f.\ 21}$. 47
44^{9-20} . 131
$44^{26ff.}$. 46
44^{28} . 46, 361
45^{1} . 46, 361
45^{1-7} . 130
47^{1-5} . 46
47^{4} . 125
47^{6} . 46
48^{14} . 46
48^{20} . 46 f.
49^{1-6} . 47, 362, 468
$49^{5f.}$. 362
50^{4-9} . 47, 131, 362, 468
$51^{9f.}$. 128, 536
51^{11} . 46
52^{2} . 46
52^{7} . 515
52^{7-10} . 130
$52^{11f.}$. 46
52^{13-15} . 362
52^{13}–53^{12} . 47, 362, 468
53 . 47, 362, 415, 470
53^{1-9} . 131
53^{3} . 469
53^{4} . 469
53^{7} . 469
$53^{7f.}$. 469
53^{10} . 531
53^{12} . 469
54 . 46
55 . 362

ISAIAH—(*continued*)
56 . . . 372
56–66 . . 47, 362, 468
56^{5-7} . . . 47
56^{7} . . . 491
56^{12} . . . 124
57^{3-7} . . . 47
58^{6} . . . 469
59–62 . . . 362
59^{20} . . . 518
60^{4-22} . . . 375
60^{6} . . . 515
60^{7} . . . 47
60^{10} . . . 47
61^{1} . . . 469
$61^{1f.}$ . . 469, 515
61^{2} . . . 490
61^{5-7} . . . 375
63^{7}–64^{12} . . . 133
66^{18-21} . . . 375

JEREMIAH :
1–25 . . . 47
$1^{11f.\ 13f.}$ . . . 130
2^{5b-13} . . . 130
4^{5}–6^{30} . . . 130
4^{11} . . . 198
7^{1-15} (–8^{3}?) . . . 129
7^{11} . . . 491
9^{17-22} . . . 124
10^{1-16} . . . 48
11^{10} . . . 72
13^{1-11} . . . 130
14^{1}–15^{3} . . . 133
14^{2-9} . . . 132
15^{10-21} . . . 132
15^{15-21} . . . 360
16^{1-9} . . . 130
17^{5-8} . . . 131
17^{10} . . . 427
17^{12-18} . . . 132
17^{21-27} . . . 48
18^{18-25} . . . 132
18^{19-23} . . . 360
$20^{7ff.}$ . . . 132
20^{7-18} . . . 360
22^{18} . . . 124
23^{28b} . . . 133
24^{2b-10} . . . 130
25^{12} . . . 360
25^{13} . . . 48
26–29 . . . 128
26–45 . . . 47
26^{18} . . . 51
26^{20-23} . . . 359
29 . . . 360
29^{1-23} . . 72, 129
29^{2} . . . 312
29^{10} . . . 360
29^{24-28} . . . 129
30 f. . . . 48
31^{27-34} . . . 48
31^{29} . . . 133
$31^{29f.}$ . . . 61
31^{31-34} . . . 360
32–45 . . . 128
34^{5} . . . 124
34^{18} . . . 355
36 . . 44, 265
36^{32} . . . 48
38^{4} . . . 265
38^{13-21} . . . 265
$40^{11f.}$ . . . 310
$42^{16ff.}$ . . . 313
43^{8-13} . . . 313
44 . . 222, 313
46–51 . . . 47
49 . . . 51
$49^{9.\ 10a}$ . . 45, 51
49^{14-16} . . 45, 51
50 f. . . 48, 312
52 . . 48, 144
52^{21} . . . 578
52^{30} . . . 309

LAMENTATIONS :
1 . . . 61
2 . . . 61 f.
2–4 . . . 61
2^{9} . . . 61
2^{19} . . . 571
3 . . . 61 f.
3^{64-66} . . . 61
4 . . . 61 f.
4^{17} . . . 61
5^{7} . . . 61

EZEKIEL :
1–24 . . . 48
1–32 . . . 575
3^{15} . . . 312
3^{16} . . . 130
$3^{16ff.}$ . . . 124
$4^{1-3.\ 7}$ . . . 130
4^{13} . . . 312
5^{1-17} . . . 130
8 . . . 361
8^{1} . . 312, 368
10^{14} . . . 126
11^{1} . . . 361
13^{2b-15} . . . 130
14^{1} . . 312, 368
16^{44b} . . . 133
17^{2-14} . . . 130
17^{3-10} . . . 126
18^{2b} . . . 133
19^{2-9} . . . 126
19^{2-14} . . . 130
20 . . . 129
21^{21} . . . 543
23^{2-35} . . . 130
25–32 . . . 48
25^{3b-17} . . . 130
27^{3} . . . 125
28^{1} . . . 125
28^{2-10} . . . 128
28^{11-19} . . . 128
30^{2b-4} . . . 125
33–39 . . 48, 575
33^{7-9} . . . 124
33^{30-33} . . 312, 368
37 . . . 361
38 f. . . . 374
40 ff. . . . 542
40–48 . 49 f., 361, 534, 575
40^{5} . . . 578
45^{12} . . . 579
45^{14} . . . 578
45^{24} . . . 578

DANIEL :
1–6 . . 65, 375
1^{1} . . . 64
1^{1}–2^{4a} . . . 65
2 . . . 64
2^{4b}–7^{28} . . 16, 63
3^{23} . . . 75
$4^{1ff.}$ . . . 129
4^{1-18} . . . 129
$6^{23ff.}$ . . . 127
7 . . 64 f., 458, 463 f., 467 ff., 471
7–12 . . . 65
7^{7} . . . 463
7^{8} . . . 64
7^{13} . 82, 414, 506
$7^{13f.}$ . . 375, 463
7^{18} . . . 375
7^{21} . . . 463
7^{25} . . . 64 f.
7^{27} . . 375, 463
8–12 . . . 65
$8^{9ff.}$ . . . 64
8^{13} . . . 64
9 . . . 64
9^{27} . . . 64 f.
11^{31} . . 64, 222
11^{45} . . . 64
12^{2} . . . 65
12^{7} . . . 65
12^{11} . . . 64
12^{12} . . . 375

HOSEA :
1 . . . 49
1^{4-8} . . . 124
2^{8} . . . 356
2^{14-20} . . . 430
2^{14-23} . . . 357
3 . . . 49
3^{2} . . . 578
3^{4} . . . 542
4^{1-6} . . . 356
4^{15} . . . 126
8^{7a} . . . 133
9^{7} . . . 359
11^{1} . . . 470
11^{1-9} . . . 430
$11^{8f.}$ . . . 49

JOEL:
1^{1}–2^{27} . . . 133
$1^{9.13}$ . . . 50
$1^{13f.}$ . . . 50
2^{12} . . . 50
2^{14} . . . 50
2^{27} . . . 50
2^{28} . . . 50
$2^{28f.}$ . . . 363
3^{2} . . . 50
3^{6} . . . 50
$3^{16f.}$ . . . 50

AMOS:
1 f. . . . 50
1^{3}–2^{16} . . . 130
$2^{4f.}$ . . . 50
3–6 . . . 50
$4^{4f.}$ . . . 130
4^{7} . . . 198
5^{2} . . . 124
$5^{4f.}$ . . . 130
5^{5} . . . 31
5^{6} . . . 130
5^{15} . . . 357
5^{16} . . . 124
6^{1-7} . . . 130
7–9 . . . 50
7^{1-9} . . . 130
7^{10-17} . . . 50
$7^{12f.}$ . . . 359
7^{15} . . . 423
8^{14} . . . 31
9^{1-4} . . . 51
9^{7} . . . 357
9^{8b-10} . . . 51
9^{11-15} . . . 51

OBADIAH:
1-4 . . . 45, 51
1-10 . . . 51
1-14 . . . 51
3 . . . 203
5f. . . . 45, 51
11 . . . 51
11-14 . . . 51
15-21 . . . 51
16-18 . . . 51
19-21 . . . 51

JONAH:
2 . . . 51
2^{1-10} . . . 127
2^{2-9} . . . 51
3^{3} . . . 51

MICAH:
1–3 . . . 52
1^{2} . . . 126
3^{8} . . . 423
3^{12} . . . 358
4 f. . . . 52
4^{1} . . . 85
4^{1-3} . . . 45
4^{1-4} . . . 144, 358, 366
4^{2} . . . 133
5^{1-5a} . . . 358
6 f. . . . 52
6^{1-8} . . . 52, 130
6^{7} . . . 532
6^{8} . . . 423
7^{6-20} . . . 133
7^{7-10} . . . 132
7^{7-20} . . . 52
7^{14-17} . . . 132

NAHUM:
1^{2}–2^{2} . . . 52
2^{2}–3^{19} . . . 52
3^{8} . . . 52

HABAKKUK:
1 f. . . . 52 f.
1^{2-4} . . . 132
1^{6} . . . 52
2^{1-4} . . . 124
2^{4} . . . 420
2^{5} . . . 52
3 . . . 52 f.

ZEPHANIAH:
1^{1} . . . 53
2^{3} . . . 130
2^{13} . . . 53
2^{15} . . . 53
3 . . . 53
3^{1-8} . . . 130
3^{14-20} . . . 53

HAGGAI:
2^{3} . . . 542
2^{20-23} . . . 372

ZECHARIAH:
1–6 . . . 363
1–8 . . . 53
$1^{1.7}$ . . . 54
$2^{6f.}$ . . . 315
3 . . . 533
4^{6-10a} . . . 372
4^{9} . . . 317
4^{10} . . . 363
7^{1} . . . 54
8^{20-23} . . . 375
9–11 . . . 54
9–14 . . . 53 f.
9^{9} . . . 444, 468 f.
$9^{9f.}$ . . . 363
9^{11} . . . 85
9^{14} . . . 54
10^{2} . . . 543
12–14 . . . 54
13^{7} . . . 481, 515

MALACHI:
1^{8} . . . 54
1^{10} . . . 54
1^{11} . . . 570
2^{4-9} . . . 54
2^{10-16} . . . 54
3^{1} . . . 54
3^{3} . . . 54
3^{10} . . . 54

APOCRYPHA AND PSEUDEPIGRAPHA

2 ESDRAS (4 EZRA):
3–14 . . . 81
7^{35} . . . 81
15 f. . . . 81

TOBIT:
4 . . . 74
4^{15} . . . 74

JUDITH:
10^{4} . . . 76
16^{17} . . . 76

ADDITIONS TO ESTHER:
13^{8}–14^{19} . . . 77

WISDOM OF SOLOMON:
1^{1}–2^{1} . . . 80
1^{3} . . . 80
2 . . . 80
2^{1-9} . . . 124
2^{12-20} . . . 80
2^{18} . . . 471
5^{1-9} . . . 80
9^{17} . . . 80
11^{2-19} . . . 80

ECCLESIASTICUS:
4^{10} . . . 471
$43^{13f.}$ . . . 75
44–49 . . . 63 f.
50^{5-21} . . . 539
50^{27} . . . 75

BARUCH:
1^{1}–3^{8} . . . 80
1^{13} . . . 80
3^{9}–4^{4} . . . 80
4^{5}–5^{9} . . . 80

SUSANNA:
20f. . . . 78
64 . . . 78

BEL AND THE DRAGON:
1-22 . . . 78
23-27 . . . 78

1 MACCABEES:
$1^{25ff.\ 36ff.}$ . . . 79
1^{54} . . . 65
$2^{8ff.\ 44}$ . . . 79

1 MACCABEES—(*continued*)
4^{36-39} . . . 538
$6^{49.\ 53}$ . . . 573
7^{17} . . . 79
8^{22-32} . . . 129
9^{22} . . . 79
9^{41} . . . 79
$11^{3.\ 7}$ . . . 79
13^{51} . . . 21
14^{1} . . . 186
$14^{16ff.}$ . . . 79
$14^{18.\ 27}$ . . . 79
16^{24} . . . 79

2 MACCABEES:
$2^{4f.}$ . . . 541
11^{21} . . . 570
11^{30} . . . 570

3 MACCABEES:
7^{6} . . . 84

JUBILEES:
$6^{17ff.}$ . . . 84
6^{18} . . . 84

ASCENSION OF ISAIAH:
1^{1}–3^{12} . . . 87
3^{13}–5^{1} . . . 87
5^{1-14} . . . 87
6^{1}–11^{40} . . . 87

1 ENOCH:
1–5 . . . 82
12–36 . . . 82
37–71 . . . 82, 464
70 f. . . . 82
72–82 . . . 82
83–90 . . . 82
91–104 . . . 82
91^{12-17}, 93 . . . 82

2 ENOCH:
22^{6-16} . . . 86
59^{2} . . . 86

TESTAMENTS OF THE XII PATRIARCHS:
Levi 18^{12} . . . 83
Judah 20 . . . 83
25^{3} . . . 83
Naphtali 5^{4} . . . 21
Asher 1^{3} . . . 83

ASSUMPTION OF MOSES:
10^{1-10} . . . 86

2 BARUCH:
76^{3} . . . 88

PSALMS OF SOLOMON:
17^{23} . . . 85
$17^{25.\ 27}$ . . . 85
17^{30} . . . 85
17^{31} . . . 85
17^{41} . . . 85
17^{47} . . . 85
18^{6} . . . 85

APOCALYPSE OF ABRAHAM:
9–22 . . . 87

NEW TESTAMENT

MATTHEW:
1^{1-17} . . . 135
1^{4} . . . 137
1^{18}–2^{23} . . . 135
1^{21} . . . 418
1^{23} . . . 95, 124
$2^{6.\ 15f.}$ . . . 95
2^{22} . . . 232
2^{23} . . . 95
3–27 . . . 135
3–28 . . . 135
3^{2} . . . 95
3^{6} . . . 561
3^{9} . . . 441
3^{12} . . . 136
3^{14} . . . 560
3^{17} . . . 469
4^{12} . . . 482
4^{14} . . . 95
5 . . . 429
5–7 . . . 142, 509
5^{3-10} . . . 86
$5^{13f.}$ . . . 490
5^{15} . . . 578
5^{17} . . . 488
5^{17-20} . . . 95, 488
5^{17-48} . . . 119
5^{21-37} . . . 139
5^{26} . . . 580
5^{28} . . . 431
$5^{31f.}$ . . . 479
5^{38} . . . 429
5^{41} . . . 578
5^{45} . . . 85
5^{48} . . . 429
$6^{2.\ 5}$ . . . 22
6^{9-13} . . . 482
6^{10} . . . 456
6^{16} . . . 22
6^{27} . . . 23
7^{17} . . . 136
7^{21} . . . 480
8^{4} . . . 487
8^{11} . . . 457, 481, 492
8^{17} . . . 95, 469
8^{20} . . . 465
$8^{21f.}$ . . . 479
9^{36} . . . 481
10^{2} . . . 482
$10^{5ff.}$ . . . 95
10^{6} . . . 490
10^{15} . . . 490
10^{23} . . . 95, 457, 492
10^{29} . . . 579
10^{32} . . . 489
$10^{32f.}$ . . . 459
10^{34} . . . 477
$10^{35f.}$ . . . 479
10^{40} . . . 482
11^{2} . . . 482
11^{2-6} . . . 442, 454, 469, 483
$11^{5f.}$ . . . 490
11^{12} . . . 488
$11^{12f.}$ . . . 454
11^{19} . . . 465
$11^{21f.}$ . . . 490
11^{25-27} . . . 472
$11^{28f.}$ . . . 487
$11^{31f.}$ . . . 136
12^{1-8} . . . 485
12^{5-7} . . . 485
12^{9-14} . . . 485
12^{11} . . . 486
12^{17} . . . 95, 469
12^{22-30} . . . 442
12^{24-28} . . . 136
12^{27} . . . 482
12^{28} . . . 452
12^{32} . . . 465
$12^{38f.}$ . . . 442
12^{39-41} . . . 491
12^{41} . . . 490
$12^{41f.}$ . . . 454
13 . . . 95
$13^{16f.}$ . . . 454
13^{24-30} . . . 480
$13^{31f.}$ . . . 455, 481
13^{33} . . . 455, 579
13^{35} . . . 95
13^{47-50} . . . 480
14^{1} . . . 233
14^{25} . . . 570
15^{1-20} . . . 486
15^{21-28} . . . 489
15^{24} . . . 490
16^{1-4} . . . 442
$16^{13ff.}$ . . . 546
16^{17} . . . 462
16^{18} . . . 95, 480, 548
16^{28} . . . 457
17^{26-30} . . . 136
18^{12-14} . . . 481
18^{12-20} . . . 95
18^{15-17} . . . 479
18^{15-18} . . . 480
18^{17} . . . 548
19^{4} . . . 431
19^{9} . . . 479
19^{17-19} . . . 487
19^{21} . . . 488
19^{28} . . . 467, 481
20^{2} . . . 579

MATTHEW—(*continued*)
21^{4} 95
$21^{12f.}$ 491
21^{18-20} 481
21^{33-41} 458, 481
21^{42} 548
22^{1-10} 481
22^{2-13} 458
22^{23} 397
22^{31} 475
22^{34-40} 486
22^{35-40} 419
23 476
23^{1-36} 486
$23^{2f.}$ 95, 487
23^{4} 487
23^{13} 480
23^{15} 401, 492
23^{23} 566
23^{37} 444
24 f. 95
24^{14} 492
24^{28} 139
25^{1-13} 458
26^{13} 492
26^{15} 234
26^{26-28} 565
26^{28} 491
26^{29} 456, 481
26^{31} 481
26^{52} 477
27^{9} 95
27^{12-15} 238
27^{49} 179
28 135
28^{1} 570
28^{11-15} 271
28^{18-20} 95, 483
28^{19} 491

MARK:
1^{1} 137, 461
1^{1}–5^{30} 170
1^{5} 561
$1^{7f.}$ 136
1^{11} 469
$1^{14f.}$ 482
1^{15} 452
1^{20} 479
1^{44} 487
2^{1-12} 140
2^{10} 465
2^{14} 235
$2^{15ff.}$ 92
2^{18} 482
2^{18-20} 441
2^{23-28} 140, 485
2^{28} 465
3^{1-3} 485
3^{1-5} 421
3^{1-6} 140
3^{11} 461, 471
3^{14} 429
$3^{14f.}$ 482
3^{14-18} 443
3^{22-27} 442
$3^{28f.}$ 465
3^{31-35} 430, 479
4 442, 483
4^{10-12} 442
4^{22} 136
4^{26-29} 455
4^{30-32} 455, 481
5^{7} 461
5^{37} 443
6^{3} 114, 439 f.
6^{7} 482
6^{14} 233
6^{14-16} 443
6^{27} 21
6^{30} 482
6^{30}–7^{23} 135
6^{34} 481
6^{39} 439
6^{50} 473
7^{1-23} 486
7^{2} 566
7^{4} 578
7^{11} 478
7^{11-13} 486
7^{24} 443
7^{24-30} 489
7^{27} 489
7^{27-29} 136
7^{31} 443
8^{1-26} 135
$8^{11f.}$ 442
$8^{22, 27}$ 443
8^{29} 461
8^{31} 465
8^{33} 441
$8^{34f.}$ 94
8^{38} 466
9^{1} 453, 456 f., 518
9^{2} 443
9^{12} 469
9^{13} 465
9^{30} 443
9^{31} 465
9^{37} 136
9^{38-41} 482
9^{41} 461
9^{47} 480
9^{50} 490
10^{1} 444
10^{6-8} 478
10^{11} 479
$10^{13ff.}$ 92
10^{17-22} 419
10^{21} 488
$10^{29f.}$ 430
10^{35} 136
10^{35-40} 443, 461
10^{45} 465, 469
10^{46-52} 444
10^{47} 456
$10^{47f.}$ 440
$11^{13f. 20}$ 481
11^{15-18} 491
12^{1-9} 458, 481
12^{6} 473
12^{13-17} 235
12^{17} 475
12^{18-27} 478
$12^{28f.}$ 487
12^{28-34} 419, 486
12^{29} 386
12^{34} 488
12^{35} 462
12^{35-37} 440
12^{38-40} 486
12^{42} 580
13 3, 137, 457
13^{6} 473
$13^{7f.}$ 139
13^{9} 457
13^{10} 457, 492
$13^{9ff.}$ 114
13^{14} 519
13^{14-20} 139
13^{21} 461
13^{24-27} 139
13^{30} 457
13^{32} 457, 472
13^{35} 570
14 446
14^{2} 566
14^{3} 567
14^{9} 492
14^{12} 447, 566
$14^{14, 16}$ 566
14^{21} 465
14^{22-24} 565
14^{24} 491, 566
14^{25} 456, 481
14^{27} 481, 515
14^{33} 443
14^{41} 22, 465
14^{47} 566
14^{49} 515
14^{58} 446
14^{61} 461, 471
14^{62} 458, 461, 466
15^{1} 448
15^{5} 469
$15^{7, 27}$ 461
15^{29} 446
15^{32} 462
15^{39} 461, 471
15^{43-45} 566
16^{8} 437

LUKE:
1^{1} 279
1^{1-4} 95
1^{3} 135
1^{4} 561
1^{32} 461
1^{69} 461

LUKE—(*continued*)
2^{1} . . . 227
2^{2} . . . 235
2^{24} . . . 487
2^{25} . . . 461
$2^{27f.}$ . . . 487
2^{32} . . . 96
2^{38} . . . 461
2^{51} . . . 440
3^{1} . . . 232
3^{6} . . . 96
3^{8} . . . 441
3^{9-13} . . . 441
3^{23} . . . 439
4^{14} . . . 483
$4^{14ff.}$ . . . 96
$4^{16ff.}$ . . . 515
4^{16-30} . . . 469
4^{19} . . . 490
4^{25-27} . . . 491
5^{14} . . . 487
6^{1-5} . . . 485
6^{6-11} . . . 485
6^{13} . . . 482
6^{20-26} . . . 139
6^{31} . . . 430
6^{36} . . . 429
7^{18} . . . 482
7^{18-23} 454, 469, 483
7^{19-23} . . . 442
7^{22} . . . 490
7^{34} . . . 465
9^{7} . . . 233
9^{10} . . . 482
9^{27} . . . 459
9^{31} . . . 516
9^{51}–18^{34} . . . 444
9^{58} . . . 465
$9^{59f.}$ . . . 479
10^{12} . . . 490
10^{13} . . . 189
$10^{13f.}$ . . . 490
10^{16} . . . 482
10^{22} . . . 472
$10^{23f.}$ . . . 454
10^{25} . . . 419
10^{25-28} . . . 486
10^{25-37} . . . 490
10^{29-37} . . . 430, 476
11^{1} . . . 441
11^{2} . . . 456
11^{2-4} . . . 482
11^{14-26} . . . 442
11^{16} . . . 442
11^{20} . 452, 454, 482
$11^{27f.}$ . . . 479
11^{29-32} . . . 442, 491
$11^{30f.}$ . . . 454
$11^{31f.}$ . . . 490
11^{32} . . . 454
11^{37-52} . . . 476
11^{37}–12^{1} . . . 485
11^{46} . . . 487
$11^{49f.}$ . . . 482
11^{52} . . . 480
12^{6} . . . 579
$12^{8f.}$ . . . 459, 489
12^{10} . . . 465
12^{14} . . . 475
12^{32} . . . 481, 548
12^{38} . . . 570
12^{49} . . . 136
12^{50} . . . 483
12^{52} . . . 479
12^{59} . . . 580
$13^{1f.}$ . . . 236
13^{1-3} . . . 490
13^{4} . . . 236
13^{6-9} . . . 481
$13^{18f.}$ . . . 455
$13^{18ff.}$ . . . 481
$13^{20f.}$ . . . 455
13^{21} . . . 579
13^{28-30} . . . 490
13^{29} . 96, 457, 481
13^{31-33} . . . 443
13^{32} . . . 449
13^{34} . . . 444
14^{5} . . . 486
14^{15} . . . 567
14^{15-24} . . . 481
14^{16-24} . . . 458
14^{34} . . . 490
15^{3-7} . . . 481
$15^{11ff.}$ . . . 96
15^{11-32} . . . 429
16^{6} . . . 579
16^{7} . . . 579
16^{16} . . . 454, 488
16^{18} . . . 479
16^{19-31} . . . 416
17^{3} . . . 479 f.
17^{5} . . . 482
17^{11-19} . . . 444
17^{16} . . . 490
$17^{23ff.}$ . . . 93
18^{8} . . . 458
18^{12} . . . 572
18^{20} . . . 487
18^{22} . . . 488
$19^{1f.}$ . . . 235
19^{1-10} . . . 487
19^{8} . . . 23
19^{10} . . . 465
19^{17-20} . . . 230
$19^{39f.}$ . . . 445
$19^{45f.}$ . . . 491
20^{9-16} . . . 481
20^{9-19} . . . 458
20^{13} . . . 473
20^{25} . . . 475
21^{2} . . . 580
21^{32} . . . 457
22^{14} . . . 482
22^{15} . . . 566
$22^{17f.}$ . . . 483
22^{17-20} . . . 565
22^{18} . . . 456, 481
22^{22} . . . 466
22^{25} . . . 231
$22^{29f.}$ . . . 481
22^{35-38} . . . 476
22^{37} . . . 469
22^{48} . . . 467
23^{7} . . . 231
23^{9} . . . 469
22^{42} . . . 456
24 . . . 135
24^{13} . . . 578
$24^{30-35, 41-43}$ . . . 567
24^{42} . . . 567
24^{44} . . . 68
24^{47} . . . 96

JOHN:
1^{13} . . . 439
$1^{35, 37}$ . . . 482
2–12 . . . 136
2^{1-10} . . . 567
2^{4} . . . 479
2^{6} . . . 579
2^{15} . . . 477
2^{19} . . . 446
2^{20} . . . 542
3 . . . 483
3^{18} . . . 520
3^{19} . . . 520
$3^{22f.}$ . . . 441
3^{22-30} . . . 483
3^{23} . . . 496
3^{24} . . . 483
3^{25} . . . 482
3^{27-36} . . . 136
4^{1} . . . 441
$4^{1f.}$ . . . 483
4^{1-3} . . . 483
$4^{38ff.}$ . . . 496
4^{48} . . . 443
5^{24} . . . 520
5^{25} . . . 520
$6^{4ff.}$ . . . 565
6^{30} . . . 443
6^{32-58} . . . 565
6^{40} . . . 520
8^{11} . . . 487
8^{41} . . . 439
8^{58} . . . 473
10^{1-16} . . . 481
$10^{7ff.}$ . . . 548
11^{9} . . . 570
$11^{25f.}$ . . . 520
12^{2} . . . 567
12^{3} . . . 579
12^{13} . . . 21
12^{31} . . . 520
12^{32} . . . 493
12^{34} . . . 468
12^{38} . . . 516
12^{48} . . . 520

JOHN—(*continued*)
13–17 . . . 136
13^{34} . . . 419
14–16 . . . 137
15 . . . 489
15^{12} . . . 419
16^{33} . . . 520
17 . . . 129
17^{3} . . . 520
18–20 . . . 136
$18^{31-33.\ 37.\ 38}$ . . . 278
$18^{36f.}$ . . . 456
19^{9} . . . 469
19^{14-31} . . . 566
19^{29} . . . 180
19^{31} . . . 566
19^{39} . . . 579
20^{31} . . . 137
21 . . . 136, 567
21^{24} . . . 115
21^{9-13} . . . 567

ACTS :
1^{1} . . . 95
2 . . . 382
2^{23} . . . 514
2^{31} . . . 563
2^{40} . . . 495
2^{42} . . . 568
2^{46} . . . 548, 568
3 . . . 515
3^{12-26} . . . 506
$3^{17f.}$ . . . 514
3^{19-21} . . . 518
4^{33} . . . 90
5^{11} . . . 546
$5^{30f.}$ . . . 514
5^{31} . . . 563
5^{36} . . . 238
5^{37} . . . 233
6^{1-6} . . . 550
6^{2} . . . 550
6^{6} . . . 563
7 . . . 517
7^{22-39} . . . 444
7^{38} . . . 516
7^{56} . . . 464
8^{1} . . . 548
8^{17-19} . . . 563
8^{26-40} . . . 469
8^{27} . . . 21
8^{36} . . . 560
8^{37} . . . 91, 142
$9^{26ff.}$ . . . 101
10^{1} . . . 229
$10^{36ff.}$ . . . 90
10^{43} . . . 563
10^{44} . . . 563
10^{47} . . . 560
11 . . . 576
11^{14} . . . 559
11^{17} . . . 560
11^{19-27} . . . 224
11^{20} . . . 101
11^{27-30} . . . 102
11^{28} . . . 238
11^{30} . . . 102, 551
12^{1-5} . . . 238
12^{5} . . . 546
12^{17} . . . 440
12^{20-23} . . . 238
12^{25} . . . 101
13 f. . . . 100
13^{1} . . . 548, 553
13^{3} . . . 563
13^{7} . . . 226, 244, 271
13^{14}–14^{21a} . . . 102
13^{38} . . . 563
$14^{21f.}$ . . . 96
14^{21b-23} . . . 102
14^{23} . . . 551
14^{27} . . . 548
15 . . . 101, 384
15^{2} . . . 102, 551
15^{3} . . . 548
$15^{4.\ 6}$ . . . 551
15^{13} . . . 440
$15^{22f.}$ . . . 551
15^{41} . . . 548
16^{2} . . . 101
16^{4} . . . 551
16^{6} . . . 100
16^{9-18} . . . 96
16^{11} . . . 137
16^{15} . . . 559
16^{20} . . . 230
$16^{20ff.}$ . . . 96
16^{33} . . . 559
$17^{1ff.}$ . . . 108
$17^{5ff.}$ . . . 96
17^{6} . . . 230, 272
17^{19} . . . 230
18^{1-18} . . . 98
18^{2} . . . 238
18^{8} . . . 559
18^{12} . . . 226
$18^{12ff.}$ . . . 96
18^{18-21} . . . 98
18^{22} . . . 102
18^{24} . . . 22
18^{25} . . . 561
18^{26} . . . 98
19^{1-7} . . . 441
19^{6} . . . 563
19^{10} . . . 107
19^{21} . . . 104
$19^{21f.}$ . . . 97
19^{22} . . . 104
$19^{23ff.}$ . . . 96
19^{31} . . . 231
19^{32} . . . 546
19^{35} . . . 230
$19^{39.\ 41}$ . . . 546
$20^{1ff.}$ . . . 97
20^{3} . . . 97
20^{4-16} . . . 96
20^{7} . . . 568
20^{18-35} . . . 137
20^{19} . . . 103
20^{28} . . . 551, 554
20^{35} . . . 137, 140, 279
21^{1-8} . . . 96
21^{8} . . . 504
21^{18} . . . 551
$21^{27ff.}$ . . . 96
$21^{32f.}$ . . . 96
21^{33} . . . 229
21^{38} . . . 238
22^{16} . . . 562
23^{8} . . . 397, 402
$23^{12f.}$ . . . 96
23^{23} . . . 229
24^{24} . . . 238
25 f. . . . 330
25^{13} . . . 240
25^{16} . . . 242
25^{33} . . . 229
$26^{31f.}$ . . . 96
27^{1} . . . 229
27^{1}–28^{16} . . . 96
27^{28} . . . 578
28^{7} . . . 230
$28^{14f.}$ . . . 557
28^{16} . . . 240
28^{28} . . . 96
28^{30} . . . 240
$28^{30f.}$ . . . 103

ROMANS :
1–14 . . . 98
1^{1}–3^{20} . . . 98
1^{3} . . . 440
$1^{3f.}$ . . . 142
1^{7} . . . 97
$1^{9ff.}$ . . . 97
1^{15} . . . 97
1^{16} . . . 493
$1^{16f.}$ . . . 97
1^{17} . . . 420
1^{29-31} . . . 142
2 . . . 98
2^{20} . . . 508
2^{29} . . . 562
3^{21}–8^{39} . . . 98
4^{5} . . . 512
4^{11} . . . 563
4^{13} . . . 562
5^{5} . . . 434
$5^{10f.}$ . . . 512
6^{4} . . . 561
6^{4-23} . . . 420
6^{6-8} . . . 562, 568
$6^{11.\ 13}$ . . . 568
6^{11-14} . . . 568
6^{17} . . . 143
7^{6} . . . 568
7^{12} . . . 428
$7^{21ff.}$ . . . 434
$8^{3f.}$ . . . 547

ROMANS—(*continued*)
8^{11} 520
8^{15} 85
8^{21} 513
9–11 98
10^{9} 119, 142
$10^{9f.}$ 90, 561
10^{15} 515
10^{16} 516
11^{13} 498, 554
11^{25} 518
11^{26} 518
12 f. 91
12–15 98
12^{1} 433
12^{1}–13^{10} 509
$12^{4f.}$ 547
12^{6-8} 553
13^{1-7} 501 f.
13^{14} 509, 562
14 97
14^{7} 548
14^{10} 511
14^{23} 97
15 97 f.
15 f. 97
15^{1-13} 97
15^{13} 97 f.
15^{16} 554
$15^{23ff.}$ 97
15^{24} 97
$15^{24ff.}$ 103
15^{26} 101
16 97 f.
16^{1} 548, 551
$16^{1f.}$ 98
16^{1-23} 137
16^{3-5} 98
16^{4} 548
16^{5} 548
16^{16} 548
16^{22} 138
16^{23} 272
16^{24} 97
16^{25-27} 97, 137

1 CORINTHIANS:
1–4 99
1^{2} 548
1^{10} 548
1^{16} 559
1^{23} 444
2^{3} 434
3^{5} 554
3^{9} 548
4^{17} 104, 106
5 99
5 f. 99
5^{7} 516
5^{9} 98, 100
$5^{10f.}$ 142
6^{1-11} 142
$6^{9f.}$ 435
6^{11} 561 f.
6^{14} 519
$6^{19f.}$ 435
7 99, 105
7^{10} 140
8–10 99
8^{5} 25
8^{6} 91
9^{21} 418, 508
$10^{1ff.}$ 516
10^{16} 547
10^{16-22} 568
11 25
11–14 99
11^{17-24} 568
11^{23} 138
$11^{23ff.}$ 91, 508
11^{23-25} 484, 565
11^{23-26} 437
11^{25} 567
11^{26} 141, 457, 567
12^{3} 142
12^{4-6} 91
12^{12} 547
$12^{12ff.}$ 547
12^{27} 547
12^{28} 550, 552 f.
13 431
14^{33} 548, 564
14^{40} 561
15 99, 508
15^{3} 91
$15^{3f.}$ 90
15^{3-6} 142
15^{3-8} 138, 437, 451
15^{3-11} 507
15^{6} 141
15^{7} 440
15^{11} 508
$15^{30ff.}$ 103
15^{32} 106
15^{36} 455
15^{43} 456
$15^{51ff.}$ 519
16 99
16^{1} 101
16^{3} 137
$16^{3ff.}$ 104
16^{8} 98
$16^{10f.}$ 104, 106
16^{19} 548
16^{21} 138

2 CORINTHIANS:
1–9 99 f., 137
1^{1} 548
$1^{8ff.}$ 103
1^{22} 22, 563
1^{23} 99
2^{1} 99
2^{3} 99
$2^{3f.}$ 99
$2^{5ff.}$ 99
2^{13} 98
2^{14}–7^{4} 100
3^{1} 137
3^{6} 434, 554
4^{1} 554
4^{14} 519
5^{1} 511
5^{2} 520
$5^{2f.}$ 520
5^{10} 511
5^{14} 434
5^{17} 510, 562 f.
$5^{18f.}$ 512
$6^{14ff.}$ 100
6^{14}–7^{1} 100
8^{12} 99
8^{23} 556
10–13 99 f., 137
10^{1} 99
11^{2} 117
11^{23} 103
12^{14} 99
12^{20} 435
13^{1} 99, 138
13^{2} 99
13^{10} 99

GALATIANS:
1^{2} 100
1^{13} 546
1^{18} 141
$1^{18f.}$ 508
2 101 f.
2^{1} 102
2^{20} 511
3^{11} 420
3^{27} 509, 562
4^{4} 439
$4^{4f.}$ 547
4^{13} 101 f.
$5^{19f.}$ 142
5^{19-21} 434
$5^{22f.}$ 142
5^{22-25} 435
6^{2} 418, 508
6^{6} 561
6^{11} 138
6^{15} 562 f.
6^{16} 443

EPHESIANS:
1^{1} 106
1^{3-14} 141
1^{7} 563
$1^{9f.}$ 513
1^{13} 563
1^{14} 22
1^{22} 547
$1^{22f.}$ 546
1^{23} 105
2^{10} 512
$2^{20ff.}$ 517
2^{20-22} 548

EPHESIANS—(*continued*)
$3^{3ff.}$ . . . 105
3^{9-11} . . . 547
4^{1} . . . 433
4^{11} . . . 550, 552
4^{16} . . . 104 f.
4^{22-24} . . . 509
4^{24} . . . 562
4^{30} . . . 563
5^{10} . . . 435
5^{14} . . . 91, 141
5^{19} . . . 545
5^{22}–6^{9} . . . 142
5^{23-32} . . . 547
5^{26} . . . 563
5^{32} . . . 547

PHILIPPIANS:
1 f. . . . 107
1^{1} . . . 110, 550 f., 553
$1^{12ff.}$ . . . 106
1^{13} . . . 102
$1^{14ff.}$ . . . 103
$1^{21ff.}$ . . . 519
1^{26} . . . 103 f.
$1^{29f.}$ . . . 107
2^{5-11} . . . 469
2^{6-11} . . . 91, 506
2^{11} . . . 561
2^{12} . . . 433
2^{17} . . . 103
2^{19} . . . 104
$2^{19ff.}$ . . . 106
2^{24} . . . 103 f.
2^{25} . . . 556
$2^{25ff.}$ . . . 106
3^{1} . . . 107
3^{1}–4^{9} . . . 107
3^{2} . . . 107
$3^{2f.}$ . . . 562
$3^{2ff.}$ . . . 107
3^{2-21} . . . 137
3^{2}–4^{3} . . . 107
$3^{8f.}$ . . . 512
3^{20} . . . 223
$3^{20f.}$ . . . 519
4^{4-23} . . . 107
4^{8} . . . 22
4^{10} . . . 103
$4^{10ff.}$ . . . 106
4^{10-20} . . . 107
$4^{15.\ 17f.}$ . . . 22
4^{22} . . . 102
$4^{22ff.}$ . . . 107

COLOSSIANS:
$1^{7f.}$ . . . 107
1^{14} . . . 563
1^{15-20} . . . 91, 141
1^{18} . . . 105, 546 f.
1^{20} . . . 513
1^{24} . . . 546 f.
1^{27} . . . 105, 511
$2^{8ff.}$ . . . 108
2^{8}–3^{4} . . . 107
$2^{9f.}$ . . . 108
2^{10} . . . 105
2^{11} . . . 108, 562
2^{12} . . . 561 f.
$2^{14.\ 16}$ . . . 108
2^{18} . . . 23
$2^{18f.}$ . . . 108
3^{3} . . . 562
3^{5} . . . 433
3^{5-12} . . . 433
3^{9} . . . 562
$3^{9f.}$ . . . 509
3^{14} . . . 434
3^{16} . . . 545
3^{18}–4^{1} . . . 142
3^{20} . . . 435
4^{16} . . . 137
4^{18} . . . 138
4^{19} . . . 107

1 THESSALONIANS:
1^{1} . . . 548
$2^{1ff.}$ . . . 109
$2^{15f.}$ . . . 109
2^{17}–3^{6} . . . 110
$3^{1ff.}$ . . . 109
4 f. . . . 109
4^{1} . . . 107
$4^{1ff.}$ . . . 91
4^{1-10} . . . 109
4^{1-12} . . . 142
4^{13}–5^{11} . . . 109
$5^{1ff.}$ . . . 109
$5^{12ff.}$ . . . 109
5^{14} . . . 109
$5^{17f.}$ . . . 564

2 THESSALONIANS:
1^{1} . . . 548
2 . . . 109
2^{2} . . . 109, 138
2^{15} . . . 135
3^{6} . . . 91
$3^{14f.}$ . . . 137
3^{17} . . . 110, 138

1 TIMOTHY:
2^{8-15} . . . 142
3^{1-15} . . . 142
3^{8-13} . . . 550
3^{16} . . . 91, 141 f.
$4^{1ff.}$ . . . 111
4^{14} . . . 563
5^{3-22} . . . 142
$6^{1f.}$ . . . 142
6^{11} . . . 142
6^{12} . . . 420, 561

2 TIMOTHY:
1^{6} . . . 563
$1^{13ff.}$ . . . 111
2^{8} . . . 440
$2^{11f.}$ . . . 142
2^{11-13} . . . 91
4^{20} . . . 272

TITUS:
1^{5}–2^{10} . . . 142
1^{7} . . . 551
$2^{1f.}$ . . . 111
$2^{13f.}$ . . . 142

PHILEMON:
^{16} . . . 108
^{22} . . . 103

HEBREWS:
2^{5} . . . 112
3^{1} . . . 555
$3^{7ff.}$ . . . 516
6^{2} . . . 563
7^{26-28} . . . 141
$8^{6ff.}$ . . . 112
10^{22} . . . 563
$10^{32ff.}$ . . . 114
10^{38} . . . 420
11^{1} . . . 22
11^{23-27} . . . 444
13^{9} . . . 135
13^{22} . . . 137

JAMES:
1^{2-12} . . . 432
1^{3} . . . 22
1^{9-11} . . . 432
$1^{19ff.}$ . . . 113
1^{25} . . . 509
1^{27} . . . 113, 432
$2^{1ff.}$ . . . 113
2^{2} . . . 113
2^{5-7} . . . 432
2^{8} . . . 509
$2^{10ff.}$ . . . 113
2^{12} . . . 509
$2^{14ff.}$ . . . 113
3^{15-17} . . . 432
$3^{6ff.}$ . . . 113
3^{8-12} . . . 432
$3^{13ff.}$ . . . 113
3^{14-16} . . . 432
$3^{17f.}$ . . . 432
$4^{1ff.}$ . . . 113
$4^{1-3.\ 11f.}$ . . . 432
$5^{1ff.}$ . . . 113
5^{1-6} . . . 432
5^{3} . . . 113
5^{4} . . . 113, 432
$5^{19f.}$ . . . 432

1 PETER:
1^{1} . . . 113
1^{3}–4^{11} . . . 114, 142
1^{7} . . . 22
1^{11} . . . 515

I PETER—(*continued*)
$1^{15f.}$ 433
1^{15-22} 142
1^{19} 516
1^{20} 142
$1^{22f.}$ 433
2^{1} 433
$2^{4ff.}$ 517
2^{5} 548, 550
2^{9} 548, 550
2^{10} 113, 548
2^{11} 433
2^{11}–3^{12} 433
2^{13-17} 433
2^{15-18} 433
$2^{21ff.}$ 114
2^{21-24} 141
3^{14} 429
$3^{18f.\ 22}$ 142
3^{19} 180
4^{3} 113
4^{12}–5^{11} 142
4^{14} 429
5^{12} 114

2 PETER:
1^{5-7} 142
2 114
2^{4} 114
$2^{10b.\ 11}$ 115

I JOHN:
1^{6} 117
1^{8} 117
2^{4} 117
2^{6} 117
2^{19} 117
2^{20} 117
2^{27} 135
3^{14} 420
3^{23} 117
$4^{1ff.}$ 117
4^{2} 117
4^{5} 117
4^{7-12} 435
$4^{10ff.}$ 117
4^{12} 117
4^{19} 435

2 JOHN:
1 117
8-10 117
12 138
13 117

3 JOHN:
9 554
9f. 118
11 118
13 138

JUDE:
1 114
3 361
4-16 114
5 516
6 114
9 114
14 81
17 114

REVELATION:
1^{4} 118, 548
1^{6} 550
1^{9} 118
1^{10} 564
1^{11} 548
1^{13} 464
2^{10} 241
2^{13} 241
4 91
$4^{8.\ 11}$ 142
5 91
5^{5} 440
$5^{9f.}$ 142
$5^{13f.}$ 142
6^{6} 578
7^{3-8} 563
7^{12} 142
7^{15-17} 141
9^{11} 11
$11^{1f.}$ . . . . 118 f.
11^{3-13} 118
$11^{17f.}$ 142
12^{14} 504
13^{10} 141
13^{14} 241
14^{6} 493
14^{8} 312
14^{14} 464
$15^{3f.}$ 141
17 502
$17^{9ff.}$ 118
18 141
$19^{1.\ 4-6}$ 142
22^{9} 118
22^{20} 142

II. AUTHORS

Abba, R., 10
Abel, F.-M., 204
Ackroyd, P. R., 162
Adam, A., 558
Adams, A. W., 162
Aeschylus, 19
Aland, K., 165, 181, 560, 562
Albright, W. F., 36, 248, 256, 258, 261, 280, 332, 380
Alcuin, 174
Allegro, J. M., 280
Alt, A., 37, 134, 252, 264, 336
Ambrosiaster, 170
Anderson, B. W., 332
Anderson, G. W., 70
Aphraates, 164, 170
Aristides, 561
Ariston of Pella, 503
Aristotle, 19, 435, 472
Arndt, W. F., 26
Athanasius, 4, 120, 167, 175, 357, 557
Audet, J.-P., 561
Augustine, 71, 135, 418, 562, 564

Baldi, D., 204
Balla, E., 53, 55
Baly, D., 204
Barr, J., 25 f.
Barrett, C. K., 332, 521
Barrois, A.-G., 280, 580
Bartlet, J. V., 561
Barton, D. M., 70
Bauer, H., 18
Bauer, W., 24, 26
Baumgartner, W., 65, 184
Beasley-Murray, G. R., 569
Beek, M. A., 219
Begrich, J., 134
Bengel, J. A., 177
Bensly, R. L., 81
Bentley, R., 177
Bentzen, A., 70, 134
Berliner, A., 158
Berossus, 249
Bewer, J. A., 70
Beza, T., 176
Billerbeck, P., 561
Birdsall, J. N., 167
Black, M., 24, 26, 136, 143, 161, 174, 280, 558
Blake, R. P., 169, 175
Blass, F., 21, 25
Boman, T., 26
Bonsirven, J., 417
van den Born, A., 49
Bornkamm, G., 100, 494
Bousset, W., 391, 417
Bover, J. M., 181
Box, G. H., 565
Brandon, S. G. F., 521, 537
Breasted, J. H., 219
Briggs, C. A., 18
Bright, J., 332, 538
Brockelmann, C., 18
Brooke, A. E., 157
Brown, F., 18
Browne, L. E., 49
Bruce, F. F., 162
Bryennios, P., 552
Budde, K., 41, 53, 60, 339
du Buit, M., 204
Bultmann, R., 140, 143, 521
Burgon, J. W., 9
Burkitt, F. C., 168, 174, 565 f.
Burrows, M., 280
Burton, E. D., 102

Caird, G. B., 521
Calvin, J., 9
Cannon, W. W., 53
Cantineau, J., 13, 18
Cary, M., 244
Cassiodorus, 174
Castro, P., 159
Cazelles, H., 18
Cerfaux, L., 547
Charles, R. H., 71, 82, 89
Charlesworth, M. P., 245
Cheyne, T. K., 58
Chrysostom, 167, 178
Cicero, 243
Cirlot, F. L., 565
Clark, A. C., 171
Clement of Alexandria, 121, 164, 168, 170, 171, 178
Clogg, F. B., 122
de Colines, S., 176
Colwell, E. C., 172
Contenau, G., 219
Cooke, G. A., 49
Cornill, C. H., 41, 62 f.
Cowley, A., 18
Creed, J. M., 561
Crehan, J. H., 538, 561
Cross, F. L., 142
Cross, F. M., 153, 162
Crowfoot, J. W., 262
Cullmann, O., 143, 521, 557, 560, 562 f.
Cunliffe-Jones, H., 10

Cyprian, 164, 170, 178 f., 561
Cyril of Alexandria, 167
Cyril of Jerusalem, 169, 562

Dahood, M., 62
Dalman, G., 65
Daube, D., 562 f.
Davies, W. D., 143
Davies, J. G., 551
Debrunner, A., 21, 25
Deissmann, A., 26
Delitzsch, F., 60, 62
Demosthenes, 19
Denney, J., 110
Dibelius, 143
Didymus, 167
Dix, G., 555 f., 558, 563, 565
Dodd, C. H., 10, 26, 92, 98, 106, 118, 136, 141, 143, 435, 494, 507, 522, 554
Drews, A., 565
Driver, G. R., 18, 280, 528
Driver, S. R., 18, 70, 543
Dugmore, C. W., 10, 564 f.
Duhm, B., 52 f., 55
Duncan, G. S., 122
Dupont-Sommer, A., 18, 280, 417

Edersheim, A., 540, 545
Ehrhardt, A., 563
Ehrlich, E., 332
Eichrodt, W., 380
Eissfeldt, O., 35, 39, 41, 70, 134
Engnell, I., 38, 537
Ephraem Syrus, 164, 170
Epictetus, 21
Epiphanius, 560
Erasmus, 176
Erman, A., 219
Estienne, R., 176
Euripides, 19
Eusebius, 116, 120, 138, 156, 168, 169, 173, 432, 503
Euthalius, 173
Ewald, H., 60

Farrer, A. M., 555
Fascher, E., 143
Fell, J., 177
Ferrar, W. H., 179
Field, F., 155
Filson, F. V., 204
Fisher, W. B., 204
Flemington, W. F., 569
Flew, R. Newton, 494
Foakes-Jackson, F. J., 23, 565
Fohrer, G., 49
Fotheringham, J. K., 576, 580
Frame, J. E., 109
Frank, T., 244
Frankfort, H., 280, 537
Freer, C. F., 168
Frere, W. H., 566

Friedrich, G., 26
Frumentius, 175
Funk, R. W., 25

Gadd, C. J., 265
Galling, K., 62, 68
Gardner-Smith, P., 116, 122
Garitte, G., 175
Garrod, D., 246
Garstang, J., 261
Gärtner, B., 567
Gaster, T. H., 280, 558
Gavin, F., 565 f.
Geiger, A., 565
Gese, H., 258
Gesenius, W., 18
Gingrich, F. W., 26
Ginsberg, H. L., 62
Glueck, N., 257 f., 261 f., 280
Goguel, M., 565
Goodspeed, E. J., 105
Gordis, R., 62
Gordon, C. H., 280
Gottwald, N. K., 62
van Goudoever, J., 580
Graf, K. H., 33
Granild, S., 68
Grant, F. C., 143, 161
Grant, M., 245
Gray, G. B., 57 f., 545
Grayston, K., 110
Greenberg, J. H., 18
Greenlee, J. H., 169
Greenslade, S. L., 558
Gregory of Nyssa, 564
Grenfell, B. P., 278
Gressmann, H., 417
Griesbach, J. J., 169, 177
Griffith, G. T., 244
Grollenberg, L. H., 204
Gunkel, H., 55, 134, 139, 274
Guthrie, D., 110

Hahn, H. F., 70
Haldar, A., 535
Haller, M., 65
Hänel, J., 68
Harding, G. L., 271
Harnack, A., 96, 552 f., 555
Harris, R., 179
Harris, Z. S., 18
Harrison, P. N., 110
Hastings, J., 89, 161
Hebert, A. G., 10
Hegesippus, 557
Hempel, J., 134
Henshaw, T., 122
Hentschke, R., 258
Herbert, A. S., 380, 523, 532, 536, 545
Herdan, G., 110
Herder, J. G., 62
Herford, R. Travers, 565
Herklots, H. G. G., 162

Herntrich, V., 49
Herodotus, 19
Hesychius, 156, 166, 168, 177, 179
Higgins, A. J. B., 569
Hill, G. F., 580
Hippolytus, 164, 408, 560 f., 564, 568
Hölscher, G., 37, 48, 65
Homer, 19
Hooke, S. H., 535, 537
van Hoonacker, A., 58
Hort, F. J. A., 166 f., 170, 177 ff., 180 f., 546, 549
Hoschander, J., 63
Howard, W. F., 22
Howie, C. G., 49
Hudson, D. F., 25
Hug, J. L., 177
Humbert, P., 52 f.
Hunt, A. S., 278
Hunter, A. M., 122, 143, 522

Ingholt, H., 258
Irenaeus, 94, 164, 170, 178 f., 550, 557, 564
Irwin, W. A., 48, 162

Jaubert, A., 569, 571, 580
Jay, E. G., 25
Jensen, P., 63
Jeremias, J., 111, 494, 559 f., 562, 566
Jerome, 71, 77, 79, 164 f., 168 f., 173 f.
Johnson, A. R., 55, 134, 535, 537, 545
Johnston, G., 547, 558
Jones, A. H. M., 244 f.
Josephus, 21, 79, 268 f., 309, 319, 323, 326, 331, 381, 388 f., 396 f., 399, 401 ff., 408, 436, 460, 534, 538, 544, 571
Judge, E. A., 559
Jülicher, A., 165
Justin Martyr, 135, 142, 164, 170, 178, 562, 564, 568
Juvenal, 242

Kahle, P., 149, 162, 248
Kahle, P. E. (Jr.), 165
Kant, Immanuel, 420
Kapelrud, A. S., 50
Kappler, W., 157
Kaufmann, Y., 380
Kautzsch, E., 18
Kemp, E. W., 557 f.
Kennedy, A. R. S., 41 f.
Kennett, R. H., 37, 56, 533
Kent, A. F., 65
Kenyon, 156, 162, 166, 179, 182
Kenyon, K., 246, 256, 280
Kilpatrick, G. D., 181
Kirby, J. C., 142
Kirk, K. E., 534 f.
Kittel, G., 26
Kittel, R., 150, 547

Klijn, A. F. J., 181 f.
Knox, W. L., 141, 143
Kraus, H. J., 380
Kraeling, E. G., 70, 204
Kraetzschmar, R., 48
Kramer, A. N., 133
Kuenen, A., 33
Kuhl, C., 134

Lachmann, K., 167, 177
de Lagarde, P., 63, 158
Lagrange, M. J., 417
Lake, K., 23, 107, 120, 122, 167, 169, 179, 181, 565
Lake, S., 122, 167, 169
Lamarche, P., 54
Lampe, G. W. H., 563
Langdon, S., 62, 580
Langton, S., 77
Leander, P., 18
Legg, S. C. E., 180
Lemaire, P., 204
Leo XIII, 7
Leon, H. J., 245
Lewy, H., 580
Lietzmann, H., 565
Lightfoot, J. B., 106, 120 ff., 549 ff., 553, 556 f.
Lightfoot, R. H., 116, 143
Lillie, W., 435
Lods, A., 332
Lofthouse, W. F., 435
Lohmeyer, E., 107, 141
Lindars, B., 522
Lloyd, S., 280
Lock, W., 110
Löhr, M., 37
Lucian, 72, 156, 166 ff., 174, 176, 177 ff., 278
Luther, Martin, 62
Lyonnet, S., 175

Macadam, L., 264
McArthur, A. A., 569
McGiffert, A. C., 109
McHardy, W. D., 175
McLean, N., 157
McNeile, A. H., 62, 122,
Machen, J. G., 25
Madden, F. W., 580
Manson, T. W., 113, 136, 143, 157, 398, 435, 494, 522, 551, 554, 556, 566 f.
Manson, W., 112, 494
Marcion, 97, 119, 138, 163 f., 170 ff.
Margolis, M., 157
Marti, K., 53
Masson, C., 141
Matzkow, W., 165
May, H. G., 162, 204
Meek, T. J., 60
Meinhold, J., 65
Meissner, B., 63

Mendenhall, G. E., 338, 380
Merk, A., 180
Messel, N., 49
Messina, G., 164
Metzger, B. M., 26, 77, 89
Micklem, N., 566 f.
Milburn, R. L. P., 568
Milik, J. T., 280
Mill, J., 177
Milligan, G., 26
Mitton, C. L., 105
Moffatt, J., 22, 98, 104, 108, 111, 114, 122
Molitor, J., 175
Molland, E., 557, 560
Montefiore, C. G., 565
Montgomery, J. A., 65
Moore, G. F., 417, 565
Morgenstern, J., 35
Moscati, S., 219
Moule, C. F. D., 26, 142, 522, 555, 569
Moulton, J. H., 26
Mowinckel, S., 37, 55 f., 380, 536
Muilenburg, J., 380, 435
Munck, J., 522

Nairne, A., 111
Neill, S., 555
Nestle, E., 181
Newman, J. H., 577
North, C. R., 38
Noth, M., 37 f., 39, 264, 332
Nougayrol, J., 272

O'Callaghan, R. T., 219
Oesterley, W. O. E., 35, 44, 54, 56 f., 67 f., 70, 245, 332, 417, 544 f., 565 f.
Oestreicher, T., 37
Olmstead, A. T., 219
Origen, 97, 119, 121, 155 f., 163 f., 166 f., 168 f., 170 ff., 177 ff., 564
Orlinsky, H. M., 332
Otto, R., 524

Packer, J. I., 10
Pamphilus, 156, 166, 168
Papias, 94, 117, 138, 500
Parrot, A., 540
Parvis, M. M., 182
Peake, A. S., 58, 161
Pedersen, J., 349, 380
Pelagius, 170
Petrie, W. M. Flinders, 247
Pfeiffer, R. H., 35, 51, 53, 63, 68, 70, 89
Philo, 21, 23, 267, 383, 388, 406, 408, 411 f., 544
Photius, 167
Pindar, 19
Plato, 19, 137, 243, 411
Pliny the Elder, 405 f., 564
Pliny the Younger, 436, 577
Plummer, A., 99
Plutarch, 21
Polybius, 21
Polycrates, 504
Porteous, N. W., 435
Posidonius, 243
Preisker, H., 142
Preiss, T., 567
Price, I. M., 162
Pritchard, J. B., 219, 280, 332
Ptolemy (the astronomer), 254

Rabbula, 174
von Rad, G., 35, 67, 380, 524, 537
Rahlfs, A., 157
Rahtjen, B. D., 107
Ranston, H., 62
Rawlinson, A. E. J., 555
Redlich, E. B., 143
Reicke, B., 559
Reid, J. K. S., 10
Reifenberg, A., 580
Reisner, G. A., 262
Renan, E., 565
Richardson, A., 10, 522, 547
Riesenfeld, H., 143
Roberts, B. J., 162
Robertson, E., 37, 159
Robinson, H. W., 47, 55, 162, 380, 435
Robinson, J. A., 106, 550, 552 f.
Robinson, T. H., 35, 44, 54, 67 f., 70, 245, 332
Ropes, J. H., 170
Rosenthal, F., 18
Rostovtzeff, M., 244
Rothstein, J. W., 68
Rowley, H. H., 10, 18, 26, 40, 65 f., 70, 89, 161, 280, 332, 380, 417, 435, 544, 558
Rudolph, W., 37, 51, 68

Saggs, H. W., 280
Salmon, E. T., 244
Sappho, 19
Sayers, D., 77
Schaeffer, C. F. A., 272
Schlatter, A., 115, 522
Schmidt, K. L., 141, 143, 547, 549
Schoeps, H. J., 522
Schürer, E., 417
Schweitzer, W., 10
Scott, C. A., 435, 522
Scott, R. B. Y., 580
Scullard, H. H., 244
Segal, J. B., 580
Segert, S., 18
Sellin, E., 32, 36, 42, 51, 57, 61 f.
Selwyn, E. G., 143
Semler, J. S., 177
Sherwin-White, A. N., 245
Siegfried, C., 62
Simon, M., 417, 546
Skinner, J., 30

Smend, R., 55
Smith, C. R., 435
Smith, G. A., 204
Smith, J., 49
Smith, S., 265
Smith, W. R., 527
Snaith, N. H., 424, 537, 571
von Soden, H., 164, 179 f., 181, 576
Sohm, R., 549
Sophocles, 19
Souter, A., 3, 180, 182
Sparks, H. F. D., 122
Sperber, A., 158
Spitta, F., 565
Stauffer, E., 494, 522, 559 f.
Stendahl, K., 559
Stephanus, *see* Estienne, R.
Strabo, 21
Strachan, J., 100
Strauss, D. F., 565
Streeter, B. H., 142, 167 ff., 179 f., 553 f., 556
Suetonius, 436
Suggs, M. J., 168
Sukenik, E. L., 271
Swete, H. B., 157, 550

Tacitus, 436
Tarn, W. W., 244
Tasker, R. V. G., 168
Tatian, 163 ff., 170, 172, 179
Taylor, V., 122, 140, 143, 182, 494
Tcherikover, V., 245
Telfer, W., 557, 569
Tertullian, 170, 178, 561, 564
Thackeray, H. St J., 157, 572
Theodulf, 174
Thiele, E. R., 580
Thomas, D. W., 280, 332, 570
Thornton, L. S., 555
Tirard, H. M., 219
Tischendorf, L. K. F., 167, 179 f.
Torrey, C. C., 23, 47 ff., 65, 68, 118
Tregelles, S. P., 167

Turner, C. H., 179, 552 f., 579
Turner, H. E. W., 494
Turner, N., 25 f.

Ulfilas, 167
Ullendorff, E., 18
van Unnik, W. C., 142

Vaganay, A., 181
Vaillant, A., 86
de Vaux, R., 271, 380, 537, 540, 545
Vernet, F., 557
Vincent, H., 270
Virolleaud, H., 272
Vogels, H. J., 164, 181
Volz, P., 37
Vööbus, A., 164, 174 f., 182

Weingreen, J., 18
Weiser, A., 70, 134
Welch, A. C., 37, 65, 67
Wellhausen, J., 33
Westcott, B. F., 115, 167, 177 ff., 181
Westermann, C., 364
Wetzstein, J. G., 60
Wikgren, A. P., 162, 182
Williams, C. S. C., 3
Wilson, J. A., 280
Wiseman, D. J., 265
Wolfson, H. A., 417
Woolley, L., 249
Wright, G. E., 204, 280
Würthwein, E., 162

Ximenes, Cardinal, 176

Yadin, Y., 111, 261 ff.

Zahn, T., 97
Ziegler, J., 157
Zimmern, H., 63
Zuntz, G., 168, 171 f., 175, 182
de Zwaan, J., 23

III. GENERAL

Aaron, 31, 33, 112, 407, 517, 533, 541
Aaronites, 533 f.
Abana, 187
Abarim, 203
Abba, 471
Abda, 196
Abel, 525, 529
Abel-beth-maacah, 188
Aberdeen Codex, 149
Abiathar, 300, 351, 533, 535 f., 543
Abimelech (in Genesis), 27
Abimelech (king), 40, 296 f.
Abisha Scroll, 159
Abner, 42, 299
Abomination of Desolation, 64 f., 519
Abraham, 27 f., 31, 84, 112, 197, 214, 248 f., 255, 259 f., 269, 283 f., 285 f., 335 f., 352, 447, 524 f., 546
Abraham, Apocalypse of, 87
Abraham, Testament of, 87
Absalom, 300
Accho, 188 ff., 190
Acclamations, 124
Achaemenids, 218
Achaia, 101, 226, 272, 499 f.
Achish, 299
Achmimic version, 165
Acrostic poems, 52
Actium, 225
Acts, Book of, 90, 95 f., 97, 101, 110, 114, 137, 166, 171, 173, 175 f., 230, 239, 241, 271, 278 f., 437, 468, 483, 489, 498, 507, 546, 551
Adad, 213
Adad-apla-idin, 216
Adad-nirari I., 216
Adam (place), 188, 192
Adam, 525
Adam and Eve, Books of, 87
Adana, 255
Address, 128
Adonai, 386, 410
Adonijah, 300, 533
Adonis, 60
Adultery, 428, 479
woman taken in, 487
Adysh Gospels, 175
Aedile, 272
Aelia Capitolina, 332
Aegean Sea, 19, 213 f.
Aegina, 267
Agapē, 549
Afra, 164
Africa, 164, 172
Africa (province), 224, 226
Agrippa, Herod, *see* Herod Agrippa
Agur, 56 f.
Ahab, 34, 44, 211, 214, 217, 258, 262 f., 303 f., 423
Ahasuerus, 63
Ahaz, 46, 52, 304, 359, 536
dial of, 570
Ahijah, 302, 351
Ahikar, 73, 133, 217
Ahiram, 124
Ahriman, 374
Ahura Mazda, 218, 374
Ai, 292, 524
'Ain Feshkha, 268
'Ain et-Tabigha, 567
Aijalon, Valley of, 192, 194
Akhenaton, 208 f., 282
Akhlamu, 216
Akiba, 145, 331, 401
Akkad, 205, 249
Akkadian, 12 f., 15, 205, 208, 210, 218, 248, 255, 257, 339, 540
Akkadians, 129, 282
Alalakh, 129
Alcimus, 325
Aleppo, 185, 197, 213, 272
Aleppo Codex, 149 f.
Alexander the Great, 20, 46, 52, 64, 66, 208, 218, 220 ff., 317, 320, 321, 376
Alexander (4th cent. A.D.), 557
Alexander Jannaeus, *see* Jannaeus
Alexandria, 77, 79 f., 83, 85 f., 88, 154, 166, 168, 171 f., 173 f., 178 ff., 221 ff., 237, 254, 321 f., 382 ff., 386, 388, 498, 557 f.
Alexandria Troas, 121
han-Allat, 266
Allegory, 130
Alphabet, 250, 255, 273
Altar(s), 272, 525 ff., 532 f., 535
of incense, 541
Amalekites, 36, 217
Amanus, 197
Amarna Age, 255, 261, 287
Amarna Letters, 12, 129, 214, 247, 254, 257 f., 273, 282, 291
Amittai, 51
'Amman, 258, 264
Ammon, Ammonites, 41, 127, 203, 211, 217, 257 f., 266, 284 f., 296 f., 300, 309 f., 318
Amon (god), 209, 282
Amon (king), 306

Amorites, 13, 127, 205, 210, 213 f., 216, 250 f., 256 f., 259, 282, 284, 543
Amos, 304, 356 f., 359, 363, 423 f., 440, 535
Amos, Book of, 45, 50 f.
Amphictyony, 281, 287, 294 f.
Amurru, 213, 256
Amyntas, 231
An, 206
Anat, 214
Anath, 126, 272
Anatolia, 185, 197, 205, 207 f., 210, 215, 217, 250, 255, 258 f., 498
Anatolian Piedmont zone, 185, 197
Anecdotes, 128
Anencletus, 557
Angels, 218, 269, 397, 402, 409, 410 ff.
Anna, 140, 461
Annals, Court, 128, 253
Annas, 503
Anthropomorphism, 29
Antichrist, 109, 119, 503
Antigonids, 221
Anti-Lebanon, 186 ff., 196, 199 f.
Antioch, 98, 100, 120, 165, 167, 172, 174, 179, 185, 197, 224, 236, 382, 497 f., 548
Antiochus III., 219, 221 f., 323
Antiochus IV. (Epiphanes), 64 f., 76, 79, 85, 222, 323 ff., 327, 375 f., 397 f., 403, 538, 542
Antipas, Herod, *see* Herod Antipas
Antipas (martyr), 241
Antipater, 224, 232, 328
Anti-semitism, 382
Antonia, 234, 239, 270 f.
Antony, Mark, 225, 328 f.
Anu, 206, 213, 215
Apamea, 235
'Aperu, *see* 'Apiru
Aphek, 192
'Apiru, 214, 261, 287
Apocrypha, 3, 69, 71 ff., 151, 409 f.
  and Wisdom Literature, 370
Apocalypse, Little, 457
Apocalypse of Ezra, *see* Ezra Apocalypse
Apocalypse of Weeks, *see* Weeks, Apocalypse of
Apocalypses, 72, 138
Apocalyptic, 83, 118, 269, 374 f., 413, 440, 452 f., 463 f., 468, 519
Apodictic law, 129
Apollos, 112
Apologetic, Christian, 513 ff.
Apophthegma, 140
Apostle (term), 443, 482
Apostles, Preaching of, 507
Apostolic age, 489
  history of, 494 ff.
  doctrine of, 506 ff.
Apostolic Decree, 384
Apries, 208, 309
Aqhat, 277
'Aqaba, 185, 262
Aquila, Version of, 98, 155, 548 f.
Aquitania, 226
Arabah, 194 ff., 257, 261 f.
Arabia, 185 f., 201, 203, 205, 212, 233, 251, 256, 266, 301, 309, 328
  South, 258
Arabic, 13, 15
Arabic versions, 81, 164
Aram, 34, 44, 127
Aram Naharaim, 197
Aramaic, 11, 13, 16 f., 19 f., 23, 63, 64 f., 66 f., 72 f., 81 ff., 86, 88, 92, 94, 118, 136, 145 ff., 148, 154, 157, 174, 215, 217 f., 266, 314, 322, 391, 440, 471, 480, 492, 545
Aramaeans, 129, 210 f., 213 f., 215 ff., 250, 252, 255 f., 258 f., 263, 284 f., 300 f., 303 f.
Archelaus, 232, 234, 329 f.
Archaeology, and Biblical events, 259 ff.
  and culture of Israel, 272 ff.
  and literature of the Bible, 217 f.
  and neighbours of Israel, 254 ff.
  and religion of Israel, 274 ff.
  and text of New Testament, 278 ff.
  Biblical, 246 ff.
  Egyptian, 247 f.
  Mesopotamian, 248 ff.
  Near Eastern, 246
Aretas, 233 f., 328
Aristarchus, 107
Aristeas, Letter of, 154, 322, 386
Aristobulus I., 326
Aristobulus II., 222, 224, 326, 328
Arisu, 260
Ark (of Covenant), 36, 41 f., 66, 295, 297, 300, 344, 347, 351, 353, 365, 533, 535, 537, 540 f., 544
  Song of, 125, 344
Ark (Noah's), 28 f., 249
Armageddon, 88
Armenia, 210 f.
Armenian version, 81, 154, 164, 175 f.
Arnon, 194, 202, 258
Arpad, 17, 215, 258
Artaxerxes I., 66, 218, 317 ff.
Artaxerxes II., 63, 66, 218, 318
Arvad, 214
Aryans, 210, 217
Asa, 536
Asaphite psalms, 540
Ascension of Christ, 96, 451
Asenath, 88
Ashdod, 46, 193, 216
Asher (tribe), 287
Asher (district), 190
Asherah, 214, 542
Ashkelon, 193, 216, 256
Ashtart, 214

Ashtoreth, 214
Ashur (god), 210, 213
Ashur (city), 210, 212, 250
Ashurbanipal, 211, 571
Ashurdan III., 253, 573
Ashur-etil-ilani, 211
Ashurnazirpal, 211
Ashur-nirari V., 253
Ashur-uballit I., 210
Ashur-uballit II., 212
Asia, 208, 221
Asia (province), 101, 103, 107, 118, 224, 226, 499, 504, 520, 548, 551, 553
Asia Minor, 98, 100, 113, 218, 221, 223, 267, 271, 282, 298, 310, 321, 336
Asiarch, 231
Asmodaeus, 73 f.
Assouan, 247
Assyria, 17, 50, 76, 129, 133, 196 f., 205, 208, 210 f., 215, 217, 250 f., 253 f., 258 f., 262, 264, 267, 272, 276, 282 f., 303 f., 305 ff., 320, 356 f., 359 f., 375
  history of, 210 f.
  oracle on, 36, 52,
Astarte, 272, 542
Astyages, 218
Aten, 209
Athaliah, 303
Athens, 19 f.
Athlit, 267
Athos, Mt., 173
Athtar, 259
Atonement, 511 ff., 527
  Day of, 389, 392, 538
Atrahasis, 128, 249
Augusta, 232
Augustus, 220, 225 ff., 229 ff., 234 f., 236, 241, 269, 271, 329
Augustus' band, 229
Austria, 226
Autobiography, 128
Avaris, 208
Avesta, 218
Azariah, 303 f.
Azarias (in Tobit), 73
Azekah, 193, 265

Baal, 126, 214, 217, 272, 274 f., 277, 337, 349, 355, 542
Baal Shamin, 259
Baalbek, 186
Babbar, 206
Babel, Tower of, 11, 248, 373
Babylon, Babylonians, 46, 48, 64, 73, 146 f., 158, 212, 215, 222, 249 f., 252, 254, 265 f., 272, 275, 282, 305 ff., 309 ff., 360, 516, 527, 533, 536, 538, 544, 572
Babylonia, 17, 48 f., 50 f., 55, 59 f., 62 f., 65, 78, 133, 205, 208, 210 f., 215 f., 217 f.
  history of, 205, 211 f.
  literature of, 212
  religion of, 206, 212
  social conditions of, 212
Babylonian Chronicle, 251, 265
Bacchus, 243
Bactria, 20, 226
Baghdad, 249, 252
Bagoas, 319
Balaam, 34, 36
Balikh, 197
Balkans, 228, 499
Banquet, Messianic, 456 f., 481, 490 ff., 567
Baptism, administration of Christian, 561
  Jewish proselyte, 560 ff.
  of Christians, 142, 482 ff., 507, 509, 516, 556, 560 ff.
  of infants, 559 f.
  of Jesus, 140, 441, 414, 469, 472
  of John, 441
  1 Peter and, 114
Bar Cochba, 145, 281, 331
Bar Koseba, 331
Barabbas, 449, 461
Barada, 187
Barak, 190
Barnabas, 112, 497 ff., 551
Barnabas, Epistle of, 120 f., 170
Bar-Rekub, 217
Baruch, 45, 48, 80, 87, 128, 265
1 Baruch, 80 f.
2 Baruch, 86 f., 374
3 Baruch, 88
Bashan, 187, 189, 202
Baths of Essenes, 407
Bathsheba, 351
Beatitudes, 86, 92, 428 f.
Beelzebub, 93, 479
Beersheba, 27, 31, 127, 185, 191, 195, 284, 337, 525
Behemoth, 58
Beirut, 186, 188
Bel, 213
Bel and the Dragon, 78
Belgica, 226
Beliar, 83
Belshazzar, 64, 212
Ben Asher, 148 ff.
Ben Chayyim, Jacob, 149 f.
Ben Naphtali, 148 f.
Ben Sira(ch), 57, 74 f., 134, 370
Benedictions, Eighteen, 392
Benedictus, 135, 158, 461
Ben-Hadad I., 217
Ben-Hadad II., 217
Bene Ammon, 258
Benefactor, 231
Benghazi, 267
Beni-shamali, 260
Beni-yamini, 259
Benjamin (tribe), 36, 39 f., 215, 260, 294 f., 300, 302, 497

Benjamin (district), 194
Beqa'a, 187 f., 196
Bernice, 240, 330
Berytus, 186
Bes, 209
Bethany, 446, 448, 492
Betharamphtha, 233
Bethel, 28, 30 f., 127, 260 f., 292, 306, 336, 346, 353, 359, 524 f., 533, 542
Beth-horon, Ascent of, 192
Bethlehem, 269, 358, 440
Bethlehem-judah, 533
Beth-Rehob, 216
Bethsaida, 233, 270, 443
Bethshan, 188 ff., 216, 255, 261, 272, 298
Beth-shemesh, 193
Bethsur, 276 f.
Beyond the River, 266, 284, 316, 319
Bhagavadgita, 7
Bibelanstalt of Württemberg, 181
Bible, and history, 5
 and other sacred writings, 5
 archaeology and the literature of, 277 f.
 authority of, 3 ff.
 background of, 205 ff., 220 ff.
 inspiration of, 6 ff.
 languages of, 11 ff., 19 ff.
 nature of, 3 ff.
 not free of error, 5 ff.
 standard of faith, 3
 unity and diversity of, 4 f.
Bibles, Printed, 149
 Rabbinic, 149
Biography, 128
Birth narratives of Jesus, 438
Birth pronouncements, 124
Bishops, 550 ff.
Bithynia, 226
Black Sea, 224
Blessing, 131
Blood, 526 f., 530 f.
Boasts, 125
Bodmer Papyri, *see* Papyri
Bodleian Library, 148, 165
Boghazköi, 215, 254
Bohairic version, 165, 167 f., 177 f.
Booths, Feast of, *see* Tabernacles, Feast of
Brazen Serpent, 195
Bridge of Jacob's daughters, 188
Britain, 237
British and Foreign Bible Society, 150, 181
British Museum, 148 f., 156, 158, 251
Bronze age, 261 f., 272
Brothers, Tale of Two, 209
Buddhist ethics, 435
Bulgaria, 226
Bull images, 353, 543 f.
Bush, Burning, 291
Byblos, 186, 200, 213, 259, 273
Byzantium, 167 f., 171, 173 f., 176, 178 ff.

Cadiz, 241
Caesar, 220, 226
 appeal to, 226, 239, 242, 242, 501
 worship of, 119
Caesar, Julius, *see* Julius Caesar
Caesar's household, 102, 104
Caesarea, 103, 167 ff., 172, 175 f., 179 f., 229, 232, 234, 236, 238 f., 270, 329 f., 504, 546
Caesarea Philippi, 188, 233, 437, 442, 444, 451, 453, 461 f., 464 f., 470 f.
Caiaphas, 236, 270, 566
Cain, 525, 529
Cain (king of Kedar), 266
Cairo Codex, 149
Cairo Genizah, *see* Genizah
Cairo synagogue, 147 ff., 157
Caleb, 19, 33, 38
Calendar, 447, 538, 570 ff.
 Deuteronomic, 343
 of Jubilees, 84
Calf, Golden, 544
Caligula, 233, 237, 330
 see also Gaius
Callistus, 567
Cambridge University Library, 148
Cambyses, 208, 218, 313, 315
Camel, 258
Cana, 270
Canaan, 257, 272 ff., 294, 336 f., 347, 424, 516, 524 ff., 532, 536 f., 538 f., 542 f.
 conquest of, 39 f., 291 ff.
 kingship in, 296
 literature of, 126 f.
 religion of, 295 f.
 spying of, 29
Canaan (son of Ham), curse of, 127
Canaanite language, and Hebrew, 11
Canaanites, 62, 213, 217, 247, 252, 256 f., 259, 301
 influence of, 37
Cananaean, 443
Canon, and Hebrew literature, 12
 Daniel and, 64, 69
 early Christian writing outside, 120 ff.
 growth of, 3 f.
 idea of, 3
 of Marcion, 163
 of New Testament, 119 f., 280
 of Old Testament, 66, 68 ff., 331, 335, 368
Capernaum, 235, 270, 443, 567
Cappadocia, 244
Cappadocian tablets, 259
Carchemish, 197, 208, 212, 215, 309, 360

Carites, 66
Carmel, 32, 185, 188, 190 f., 192, 246
Carthage, 170, 179, 214, 224
Casiphia, 312
Casius Mts., 197
Casuistic law, 129
Catechetical teaching, 142 f., 509
Caucasus, 210
Cenchreae, 548, 551
Cenomanian limestone, 191 f., 195, 204
Census, 227, 235
Central Rift, 189, 191, 194 f., 196, 200 f., 203
Central Valley of Palestine, 185
Centralization of worship, 32 f., 43, 306 f., 312, 368, 527, 531, 534, 539
Centurion, 228 f.
Centurion's servant, healing of, 489
Cephas, 90
  see also Peter
Cereal offering, 529, 539
Certainty of hearing, 133
Chalcis, 239
Chaldaeans, 52 f., 61, 64, 211, 216
Chaos, 275
Charisma, 552
Chebar, 361
Chemosh, 217, 364
Chenoboskion, 279
Cherubim, 540, 544
Chester Beatty papyri, *see* Papyri
Chicago Field Museum, 248
Chicago Oriental Institute, 253
Chief Musician, 56
Chloe, 99
Chorazin, 189, 270, 443
Chrestus, 238
Christ, church as body of, 547, 549, 568
  exaltation of, 105
  imitation of, 509
  saving work of, 433 f., 511 ff.
  see also Jesus
Christianity, and Judaism, 378 f.
  Jewish, 487
Christians, persecution of, 240
Christology, 105 f., 111 f., 116 f.
Chronicler, 42, 67 f., 84, 304, 307, 314, 316 ff., 320 f.
Chronicles, Books of, 44, 66 ff., 73, 128, 534
Church, and Bible, 3 ff.
  and New Israel, 5
  and priesthood, 516 ff.
  and sayings of Jesus, 140
  and Temple, 516 ff.
  apologetic of Early, 513 ff.
  Bible of Early, 154
  doctrine of Early, 105, 506 ff.
  early history of, 494 ff.
  first gospel of, 95
  hope of Early, 518 ff.

  Jesus and the, 480 ff.
  nature of, 545 ff.
  organization of Early, 549 ff.
  the body of Christ, 547, 549, 568
  worship in primitive, 559 ff.
Churches, Letters to seven, 504
Cilicia, 548
Cilician Gates, 197
Cimmerians, 211
Circumcision, 127, 384, 393, 398, 498 f., 561 ff.
Citizenship, Roman, 226 f., 230, 237, 241 f.
Claros, 23
Claudius, 237 ff., 242 f., 272, 498, 500
Clement of Rome, 112, 120 f., 557
1 Clement, 120, 143, 557 ff.
2 Clement, 120
Clement VIII., 176
Cleopas, 140
Cleopatra, 329
Climate of Palestine, 197 ff.
Coast plain of Palestine, 185, 199, 203
Codex Alexandrinus, 97, 156 f., 167, 177
Codex Bezae, 171, 176
Codex Bobiensis, 164
Codex Boernerianus, 97
Codex Brixianus, 164
Codex Cantabrigiensis, 164
Codex, Coislinianus, 173
Codex Colbertinus, 164
Codex Corbeiensis II., 164
Codex Ephraemi, 156, 167, 177
Codex Euthalianus, 173
Codex Floriacensis, 164
Codex Gigas, 164
Codex Koridethi, 168
Codex Monacensis, 164
Codex Palatinus, 164
Codex Regius, 167, 173
Codex Rehdigeranus, 164
Codex Sinaiticus, 156 f., 166 f., 171, 173, 177, 278
Codex Vaticanus, 156 f., 163, 166 f., 171, 173, 177, 278
Codex Vercellensis, 164
Codex Veronensis, 164
Coele-Syria, 187, 221, 309
Cohort, 228 f.
Coinage, 230, 235 f., 579 f.
Colonies, Roman, 230
Colossae, 103, 107, 556
Colossians, Epistle to, 102 ff., 106, 107 f., 137, 547
  and Ephesians, 104 ff., 108
Commandment, The Great, 486 f.
Concubinage, 260
Confession, 131 f.
  of Peter, 437, 453, 461 f., 464 f., 470 f., 546
Confucian ethics, 435
Conjectural emendation, 160

Constantine, 502
Constantinople, 20, 156, 167, 177
Continual sacrifice, 539
Coponius, 236
Copper, 195
Copper Scroll, 85
Coptic, 21
Coptic Gospels, 279
Coptic version, 81, 154, 160, 165
Corban, 478, 486
Corinth, 97 ff., 103, 108, 120, 137, 272, 435, 499 f., 507
  church at, 98 ff., 107
Corinth, Epistles to, 98 ff., 102
  1 Corinthians, 168, 447, 519
  2 Corinthians, 519 f.
Cornelius, 229
Corsica, 224, 226
Covenant, 91, 126, 129, 142, 276 f., 295, 341 f., 345, 536
  Israel's response in, 421
  meaning of, 350
  New, 91, 481, 546, 565, 567
  of Damascus, 268
Covenant, Book of, 129, 252, 265, 343, 422
Crassus, 224, 328
Creation, 28, 249, 373
Creation epic, 212
Creed, 142
Crete, 216, 226, 551
Crispus, 559
Crucifixion of Jesus, 90, 96, 112, 114, 236
  date of, 439, 576
Crusaders, 189, 195, 576
Cult, 130, 131 ff., 312
  and psalms, 56
  imperial, 230
  Israelite objects of the, 542 ff.
  sites, 337
Cumanus, Ventidius, 238 f.
Cuneiform, 205, 214, 250 f., 266, 273
Curetonian Syriac, 165, 179
Curse, 131
  of Canaan, 127
Cush, 207
Cyaxares, 212, 217
Cybele, 244
Cynics, 243
Cyprus, 197, 226, 271, 294, 498, 541
Cyrenaica, 267, 382
Cyrene, 226 f.
Cyrenius, 235
Cyrus, 46, 64, 66, 68 ff., 78, 212, 218, 251, 266, 309 f., 314 ff., 361
  Edict of, 314 f., 316

Dagon, 256
Dalmatia, 226
Damascus, 17, 187 f., 196, 200, 211, 216 f., 258, 263, 300 f., 303 f., 328, 497
Damascus Document, 89
Damasus, Pope, 173
Dan (tribe), 188, 294, 533
Dan (city), 27, 39, 188, 302, 353, 533
Dan'el, 273
Daniel, 13, 64, 127
Daniel, Book of, 63 ff., 69, 138, 221, 248, 310, 325, 374 f., 415
  Additions to, 75 f., 77 f.
Danube, 228
Darb es-Sultan, 196
Daric, 66
Darius the Mede, 64
Darius I. (Hystaspis), 53, 66, 73, 218, 314 ff., 317
Darius II., 318
Darius III., 318
David, 34, 41, 61 f., 67, 85, 128 f., 193 f., 215 f., 258, 261 f., 265, 274, 291, 296 ff., 307, 326, 350 f., 352 ff., 366, 413 f., 423, 454, 470, 517, 533, 535 f., 543
  and Goliath, 127
  and Messiah, 85
  and Psalter, 55
  court history of, 41 f., 128
  his elegy on Saul and Jonathan, 38, 42, 124
  house of, 132, 302 f., 312, 314, 320 f., 350, 354, 358, 365, 372, 378, 452, 460, 507
  Jesus and, 440
  reign of, 299 ff.
Davidic Psalter, 540
Day of Yahweh, *see* Yahweh
Deacons, 550 ff.
Dead, Book of, 209
Dead Sea, 113, 151, 188, 191, 194 f., 202 f., 217, 257, 269, 292, 329, 331, 404, 406
Dead Sea Scrolls, *see* Qumran
Debir, 260, 540 f.
Deborah, 13, 40, 76, 125, 294
Decalogue, 340, 342, 345, 356, 371, 384, 422, 541, 564
  Ritual, 572
Decapolis, 190, 503 f.
Decurions, 229
Dedication, Feast of, 85
Deir el-Bala'izah, 165
Deir ez-Zor, 186
Delaiah, 320
Delos, 267
Delphi, 272
Delta, 247, 338
Demas, 107
Demetrius, 224
Demons, 318, 397, 410 ff.
Denarius, 235, 579
Department of Antiquities, Israeli, 269
  Mandatory, 267
Derbe, 100

Dereliction, cry of, 450, 469 f.
Deutero-Isaiah, 37, 46 f., 62, 95, 130, 313 f., 316, 361 f., 363
Deutero-Zechariah, 54
Deuteronomy, 356 f., 368, 424 f., 534
and Chronicles, 67
and historical books, 37 f., 39 f., 41 f., 43 f., 67, 259, 263, 311, 313 f.
Code of, 129
date of, 32 f., 37
Dead Sea Scrolls of, 153
style of, 30 ff.
Diadochoi, 221, 322
Diaspora, 46, 50, 116, 154, 222 f., 225, 235, 247, 267, 331, 381 ff., 387, 390 f., 401, 412, 428, 496, 567
Diatessarōn, 163 ff., 170, 175 f., 179
Diatribe, 22, 137
Dibon, 194, 258
Didache, 95, 120 f., 170, 552 f., 559, 561, 568
Didrachmon, 388
Diognetus, Epistle to, 122
Dionysus, 274
Diotrephes, 118, 553 f.
Dirges, 124
Disciples, Twelve, 443 f., 481 f., 492, 546
Dispersion, *see* Diaspora
Disruption of the kingdom, 302, 352
Dittography, 160
Dives, 416
Divination, 543
Divorce, 431
Jesus and, 479 f.
Doeg, 533
Dominus Flevit, 271
Domitian, 118 f., 120, 240, 433, 502
Dor, 256, 263
Dothan, 264, 283
Dragnet, Parable of, 480, 548
Dragon, 128
Drink-offering, 525, 539 f.
Drinking songs, 124
Druids, 243
Drusilla, 239
Druzes, 190
Dualism, 269, 408
Duccio, 568
Dumuzi, 206
Duplicated passages of the Old Testament, 144
Dur-Sharrukin, 253
Du'ru, 263
Dying and rising god, 139, 206, 213, 275

E (Pentateuchal source), 31, 32 f., 34 f., 39, 41, 338, 524 f.
Ea, 206, 213, 215
Easter, the first, 495, 546, 564
Eastern Highlands of Palestine, 185, 202 f.
Eastern text, 165
Ebal, 192
Eber, 285
Ebionites, 504
Ebionites, Gospel of, 560
Ecbatana, 73 f.
Ecclesiastes, 62, 134, 371, 427
Ecclesiasticus, 63, 74 f., 80, 370, 426
Ecclesiology, 106
Ecstatic prophecy, 276, 353 f.
Eden, Garden of, 28, 525, 540
Edessa, 165, 170, 174
Edicts, Royal, 129
Edom, Edomites, 27, 46, 51, 185, 195, 199, 202 f., 211, 217, 257 f., 261, 264, 267, 269, 284 f., 292, 296, 300 f., 304, 326, 533
Education, 393
Egypt, 28, 61 f., 124, 126, 129, 156, 163, 165 ff., 170, 172, 186, 193, 195, 199, 202 ff., 210 ff., 213, 215, 218 f., 221, 223, 226 f., 237, 244, 246 ff., 254 ff., 259 f., 263 f., 265, 273 f., 279, 282 ff., 294, 298, 301 f., 305 ff., 309 f., 312 f., 315 ff., 324, 338 ff., 346, 356, 358, 363, 365, 369, 373, 375, 382, 385, 387, 406, 504, 516, 524 f., 531, 533, 536 f., 568
history of, 207 f.
kingship in, 247
literature of, 208 f.
religion of, 209 f.
Wisdom literature of, 57
Egyptian recension of New Testament, 166 f., 170, 172
Ekron, 193, 216
El, 214, 259, 337, 410, 525 f., 544
El Bethel, 525
El 'Elyon, 525
El Ro'i, 525
El 'Olam, 525
El Shaddai, 28, 339, 525
Elah, Valley of, 193, 268
Elam, Elamites, 63, 205, 210 f., 252
Elamite language, 218
Elath, 304, 544
Eleazar (son of Aaron), 533 f.
Eleazar (in 2 Maccabees), 85
Election of Israel, 358, 374, 387, 452, 538
Elephantine papyri, *see* Papyri
Eli, 295, 297, 528, 532 f.
Eliakim, 307
Eliashib, 67, 318 f.
Elihu, 58
Elijah, 32, 44, 127, 303, 351, 355, 363, 423, 440, 444, 490
Elisha, 44, 127, 303, 351, 490
Elkanah, 532
Elohim, 31, 54 f., 410
in Psalter, 144
Elymas, 244

Elyon, 259
Elzevir brothers, 176
Emendation of text, 159 ff.
Emmaus, 135
Emperor worship, 138
Encaenia, 538
Engedi, 194, 331, 405
Enki, 206
Enkomi, 541
Enlil, 206, 213, 215
Enoch, 72
1 Enoch, 81 ff., 88, 278, 374, 409, 464, 471
Similitudes of, 464
2 Enoch, 86
Enosh, 525
Enthronement Festival, 55
see also New Year Festival
Enthronement Hymns, 132
Entry, Triumphal, 445, 455 f., 461, 469
Eocene limestone, 191 ff., 204
Epaenetus, 97
Epaphras, 107
Epaphroditus, 106
Ephesus, 98, 102, 103 f., 107, 118, 121, 137, 230, 499, 504, 549
Ephesians, Epistle to, 102 f., 104 ff., 106, 137, 142 f., 547 f.
and Colossians, 104 f.
Ephod, 130, 543
Ephraim (son of Joseph), 88
Ephraim (tribe), 534
Ephraim (district), 191, 202, 204, 298
Ephron, 255
Epics, 273
Epicureans, 62, 342, 397
Epigraphy, 273
see also Inscriptions
Epimanes, 79
Epistola Apostolorum, 170
Epistles, Catholic, 91
of Paul, 91, 97 ff.
of New Testament, 91, 430
text of, 167, 173
Eponym, 251, 253
Erastus, 272
Erech, 206, 248
Eridu, 206
Esarhaddon, 208, 211, 258, 264, 316
Esau, 36, 127, 285
Eschatology, 93, 95, 105, 111 f., 116, 139, 367, 377, 409, 412 ff., 452 ff., 474 ff., 489 f., 492 f., 518 ff.
Esdraelon, 125, 190, 203, 298
Eshcol, 33
1 Esdras, 72 f.
2 Esdras (4 Ezra), 72, 81, 87, 375
Eshbaal, 299
Eshmunazzar, 267
Eshnunna, 210, 252
Essenes, 268, 277, 323, 327, 377, 379, 396, 404 ff., 410, 414, 504, 559
baths of, 407
ethics of, 408 f.
Esther, 13, 63, 77
Esther, Book of, 63, 128, 151, 248
Additions to, 77
Ethbaal, 214
Ethics, basis of New Testament, 91
Biblical, 418 ff.
of Essenes, 408 f.
of Jesus, 473 ff.
of primitive Church, 508 ff.
Ethiopia, 175, 208
Ethiopian eunuch, 81 ff., 87, 154, 160, 164, 175
Ethnarch, 224, 232, 237, 329
Eucharist, 142, 437, 448, 457, 483 f., 547, 549, 556, 563 ff.
Euergetes, 231
Euphrates, 186, 196 f., 202, 208, 212, 216, 220, 235, 241, 247, 250, 265, 284, 335
Execration texts, 256, 259
Exhortation, 130, 142 f.
Exile, 309 ff., 374, 510, 544
and the Canon, 368
significance of, 8
Exodus from Egypt, 40, 286 ff., 295, 447, 516, 531, 536 f.
significance of, 5, 8
Exodus, Book of, 27 ff., 341, 418
date of, 260 f., 283
route of, 288 f.
Evil-merodach, 43, 212, 309
Ezekiel, 37, 126, 130, 313 f., 361, 363, 535
and priesthood, 33 f.
Ezekiel, Book of, 45, 48 f., 248, 312, 368, 534
Ezion-geber, 195, 301, 304
Ezra, 61, 64, 66 f., 72, 75, 218, 267, 312 f., 315, 319 f., 321
and the Priestly Code, 34, 39, 54
period of, 317 f.
Ezra, Book of, 66 ff., 72 f., 267
Ezra Apocalypse, 81, 87
4 Ezra, *see* 2 Esdras

Fables, 126
Fadus, Cuspius, 238
Faith, in Pauline thought, 434
Family, Judaism and the, 393 f.
Farwardigan, 63
Fat, 526 f., 530
Fatherless, 424
Fayyum, 156
Fear of Isaac, 336
Felix, 239, 242
Fertility cult, 275, 542
Festivals, 538
Festus, Porcius, 239, 330
Fig-tree, Parable of withered, 481
Firkowitch, A., 148
Firstfruits, 529

Firstlings, 529
Five thousand, Feeding of, 443, 483
Flood, 38 f., 212, 248 f., 252 f., 373, 527
Florus, Gessius, 239
Folk-tales, 127
Food laws, 486, 499
Form criticism, 90 ff., 138 ff., 437
of Gospels, 139 ff.
of New Testament, 135 ff.
of Old Testament, 123 ff.
outside Gospels, 141 ff.
Formgeschichte, 139
France, 226
Freedom, human, 374
Freer Gospels, 167 f., 173, 248
Freewill offerings, 528
Freising fragments, 164
Frömmigkeit des Gesetzes, 391
Future life, 206, 210

Gabael, 73
Gabbatha, 270
Gabriel, 410
Gadara, 230
Gaius (of Derbe), 101, 118
Gaius (Emperor), 233 f., 237, 519
see also Caligula
Galatia, 100 f., 226, 231, 235, 498 f.
Galatians, Epistle to, 98, 100 ff.
Galba, 118
Galilee, 186, 188, 202, 222, 230, 233, 236, 261, 263, 268, 270, 328 ff., 390, 440, 444 ff., 452, 461, 477, 483, 490, 587
Lake of, 189, 233, 270, 443
Gallia Lugdunensis, 226
Gallia Narbonensis, 226
Gallio, Lucius Junius, 226, 272, 500 f.
Gamala, 235
Gashmu, 266
Gath, 41, 193, 216, 299
Gathas, 218
Gattungsgeschichte, 139, 141 f.
Gaul, 19, 164, 170, 179, 227 f., 232, 234, 241
Gaulanitis, 235
Gaumata, 218
Gaza, 193, 200, 216, 294
Gebal, 213 f.
Gedaliah, 265 f., 310 f., 315
Gehenna, 83, 492
Gemara, 373
Genealogy of Jesus, 439
Genesis, 27 ff., 84, 205, 248 ff., 252, 259, 335, 337 f., 418, 525
Genesis, Little, 84
Genizah, 71, 74, 148 f., 150, 157
Gentiles, and Church, 497 ff., 546
court of, 446, 491
Jesus and, 489 ff.
Jews and, 382, 384 f.
Georgian version, 81, 164, 175 f.
Geography of Palestine, 185 ff.
Gerar, 28, 286
Gerizim, 192, 237, 320, 387
Germany, 226
Gershom, 533
Geshem, 266, 318
Geshur, 216
Gethsemane, 439
Gezer, 262, 264, 268, 542
Calendar, 12, 570
Ghab, 186, 197
Ghouta, 187
Gibeah, 260, 298
Gideon, 190, 294, 296, 350, 424
Gihon, 264
Gilboa, 190, 298
Gilead, 34, 191 f., 202 f., 263, 296
Gilgal, 38, 346
Gilgamesh, 128, 212, 215 f., 248, 250, 252, 277
Gilzau, 263
Girgashites, 216
Gishem, 266
Gnomic writers, 62
Gnosticism, 82, 99, 108, 111, 114, 117, 119, 139, 279 f., 410, 496, 557
Gobryas, 310
God, and anthropomorphism, 29
and Job, 59
in Israel's theology, 252
Judaism and, 385
Kingdom of, *see* Kingdom of God
of the fathers, 336 f., 339
revelation of, 6, 291, 418
sons of, 128
see also Yahweh
Golden Rule, 74
Golenischeff Papyrus, *see* Papyri
Golgotha, 271
Goliath, 127, 193, 543
Gomer, 49
Gomorrah, 194
Good Wishes, 124
Goshen, 287
Gospel(s), 90, 135 ff., 163 f., 165, 175, 230, 430, 436 f., 471
Apocryphal, 279
Fourth, 115 ff.
Synoptic, 93 ff.
Theology of, 438, 468 ff.
Gospel of Philip, 279
Gospel of Thomas, 279
Gospel of Truth, 279 f.
Gothic version, 164, 167, 177
Göttingen Septuagint, 156 f.
Gozan, 259
Graeco-Roman world, 220 ff.
Gratus, Valerius, 236
Greece, Greeks, 50, 54, 62, 97, 218, 220 f., 271, 317, 321, 385
Greek (language), 19, 154, 383, 392, 430, 434, 440, 452 f.
Bible, 3, 20

Greek (language)—(*continued*)
compositions in (Apocrypha, etc.), 77, 79 f., 84 ff.
dialects of, 19, 21
Gospels composed in, 23
Hellenistic, 20 ff.
New Testament, 22 f.
Versions of Old Testament, 60 f., 69, 72, 75, 77, 79 f., 84 ff.
Greek culture, 322 f.
kingdoms, 254
rule, 321 ff.
Guilt-offering, 530 f.
Gutians, 205

Habakkuk, 360
Habakkuk, Book of, 52 f., 133
Commentary on, 52 f., 88
Habiru, 214, 247, 285, 287, 291 f.
Hadad, 217, 259, 272, 274
Hades, 408
Hadrian, 331
Haftarah, 545
Hagar, 260
Haggadah, 485
Haggai, 315 f., 362, 372
Haggai, Book of, 53, 66, 314
Haifa, 267
Halakah, 440, 442, 485
Hama, 258 f.
Haman, 63
Hamath, 17, 185 f., 196 f., 201, 215, 217, 255, 258
Hamman, 63
Hammurabi, 210, 212, 250, 282
Code of, 252, 260
Hananiah, 306
Hands, Laying on of, 563
Hannah, 42
Hanukkah, 538
Hapiru, 214
Haplography, 160
Har(r)an, 250, 259, 265, 284
Harklean Syriac, 164, 174 f.
Harvest songs, 126
Hasidaeans, 326
Hasidim, 326, 397, 405, 440
Hasmonaeans, 79, 217, 219, 222, 268, 324 f., 326 ff., 376, 389, 406
Hatti, 215
Hattusas, 215
Hattusilis I., 215
Hattusilis III., 215
Haustafeln, 142
Hazar-enan, 196 f.
Hazor, 188, 261 f., 263, 272, 301, 538
Heave-offering, 528
Hebat, 215 f.
Hebrew, a " mixed " language?, 11 f.
Canaanites and, 11
dialectal forms of, 13
in Diaspora, 322
loan-words, in, 18
meaning of term, 338
nature of, 13 f.
noun in, 14 f.
numbers in, 15
original language of mankind?, 11
pronunciation of, 12 f.
script of, 18
syntax of, 15
triliterality of, 14
vocabulary of, 16
vocalization of, 12 f.
Hebrews, Epistle to, 22, 111 f., 137, 168, 278, 280
Hebron, 31, 33, 38, 191, 194, 255, 266 f., 269, 283 f., 299, 300, 336 f., 398, 524
Heilsgeschichte, 524
Hellenism, 219, 221 ff., 232 f., 322 ff.
Hellenists, 496 f., 503, 516 f.
Heliopolis, 209
Hell, 416
Henotheism, 525
Heracleitus, 62
Heraclius, 174
Hermas, Shepherd of, 120 f.
Hermon, 187
Hero tales, 127
Herod the Great, 217, 224, 231 ff., 238, 267, 269, 271, 328 ff., 381, 388 f., 541
Herod Agrippa I., 233 f., 238 f., 330
Herod Agrippa II., 239 f., 330, 534
Herod Antipas, 233 f., 237, 270, 329 f. 443, 449
Herodians, 233, 446
Herodias, 233
Herodium, 269
Heshbon, 35, 193, 257
Hesiod, 62
Hexapla, 155 f.
Hexateuch, 39
Hezekiah, 32 f., 37, 46, 53, 56 f., 128, 208, 247, 264, 305, 357, 359, 536, 544
Hezekiah, Testament of, 87
Hiel, 532
Hieroglyphs, Hittite, 215, 255
High-God, 525 f.
Hill shrines, 538
Hillel, 387, 399, 479, 561
Hiram, 213, 300
Hispania Tarraconensis, 226
Historical narrative, 128, 137
Hittites, 129, 208, 210, 212, 213 f., 215 f., 254 f., 276, 282 f., 298
hieroglyphs of, 215, 255
history of, 215
treaties of, 342
Hivites, 216
Hofstil, 274
Holiness, 425 f.
Holiness Code, 35, 129, 313, 425
Holofernes, 76

Holy Spirit, 6 f., 96, 105, 110, 498, 507, 510 f., 518, 520 f., 522, 563 f.
testimony of, 10 f.
Holy of Holies, 224, 365, 389, 491, 539, 541
Holy Place, 491, 539
Holy War, 293
Homily, 137
Homo, 185 f., 196
Homoeoteleuton, 160
Hope of Early Church, 518 ff.
Hophra, 208, 309
Horeb, 289, 291
Horemheb, 260
Horites, 215 f., 254, 282
Horns, 209
Horns of Hattin, 189
Hosea, 262, 304, 356 f., 359, 363, 423 f.
Hosea, Book of, 45, 49
Hoshaiah, 264
Hoshea, 263, 305
Huleh, 188
Humour, 136
Huna, Rab, 562
Hungary, 226
Hurrians, 208, 210, 214 f., 216, 254 f., 260, 282, 284
Huru, 216
Hyksos, 208, 214, 216, 260, 282, 284, 287
Hymns, 56, 132, 141
early Christian, 91
Hymns Scroll, 88, 269, 280, 377
Hyrcanus I., John, 79, 217, 320, 325 f.
Hyrcanus II., 222, 224, 326, 328

Iconium, 100
Iddo, 67
Idols, Judaism and, 386
Idumaea, Idumaeans, 217, 222, 224, 232, 326, 328 f., 288
Ignatius, Epistles of, 120 f., 551, 554, 568
Ijon, 188
Illyricum, 499
Images, 232, 237, 533, 543 f.
Immorality, sexual, 423, 427, 431, 434
Inanna, 206, 212
Incantations, 206, 250
India, 20, 221, 223, 282, 321, 538, 544
Indo-Aryans, 282
Indra, 216
Infancy narratives of Jesus, 487
Ingathering, Feast of, 537, 539
Initiants, Hymn of, 512
Inscriptions, Greek, 269
Hittite, 255
Karatepe, 255
Latin, 269
Moabite, 258
Nazareth, 271
Inspiration of the Bible, 6 ff.
Inter-testamental literature, 71 ff.
Ira, 536
Iran, 205, 210, 218, 248
Iraq el-Amir, 266
Iron, Philistines and, 298
Iron Age, 260, 272
Isaac, 27 f., 36, 214, 285 f., 335, 524 f., 532
Isaiah, 13, 44, 46, 51, 126, 276, 304 f., 353, 357 ff., 363, 423, 468, 535
Isaiah, Book of, 45 ff., 67, 91, 248
Qumran scrolls of, 88, 152 f.
Isaiah, Ascension of, 87
Isaiah, Deutero-, *see* Deutero-Isaiah
Isaiah, Martyrdom of, 87
Isaiah, Trito-, *see* Trito-Isaiah
Isaiah, Vision of, 87
Isin, 210, 249
Isis, 210, 244
Ishmael, Ishmaelites, 28, 217
Ishmael (murderer of Gedaliah), 266, 310
Ishtar, 63, 206, 213, 215 f.
Descent of, 212
Islam, 544
Israel (people), 34, 185, 188, 191 ff.
and Canaanite practices, 349
and culture of neighbours, 275
and redemption, 95
archaeology and the culture of, 272 ff.
archaeology and the religion of, 274 ff.
culture of, 246, 250
distinctive character of, 252 f.
conversion of, 518
election of, 358, 374, 387, 538
history of, 246, 251, 257 ff., 281 ff.
meaning of name, 281
monarchy in, 296 ff.
Moses and faith of, 328 ff.
neighbours of, 205 ff., 254 ff.
religion of, 335 ff.
settlement of, 256 f., 260 f., 274, 289 f., 291 ff.
stele, 261
the New, 5, 281, 443, 482, 485
Israel (kingdom), 49 f., 211, 217, 262, 274, 302 ff., 358
Itala version, 164
Italian band, 229
Italy, 164, 170, 179, 224 f., 228, 231, 242, 271
Ithamar, 533 f.
Ituraea, 232

J (Pentateuchal source), 31, 32 f., 34 f., 39, 41, 338 f., 351 f., 524
Jaazaniah, *see* Yaazaniah

Jabbok, 192 f., 202
Jabesh-gilead, 40
Jacob, 28, 36, 127, 214, 247, 260 f., 281, 285 f., 335 f., 338, 524 f., 534, 542 f.
  Blessing of, 36, 83
Jaddua, 66
Jaffa gate, 270
Jairus (name on an ossuary), 271
James the Just, 95, 101, 112, 137, 432, 436, 440, 451, 503, 507 f., 551, 553
James, (son of Zebedee), 238, 443, 445, 479
James, Epistle of, 22, 91, 112 f., 137, 432, 508
Jamnia, 68 ff., 331
Jannaeus, Alexander, 222, 326 f., 328, 440
Jashar, Book of, 34, 38 f., 125
Jason (High Priest), 223, 323 f.
Jason of Cyrene, 79
Javan, 218
Jaxartes, 221
Jebel Bishri, 186, 196
Jebel Buweida, 196, 201
Jebel Druze, 190, 199 ff.
Jebel Fureidis, 269
Jebel Usdum, 194
Jebus, 194
Jebusites, 216, 300, 352, 366, 544
Jeconiah, 80
Jehoahaz, 265, 307
Jehohanan, 318
Jehoiakim, 64, 265, 307 f.
Jehoiachin, 43 f., 47, 265 f., 307 f., 309, 311 f.
Jehoram, 51
Jehoshaphat, 129
Jehoshaphat, Valley of, 50
Jehu, 90, 211, 263, 303
Jephthah, 296 f., 424, 532
Jerahmeelites, 217
Jeremiah, 13, 37, 44, 47, 49, 80, 87, 126, 130, 222, 297, 306, 308, 310, 312 f., 360 f., 363, 535
  and Lamentations, 61
  confessions of, 360 f.
Jeremiah, Book of, 45, 47 f., 51, 91, 248, 265, 276
  Dead Sea Scrolls of, 153
Jeremiah, Epistle of, 72
Jericho, 34, 192, 235, 246, 256, 261, 266, 268, 290, 292, 444, 532
Jeroboam I., 36, 43, 262, 302, 351 ff.
Jeroboam II., 34, 36, 50, 51, 303 f., 423
Jerusalem, 36, 45, 46 f., 48 f., 52 f., 56, 64, 66 f., 73, 85, 97, 141, 147, 191, 194, 199 f., 212, 218, 222 f., 224 f., 229, 234, 236 f., 256, 259, 264 ff., 270 f., 274, 292, 300 ff., 305 ff., 311, 313 f., 316 ff., 320, 324 f., 330 f., 350 f., 352 f., 359 f., 365 f., 368, 384, 390, 425, 495 ff., 500, 503 f., 507, 514, 517, 533 f., 544, 548 f.
  centralization of worship and, 386
  church of, 440, 451, 489, 497, 499, 503, 551, 553
  Council of, 101 f., 489, 498, 504
  fall of (597 B.C.), 251
  fall of (586 B.C.), 48, 50, 51, 54, 80, 309 f., 361, 371, 388
  fall of (A.D. 70), 94, 114, 137, 146, 239, 268 f., 277, 379, 391, 460, 503
  Hebrew University of, 150
  Jesus and, 443 ff.
  New, 375
  Paul's visits to, 101 f.
  pilgrimage to, 382
  priesthood of, 33 f., 151, 532 ff.
Jeshimon, 193 f.
Jeshua, 53, 314, 316, 460, 533
Jesus, accounts of, 4, 6
  and Caiaphas, 270
  and fulfilment of law, 379
  and Gospels, 135 f.
  and Jewish law, 485 ff.
  and Kingdom of God, 451 ff.
  and Pilate, 270
  and prophecy, 95
  and purpose of God, 378
  and the Church, 480 ff.
  and the Gentiles, 489 ff.
  and uniqueness of the Bible, 5
  and Zealots, 377
  ascension of, 451
  baptism of, 441, 444, 469, 472
  came in fulness of time, 4
  chronology of life of, 438 f., 447
  death of, 236 f., 450
  ethical teaching of, 474 ff.
  in early Christian theology, 506 ff.
  in early preaching, 90 f.
  in Hebrews, 111 f.
  is the unity of the Bible, 4
  Last Supper of, 447 f., 455 f., 483 f., 565 ff.
  life of, 436 ff.
  ministry of, 92 ff.
  passion of, 445 ff., 459, 464 ff.
  resurrection of, 437, 444, 446, 450 f.
  sayings of, 24, 139 f., 278 f.
  stories about, 140
  taught in Aramaic, 19
  teaching of, 139, 419, 427 ff., 436 ff.
  titles of, 459 ff.
  tomb of, 271
  trial of, 236 f., 448 f., 469
Jesus ben Sira, *see* Ben Sira(ch)
Jethro, 339, 532
Jewish War (A.D. 66–70), 311, 330 f., 406

Jews, 221 ff.
  and Samaritans, 232, 239
  Roman policy towards, 223 f., 225
Jezebel, 214, 303
Jezreel, 190
  Valley of, 190
Joab, 299
Joachim, 77
Joash, 49
Job, Book of, 57 ff., 134, 250, 276, 370 f., 427
Job, Babylonian, 59 f.
Joel, 49 f., 362 f.
Johanan, 67, 318 f.
John of Gischala, 331
John the Baptist, 93, 136, 233, 269, 439 ff., 443, 454, 459, 465, 469, 482 f., 488, 490, 496, 515
John the Elder, 116
John (the son of Zebedee), 118, 137, 443, 445, 479
John, Gospel of, 115 ff., 165, 169, 278, 280, 438 f., 441, 443 f., 447, 449, 451, 456, 461, 468, 471 ff., 477, 483, 487, 520, 565 f.
  and Qumran, 89
  and Synoptics, 115 f.
  prologue to, 23
John, Epistles of, 117 f., 137, 280
Joiada, 318
Jonah, Book of, 51, 93, 127, 222, 370 f., 491
Jonathan (son of Saul), 38, 124, 192, 299
Jonathan (5th century), *see* Johanan
Jonathan (the Maccabee), 325 f.
Jonathan ben Uzziel, *see* Targum
Jordan, 38, 185, 188, 190 ff., 199, 202, 213, 216, 235, 257, 266, 268, 290, 292, 294, 304, 326, 347, 444
Joseph (patriarch), 18, 28, 31, 34, 36, 73, 88, 128, 260, 283, 287, 338, 540
Joseph (husband of Mary), 220
Joseph and Asenath, 88
Joshua, 29, 31, 33, 40, 127 f., 192, 291 f., 345 ff., 353 f.
Joshua (High Priest), *see* Jeshua
Joshua, Book of, 34, 38 f., 40, 157, 260, 264, 292
Josiah, 32, 72, 251, 264 f., 305 ff., 311, 357, 367, 424, 527, 531, 534, 539, 544
Jotham, 126, 296
Jozadak, 460
Jubilate, 141
Jubilees, Book of, 83 f., 88, 374, 409, 485, 571
Judaea, 191, 221 f., 224 f., 226 ff., 230, 232 f., 235, 237, 269, 324, 329, 483, 489, 495 ff., 501, 504
  under procurators, 330 ff.
  wilderness of, 193, 201, 299, 311
Judah (son of Jacob), 31
Judah (tribe), 36, 300 ff., 339, 344, 507, 517, 534
Judah (district), 193 f., 203 f., 208, *see also* Judaea
Judah (kingdom),49 f., 208, 211, 217, 242, 251, 258, 262, 264 ff., 274, 295 f., 302 ff., 365 ff., 309, 350, 358 ff.
Judah (province), 310 f., 315, 319
Judah the Galilaean, 402 f.
Judaism, 50, 112 f., 119, 145 f., 148, 151, 153 f., 217, 219, 222, 239, 375 ff., 381 ff., 445 f., 465, 485 ff., 500 f., 544, 564
  and Christianity, 378 f.
  beliefs of, 384 ff.
  ethics of, 418 ff., 431
  parties in, 326 f.
  sects of, 394 ff., 404 ff.
Judas Maccabaeus, 79, 222 f., 268, 324 f., 526, 538, 542
Judas Iscariot, 443, 447 f., 467, 495
Judas of Gamala, 235
Jude, 137
Jude, Epistle of, 81, 114 f., 137, 516
Judgment, day of, 481
  Last, 415, 511, 519
  prophets and, 357 f., 360
Judges, 349, 354, 534
  period of, 256
Judges, Book of, 39 f., 61, 292, 295, 297, 348 f., 533
Judith, 76, 128
Julias, 233
Julius Caesar, 224 f., 228, 230, 232, 328
Jupiter Capitolinus, 239
Justice, 424
Justification, 105, 511 ff.
Justinian, 174

Kadesh, 289 f., 337, 339, 347
Kalhu, 276
Kanesh, 259
Kara Huyuk, 259
Karatepe, 255
Karnak, 262
Kassites, 210
Kedar, 266
Kefr Kenna, 270
Kenite(s), 36, 217, 291
  and Yahweh, 339
  source of Pentateuch, 35
Kenizzites, 217, 261
Kerak, 194
Keret, 273, 277
Kerygma, 90, 92, 95, 98
Khabur, 216, 254, 259
Khafajeh, 248
Khirbet Kerazeh, 270
Khirbet Qana, 270

Khirbet Qumran, 268, 271
Khorsabad, 253
Kidron, 264
Kiev, 173
Kingdom of God, 413, 420, 428 f., 442 f., 451 ff., 459 ff., 474 ff., 479 f., 487 ff., 546, 548
parables of, 95
Kings, Books of, 43 f., 45, 66 f., 84, 251, 258 f., 263
Kingship, and cult, 535 ff.
in Egypt, 247
in Israel, 274, 350 ff., 365, 423
in Near East, 273 f., 296
Kinsman of Isaac, 336
Kir-hareseth, 194
Kiriath-sepher, 260
Kirkuk, 251
Kish, 205, 248 f.
Kishon, 190
Knights (Roman), 226
Koinē, 20 f., 23 ff., 138, 171, 177
Korahites, 534, 540
Kultfrömmigkeit, 391
Kumarbi, 216
Kurnab, 195
Kypros, 269

L (source of Luke), 93, 136
L (Old Testament source), *see* Lay Source
Laban, 285, 525, 542
Labashi-Marduk, 212
Lachish, 129, 193 f., 261 f., 265 f., 305
letters, 12, 265, 308
Lagash, 205
Lamb, Passover, 447
Lamech, Song of, 35, 125
Lamentations, Book of, 61 f., 276
Laments, 56, 132 f., 250
Laodicea, 137
Larnaka, 541
Larsa, 206, 210, 249
Last Day, 358, 366, 377
see also Judgment
Last Supper, 91, 439, 447 f., 455 f., 469, 481, 483 f., 491, 546, 565 ff.
date of, 447, 566, 571
Latin, 21, 72, 75, 79, 81, 87, 163, 383, 440
versions, 97, 154, 158, 164, 170, 173 f., 178
Law, administration of Roman, 230
apodictic, 252
Canaanite, 273
canonization of, 68
casuistic, 252
Deuteronomic, 356 f.
in post-exilic age, 372
interpretation of, 390 f., 393, 396, 428
Israelite, 291, 335, 356
Jesus and Jewish, 485 ff.
Mesopotamian, 335
Near Eastern, 343, 356
obedience to, 373, 383, 398
Old Testament, 112
ritual and, 387, 391
Laws, 129 f.
codes of, 205, 212, 215, 252
Lawsuits, 130
Lay source of Old Testament, 35, 39 f., 41
Lazarus, 140, 416
Leah, 261, 534
Leaven, Parable of, 455
Lebanon, 186 ff., 196, 199 f., 239
Legates, 226
Legends, 127, 140, 273
Legion, Tenth, 239
Legions, 228 f.
Leipzig, 156
Lemuel, 56 f.
Leningrad, 148, 173
Codex, 149 f.
Leontopolis, 387
Leper, Cleansed, 487
Letters, 129, 137
Levant, 185 ff., 197 ff., 202
Levi (tribe), 339, 344, 348, 534
Levi (Matthew), 235
Leviathan, 58, 214, 502
Levirate marriage, 61
Levites, 29, 32 f., 54, 66, 131, 312, 368, 375, 378, 388 f., 424, 528, 533 ff.
Lex talionis, 429
Libnah, 193
Libya, 207 f.
Link Expedition, 270
Linus, 557
Lipit-Ishtar, 252
Lisan Peninsula, 194 f.
Lists, 129
Litani, 186 ff.
Liturgy, 125, 132 f., 142, 248, 274 ff.
prophetic, 52 f., 133
Livia, 233
Livias, 233
Logos, 116, 412, 521
Lord's Supper, 91, 508
Lot, 194
Lotan, 214
Love songs, 126
Lugdunum, 557
Luke, 95 f., 107 f., 111 f., 279
Luke, Gospel of, 93, 95 f., 116, 165, 167, 170, 181, 278 f., 416, 438 ff.
Infancy hymns of, 23
style of, 22
Lusitania, 226
Luwian, 215
Luz, 28
Lycaonia, 100
Lycia, 237
Lycus, 107

Lydia (person), 559
Lydia (province), 217 f., 222, 310
Lyons, 557
Lysanias, 239
Lysias, Claudius, 239

M (source of Matthew), 93, 136
Ma, 244
Maacah, 216
Maccabaean age, 55, 62 f., 76, 277, 375
  martyrs of, 85
  revolt of, 219, 268, 324 ff., 397 f., 405, 463
Maccabees, The, 376 f.
Maccabees, Books of, 223
  1 Maccabees, 79, 326 f.
  2 Maccabees, 79, 85, 375
  3 Maccabees, 84
  4 Maccabees, 85
Macedon, 208, 218, 221, 230
Macedonia, 98, 101, 103, 224, 226, 499
Machaerus, 269
Magdala, 189, 270
Magians, 218
Magic, 131, 206, 209 f., 215, 277
Magna Mater, 243
Magnesia, 121
Magnificat, 135
Mahanaim, 298
Majdal, 270
Malachi, Book of, 51, 362
Malatya, 215
Malta, 230
Mammon, 445
Mamre, 269, 538
Manasseh (son of Joseph), 88
Manasseh (district), 192, 204
Manasseh (king), 32, 47, 48 f., 52, 264, 304 f., 359, 536
Manasseh, Prayer of, 76 f.
Manual of Discipline, 88, 268, 280, 409, 512
Manuscripts, Gothic, 164 f.
  Greek, 97, 106, 120, 164 f., 166 f., 168 f., 175, 176 f., 178, 180 f.
  Hebrew, 149
  Latin, 164 f., 174, 176
  Sahidic, 165
  Syriac, 175
Marathon, 218
Marcus Aurelius, 122
Marduk, 63, 213, 218, 250, 275, 308, 315
Mari, 129 f., 196, 210, 212 f., 214, 250 f., 259 f., 272, 276, 282, 284, 335, 353
Mariamne, 329
Marissa, 268
Mark, 107, 113, 138, 500
Mark, Gospel of, 93 f., 116, 138, 141, 163, 368, 173, 180, 437 f., 441 ff., 500, 566
  ending of, 437
Marriage, 105
Martha, 140
Martha (name on ossuary), 271
Martyrs, Acts of the Pagan, 237
Mary (the Virgin), 439 f., 461
Mary Magdalene, 140
Mary (sister of Martha), 140
Mary (name on ossuary), 271
Masada, 194, 269, 329, 331
Mashti, 63
Maskil, 56
Massoretes, 13, 145, 151
Massoretic text, 145 ff., 151 ff., 155, 160, 277 f.
Mattaniah, 308
Mattathias, 324
Matthew, Gospel of, 93, 94 f., 116, 167 f., 170, 180, 279, 438 f., 441, 454 ff.
  its use of the Old Testament, 95
Mauretania, 237
Mazdeans, 408
Meal-offering, 529
Meals, 394
Measures, 578 f.
Medes, 64, 211 f., 217 f., 307, 310
Media, 73
Mediterranean, 185, 187 f., 194 f., 198 f., 201, 211, 220, 223 f., 267, 289, 294, 332, 499
Megiddo, 190, 262 f., 265, 272, 301, 307
Meirun, 261
Melchizedek, 35 f., 112, 517
Melek, 532
Melkart, 259
Memphis, 207, 209, 222
Memra, 412
Menahem, 263, 304
Menelaus, 323 f.
Mercy, 424
Merj Ayoun, 188
Merneptah, 208, 261, 283, 298
Merodach-Baladan, 211
Merom, 189, 261
Mesas, 196
Mesha, 18, 217, 258, 364
Mesopotamia, 186, 202, 205, 207, 210, 213, 215 ff., 246 ff., 258 ff., 267, 273, 275, 277, 282, 285, 298, 321, 335 f., 346 f., 353, 364, 369, 536 f., 541
  history of, 210 f.
Messiah(s), 46 f., 54, 83, 85, 87, 112, 237 f., 268, 314, 358, 374, 378, 402, 413 f., 440 f., 443 ff., 460 ff., 495 f., 506, 513, 515, 517
  Jesus the, 94, 96, 116
  of Aaron and Israel, 460
  two, 83, 89, 112
Messianic beliefs, 412 ff., 500
Meter in Old Testament, 123
Micah (in Judges), 533, 543

Micah (prophet), 304, 357 f., 423
Micah, Book of, 51 f.
Michael, 112, 410
Michael ben Uzziel, 149
Michal, 299, 543
Michigan, University of, 278
Midian, Midianites, 28, 190, 217, 294, 296, 339, 532
Midrash, 67, 84, 565
Miktam, 56
Milan, 564
  Edict of, 156
Miletus, 267
Milid, 215
Milkom, 217
Millennium, 86
Minet el-Beida, 272
Minaeans, 534
Ministry of the Church, 550 ff.
Minoan empire, 216
Minor Prophets, 91, 248
  Scroll of, 135
Miracles of Jesus, 442 f., 454, 492
Miriam, Song of, 36, 125, 341
Miriam (name on ossuary), 271
Mishnah, 16, 145 f., 373, 392, 399, 539 f., 545, 561
Mishor, 203
Mitanni, 208, 210, 215 f., 254, 282
Mithras, 216, 218, 244
Mithridates, 224
Mizpah, 262, 265 f., 310 f.
Moab, Moabites, 61, 127, 188, 193 f., 202 f., 211, 217, 257 f., 261, 264, 284 f., 292, 294, 296, 309, 364, 532
  Sites of, 35
Moabite stone, 217
Modein, 324
Moesia, 226, 228
Molech, 532
Monarchy, Israelite, 296 ff.
Monasticism of Essenes, 406
Mon-episcopos, 553, 558
Money, 579 f.
Monologues, 129
Monophysites, 174
Monotheism, 384, 398, 525
  Judaism and, 386 f., 390
  of Akhenaton, 208
  Persian, 218
  Rome and, 244
Montanists, 119, 121
Months, names of, 570 f.
Mordecai, 63, 77
Moreh, 190, 524, 538
Morning star, 128
Moscow, 173
Moses, 27 f., 47, 56, 84, 111, 195, 232, 237, 352 ff., 359, 372, 376, 378, 386, 432, 444, 533, 535, 544 f.
  and authorship of the Pentateuch, 30 f.
  and Decalogue, 422
  and Israelite faith, 388 ff.
  Blessing of, 36, 348
  law of, 381, 389, 399
  New, 143
  sin of, 345
  Song of, 36 f., 133
  work of, 290 f.
Moses, Apocalypse of, 87
Moses, Assumption of, 85 f.
Moses, Testament of, 86
Mosul, 253
Mot, 214, 274 f.
Mountain, sacred, 340 f.
Murabba'at, 145
Murashu sons, 267
Muratorian Canon, 121
Mursilis I., 215
Mustard seed, Parable of, 455, 481
Muwatallis, 215
Mycenaean pottery, 256
Mysteries, Villa of, 244
Myth(s), 128, 140, 248, 277
  and ritual, 206

Naaman, 490
Nabataeans, 195 f., 203, 217, 328
Nablus, 159, 260, 272
Nabonidus, 64, 212, 309 f., 312
Nabonidus, Prayer of, 310
Nabopolassar, 211, 256, 306 f.
Nabu, 213
Nabunaid, 309
Nag Hammadi, 279
Nahor, 259
Nahr Auja, 263
Nahum, 13, 360
Nahum, Book of, 52
Nanna, 206
Naphtali, 261
Naramsin, 249
Narratives in Old Testament, 127 f.
Nash Papyrus, *see* Papyri
Nathan, 8, 126, 300, 350 f.
Nathanael, 140
Nazarenes, 504
Nazareth, 189, 238, 270 f., 440, 469, 490 f., 506 f.
Near East, culture of, 131
  poetry of, 126 f.
  treaties, of 129
Nebo, 213
Nebuchadnezzar (or Nebuchadrezzar), 64, 76, 208, 212, 214, 251, 266, 307 f., 309, 360
Necho, Pharaoh, 196, 208, 212, 265, 307
Negeb, 195, 201, 203
Nehemiah, 47 f., 54, 61, 66 f., 128, 218, 266, 315, 318 ff.
  period of, 317 f.
Nehemiah, Book of, 66 ff., 72 f.
Nehushtan, 544

Neighbour, love of, 386 f., 419 ff., 429, 476, 489
Neo-Babylonian empire, 52, 64, 211 f. 216, 251
Neofiti I., 157 f.
Neo-Levitical code, 142
Neo-Pythagoreans, 243
Nergal-shar-usur, 309
Neriah, 80
Neriglissar, 212, 309
Nero, 114, 118 f., 239 ff., 331, 433, 436, 500 ff.
Nero redivivus, 502
Neutral text of New Testament, 178 f.
Newcastle, 241
New Moon, 539
New Moon festival, 366
New Testament, and Old Testament Canon, 68
  literature of, 90 ff.
  Canon of, 119 f., 280
  three parts of, 3
  transmission of text of, 163 ff.
New Year Festival, autumn, 274 f.
  Babylonian, 55, 63, 213
  Israelite, 55, 365, 392, 536 f., 538
  Near Eastern, 365
  spring, 250, 275
  see also Tabernacles, Feast of
Nicanor Gate, 526, 540
Nicene Creed, 385
Nicodemus, 140, 483
Nicolaitans, 504
Night Visions of Zechariah, 54
Nikkal, 259
Nile, 207, 220, 247 f., 286, 313
Ninurta, 213
Nineveh, 73 f., 93, 211 f., 246, 248 f., 251, 264 f., 307
  fall of, 51 ff.
Nippur, 206, 248, 252, 267
Noachic commands, 384
Noah, 28 f., 84, 249, 525
Noah, Book of, 82
Nob, 533, 543
Noricum, 228
Novella, 127
Novellen, 140
Nubia, 175, 207
Nubian sandstone, 195
Numbers, Book of, 29 ff., 146, 292
Nunc Dimittis, 135
Nuseiriyeh, 197, 200
Nuzu, 250, 260, 282, 284 f., 335
Nyasaland, 185

Oaths, 125 f., 129
Obadiah, 51, 362
Obed-edom, 535
Oblation, 531
Octavian, 225, 328 f.
Offerings, 525 f.
el-ʿOla, 534
Old Testament, and Near Eastern culture, 131
  inherited from Judaism, 3
  literature of, 27 ff.
  threefold division of, 3, 27
  transmission of text of, 144 ff.
  versions of, 154 ff.
  worship in, 523 ff.
Olives, Mt. of, 271, 448
Omri, 6, 192, 258, 262, 274, 302 f.
On, 88
Onesimus, 102, 104 f., 107 f.
Onias III., 323
Onias (of Leontopolis), 387 f.
Onkelos, *see* Targum
Oppression in Egypt, 287 f.
Oracles, 130
Oral tradition, 35, 38
  Jewish, 442
Orontes, 186, 254, 257, 259, 263, 497
Orthopraxy, 385, 387
Osiris, 209 f., 274
Ossuaries, 271
Othniel, 261
Oxford University Expedition, 248

P (Pentateuchal source), 67, 338
Paddan-aram, 197, 284 f.
Palestine, 64, 66, 85, 92, 111, 113, 116, 141, 146 f., 154, 166, 170, 173, 205, 207 f., 213, 215, 218, 220 ff., 232, 234, 236, 247, 251, 254 ff., 259, 262, 264 ff., 269, 273, 282 f., 286, 294, 298, 307, 309 ff., 336, 338, 347, 350, 353, 369, 381, 392, 403, 412, 496, 538
  Church in, 503 ff.
  geography of, 185 ff.
  Greek rule of, 321 f.
  Hebrew settlement of, 246 f.
  Roman rule of, 328 ff.
Palestinian recension, 168 f.
Pallas, 239
Palmyrene, 196
Pamphylia, 238
Panias, 233
Pannonia, 226, 228
Paphos, 272
Papyri, Aramaic, 66, 217
  Bodmer, 165, 172, 180, 278
  Chenoboskion, 279
  Chester Beatty, 97, 156, 168, 171, 175, 180, 248, 278
  Elephantine, 17, 64, 67, 129, 217, 222, 266 f., 313 f., 315, 318
  Golenischeff, 273
  Greek, 21 ff.
  Magical, 410
  Nash, 247
  Oxyrhynchus, 81, 278
  Rylands, 117, 248

Parables, 93
  of Enoch, 82
  of Jesus, 429 f., 442, 455, 458, 462, 476, 481
  of Old Testament, 126
Paradigm, 140
Paradise, 416
Parallelism, 15, 123 f., 127, 136
Paris, 156, 173
Paronomasia, 125
Parousia, 109, 141, 453, 456, 458 f., 472, 507, 510 f., 518 ff.
Parthians, 235, 328
Passion of Jesus, 92, 141, 437, 445 ff., 459, 464 ff., 469 f., 473, 477, 491
Passover, 133, 142, 270, 288, 341, 343, 347, 366, 392, 439, 445 ff., 531 f., 565 f., 571
Pastoral Epistles, 110 f.
Patmos, 118
Patriarchs, 84, 250, 259 f., 283 ff., 293, 335 ff., 373
  sacrifices of, 538
  worship of, 524 ff.
Paul, 90 ff., 95 ff., 114, 137 ff., 141, 178, 220, 223, 230, 239 f., 330, 415, 433 ff., 437, 443, 448, 457, 469, 483 f., 486, 488, 491, 497 ff., 506 ff., 518 f., 544, 547 ff., 557, 564, 566
  Epistles of, 91, 97 ff., 163, 247, 267 f., 278 ff., 433.
  journeys of, 271 f.
  prison epistles of, 102 ff.
  style of, 22
  teaching of, 510 ff.
  visits to Jerusalem of, 101 f.
Paulus, Sergius, 226, 244, 271 f.
Peace-offerings, 528
Pekah, 217, 304
Pella, 503 f.
Pentateuch, 27 ff., 39, 111 f., 150 ff., 335, 373, 537, 545
  canonization of, 68
  poetical passages in, 35 f.
  Samaritan, 159
  Samaritans and, 320
  Syro-palestinian version of, 174
Pentecost, 84, 96, 142, 346, 392, 456, 483, 495, 546, 564
Penuel, 127
Peraea, 203, 222, 233, 328 ff., 444
Pergamum, 241
Pericles, 19
Perizzites, 216
Persepolis, 321
Persia, 17, 20, 53, 62 f., 64 f., 73, 129, 186, 205, 208, 212, 217 f., 222, 244, 251, 254, 266 f., 269, 282, 310, 315 f., 319, 321, 372, 374, 385, 398, 401, 411, 538
Persian Gulf, 218, 249
Persian language, 21
Persian religion, 218
Peshitta, 154, 158 f., 160, 174, 178
Peter, 90, 101, 137 f., 141, 238, 240, 441 ff., 450, 461 ff., 468, 477, 480, 499 f., 503, 506 ff., 514 f., 546, 557
  and Mark, 94, 113
Peter, Epistles of, 280
  1 Peter, 22, 113 f., 142 f., 278, 432 f., 548
  2 Peter. 22, 114 f., 138
Peter, Apocalypse of, 279
Peter, Gospel of, 170, 450
Pharaoh, 193, 207, 260
Pharisees, 75, 79, 84 ff., 89, 93, 224, 233, 235, 269, 323, 326 f., 376, 378 f., 396, 397 ff., 404, 409, 416, 418, 429, 440, 442 f., 446, 476, 485 ff., 492, 497, 572
Phasael, 328
Philadelphia, 121, 568
Philemon, 103
  Epistle to, 104, 107 f., 137
Philip (disciple), 140, 233
Philip (the Evangelist), 267, 468, 496, 504
Philip (the tetrarch), 232 ff., 239, 329
Philip of Macedon, 20, 321
Philippi, 103, 108, 121, 230, 506, 551, 559
Philippians, Epistle to, 102 f., 106 f., 519
Philistines, 41, 185, 193, 204, 208, 211, 216, 254, 256, 261, 263, 266, 294 f., 297 ff., 349 f., 525, 533
  language of, 17
Philology, 246
Philomelium, 121
Philosophy, Bible and, 383
  Greek, 80
  Hebrew, 85
  Philo and, 411
Philoxenian version, 174 f.
Phinehas, 533 f.
Phoebe, 98, 137, 551
Phoenicia, Phoenicians, 62, 185 f., 200, 207 f., 211, 213 f., 215, 259, 267, 271, 303, 336, 364, 423, 538
  exports of, 214
Phoenician, 13
Phrygia, 100, 222, 243 f.
Pilate, Pontius, 233 f., 236 f., 270 f. 330, 436, 439, 446, 449, 456
  wife of, 140
Pilgrimage, 382
  songs, 133
Pirke Aboth, 401, 428
Pisgah, 203, 541
Pisidia, 100
Pithom, 287
Pius I., 121
Plagues of Egypt, 288
Plain, Cities of the, 194

Pledges, 530
Poetry, Canaanite, 273
of the Old Testament, 123 ff.
Police, Temple, 448, 496
Politarchs, 272
Polycarp, Epistle of, 117, 121
Polycarp, Letter to, 121
Polyglotts, 157, 176
Polytheism, 336
Pompeii, 244
Pompey, 219, 222, 224, 528
Pontus, 224
Poppaea, 239, 501
Porta Maggiore, 244
Portugal, 226
Pothinus, 557
Potiphar, 28
Potiphera, 88
Pottery, 247, 261
Praetorian Guard, 102, 104, 229, 240
Praetors, 226
Prayer(s), 129, 250, 360, 364, 366 f.
in Christian worship, 564 f.
Lord's, 456, 471, 484
Prefects, 226, 229, 240
Presbyters, 550 f.
Priene, 267
Priest, High, 234, 236 f., 239, 389, 414
Priestly Code, 129, 131, 313 f., 527
age of, 32 ff.
and Joshua, 39
characteristics of, 30 f.
Ezra and, 34, 39, 54
style of, 30
see also P
Priests, 29, 33, 54, 388 f.
dues of, 528 ff.
Mesopotamian, 275 f.
Princeton Theological Seminary, 270
Prisca, Priscilla, 98, 112, 548 f.
Proconsuls, 226
Procurators, 226, 228, 230
of Judaea, 234, 238, 330 ff.
Pronouncement stories, 92, 140
Prophecy, argument from, 514 ff.
Prophets, 303 f., 353 ff.
and faith in God, 359
and judgment, 357 f., 360
and morality, 424
and politics, 357
and restoration, 361 f.
and social righteousness, 355
cultic, 131, 535
false, 100
in ancient Near East, 353 f.
in Early Church, 552 f., 559
Israelite, 355 ff.
Mesopotamian, 276
post-exilic, 362 f.
Prophets, Books of, 44 ff., 130 f.
canonization of, 68 f.
Minor, 49
Proselytes, 384, 401, 413
Prostitution, sacred, 32, 425
Protestantism, Liberal, 10
Protestants and Scripture, 9
Proto-Luke, 93, 438
Proverbs, Book of, 56 f., 58, 75, 80, 133, 370 f., 426
Providentissimus Deus, 7
Psalms, 54 ff., 91, 131 f., 274 f., 277, 296, 426, 539 f., 545
and Wisdom Literature, 368
and worship, 364, 367 f., 392
royal, 426
Psalms of Solomon, 85, 460
Psammetichus I., 208, 306
Psammetichus III., 208
Pseudepigrapha, 71 f., 81 ff., 151, 409
Pseudo-Clementine Homilies, 560
Ptah, 209
Ptah-hotep, 57
Ptolemais, 189
Ptolemies, 62, 64, 208, 218, 221, 322 f.
Ptolemy I., 221 f., 332
Publicans, 227
Punon, 195
Purim, 63, 528
Pur-Shagale, 253
Pyramids, 207
Pythagoreans, 408

Q (Gospel source), 93 ff., 113, 136, 279, 438, 441, 444, 453 ff., 457, 459, 465 f., 471 f., 479 ff., 486 f., 490 ff.
Qadesh, 208, 215, 254
Qainu, 266
Qaraites, 74, 147
Qarn Sartaba, 269
Qarqar, 196, 211, 217, 263, 303
Qatna, 213, 254, 257
Qua, 165
Quadratus, Ummidius, 239
Queen of Heaven, 313
Quelle, 93
see also Q
Quirinius, 227, 235 f.
Qumran, 150 ff., 155, 160, 268, 280, 405, 409
sect, 111, 327, 405, 414, 440 f., 468, 558 f., 571
Scrolls, 12, 52 f., 63, 73, 74, 79, 82 ff., 88 f., 116, 142 f., 144 f., 147, 153, 268 f., 271, 277 f., 326 f., 374, 377, 379, 405 f., 408 ff., 439, 447, 460, 512

Raamses, 287
Rabbath Ammon, 193, 258
Rabbis, 391 f., 399, 427 f., 485 ff.
Rabbula, 174
Rabshakeh, 128

Rachel, 525, 543
Rages, 73 f.
Raguel, 73
Rainfall of Palestine, 198 ff.
Ramat el-Khalil, 269
Rameses II., 208, 215 f., 283, 288, 298
Rameses III., 256
Raphael, 74, 410
Ras Shamra texts, 12, 213, 250, 254 f., 272 f., 275, 277, 541
Re, 207, 209
Rebekah, 36
Recensions of the New Testament, 166 ff.
  Egyptian, 166 f., 174
  Lucian's, 167 f.
  Palestinian, 168 f.
Rechabites, 423
Reconciliation, 512 f.
Red Sea, 36, 195, 214, 300 f., 304, 516
Redemption in Christ, 98, 108
Reeds, Sea of, 125
Rehob, 33
Rehoboam, 262, 302, 351 ff.
Religion, of Israel, 315 ff.
  of patriarchs, 335 ff.
  Roman, 230 f.
Remnant, 33, 463, 467 f., 481 f.
Rephaim, 300
Reshef, 259
Resurrection, belief in, 75, 90, 96, 99, 112, 114, 238, 351 ff., 397, 401, 408, 415, 519 f.
  of Jesus, 138, 420, 437, 444, 446, 450 f., 455 f., 459, 462, 465, 483, 485, 489, 491, 494 ff., 506 f., 511, 520, 546, 563 f.
Return, 46 f., 51, 55, 68, 218, 314 ff.
Reuben, 31
Revelation, Book of, 91, 95, 118 f., 138, 178, 241, 278, 280, 412, 492 f., 502, 504, 517, 520
  style of, 22
Rezin, 217
Rezon, 304
Rhaetia, 226, 228
Rhine, 226, 228
Rhodes, 268
Rhythm, 15
Riblah, 196, 308
Rich Young Ruler, 487 f.
Riddles, 125
Righteousness, 424 f., 511 f.
  of God, 98
Ritual, 130
  and prophecy, 52 f.
  and psalms, 55
Roads, of Palestine, 187 ff., 192 f. 197, 202
  Roman, 271
Robbers, Valley of, 189
Roma, 231
Roman citizenship, 497, 501
Romans, Epistle to, 97 f., 102, 137, 143, 278 f., 520
Rome, Romans, 20, 94, 96 ff., 103, 106, 120 f., 137, 145, 156, 163 f., 166, 208, 219 f., 224, 226, 230 f., 236, 239 f., 254, 269, 331, 376, 378, 382 f., 436, 498, 500 ff., 542, 549, 554, 557, 568
  achievements of, 243
  administration of, 100 f., 227 ff., 241, 446, 449, 475, 493, 500, 513 f.
  and Antiochus IV., 324
  and monotheism, 244
  empire of, 220, 241
  fire of, 502
  gospel in empire of, 499 ff.
  Jewish revolt against, 503
  Palestinian administration of, 271, 328 ff., 381, 389
  Paul's imprisonment in, 103, 110
  religion of, 243 f.
Royal psalms, 56, 132
Rufus, Annius, 236
Rule of the Community, *see* Manual of Discipline
Ruth, Book of, 60 f., 127
Rylands, Library, 148, 278
  papyri, *see* Papyri

Sabbath, 225, 239, 319, 343 f., 347, 366, 392 f., 465, 485 f., 539, 541, 545, 549, 564, 566, 571
Sabbath psalms, 540
Sacaea, 63
Sacred meal, 528, 530
Sacrifice, in Israel, 348 f., 350 f.
  in Judaism, 387 f., 525 ff.
  Servant of Yahweh and, 362
Sadducees, 75, 224, 323, 327, 376, 396 f., 401, 409, 412, 416, 478
Safed, 261
Sahak, 175
Sahar, 259
Sahara, 241
Sahidic version, 165, 167 f., 178 f.
Sailor, Shipwrecked, 209
Sais, 208
Saladdin, 189
Salamis, 218
Salome Alexandra, 326, 328
Salutations, 124
Salvation, oracles of, 130
Sam'al, 17, 215, 217
Samaria, 67, 192, 211, 222, 232, 262 f., 264, 266, 268 f., 274, 303, 305 f., 311, 313, 315 f., 318, 320 f., 326, 328 f., 444, 492, 496
  fall of, 34, 49, 359
Samaritan, Parable of Good, 429, 476
Samaritan Pentateuch, 159
Samaritans, 13, 68, 232, 237, 239, 330, 387, 395 f., 490, 504
  schism of, 320

Samson, 125, 129, 193, 294, 298
Samuel, 37, 41, 128, 295, 297 f., 349 ff., 532, 534
Samuel, Books of, 40 ff., 66 f., 84, 352
Scrolls of, 153, 155
Sanballat, 67, 266, 315, 318 f., 320
Sanhedrin, 234, 236, 239, 381, 389 f., 394 f., 496, 514
Sarah (in Tobit), 73
Sardinia, 224, 226, 236 f.
Sargon I., 205, 249
Sargon II., 211, 263
Satan, 58, 86, 241, 409
Satire, 131
Saudi Arabia, 188
Saul, 27, 36, 40 ff., 67, 133, 261, 297 ff., 300, 350, 352, 354, 366, 527, 532
Saul (Paul), 497
Scotland, National Bible Society of, 181
Scorpions, Ascent of, 196
Scribes, 390 f., 419
Script, Hebrew, 146, 153
Scripture, Protestants and, 9
Roman Church and, 7, 9
Scythians, 53
Scythopolis, 190
Sea, Song of the, 125
Sea peoples, 208, 213, 215 f., 254, 261, 283, 294, 298
Seals, 265
Sebaste, 232, 234, 329
Second Advent, *see* Parousia
Secret, Messianic, 442, 462
Secundus, Quintus Aemilius, 235
Seder, 545
Seed growing secretly, Parable of, 455
Seffuriyeh, 270
Seilun, 260
Sejanus, 236
Selah, 540
Seleucids, 62, 64, 218, 221 f., 268, 322 ff.
Seleucus I., 322
Semitisms in New Testament, 23 f.
Senate, Roman, 224 f., 227, 235 f., 269, 329
Seneca, 501
Sennacherib, 46, 73, 125, 208, 211, 264, 305
Sennonian chalk, 191, 193
Sepphoris, 230, 233, 270
Septuagint, 20, 23 f., 40, 57, 66, 72, 75, 77, 89, 145, 153, 154 ff., 160, 166, 170 f., 222, 248, 384, 469, 472, 516
Sepulchre, Holy, 270 f.
Sergius Paulus, *see* Paulus, Sergius
Sermon on the Mount, 268, 419, 428, 477 ff., 488, 509
Sermons, 129
Serpent, Brazen, 127, 544
Serug, 259
Servant, Songs, 47
of Yahweh, *see* Yahweh, Servant of
Suffering, *see* Yahweh, Servant of
Seth, 210
Seti I., 261
Settlement of Israel, 345, 536
Shallum, 304, 307
Shalmaneser (in Tobit), 73
Shalmaneser I., 211
Shalmaneser III., 211, 217, 262
Shalmaneser V., 211
Shamash, 259
Shamash-shum-ukin, 211
Shammai, 399, 479, 561
Shamshi-Adad I., 210
Sharon, 192, 200, 256, 263
Sheba, Queen of, 93, 301, 490
Shechem, 31, 192, 247, 254, 259, 262, 273, 287, 292, 302, 311, 336 f., 339, 346, 524 f., 534, 538, 543
Sheep, Parable of the lost, 481
Shekinah, 412
Shelemiah, 320
Sheol, 6, 415 f.
Shephelah, 193, 204
Sheshbazzar, 314 f.
Shield of Abraham, 336
Shiloh, 39, 126, 260, 302, 311, 346, 532 f.
Shishak, 208, 302
Shoshenq I., 208, 262
Shrines, 525
Shulammite, 60
Shuruppak, 248 f.
Sibylline Oracles, 83
Sicily, 19, 224, 226
Sidon, 184, 188, 200, 211, 213 f., 257, 267, 423, 490
Sihon, 35
Silas, 112
Siloam, 236, 264
inscription, 12
Silvanus, 114
Simanu, 253
Simeon (tribe), 339, 534
Simeon (Luke 2), 140, 461
Similitudes of Enoch, 82, 415
Simon (High Priest), 539
Simon bar Jonah (on ossuary), 271
Simon Maccabaeus, 222, 325
Simon Magus, 496
Simon of Cyrene, 450
Simon the Zealot, 443
Sin (god), 212, 249, 259, 309
Sin, 529 f.
Sin offering, 529 f.
Sinai, 35, 84, 273, 276, 289 f., 338 f., 341, 345, 374, 387, 526
desert of, 193, 201
Sinaitic Syriac, 165, 178 f.
Sin-sharra-ishkum, 211
Sin-shum-lishir, 211

Sinuhe, 208
Siphrê, 146
Sippar, 206
Sirach, *see* Ben Sira(ch)
Sirocco, 198
Sisera, 190
Sitz im Leben, 139
Slaves, release of 29
New Testament advice to, 433 f.
Slavery, Roman, 242
Smyrna, 121, 241
Snow, 199
Sodom, 185, 194 f.
Sogdian, 175
Sol invictus, 538
Solomon, 32, 34, 43 f., 56, 60, 62, 67, 72, 85, 128 f., 195, 208, 213, 216, 255, 262 f., 270, 274 f., 291, 296, 300, 326, 352, 365 f., 389, 413 f., 423, 454, 470, 533, 536, 538, 542
Acts of, 128
reign of, 128
Solomon, Psalms of, *see* Psalms of Solomon
Solomon, Wisdom of, *see* Wisdom of Solomon
Son of God (title), 470 ff., 506, 520
Son of Man, 82, 375, 414 f., 444, 458 ff., 463 ff., 481, 518 f., 548
Song of Songs, 60, 126
Sorcery, 55
Sorek, Vale of, 193, 268
Soteriology, 106
Soul, immortality of, 408
South Arabian, 13
Spain, 19, 97 f., 103, 150, 164, 170, 176, 224, 226, 499
Speculum de divinis scripturis, 164 f.
Spirit, Holy, *see* Holy Spirit
Spirits, evil, 411
two, 408
Standards, 236
Stater, 236
Stephen, 496 f., 516 f.
Stephanas, 559
Stoics, 62, 243, 402, 431
Stories, about Jesus, 140
about people, 140 f.
Straton's Tower, 271
Strong One of Jacob, 336
Strophes in the Old Testament, 123
Subeita, 196
Succoth, 266
Sudan, 247, 264
Suez, Gulf of, 289
Sufferer, Plaint of the, 274
Sumer, 248 ff.
Sumerian culture, 205 f.
love songs, 126
treaties, 129
Sunday, 564
Sun-god, Hymn to, 209
Supper, Last, *see* Last Supper
Lord's, *see* Lord's Supper
Suppiluliumas, 215
Susa, 252, 317, 321
Susanna, 77 f.
Symbolism, 130
Symmachus, 155
Synagogue, 20, 71, 85, 98, 113, 223, 238, 267, 368 f., 384, 386, 389 ff., 504, 544 f., 551, 555, 564 f.
and Temple, 391
rise of, 368 f.
Synchronisms, 254
Syncretism, 262
Synoptic Gospels, 93 ff.
and Fourth Gospel, 115 f.
Syria, 79, 156, 166 f., 170, 185 f., 201, 207 f., 211, 213, 215 f., 218, 221 ff., 226 f., 229, 234 ff., 239, 247, 249, 251, 254 ff., 259, 263 f., 266, 273, 285, 298, 307, 321, 328, 336, 353, 364, 376, 504, 548, 553, 568
Syriac, 147, 163 f.
versions, 72, 75, 79, 81, 86 f., 88, 154, 158 f., 164 f., 174 f., 178
Syrian Saddle, 197
Syrophoenician woman, 489 f.

Taanach, 254, 272 f.
Tabernacle, 28 f., 111, 344, 387
Tabernacles, Feast of, 29, 34, 346, 445, 540
et-Tabigha, 270
Tabor, 190
Talmud, 11, 145 f., 373, 392, 399, 436, 439, 528, 544, 555
Tammuz, 60, 126, 206, 213, 274
Tares, Parable of, 480, 548
Tarsus, 497
Targum(s), 148, 154, 157 f., 160
Fragment, 158
Jonathan, 158
Onkelos, 158
Palestinian, 158
Taurus, 113
Tattenai, 316
Taxation, Roman, 227, 235
Teacher of Righteousness, 406, 414
Telepinus, 215
Tell Abu Hawam, 367
Tell Abu Hirmil, 252
Tell el-Ajjul, 273
Tell Beit Mirsim, 260 f., 273
Tell ed-Duweir, 261 f., 265, 273
Tell Fara, 248 f.
Tell el-Far'a (Tirzah), 262 f., 272
Tell el-Far'a (Wadi Ghazzeh), 272
Tell el-Ful, 260 f.
Tell Halaf, 259
Tell Hariri, 250
Tell el-Hesy, 247
Tell Hum, 270

Tell Jemmeh, 264, 273
Tell el-Kheleifeh, 262
Tell Maskhutah, 266
Tell en-Nasbeh, 262, 265 f.
Tell Tainat, 272
Tema, 64, 212, 309
Temple, Solomon's, 32 f., 36, 40, 43 f., 56, 67, 214, 272, 275, 301, 305 f., 311 f., 314, 357, 361, 365 ff., 388, 425, 537, 538 f., 541
second, 47, 50, 53 f., 65 f., 73, 75, 151, 222 f., 319, 328, 368, 372, 382, 387 f., 526, 531, 539, 541 f.
Herod's, 86, 111, 232, 234, 237 f., 269 f., 329, 331, 388, 448 f., 495 f., 501, 519, 542, 549
and synagogue, 391 ff.
choirs of, 540
Church and, 517 ff.
Cleansing of, 445 f., 448, 455, 477, 491
destruction of (586 B.C.), 541
destruction of (A.D. 70), 369, 485, 503 f., 544
Essenes and, 407 f.
furnishings of, 540 ff.
manuscripts in, 146
personnel of, 522 ff.
rebuilding of, 314 ff.
service of, 388
singers in, 535
tax, 34, 225, 235, 239, 388
worship of, 538 ff.
Temple, Samaritan, 320, 326
Temple of Leontopolis, 387 f.
Temptation of Jesus, 140, 441, 461, 471
Ten Commandments, *see* Decalogue
Tent of Meeting, 28 f., 344, 541
Terah, 259
Teraphim, 260, 525, 542 f.
Terra rossa, 191, 204
Teshub, 215 f.
Testaments of XII Patriarchs, 83, 88, 409
Testimonies, 91
Tetragrammaton, 410
Tetrapla, 156
Tetrarch, 232 f.
Tetrateuch, 38
Text, of New Testament and archaeology, 278 ff.
of Old Testament and Ras Shamra, 277
of Old Testament and Dead Sea Scrolls, 277 f.
transmission of, 144 ff., 163 ff., 246, 265
Textus Receptus, 167, 176 f., 180 f.
Thank-offerings, 528 f.
Thanksgiving(s), 56, 132
psalms of, 51
Thebes, 52, 208 f., 262, 306
Theognis, 62
Theology of Early Church, 506 ff.
Theophilus, 137
Theos Hypsistos, 223
Therapeutai, 406
Thessalonians, Epistles to, 108 ff.
1 Thessalonians, 518 f.
2 Thessalonians, 519
Thessalonica, 108, 110, 230, 500
Theudas, 238
Thomas, Gospel of, 170
Thrace, 237
Threats, 130
Thummim, 130, 532, 543
Thutmosis I., 208, 282
Thutmosis III., 208, 282
Tiamat, 250, 275
Tiberian vocalization, 147 f.
Tiberias, 230, 233, 270, 443
Tiberias, Lake, 235
Tiberius, 229, 233 f., 236 f., 244
Tiglath-pileser I., 211
Tiglath-pileser III., 211, 217, 263, 304
Tigris, 74, 205, 210, 220
Time, divisions of, 570 ff.
Timothy, 558
Epistles to, 110 f., 137
Timnah, 193
Tirhakah, 211, 247, 264
Tirzah, 188, 192, 263
Tithes, 54, 566
Titus (emperor), 240, 331, 542
Titus, 558
Epistle to, 21, 110 f., 137
Tobiah, 266, 318 f.
Tobias, 74
Tobit, 73 f.
Tobit, Book of, 73 f., 76, 88
Tocra, 267
Tomb, Empty, 450 f.
Toparchy, 230
Torah, 84, 139, 373 f., 376 f., 399, 428 ff., 485, 511, 513
Tosephta, 540
Totemism, 527
Trachonitis, 190, 232, 329
Tractarians, 534
Tradition, in Roman teaching, 7, 9
oral, *see* Oral tradition
Tralles, 121
Transfiguration of Jesus, 444, 451, 456, 472
Transjordan, 213, 217, 261, 263, 299, 504
Treaties, 129
Hittite, 276 f.
Near Eastern, 341
Trees, sacred, 538
Trent, Council of, 7, 70
Trespass, 530
Tribal league, 345 ff.

Tribute money, question of, 446, 475
Tripoli, 185 f., 196
Tripolis, 186
Trito-Isaiah, 47, 62, 486 f.
Trust, psalm of, 133
Tueris, 209
Tukulti Ninurta I., 211
Tunisia, 224
Turin, 173
Turkey, 188
Turks, 270
Two spirits, 83, 89, 121
  ways, 83, 89
Typology, 515 f., 555
Tyre, 127, 186 ff., 212 f., 214, 257, 301, 309, 321, 490

Ubaid, 249
Ugarit, 129, 196, 213 f., 255, 337, 544
Ugaritic language, 12 f., 15
  literature, 214
Ulfilas, 167
Umma, 205
Universalism, 376, 384
  of Luke, 96
  of Matthew, 95
Unleavened bread, 531
Unleavened Bread, Feast of, 267, 343, 346, 537, 539
Upper room, 447
Ur, 133, 205, 210, 248 ff., 252
Urartu, 211, 217
Uriah (Hittite), 255, 300
Uriah (prophet), 308
Urim, 130, 532, 543
Ur-Nammu, 252
Uruk, 206
Utnapishtim, 249
Utu, 206
Uzziah, 47, 303 f., 536

Van, Lake, 254
Varuna, 216
Vashti, 63
Vatican City, 240
  Library, 157
Venus, 206, 259
Versions, of New Testament, 173 ff.
  of Old Testament, 154 ff.
Vespasian, 240, 331, 502 f.
Vineyard, Parable of, 481
Virgin Birth, 439 f.
Visions, 130
Vitellius, Lucius, 234, 237
Vows, 133, 528
Vulgate, 72, 77, 81, 154, 158 f., 160, 164, 173 f., 177

Wadi el-Afranj, 268
Wadi el-Ammud, 261
Wadi Far'a, 192
Wadi, Fari'a, 188
Wadi Ghazzeh, 264, 272
Wadi el-Hesa, 258
Wadi Kabir, 197
Wadi Lemmun, 189
Wadi Mujib, 258
Wadi Murabba'at, 278
Wadi Murra, 196
Wadi Sirhan, 188
Wailing wall, 270
War cries, 125
War, Jewish, 112 f.
War Scroll, 88, 268 f., 374
Warka, 248 f.
Wave-offering, 528
Way, The, 495 f.
Weddings, 393
Weeks, Apocalypse of, 82
Weeks, Feast of, 84, 346, 537, 539
Weights, 579
Well, Song of, 35, 124
Wells, sacred, 538
Wenamon, 208, 256
Western Highlands of Palestine, 185, 191, 193, 200
Western text, 142, 163 f., 165, 167 ff., 169 ff., 175, 177 ff.
Westminster Confession, 8
Whole-offering, 526 f., 529, 532, 539
Wicked Husbandman, Parable of, 472 f.
Widow, 424
Wilderness, wandering in, 289 f.
Wisdom, personification of, 56
Wisdom literature, 57 f., 75, 79, 133 f., 247 f., 275, 369 ff., 426 f.,
  in Apocrypha, 370
  in Babylon, 212
  in Near East, 369, 371
  of Egypt, 57
Wisdom of Solomon, 79 f., 370, 426
Women, Court of, 541
Worker's song, 124
Worship, centralization of, 368
  day of Christian, 563 f.
  Early Christian, 91, 559 ff.
  in Judaism, 387 ff.
  in Near East, 336
  in Northern Israel, 352 f.
  in Old Testament, 523 ff.
  in post-Settlement period, 348
  in wilderness period, 344
  Israelite, 363 ff.
Writings, canonization of, 68 f.
Württemberg Bibelanstalt, 181

Xerxes, 63, 218, 317
Xisuthros, 249

Yaazaniah, 265 f.
Yabneh, 264
Ya'diya, 215
  see also Ya'udi
Yahu, 313

Yahweh, active and righteous, 341, 348
acts of, 421
altars of, 29, 32
and Canaanite religion, 345 f.
and covenant, 350
and Elephantine, 313
and Exodus, 516
and guidance of Israel, 364, 372
and Judges, 39
and judgment, 357 f., 360
and Kenites, 339
and king, 298
and Messiah, 85
and New Year Festival, 536
and prophets, 130, 354 ff.
and Sinai, 35
and Tent of Meeting, 344
and Torah, 130
and war, 293 f.
and Yaw, 259
and Zeus, 222
anger of, 364
Ark and, 540
Book of Wars of, 125
called Theos Hypsistos, 223
centralization and, 306 f.
character of, 340 f., 345
covenant with, 295
Day of, 50, 53, 314, 413
delight in, 373
His election of Israel, 374
His name not to be uttered, 386
Kingdom of, 413, *and see* Kingdom of God
meaning of name, 339 f.
Moses' encounter with, 340 f.
only Lord of Jews, 381
power of, 341
prophets' faith in, 359
replaced by Jupiter Capitolinus, 239
requirements of, 418, 421 f.
revelation of name of, 28, 338 f.
reverence for, 427
Sanballat and, 320
Saviour of Israel, 524, 537
Servant of, 47, 55, 82, 95, 141, 361 f., 415, 441, 460, 468 ff., 478, 506, 515, 531
triumph of, 125
uniqueness of, 523
universal rule of, 375 f.
use of name in Pentateuch, 28, 30
use of name in Psalter, 54 f., 144
worship of, 363 ff., 523 ff.
see also God
Yarkon, 263
Yarmuq, 189, 202
Ya'udi, 258 f.
see also Ya'diya
Yaw, 259
Year, divisions of, 570 ff.
Sabbatical, 572 f.

Zacchaeus, 23, 140, 235, 487
Zadok, 300, 351, 396, 517, 533, 535 f., 544
and priesthood, 33
sons of, 405, 407
Zadok (Pharisee), 235
Zadokites, 533 f.
Zakir, 217
Zarathustra, 218, 374
Zarephath, 491
Zealots, 113, 235, 239, 330, 377 f., 382, 396, 402 ff., 409, 440, 443, 460
Zebedee, 115, 238
Zebulun, 287
Zechariah, 315 ff., 362 f., 372
Zechariah, Book of, 53 f., 66, 314, 375
Zedekiah, 308, 310, 312, 360
Zeno, 266
Zephaniah, 53, 360
Zered, 194 f., 202 f., 258
Zerubbabel, 47, 53 f., 61, 66, 73, 267, 314 ff., 372, 460
Zeus, 222
Zeus Olympios, 324
Zimrilim, 250
Zion, 358, 366, 518, 535, 537, 542
Sisters of, 270
Songs of, 132
Ziqqurats, 248
Ziusudra, 249
Zobah, 216
Zophar, 59
Zoroaster, 218, 374
Zoroastrianism, 269

IV. LATIN, GREEK, AND ORIENTAL WORDS

'ābhîr, 336
adelphos, 25
agapaō, 430
agapē, 24, 430
agora, 272
aiōnios, 25
ala, 229
'am hā'āreṣ, 306, 311, 385, 393, 416
'āmîth, 530
apechō, 22
'^{a}phuddāh, 543
apolutrōsis, 24
apostolos, 25, 555 f., 558
apsu, 541
'ar'ā', 16
'arḳā', 16
'^{a}ṣereth, 539
'^{a}rōn, 344
arrhabōn, 22
artos, 566
as, 236
'āshām, 539
'āshām tālûy, 531
'^{a}shērîm, 32, 542
'āsîph, 539
aureus, 235
autobasileia, 459
auxilia, 328 f.

'b, 14
baptisma, 24
baru, 275
bayith, 560
b^{e}khôrôth, 525, 529
bēma, 272
birkath ham-mînîm, 504

charis, 24
charisma, 274
cohors Augusta, 229
cohors Italica civium Romanorum, 229
cohors Sebastenorum, 229

dallath hā'āreṣ, 311
dawidum, 215
d^{e}bhîr, 538
denarius, 235
diakonos, 110, 550
didachē, 556
dm, 14
duoviri, 230
dynameis, 411

e-gal, 538
'êkhāh, 124
ekkalein, 546
ekklēsia, 24, 391, 507, 546
ekklētos, 546
'ēlleh, 16
ellogimoi andres, 558
embateuō, 23
embateuōn, 23
enuma elish, 212 f., 249 f., 536
episkopē, 551, 554
episkopos, 25, 110, 120, 551 f., 553 f., 558
equites, 226, 239
'ēshel, 525
euangelion, 25, 215

gal 'ēdh, 17
gālāh, 71
Galatai, 101
Galli, 101
gānaz, 71
gānûz, 71
gens in qua nemo nascitur, 406
gō'ēl, 61
gôyîm, 401

ḥ^{a}bhērîm, 566
ḥ^{a}bhûrāh, 565 f.
hag-gilyônîm, 71
ḥ^{a}khāmîm, 75
ḥ^{a}môr, 15
ḥāṭā', 530
hay^{e}wānî, 52
hayyayin, 52
hē basileia tou Theou, 24
hē dikaiosunē tou Theou, 24
hēkhāl, 538
ḥesedh, 421
hithpa'ēl, 16
ho huios tou anthrōpou, 24
hodos, 24
homologoumena, 119
hôy 'āḥî, 124
hôy 'āḥôth, 124
hôy 'ādhôn, 124
hypostasis, 22

'ibhrîm, 11
'ibhrîth, 11
imitatio Dei, 429, 433
impulsore Chresto, 238
'ishshāh, 526
'iṭṭûrê has-sôph^{e}rîm, 147

ḳādhôsh, 224
ḳāhāl, 546